CAMBRIDGE LIBRA

Books of enduring scholarly value

Maritime Exploration

This series includes accounts, by eye-witnesses and contemporaries, of voyages by Europeans to the Americas, Asia, Australasia and the Pacific during the colonial period. Driven by the military and commercial interests of powers including Britain, France and the Netherlands, particularly the East India Companies, these expeditions brought back a wealth of information on climate, natural resources, topography, and distant civilisations. Their detailed observations provide fascinating historical data for climatologists, ecologists and anthropologists, and the accounts of the mariners' experiences on their long and dangerous voyages are full of human interest.

Hakluytus Posthumus or, Purchas His Pilgrimes

Richard Hakluyt's 12-volume *Principal Navigations Voyages Traffiques and Discoveries of the English Nation*, originally published at the end of the sixteenth century, and reissued by the Cambridge Library Collection in the edition of 1903–5, was followed in 1625 by *Hakluytus Posthumus or, Purchas his Pilgrimes*, now reissued in a 20-volume edition published in 1905–7. When first published in four folio volumes, the work was the largest ever printed in England. An Anglican priest, Samuel Purchas (1577–1626) was a friend of Hakluyt, and based his great work in part on papers not published by Hakluyt before his death. As well as being a wide-ranging survey of world exploration, it is notable as an anti-Catholic polemic, and a justification of British settlement in North America. Volume 14 describes voyages to Greenland, Scandinavia and Russia (including a journey of two Cossacks to China), and begins an account of the West Indies.

Hakluytus Posthumus
or, Purchas His Pilgrimes

*Contayning a History of the World
in Sea Voyages and Lande Travells
by Englishmen and Others*

VOLUME 14

SAMUEL PURCHAS

CAMBRIDGE
UNIVERSITY PRESS

CAMBRIDGE
UNIVERSITY PRESS

University Printing House, Cambridge, CB2 8BS, United Kingdom

Cambridge University Press is part of the University of Cambridge.
It furthers the University's mission by disseminating knowledge in the pursuit of
education, learning and research at the highest international levels of excellence.

www.cambridge.org
Information on this title: www.cambridge.org/9781108079990

© in this compilation Cambridge University Press 2014

This edition first published 1906
This digitally printed version 2014

ISBN 978-1-108-07999-0 Paperback

Hakluytus Posthumus

or

Purchas His Pilgrimes

In Twenty Volumes

Volume XIV

GLASGOW

PRINTED AT THE UNIVERSITY PRESS BY
ROBERT MACLEHOSE & COMPANY LTD. FOR
JAMES MACLEHOSE AND SONS, PUBLISHERS
TO THE UNIVERSITY OF GLASGOW

MACMILLAN AND CO. LTD.	LONDON
THE MACMILLAN CO.	NEW YORK
THE MACMILLAN CO. OF CANADA	TORONTO
SIMPKIN, HAMILTON AND CO.	LONDON
MACMILLAN AND BOWES	CAMBRIDGE
DOUGLAS AND FOULIS	EDINBURGH

MCMVI

Hakluytus Posthumus

or

Purchas His Pilgrimes

Contayning a History of the World
in Sea Voyages and Lande Travells
by Englishmen and others

By

SAMUEL PURCHAS, B.D.

VOLUME XIV

Glasgow
James MacLehose and Sons
Publishers to the University
MCMVI

THE TABLE.

[Chap. II.

v

THE TABLE

The Contents of the Chapters—*Continued.* PAGE

THE TABLE

THE TABLE

The Contents of the Chapters—*Continued.*

CHAP. IX.

THE TABLE

The Contents of the Chapters—*Continued.*

THE TABLE

The Contents of the Chapters—*Continued.*

THE TABLE

THE TABLE

THE TABLE

xiii

THE TABLE

THE TABLE

The Contents of the Chapters—*Continued.*

THE TABLE

xvi

THE TABLE

The Contents of the Chapters—*Continued.*

THE TABLE

The Contents of the Chapters—*Continued.*

ILLUSTRATIONS

THE FOURTEENTH VOLUME

OF

Purchas His Pilgrimes

Contayning English Northerne Navigations and
Discoveries, relations of Greeneland, Groen-
land, the North-West Passage and other
Arctike Regions, and later Russian
Occurrents ; with a Description
of the West Indies by
Antonio de
Herrera

English Northerne Navigations,

and Discoveries, relations of Greeneland, Groenland,
the North-West Passage, and other Arctike
Regions, with later Russian occurents.

THE FOURTH BOOKE.

Chap. I.

A Voyage set forth by the Right Worshipfull Sir
Thomas Smith, and the rest of the Muscovie
Company, to Cherry Iland : and for a further
discoverie to be made towards the North-Pole,
for the likelihood of a Trade or a passage that
way, in the Ship called the Amitie, of burthen
seventie tuns ; in the which I Jonas Poole was
Master, having fourteene men and one boy :
A.D. 1610.

He first of March 1609. I wayed at *A.D. 1609.*
Black-wall and went to Gravesend. The *Secund.*
third day I went downe to the Noore- *Comput. Ang.*
head. The ninth, wee wayed and put out
to Sea (blessed bee God:) and by the
fifteenth day I was in the Bay of Rosse,
on the Coast of Norway, in Latitude 65.
degrees : at what time the wind came Northerly, and blew

extreame fierce, with great store of Snow and Frost. The sixteenth day, wee had the like weather and winds, so that wee could not maintaine a * mayne-course, and we lost some of our Beere. The seventeenth day, we had Snow, and all the Beak-head was so laden with Ice, that it seemed a firme lumpe, and the wind at North, which blew so fierce that we could not maintaine a * fore-course, and drave us backe to the altitude 63. degrees, 56. minutes. The storme continued so exceeding violent, that I was faine to spoone before it fortie eight houres, and the same wind and weather continued till the twentie one day, and in that time wee were driven as farre to the Southwards as Shottland. And being faire by the Land, and seeing no likelihood of faire weather, I got a Fisher-man to conduct mee to a good Harbour, called Hamersound, not so much to eschew the stormy weather, as to stop some leakes, and to amend our tackling. I tarryed in Shottland till the twelfth of April 1610. at which time the wind was Southerly. The former wind came to the North at midnight, with great store of Snow, which froze as fast as it fell: which wind continued till the fourteenth at noone. At two of the clocke it came to the East north-east, and I stood to the Northwards, after many stormes, much cold, Snow, and extreame Frosts. I had sight of the North-cape the second day of May. Then I stood towards Chery Iland, the winde being at West North-west. The third day at noone, the Cape bare South South-east; seaventeene leagues off, we had much Snow with Frost. The fourth day, it was thicke weather with great store of Snow and Frost, the winde at North-west and by North. The fift day, it was faire weather, the winde at North North-east. The sixt day, at two of the clocke in the morning, I met with some Ice, but not very thicke, so that I held my course toward Chery Iland, the winde being at South: at five of the clocke, I saw the Ice so thicke, that I could not possibly get through it. Then I stood to the West wards with a short sayle, and sounded, but had no ground at a hundred fathome: thicke foggie weather, at eight of the

The Mainsayle without a Bonnet.

The foresayle without a Bonnet.

Hamersound in Shotland.

North Cape in 71. degrees 20. minutes. May the second.

[III.iv.700.]

Chery Iland. Ice.

clocke it began to cleere up, and I stoode into the Ice finding it scattered in some places; and at twelve at noone, I found the Pole elevated above the horizon 74. degrees 7. minutes, and sounded, but had no ground at one hundred and seaventie fathomes. From twelve till foure, I ran North North-west two leagues, and sounded, and had a hundred and sixtie fathomes. Then Chery Island did beare, as I judged, North North-west, about fifteene leagues off or more: from foure till eight it was calme, at eight of the clocke the winde came Southerly, and I stood towards the Iland and found the Ice so thicke, that the Ship had no roome to wend, and withall such a fogge that I could not see one Cables length; in which time the Ship had many a knocke, but thankes be to God, no harme was done. By twelve of the clocke, the seaventh day, I got out of the Ice and lay a hull till the North Sunne, at which time it began to be cleere weather: then I set saile, and stood to the Eastwards, cold frosty weather.

The sixt day of May wee were in 74. degrees 7. minutes.

The eight day it was very foggie, the winde at North and by East, with Snow and Frost: I stood to the Eastwards, in hope to get the Easter end of the Ice, and so to Chery Island; and I ranne into a Channell betweene two firme bankes of Ice, and could finde no way through, but lay in the Ice till the ninth day at a South Sunne. Then I observed, and found the Ship in the altitude 74. degrees and 17. minutes, the winde being at North North-west, very faire weather, but frostie.

I sailed in the abovesaid Ice, one while one way, and another while another, in hope to finde some opening towards the Iland: but which way soever I stood, I saw all the Sea covered with Ice. At a South Sunne, the tenth day, I observed both with my Astrolabe and Crosse-staffe, and found the Poles height 74. degrees and 15. minutes: and the variation 13. degrees and 30. minutes the North point Westerly: by a North Sunne I got out of the Ice into the open Sea, and to write each course, way, and winde, with all other accidents, would be too tedious: but the thirteenth day of May, at midnight, I sounded,

Abundance of Ice.

74. degrees 15. minutes, variation 13. degrees 30. minutes.

3

The Lyonesse was sent to Chery Iland.

being in very thicke Ice, and had a hundred thirtie eight fadoms; there presently I espied the Lionesse standing into the Ice, I kept her company till eight of the clocke at night, and then I steered as followeth, from eight above said till twelve at noone: The foureteenth day I sailed North-west and by North twelve leagues, the winde at South South-east, thicke foggie weather: from twelve till foure at night, I sailed seaven leagues North, the same winde and weather with raine. And by the fifteenth day at foure of the clocke in the morning, I had sailed North twentie seaven leagues, the same winde and weather: at what time I supposed, that I was not farre from land,

* As Cobodines wildgeese and Willocks.

because I see great store of Sea-Foule * about the Ship: at eight of the clocke I sounded, but had no ground at a hundred and fortie fathome: very foggy weather: likewise I sounded at twelve of the clocke at noone; no ground at

Ice.

a hundred thirtie five fathomes, where I met with Ice and great store of Fowle, as before, winde at South, and foggie weather.

I stood through the Ice, till eight of the clocke at night, holding no course by reason of it, at which time I sounded, and had ninetie five fathom greene oze, the weather being all one, and very much Ice from eight, till ten of the clocke. I sayled North, one league and a halfe, and had seventie five fathoms rockie ground. From ten till twelve at midnight I sayled North one league and a halfe, and sounded, and had thirtie seven fathoms, the wind being at South, with great store of raine and fogs, and abundance of Ice round about, but something broken. Then I stood off West and by South, and tooke in all the Sayles, except the fore-saile and maine top-saile: and at one of the clocke the sixteenth day sounded, and had fortie fathomes oze: likewise I sounded at two of the clocke, and had fiftie two fathomes: I could neither perceive Current nor Tide in

Much raine.

all this time, and it did raine as fast as I have commonly seene in England: then I stood to the Eastwards, and at three of the clocke sounded, and had fortie fathomes oze: and thus I sailed among the Ice East and East and by

South, and East North-east, keeping no certaine course, by reason of the Ice, and had these depths following, 30. 20. 19. 16. and fifteene fathomes, and then I saw the Land *Land the* 16. within two leagues and lesse of me, bearing betweene the *day of May.* South and by East, and the North-west: then I stood in East and by South, supposing to have found a harborough within a ledge of rocks that lay off a low point, which seemed like an Iland, and standing in, I found depths, 10. 9. 8. 7. 6. 7. 4. and three fathomes, standing in it a shoald bay, and full of rockes.

Then I steered away North-west and by West, and had six, seven, eight, and ten fathome foule ground; this part of this Land is foule ground a great way off, therefore come no neerer this place then ten fathome, and that will carry you cleere of all dangers that I could see. Towards noone it cleered up, and I did looke the Meridian altitude of the Sunne, which was 34. degrees and 20. minutes, the *Note.* declination being 21. degrees and 10. minutes North, the Equator must bee 13. degrees and 10. minutes above and [III.iv.701.] beneath my Horizon. The Complement being 76. *76. degrees* degrees and 50. minutes, the Poles height. Likewise I *50 minutes,* found by true observation the Compasse to vary 16. *Pole height.* degrees, and before I had sayled foure leagues I saw a *degrees.* Sound that lay East and by South in, the winde comming *The North* to the East South-east; then I sent the Skiffe on land in *point westerly.* the mouth of the Sound, because I supposed I had seene Morses on the land, but they proved Rocks. I followed *Rockes.* into the said Bay with the ship, but standing in I had a stiffe gale of winde off the shoare, which drave abundance of Ice out of the Sound, through the which I enforced the ship, in hope there to have found an Harbour; in turning in I found these depths, thirtie five, thirtie, twentie, and eighteene fathoms. The Boat came aboard about a North-west Sunne, and the men told me they found deepe water within and foule ground; they saw great store of Mohorses lying on the Ice, but none on land, and they *Mohorses or* brought a piece of a Deeres horne aboord, therefore I *Morses.* called this Sound Horne Sound, and a Mount that lyeth *Hornsound.*

foure leagues to the South of it, the Muscovy Companies Mount, because it was my first landfale.

Then finding no benefit here to bee had, nor Haven for the ship, I stood to Sea, and sayled North-west and by North foure leagues: at midnight it blew very hard, and I stood to the Westwards with a short sayle, and sayled foure leagues West by eight of the clock the seventeenth day. Then I stood to the Landwards, the winde being at South South-west thick weather: and three leagues from

me I saw a Point, which I named the Ice Point, because there lay abundance of Ice upon it. Then I saw another Point beare North North-west five leagues off, which I

named Bell Point, because of a Hill formed like a Bell on the top, and to the Northwards of Bell Point goes in a great Bay with two Sounds in it, the one lieth in East South-east, the other North-east and by East; the last Sound you can hardly discerne, by reason there is a long Iland lying in the mouth of it. But the going into the said Sound is on the North side, yet there is an Inlet

under Point-partition, but very narrow and full of Rocks, and an exceeding strong Tyde setteth in there. This day I found the weather very warme and farre temperater then I have found it at the North Cape at this time of the yeere: this place lying in 77. degrees and 25. minutes, and the Cape in 71. degrees and 20. minutes; this place being to the Northwards of the Cape 6. degrees and 5. minutes: and note, two leagues to the Southwards of Bell Point is a ledge of Rocks three miles off the shoare, and come no neerer the shoare then fifteene fathom: upon the North side of the Bay is low land, which I named

Lownesse Iland. I called the North Sound Lowe Sound. Into the Bay I turned, the winde at East North-east faire weather; turning in I had no lesse then fortie fathoms close by the shoare, and in the middest no ground at sixtie fathoms, and being neere the Point that parteth both the

Sounds, the winde increased with raine. Then I saw the Sound frozen over from side to side, and upon the Ice a Beare and great store of Mohorses, but the winde blew so extreme hard, that the Boat could not row to windwards, to trie if we could kill some of them. The fogs and raine *Very thicke fogs.* continued till ten of the clock the nineteenth day, at which time the raine ceased, and it did freeze with snow and winde and fogs, as before.

From twelve at mid-night the nineteenth day, till foure in the morning the twentieth day, I sayled three leagues South-west and by South, then I found the Ice thicker then before. It was very thick fogs, with winde, frost, *Extreame cold weather.* and snow, and cold, that I thinke they did strive here which of them should have the superioritie. I put into the Ice aforesaid in hope to get through, and after many a sore stroke with the ship in it, I got through at a South-west Sunne, at what time it began to be faire weather. Then I stood through the Ice towards the land againe, in hope that that land would prove worth the labour and travell; and going to set the mayne top sayle, it was frozen *Sailes frozen.* as hard as ever I saw any cloath in all my life time, so that all my company could very hardly set it; and whereas I supposed, and have often said, that this climate is not so subject to foggs in May and June, as it is in July and August, it is contrarie; for I have not seene the Sunne on the Meridian these five dayes, nor seene it at all in sixtie houres: I had not sailed three leagues North-east, when it was as thicke as it was before with Frost and Snow: yet I stood still towards the Land.

The twentie one, I saw the Land at an East Sunne, and stood towards it, and at a South and by West Westerly, I observed the Sunne, and found the Meridian altitude of it 33. degrees 30. minutes, the declination being 21. degrees 56. minutes, &c. the altitude of the Pole was 78. degrees 26. minutes. The winde at North North-east: cold frostie weather: This place I called the Black-point *Blacke-point Ile.* Ile: I called a point (that lyeth foure leagues to the North-west of Black-point) Cape cold, and to the South-east *Cape-cold.* of Black-point is a great sound, which because it was covered with Ice, I called Ice-sound, and standing neerer *Ice-sound.* to the shore, I could not see any Sound or Harbour open;

therefore I determined to stand to the Northwards to seeke what good might be done that way to profit the Merchants, and also to get some Wood, for we had but little left. I sounded at the Black-point, and had twentie three fathomes streamy ground. At two of the clocke I stood off, and at midnight stood to the shore againe, cold weather with frost, the winde at North and by East. The two and twentieth day, at an East Sunne, I was faire by the Land, betweene Cape-cold and Black-point, a league off where it fell calme, and I sounded there, and had twentie eight fathoms, where I tried for Fish, but could take none.

[III. iv. 702.] The three and twentieth day, at an East North-east Sunne, I was within three leagues of Capecold: this day it was faire weather, and I tooke the Sunnes height at twelve of the clocke, and found it to be 33. degrees 30. minutes, the declination being 22. degrees 13. minutes, the distance of the Pole from my Zeneth, was 11. degrees 17. minutes, the complement thereof being 78. degrees and 43. minutes, the Poles altitude. All this day it was calme

Faire weather. all the forenoone, warme sunshine weather, and whereas I named this place Cape-cold, if I had falne with it this day, or the like, I should have given it another name. Here I tried to take fish, but could perceive none. Item, there is a point that beareth from Cape-cold North & by West

Fayer-forland. which I called Faire-forland: this Forland, and Cape-cold, and Black-point, are all one Iland. At sixe of the clocke at night, the winde came to the North North-west, then I determined to view the Ice-sound better; but comming neere it, I perceived it packt ful of Ice, so that I could see no end thereof at the Top-mast-head, neither could I see any open water in it. At a North Sun, the wind came to the North-east, and by North, then I stood to the Northwards, as before.

The foure and twentieth day, at a North-east Sunne, the wind came to the South-west, faire weather and warme. At a North north-east Sun, I tooke the Meridian Altitude, which was eleven degrees above the Horizon, and by working accordingly, I found the elevation of the Pole

8

above the Horizon, to be 78. degrees, 37. minutes. The five and twentieth day, at an East-south-east Sun, I set the boat to the land, neere Fayer-forland, and it being calme I sounded fortie five fathoms, where I proved for fish, but could find none, and within one league of the shoare I had *No fish.* five and thirtie, and thirtie fathome streamy ground. At a South-east Sunne, the Boat came aboord laden with *In all this* Wood, and some Whales fins. The men told mee there *land by the sea side is good* was great store of Morses in the Sea, about the shoare *store of Drift-* side, and about thirtie on Land. Immediately I sent my *wood, but none* Mate, Nicholas Woodcock with the Boat on Land againe, *groweth here.* to see if they could kill any of the said Mohorses, and also *N. Woodcock.* to search what other thing they should hap to find that *Whale-fins.* might prove beneficiall. Moreover I was certified, that all the Ponds and Lakes were unfrozen, they being Fresh-water, which putteth mee in hope of a milde Summer here, after so sharpe a beginning as I have had, and my opinion is such (and I assure my selfe it is so) that a passage may bee assoone attayned this way, by the Pole, as *Hope of a* any unknowne way whatsoever, by reason the Sun doth *Polare* give a great heat in this climate; and the Ice, I meane that *passage.* that freezeth here, is nothing so huge as I have seene in 73. degrees.

The sixe and twentieth day, at a North-east Sunne, the Boat came aboord againe, having slaine but two Morses, at twelve at midnight the wind came to the North, and blew so hard, that I was enforced to try with a Mayne-course, cold frosty weather, with snow. The sayd wind and weather continued till a South Sun, the seven and twentieth day, at eight of the clocke at night, the wind came to the North-west and by West faire weather, then I stood towards the Land again. And at a South-east sun, the eight & twentieth day, I was within three leagues of Fayer-forland, and standing in I sounded divers times, and had these depths, 15. 17. 19. and 18. fathoms, within five, sixe, and seven myles of the shoare, and when Fayer-forland did beare South and by East by the Compasse. It being two miles from me, I saw the Land beare North-east

and by North, about nine leagues off, the which because it
was full of knottie Mountaines, I called Knottie-point,
and betweene Knottie-point, and Fayer-forland, I saw a
great Bay, which because it was foggy on the sudden, I
could not discover. In the Sea, about the Forland, I
saw great store of Mohorses and Sea-fowle, I sounded in
the Bay and had ninetie five fathomes rockie ground. I
stood to Sea, and had very foule weather, with snow, and
fogs, and frost, which weather continued till the thirtieth
day, at foure of the clocke in the morning, at which time I
was within one mile of Fayer-forland in nine fathomes,
and then I sayled East North-east about two miles, and
had these depths, 18. 17. 16. 14. and 12. fathomes all
rockes. Then I steered South with the like depths and
grounds, but when I had runne South South-east three
miles further, I had sandie ground, then did Fayer-forland
beare West and by North, about three leagues of, the
next cast I had tenne fathomes foule ground, and from
thence I steered two leagues South and by East, having
these depths, 10. 9. 8. and 7. fathomes, then I saw the
Bay covered over with Ice. I turned out the wind at
North. ·This Sound I named Fowle-sound, for in this
Bay are three Sounds; this I spake last of, which lyeth in
South, and goeth out at Black-point: another lyeth in
East South-east, which I named Deere-sound: another
goeth in North, which is called Closse-cove, and being
neere the point betweene Fowle-sound and Deere-sound,
it fell calme, and I sent the Skiffe on Land, and standing
after, with a little wind at West, I found the sayd Point
very shoale, with a ridge of Rockes, where I had these
depths, 4. 5. 6. 7. 9. 10. 18. and then 30. fathomes. At a
South Sun, the Boat came aboord and brought Wood, and
some Whale-fins.

The last of May, at an East North-east Sun, I was
within three leagues of Knotty-point, at which time I saw
Ice all the Sea over betwixt the West and the Land: then I
saw another Point foure leagues distant from Knotty-
point, the one bearing of the other North and by East,

and South and by West, and it is smooth Land, the which
I named the Gurnerds-nose, indifferent warme weather: *Gornerd-nose.*
and finding the Ice to bee so thicke that I could not passe
it, and the wind comming to the West, I stood to the
Southwards againe, determining to search the Sounds
better for a Road, and for commodities, because I saw no [III. iv. 703.]
good to bee gotten in keeping the Sea amongst the Ice,
and at a North Sun, I was in the entrance of Close-cove, *Note.*
where I had no ground at one hundred & twenty fathomes,
and yet I was within two Cables length of a sunken ledge
of Rockes, that lyeth on the Larboord side of the Bay a
mile from the shoare.

The first of June I found a good Road in Close-cove, *June.*
on the South-west side, where I rid in seven fathomes
sand mingled with oze, at an East Sun I sent a Skiffe to a
low Point, that lyeth on the North side of the Bay, where
they found some Whales fins, and three pieces of Mohorse
teeth, and upon a little rockie Iland, they saw neere one
hundred Mohorses, which were there sleeping. In this
time I went towards the bottome of the Sound, and slue a *A Beare*
white Beare. At a South-west Sun, I went towards the *slaine.*
rocke, to see if I could kill any of the Morses that lay
there, and as wee went by the shoare side I espied Deere, *Foure Deere*
three of them I slue, and one of my company one. But *slaine.*
when I came to the rocke, the Ice that the beasts lay on
was hollow, and the rocks that was betwixt the Ice and
the sea stood sloping toward the Sea; the which when I
saw, I determined to go aboord and let them alone, yet
afterward I went on the rocke betwixt the Ice and the Sea:
and as I with the rest of my company were killing them,
the Ice brake, and Ice and beasts slid into the Sea together,
and carryed one of the men with them, so that he escaped
out of that danger very hardly; for besides the weight of
dead Mohorses, and Ice that bruised him, the beasts that
were alive strook at him in the water, and bruised him very
soare. I had beene in the same case, if I had not beene
the nimbler, and slipt on one side. I killed three Morses,
whose teeth I tooke off. Then I espied the Beare, which

*His name was
Tho. White-
man.
A Beare
slaine.*
my Mate had hurt before with a shot; hee went into the Sea, when hee saw the Boate, where I slue him with a Lance, and brought him aboord.

The second day at a North and by East Sunne. At a South Sunne, I went to the South shoare of Deere-sound, where I found a good quantitie of Fins, and came aboord, at a North North-west Sunne. The third day, being Sunday, I rid still, having the wind at West South-West much wind. Then upon the side of a Hill, a mile to *A crosse set up.* the Westwards of the Road, I set up a Crosse, with a writing upon it, signifying the day of my arrivall first in this Land, by whom I was set out, and the time of my *Crosse road.
A good Road
for all winds.* being heere. This Road I called Crosse-road. At a South-east sunne the fourth day, I wayed the wind at West South-west, and when I was almost out, the wind increased with fogs, which made me put back into the Road, where I anchored the same day at six of the clocke, at afternoone. The fifth day, at a North-east and by East sunne I wayed, and it fell calme, then I went to the East *There is great
store of Fowle
in this Land.* side, and killed some Fowle, which I found in great abundance: and when I was readie to go aboord, I saw fourteene Deere, at which time I spent all my powder, *A Buck slaine.* and shot but one shot, with the which I slue a fat Buck. The same day, at a South sun, I went on Land and slue *Three Deere
slaine.
A fawne
taken.* two Deere more. And at a South-west sun I went on Land and slue a Doe, and took the Faune alive, and brought it aboord, but it dyed the next day. The calme continued till the sixth day, at an East North-east sunne (and we drove in the Bay, with a little soaking tyde that runneth there.) Then I sent the skiffe to the rocke afore-said, to see what store of Mohorses were there; at three of the clocke they came aboord, and told mee there was neere two hundred beasts. I tooke both the boat and skiffe, with all my company, and went to the rock, and in *Beares slaine.* going thither I slue a Beare: but when I came to the rocke, the beasts began to goe into the sea, then I presently went on land, with all my company, and slue eightie *Mohorses.* beasts, whose teeth I tooke, and in going aboord slue

another Beare, and came aboord the seventh day, at a
North-east sun. Then I saw two white fishes, which at *White fishes.*
the first sight I supposed to be Beares, they had long
snouts like Sturgeons, two flat Fins close by their gils, flat
bodied, small towards their tailes, and a broad taile.

The tenth day, I went on shoare and slue five Deere, *Five Deere.*
with the which, and them that I slue before I have
lengthened out my victuals, blessed be the Creator of the
World,* which hath not made any part thereof in vaine, **Isa. 45. 18.*
but so that in these parts (which hath seemed unpossible
to our Ancestors to bee travelled unto, by reason of the
extreame cold which they supposed to bee here) I find the
ayre temperate in the Lands, and nothing so cold as I have
found at Chery Iland in five severall Voyages. Moreover, in this Land I have seene great store of Deere, which
have neither bush nor tree to shelter them from the
nipping cold of Winter, nor yet any extraordinarie pasture
to refresh them. If these (I say) having nothing but the
Rockes for a house, and the Starry Canopie for a covering,
doe live here; why may not man, which hath all the gifts
of God bestowed upon him for his health and succour?

The eleventh day in the morning, I sent the skiffe to a
Beach, that lyeth Northwards from the Rocke where we
slue our beasts, but when they came to the Rocke, it
beganne to blow hard at North North-west, that they
could not proceed any further, upon the Rocke they found
a Beare, and slue him, and came aboord. In which time
I tooke the boate and went to the East side, and slue two *Two Beares,*
Beares and two Deere. *and two Deere*

The twelfth day, at a North-east sunne I wayed, and *slaine.*
having very little wind, I sent the skiffe to goe to the
place abovesayd, at a North sunne, they came aboord and
brought some Whales Finnes and a Beare, and told mee
that it did blow very much wind at Sea, yet I had it all *[III.iv.704.]*
this time calme in the Bay. Yet before I could get out
of the Sound, the wind came to the North-west, and blew
very hard, which made mee to put roome for Crosse-road, *Crosse-road.*
where I rid till the fourteenth day, in which time I caused

both the boates to bee trimmed, and the thirteenth day at
noone, I observed on Land, in this place, and found the

Poles height
in 79. degres
15 minutes.
Compasse vary
18. degrees
16. minutes.

Poles height 79. degrees, fifteene minutes, and the variation of the Compasse 18. degrees, 16. minutes North-
west: the same day I slue a Bucke.

The fourteenth day, at a South-east Sunne I wayed,
the wind at South-west foggie weather, at a South-west
Sunne, I went on Land and slew a Buck.   The fifteenth
day, at East Sunne, I got out of the Bay, at which time

Ice.

I saw abundance of Ice to the Sea-wards, but the wind
came to the South-east, and I sayled betwixt the Ice and
the shoare.   At a North-west Sunne, I sent the skiffe
(with seven men in it) to the Land under Knottie-point,
at which time the wind came to the North-east, and I stood
to the North-wardes, where I had these depths, fifteene,
thirteene, and eleven fathomes foule-ground.   These
depths were about a league, and to the Northwards of

Great store of
Whales.

Five Deere
slaine.

Knottie-point, I saw great store of Whales, the like I
saw in Deere-sound.   The sixteenth day, the Skiffe came
aboord, and brought a few Finnes, and five Deere, and
they told mee that within the Bay, that lyeth betwixt
Knottie-point and Gurnerds-nose is a Haven, in the
entrance whereof is an Iland, and seven fathomes going
in, but within eight, nine, fifteene, and twentie fathomes
good ground.   This maketh Gurnerds-nose, an Iland, for
this Haven goeth out on the North-west side of Gurnerds-

Faier-Haven.

nose.   I named this Haven, the Fayre-haven; I found a
great tyde heere, which runneth South South-west, the
floud commeth from the Southwards.

Then standing to the Northwards, I saw the Sea covered

Abundance of
Ice.

79. degrees
50. minutes.
the Latitude of
Gornerds nose.

with Ice, which lay close to the Land which made me
stand to the Southwards again, I observed at Gurnerds-
nose, and found the Poles height 79. degrees, 50. minutes.
At a North-west Sun, the same day, I sent the skiffe on
Land to search the Coast to the Southwards of Knottie-
point, where I sounded and had twenty foure fathomes
Foule-ground, and in the Fayre-way I sounded, having
these depths, 30. 35. 45. and 48. fathomes all Rocky-

ground. By the seventeenth day, I was in the entrance *The farthest* of Close-cove, at a South Sun, at which time the Skiffe *place of my* came aboord, and brought a Beares skin, and a Buck, and *being this* a good quantite of Whales Fins and an Unicornes horne, *This Unicorns* which was five foot and seven inches long, and in the *horne is the* biggest part of it, it was seven inches and a halfe about. *Horne of a fish* The eighteenth day, at a South Sun, I came into the Road, *of which see* where I rid all that day, having very much wind and raine *discovery.* that wee could doe nothing. At a North Sunne, I sent my Mate, with the Skiffe, and sixe men to seeke for more Fins, &c. The ninteenth day, at a North Sun, they came aboord, having slaine ten Beares, three of their skins and *Ten Beares* fat they brought aboord, and a good quantitie of Fins, and *slaine.* six paire of teeth. The twentieth day, in the morning, I sent both the Boat and Skiffe to flay the other seven Beares, the wind being at North faire weather. But they were no sooner gone, but it blew very hard at North, which brought abundance of Ice out of the bottome of the Sound, but did the Ship no hurt. At a West South West Sunne, the Boats came aboord with the Beares skins, the wind abovesaid set so much Ice out of the sound upon the Ship, that it inforced mee to set sayle.

The one and twentieth day, at a North Sun, I stood towardes Fayer-forland, and sent out the skiffe. The two and twentieth day, at a South-east sunne, they came aboord, with the skiffe laden with Fins, and killed five *Five Deere* Deere. Then I went on Land to search what I could find, *slaine.* and I slew a Beare, and tooke a young one alive, and at *A yong beare* three of the clocke in the afternoone I came aboord with the *taken.* skiffe laden with Fins. The three & twentieth day, at a South-east sun, the Boat came aboord, and brought a good quantitie of Finnes, and a Beares skinne. Then I stood *A Beare* toward Cape-cold, and the same day, at a South sunne, I *slaine.* sent the skiffe on Land to the North-wards of the Cape, where they found sixteene Mohorses on a rocke, which they slue; and at a North-east sun, the foure and twentieth day, they had brought all the teeth and blubber of them *Take heede of* aboord; at which time the wind came to the North-west, *this point.*

and blew verie hard: then I stood towardes the Ice-sound
to seeke what commodities it would yeeld.   At a North
sunne I was neere Black-point, which hath a great many
sunken Rockes lying on the southermost end of it, therefore
you must come no neerer that shoare then twentie five
fathomes.   The five and twentieth day, till a South sun,
it was calme, and the tyde drove the ship so farre from the
Land, that I could not send the boat on shoare.

The sixe and twentieth day, at a South South-west
Sunne, I came aboord, more laden with travell then com-

modities, at which time I slue a Buck.   Then I stood
toward Ice-sound, and at a Point which parteth Foule-
sound and Ice-sound, I had thirtie fathomes oze, & so to
ten fathomes Rockes, then I steered East along the shoare,
and had betwixt thirtie and fifteene fathomes oze and
sand.   In fifteen fathomes I anchored, having the wind at
North North-west, faire weather at a North-west sun, at
a North sun, I sent the skiffe to the shoare to search for
commodities.   The seven and twentieth day of June, at
an East North-east sun, they came aboord, and brought
a good parcell of fins.   At six of the clock I sent the
Skiffe to the Land againe, and set sayle with the ship;
but it being calme, and the tide setting the Ship towards

a ledge of rocks, made mee to anchor againe.   At a South
South-east Sun, they came aboord againe, and brought a
good quantitie of fins: at a South Sunne I sent the Skiffe
towardes the mouth of Ice-sound, and in the entrance
thereof I found a Cove in the which was twentie fathomes,
and so to thirteene, but by reason of the tyde, and edy-
winds, I could not get into it; here the Skiffe came aboord
and brought a few finnes.   Then I steered to another
Sound, in the South side of Ice-sound, where I anchored
in twentie fathomes oze, the same day at a North Sun.
The eight and twentieth day I stayed at the place abovesaid, and tried the Beares grease to bring it into oyle, and

when we were all busied, a Beare came swimming over
the Bay, towards the ship, which I slue, and split my
Peece, the winde being at West.   The nine and twentieth

16

day, at a South-east Sunne, I sent the skiffe to search the
Coast to the Westwards of this Bay, the wind at North-
west. The last of June, the skiffe came aboord, at a
South-east Sunne, and brought a few Finnes, and a Bucke, *A Bucke.*
the wind at North.

The first of July, being Sunday, I rid at the place above- *July the first.*
said, in hope to have more Mohorses on Land; I observed
heere and found this place in 78. degrees, 24. minutes, and *78. degrees,*
the variation Westwards, seventeene degrees. Then I *24. minutes,*
sent the skiffe to see if any more beasts were on Land. *var. 17. deg.*
The wind at North-west, faire weather. The second day, *W.*
at a North North-east Sunne, they came aboord and
brought two Deere. The third, wee slue a few Morses, *Two Deere*
whose teeth and blubber wee brought aboord, at a North- *slaine.*
west Sunne, at which time I slue a Pricket: this place I
named the Green-haven. Immediately I sent the skiffe *Greene-*
to take the teeth, and fat of seven beasts, which lay slaine *harbour one*
in another place. The wind at West, thicke foggie *Deere slaine.*
weather. It floweth here on the Change day South, and
by West, and hyeth sixe foot water, and runneth halfe
tyde halfe quarter. The fourth day, we rid still the wind
at South-west with fogs and raine, and very much wind:
at the same time I saw great store of Ice in Ice sound. *Ice.*
The fifth day, at a North-east Sunne I¹wayed, the wind
at West thicke weather, and in standing out wee slue a *A Beare*
she Beare, and tooke her two young ones. Indifferent *slaine, two*
faire weather, we lay becalmed all this day. *yong ones*
taken.

The sixth day, I was off Lownesse (at a South Sunne)
the wind being at East blew so hard, with raine and thicke
weather, that I was enforced to take in all the ʼsayles save
a Mayne-course, which storme continued till eight at
night, at which time I set more sayle, and stood to the
Southwardes, hoping to get some goods that way. The
seventh day, at noone the wind came to the North-east,
and then it began to bee cleere weather, at what time I
saw the Land of Bel-sound, whither I purposed to goe,
yet could not by reason of abundance of Ice, which lay *Ice.*
above three leagues from the Land, which I could not

possibly passe. At a North-west and by West sun, I
saw abundance of Ice all along the Land, to the Southwards of Bel-sound. The eight day, at twelve at noone,
I stood into the Ice, in hope to get to the shoare, the
wind at North and by West hasie weather, Horne-sound
bearing East North-east, nine leagues of, I stood to the
landwards till foure of the clocke, at which time I found
the Ice so thick that I was forced to stand to the Southwards to eschew it. I sayled by, and amongst the Ice,
till a North North-west Sunne, at which time I was within
three leagues of the shoare. Then I sounded, and had
thirtie sixe fathomes. Then I stood to the Westwards,
and finding all this part of the Land full of Ice, I purposed
to stand to the Northwards againe to search for commodities that way: the wind being at North-west, I turned
to windwards, till the tenth day, at eight of the clocke
before noone, at which time wee found a part of a dead
*A dead
Whale.* Whale, which I caused to bee made fast to the Ship,
determining to get into some Harbour, there to make the
best of it I could. Before I could get into Bel-sound, at
which time I saw all the bottom of the Sound full of Ice,
so that there was no refuge for the Ship. Then I was
faine to turne out with the winde at West, and beganne
to blow verie hard. At a North-west Sunne, it was fayre
weather, and I sent my Mate with the skiffe to search
the Coasts towardes Bel-point. The fourteenth day, at a
North-east Sunne, the skiffe came aboord, and brought
*Three Beares
slaine.* three Beares, which they had slaine. Immediately I sent
the Boat for water and wood, and then I stood through
the Ice, and got through it by a North Sun the fifteenth
day, the wind at North-west foggie weather. Then I
turned to windwards, to double Lownesse, and got cleere
of it: at sixe of the clocke at night thicke foggie weather.
The sixteenth day, at five of the clocke in the afternoone, I got to Black-point, the wind comming to the
South, thicke weather. Then I sent the skiffe to range
the Coast, and to search what they might find. The
seventeenth day, at ten of the clocke they came aboord,

and brought some Fins, and three Deere. Then I stood *Three Deeres slaine.* towards Crosse-road, and anchored there at a North-sun, the wind and weather as abovesaid. The eighteenth day, about five of the clocke in the morning, I sent the skiffe to see if they could find any Morses on Land, on the Rocke, or in Deere-sound, and in the meane time, I, with the rest of the company got drift-wood and water readie, and about a South sunne, a Beare with two young ones; *A Beare with two young ones taken.* the Dam I slue, and tooke the young ones aboord the ship, the wind Northerly, cold, foggie weather. The nine and twentieth day, in the morning, I went to the East side, to see if any Mohorses were on land; there I slue foure exceeding fat Buckes and a Doe. In which time *Five Deere slaine. Two Beares slaine. Sea-coales.* the skiffe came aboord and brought two Beares skins, but found no beasts, and in Deere-sound they found Sea-coales, which burnt very well.

The twentieth day, I sent the Skiffe into the bottome [III. iv. 706.] of Closse-cove to search it for commodities, the wind at South close weather with raine: at eight of the clock at night they came aboord, but found nothing; immediately I got wood and water aboord, which was ready before, preparing to set sayle the wind and weather abovesaid, we slue three Deere. The one and twentieth, I wayed, the wind at North faire weather. The two and twentieth day, the wind came to the West, and then I stood to the Northward, at eight of the clocke hasie weather. At twelve of the clocke at noone the wind came to the North, and I stood to the Southwards by Fayer-forland. The three and twentieth day, at an East north-east Sunne, the Boat brought some Whales finnes, and three Buckes, and one *Three Bucks slaine.* Doe: In which time I thought I had seene Land beare West from me. I stood to the Westwards, and by a South South-east sunne, had run fifteene leagues West and by South, then I perceived it to be fogs. The foure and twentieth day, at seven of the clocke in the afternoone I came into Bel-sound and found but little Ice, then I sent the Skiffe to seeke for a Road for the Ship, and also for commodities. The five and twentieth day, at three of

No good
chanell.

the clocke in the morning, the Skiffe came aboord, having
beene in the mouth of the North Inlet, which I call Low-
sound, they went into it by Point-partition, but there is
no good Channell that way for a Ship: neverthelesse there
seemeth to bee an Inlet or Channell, but it is full of Rockes
from side to side, and the men told mee, that upon the
Land lay some Mohorses, which I sent them to kill.   At
eight of the clocke, the Skiffe came aboord, and brought
the teeth of the sayd beasts, and some blubber.   Immediately I sent them into Bel-sound, to seeke for a Road for
the Ship, the wind at West thicke foggie weather.   About
an North West Sunne, I anchored in Bel-sound, in sixteen
fathomes ozie ground, this Harbour lyeth about two
leagues above Point-partition on the South-side of it, and
here a ship may ride safe from all windes.   At a North

A Beare
slaine.

Sunne my Mate slue a Beare.   The six and twentieth
day in the morning, it blew hard, and I went on Land

A fat Bucke.
And although
I have not
written of the
fatnesse of the
rest, yet the
most of them
were two and
three inches
thicke of fat.

and slue a Beare, and a Bucke which had three inches and
an halfe in thicknesse of fat on the haunches.   At nine of
the clocke I sent both the Boats to fetch the fat of those
Mohorses which were slaine the day before, and likewise
to search if they could find any more, the wind at North
with fogs.   At six of the clocke at night the Boats came
aboard with the fat, and brought two Buckes, but found
no beasts on Land.

The seven and twentieth day, at a South South-east
Sunne I weighed, the winde being at North and by West
faire weather, and I steered out (betwixt an Iland and the
point where I rid) South-west and by West, having these
depths, 10. 7. 6. 5. and 4. fathomes: then I was in the
middest betwixt the said point, and a shoald which lay
South and North, one of the other, and after keeping the
same course, I had these depths, 5. 6. 7. 8. 9. 10. 12. and
13. fathomes, in all these depths I had sand, and after
oze.   At sixe of the clocke the wind came to the South-
west with fogges, and I turned to the wind-wards.   And
at twelve, the eight and twentieth day Lownesse did beare
North-east about foure leagues off, where I sounded

having thirtie two fathomes streamie ground with blacke
stones, at which time it was calme, and continued so till
the nine and twentieth day at sixe of the clocke in the
morning, then the wind came to the North with fogges,
and I stood to the Southwards, and to see what Commodities I could find that way.

At nine of the clocke I was neere the Ice-point, where *My departure*
I met with much Ice, which put mee from the Land, and *from the land.*
I was enforced to steere South-west and by South to *Ice.*
shunne it, the winde at North-west which blew hard with
fogges.   The wind increased, I stood towards Cherrie
Iland (if possible I could attayne it) for fogges and Ice.
The thirtieth day, at foure of the clocke in the morning
I saw no Ice, having kept no certayne course, by reason of
the Ice which I had past, the winde at North and by West,
cold foggie weather with raine.   From the time abovesaid till twelve of the clocke at noone I sayled South
South-east, and ranne fifteene leagues, the same wind and
weather, at which time I sounded & had eightie fathoms
greene oze like Kowes dung.   I sounded at two of the
clocke, and at foure of the clock, the first, eightie eight,
the second, eightie two fathomes, and sayled sixe leagues,
the former course wind and weather.   At which time I
heard a breach which proved Ice, then I steered West to
eschew it, the fogges being so thicke that I could not see
one Cables length.

The last of July at noone, I had sayled South and by
East halfe a point Southerly eight leagues having little
wind, and sounded, and found one hundred and fortie
fathomes thicke foggie weather, and in haling up the Lead,
a fish followed it to the top of the water: then I tryed *A fish seene.*
to take fish but could not.   At foure of the clocke in the
afternoone, the winde came Southerly, and I stood to the
Westward, by reason the Ice lay both to the South and
East of us, at a North Sunne it was cleere weather, and I *Ice & fogs two*
saw the Ice round about us, cold weather with frost. *of the greatest*
hinderances in
The first of August, we beat in the Ice till noone, but *the Northerne*
could finde no end thereof, because it was so foggie, and *Navigations.*

the Ice packed very close; yet after many intricate courses, I got to the Westwards of it at mid-night the same day, the winde at South-east, cold weather with raine and fogges. And after I had seene so much Ice that I could not come neere Cherry Iland, to prosecute the rest of my *I stood towards* Voyage, I determined to stand for England, as God would *England.* give me leave. From mid-night the first day, till eight of the clocke the second day before noone, I sayled South-west and by South five leagues, the wind at East South-[III.iv.707.] east, thicke fogges with raine. From the second day at eight of the clocke, till the third day at twelve of the clock at noone, I sayled West South-west fifteene leagues, the wind at South and by East, wet foggie weather. From noone abovesaid, till twelve at noone the fourth day, I sayled foure leagues South, the winde variable, and the most part of that time calme, and so continued till eight of the clocke at night, at which time the wind came to the South and by East, and blew very hard; from the fourth day at noon till the fift day at noone I sayled South-west Westerly seven leagues. The sixt day, the winde was at South-east cleere weather, at noone I found the shippe in 73. degrees, the North Cape bearing by my computation, East South-east Easterly. The seventh day at noone, I found the ship in 72. degrees 22. minutes, indifferent faire weather. And from the seventh day at noone, till the eight day at noone I sayled foure and twentie leagues, the course South South-west, the wind at South-east and by East, at which time it beganne to be very foggie, and the winde came to the South, but immediatly it was calme, and continued so till mid-night. Then the wind came to the North, little wind, and at a South Sunne the ninth day, I had sayled South seven leagues. From the ninth day at noone till the tenth day at that time I sayled South, and ranne seven leagues South, it being calme most part of the day, with much rayne and fogges. From twelve the tenth day, till noone the eleventh day, I sayled South and by West, and ranne seventeene leagues, the wind Northerly. And from the eleventh day at noone, till the twelfth at that time, I sayled South and by West eighteene leagues, the winde at North North-west faire weather. From noone the twelfth day, untill twelve at noone the thirteenth day, I sayled South and by West fortie eight leagues, the wind betweene the North, and the West North-west gustie weather. From the thirteenth at noone, till the fourteenth at noone, I sayled South and by West fortie five leagues, the wind betwixt the West North-west, and the West South-west gustie weather, latitude 64. degrees 21. minutes. From the fourteenth day at noone, till the fifteenth day at that time, I sayled South and by West nine and twentie leagues, at which time I observed and found the ship in 62. degrees 53. minutes faire weather, the wind at North. *In 62. degrees* At foure of the clocke the same day, I saw Skutsnesse in *15. minutes.* Norway seventeene leagues off, and bearing South-east, from whence I hold it superflous to write it, being a place well knowne. The last of August I arrived at London, Blessed be God for ever and ever. Amen.

A briefe note what Beasts, Fowles, and Fishes were seene in this Land.

BEasts : Buckes, and Does, white Beares and Foxes, of colour dunne and grey.

Fowles : white Partridges, a small land Bird, like a Sparrow, partly white, and partly browne, a Fowle with a combe and a tayle like a Cock, a redde Fowle of the bignesse of a Pidgeon ; a white Fowle with a greene bill, the top of the bill of it and the eyes were redde, with blacke feet. Wild Geese, Coluidines, Gulls, Sea-mewes, *The Coluidine* Willockes, Noddies, Ice-birds, Reeks, and Sea-pidgeons. *is as big as a*

Fishes : great store of Whales, Gramposes, Mohorses, *Mallard, the* the white fish I spake of the seventh of June, a small *male is neerer* fish like Cuplen, likewise I saw the bones of Cods, or *of the colour,* Haddocks ; but could take no fish : I often looked for *and the female browne.* Shel-fish, but could take none : divers of my company did see two Beavers.

23

Chap. II.

A Commission for Jonas Poole our Servant, appointed Master of a small Barke called the Elizabeth, of fiftie tunnes burthen, for Discoverie to the Northward of Greenland, given the last day of March 1611.

I N as much as it hath pleased Almightie God, through the industry of your selfe and others, to discover unto our Nation a Land lying in eightie degrees toward the North-pole: We are desirous not only to discover farther to the Northward along the said Land, to find whether the same be an Iland or a Mayne, and which way the same doth trend, either to the Eastward or to the Westward of the Pole, as also whether the same be inhabited by any people, or whether there be an open Sea farther Northward then hath beene alreadie discovered. For accomplishing of all which our desires, we have made choice of you, and to that end have entertayned you into our service for certayne yeares upon a stipend certayne: not doubting, but you will so carrie your selfe in the businesse, for which you were so entertayned, as God may be glorified, our Countrey benefited, your selfe credited, and we in our desires satisfied. And for your better instruction to proceed in this your Voyage, we have thought good to set downe our opinions what course wee thinke fit to be observed in the same: which is, That forasmuch as by your owne report of the great store of Whales in those Seas, wee are at an extraordinary charge this yeare, of setting out a ship and men for that purpose, which ship is called the Marie Margaret of London, in burthen one hundred and fiftie tunnes or thereabout: Our meaning is, that you doe keepe company with the said ship, and not to leave her, till God send you to the places,

Poole entertayned by a certaine stipend. He was as I have heard, miserably and basely murthered betwixt Ratcliffe and London after his returne from this Voyage.

[III.iv.708.]

where she may make her Voyage : which by your report should be at a place named by you the last yeare 1610. Whale Bay.

And God sending you to the said place, we would have you to stay there the killing of a Whale, or two or three, for your better experience hereafter to expedite that businesse, if through extremitie of the Ice you should be put from your Discoveries. And in the meane time while you are staying about killing of the Whale, you may cause some of your people to bee searching the Coast with their Shallops for Whale finnes, Morses teeth, Ambergreese, or any other commodities, that may be found upon that Coast. And having thus stayed a convenient time with the said great ship for the purpose above specified, wee would have you then to proceed on your Discoverie for the satisfying of our expectations formerly mentioned, which is, to discover further to the North Pole as farre as *Further dis-* possibly you can, and how the Land alreadie discovered *coverie to the* .doth trend, and whether there be any inhabitants in the *North.* said Land, and whether there be an open Sea to the Northward beyond the said land. And in this your coasting the land, we doubt not but you will endeavour with your Shallops to gather up all the Whale finnes you can finde, to kill the Morses which you can come by on land, and to reserve the teeth and blubber to the most advantage that may bee, the better to beare out the great charge which you know we are at in these Discoveries. And to that end we have laden in you eleven Tunnes of emptie caske.

And having spent so much time in this your Discoverie, and in gathering up of such commodities as that Coast will affoord, and as the season of the yeere will permit you, then we would have you returne for England, and in your way homeward to touch at the place where you left the Mary Margaret, to see if shee be not gone ; and finding her there, and that the time of the yeere will permit, wee would have you melt your Blubber into Oile before your comming from thence, to avoid the great trouble and inconvenience you know we fell into the last yeere 1610. by bringing the same hither in Blubber. But if the said ship should chance to be full fished, and so to be gone before your comming thither, yet we would have you stay there, or at Cherie Iland some small time to melt your Blubber : to which end we have appointed Thomas Edge our servant in that ship to leave a Copper, and such necessaries as shall serve your turne, for the performing of that businesse, behinde him ; and have delivered him likewise advertisements at that place of their proceedings in the voyage, and of their intent, what course they purpose to take, together with their opinions, what course they would have you take.

Thomas Edge.
See sup. l. 3.
c. 2.

In these matters of Discoveries and uncertaine Voyages, the varietie of occurrences and Sea dangers is such, as we cannot directly prescribe a course certaine to be held : yet we hold it fitting to set downe Our opinions of the needfull : which are, that at your first departure out of England you keepe counsell together, and agree upon your places of meetings, if by tempest of weather you chance to bee separated ; still shaping your course directly for Chery Iland, where we would have you stay. And if at your comming thither, you finde the same cleere of Ice, and that there be Morses on shoare, then wee would have you to worke upon them, as time and opportunitie will permit, alway having respect to your intended voyage. And having dispatched your businesse in that place, wee would have you depart in company together for The Whale Bay, as aforesaid, and to follow our instructions formerly set downe to be done in that place. And having performed what may be done in the parts beyond Cherie Island, and so returning backe againe for England, we hold it fit you make your Rendezvous againe at the said Cherie Iland, and there to stay the one for the other, and to be killing of the Beasts there till the last of August, if neede bee. And if it happen that one ship doe arrive there before the other, and no Morses come on shoare, then wee would have them spend the time in searching for the Lead Ore,

Cherie Iland.

or any other Minerall matter that may be like to be of
worth upon the said Land.   And thus having stayed at
Cherie Iland till the last of August the one for the other,
and not meeting together, the ship so staying having
made her Voyage, wee would have her to returne directly
for England, and to leave a Note in writing of the day of
her departure.   This is our opinion.   Notwithstanding,
if upon better grounds you shall among your selves finde
a convenienter course to be held for the good of the
Voyage, and the benefit of us the Adventurers, wee leave
it to your selves to agree upon, as time and opportunitie
shall serve.

And for the avoyding of an Objection heretofore used,
That the want of sufficient victuals hath beene the cause
of the overthrow of the Voyages by speedier returne
home, then otherwise they would; wee have thought fit
to set downe the quantitie of victuals delivered aboord
your ship in this our Commission, to the intent to cleere
our selves and our Agent of that imputation, and to lay
the blame on your selves, if by default the same be evill
husbanded.   The particulars are these.   Beefe, 22.^{c} 3.
quarters, 18^{li}.   Bisquit 30.^{c} Beere 14. Tunnes.   Fish, 200.
of Haberdin, and halfe an hundred Lings.   Cheese 300.^{c}
weight.   Butter three Firkins.   Oyle three Gallons.
Pease ten Bushels.   Oate-meale five bushels.   Candels,
sixe dosen.   Aquavitæ, thirtie Gallons.   Vinegar one
rundlet of twentie Gallons.   This proportion of victuals
will last you seven or eight moneths with good husbandry,
together with the helpes of Fish, Fowle, and Beasts that
are to be had in abundance upon those Coasts.   So that
we hope you shall have no cause to the contrary, but
cheerfully to goe forward in your businesse, whereby not
onely the small Barke you goe in, but the great Ship may
come home fully laden with one commoditie or other,
which we doubt not but by your diligence and good
endevours you may attayne unto.

But if you shall chance by extremitie of Ice, or other-   [III. iv. 709.]
wise to be put backe from your discoverie, or from

obtayning commodities upon the coast of Greenland, whereby to lade both ships; then we would have you stay at Cherie Iland, or other Ilands thereabout so long time as possibly you can, and as the season of the yeere will permit you, to finish the rest of your voyage. And if there bee sufficient lading betweene you both to lade the bigger ship, wee would have her to bee dispatched from thence with all speede, and you to stay there as long as you may conveniently for the good of the Voyage: which the more beneficiall it prooveth, the more it will be for your credit, and we will not be unthankefull at your returne.

We would have you at every place of meeting with the Mary Margaret, to deliver to Thomas Edge our servant a particular Note of what goods you have taken into your ship. And at your last lading place we would have you make a generall invoyce of the whole Cargason of goods laden in your ship, and having signed the same, to seale it up, and direct the same to our Agent resident in London. And if you doe chance to meete with the Mary Margaret at or after your last Port of lading, we would have you deliver a Copy of the said invoyce to our servant Thomas Edge for our better satisfaction, what casualtie soever might happen by the way, and at any hand to have such an invoyce ever readie sealed, and for mortalities sake put up in some sure place of custodie.

We hold it fit, that you Jonas Poole should be as grand Pilot in this voyage to the Northward. And therefore we would have you to accompany the great ship, and to bring her to the places of fishing for the Whale; or to any other place, which you out of your experience shall thinke fit to bring her for the good of the Voyage and benefit of the Adventurers. And our will is, That Steven Bennet Master of the said great ship together with the rest of the company in that ship, doe follow the said Jonas Pooles directions, as they will answer the contrarie upon their perils at their comming home.

And for that heretofore the Company have beene abused

by lewd and bad people, who have imbeseled part of that which by our great charges and adventures hath beene obtayned : Our minde and will is, That you Jonas Poole doe make search in your owne ship, that none of our Whale finnes, Morses teeth, Oyle, or any other commodities gathered at our charge, be imbeseled or carried away by any of the Mariners, who will looke to have the uttermost of their wages paid them, and to bee fed with meate and drinke sufficient. And God sending you into England, we would have you suffer none of your people to goe on shoare unsearched : neither would we have you to leave the ship till your comming into the River of Thames, that we give you order to the contrarie. And if you chance to be winde bound upon the coast, you may send up one of your people with your Letter, but not to come your selfe on shoare till our farther order, as aforesaid.

The like order we would have Steven Bennet to use in his ship, by vertue of this our Commission, which we have ordered to Thomas Edge our servant to see performed accordingly.

And in as much as we have agreed here with a Tanner for all the Morses hides which wee kill and bring into England, and have sent men of purpose for the flaying, salting, and ordering of the same, whereof we have appointed one to goe in your ship: We would have you reserve the said hides, and floore your ship therewith in stead of ballast. And if you obtayne a greater quantitie then you can bring away with you, having alwayes regard to commodities of more value, which are Oyle, Teeth, and Whales finnes, that none of them be left behind ; We would have you leave the said overplus of hides in some convenient place, till the next yeere, that we send more store of shipping.

Agreement with a Tanner for Morses hides.

[A Commission

A Commission for Thomas Edge our servant, appointed to goe as our Factor in the Ship called the Mary Margaret, of the burthen of one hundred and fiftie Tunnes, for the killing of the Whale and Morses upon the coast of Greenland, or any other place in the North Ocean: Given the 31. of March, 1611.

Adventures and losses in first Discoveries.

YOu are not ignorant of our imploying you heretofore in two severall Voyages to Cherie Iland. The first whereof, by reason of one Duppers going thither, together with certaine men of Hull, glutting the said place, prooved to us a thousand pound losse of our principall. As also in the second Voyage, because you could not come to set footing upon the said Iland, by reason of the abundance of Ice lying round about the same sixteene leagues compasse till the twentie eight of July, by which occasion our whole charge of setting out that yeeres adventure had beene lost, if the refuge to lade our ship backe againe from Saint Michael the Archangel in Russia had not holpen us: yet notwithstanding that helpe, wee lost by that voyage above five hundred pounds. We entring into due consideration of the premisses, doe not impute the cause of these our losses unto you; but to the accidents then happening contrarie to our expectation: yet these losses growing upon us in the times of your imployment, we can doe no lesse then put you in minde thereof, to the intent to incourage and stirre up your minde to doe your uttermost indevour to further the businesse in this your third imployment, that we may recover our selves of the losses formerly sustained. And for that end we have made choice of you againe to goe as our Factor in the Ship Mary Margaret, of one hundred and fiftie Tunnees, the Master being Steven Bennet, for the killing of the Whale: And to that end, as you well know, have bin at charge of

[III.iv.710.] procuring of six men of Saint John de Lux, accustomed to that function: whose names are as followeth: videlicet, Juan de Bacoyne, Juan de Agerre, Martin de Karre, Marsene de Horisada, Domingo de Sarria, and Adam de Bellocke: which men wee would have to be used very kindely and friendly during this their voyage, whereby being strangers and leaving their owne Countrie to doe us service, they may have no just cause of complaint, but rather to be incouraged to doe us service hereafter, if there be cause. And although it be our meaning they should be encouraged by all good and curteous usage to be readie to doe us service, yet we will have you together with our owne people and Mariners imployed in this Voyage, to observe and diligently put in practise the executing of that businesse of striking the Whale, as well as they: And likewise to know the better sorts of Whales from the worser, whereby in their striking * they may choose the good, and leave the bad. And to that end we doe set you downe here under, the severall sorts of Whales, together with the differences of goodnesse betweene the one and the other, as we have gathered the same by information from men of excellencie in that businesse: who make knowne unto us, that there are eight severall kindes of Whales, all differing the one from the other in quantitie and qualitie. Which for your better instruction, we have thought good to set downe in this our Commission.

Sixe Biscainers procured for killing of the Whale (as I have heard) by Woodcocks advise, who had lived and been imployed with them in Grand Bay, &c.

*This was a conceit, as if all places had choice of all kindes, which experience hath since taught otherwise.

The first sort of Whales, is called the Bearded Whale, which is black in colour, with a smooth skinne, and white under the chops; which Whales is the best of all the rest: and the elder it is, the more it doth yeelde. This sort of Whale doth yeelde usually foure hundred, and sometimes five hundred finnes, and betweene one hundred and one hundred and twentie Hogsheads of Oyle. The second sort of Whale is called Sarda, of the same colour and fashion as the former, but somewhat lesse, and the finnes not above one fathom long, and yeeldeth in Oyle, according to his bignesse, sometimes eightie, sometimes a hundred Hogsheads. The third sort of Whale is called

See of the kinds of Whales sup. 471. I have added this to be compared with that, for further light.

Trumpa, being as long as the first, but not so thicke, of colour Grey, having but one Trunke in his head, whereas the former have two. He hath in his mouth teeth of a span long, and as thicke as a mans ·wrist, but no fins: whose head is bigger then either of the two former, and in proportion farre bigger then his body. In the head of *Spermaceti or* this Whale is the Spermaceti, which you are to keepe in *Permaciti as* Caske apart from your other Oyle: you may put the Oyle *the vulgar·call* you finde in the head and the Spermaceti altogether, and *it.* marke it from the other Oyle, and at your comming home, we will separate the Oyle from the Spermaceti. The like is to be done with the Oyle of this sort of Whale, which is to be kept apart from the Oyle of the other Whales. The reason is, that the Oyle of this sort of Whale being boyled, will be as hard and white as Tallow, which to be mingled with the other Oyle being liquid, would make the same to shew as footie Oyle, and so consequently spoyle both, and be of little value: you are therefore to be very carefull to keepe the Oyle of this sort of Whale apart, as well of the head as of the body, for the reasons before mentioned. In this sort of Whale is likewise found the *Ambergreese.* Ambergreese, lying in the entrals and guts of the same, being of shape and colour like unto Kowes dung. We would have you therefore your selfe to be present at the opening of this sort of Whale, and cause the residue of the said entrals to be put into small Caske, and bring them with you into England. We would have the Master also to be by at the opening of this Whale, and to be made privie of the packing of those Barils. And although it be said, that the Ambergreese is onely in this Whale and in none other, yet we would not have you be absent at the opening of any other: but if you see cause to make a reservation of the entrals of every Whale, that you shall perceive to be cause of the least suspect to have any of the said Ambergreese, being a matter, as you know, of good worth, and therefore not slightly to be regarded. The Teeth likewise of this sort of Whale we would have you cause to be reserved for a triall; as also any other matter extraordinarie that you shall observe in the same. This Whale is said to yeelde in Oyle fortie Hogsheads, besides the Spermaceti. The fourth sort, &c. as sup. 471. 472.

And in as much as industrie and diligence are two principall steps to atchieve great enterprises, and negligence and idlenesse are enemies to the same; we would have you in this charge committed unto you, to imbrace the one, and to avoide the other: and to shew that example of paines taking to the rest of the company of your Ship in your owne person, as well in setting them on worke, as in putting your owne hand to the businesse when neede requireth, as that there be no idle time spent, but that every one be imployed in some businesse or other in helping to kill the Whale, or in searching the Bayes along the coast for Whales, Ambergreese, Morses teeth, or any other strange thing, that may be found upon that coast, or in killing the Morses, Beares, or anything that may make profit toward our great charges.

Touching directions for your keeping company together with the Elizabeth, and of the course we thinke fitting for the Master of that Ship to observe, we have set the same downe at large in our Commission delivered to Jonas Poole, a Copie whereof we deliver you herewith, for your better instructions, to observe what is to be done on both your behalfes for the good of the Voyage: which our Commission, we would have you strictly observe, unlesse upon some speciall occasion to us unknowne, and by the consent of the principall Officers in both the Ships, you shall see just cause to the contrary.

You have with you an order set downe by the Lords of his Majesties privie Counsell, for the maintaining of our Charter: which we would have you make knowne to any of our Nation, that you may chance to meete withall either at Cherie Iland, or upon any of those coasts. And if any stranger doe offer you violence, or doe disturbe you in your trade, you may both defend your selves, and maintaine your trade to the uttermost of your powers, &c.

The rest as not so necessary to the publike is omitted.

[III.iv.711.]

Chap. III.

A briefe Declaration of this my Voyage of discovery to Greeneland, and towerds the West of it, as followeth : being set forth by the right Worshipfull Sir Thomas Smith, Governour of the right Worshipfull Company of new Trades, &c. written by Jonas Poole.

Foure Ships.

Ee set sayle at Blacke-wall the eleaventh of Aprill, 1611. with foure Shippes: The one called the Mary-margaret, of burthen one hundred and fiftie Tuns, with nine and fortie Men and Boyes. The next the Elizabeth, of burthen sixtie Tuns, with eighteene Men and Boyes. The third was called the Amitie, of burthen seaventie Tunnes, with foure and twentie Men and Boyes. The fourth was called the Resolution, with about sixteene Men and Boyes: the Resolution was appointed to goe to Saint Nicholas in Russia, in hope to make two Voyages thither *See Sup. l. 3.* this yeare. The Amitie was to goe to Pichora or Nova-zembla, there to see if they could make a Voyage by way of trade, or by killing of Mohorses, &c. The Mary-margaret was appointed to keepe the Elizabeth companie to Greeneland, abovesaid, there to kill the Whale, for which purpose we had sixe men of Saint John de Luz, with all things fitting for that purpose. The Elizabeth was appointed to see if it weare possible to passe from Greeneland towards the Pole, and to search in those Seas what likelihood of a passage that way, &c. But before we were as farre to the Northwards as the latitude of sixtie *The Ships separated.* five, we were all separated, by reason of contrarie windes and foule weather: the Elizabeth, in which Ship I was, was stoked, that the water which was in her could not come to the Pumpe, but lay upon the balast, which was the cause we could beare no sayle to keepe the Mary-margaret companie.

Yet by the thirteenth day of May I came to Cherie Iland, and the foureteenth I spake with the Amitie. The sixteenth day I met with the Mary-margaret, which kept mee companie to Greeneland, but in our passage thither we saw a banke of Ice to the East wards of us, above fortie leagues long. The nine and twentieth of May, we anchored in a place named (by me the last yeare) Cross-road, but before we got thither, wee were much troubled with Ice and contrarie windes, and we found almost all the sounds full of Ice, that the Biscainers could not strike one Whale, although they saw divers, which as they said were of the best kinde of Whales.

Cherie Iland.

Crosse Rode.

Ice a hinderance to Whale killing and discovery.

I staid there till the sixteenth of June, in which time we set up our shalops and ranged some part of the Coast, but found little, by reason the beaches were covered with Snow and Ice. Likewise in the same time, I was put out of the roade with Ice, and stood out West and by North into the Sea about foureteene leagues, where I found a banke of Ice; then I stood into the sound againe and got off the Shalop which was in the roade, at which time (which was about the eleaventh of June) I stood to the Sea againe and had a storme at South, which sunke our Shalop, and I saw the Ice lye close to the Land in 80. degrees. Then I went into Crosse roade againe, and had a Shalop from the Mary-margaret, and because I perceived the Ice above said to lye close to the land, and unpossible to passe that way there running verie strong Tides, in the which it is dangerous dealing with the Ice : I determined to stand to the Southwards alongst the said Ice, to see if I could finde the Sea open that way, and so get to the Westwards of the said Ice, and then proceeded on my Voyage : but I found it to lye the next hand South South-west and South-west and by South, and ranne alongst it about one hundred and twentie leagues, at which time I supposed my selfe neere Groenland, as it is laied downe by Hudson and others, and called Hold with

80. Degrees.

New discovery. Hold with Hope.

hope: I ranne neere fortie leagues to the Westwards of the Eastermost part of the said Land, as it is laid downe, and by my accounts I was to the Southwards of it, neere *Store of* the latitude 74. degrees, where I saw abundance of Whales *Whales.* by the sides of the Ice; for I sailed all this time sometimes in, and sometimes by the said Ice, and sounded most commonly each watch, but had no ground at 160. 140. 180. and 200. fathomes.

Then the winde came to the North-west, and I perceiving the Ice to trend still to the Southwards, determined to stand to Greeneland, from whence I came, there to make my Voyage and likewise to try the certaintie concerning the misplacing of the Land, but the next day, being about the seaven and twentieth of June, the winde came to the North, and I stood for Cherie Iland, and came to it the nine and twentieth of the same Moneth, where I found that place of my being, when I supposed I should have *Cherie Iland.* found Land, did beare from Cherie Iland West and by South, above one hundred twentie five leagues. When *Three hundred* I came to the Iland I saw about three hundred Morses *Morses.* on land, but a storme comming they went all into the Sea.

The twelfth of July, we slue above two hundred; and by the three and twentieth day wee had taken all their fat Hides and Teeth, which with the Victuals we had laded the ship: then I determined to hale up a shalop to goe to Greeneland, to search if I could finde any Land or Ilands, that might prove beneficiall the next yeere, and likewise *[III.iv.712.]* to search for Teeth and Whales Finnes. The foure and twentie, and five and twentie dayes, it was very much wind at North, which caused the Sea to go so high that we could not land. Yet at eight of the clock at night the wind ceased, and I went on land where I found *Mary* certayne of the Marie Margarets men, by whom I under-*Margaret lost.* stood, that the said ship was cast away, and that Master Thomas Edge servant to the right Worshipfull Company, &c. with Stephen Bennet Master of the said shippe, and others to the number of thirtie persons, were arrived on

36

the South side in three Boats, and that they parted from two Boats in Greenland with nine men in them.

Immediately Master Edge and Master Bennet came aboard, and I weighed and stood to the West side of the Iland, and anchored there, and put neere one hundred Morse-hides on land, and some emptie caske, and haled up a shallop. The six and twentieth day about noone, we weighed and stood to the South-west side of the Iland, and sent men on land to hale up two shallops there. And at mid-night I set sayle for Greenland, carrying with mee two Biscaine shallops, determining there to try the Blubber of those Morses we had killed, and bring it to Oyle, and to bring all the Oyle, Teeth, and Finnes which they had gotten in that Countrey. And after divers winds, but indifferent faire weather, I arrived at Blacke-point the last of July, and having the wind at North, I was per-swaded by divers that had gone that way to go betwixt the Iland and the Mayne, but when I was almost through, and in sight of that place where the Mary Margaret lyeth sunke, I could not find water enough for the ship, yet I was told there was enough by divers that had gone that way in the shallops. Here we stayed two dayes to buoy the channell, which is shoald and narrow, for we had at three quarters floud, but eleven foot water.

The third of August I got over, and about eight of the clocke at night, I anchored neere the Mary Margaret, the Sunne being in 79. degrees, and there I found a shippe of Hull conducted thither by one Nicholas Woodcock, he *Ship of Hull.* being in one of the Boats which stayed in Greenland, when those came from thence that came to Cherrie Iland. The ships name was called the Hopewell, one Thomas Marmaduke being Master. Here we found that hee had slaine above one hundred and thirtie Mohorses, which were left on land when Master Thomas Edge came from thence with the Boats aforesaid, and we did determine to kill at my arrivall. Assoone as the ship was moored, wee got out Blubber and sent it on land to bee brought into Oyle, and wee followed our worke till the seventh of

August at noone, at which time having Oyle by the ships side, we put out all the Blubber which was in hold, save two tuns and a halfe, supposing the ship had ballast enough in her, for there was above twelve tuns of Hides, which were the chiefest cause of the losse of the ship, and nine tunnes of Oyle, and above seven tunnes of ballast, a Hogshead and a Barrell of Teeth: besides halfe a tunne of stones, all which was about nine and twentie tunne weight, and to any unpartiall mans judgement, sufficient to shift a Barke of sixtie tunnes. But as the last But went out of her, the ship began to held, and with all a great many men went to leeward, there being at that time above forty aboard. Then the hides which lay in hold, slid to leeward, and brought her altogether downe, then every man made shift to save his life, and I being farre from the hatches, could not get up so soone as others did.

Double danger. At which time I saw death before mine eyes two wayes, one if I stayed in hold, I was sure to be drowned: the other if I went up the hatches, I was in election to be slaine; for downe at the hatches fell hogsheads of beere and divers other things, the least of them being sufficient to beate a mans bones, and in attempting to get up, I was beaten downe twice and hurt. But it was not the will of God to take my life from mee then, but to revive me, to plucke me even from the jawes of death, and by swimming and crawling I got into the Sea cleere of the ship where a Boat tooke me up, and blessed bee God, no man perished at that so dangerous an accident. We being all got into three Boats, went to the Hull ship, where we found but small comfort: for Duke told us plainly, wee should not come aboard his ship, and caused Pikes and Launces to bee brought to keepe us out. Then Master Edge and divers others desired him to let mee come aboard, which hee did, and with much adoe I got aboard, having mine head broke to the skull, and my brow that one might see the bare bones, and by mine eare I had a sore wound, likewise the ribs on my right side were all broken and sore bruised, and the collar bone of my left shoulder is broken, besides my backe was so sore, that I could not suffer any man to touch it.

That which followeth, being further accusation of Marmaduke, is omitted. And I have here added out of his Brother Randolph Poole their returne; omitting the former part of his Relations of the same Voyage.

In this our great distresse, Thomas Marmaduke Master of the shippe of Hull, professed great kindnesse towards us, promising us passage, and that he would try if he could recover our ship: but hee deferred the time one whole weeke, till shee was full of oze, so that when wee came to weigh her, but her Cables burst, and so we left her to all our sorrowes, without hope of recoverie. Then we went aboard the ship of Hull, which God had prepared for our succour, where our Merchant agreeing for the fraight, we got the goods aboard; namely, about twentie, or one and twentie tunnes and an halfe of Oyle, and a Barrell of Beares Oyle, about tenne tunnes of Whales Finnes bound up in an hundred and six bundels, in every one thirtie Finnes, and in some more, five Hogsheads of Morses Teeth, and one and twentie odd paire. And if our ship had not miscarried, the Voyage had beene much better.

The nineteenth of August, we directed our course for England, the weather being reasonable faire, and the wind for the most part betwixt the North and the West: and wee continued our course homeward all that moneth. [III. iv. 713.]

Upon Tuesday the third of September, about two of the clocke in the morning, we were imbayed with land, and were neere the shoare before we were aware. Wee steered backe North and by East: and at twelve of the clocke we found our selves to be on the West side of the Iles of Orkney, and steered East into a great sound, called Pentlow Fryth, where wee beeing entred there came a Boat from the shoare, which brought us fresh meat, and one of the men directed us through the Sound. This Sound lyeth in the latitude of 58. degrees and 36. minutes, and the course through, is East North-east, and West South-west, it floweth there on the change day, South

They returne homeward. September 3.

Orkney Ilands. Pentlow Fryth, in 58. degrees 36. minutes.

39

South-east and North, North-west halfe a tyde, nine foote
high or thereabout. At the entrance in on the North side,
there is an high red Mountayne, and the Sound there is
twelve miles over: but farther in the land is somewhat
lower, and the Sound narrower. You may sayle along the
North shoare two miles off the land in fortie or fiftie
fathomes; and on the said shoare about foure miles East
South-east. From the red Cliffe there is a Bay, into
which you may steere North by West, giving the West
point of the entrance into the said Bay a good birth: for
there the water is shoald and fowle ground: but in the
middle of the entrance, 30. 20. 18. 12. 10. 6. and 5.
fathomes: but wee anchored in 10. fathomes, fine sandie
ground.

The fift of September at an East South-east Sunne wee
set sayle, keeping our course above mentioned, leaving
five small Ilands on our larboord side, and one Iland on
our starboord side: and so keeping an high Cliffe, which
lyeth into the Sea on Scotland side, open of a low Land in
the sound on the same shoare, we sayled out as before is
said.

Upon the   day at a North Sunne, we anchored in
Humber mouth: there it floweth on the change day West
South-west. Upon the eight day we arrived at Hull,
safely and well in body, but much distressed and impayred
in our states, which God at his good pleasure can restore.

At our first comming to this Country of Greenland, the
Mountaynes and Valleyes thereof, except it were some
few places, were all covered with snow: but ere we went
away, the tops of the high Hils, and the lower Plaines
appeared greene with Mosse, and some little quantitie of
grasse. This Countrey, and likewise the seas in these
parts, are subject to marvellous thicke and mistie weather,
especially when the sunne, with his most forcible heat
Many fat melteth the Ice and snow, whose vapours obscure the light
Deere, white of the sunne, making small difference betweene the day
Beares, white, there, and the irkesome night in other places.
grey, and dun We found in this Countrey many fat Deere, which we
Foxes.

40

killed with our Peeces and Dogges at our pleasure, which was a great refreshing to us in that unquoth place : many white Beares, with white, grey, and dunne Foxes. We found also abundance of Fowle : namely, Culuidines, sea *Abundance of* Pidgeons, white land Partridges, wild Geese, Willockes, *sundry* and many other Fowles. Among which I noted the nature *Fowles.* of one, which we called an Allen; who (like to the great *Allen a* fishes, which eate up the small, or like to some great men, *devouring* which devoure all the labours of the poore) when some *Fowle.* smaller Birds have gotten any thing, then he leaveth not beating of them, till they have cast up what they have eaten, which he laying hold of devoureth up : and so with little meate in their gorges, and few feathers on their backes, he leaveth them to get more, not for themselves but for him. We found on the shoares many huge *Many huge* Morses. *Morses.*

There is great store of fresh water in every Valley, which proceedeth most of the melted snow. On every Beech is great plentie of drift wood, but never a bush nor tree groweth in those quarters, as farre as we have hitherto discovered.

Chap. IIII.

A Relation written by Jonas Poole of a Voyage to Greenland, in the yeere 1612, with two ships, the one called the Whale ; the other the Sea-horse, set out by the Right Worshipfull the Muscovie Merchants.

He seventh of Aprill, 1612. wee set sayle at Blacke-wall, and went to Gravesend.

The third of May we came to Cherie *Chery Iland.* Iland, where we found a ship of Holland, in which one Alan Salowes an English-man was Pilot. The same day about a North sunne we anchored on the West side of the Iland.

The fourth, we trimmed a shallop which I left there the

last yeere : and Alan Salowes went aboard our Admirall, and Master Russell sent for Master Thomas Edge, Master Arthington, John Mason, and my selfe : where wee had some speech about detayning him, and to have brought him into England : but in the end hee was let goe. At a North sunne we sent our shallop to the South-east side of the Iland to fetch a shallop, which was left there the last yeere : but they could not get thither for Ice, and came [III.iv.714.] aboard againe at an East North-east Sunne the fift day : at which time we weighed, and stood to the Westward, but immediatly we altered our course, and stood toward the Iland againe among the Ice ; and about a West North-west Sunne wee sent our Skiffe and Shallop to fetch the Shallop aforesaid. The winde was at North and by West, frostie weather with snowe.

The eight, wee stood toward Cherie Iland againe, and were faire by it at a South sunne : at which time the winde came to the South-east, and wee saw the Hollander standing with us. Then we altered our course, and sayled West North-west, determining, if hee followed us, to stay for him. At ten of the clock at night hee came to us : and the Admirall sent his shallop aboord of him to command him to be gone out of our companie : and at a North sunne hee stood away from us, and sayled North and by East, and we lay by the lee.

The twentieth at a South Sunne we saw our Consort, and spake with them, and they told us, that they had almost split their ship with a piece of Ice, which brake nine of their Timbers, so that they had five foot water in hold.

The one and two and twentie dayes, wee plyed to windward, the winde being at North faire weather. And at Blacke Point wee saw great store of Ice driving to the South. At eight of the clocke at night Blacke Point did beare from mee East and by North nine leagues. And the three dayes past we saw great store of Whales within ten or twelve leagues off the Land.

Blacke point.

Great store of Whales.

Cape Cold.   The three and twentieth we were faire off Cape Cold ;

where Master Edge and Master Arthington went with
the Basks in their Shallops for Crosse-rode, in hope to
kill some Whales. And we saw store of Whales in the
Sea.

The five and twentieth we got into Foule Sound, all *Foule Sound.*
the Sounds being full of Ice; and the Shallops came
aboord and brought some Venison, which was very leane.
And at six of the clock the Basks went with the Shallops
to Faire Foreland, to see if they could kill a Whale : and *Faire*
at a North-west Sunne Master Edge went with a Shallop, *Foreland.*
to see if Crosse-rode were open.

The six and twentieth, the two ships abovesaid came
into Foule Sound : one of them was that Hollander before
mentioned; the other was a ship of London, called The
Diana, whereof one Thomas Bustion dwelling at Wapping *The Diana of*
wall, was Master. *London.*

The seven and twentieth, Alane Salowes came aboord
of our ship, and told us, that his Merchant had broke his *Dutch Mer-*
necke downe a Cliffe. The same day the Hollander and *chant brake his*
the Diana stood to the Southward. The winde was at *necke.*
North North-west, and Northwest, which kept the Ice in
the Sounds. The twentie eight, we sent the long Boat
and our Shallop to Brokennesse, with a Shallop of ten
Tunnes, there to be set up. The winde was at West with
snowe and frost. The same day the Basks came aboord, *Six*
but could kill never a Whale. The winde came to the *Biscayners.*
South South-west, with frost and snowe.

The nine and twentieth, the winde was at South with
much snowe. The same day one of our men dyed,
named John Butcher, having layen sicke about three
weeks. The thirtieth, one Michael Perkins dyed aboord
The Whale. The last of May, the winde was at South;
and wee stood toward the Foreland in 79. degrees. The
same day at midnight, the Chyrurgeon of The Whale
dyed.

The first of June, we stood into Foule Sound, where *June.*
wee saw abundance of Ice drive out with the winde at
East. The second day, the winde was at North and by

*Tho.
Marmaduke.*

*Marmadukes
Discoverie to
82. degrees.*

East, cold frostie weather. All which day wee lay under saile in the mouth of the Sound. The third day, wee spake with Thomas Marmaduke of Hull, in a ship called The Hope well. Wee sent for him to come aboord, but he answered, that he was not well, and sent his Mate Christopher Nayler. The same day, we stood to the mouth of the Sound, but it was covered with Ice. And Marmaduke stood to the Northward; and as we were afterward informed, discovered as farre as 82. degrees; two degrees beyond Hakluyts Headland. The fourth, we sent our shallop on shoare in Foule Sound, to see if any harbour were open to ride in, and to put our Admirall on ground to stop her leake. The same day, our long Boate came to us from Brokennesse. And we turned into the Sound, because we saw the Ice drive out with the winde at South, and blew hard. The fift, we anchored in Foule Sound in seventeene fathoms water and sandie ground, where we saw the place where both the ships lay which wee lost the last yeere, covered with Ice. The same time wee sent our shallop with our Carpenters, to finish the aforesaid shallop at Brokennesse. The winde continued at South; and the Whale turned into the Sound by us, and anchored there at a South-west by South Sunne. The ninth, the Admirals Boate and ours went with provision and men to worke upon a Whale, which the Basks had killed; and we stood toward the Foreland with the ships, where the Whale was killed, the winde at South, thicke foggie weather. And by an East North-east Sunne wee anchored in the mouth of Foule Sound in fifteene fathoms, gray sand with some shells. At a West sunne the Boate came aboord for caske and other provision, and told us, that the Basks had killed two other Whales.

The seventeenth, one Baske named Chapel, tooke five of our English men to him, and they trimmed the shallop to kill the Whale. About a West North-west sunne they went away, the winde at South. The twentieth, the Biscaine shallop came aboord of us from the Foreland,

and told us that they had strooken three Whales, which brake away.

The two and twentieth wee rid still, the winde being at North-west, with snowe and frost. The five and twentieth, we got the Whale on flote, having stopped her leake. We were no sooner off, but it blew most fiercely, so that the Whales long Boate and our shallop brake from the Whales sterne, and were split in pieces on the Ice, that lay on shoare. The same day about a South sunne two men came from Faire Foreland, and told us that Master Edge was come from the South in the Pinnasse, and had spoken with one Nicolas Woodcock an Englishman, which was my Mate to this Countrey of Greenland in the yeere 1610. The said Woodcocke was now Pilot of a ship of Saint Sebastian in Biscay, and rid in Ice Sound. Moreover, they spake with the men of the Boate of the Diana, and saw the Hollanders Boate, but spake not with their men. The two men abovesaid told us likewise, that John Chapel our Baske with five English men had killed a Whale: and betwixt them and another shallop they had slaine another, and had them both on shoare.

The seven and twentieth we rid still, and our Carpenter went to worke to mend the knee of our beake-head. And I went to see what Morses were on Land, where I found neere one hundred and fiftie. The eight and twentieth, the shallop that had all English men in her save one Baske, came aboord for provision, and told me, that they and Johannes Chapel, had slaine a great Whale close by our ship, which towed them off into the Sound, and our long Boate followed them. At the same time we saw sixe Whales close by the ships side as we rode in harbour: and we saw great store in the Sound, and within one houre there were so many about our ships and in the Sound, that we could not count them. About a North-west sunne our long Boate brought the men that strooke the Whale abovesaid, and towed their shallop on land: for the said Whale had sunke her with his taile. The same time our Carpenter went to worke on the broken shallop, and I went

[III.iv.715.]

Woodcock Pilot of a Biscay ship.

The fourth and fifth Whales killed.

The sixt whale killed.

Three hundred Morses.

Biscainers envie.

The seventh Whale killed.

The eight Whale killed.

to the place where the Morses lay, where I found about three hundred on land. Then I went aboord the Whale to get some harping Irons: for they had all, but I could get but one, because the rest of the Basks had laid them up, envying that one Baske, that went with all English men, had done so much, because by their good wills they would not have us to have any insight into this businesse. Moreover, hee that had the chiefest command in this voyage, did greatly condemne the going of so many English men with that one Baske, either for feare they should kill none, and lose all their provision for the said use, or for feare that our men should kill the Whale aswell, and as soone as they; yet was there none of the other Boates but had lost more then they had lost. And as for killing, there was not one Whale killed with one Boate alone, save ours, with all English save the Baske aforesaid, which slue three without the helpe of any other Boate. This day the Basks slue another Whale at the Foreland.

The nine and twentieth, the broken shallop was mended, and I went to the Foreland, to see whether the other shallops would come where the ships rode in harbour, where abundance of Whales were still. The same time the Basks killed another Whale. Then I romaged my ship, and put caske on land. All this day it was calme.

The last of June, one came from the Foreland, and told us, that the Basks had slaine two great Whales. All this day likewise it was calme: and there lay abundance of huge Whales in the harbour about our ships. One of the whales abovesaid, Johannes with the five English men slue without any of the others helpe. For they stood on the land flouting, and saying, that it was unpossible for them to kill him, and would not once lanch their Boates to helpe them: yet hee was one of the greatest that were killed this yeere. All this day the whales lay so thicke about the ship, that some ran against our Cables, some against the Ship, and one against the Rudder. One lay under our beake-head and slept there a long while. At which time our Carpenter had hung a stage close by the water, whereon his tooles lay. And wee durst not molest the said whale for feare he should have overthrowne the stage and drowned all his tooles. In the end he went away, and carried the ships head round, his taile being foule of the Cable.

The first of July, at a North North-east Sunne, the shallops came to kill whales in the harbour where we rid, and strooke three, which all brake away. The same day, Johannes strooke a whale, that smit in the side of his shallop and split it. Now wee perceived the whales to begin to goe out of the Bayes. The second day, the Basks slue three great whales faire by our ships, in lesse then foure houres; which wee with our long Boate and men towed into harbour, and made fast to our ship. And the Basks went with their shallops to Faire Foreland.

The ninth and tenth Whales killed.
The eleventh, twelfth and thirteenth Whales killed.

The seventh day, wee had abundance of Ice about our ships, which with the winde and the tyde drave out off another Sound. The eight, we rid still, and were troubled with much Ice, by reason of a storme that blue at Southwest and by west, &c. The rest is omitted as having nothing of note, but ordinarie accidents.

Chap. V.

[III.iv.716.]

A Journal of the Voyage made to Greenland with five English Ships and a Pinnasse, in the yeere 1613. Written by Master William Baffin.

Ascension day.

Y the providence of Almightie God wee departed from Queenborough the thirteenth day of May with sixe good Ships, viz. The Tigre, Admirall; the Matthew, Vice-admirall; the Sea-horse, called the Gamaliel, the Reare-admirall; the Desire; the Annula; and the Richard and Barnard; with the John and Francis shortly to follow.

The one and twentieth day, faire weather, the winde

Southward, wee still making to the Northwards. This morning wee had sight of Land on the Coast of Norway, it lying East and by North off about twelve or fourteene leagues. This day at noone, we were in the latitude of 61. degrees and 30. minutes, the variation of the Compasse at Scoutes-nes is eight degrees East, it being about ten or twelve leagues off: wee having made a North way halfe East, about thirtie leagues.

The three and twentieth at noone, in the latitude of 65. degrees and 45. minutes, in which place, the Needle of Declination doth dippe under the Horizon 63. degrees and 30. minutes by that Instrument which declineth 54. at London.

Greenland attayned in eighteene dayes.

The thirtieth day, about three of the clocke, wee espied the land of Greenland, being about eight or nine leagues off. The Southwardest part of it bare South-east and by East off it, which shortly wee perceived to bee the Land lying in 76. degrees and 55. minutes, which is called Horne-sound. This Land lyeth by our common Compasse North North-west. Within two houres after we had sight of Land, it began to snowe, and was very cold. This evening the Compasse was varied thirteene degrees West.

The one and thirtieth day, variable weather with snowe, and very cold, and the winde also variable: and in the afternoone the winde was at the North-east. In the morning, wee espied a ship, and about noone we spoke with her, and their Master and Pilot came aboord of us. And

A ship of Saint John de Luz.

Eight Spaniards on the coast.

wee knew them to bee that ship of Saint John de Luz, which had leave of the Companie to fish. And they told us, that there were eight Spaniards on the Coast. Also, wee espied another ship, which we supposed to be a French man, and had one Allan Sallas to their Pilot.

The Generall was Captaine Benjamin Joseph after slaine in fight with a Carrike.

The second of June, in the morning, about five of the clocke, our Generall sent our shallop to a small Pinke, that all this night we saw along the shoare, to bid their Master and Pilot come aboord us, which presently they did. The Masters name was Clais Martin of Horne, and his ship was for Dunkerke, and he told us that he was consorted with another ship that was his Admirall, the Captaines name was Fopp of Dunkerke, and that he was on the Coast. Wee kept the Master and Pilot aboord of us, and sent some of our men aboord of her, and brought her under our lee: and then, we sent their Master aboord againe, charging them to follow us. This afternoone we tooke their shallop with five or sixe men, whereof two were English men, and one Scot, at the Faire foreland.

The fourth day also faire weather. This morning was the first Whale killed. Wee had no night since the three and twentieth of May. The fift day, faire weather, but very cold, the winde North. Wee sayled along the Iland being about eighteene or twentie leagues in length; lying for the most part by the common Compasse North and by West halfe Westward. About nine of the clocke in the afternoone, we saw our other three ships, viz. the Gamaliel, the Desire, and the Richard and Barnard, which lay there to and fro, because they could not goe into their Harbour by reason of the Ice: and also, because there were foure other ships in a Bay or Cove, called Pooppy Bay, or Nickes Cove: and also other ships on the other side in Greene Harbour. We sayled along the drift Ice untill about one or two of the clocke in the morning, at which time, we came to an anchor in the entrance of the Sound, because the Ice came driving out so fast. *Dutch ship. No night. the 23. of May.*

The sixt day, faire weather, the winde variable, till the afternoone: at which time it came to the Northwards. About three in the afternoone we weighed anchor, and about ten of the clocke we came to the foure ships lying in Pooppy Bay: two of them being Hollanders, and one a Rocheller, and the other a ship of Burdeaux. The Masters of the Hollanders came aboord of our ship, to speake with the Generall, both of them being of Amsterdam, and brought a Commission granted by the Grave Maurice, for to fish in this Countrey. But, when they saw our Kings Majesties Commission granted to the worshipfull Companie, they told our Generall, that they would *Divers strangers.*

depart this Coast: having our Generals Ticket to shew to their Adventurers, that they were there, and had made their Port, and how he would not suffer them to fish. We anchored close by the French ship wherein was *Allane Sallas*, being readie to fight, if they refused to come aboord us. So, when we sent our shallop, the Master came presently and their Surgeon, who could speake English. At the first, they denyed that *Sallas* was aboord of them: but, being hardly urged, they confessed that hee and one *Thomas Fisher* an English man were aboord, who were both presently sent for. This *Sallas* was their Pilot, and *Fisher* was their Gunner.

[III.iv.717.]

The seventh day faire weather, we road still at an anchor. This day I observed the latitude of the place, and found it in 78. degrees 24. minutes. The variation of the Compasse is in this place 15. degrees 21. minutes West. About a North Sunne a small ship of Biscay came into the harbour where we roade.

*Lat. 78. deg.
24. minut.
Ship of Biscay.*

The eight day, for the most part snow, the winde Southward. This day the Master of the French ship, being a ship of nine score, or two hundred, called the *Jaques* of *Burdeaux*, agreed with our Generall that hee might fish on the coast: our Generall was to have halfe the Whales he could kill. Also, this day, the Master of the ship of *Rochel*, and the Master of the small ship of *Biscay*, were agreed to depart from the coast.

Snowe.

The ninth day, faire weather. This morning the *Gamaliel* our Reare-Admirall, and the *Desire* weighed anchor to goe for Greene harbour, where two ships lay, one of *Dunkerke*, and the other of Saint Sebastian in *Biscay*. The Captaine of the *Dunkerke*, called *Fopp*, had beene with our Generall, and told him that he would depart from this Coast. Our Generall gave him leave to take the Pilot of the small Pinke, and the other Dutch men he had taken of his; keeping only the English men and the Scots. Also, the two ships of Holland, with the ship of *Biscay*, and that of *Rochel* weighed anchor, and departed from this Harbour. About six of the clocke in the afternoone,

*Greene
harbour.*

came the Master of the ship of Saint Sebastian aboord of us, being brought by one of the Masters Mates of the Desire (they having taken two of his Shallops) to know our Generals pleasure, whether he should have them againe, or no. Our Generall gave them him againe, upon condition, that he would depart the Coast. About a North North-west Sunne, we weighed anchor to goe for Horne-Sound, where we heard, that there were divers ships; the wind Northward a small gale.

The tenth day, faire weather, the winde at North, being very close weather. About a North Sunne we came to an anchor in the entrance of Low Sound, where we saw *Low sound.* two ships ride at anchor. Our Generall sent our shallop to see what ships they were, who found them to bee the two ships of Holland. Also our long Boate went on shoare to set up the Kings Majesties Armes upon a low *His Majesties* point of land, lying a great way off, called Low-nesse. *Armes and a* We set up a Crosse of wood, and nayled the Armes upon *Crosse set up* it. *at Low-nesse.*

The thirteenth day, in the morning, it snowed very fast, *Snowe.* being very thicke weather, the winde variable, we standing off from the land. About seven of the clock it began to cleere up, at which time we espied three ships; and making toward them, at length we perceived them to be the three ships which came from the Bay where we road: the winde also was at East and by South, and blew a very stiffe gale. Then we stood in for the shoare, and spent most of this day in turning up Horne-Sound. And about a North North-west Sunne, at ten a clock wee espied six ships lying at anchor on the South side of the Sound, in a small Bay. The one of them was Captaine Fopp the Dunkerker, who came in before us, and was appointed by our Generall to come into this harbour, and there to stay for us, and to goe to the Foreland, to have his other ship which we kept there. Foure of them were Biscaines of Saint Sebastian; *Thomas* and one of them was in the harbour where we road and *Bonner* found the French ship: The sixt was a ship of Amsterdam, *Englishman,* wherein Thomas Bonner was Master and Pilot, and above *Master and* *Pilot,* twentie English men more. All the Biscaines came aboord of us as soone as we were at an anchor: but Thomas Bonner refused to come, being sent for by our Generall. Our Generall commanded our Gunner to shoot at him, he himselfe discharging the second Ordnance. Then presently he began to set saile, and cut his cable, thinking to get from us: but wee having shot him through three or foure times, they began to weave us, so we sent our shallop and he came aboord. There were five or sixe more of the English men fetched aboord, and some of our men sent to bring her to an anchor, where shee might ride safe: for, shee was almost run ashoare. This was about a North sunne, or eleven a clocke. The Biscaines were charged presently to depart, so soone as they had filled fresh water, which, they said, they wanted; and to bring what Whale finnes they had found, or had taken, or other things.

The fourteenth day, faire weather, the winde at East North-east. This morning one of the Biscaines brought a few Whale finnes aboord of us, and the skin of a Beare, which they had killed. Then was our Boat-swaine sent aboord of them to search their ships, and to bid them depart. Our Generall kept the Holland ship, wherein was Thomas Bonner, to the use of the Companie. This day I observed the latitude of this place by a Quadrant of foure foote Semidiameter, and found it to stand in 76. degrees 55. minutes: the Declination of the Needle under the Horizon, is 67. degrees 30. minutes, pointing to the Northwards: but pointing to the Southwards, it is 80. degrees. The variation of the Compasse is 12. degrees 14. minutes west from the true Meridian: but from our common sayling Compasse it is 17. degrees, because the Compasse is touched five degrees and a halfe to the Eastward, and the variation is to the Westward.

This day in the afternoone, the foure ships of Biscay departed from this Harbour, which is called Horne-Sound: and about a North sunne, I, with the Master Thomas Sherin went ashoare with other, to set up another

76. deg. 55. min. declination 67. deg. 30. min. Variation 12. deg. 14. min.

[III.iv.718.]

Crosse with the Kings Majesties Armes, cast in Lead,
nayled upon it. Then I observed the Sunne upon his
North Meridian, by my foresaid Quadrant, and found it
elevated above the Horizon 10. degrees and thirtie
minutes: but because his heigth at the South Meridian,
and his heigth at the North did not agree, in finding of
the Latitude, I did abate five minutes from each, as the
meane betwixt both: for his altitude at the South Meridian
was 36. degrees 40. minutes, the declination 23. degrees
and 29. minutes.

The fifteenth day, faire weather, the winde in the morning South, but almost calme. This day about noone we
weighed anchor with the ship of Amsterdam, and divers
of her men were fetched aboord us with their Shipper,
and some of our men were sent aboord her with one of
our Masters Mates, called Master Spencer. All this day
it was so calme, that wee were faine to towe our ship.
Our Carpenter did trim up two of the Biscaine Shallops
which they did leave behinde them, and they did leave
divers Hoopes and Caske staved ashoare.

The eighteenth day, faire weather, the winde variable,
we stearing away Northward. This afternoone wee met
with another ship of Biscay, being a ship of two or three
hundred Tunnes. Our Generall, as he did to the rest,
caused her Master and Pilot to come aboord us, to whom
he shewed his Commission, charging them to depart this
Countrey. They, seeing no remedie, were content, so
soone as they had filled fresh water. Wee met with them
off the Southward part of the Iland. Our Generall being
so neere Greene Harbour, where the Gamaliel and the
Desire road, wee went into the Sound to see them, with
this great ship of Biscay, and the ship of Amsterdam.
We found that the entrance of Greene Harbour was quite
stopped with Ice; and ran our ship into it, thinking to get *Abundance of*
through, but wee could not. Then wee got her out *Ice.*
againe, and came to the Bay where wee roade on the other
side of the Sound in Pooppy Bay, or Niches Cove.

The nineteenth day, faire weather, the winde Northward. This day about twelve of the clock we came to an anchor in the foresaid Bay. This afternoone there came another ship of Saint Sebastian into the Bay where wee roade : and about seven of the clocke, the Captaine came aboord of us, who told us that he had lost six of his men and a shallop upon the coast of Groineland, upon an *An Iland in* Iland in the latitude of 72. degrees or thereabouts. This *72 degrees on* was the Master which had beene here the last yeere, and *the Coast of* made a great voyage, Master Woodcocke being their *Groinland.* Pilot. His making so great a voyage, was the cause that so many ships were here this yeere.

The twentieth in the morning, we had newes that the John and Francis was come about two dayes agoe, and *Three and* that they had killed one and twentie Whales at the Fore-*twentie whales* land, and had also killed two at Greene harbour. This *killed.* day it was very close weather with some snowe; the winde North-west. This afternoone the Captaines of the two Biscay ships were commanded to depart this Coast.

The one and twentieth, wee perceived another ship standing toward us. Wee lessened our sailes and stayed for her to see what shee was. At length, we perceived her to bee another Biscaine. About a North sunne we came to an anchor in Greene harbour, by the Gamaliel, and the Desire, and the ship of Burdeaux : and the Biscaine followed us. So soone as they were come to an anchor, their Captaine came aboord of us, to whom our Generall shewed his Commission as he had done to the rest, charging him to depart those Coasts, and told him, that hee would take away some of their shallops. They earnestly intreated him not to take them away, and they would depart : the Captaine offering his bond to our Generall, that if he stayed either in Greenland, Groineland, or Cherie Iland, he would willingly forfait all he was worth. There was another Whale killed in Greene-harbour, in the *A man slaine.* killing whereof there was a man slaine, and a Boate overwhelmed, by too much haste of following him, after the harping Iron was in him.

The three and twentieth day, faire weather, the winde
Northward. This day, and the last night I observed the
latitude of the place where we roade, and found it by both,
to bee in the latitude of 78. degrees 7. minutes: the skie
at both observations being very cleere, where I finde that
there is no sensible error betweene a South observation
and a North, the skie being cleare. But if the skie be
hasie, there will be some difference, as of eight or ten
minutes, being observed on shoare by some large Quadrant
or other Instrument for the purpose, also a South South-
west Moone by the common Compasse, maketh a full Sea
in this place.

Latitude 78.
deg. 7. min.

Note.

*A South South
west Moone
maketh a full
Sea here.*

The ninth of July, faire weather, the winde at North.
This day wee stood to the Southward along the Iland:
but, toward night it fell calme, and then the winde came
to the West. The tenth day, faire weather, but thicke and
close, the winde South South-west. All this day we stood
for Bell-Sound. Our Generall went on shoare this afternoone, and killed foure Deere, and brought a young Morse
alive with him aboord.

The eleaventh day faire weather, but calme. This
afternoone wee perceived five shippes in a Bay in Bel-
sound. The winde was so calme, that we were faine to
towe in our shippes, and about a North North-west sunne,
we came to an anchor by them, with our three ships, viz.
the Tigre Admirall, the Mathew Vice-Admirall, and the
Richard and Barnard, having made all things readie for to
fight. These five shippes which rid here, the one was a
great shippe of Biscay of seven hundred Tunnes, and the
two Hollanders, which we found the sixt of June in
Pooppy-bay, and one small Pinke of Amsterdam, and
another small shippe of Rochell. This great shippe of
Biscay, which we expected would have fought with us,
sent their Captaine aboord of us before we came to an
anchor, and submitted themselves unto the Generall. The
two ships of Amsterdam, whose Masters names were these,
viz. Cornelius Calias, William Vermogon, Admirall, and
John Jacob Vice-Admirall, these two would gladly have

[III.iv.719.]

*A Biscayan
ship of 700.
tuns.*

55

stood out with us, if the Biscaine would have assisted them.

The twelfth day faire weather. This day the ship of John Jacobo was unladen of such goods as shee had in her; as Oyle, Blubber, and Morses skinnes. The thirteenth day I was sent in a shallop to Greene Harborough.

The fourteenth day, thicke close weather, the winde Northward; but toward noone it began to cleare up, and then it blew more winde. About a West sunne, we came to a small Iland, or rather a Rock, where Morses use to come: where we found seaven which we killed, and knocked out their teeth, and let them lye. In this place *Many rockes* are many of these rockes, where are great multitudes of *full of Fowle.* foule, and they are called Lizets Ilands. The Land all *Lisets Ilands.* along is so full of Rockes, that it is unpossible for any shippe to come neere the Maine, but in the Sands which are very deepe, and good to come in. All this evening and night wee rowed betweene this Iland and Ice-sound.

The fifteenth day, about nine or tenne a clocke, we came to the shippes in Greene-harborough, where we *Eighteene* found, that they had killed eighteene Whales in all. *Whales killed.* Foure of these ships were Frenchmen, which had killed eight Whales for the Companie according to the agreement which the Generall had made with them: which was, that they should kill eight for us, and after, what they could kill, should be for themselves. Our English men *Three Whales* had killed three in this place, and the Baskes in the Desire *killed by the* also three. The Desire had taken in an hundred tunnes *English.* of Oyle when wee came there, and she was to be laden so soone as she could.

The seaventeenth day also faire weather, the winde Northward. This day, toward a West Sunne, the Master of the French shippe came from Sea-horse Bay, who went thither to speake with our Generall: because Master Mason and Master Cooper had stayed his Shallops from going to Sea, in regard they would not observe the orders which the Generall had appointed them: which were, that those Whales which our Englishmen did chase, they should not follow, nor our men should not follow the Whales they chased. For the order of the Biscaines is, that who so doth strike the first Harping Iron into him, it is his Whale, if his Iron hold. This evening, I say, he returned from Sea-horse Bay, having lost his labour: for the Generall and Master Edge were in Bell-sound. We understood by him, that they had killed some eight and thirtie Whales in all; and that there was one hundred and sixtie tunnes of Oyle ready made.

The five and twentieth day in the morning, the Desire weighed Anchor to go to the Generall, and the Master of the French ship also this morning went from thence to speake with the Generall, because of a Whale which was in strife betweene his Biscaines and ours: when for pilfering and for some peremptorie speeches, two of the Rochellers were ducked at our Yard arme, the one on the one side, and the other on the other. This day I also observed the latitude of this place, and found it to be 77. degrees 40. minutes. Also, the variation of the Compasse is 13. degrees 11. minutes West. This variation was observed the third of August in the morning: the height of the sunne above the Horizon was 17. degrees 24. minutes, and the declination was 14. degrees 41. minutes North in the latitude of 77. degrees 40. minutes, and his Magnetical azimuth was 63. from South to East. The ninth day wee had sight of Master Bonners Ship, wherein was Master Marmaduke, who had beene to the Northward as farre as Faire-haven: and now, as he said, he was bound to the southward to discover beyond Point Looke-out, having his direction from Master Edge, as he said. Our Generall told him, that hee had hindered the Voyage more by his absence, then his discoverie would profit; and that it were best that he went backe with him to the Fore-land, and that he would give no licence to goe now for Discoverie, because the yeare was farre spent: but bad him, according to his Commission, so to proceede. The twelfth day I observed, and found the latitude of this place by an exact

August 1.

Latitude 77.
degrees, 40.
minutes.
Variation, 13.
degrees, 11.
minutes.

Latitude 79.
degrees, 14.
minutes.
This was Ma.
Cudners ship
of London.

observation to be in 79. degrees 14. minutes. They in
the Pooppy-Bay had seene a ship of England off Black-
point, and had spoken with her, who told them that they
were come from Kildeene.

The foureteenth day faire weather, the Winde at North
North-east. This day about tenne a clocke in the fore-
noone, we waied anchor to goe homeward, being sixe ships
in company, viz. the Tigre Admirall, the Gamaliel Vice-
Admirall, the John and Francis, the Annula, the ship of
Burdeaux which the Generall agreed with to fish in
Greene-harborough, and the Biscay ship which fished in
Sir Thomas Smiths Bay.

The fifteenth day very faire weather, all the forenoone
almost calme : in the afternoone, an easie gale at North-
east. This day about twelve a clocke at noone, wee were

against Faire Foreland, which is in the latitude of 79.
degrees 8. minutes. This night was very cleere and faire
weather, and also calme, by which meanes I had very good
opportunitie to finde the sunnes refraction. For behold-

ing it about a North North-east sunne, by the common
Compasse, at which time the sunne was at the lowest, it
was but one fift part of his body above the Horizon,

having about foure fifth parts below, so neere as I could
gesse. His declination for that instant was 10. degrees
35. minutes North, being at noone in the 2. degree 7.
minutes of Virgo, his daily motion was 58. minutes:
whose halfe beeing nineteene to bee added to the former,
because it was at twelve houres afore noone. I say his
place at that instant was 2. degrees 26. minutes of Virgo,
whose declination was as before 10. degrees 35. minutes:
the Latitude of the place was 78. degrees 47. minutes,
whose complement was 11. degrees 13. minutes, the
declination being substracted from the complement of the
Poles elevation, leaveth 38. minutes, foure five part of

which 12. minutes; which being substracted from 38.
leaveth 26. minutes for the Refraction. But, I suppose
the Refraction is more or lesse, according as the ayre is
thicke or cleare, which I leave for better schollers to dis-

cusse: but this I thought good to note, for the better helpe of such as doe professe this studie.

The sixteenth day also very faire weather, and for the most part calme: the winde that was, was at North-west. This morning, we espied a ship out in the offen, over against Cold-cape, which we stood with, and she also stood with us. And when we came to her, wee found her to be the Desire, a shippe of Alborough. Our Generall sent for the Master and Merchant aboard of us, who certified him that they came from Killedeeve, and that they had made but a bad Voyage of fish: and they were come to see, if we could fraight them home. The Merchant was of London, whose name was Master Cudner; the Masters name was Fletcher, who also brought sixe men which Thomas Bonner had left at Cherie Iland. These sixe men had killed but one Morse all this yeere at the Iland: who also told us, that William Gourdon was gone to the North-wards. At noone, the three and twentieth day, I observed the variation of the Compasse, and found it to be one degree 5. minutes East.

M. Cudner of London.

William Gourdon.

Variation 1. degree 5. min.

The three and twentieth day faire weather, with a fine gale at North and by East. We stearing away South and by West halfe South: being at noone, by supposition, in the latitude of 69. degrees no minutes. Having sailed since yesterday noone, some thirtie leagues South, true.

The foure and twentieth day, very faire weather and cleere, the winde all the fore-noone Northwards, but about noone it came to the South-east. This morning I observed the middle starre in the Great Beares tayle, and found it to bee in the latitude of 68. degrees 24. minutes about two a clocke, at which time that starre was on the Meridian under the Pole. Also I observed the starre in the Beares Rumpe about one a clock, and found the like latitude. Also all this day we had sight of Rost Ilands, being about ten or eleven leagues off us. Also at noone I observed the latitude by the Sun, and found us to be in the latitude of 68. degrees no minutes, which did agree with the former Observations by the starres. Also the

Rost Ilands or Rosten.

68. deg. no min.

The variation 4. degrees 8. minutes East.

variation of this place is 4. degrees 8. minutes East from the true Meridian, wee having runne since yesterday noone some two and twentie leagues South and by West. Almost all the afternoon it was almost calme.

The five and twentieth day also very faire weather, the winde this morning came to the East South-east a fine easie gale. We steered away South and by West halfe West ten leagues, being at noone in the latitude of 67. degrees *Variation 5.* 5 minutes. The variation of this place is 5. degrees 3. *deg. 3. minutes* minutes East, neere to the set of our Compasse. This *East.* Evening the winde came to the South South-west, which continued about two Watches.

The nine and twentieth day faire weather, with a good gale of winde at North North-east. From two this last night to sixe, we stood away South-west and by South, and at sixe we steered away South South-west, being at noone *The lying of* by observation, in 62. degrees no minutes. The land *the land about* about Scoutesnesse lyeth in this sort: from sixtie three *Scoutsnesse.* toward sixtie two, it is nineteene leagues South South-west halfe Westward: from thence tenne leagues South and by West, which is two or three Ilands, which are the Westwardest land in Norway, lying in the latitude of 62. degrees 44. minutes. But whether these Ilands, or a Point of land, which lyeth about three or foure leagues more to the North, be called Scoutesnesse, I know not. The sixt of September we entred the Thames.

Chap. VI.

A Voyage of Discoverie to Greenland, &c. Anno 1614. Written by Ro. Fotherbye.

He ship Thomasine went downe from Black-wall to Woolwich the sixteenth of Aprill, and from thence to Gravesend the three and twentieth, where shee remayned untill the eight and twentieth of the same; and weighing from thence she anchored againe in Tilberie Hope, with ten ships more of good burthen, and two Pinnasses all of the Green-land Fleet, set forth also at the charge of the said Company, under the command of Master Benjamin Joseph, Chiefe Captayne and Generall of the said Fleet.

We set sayle out of Tilberie Hope the fourth of May, [III.iv.721.] and came to an anchor the same day in Lee Road, where we stayed till the next morning, then wee set sayle againe and went forth to Sea before night.

We went forth to Sea.

We proceeded in company of the Fleet, and met with *We met with* stragling Ice the five and twentieth of May in the latitude *Ice in 75. deg.* of 75. degrees 10. minutes, through which wee passed *10. minutes.* without danger, holding on our course all that day, till time of mid-night; then we found the Ice so close packt together, that we were forced to tacke about, and stand to the Westward, till wee found more open passage, wee plyed through it without any great danger, till the eight and twentieth day: but then being in sight of Land, we passed amongst very much Ice all the fore-noone, which lay in great abundance on both sides of us: but a desire (as it seemes) to get through it, drew us on to be the more intangled with it, for about noone we could neither find a passage to goe forward, nor way to retyre backe againe, but being nine ships and two Pinnasses (for the Prosperous and the Desire lost Company through foule weather, the one and twentieth of May, otherwise we had beene thirteene sayle) we began very suddenly to bee inclosed

and shut up with Ice. Now every one wrought the best
meanes he could for the safetie of his ship; Our Master in
the Thomasine, caused a Hauser and a Grapnell to be
carried forth, and laid upon a great Iland of Ice, and so we
rid as at an Anchor, and by that meanes wee stayd from
forceable rushing against other peeces; afterward we laid
forth an anchor for surer hold, and made fenders of an old
Cable, which was hung over the ships sides to keepe the
Ice from piercing of her plankes. Wee rid thus from the
eight and twentieth of May till the second of June, still
floating as the wind drove us with our anchor, holding
Iland, which now we accounted as the shoare, and made
use thereof accordingly, for upon it our Carpenter sealed
and trimmed our lesser shallop.

On the second of June we had a great homeming Sea,
the wind being at North-west, whereby we judged we
were not farre from an open Sea to windward of us; there
wee resolved to make tryall what we might doe, to free
our selves out of the Ice. In the afternoone about three a
clock we got aboard our Anchor, letting fall our fore top-
sayle, and putting forth our Mizen; and so drove a sterne
for a while, till the floating Iland gave way; then wee filled
our top-sayle, and attempted divers places where to passe,
but had repulse and fell asterne againe; notwithstanding at
the length we prevayled, and with much adoe we attayned

an open Sea at a North, and by West Sunne, parting very
gladly from these ill neighbouring Ilands; which at our
parting from them, gave us, or rather received from us
some knockes, but whilest we remayned amongst them
they seemed much more perillous then they proved hurtfull, so wee praysed God for our safe deliverance, wishing
that the rest of the ships which we left in the Ice, were as
cleere out of it as was the Thomasine.

Having attayned the open Sea to the Westwards, we
proceeded to the Northwards; keeping the Ice still on our

starboord side, and met with the Mary An-Sarah, that got
also free of the Ice the same day that we came forth of it;
we kept company together till the next day, when being as

high as Prince Charles Iland, we both stood in for the shoare, the Mary An-Sarah going for Bel-sound, her assigned Harbour; but we proceeded to the Fore-land, *We came to* where when wee came the sixt of June, wee met with two *the Fore land.* shallops that belonged to the Desire, wherein was Cuthbert Appleyard, and William Simmes Harponiers; by whom we understood, that the Prosperous and the Desire had more desiredly prospered, then all the rest of the Fleet, they escaped the danger that all the rest fell into, and came to the Fore-land the third of June, finding the Harbour open.

Here was yet no worke begunne, for they had not seene one Whale since their comming into the Harbour; so that for us there was no cause of stay to bee helpfull unto them, and therefore we proceeded to the Northward, *We proceeded* hoping to find the shoare still as free from Ice, as it was *to the North-* at this place; but it fel out contrary to our expectations, *wards.* for being come as farre as Maudlen Sound, in the latitude *Maudlen* of 79. degrees 34. minutes, we met with some stragling *Sound.* Ice, and from the mayne top we saw much Ice lye betwixt us and Hackluyts Head-land, which seemed to bee close to *Hackluyts* the shoare, therefore we sent some men in a shallop to *Head-land.* Maudlen Sound, to see if it were open, that wee might *We anchored* harbour our ship there, and search for a leake which wee *in Maudlen* found her subject unto in foule weather. *Sound.*

The Sound was open, and we anchored in a good Harbour, but the Ice was not gone cleere from the shoare, therefore we could not hale our ship aground, but we carined her and set up our Biscaine shallop which we carried with us out of England in pieces.

The next day after our comming hither I went forth in *I went forth* a little shallop (the other being then unset together) to *in a shallop.* see how the Ice lay at Hackluyts Head-land, and whether we might passe with our ship that way or no. Being come forth of the Harbour, we perceived, that it was very foule weather at Sea, notwithstanding I proceeded into Faire Haven, where the South Harbour was then open, but much Ice lay then in the Sound unbroken from shoare to shoare; otherwise wee might have passed that way to Hackluyts Head-land, betwixt the Iland and the mayne Land; we stayed here till the next morning, then the weather beganne to cleere up, and wee put forth to Sea againe, intending to goe without the Ilands: but being out of the Harbour wee found the foule weather to be such, as our little weake shallop was not able to endure, therefore we returned againe to our ship into Maudlen Sound, where we killed two Female Morses, and took their Teeth, Hides and Blubber.

We set sayle out of Maudlen Sound and followed the Ice.

[III.iv.722.]

On the tenth of June we set sayle out of Maulden Sound, and coasted along to the North-ward, till we were past Hackluyts Head-land, but then we saw the Ice lye before us, extending close to the shoare, so that for us to passe further that way, it was not possible: therefore wee turned to the Westward, to see if wee could find passage further from the shoare. Wee sayled as the Ice trended West and West South-west till the thirteenth day, and keeping still alongst it, we found it to trend neerest South and South South-west, we proceeded well thus far, till we came under the latitude of Prince Charles his Iland, in 78. degrees 40. minutes, being eight and twentie leagues from shoare, but then we altered our course, and stood in for the Foreland, to goe and be helpfull to the other ships there for the furthering of their Voyage according to our Instructions (as some did understand them) but contrary I am sure to some of our desires. When we came neere the Fore-land, we saw eleven ships of Hollanders under sayle, plying to the Southwards: one of them came roome towards us, and strucke her top-sayles twice, whereby we supposed they tooke us for some of their Fleete, which they wanted, but wee held on our course still into Sir Thomas Smiths Bay, where we came to an anchor the fifteenth of June, by the John-Anne-Francis, and the Desire, the Mary Margaret being then under sayle to go to the Fore-land.

Prince Charles Iland in 78. degrees 40. minutes. Wee stood againe for shoare.

Eleven Holland ships.

We anchored in Sir T. Smiths Bay.

Here was yet no need of any helpe that we could make them, for they had hitherto neyther killed nor seene one

Whale since their first comming in hither; therefore we thought it best not to stay here, but rather goe to Faire Haven, where wee should bee more readie to proceed on our Discoverie when the Ice would give us leave, and in the meane-time wee might bee helpfull to the two ships thither assigned for the making of their Voyage, and so much the rather wee hasted, because we understood that the Hollanders also set forth a ship on Discoverie.

We set sayle the seventh of June, and met with the Prosperous, that came from Crosse-road, and was going into Sir Thomas Smiths Bay, there to get some Bricke and Lime to mend their Fornace, as Nicholas Woodcocke the Master told us; then we went forth to Sea, and being about foure leagues from the shoare, the winde began to blow so hard from the North-west, that wee were forced back againe to seek Harbour, and came to an anchor the nineteenth of June, in Crosse-road. Here we stayed two dayes, much wind blowing at the North North-east, till the one and twentieth of June, and then in the after-noone the wind came to the East and by South, and the weather was faire, therefore at a North North-west Sunne, we weighed and set sayle againe, and so did the Thomas Bonaventure, that came to an anchor by us this morning, beeing also bound for Faire Haven.

We went forth of Sir T. Smiths Bay.

We were driven backe againe into Crosse-road.

We set sayle out of Crosse-road.

This next day in the afternoone we were thwart of Maudlen Sound, and the weather being faire and calme, we sent a shallop to the Northward, to see what alteration there was amongst the Ice, and to seeke out some good Harbour for a ship, and also to set up the Kings Armes at Hackluyts Head-land, or some other convenient place.

When Master Baffin was gone from the ship in the foresaid shallop, I went presently into the other shallop into Maudlen Sound, there to set up the Kings Armes; and also to see if there were any Morses come ashoare; when I was within the Sound, I found no Beeches bare for Morses to come upon: for Ice and snow lay yet undissolved from the shoare side, but I went to the Harbour, and there caused a Crosse to be set up, and the Kings

One shallop to the Northward. The other into Maudlen Sound.

Armes to bee nayled thereon; under which also I nayled a piece of sheet Lead, whereon I set the Moscovie Companies Marke, with the day of the moneth and yeere of our Lord. Then cutting up a piece of Earth, which afterward I carried aboard our ship, I tooke it into my hand and said, in the hearing of the men there present to this effect.

I take this piece of Earth, as a signe of lawfull possession (of this Countrey of King James his New-land, and of this particular place, which I name Trinitie Harbour) taken on the behalfe of the Company of Merchants, called the Merchants of New Trades and Discoveries, for the use of our Sovereigne Lord James by the grace of God, King of great Brittaine, France, and Ireland, whose Royall Armes are here set up, to the end that all people who shall here arrive may take notice of his Majesties Right and Title to this Countrey, and to every part thereof. God save King James.

Trinitie
Harbor is
under the
parallel of
79. degrees
34. minutes.
We came to
an anchor in
Faire Haven.

This is a good safe harbour, and is under the latitude of 79. degrees 34. minutes, as I have found by good observation, and have of Westerly variation 25. degrees. When I had here set up the Kings armes, I returned toward our ship, which was come to an anchor at the entrance of Faire haven, staying till the floud came, because that at the Tide of Ebbe, there runnes a great current out of the Sound; so at the next floud, we came into Faire haven and anchored by the Gamaliel and the Thomas Bonaventure, the three and twentieth day of June.

Then John Mason, Master of the Gamaliel, came aboord of our ship, and I asked him if he had any worke for our men, for I would cause them to come a shore:

No Whales
were yet come
in.
[III.iv.723.]
The shallop
returned from
the North-
wards.
Cape Barren.

he told me, that hitherto he had not seene a Whale come in, but his Furnaces and Coppers were already set up, and therefore as yet he had no neede of helpe, but when occasion served he would imploy them. This day about eleeven a clocke Master Baffin returned in the Shallop from the Northwards: he said that he had beene at Cape Barren, which is the point of an Iland three or foure leagues from Hackluits head-land, but further then that he could not passe for Ice which lay close to the shore, and he had not set up the Kings armes in any place.

On Munday the seven and twentieth day of June, I went forth againe in the Shallop to the Northward, partly to see what alteration there might be in the Ice, with the Easterly windes which had blowne hard since the Shallop last returned, but chiefely to set up the Kings armes in some places convenient, because there was none set up to the Northwards of Maudlen sound.

We rowed to Cape Barren, where formerly Master Baffin had bin, and finding the Ice there gone from the shore, we proceeded further to an Iland which now we call the Saddle, in respect of the forme thereof, more then a *Saddle Iland.* league distant from Cape Barren. In our way thither it began to snow, and grew to be a great and vehement storme from the West North-west, therefore we hasted and *A Storme.* got to the lee side of the aforesaid Iland, and there made fast our Shallop with a grapnell laid upon the Icie shore, using the best meanes we could with our shallops saile to keepe us from the extremitie of so cold an harbour: we staid here eight houres, and the storme continued driving the Ice still Eastward in great abundance and with wonderfull swiftnesse: when the weather began to cleere, I caused the men to rowe to Leewards to another Iland a league distant, which seemed then to be a Cape of the maine land, purposing there to set up the Kings armes; but afterwards wee found it to be an Iland, and to the maine wee could not come for broken Ice.

This stormie weather continued from Munday night till Friday morning, during which time we had beene but eleaven leagues at the furthest from our ship, yet went we so farre as we could have gone, had the weather beene never so faire; for at foure leagues distance from Cape Barren, the Ice lay firme and unbroken two or three miles from the shore, and close againe to it lay the shattered Ice thronged together with this present storme.

On Friday morning we came backe againe to Hackluits *Julie.*

headland, and there I set the Kings armes in the like manner as at Trinitie Harbour: from thence we rowed towards our ship, and as we entred into Faire-haven, there

The Whales began now to come in.

came a Whale that accompanied us into the harbour leaping and advancing himselfe almost quite out of the water, falling headlong downe againe with great noise; we hasted aboord our ship, and I sent forth both our Shallops to strike this Whale if they could, and told Master Mason of her comming in, who also went forth in his Shallop: but it seemes the Whale past under the Ice which lay yet unbroken betwixt the North harbour and the South harbour, for they could not see her againe.

The next day there came more Whales in, and Robert Hambleton, our Masters mate strucke two, which

Two Whales escaped.

unluckily escaped; the first for want of helpe, the Gamaliels Shallop being in chase of another Whale, and our owne little Shallop not able to row against a head-sea to assist the other: so that at length the Whale having towed the Shallop forth to Sea, the harpingiron came out: the second was also strucken within the sound, and ranne under the Ice, which lay yet unbroken at the East end of the Sound, and drew the Shallop upon it cleare out of the water; by which meanes the Harpingiron came forth. Here we remained till the sixt of Julie, our men and Boates being helpefull at all times to further the Voyage.

We came forth of Faire haven.

The sixt of Julie we set saile forth of Faire-haven, intending to make triall if wee could to get to Westwards of the Ice, and so proceede to the Northwards, having sent away one of our Shallops the day before, provided with twentie dayes Bread, to coast alongst the shoare, search the Beach for Commodities, and set up the Kings Armes at places convenient, hoping thereby to prevent the Hollanders, who now rid in the North harbour of Faire-haven, and were ready for the first opportunitie, to discover and take possession of other harbours, having two Ships to goe forth onely upon Discovery.

We met with Ice and stood to the North-wards.

We sailed Westwards from Faire-haven seven leagues, and then met with a maine banke of Ice which trended

68

North & South, the Sea appeared to the Northwards to be
open so far as we could see, therfore we plied that way:
when we had run seven or eight leagues more, the Ice lay
so thick on every side, that we were bard from proceeding
any further; then we stood in toward the shore, and being
a little to the Northwards of Cape Barren, our Shallop had
sight of us, & came rowing to us through the broken Ice.
Master Baffin told us the shore to the Eastward was much
pestered with Ice, and he had set up the Kings armes at
the entrance of a faire Sound, about foure leagues distant
from Cape Barren.

Our Shallop came to us.

Now the weather being faire and calme, Master Sherwin,
Master Baffin and I, went in the Shallop to the place where
the Kings Armes were set up, purposing (because the ayre
was very cleere) to goe upon some high mountaine, from
whence we might see how the Sea was pestered with Ice,
and what likelihood there was of further proceeding.
According to this our intent, we ascended a very high hill,
and from thence we saw the Ice lye upon the Sea so farre
as we could discerne, so that the Sea seemed to be wholly
toured with Ice, save onely to the Eastwards: we thought
that we saw the water beyond the Ice, which put us in
some hope that we should ere long get passage with our
Shallops along the shore, if we could not passe with our
shippe. Being thus satisfied, we returned abord our ship
and plyed towards Faire haven, advising amongst our
selves of the best course we could to further the businesse
committed unto us.

[III.iv.724.]
We returned towards Faire haven.

We resolved to make our discovery along the shore with
both our Shallops, and to carry with us our provision for
the Whale-killing, conceiving good hopes besides, of
profit which the beaches would afford us; therefore we
intended when our ship was brought safe into harbour
againe, to goe from her with both our Shallops, and to put
in practise this our late resolution. But the weather falling calme, and a fogge succeeding, which continued three
dayes, so that our ship came not into harbour till the
twelfth of July; I went from her the eleventh day, intend-

We intended to discover in Shallops.

I went forth in the one Shallop.

ing to search the Beaches, till Master Baffin came to me with the other Shallop, and then we to proceede both together : but before he came, I had gone so farre as that the Ice would not suffer mee to passe a Boates length further, and I had also searched a very faire Beach which was altogether fruitlesse.

Master Baffin came to me in the other Shallop.

Master Baffin came to me at a place appointed the foureteenth day of Julie, in the other Shallop, and we proceeded both together to the Eastwards againe, and found passage amongst the Ice about a league further then I had lately beene, so that we came to the firme Ice, that lay almost two miles from the shoare of Red-beach, unbroken up this yeare. Here wee haled up our Shallops out of the water, lest the broken Ice which is carried to and fro with the winde, might split them or bruse them : then Master Baffin and I with foure men more walked over the firme Ice and went ashore on Red-beach, where we travelled about the space of three miles by the shore side, but found no commodities as we expected to have done; for here had the Hulmen been in 1612. as we might know by fires that they had made, and gathered the fruites that many yeares before had brought forth. Thus as we could not finde that which wee desired to see, so did we behold that which we wished had not beene there to be seene, which was great abundance of Ice, that lay close to the shore and also off at Sea so farre as we could discerne; wherefore being thus satisfied, and more wearie to know that we could passe no further, then with travailing so farre, we returned to our Shallops, and went aboord of our Ship in Faire haven on Sunday the seventeenth of July, passing the neerest way betwixt the Ilands and the maine Land, for now the Ice was broken betwixt the South-harbor where we rid, and the North harbour, where the Hollanders rid.

Red-beach.
We hailed our Shallop upon the Ice.

We returned to our Shallop.

The next day we sent our Shallop to the North-east side of Faire haven, there to lye for the comming of the Whales over against the Gamaliels two Shallops that lye on the other side for the same purpose.

ROBERT FOTHERBY

The twentieth of July, wee were under saile to goe forth of Faire haven with the Gamaliel, purposing to have taken two Ships that rid at the entrance of Maudlen-Sound, with John Mason, who first descried them, supposed to be the one a Bask, and the other an English man; but the winde blew right into the Harbour, so that we could not get forth, and therefore we came to an anchor againe where we rid before.

We were under saile and came to an anchor againe.

On the one and twentieth of July, our Harponiers killed a Whale, which split one of our Shallops and strucke the Harponier that was in her overboord: but both hee and the rest of the men were relieved and taken into an other Shallop: then we sent our Carpenter to mend the Shallop that was split: and on the five and twentieth day they helpt to kill another Whale.

We killed a Whale.

On the sixe and twentieth of July, I drew the plat of Faire haven, as it is here projected (but here too costly to insert.)

When this Scoale of Whales were past, we went out of Faire haven the first of August with both our Shallops, Master Baffin in the one, and I in the other, with five men more in each Shallop, thinking that now we should finde the Ice broken and cleere gone from the shore, conceiving some good hope to proceede and make some new discovery, which was the chiefe occasion of our imployment. Wee passed over Red cliffe-Sound, which we found cleare of Ice; and from thence we proceeded to Red-beach, where we also found great alteration since our last being there, notwithstanding the Ice was not cleerely voided from the shore; for in some places it was firme and unbroken off, for the space almost of halfe a mile: so we rowed alongst it, till wee came neere the North end of the Beach which lyeth furthest into the Sea, and there we found an open way to the shore with our Shallops, and went on land; but seeing in all places great abundance of broken Ice, we lay close to the shoare, and doubting that although perhaps with much adoe, we might get about the point of the Beach, yet should we still be pestered with Ice from pro-

August. We went to the North- wards with our Shallops.

We got to the shoare of Red Beach with our Shallops.

We walked over Red-beach.

ceeding any further, we resolved to walke over land, to the other side of the Beach, where we saw a hill about foure miles distant, from which we thought we should be satisfied, how much further it was possible for us to proceed: so thither we travailed, where when we came, wee saw a very faire Sound on the East side of the Beach which was open within, but there lay very much Ice at the entrance of it, which although it was extended more then halfe over Sound, yet we doubted not but if we could get our Shallops about the Beach, we should finde either one way or other to passe over the said Sound, & from the high land on the other side, we should receive very good satisfaction, if the weather continued faire and cleare as now it was, therefore we intended to make triall what we might do; but before we returned we went down to the point of the Beach, at the entrance of the Sound, and there set up a Crosse, and nailed a sixe pence thereon with the Kings Armes. This being done, we returned to our Shallops, and according to our late determination, we rowed about the point of Red-beach, and with many crooked windings amongst the Ice, at length we got over Wiches Sound (for so it is now named.)

[III.iv.725.]

The Kings armes are set up at Wiches Sound.

We passed over Wiches Sound.

As soone as we were over on the other side, about two leagues from Red-beach, Master Baffin and I clambred up a very high hill, from whence we saw a point of land bearing East North-east, by the ordinary Compasse eighteene or twentie leagues distant, as I supposed. Wee likewise saw another faire Sound to the Southwards of us, which was much pestered with Ice, but we could not see the end of it. Here upon the mountaine wee set up a Warelocke, and then came downe againe with lesse labour, but more danger then we had in getting up, by reason of the steepinesse thereof: then we walked to the shoare side, and there found many beach Finnes, whereby I conjectured that Master Marmadukes men in his first discovery, made in Anno 1612. had not beene upon this land to search the Beaches, for in all other places where we had beene heretofore, we could finde nothing at all.

We found Beach Fins.

Now therefore we resolved to make further search alongst
this shoare, and to proceede with our Shallops so farre
as we possibly could: whereupon wee returned to our
men againe whom we left with our Shallops, where we
first landed.

Having stayed here a while and observed the latitude
which I found to be 79. degrees 54. minutes, we saw a
Shallop come rowing towards the extreamest point of
this shoare, therefore we hastned towards them to see
who were therein, and found them to be Master Marmadukes men, lately come from their ship the Harts-ease,
which they said they left at Sea amongst the Ice, about
a league from Red Beach: here they were setting up a
Crosse, which they said that they found there fallen downe,
and had beene formerly set up in the time of Master
Marmadukes first discovery, by one Laurence Prestwood,
whose name I saw thereon engraven, with two or three
names more, and it had the date of the seventeenth of
August 1612. Upon this Crosse they nailed the Kings
Armes.

We met with the Hartsease Shallop.

Note.

Here we parted from them, and according to our former
determination we proceeded, some in the Shallops amongst
the Ice, and others on shoare, till wee went about foure
leagues further: in which space we found many more
Finnes, and one paire of Morses teeth, but now we found
the Ice so close packt together, that wee could not proceede
any further with our Shallops: wherefore Master Baffin
and I intended to walke over land untill we should be
better satisfied how farre this Sound went in, for wee
could as yet see no end of it, and it seemed to make a
separation of the land; so leaving our men here with the
Shallops, wee travailed almost a league further, till we
came to the point of a sandie beach, that shot into the
Sound, which was wonderfully stored with drift Wood
in great abundance. From this point we received such
satisfaction as we looked for, because we saw the end
of the Sound which lies South in about ten leagues. It
hath in it a good harbour that is landlockt, and doubtlesse

The end of Sir Thomas Smiths Inlet discovered.

it is a good place for the Whale-killing if it be not every yeare as now it is pestered with Ice. Here I saw a more naturall earth and clay then any that I have seene in all the Countrie, but nothing growing thereupon more then in other places. This Sound is that which formerly had and still retaineth the name of Sir Thomas Smiths Inlet.

We returned towards our Ship.
A storme began when we were amongst Ice.

Being thus satisfied, we came backe againe to our Shallops, and seeing no way but one, we returned towards our Ship; but before we could get to Red-beach, there arose a very great storme from the East North-east, after we had entered amongst the Ice in Wiches Sound, so that we were separated the one Shallop from the other, whereby our danger was the greater: for whiles wee were both in company together, the one might have beene helpfull to the other when neede required, and more easie it seemed to save them both, then being separated to keepe either of them from wracke; but God (who in his wonted mercie is ever ready to relieve the faithfull distressed) did not onely so provide that we met together againe, and indeede were helpfull the one to the other (otherwise I doubt the one Shallop had miscarried, for she was in great danger)

We get forth of Ice.

but also delivered us safely out from amongst these perillous rockes of Ice, which it was very hard to shun, and at the length brought us into an open Sea, where with as scant a saile as we could make, we past swiftly before the winde, the Sea comming divers times over the sternes of our Shallops, which wet our skinnes, that had scarse any dry cloathes on before to keepe them warme, by reason of a drizeling Snow which fell with the storme:

We came aboord our ship.

then we went aboord our Ship into the South harbour of Faire haven, the fift of August, with one hundred and fiftie Beach finnes, and one paire of Morses teeth, giving thanks to God for his blessing and mercifull deliverance.

The Holland Discoverers go homewards.

The ninth of August, two ships of the Hollanders, that were appointed for Northerne Discovery, were seene thwart of Faire Haven, sayling to the Southwards.

Our ship went forth to Sea.

The eleventh of August, we set sayle forth of Faire Haven, the winde at South South-west, intending to make tryall, if yet the Ice would admit us to have passage to the Northwards or the North-eastwards. We held our course from Cape Barren, North-east and by East, till seven a clocke at night, at which time having runne eight leagues from the shoare, wee met with the Ice which lay East and by South, and West and by North, and bore up alongst it to the Eastwards, for the winde was now come to the North North-west; then wee tackt about to the Westwards, and plyed off and on close by the Ice, till the thirteenth day at mid-night, still expecting a change of the weather, that we might have made some adventure amongst the shatterd Ice, for both on the twelfth and thirteenth day, the winde blew hard at North, and the weather was cold, thicke, and very winter-like with fall of snow: this winde being so contrarie, drove both the Ice and our ship to leewards towards the shoare, so that wee were forced to put into Harbour againe, and came to an Anchor the fourteenth day in the North Harbour of Faire Haven, where the Fleet of Hollanders lately rid, at which time the Hartsease was there at an Anchor.

Now was the Land both Mountaynes and Plaines wholly covered with snow; so that almost all mens mindes were possessed with a desire of returning for England: But to prevent a sudden resolution for a homeward Voyage without further satisfaction, I made motion that once againe we might goe forth with our shallops, to see what alteration there might bee found alongst the shoare. It fell out that I was to goe in one shallop for this purpose, so I tooke with me eight men, and went from our ship the fifteenth day of August.

We rowed to Red-cliffe Sound, where we passed through much Ice that was newly congealed being thicker then an halfe Crowne piece of silver, notwithstanding we broke way through it, and being over the Sound, we had a cleere Sea againe; then we proceeded to Red-beach, where finding the shoare cleere of Ice (which at my last being there was wonderfully pestered) I conceived good hope to finde passage to the furthest Land from thence

We met with Ice eight leagues from the Shore.

[III.iv.726.]
We plyed off and on the Ice two dayes.

We anchored againe in the North Harbor.

I went to the Eastwards in a shallop.

Ice was newly frozen in Red-cliffe Sound.

I intended to goe once to Point Desire.

in sight, bearing East halfe a point Southerly, nine, or ten leagues distant; to this end we put off from the shoare of Red-beach, and rowed a league and more in an open Sea, and then met with Ice which lay dispersed abroad, and was no hinderance to our proceeding, so that we continued rowing the space of sixe houres, in which time we had gotten more then halfe way over: but then we found the Ice to lye very thicke thronged together, so that it caused us much to alter our course, sometimes Southward and sometimes Northwards, and even in this time, when we thought wee stood in most need of cleere weather, it pleased God to send us the contrary, for it *A great snow* beganne to snow very fast, which made the Ayre so thick *began.* that we could not see to make choice of the most likely way for us to passe, therefore I thought good to stay here awhile, hoping that ere long the weather would bee more agreeable to our purpose; so a Grapnell being laid forth upon an Iland off, to hold fast our shallop, a Tent was made of the shallops sayle to keepe the weather from us, and we remayned here five houres, but finding no alteration in the constant weather, I willed the men to take downe the Tent, and with faire tearmes perswaded them, that notwithstanding the wet weather, it were good to be doing something, to get over to the desired shoare, where we might refresh our selves, and have fire to dry our wet clothes; they seemed well content with this motion, and *I could not* so we rowed the space of foure houres more, the Ice still *passe for Ice.* causing us to hold a South and South South-east course, which carried us further into Sir Thomas Smiths Inlet, and put us from the place where we wished to be.

The thicke snowie weather continued all this time, which was very uncomfortable to us all, but especially to the men that rowed; and as the snow was noysome to their bodies, so did it also begin to astonish their mindes, as I well perceived by their speeches, which proceeded upon *The originall* this occasion. The snow having continued thus long, *cause of Ice at* and falling upon the smooth water, lay in some places an *Sea.* inch thicke, being alreadie in the nature of an Ice compact, though not congealed, and hindred sometimes our shallops way; this I say caused some of them, not altogether without reason to say, that if it should now freeze as it did that night when we came over Red-cliffe Sound, we should be in danger here to be frozen up. Howsoever this search might bee a meanes to discourage the rest, that considered not of such a thing till they had heard it spoken of : yet true it is, that I saw no likelihood, by reason of the Ice, how to attayne my desire at this time, and therefore I bade them row toward the shoare *I went backe* of Red-beach againe, where I intended to stay till the *againe to Red-* weather might happily be more convenient. So holding *beach.* a West North-west course, so neere as the Ice would suffer us, wee came to the East-side of Red-beach, having beene eighteene houres amongst the Ice, during all which time the snow fell, and as yet ceased not. When we had been here about an houre it began to cleere up, and the wind to blow hard at East, which rather packt the Ice close together in this place then disperst it, so that I was now out of hope to get any further then I had beene alreadie : wherefore I returned toward our ship, intending as I went *I returned* to make a more particular Discoverie of Broad-bay, and *towards our* Red-cliffe Sound, hoping that one place or other would *ship.* afford some thing worthy of the time and labour. When we were come to the West side of Red-beach, it began to blow much wind, where withall the Sea growing to be great, all men advised to passe over Broad-bay, whilst the winde and weather would serve us to sayle, for they said it was like to be very foule weather : so seeing that it was no convenient time for coasting, we came over the Bay to Point Welcome (which I so named because it is a *Point* place, where wee oftentimes rested, when wee went forth *Welcome.* in our shallops) it is about foure leagues distant from the North end of Red-beach.

At this point the Hollanders had set up Prince Maurice his Armes, neere unto a Crosse which I had caused to bee set up above a moneth before, and had nayled a six pence thereon with the Kings Armes, but the men that [III.iv.727.]

were with me, went (without any such direction from mee) and pulled downe the said Princes Armes, whilst I was gone up a Mountayne to looke into the Sea, if I could see any Ice: and when I came downe againe they told me, that the six pence was taken from the Crosse that I had set up, and there was another post set by it, with the Hollanders Armes made fast thereon, which they had pulled downe; so, because the six pence was taken away, I caused one to nayle the Kings Armes cast in Lead upon the Crosse: which being done we rowed to the bottome of Red-cliffe Sound, and as we coasted alongst the shoare, we searched two little Beaches, which had some wood on them, but nothing that we found of better value.

The Kings Armes are set up againe at Point Welcome. I went into Red cliffe Sound.

About two leagues within the Sound, on the East side there is an Harbour where shippes may ride in good ground Land-lockt, but if other yeeres be like this, I cannot say that it is an Harbour fitting for ships, because it is late ere the Sound breake up; for even now there lay much Ice at the bottome of it, insomuch, that I was forcst to leave the shallop, because I could not passe with her for Ice, and walke two miles over stonie Mountaynes, with another man in my company, to bee satisfied concerning a point of Land that shot into the Sound, whether it were an Iland or no, as by all likelihood it seemed to bee: but when I came to the farthest part of it, I saw it joyne to the mayne Land, wherefore I called it Point Deceit, because it deceived mee so much. From hence wee proceeded toward our shippe, and came aboord of her in the North Harbour of Faire Haven, on Friday night being the nineteenth of August, where she rid alone; for Master Marmaduke was gone forth to Sea that day.

Point Deceit.

I came aboord our ship.

The two and twentieth of August, John Mason Master of the Gamaliell, came over from the South Harbour for helpe to hayle up a Whale which had beene sunke fourteene dayes, in one hundred and twentie fathome depth, or else to pull the Warpe and Harping Iron out of her, for now it was time to take her or forsake her. Master

A Whale lay sunken fourteene dayes.

78

Sherwin our Master caused our long Boate to bee manned
and went with him; when they came where the Whale
was sunke, they haled, and shee presently rose, bolting
suddenly up with a thundring cracke made with the burst-
ing of her bodie; and notwithstanding shee had layen so
long, yet had shee all her Finnes fast. Whilst this was
in doing, the Hartsease was comming into the Harbour *The Hartsease*
from the Northward, and anchored by our ship an houre *anchored by us.*
after.

Here wee stayed till the seven and twentieth of August,
and since my last returne hither in the shallop from the
Eastwards, the weather hath beene commonly warme, and *Warme*
the Mountaynes were now more cleere of Snow, then they *weather in the*
had beene any time this yeere, notwithstanding there had *end of August.*
much snowe fallen since the beginning of this moneth,
but it was quite consumed, and a greater signe of warmth
and thaw was now to bee observed then any time of the
yeere heretofore; namely, by the often falling of the Ice
into the Sea from the huge snowie bankes, making a
noyse like Thunder, so that the time was very hopefull,
but thus wee made use of occasion offered.

The seven and twentieth of August, it was faire and
warme weather, calme till noone, then had wee a gale
of winde from the South South-west, wherewithall wee
set sayle out of Faire-haven in the company of the *We set sayle to*
Hartsease, with whom wee had beene in termes of *the Eastward.*
consortship, but nothing was concluded. About sixe a
clocke at night wee were sixe leagues from Cape Barren,
which bore from us South-west and by South.

Wee proceeded still to the North-eastward, and on the
eight and twentieth day in the morning wee had runne
about twentie leagues from Cape Barren, in an East North-
east way by the ordinary Compasse, being open of Sir
Thomas Smiths Inlet, nine or tenne leagues from the
shoare; at which time wee were come to the Ice that
trended East South-east, and West North-west, but the
Sea being very rough, wee stood off againe from the Ice;
in the afternoone it fell calme, and at night we had a gale

of winde at East, and the ship was steered West, and
then South-west homewards.

The nine and twentieth day, the winde Easterly an
easie gale; at foure a clocke in the afternoone Hackluyts
Head-land bore from us South east by East foure leagues
distant: this Evening was very warme.

The thirtieth day, the winde at North-east an easie gale,
at foure a clocke in the afternoone, Maudlen Point bore
East North-east halfe a Point Easterly about three leagues
distant: towards the Evening it fell calme, the weather
not cold.

The thirtieth day, faire Sunne-shine weather and calme
till noone, and then we had a good gale of winde from
the North-east, being five leagues distant from the Foreland, which bore South-east; now wee altered our course
and stood to the West-ward: therefore to keepe us still
in the parallel that now wee were in which was 79. degrees
We stood to
the westwards.
8. minutes, West North-west course was directed, in
respect of the Variation, to make good a true West way.

This course wee held till we had runne about twentie
leagues, and then wee ranne twentie leagues more in a
West and by North course till one a clocke on Friday
morning; at which time it fell calme; and wee heard the
Sea make a great noyse, as if wee had beene neere Land,
but wee rather judged it to bee Ice, as indeed it proved
[III.iv.728.]
to bee, for in the morning when it was light and cleere, wee
saw the Ice about a league from us, which trended
Southerly; having now a gale at East North-east, wee
steered away South and South South-east, but in the
Wee met with
Ice.
afternoone we were embayed with a long banke of Ice,
which wee could not weather, therefore wee were faine
to tacke about, and the winde having come more Southerly
then it was in the morning, wee stood off from the Ice
North-east and North-east and by North, and then to the
Southwards againe, making sundrie boardes to get forth
to wind-wards of the Ice.

The third day before noone, wee had sight againe of
Ice to Westwards of us, and at noone were under the

parallel of 78. degrees 27. minutes, according to my Observation: then wee stood a way South to keepe cleere of the Ice, for wee had a great homing Sea, although but little winde; and therefore durst not be to bold to edge too neere it, especially the wind being Easterly as then it was.

On the fourth day our men saw the Ice againe from the mayne top-mast head, and therefore wee still maintayned a Southerly course: the next day it began to be foggie, and continued close weather and hazie for three dayes, so that wee had no more sight of the Ice; neyther *We left the* could wee at this time receive any further satisfaction *Ice and came* concerning the same: therefore wee kept a Southerly *for England.* course so neere as wee could, although wee had but little winde, and the same very variable till the ninth day, but then wee had a good gale of winde at West North-west.

On the tenth day beeing Saturday, wee were by my reckoning fiftie leagues distant from Low-foot, which bore from us East South-east halfe a Point Southerly: this day the wind shifted to the South-west, and at night came to the South with much raine; then came backe againe to the West North-west and began a great storme. *A storme*

This night the Master and others saw a light upon the *beganne.* Fore-bonnet, which the Saylers call a Corpo Santo: it *A Corpo* appeared like the flame of a Candle, and (as Sea-men *Santo.* observe) it always presageth an ensuing storme; which *It is often seen* to verifie, this foule weather continued the next day, and *at the end of* grew to be so vehement on Sunday night, that the Sea *stormes.* oftentimes over-raked our ship, and wee were faine to lye atry with our fore course onely, and our Mayne topmast also strucke, which last thing (as Sea-men say) is seldome done at Sea, then about one a clocke we were forced to take in our fore course, and to lye a-hull for five houres.

The fourth day of October, the shippe came to Wapping with the whole number of men that shee carryed forth (my selfe excepted that was come before) being sixe and twentie, all in perfect health.

Chap. VII.

A true report of a Voyage Anno 1615, for discoverie of Seas, Lands, and Ilands, to the
Northwards ; as it was performed by Robert
Fotherbie, in a Pinasse of twentie tunnes called
the Richard of London : set forth at the charge
of the Right Worshipfull Sir Thomas Smith,
Knight, my very good Master, and Master
Richard Wiche, Governours : and the rest of
the Worshipfull Company of Merchants, called
the Merchants of New Trades and Discoveries,
trading into Moscovia, and King James his
New Land.

Y the providence of Almightie God I
went forth of Harwich Harbour in the
foresaid Pinnasse, the twelfth of May, in
the company of eight shippes of the Fleet,
for King James his New Land, who in
foule weather out-sayled me in the latitude 71. degrees, or thereabouts. So I
proceeded alone towards King James his New Land : and
met with Ice in latitude 73. degrees 30. minutes, I stood
North-eastwards for the west of King James his New
Land, and had sundry conflicts with the Ice in rainie and
wet foggie weather, and had sight of Land the eleventh
of June, and on the nineteenth of the same I anchored
in Faire Haven. Here I stayed till the third of July,
for the Pinnasse had received some hurt amongst the Ice,
which to amend, I was faine to hale her aground, besides
divers other things necessary to be done, which detayned
mee longer then willingly I would have stayed there.

From hence I sayled Northward, but met with Ice in
Hackluyts latitude 79. degrees 50. minutes, being six leagues from
Headland. Hackluyts Head-land, then I coasted the Ice as it lay in

82

Points and Bayes to the Westwards and South-westward, and being thirtie leagues from the Land in latitude 79. degrees 10. minutes, I found it to trend Northward and North-westwards, and coasted it to the latitude of 79. [III.iv.729.] degrees 50. minutes, but then I was embayed with Ice, and was faine to stand out againe and sailed above ten leagues before I got cleere: when I was out of this Bay, I proceeded South Westerly with the Ice on the starboord to the latitude 78. degrees 30. minutes, where being fortie leagues from the shoare, I was againe embayed with the Ice, and having had faire Sun-shine weather all the day, which made mee the bolder to stand so neere it, the weather on a sudden fell foggie, and the wind beganne to blow hard at South, which put us to great trouble and no small perill: but the Almightie power who hath mercifully *Perill and* delivered us heretofore out of as great dangers, preserved *escape.* us also from this: when wee were gotten cleere off the Ice, we had the Sea much growne, and the storme increasing, but beeing desirous still to keepe the Sea, I stood close by the wind under a payre of coarses, till the Pinnasse waxt leake with bearing too much sayle, and there was forced to lye atry under a mayne coarse only: and although shee stemmed South-east and South-east by South, yet was she hurried violently to the North-eastwards, and by the mercifull providence of God we fell right with the Fore-land, in latitude 79. degrees, then I stood over Sir Thomas Smiths Bay for harbour in Crosse-road, where I anchored the thirteenth of July being Thursday. I stayed here foure dayes, in which time my men mended the Sayles and ships tackling that had received hurt by the late storme, and made a new mayne Sayle to serve in time of need, and on the seventeenth of July I weighed out of Crosse-road, and sayling Westwards from thence came to Ice againe in latitude 78. degrees 40. minutes, which I coasted as it lay neerest South-west, or more Westerly, but with many Points & Bayes, wherewith I was sometimes intangled, yet, God be thanked, got cleere againe, either by helpe of Oares or Sayles without any hurt. In this sort I proceeded with good satisfaction, although not with so good content, till I came to the latitude of 76. degrees, beeing above one hundred leagues from Point Looke-out, but then was crossed with a contrarie storme from the South-west and South South-west, which drove me to the South-east ward, till I came in the latitude of 74. degrees, and then I made my way Westward againe, so neere as I could lye, close by the winde, and over-ranne the formerly supposed Land of Groynland, which some have layd downe in plats and extended to 75. degrees. When I came into the latitude of 73. degrees, I stood West and North-west, and fell with Ice againe in latitude 73. degrees 50. minutes, and thought indeed at that time that I was neere Land by abundance of Fowle, which we saw in great flockes : but such thicke fogges have continued for three or foure dayes together, that we might sooner heare the Land if any were, then see it, and so did we first find this Ice by hearing the rut, thinking till we saw it, that it had beene Land, so that we were embayed with it, before we thought that we had beene neere it ; then I stood out againe and coasted the Ice still to the Westwards Southerly, but could see no Land, as I expected to have done, untill wee came under the latitude of 71. degrees thirtie minutes, and then we espyed a snowie Hill very high in the cloudes, for this day was very cleere at Sea, but the fogge was not yet cleered from the Land, so that we could see no part of it, but only the top of a snowie Mountayne, which appeared very high although wee were fourteene or fifteene leagues distant from it, bearing off us South-east and by South.

Then I stood in for the shoare, supposing it had beene part of the Mayne of Groynland : for the fogge lay on each side of this Mount, as if there had beene a great Continent under it, but it proved otherwise, for as we came neerer to it, the fogge dispersed more and more, and when wee were five leagues distant, the Land appeared in forme like an Iland.

Note.
Errour of
Gronland.

Fogges.

High Hill.

When I came neerer the shore, I could find no Harbor
to anchor in.   Notwithstanding, the weather being faire
& calme, I hoist out my Boat & went ashore with three
men more, and set up the Kings Armes : then we searched
a Sandie Beach, which was abundantly stored with drift *Drift wood.*
wood, but yeelded no other fruits, that we could find
worth the taking up, so I returned aboord againe, and
sent ashoare my Boat to fetch some wood.   But before
the men had laid into her the little quantitie that she was
able to carrie, they came aboard againe, for the wind began
to blow hard, and the Sea to goe loftie, so that here was
no place for us to abide any longer, otherwise I was purposed to have searched further alongst the shoare, but this
gale of winde comming Northerly I stood from hence to
the Westwards, being desirous to see more Land or finde
a more open Sea.   And having sayled about fifteene or
sixteene leagues I met with Ice again, in latitude 71.
degrees, and coasted it eight or nine leagues further Westward, and South-westward as it lay, but then the wind
came to the South-west, and we stood close by it a while
to the Southwards, but finding the gale to increase, and
considering that it was the most contrary winde which
could blow against my further proceeding (for the Ice as
we found did trend neerest South-west, and besides if
there had beene any high Land within twentie leagues of
us, wee might perfectly have made it, the weather was
so faire and cleere.)   In these respects, and for the Reasons
following, I tooke the benefit of this wind to returne to
the North-eastwards againe, being now about two hundred
leagues from King James his New Land in latitude 71.
degrees.   *Note.*
   First, I purposed to sayle alongst the South-east side
of the Land that I had discovered, to bee better satisfied
what Harbours there were, and what likelihood of profit
to ensue ; and from thence to proceed to the place where
I first fell with Ice in latitude 73. degrees when I was
driven to the South-eastwards with a Westerly storme,
for I am yet verily perswaded, that being there we were [III.iv.730.]

not farre from Land, although wee could not see it by
reason of thicke foggie weather. Then my further intent
was, if I found no good occasion to spend my time there,
for to coast the Ice, or try the open Sea to the Northwards,
betwixt 73. and 76. degrees, where formerly I had not
received desired satisfaction by reason of a storme that
drave me off, and then I purposed, if time might seeme
convenient, to proceed to the North Coast of King James
his New Land, to have seene what hope was there to be
had for passage Northward, or for compassing of the
Land, which is most like to be an Iland.

I stood away East and by South, and being neere the
foresaid Iland, the winde came to the West and blew a
very hard gale, wherewith I passed alongst the South-east
side of the Iland under a paire of coarses, but without
that satisfaction which I expected: for the winde blowing
so stormie, and the Sea growne very great, I was forced
to stand further from the shoare then willingly I would
have done, and besides there was a thicke fogge upon
the Land, whereby I could not be satisfied what Harbours
or Roads were about it, yet might we see three or foure
Capes, or Head-lands, as if there went in Bayes betwixt
them. I sayled about it, and then stood to the Northward againe, and being now assured that it was an Iland,
Sir T. Smiths I named it Sir Thomas Smiths Iland.
Iland.

This Iland is about ten leagues in length, and stretcheth
North-east and South-west: it is high Land, and at the
North end of it there is a Mountayne of a wonderfull
height and bignesse, all covered with Snow, which I called
Mount Mount Hackluyt; the base or foot of it on the East side
Hackluyt. is almost foure leagues long, it hath three such sides at
the base lying out to the Sea, and from the fourth side
doth the rest of the Iland extend it selfe towards the
South-west, which is also, as it were, a place fortified with
Castles and Bulwarkes, for on each side there bee three
or foure high Rockes which stand out from the Land,
appearing like Towres and Forts. It lyes in the parallel
of 71. degrees, where the Needle varieth from the true

Meridian Westwards eight degrees. The Land is generally so farre as I have seene, Rockie and very barren, and
worse then the Land that I have seene in King James
his New Land, under eightie degrees, for there is no
grasse but mosse, and where I first landed upon low
ground, all the stones were like unto a Smiths sinders
both in colour and forme, the sand is generally mixed
with a corne like Amber; the Beaches are abundantly
stored with drift wood and many stones, light like Pumis,
which will swimme on the water. I saw many traces of
Foxes and the footing of Beares, but not any signe of
Deere or other living creatures, and very small store of
Fowle.

From hence I stood to the Northward according to my
former purpose, but was crossed with a contrarie storme
from the North-west which put me off to the Eastward:
but as the wind shifted I made my way to the North-
westwards all I could, and came againe to the Ice in latitude
75. degrees, from whence I proceeded towards King James
his New Land, and had sight of the Land the eighteenth
of August, being in latitude 77. degrees 30. minutes, and
having a hard gale of wind then at North-west, I stood
close by it under a paire of coarses, but could not weather
Prince Charles Iland, and therefore I bore up, intending
to goe into Nicks Cove, which is on the North side of
Ice-sound, there to attend a faire winde, and in the meane
time to get ballast aboard the Pinnasse, and all other things
necessary. But comming to enter into the Harbour, I
thought it not a place convenient, because I could hardly
have gotten out againe with a Southerly wind, which
would carrie me to the Northwards, and therefore I stood
over for Green-harbor, where I anchored at one a clocke
in the morning, the nineteenth of August.

Here I caused my men to launch a shallop, and to get
ballast and water aboard the Pinnasse, and before nine a
clocke at night I was readie to proceed Northward with
the first faire winde. I stayed here five dayes, during
which time it blew hard for the most part at North and

North-west, and on the foure and twentieth of August, the winde came to the East North-east as wee supposed, till we were out of the Harbour, so I set sayle to proceed Northward, and had the wind Easterly out of Ice-sound, wherewith I stood North-west towards Cape Cold, but being cleere of the high Land, we found the wind to bee at North North-east, therefore I resolved of another course, which was this.

Having perused Hudsons Journall written by his owne hand in that Voyage wherein hee had sight of certayne Land, which he named Hold-with-hope; I found that by his owne reckoning it should not be more then one hundred leagues distant from King James his New Land, and in the latitude of 72. degrees 30. minutes or there-abouts: therefore seeing I could not proceed Northward, I purposed to goe to the South-westwards to have sight of this Land, and discover it, if wind and weather would permit. So I stood away South-west, and sometimes West South-west, till I had runne one hundred and thirtie leagues, and was by account in latitude 72. degrees 30. minutes, where having the wind contrarie to proceed further Westward, I stood Eastward till I had runne thirtie leagues, in which course I should have seene this Land, if credit might be given to Hudsons Journall, but I saw not any. And having a hard gale of winde still Northerly, I conceived no course so good to be taken at this time, as to speed homewards; and so stood to the Southwards, directing my course for England, this beeing the eight and twentieth of August. After which time the wind continued Northerly till the sixt day of September, and

[III.iv.731.] then wee were on the coast of Scotland in latitude 57. degrees, and on the eight day of September had sight of the land of England on the coast of Yorkeshire. Thus by the great mercy of God have we escaped many dangers, and after a cold Summer have some taste of a warme Autumne. All glorie therefore be to God the Father, the Sonne, and the Holy Ghost. Amen.

By this briefe Relation, and by the plat wherein I have

traced the ships way upon each severall traverse it may plainly appeare, how farre the state of this Sea is discovered betwixt 80. and 71. degrees of latitude, making difference of longitude 26. degrees from the Meridian of Hackluyts Headland.

Now if any demand my opinion concerning hope of a passage to bee found in those Seas; I answer, that it is true, that I both hoped and much desired to have passed further then I did, but was hindred with Ice: wherein although I have not attayned my desire, yet forasmuch as it appeares not yet to the contrarie, but that there is a spacious Sea betwixt Groinland and King James his New-land, although much pestered with Ice; I will not seeme to disswade this worshipfull Companie from the yeerly adventuring of 150. or 200. pounds at the most, till some further discoverie be made of the said Seas and Lands adjacent, for which purpose no other Vessell would I advise unto, then this Pinnasse with ten men, which I hold to bee most convenient for that action, although heretofore I conceived otherwise, but now I speake after good experience, having sayled in her out and in above two thousand leagues.

Ro. FOTHERBY.

A Letter of Robert Fotherby to Captaine Edge, written in Cross-rode, July 15, 1615.

MAster Edge, By the mercy of God I came into Crosse-road on Thursday last, being driven from Sea neere shoare by extreme tempest. At the beginning of the storme I was unwittingly embayed with Ice above fortie leagues from land, in latitude 78. degrees and 30. minutes, but, thankes be to God, I got cleare of it, yet not without much trouble and great danger. Having plyed under two coarses to and againe so long till my Pinnasse was made leake with bearing, I tryed it under a mayne coarse and stem'd South-east and South-east and by South, notwithstanding I was hurried to the North-

ward, and fell right with the Foreland, which by reason
of the misty storme we could not see till we were within
a league of it; then I stood over the Bay and came to an
anchor here, where I must be forced to stay till our sailes
be mended, and a new mayne coarse be made, if not a
fore coarse also. Then I purpose to goe to Sea againe,
and to proceed in coasting the Ice to the Westward, if it
hinder me to proceed Northward. I have already coasted
it from Hackluyts Headland to the latitude aforesaid,
and intend to beginne againe so neare as I can at the
place where I was put off with the storme. I came from
Faire Haven the fourth of July, and then had there beene
killed twelve Whales, besides one found dead, and another
brought in by Fra. Birkes, which he found at Sea before
he came into Faire Haven.

Ships of the King of Denmarke. When I came in hither, here were three Ships and a
Pinnasse of the King of Denmarks; they rid in deepe
water about a league and a halfe from the Road, but
weighed from thence, and the Admirall came to an anchor
close by me, and sent to intreat me to come aboord of
him; I went aboord and was courteously entertayned by
the Generall, who questioned me of the Country, and
asked me by what right the English Merchants did resort
and fish in this place: I told him, by the King of Englands
right, who had granted a Patent to the Muscovie Company
of Merchants, whereby he authorizeth them, and for-
biddeth all others to frequent these places. Then he
entreated me to goe with him to Sir Tho. Smiths Bay,
to the two English ships there. I told him, it would be
losse of time to me, because I had some businesse here
to doe, and then to goe forth presently to Sea againe to
prosecute my Discovery. He said, that he would have
me goe with him to be witnesse what passed betwixt him
and you, for he had matters of importance to acquaint
you withall, which concerned our King and theirs, and
therefore intreated me to give direction presently to weigh
and set saile, for I must needs goe with him: I replyed
againe, that it would be a great losse unto me of time,

and I knew not how to answer it; but he told me peremptorily that I must goe with him. So seeing no remedie, I bad the Master be readie: then he presently weighed and kept me aboord him, but afterwards meeting with the two Captaines that came from you, he returned and anchored againe in Crosse-road. I received very courteous entertaynment of the Admirall, Vice-admirall, and of Captaine Killingham: but Captaine Killingham being aboord of me, went away as he seemed, discontented because I would not give him a young Morse I have aboord, which I denyed to doe, because I writ to my Master from Faire Haven, that such a thing I have, and will bring alive into England, if I may. When he went off aboord of me, he said, he would shoot downe my flag: And soone after there came a shot which flue over us, out of the Admirall, and I expected another; but soone after there came a man aboord of me out of the Admirall, to see if any of your men that came in the Shallop, would goe with them into the Bay, and he swore unto me that the shot was made to call their Boat aboord, because they were ready to weigh. As farre as I can perceive, their purpose is to see what Grant the King of England hath made unto the Companie, for they seeme to pretend that [III.iv.732.] the right of this Land belongs to the King of Denmarke, and neither to English nor Hollanders. Thus with my heartie commendations to your selfe, and Master Bredcake, together with my praiers for your prosperous voyage, I commit you to God.

Chap. VIII.

Divers other Voyages to Greenland, with Letters of those which were there employed, communicated to mee by Master William Heley.

An. 1616. Edges Iland was discovered, and a prosperous voyage was made, all the ships being laden, under the command of Captaine Thomas Edge. An. 1617. Witches

Iland was discovered; and what voyage was made appeareth in the Letter following, written to Master Decrow by William Heley.

Laus Deo, in Portnick the 12. of August, 1617.

Worshipfull Sir,

Y dutie remembred, May it please you to understand, that through Gods blessing our Voyage is performed in all the Harbours in the Countrie this yeere, with a greater overplus then our ships will carry: so that in some places wee must of force leave good store of Oyle and Blubber behinde for the next yeere. Wee are all for the most part readie to set sayle, being full laden: onely I desire to see the Coast cleere of Interlopers, whereby our provisions may be left in securitie. We tooke a ship of Flushing, called the Noahs Arke (Master, John Versile) in Horne-sound, having out of him two hundred hogs-heads of Blubber and two Whales and a halfe to cut up, a great Copper, and divers other provisions, and sent him away ballasted with stones. There were two more of them who were gone laden with Blubber, before we could get thither, having intelligence of our comming. There were also two Danes, who made one hundred and odde tunnes of Oyle, and laded one ship for Copen-haven, the other with halfe the Oyle and Finnes for Amsterdam, and left the Country about the sixth or seventh of August. And for Master Cudner, he rid in Portnick, where he killed eleven Whales, and made some seventie and odde tunnes of Oyle, which is laden aboord him and his Finnes. In whom, if our ships had come together thither as I desired, I would have laden fortie or fiftie tunnes of Oyle in him, and displaced his men and sent him for England: but bad weather hindring our ships getting thither, and his sudden departure after our comming in with the Pleasure, shee being laden and not sufficiently fitted to surprise him, he escaped, but I sent her away in company with him, whereby he may not doe any hurt in other places in the Country. I would have had him to have taken in some Oyle, for which I offered him fraight, so I might put some men into him to see to it, and that it might be brought safe to London: but he refused, yet protesteth, he purposeth to bring his ship and goods to London: his voyage is by the thirds, so that his men will rather dye then forget that they have got. The small ship John Ellis is returned from the South Eastward, having made some further discovery, and killed some eight hundred Seamorse, and laden the teeth, and thirtie tunnes of hides, and the rest of his lading in Oyle: he brought some Sea-horse blubber with him. He met with Thomas Marmaduke of Hull in those parts, who had not done any thing when he saw him towards making a voyage, but went for Hope Iland, and no doubt but hee will doe much spoile there. As for the Beare, shee departed for Hamborough the third of August out of Crosse-road; and the Gray-hound in company with her for England, who, I hope, is safely arrived, and by whom I hope you understand of her proceedings at full.

The Whales killed this yeere in the Country are about one hundred and fiftie in number, and the Oyle made will be about one thousand eight hundred and odde tunnes, besides the blubber left for want of caske. The lading of this ship is one hundred and eightie tunnes, as by the Bill of lading here inclosed. Thus having not further wherewith to acquaint your Worship, withall praying God to send all home in safety with a good passage; I humbly take my leave, and doe rest

Readie at our Worships command in all
dutifull service.

WILLIAM HELEY.

[A Letter

[III. iv. 733.] A Letter of Master Robert Salmon to Master Sherwin. In Sir Thomas Smithes Bay, the 24. of June, 1618.

LOving friend Master Sherwine, I kindly salute you, wishing you as much prosperitie as unto my selfe, &c. Since our comming into the Bay, we have beene much troubled with Ice and Northerly windes, so as we have not beene two dayes free of Ice. We had a storme Northerly which brought in much Ice, so as we were inclosed withall eight dayes: there went such a Sea in the Ice that did beate our ships very much for foure and twentie houres, that I did thinke we should have spoyled our ships: but I thanke God we cannot perceive any hurt at all it hath done to us; also we have broken two anchors with the Ice; we have killed thirteene Whales, but they yeeld but little, in regard of the Ice which hath much hindred us in our worke, for in ten dayes we could not doe any worke the Bay was so full of Ice: the Bay was full as low as Fox nose, and now at this present the Bay is full of shattered Ice, the windes hanging Northerly keepes it in. Here is five sayle of Flemmings which have fourteene and sixteene pieces of Ordnance in a ship; and they doe man out eighteene Shallops, so that with theirs and ours here is thirtie Shallops in the Bay, too many for us to make a voyage: there is at the least fifteene hundred tunnes of shipping of the Flemmings; we have reasonable good quarter with them, for we are merry aboord of them, and they of us; they have good store of Sacks, and are very kinde to us, proffering us any thing that we want. I am very doubtfull of making a voyage this yeere, yet I hope Crosse-road will helpe us for one ship, the Company must take another course the next yeere: if they meane to make any benefit of this Country, they must send better ships that must beat these knaves out of this Country, but as farre as I can understand by them, they meane to make a trade of continuance of it: they have every

94

one of them Grave Maurices Commission under his Hand
and Seale : we will let them rest this yeere, and let who will
take care the next yeere, for I hope not to trouble them.
I pray remember my dutie to the Captaine, and also to
honest Master Thornbush, and to John Martin; Master
Smith doth remember his love to you, and to all the rest
of his friends : we are well as this present, I thanke God :
I pray let us heare from you when you have any convay-
ance ; I hope wee shall goe home in companie together as
wee came out.   Thus with my love once againe remembred to you, beseeching God to send us all a prosperous
voyage, and joyfully to meet, I rest.

A Letter of Master Th. Sherwin : Bell-sound this 29. of June, 1618.

MAster William Heley, your Letter I received,
wherein I understand you have tooke very great
griefe, which I am very sorry for : but I am in good hope
to come to you my selfe one of these dayes, that I may
comfort you with a good couple of Hennes and a bottle
of Canary wine, but I pray bee carefull of your selfe and
keepe you warme, and take heede the Nodis doe not pick
out your eyes : but as for the Flemmings let them all go
hang themselves, and although you be not strong enough
to meddle with them, yet the worst wordes are too good
for them, the time may come you may be revenged on
them againe.   The Captaine wishes they would come all
into Bell-sound and beat us out, and carry us for Holland ;
here is a great fleet of them in this Country.   Here came
in two Flemmings, but wee handled them very honestly,
but for feare of after-claps, or had it beene the latter part
of the yeere, we would have handled them better ; now
they be gone for Horne-sound, I would that they had all
of them as good a paire of hornes growing on their heads,
as is in this Country.   As concerning our voyage, Master
Salmon can certifie you both in Horne-sound, and in our
harbour.   My brother Busse, John Martin, and I, dranke

to you, and wish you many a Venison pasty. We have so little to doe wee feare we shall all have the Scurvy, but we have pulled downe the Flemmish house, and brought it neere more fit for our turne. Thus praying you to remember my love to all at Faire-haven, I cease, with my prayers to God, to send you and us all a prosperous voyage, with all your good health, that we may goe merrily home together.

A Letter of James Beversham to Master Heley. From Faire-haven, the 12. of July, 1618.

MAster Heley, My commendations remembred to your selfe, Master Salmon, Master Smith, and Master Beymond, as also to Master Wilkenson, Mate Headland, Master Greene, and the rest of our good friends with you, wishing all your healths as my owne; I am very sorry to understand of the annoyances by the Flemmings, both with you and other places; as also of the small hope there is, in making a voyage this yeere. For our parts we are and have beene so pestered with Ice these twentie dayes, that we have not beene able to goe out to Sea with our Shallops above twice in the time, neither have we beene able to doe any good by reason of foule [III.iv.734.] weather and fogs, nor have seene any more then one Whale in all that time, which after shee was killed turned us to much trouble, by reason of foule weather, and forced us at last to leave her in the Ice, where the Beares made a prey of her, who I feare will spoyle her before shee be recovered. We have killed sixteene Whales besides, whereof the Flemmish Biscainers stole one, for which they have promised satisfaction, but they are so shut up with Ice that they are not able to stirre either Ships or Shallops. All the Sea to the Northward of Hakluyts headland, and both Eastward and Westward thereof, is packt so full of Ice, that I feare it will overthrow our voyage, and put our ships in much hazard, the Lord release us of that miserie in due time, I neither have nor will be slack to doe my

best endevours for the good of the voyage, the prosperitie
whereof I doe much wish and desire both here and in all
other places. I pray remember my love to the Captaine,
by your next convoy to the Southward, with my commendations to all the rest of our friends; thus for present
wishing your health, I kindly take my leave, and rest your
loving friend.

I had thought to have added a large Discourse of occurrents betwixt the Dutch and English in Greenland this
1618. and had prepared it to the Presse. But having
alreadie given some Relation thereof from Captaine Edge
&c. and seeing the insolencies of some of the Dutch were
intolerable to English spirits, which then suffered, or hereafter should reade them; I chose rather to passe them by;
advising my Countrimen not to impute to that Nation
what some frothy spirit vomits from amidst his drinke,
but to honor the Hollanders worth, and to acknowledge
the glorie of the Confederate Provinces, howsoever they
also have their sinks and stinking sewers (too officious
mouthes, such as some in this businesse of Greenland,
beyond all names of impudence against his Majestie, and
his Leege people, as others elsewhere have demeaned
themselves) whose lothsomnesse is not to be cast as an
aspersion to that industrious and illustrious Nation.
Every Body hath its excrements, every great House its
Vault or Jakes, every Citie some Port exquiline and dung-
hils, every Campe the baggage; the World it selfe a Hell:
and so hath every Nation the retriments, scumme, dregs,
rascalitie, intempered, distempered spirits, which not
fearing God nor reverencing Man, spare not to spue out
that to the dishonor of both, which saving the honor of
both can scarsly be related after them. A difference is
to be made of relation and personall faults, of which we
have said enough in the East India quarrels, twixt ours
and the Dutch.

[A Letter

A Letter of John Chambers to W. Heley, Bel-
sound June 16. 1619.

Terrible Disaster.

LOving and approved good friend, Master William
Heley, &c. I am forc't to write in teares unto you
for the losse of our Men, by the most uncouth accident
that ever befell unto poore men. The thirteenth of June
last we were put ashore in the Ice Bay, our Shallops being
not aboord: but as soone as wee heard of it, we made
what haste we could, and haled our shallops upon the Ice,
and went aboord our ship. By that time we had beene
there an houre, making what meanes we could to get her
out, a maine peece of the Cliffe falling, the fearefullest
sight that ever I beheld being then aboord, expecting
nothing else but death, with all the rest that were in her:
But God of his great mercie and providence deliver'd us,
that were not then appointed to dye, that were past all
hope of life; for the Ice fell so high and so much, that it
carried away our fore-Mast, broke our maine-Mast,
sproung our Bouldstrit, and fetcht such a careere that she
heaved a piece of Ordnance over-boord from under our
halfe Decke, hove me over boord amongst the Ice in all
the sea, and yet I thanke the Lord I was never hurt with
a piece of Ice, although it pleased God they were spoyled
and killed close by me. Thus having related unto you
the miserie of this our Voyage, hoping of your aide and
assistance in what you may, I shall be ever bound to pray
for you. The Captaine bid me write unto you for a five
inch Haser, which I pray you spare me and it be possible:
I have writ the particular of our wants in my Brother
Sherwins Letter, which I pray you be a meanes to further
me in. Thus ceasing any further to trouble you, I commit you unto the Lord, unto whom I pray to blesse and
prosper you in this your present Voyage, with all the
rest of your dayes.

The men that are killed are these: My Mate Money,

Nicholas Greene and Allin the Butcher.   There be many
more hurt which I hope will recover it by the helpe of
God and the meanes of a good Surgeon.

L Oving friend Master Heley, I kindely salute you, &c.
  Your Letter I received the fifth of this present:
wherein I understand of the backwardnesse of your
Voyage, the which I am hartily sorrie for: but you must
be content, seeing it is the will of God it shall be so, and
that other harbours take neighbours fare with you: our
best hopes of our Voyage was upon you, for of our selves
we doe little, in regard we are much troubled with Ice,
and have bin so this ten dayes, which hath made us hale
a shoare sixe or seaven times for it: we have had the
windes at North-east, and East North-east, and at North-
west, which now keepes in the Ice: we have killed ten
Whales, whereof eight are made into Oyle, which hath
made one hundred and eleaven Tuns & a halfe, the other
two were killed the fourth of this present, being very
large fish, not doubting but they will make sixe and [III.iv.735.]
thirtie or fortie tunnes: we have the hundred tunnes
aboord, the rest Master Barker taketh in, in regard Master
Bushes shippe is not fitted up, we shall make her fore-
Mast to serve againe and all things else for this Voyage.
The fourth of this present, George Wivelden came from
Horne-sound, where they have killed foure Whales, they
have bin much troubled with windes Easterly, also much
Ice, there is so much Ice off of Point Looke out, that
George could not get about.   This Ice hath put in young
Duke of Hull into Horne-sound, his ship being much
torne with the Ice, his Merchant is now aboord of us, his
name is Medcafe, whom the Captaine doth detaine, his
Voyage is utterly overthrowne, for he hath lost one shallop
with sixe men, and another shallop broken with the Ice,
his Ruther Irons being all broken, his Steeme broke a way
close to the Woodings, also George did meete with a
Fleming of Flushing, burthen two hundred tuns, the
which he thinkes is cast away with Ice, for the Ice did

beate her very sore. I understand by M. Catchers Letter, that there is eleaven saile of Flemmings and Danes about them, I doubt not but we shall call them to account of how many tunnes of Oyle they have made, as they did call us the last Voyage to account: my love is such unto them, that I protest I could wish with all my heart that we might goe and see them, and to spend my best bloud in the righting of our former wrongs. Also I understood by Robert Foxe, that Adrian of Flushing is one of them, I should be very glad to see him, that I might balance the account with him. The Captaine willed mee to write unto you concerning the Russe house, that if you cannot set it up, that then you should make an English house of it, and to place the post of a Deales length, and to be three Deales in length, and so much in breadth, and so to cover it with Deales the next yeare, and so he thinketh that it will make two frames: also hee could wish that you would remove the Coppers more up into the Bay. I pray you commend me to my loving friend Master Sherwine, Master Wilkinson, Master Henderson and Michael Greene; also my love remembred unto your selfe, I take my leave, hoping we shall see you at the Fore-land ere it be long: till when, I pray God to blesse you and prosper you in all your proceedings. Resting still
Your assured friend to command
ROBERT SALMON Junior.

Bell-sound the fifth of
July. 1619.

A Letter of J. Catcher to Master Heley from Faire-haven. Laus Deo, this seventeenth of June, 1620.

L Oving Brother, with my best love I salute you, wishing you better then we at this time, to have good store of Whales to make for you and us a Voyage, for we have seene small store of Whales, but have killed none as yet. In the Flemish harbour there is three Flemings

great shippes, whereof is one Statesman of Warre, who
have set to Sea eighteene shallops with three Biscaners in
everie shallop; and in our harbour two of the Kings of
Denmarkes ships, who have set to Sea seaven shallops
with three Biscainers in everie shallop: the Hollanders
have killed one Whale, and found one Whale of the last
yeares killing.   I thought good to send to you the sooner,
because we hope you have good store of Whales, that you
may send for us to you, which I pray God you may, for
we are in great doubt, but our hope is, if that you are not
yet provided to send for us, we have a great time to stay
in this Countrie, in which time, it may so please God,
that we may here make a Voyage.   For our selves, one of
our men is dead, and one other sicke, so that wee have
but one and fiftie men, which is too little as you know,
therefore if you can spare us three men, they will stand
us in good stead: if our Voyage commeth in, there is to
the Northward good store of Ice, which putteth us in good
comfort that we shall have Whales: the Danes doe report
that there is two shippes to come from Denmarke to our
harbour, but as yet are not come.   I pray you commend
us to Master Wilkinson, Master Greene, Master Hedlam,
Master Cleyborne, Master Alpho, and all the rest of our
good friends.   Humfrey Moore is very sicke, so that we
shall want a Harponiere.   I know not what to write more
to you, for with griefe I write this.   Thus kindely taking
my leave, beseeching God to blesse us, and send us a good
Voyage, with a merry meeting, I rest

Your loving brother to use

JOHN CATCHER.

A Letter of Robert Salmon from Sir Thomas
Smiths Bay, July 6. 1621.

LOving friend Master Heley, with my love I salute
you, &c.   These are to certifie you, that upon the
fifteenth of the last, we arrived at Sir Thomas Smiths
unfortunate Bay: since which time we have killed sixe

Whales, which are almost reduced into Oyle, being some
seventie tunnes or somewhat more; so within a day or
two we may goe sleepe, for I feare we have our portion
of Whales in this place: wee have not seene a Whale this
foureteene dayes, and faire weather is as scarse as the
Whales, for ten daies together nothing but blow, sometime Southerly and sometime Northerly: I doe verily
[III.iv.736.] perswade my selfe that God is much displeased for the
blood which was lost in this place, and I feare a perpetuall
curse still to remaine yet; God I know is all-sufficient,
and may, if it please him, send a Voyage in this place.
Newes from Faire-haven I can write you none, for as yet
we have not heard from him: the reason thereof I cannot
conceive; I feare his Shallop is miscarried, for certainely
else we should have heard from him ere this, or some other
cause there is: I pray God it be not so. I pray commend
me to Master John Hedlam, and tell him that the Master
and Pilot doe set both their horse together, being very
great friends: also I pray commend me to my Cosen
William Driver and Master Wilkinson, wishing them all
happinesse. I am in good hope that you have done some
good upon the Whale, not doubting but you will have
sufficient for your selves and to helpe your neighbours,
the which I desire may be. Other newes I have none to
write you. So desiring God to blesse you in your proceedings in this your Voyage, I take my leave: Resting
Your loving friend to command
ROBERT SALMON Jun.

Nine Ships were imployed Anno 1622. of which one
for Discoverie. Their disastrous successe you may reade
before, page 469. The last Fleete Anno 1623. was set
forth by the former Adventurers, under the command of
Captaine William Goodlard, William Heley being Vice-
admirall. Of the successe thereof you may read the
Letters following.

NATHANIEL FANNE

Laus Deo in Faire-Haven, the foure and twentieth
of June, 1623.

MAster Heley, your health wished, as also a happy
accomplishment of your pretended Voyage desired.
I had written you according to order, of all matters
happening since our arrivall, had not contrarie windes and
weather prevented, and therefore have taken the first
opportunitie offering at present.

Wee arrived at our harbour with both our Ships in
safetie upon the third of this present, blessed be God,
finding the yeare past to have beene a verie hard season,
in regard of the great quantitie of Snow and Ice, but yet
not very offensive to us in respect of our good harbour.
Touching our proceeding upon our Voyage, by the eight
of this present we had killed thirteene Whales, and then
were all our Shallops constrained in, by reason of foule
weather, till the fifteenth, dicto, and upon the fifteenth we
killed two more, which being all boyled but the heads,
and then estimated will hardly make past eightie Tunnes,
which is a very small quantitie. The weather continued
bad till the twentie two, dicto, and upon the three and
twentieth we killed three more, which by probabilitie will
make neere fortie Tunnes. And thus wee doubt not but
by degrees we shall accomplish our Voyage, by the grace
of God.

As touching our order for the Flemmings, wee went as
yesterday aboord them, supposing that wee should have
found the Danes there, but they are not as yet arrived,
but wee found there five sailes of Flemmings, the Admirall
five hundred Tunnes, the Vice-admirall of the same
burthen, the other three neere two hundred each Ship,
having also fiftie or sixtie persons amongst them, having
foure and twentie Shallops belonging to their five Ships,
and are building Houses and Tabernacles to inhabit, for
they make new and substantiall: also they told us, they
expected one or two Ships more everie day: after some

time we had conference concerning the order given us with the Generall Cornelius Ice, and declared unto him that the time granted them to fish upon King James his New Land was expired, and thereupon his Majestie hath granted to our Principals a Commission under the broad Seale of England for the depressing of any Interloper or Flemming whatsoever that we shall meete withall upon this Coast; yet notwithstanding it pleased our Principals to appoint us to goe aboord them, and in a loving manner to informe them hereof, which if you will condescend unto and desist fishing, you shall manifest your selves friends to our Principals; if otherwise, you shall cause them to compell by force, who had rather perswade by love. Unto which he answered, that he heard of no such matter in Holland, for if there were, it should be certified by writing: to which we answered, that Sir Nowel Carroon their Agent was not ignorant of it, who should give information: and saith he, I have a Commission from the Prince of Orange, for the making of my Voyage upon this Coast, which was procured by my Merchants for my defence: and this is that could be gotten by words from him.

Also at our first arrivall, there rode two Biskie shippes with the Flemmings, but within a day or two they waied and stood for the Southward: but inquired of the Flemmings what port they were bound for, they answered, for the North Cape; but Master Mason is perswaded they are at Greene-harbour: to which purpose I wrote to Master Catcher, that he gives order to his shallop that goes to Bel-sound, to stand in for the harbour, to give the Captaine true information. And so for present I rest, intreating you to remember me to Master Salmon and Master John Hadland: and thus contracting my sailes, lest the winde of my words carrie me into the Ocean of discourse, here I anchor: resting

Your friend
NATHANIEL FANNE.

Master Catchers Letter the nine and twentieth of [III. iv. 737.]
June, 1623.

BRother Heley, with my best love I salute you, wishing your health with a prosperous Voyage, &c. Since
our departure, we have had much foule weather and
troubled with Ice before we could get into harbour, and
after we came into harbour, we never let fall anchor, by
reason of the Ice, till the sixteenth of this month, in which
time we killed sixe Whales at the Fore-land, which made
but eighteene Tuns and a halfe; and since we have killed
sixe Whales more, which I hope will make in all upwards
of eightie Tunnes. We have fit nine Shallops verie well,
and I thanke God not one of our Men faileth, save one
that was shot accidentally with a Musket. I hope some
of the Southerne harbours will supply our wants, if there
be any, which I feare there will: our harbour, manie say
still, is unpossible to make a Voyage, by reason that the
Flemmings shed bloud there, which I pray God to take
that plague from us. For Faire-haven, I doubt not but
that you shall heare by the Letters sent you of the proceedings; but Master Sherwin writ, that there is five
Flemmings of five hundred Tunnes a peece: there was
also two Biscainers which the English nor Flemmings
would suffer to fish: therefore they departed, and said
they would goe for the North Cape; but I thinke they are
in Greene-harbour, or gone to the Eastward; which if
they be in Greene-harbour, our Shallop going to Bel-sound
shall touch there to see, and so certifie the Captaine, and
know his will what he would have done in it: I hold it
not fit that they should harbour there. There are no
Danes in the Countrie as yet, &c.

Captaine William Goodlards Letter : Bell-sound this eight of July, 1623.

Loving friend Master Heley, I kindely salute you, wishing health to you with the rest of your companie, praising the Lord for your good successe in your fishing. To certifie you of our proceedings ; wee have killed here in Bel-sound three and thirtie Whales, and lost manie more by Irons broken, yet I hope sufficient to fill our ships : we have boiled a hundred and eightie Tunnes, of which a hundred and sixtie aboord our Ship, and make account sixtie tunnes more will fill our hould. Our Whales here prove verie watrish and leane, which maketh bad Oyle, and hindereth us much in boyling. This present day our shallop came from the Fore-land, at which time they had killed fifteene Whales verie small, and are verie doubtfull of a Voyage there : if God sendeth fish into this harbour, I will not spare till I have killed sufficient to fill all our Casks, to leave for them if there be occasion. The foure and twentieth of June, there was killed at Faire-haven eighteene Whales, which prove verie small to yeelde, by their estimation one hundred and twentie *Flemmings.* tunnes : having there five Flemmings well fortified, and ships of five hundred Tuns some of them, and two more expected thither everie day, which I feare will hinder much our shippes in their fishing this yeare, and in my judgement not to be removed from thence, for they having a Commission from the States to fish upon this Coast ; were our whole Fleete there, and could put them away, yet would they flie to one of our Southerne harbours, and so should we spend our time in following of them, and lose our Voyage, &c. There were two French Ships of Saint John de Luz at Faire-Haven, which were put away by the Flemmings and our Ships, which they judge are gone for the Cape.

With a heavie heart I write you the lamentable accident which happened here the eight and twentieth of June, our shallops all out in chase, and my selfe asleepe; my brother having a shallop lying by the ships side, spide a Whale going into the Ice Bay, followed him and strucke him, and his rope being new ranne out with kinckes, which overthrew his shallop, where he lost his life with my Boy Bredrake, being as we thinke carried away with the rope (the dearest Whale to me that ever was strucke in this harbour) there was never anie losse, I thinke, went so neere my heart, &c.

Many other Letters I could have added, but doubt I have already wearied you with this uncouth Coast, whereto our English Neptunes are now so wonted, that there they have found not onely Venison but Pernassus and Helicon; and have melted a Musæan Fountain out of the Greenland Snowes and Icie Rockes. Whole Elaborate Poems have I seene of Master Heley, as also of James Presson, there composed: but we have harsher Discoveries in hand, to which wee are now shipping you. This I thought good at our parting to advertise thee, that Master Heley hath affirmed to me touching the diversitie of weather in Greeneland; that one day, it hath beene so cold (the *Cold and heat strangely variable.* winde blowing out of some quarter) that they could scarce handle the frozen sailes: another day so hot, that the pitch melted off the ship, so that hardly they could keepe their cloathes from pollution: yea, he hath seene at midnight Tobacco lighted or fired by the Sunne-beames with a *Tobacco lighted by the Sun at midnight.* Glasse. Likewise for a farewell to our Whale-storie, I thought good to deliver Stowes relation touching a Whale somewhat differing in forme from those here usually found in Greeneland: myselfe also having spoken with some diligent viewers thereof in Thanet where it was taken Julie 9. 1574. shooting himselfe on shore besides Rammesgate in the Parish of Saint Peter, and there dying forsaken of his Ocean parent. Hee came on shoare about six of the clocke at night, and died about six the next morning, before which time he roared and was heard more then a *[III.iv.738.]* mile on the land. The length was two and twentie yards, the nether jaw twelve foote in the opening: one of his eyes (which in the Greene-land Whale is verie small, not much greater then the eye of an Oxe) being taken out of his head, was more then six Horses in a Cart could draw; a man stood upright in the place whence the eye was taken. The thicknesse from the backe whereon he lay, to his bellie, which was upwards, was fourteene foote; his taile of the same breadth: three men stood upright in his mouth: betwixt his eyes twelve foote: some of the ribs sixteene foote long: the tongue fifteene foote long: his liver two Cart load: into his nostrils anie man might have crept: the Oyle of his head Spermaceti, &c.

Chap. IX.

The late changes and manifold alterations in Russia since Ivan Vasilowich to this present, gathered out of many Letters and Observations of English Embassadors and other Travellers in those parts.

§. I.

Of the reigne of Ivan, Pheodore his sonne; and of Boris.

Eader, I here present thee not what I would of Russian affaires, but what I could. We Englishmen under the government of his Majestie, have enjoyed such a Sunshine of peace, that our Summers day to many hath beene tedious; they have loathed their Manna, and longed for I know not what Egyptian flesh pots. For what else are Warres but pots set over the fire of Anger (how often of Furie, yea of Hell, the Furies or Devils blowing the coales) and boyling mans flesh? whole Families, Villages, Townes, Cities, Shires, Provinces, not onely hurried thereby in confusions of State, harried and enflamed with combustions of goods and goodnesse, but the flesh of Men, Women, and Children, but chered and as it were boyled beyond the manifold shapes of Death, unto the bones, into the Vapors, Froth, Scumme, Chaos, nothing and lesse then nothing of Humanitie! Such is the inhumanitie, the immanitie, the inanitie of Warres! And such Warres have made impressions into all our Neighbour Countries (whiles wee sit under the shadow of Beati Pacifici) have lightened on Turkie and blasted the Seraglio, have thunder-stricken Barbarie, have torne the Atlas there, and rent the Grison Alpes in Europe; have shaken France with earthquakes; have raysed Belgian stormes, Bohemian broyles, Hungarian gusts, Germanian whirlewinds (these selfe-divided in Civill, that is, the vilest, uncivillest massacres and worst of Warres) that I mention not the inundations and exundations of Poland; the Snowes and Mists of Sweden, the Danish Hailes and Frosts. But all these and more then all these Tempests, Turnado's, Tuffons have combined in Russia, and there made their Hell-mouth centre, there pitching the Tents of Destruction, there erecting the Thrones of Desolation.

Pestilence and Famine had gone two yeeres before as *A. Thuan.* direful Heralds, to denounce these dreadfull warres and *histor. l.* 135. mutations of State: the Pestilence possessing the Northerne parts of the World, and dispossessing it of many many thousands: the Famine in Russia wanting necessaries to eate, necessarily devoured all things, not onely Cats, Mice, and impure Creatures, but mens flesh also, and that in neerest necessitude, Parents revoking to their wombes by unnaturall passage the dearest pledges of Nature, which having even now dyed with hunger, were made preservatives from like death to those which first had given them life. The Mightier made sale of the Poorer, yea, Fathers and Mothers of their Sonnes and Daughters, and Husbands of their Wives, that price might bee had to buy Corne, which was now beyond all names of whatsoever price credible. But these things must be further searched.

Bloudinesse is a slipperie foundation of Greatnesse, and

the Mercifull have the promise to finde mercy: other wisedome (how ever seeming politike) is earthly, sensuall, devillish; yea, ruine to the foole-wise Consultors, as appeareth in Pharaohs working wisely, that is, cruelly, to prevent the multiplying Israelites. The greatest of Creatures on Sea and Land, the Elephant and Whale, live on grasse, weeds, and simpler diet, not on rapine and flesh or fish-devouring prey: Thunders and all tempestuous stormes trouble not the higher aiery Regions, but the lower and those next the baser earthy dregs, the sediment and sinke of the World: nor doth ancient Philosophie reckon Comets other then Meteors, or falling Starres to be Starres indeed, but excludes both from the heavenly Sphæres. Had Alexander followed this rule, and sought Greatnesse in Goodnesse (like him which is Optimus Maximus, the Great God, the great Good of the World) and in himselfe rather then others, in being Master of himselfe then Lord of large Territories; he neither had sighed after the conquests of other Worlds which Foolo-sophie had created, before he had seene the tenth part of this; nor had dyed by poyson in a forraine Countrie, forced to content himselfe with possessing, nay, being possessed of a few feet of earth: then had he beene in very deed (now but in Title) Great Alexander. Great Goodnesse is the true and good Greatnesse.

I know not how fit a Preface this may seeme to the ensuing Russian Relation; this I am sure, that they which write of Ivan Vasilowich, the Great Great Muscovite, doe lay heavie aspersions on his Father and Grand-father, but on himselfe supersuperlatives of crueltie (that I mention not other vices) both for Matter and Forme. These things are delivered particularly in the Histories of Alexander Gwagninus, Tilmannus Bredenbachius, Paulus Oderbornius, Reinoldus Heidensten and others, in large Tractates written thereof purposely. His merits of the English might procure a silence of his evils (wee of all men being in regard of respect to our Nation unworthy to speake, that which hee, if those Authours have not beene

malicious, was worthy to heare) if so dreadfull effects did
not force an Historian (that is, the Register of the execution of Acts of Gods bountie and justice decreed in the
Court of Divine Providence) to looke to the direfull
Cause in foregoing sinnes, that after Ages may heare and
feare.

I will touch a few of those which Gwagninus alone
relates. His owne brother being accused An. 1570. by
Wiskonati, is said without leave granted to cleare himselfe,
to bee put to exquisite tortures first, and after to death; his
wife stripped and set naked to the eyes of all, and then
by one on horse-backe drawne with a rope into the River
and drowned. John Piotrowich, a man of principall command, accused of treason, presenting himselfe to him, not
admitted to make any purgation, was set in Princely
accoutrements on a Throne, the Emperour standing bare-
headed before him and bowing to him, but soone after
with a knife thrusting him to the heart, the Attendants
adding other Furies till his bowels fell out; his body
dragged forth, his servants slaine, three hundred others in
his Castle executed, his Boiarens all gathered into one
house and blowne up with poulder; their Wives and
Daughters ravished before his face by his followers, and
then cut in pieces, and no living thing left in their houses
or grounds; the husbandmens wives stripped naked as
they were borne and driven into a Wood, where were
Executioners purposely set to give them their fatall entertainment. His Chancellor Dubrowsti sitting at table with
his two Sonnes, were also upon accusation without answere
cut in pieces, and the third sonne quartered alive with
foure wheeles, each drawne a divers way by fifteene men.
Miessoiedowyschly, supreme Notarie, displeasing him, his
wife was taken from him, and after some weeks detayning
was with her hand-maid hanged over her husbands doore,
and so continued a fortnight, he being driven to goe in
and out by her all that time. Another Notaries wife was
ravished and then sent home and hanged over her
husbands table, whereat he was forced daily to eate. In

*Al. Gwagnini
descript. Mosc.
George
brother to the
Emperor
done to death.
Hee addes
principal
Nobles, here
omitted.*

travelling if he met any woman whose husband he liked not, he caused her to stand with her nakednesse disclosed till all his retinue were passed. Cutting out tongues, cutting off hands and feet of his complayning Subjects, and other diversified tortures I omit; as also the guarding his father in lawes doores with Beares tyed there, that none might goe in or out, hanging his servants at his doores, torturing him for treasure; casting hundreds of men * at once into the water under the Ice; two thousand seven hundred and seventie thus and by other tortures executed at Novogrod An. 1569. besides women, and the poorer persons which Famine forced, did eate the bodies of the slaine, and were after slaine themselves; the Archbishop also set on a Mare with his feet tyed under the belly, and made to play on Bag-pipes thorow the Citie; the Monks spoyled and slaine; Theodore Sirconii, the Founder of twelve Monasteries, tortured to shew his treasure and then slaine: Wiazinsky his Secretarie, by many dayes renewed tortures dying: hee recreating himselfe with letting Beares loose in throngs of people; John Michalowich Wiskewati the Chancellor, his eares, lips and other members one after another cut off * by piece-meale, notwithstanding all protestations of his innocency; above two hundred other Nobles at the same time variously executed, one his Treasurer, two other Secretaries; the Treasurers wife set on a rope and forcibly dragged to and fro thereon (by that torturing her naked flesh to learne her husbands treasures) whereof soone after she dyed in a Monasterie, into which shee was thrust. All these are but a little of that which Gwagninus alone hath written. A taste and touch is too much of bloud, and in such immanities. He is also said in a famine to have gathered many people, in expectation of almes, on a bridge, and there guarded the bridge being cut to drowne them, as the readiest way for cheapnesse of corne. But I lothe such crudities. His last crueltie was on himselfe, dying with griefe, as was thought, for the death of his eldest sonne Ivan, whom falsly accused he struck with a staffe wrought with Iron, whereof he dyed in

*700. *women at one time; 378. prisoners at another. 500. Matrons and Virgins of noble bloud exposed to be ravished by the Tartars in his sight at another time &c.*

A Secretarie cutting off his privities he died presently; which the Emperour construing to be done purposely, caused him there instantly to eate what he had cut off.

few dayes after. Hee was a man accused for communicating in disposition with his father, and as a joyfull Spectator of his tragicall executions.

But if any delight to reade the terrible and bloudie Acts of Ivan Basilowich, he may glut, if not drowne himselfe in bloud, in that Historie which Paul Oderborne hath written of his life, and both there and in others take view of other his unjust Acts. I will not depose for their truth, though I cannot disprove it: adversaries perhaps make the worst. For my selfe I list not to rake sinkes [III.iv.740.] against him, and would speake in his defence, if I found not an universall conspiracy of all Historie and Reports against him. I honour his other good parts, his wit, his learning (perhaps better then almost any other Russe in his time) his exemplarie severity on unjust Magistrates, his Martiall skill, industrie, fortune, whereby he subdued the Kingdoms of Casan and Astracan (which also the Turke sending from Constantinople an Armie of three hundred thousand to dispossesse him of, A. 1569. besides his hopes and helpes from the Tartars, few returned to tell their disasters, and the destructions of their fellowes) besides what hee got in Siberia and from the Pole, Sweden, Prussian, extending his Conquests East, West, North, and South: yea, his memorie is savourie still to the Russians, which (either of their servile disposition needing such a bridle and whip ; or for his long and prosperous reigne, or out of distaste of later tragedies) hold him in little lesse reputation (as some have out of their experience instructed me) then a Saint.

His love to our Nation is magnified by our Countrimen with all thankfulnesse, whose gaines there begun by him, have made them also in some sort seeme to turne Russe (in I know not what loves or feares, as if they were still shut up in Russia, & to conceale whatsoever they know of Russian occurrents) that I have sustayned no small torture with great paines of body, vexation of minde, and triall of potent interceding friends to get but neglect and silence from some, yea almost contempt and scorne. They

alledge their thankfulnesse for benefits received from that
Nation, and their feare of the Dutch, readie to take advantage thereof, and by calumniations from hence to intervert
their Trade. This for love to my Nation I have inserted
against any Cavillers of our Russe Merchants: though I
must needs professe that I distaste, and almost detest that
(call it what you will) of Merchants to neglect Gods glorie
in his providence, and the Worlds instruction from their
knowledge; who while they will conceale the Russians
Faults, will tell nothing of their Facts; and whiles they
will be silent in mysteries of State, will reveale nothing
of the histories of Fact, and that in so perplexed, diversified chances and changes as seldome the World hath in so
short a space seene on one Scene. Whiles therefore they
which seeme to know most, will in these Russian Relations
helpe me little or nothing (except to labour and frustrated
hopes) I have (besides much conference with eye witnesses)
made bold with others in such books as in divers languages
I have read, and in such Letters and written Tractates as
I could procure of my friends, or found with Master
Hakluyt (as in other parts of our storie) not seeking any
whit to disgrace that Nation or their Princes, but onely
desiring that truth of things done may bee knowne, and
such memorable alterations may not passe as a dreame, or
bee buried with the Doers. Sir Jerome Horsey shall
leade you from Ivans Grave to Pheodores Coronation.

The most solemne and magnificent coronation of
Pheodor Ivanowich, Emperour of Russia, &c.,
the tenth of June, in the yeare 1584. seen and
observed by Master Jerom Horsey Gentleman,
and servant to her Majestie.

*Or Thedor.

Sir Jerom
Horsey.

The death of
Ivan Vasili-
wich 1584.
April 18.

WHen the old Emperor Ivan Vasilowich died (being
about the eighteenth of April, 1584. after our
computation) in the Citie of Mosco, having raigned fiftie
foure yeares, there was some tumult & uprore among some
of the Nobilitie and Comminaltie, which notwithstanding

was quickly pacified. Immediately the same night, the Prince Boris Pheodorowich Godonova, Knez Ivon Pheodorowich, Mesthis Slafsky, Knez Ivan Petrowich Susky, Mekita Romanowich and Bodan Jacoulewich Belskoy, being all noble men, and chiefest in the Emperours Will, especially the Lord Boris, whom he adopted as his third son, and was brother to the Empresse, who was a man very well liked of all estates, as no lesse worthy for his valour and wisedome : all these were appointed to dispose, and settle his Sonne Pheodor Ivanowich, having one sworne another, and all the Nobilitie and Officers whosoever. In the morning the dead Emperour was laid into the Church of Michael the Archangell, into a hewen Sepulchre, very richly decked with Vestures fit for such a purpose : and present Proclamation was made (Emperour Pheodor Ivanowich of all Russia, &c.) Throughout all the Citie of Mosco was great watch and ward, with Souldiors, and Gunners, good orders established, and Officers placed to subdue the tumulters, and maintaine quietnesse : to see what speede and policie was in this case used, was a thing worth the beholding. This being done in Mosco, great men of birth and accompt were also presently sent to the bordering Townes, as Smolensko, Vobsko, Kasan, Novogorod, &c. with fresh garrison, and the old sent up. As upon the fourth of May a Parliament was held, wherein were assembled the Metropolitane, Archbishops, Bishops, Priors, and chiefe Clergie men, and all the Nobility whatsoever : where many matters were determined not pertinent to my purpose, yet all tended to a new reformation in the governement : but especially the terme, and time was agreed upon for the solemnizing of the new Emperours coronation. In the meane time the Empresse, wife to the old Emperour, was with her childe the Emperours son, Charlewich Demetrie Ivanowich, of one yeares age or there abouts, sent with her Father Pheodor Pheodorowich Nagay, and that kindred, being five brothers, to a towne called Ouglets, which was given unto her, and the yong Prince her sonne, with all the

Lord Boris adopted as the Emperors third sonne.

[III.iv.741.]

Lands belonging to it in the shire, with officers of all sorts appointed, having allowance of apparell, jewels, diet, horse, &c. in ample manner belonging to the estate of a Princesse. The time of mourning after their use being expired, called Sorachyn, or fortie orderly dayes, the day of the solemniz-*The day of* ing of this coronation, with great preparations, was come, *Pheodor his* being upon the tenth day of June, 1584. and that day *coronation.* then Sunday, he being of the age of twenty five years: at which time, Master Jerom Horsey was orderly sent for, and placed in a fit roome to see all the solemnity. The Emperour comming out of his Pallace, there went before him the Metropolitane, Archbishops, Bishops, and chiefest Monkes, and Clergie men, with very rich Coapes and Priests garments upon them, carrying pictures of our Lady, &c. with the Emperors Angell, banners, censers, and many other such ceremonious things, singing all the way. The Emperour with his nobility in order entred the Church naméd Blaveshina or Blessednes, where prayers and service were used, according to the manner of their Church: that done, they went thence to the Church called Michael the Archangell, and there also used the like prayers, and service: and from thence to our Lady Church, Prechista, being their Cathedrall Church. In the middest thereof was a chaire of majestie placed, wherein his Ancestors used to sit at such extraordinary times: his roabes were then changed, and most rich and unvaluable garments put on him: being placed in this Princely seate, his nobilitie standing round about him in their degrees, his imperiall Crowne was set upon his head by the Metropolitane, his Scepter globe in his right hand, his sword of Justice in his left of great riches: his six crowns also, by which he holdeth his Kingdomes were set before him, and the Lord Boris Pheodorowich was placed at his right hand: then the Metropolitan read openly a booke of a small volume, with exhortations to the Emperour to minister true Justice, to injoy with tranquility the Crowne of his ancestours, which God had given him, and used these words following:

Through the will of the almightie and without beginning God, which was before this world, whom we glorifie
in the Trinitie, one onely God, the Father, the Sonne, and
the holy Ghost, maker of all things, worker of all in all
every where, fulfiller of all things, by which will, and
working, he both liveth and giveth life to man : that our
onely God which enspireth everie one of us his onely
children with his word to discerne God through our Lord
Jesus Christ, and the holy quickning spirit of life, now in
these perillous times established us to keepe the right
Scepter, and suffer us to raigne of our selves to the good
profit of the land, to the subduing of the people, together
with the enemies, and the maintenance of vertue. And
so the Metropolitan blessed and laid his crosse upon him.
After this, he was taken out of his chaire of Majesty,
having upon him an upper roabe adorned with precious
stones of all sorts, orient pearles of great quantity, but
alwayes augmented in riches : it was in weight two
hundred pounds, the traine and parts thereof borne
up by six Dukes, his chiefe imperiall Crowne upon his
head very precious : his staffe imperiall in his right
hand of an Unicornes horne of three foote and a halfe
in length beset with rich stones, bought of Merchants
of Ausburge by the old Emperour, in Anno 1581. and
cost him 7000. Markes sterling. This Jewel Master
Horsey kept sometimes, before the Emperour had it.
His Scepter globe was carried before him by the Prince
Boris Pheodorowich : his rich cap beset with rich stones
and pearles, was carried before him by a Duke : his sixe
Crownes also were carried by Demetrius Ivanowich Godonova, the Emperours unckle, Mekita Romanowich ·the
Emperors unckle, Stephen Vasiliwich, Gregorie Vasiliwich, Ivan Vasiliwich brothers of the bloud royall. Thus
at last the Emperour came to the great Church doore,
and the people cried, God save our Emperour Pheodor
Ivanowich of all Russia, His Horse was there ready
most richly adorned, with a covering of imbrodered
pearle and precious stones, saddle, and all furniture

agreeable to it, reported to be worth 300000. markes sterling.

There was a bridge made of a hundred & fiftie fadomes in length, three manner of waies, three foot above ground, and two fadome broad, for him to goe from one Church to the other with his Princes and nobles from the presse of the people, which were in number infinite, and some at that time pressed to death with the throng. As the Emperor returned out of the Churches, they were spred under foot with cloth of Gold, the porches of the Churches with red Velvet, the Bridges with Scarlet, & stammelled cloth from one Church to another: and as soone as the Emperor was passed by, the cloth of gold, velvet and scarlet was cut, & taken of those that could come by it, every man desirous to have a piece, to reserve it for a monument: silver and gold coine, then minted of purpose was cast among the people in great quantitie. The Lord Boris Pheodorowich was sumptuously and richly attired, with his garments decked with great orient pearle, beset with all sorts of precious stones. In like rich manner were apparelled all the family of the Godonovaes in their degrees, with the rest of the Princes and nobilitie, whereof one named Knez Ivan Michalowich Glynsky, whose roabe, horse and furniture, was in register found worth one hundred thousand markes sterling, being of great antiquitie. The Empresse being in her Pallace, was placed in her chaire of Majesty also before a great open window: most precious, and rich were her robes, and shining to behold, with rich stones, and orient Pearles beset, her crowne was placed upon her head, accompanied with her Princesses, and Ladies of estate: then cried out the people, God preserve our noble Empresse Irenia. After all this, [III.iv.742.] the Emperour came into the Parliament house, which was richly decked: there he was placed in his royall seat adorned as before: his sixe crownes were set before him upon a Table: the Bason and Ewre royall of gold held by his knight of gard, with his men standing two on each side in white apparell of cloth of silver, called Kindry with scepters and battle-axes of gold in their hands, the Princes and nobility were all placed according to their degrees all in their rich roabes.

The Emperour after a short Oration, permitted every man in order to kisse his hand: which being done, he removed to a princely seate prepared for him at the table: where he was served by his Nobles in very princely order. The three out roomes being very great and large were beset with plate of gold and silver round, from the ground up to the vauts one upon the other: among which plate were many barrels of silver and gold: this solemnitie and triumph lasted a whole weeke, wherein many royall pastimes were shewed and used: after which, the chiefest men of the Nobilitie were elected to their places of office and dignitie, as the Prince Boris Pheodorowich was made chiefe Counsellour to the Emperour, Master of the Horse, had the charge of his person, Lieutenant of the Empire, and warlike engins, Governor or Lieutenant of the Empire of Cazan, and Astracan, and others: to this dignitie were by Parliament, and gift of the Emperour given him many revenewes and rich lands, as there was given him, and his for ever to inherite a Province called Vaga, of three hundred English miles in length, and two hundred and fiftie in bredth, with many Townes and great Villages populous and wealthy: his yearely Revenew out of that Province, is five and thirtie thousand Markes sterling, being not the fifth part of his yeare Revenue. Further, he and his house be of such authoritie and power, that in forty dayes warning, they are able to bring into the field a hundred thousand Souldiours well furnished.

The conclusion of the Emperours Coronation was a peale of Ordnance, called a Peale royall, two miles without the Citie, being a hundred and seventy great pieces of brasse of all sorts, as faire as any can be made; these pieces were all discharged with shot against bulwarkes made of purpose: twentie thousand hargubusers standing in eight ranks two miles in length, apparelled all in velvet, coloured silke and stammels, discharged their shot also twise over in good order: and so the Emperour accompanied with all his Princes and Nobles, at the least fiftie thousand horse, departed through the Citie to his pallace. This royall coronation would aske much time, and many leaves of paper to be described particularly as it was performed: it shall suffice, to understand that the like magnificence was never seene in Russia.

The Coronation, and other triumphs ended, all the Nobilitie, officers, and Merchants, according to an accustomed order every one in his place and degree, brought rich presents unto the Emperour, wishing him long life, and joy in his kingdome.

The same time also Master Jerom Horsey aforesaid, remaining as servant in Russia for the Queens most excellent Majestie, was called for to the Emperour, as he sate in his Imperiall seat, and also a famous Merchant of Netherland being newly come to Mosco (who gave him selfe out to be the King of Spaines subject) called John de Wale, was in like sort called for. Some of the Nobilitie would have preferred this subject of the Spaniard before Master Horsey servant to the Queen of England, whereunto Master Horsey would in no case agree, saying, hee would have his legges cut off by the knees, before hee would yeelde to such an indignitie offered to his Soveraigne the Queenes Majestie of England, to bring the Emperour a present, in course after the King of Spaines subject, or any other whatsoever. The Emperour, and the Prince Boris Pheodorowich perceiving the controversie, sent the Lord Treasurer Peter Ivanowich Galavyn, and Vasili Shalkan, both of the Counsell, to them, who delivered the Emperour backe Master Horseys speech: whereupon he was first in order (as good reason) admitted and presented the Emperour in the behalfe of the English Merchants trading thither, a present, wishing him joy, and long to raigne in tranquilitie, and so kissed the Emperours hand, he accepting the present with good liking, and avouching, that for his Sisters sake, Queene Elizabeth of England, he would be a gracious Lord to her

Merchants, in as ample manner as ever his Father had beene: and being dismissed, he had the same day sent him, seaventie dishes of sundry kinds of meats, with three carts laden with al sorts of drinks very bountifully. After him was the foresaid subject of the Spanish King admitted with his present, whom the Emperor willed to be no lesse faithfull & serviceable unto him, then the Queene of Englands subjects were & had been, & then the King of Spains subjects shold receive favor accordingly.

All these things thus in order performed, prayses were sung in all the Churches. The Emperour and Empress very devoutly resorted on foote to many principal Churches in the Citie, and upon Trinitie Sunday betooke themselves to a progresse in order of procession, to a famous Monasterie called Sergius and the Trinitie, sixtie miles distant from the Citie of Mosco, accompanied with a huge armie of Noblemen, Gentlemen, and others, mounted upon goodly Horses with furniture accordingly.

The Empresse of devotion tooke this journey on foote all the way, accompanyed with her Princesses and Ladies, no small number: her Guard and Gunners were in number twentie thousand: her chiefe Counsellor or Attendant, was a noble man of the bloud Royall her Uncle of great authoritie, called Demetri Ivanowich Godonova. All this progresse ended, both the Emperour and Empresse returned to Mosco: shortly after, the Emperour by the direction of the Prince Boris Pheodorowich, sent a power [III.iv.743.] into the Land of Siberia, where all the rich Sables and Furres are gotten. This power conquered in one yeere and a halfe one thousand miles. In the performance of this warre, there was taken prisoner the Emperour of the Country, called Chare Sibersky, and with him many other *Chare* Dukes and Noble men, which were brought to Mosco, *Sibersky* with a guard of Souldiers and Gunners, who were received *Prince of* into the Citie in very honourable manner, and doe there *Siberia taken* remaine to this day. *prisoner &*
brought to
Hereupon the corrupt Officers, Judges, Justices, Cap- *Mosco.*

taines and Lieutenants through the whole Kingdome were remooved, and more honest men substituted in their places, with expresse commandement, under severe punishment to surcease their old bribing and extortion which they had used in the old Emperours time, and now to execute true justice without respect of persons: and to the end that this might be the better done, their lands and yeerly stipends were augmented: the great taskes, customes, and duties, which were before laid upon the people in the old Emperours time, were now abated, and some wholly remitted, and no punishments commanded to be used, without sufficient and due proofe, although the crime were capitall, deserving death: many Dukes and Noble men of great Houses, that were under displeasure, and imprisoned twentie yeeres by the old Emperour, were now set at libertie and restored to their lands: all prisoners were set at libertie, and their trespasses forgiven. In summe, a great alteration universally in the government followed, and yet all was done quietly, civilly, peaceably, without trouble to the Prince, or offence to the Subject: and this bred great assurance and honour to the Kingdome, and all was accomplished by the wisedome especially of Irenia the Empresse.

These things being reported and carried to the eares of the Kings and Princes that were borderers upon Russia, they grew so fearfull and terrible to them, that the Monarch of all the Scythians called the Crim Tartar or *Sophet Keri* great Can himselfe, named Sophet Keri Alli, came out of *Alli King of* his owne Countrie to the Emperour of Russia, accom- *the Crims* panied with a great number of his Nobilitie well horsed, *arrivall at* although to them that were Christians they seemed rude, *Mosco.* yet they were personable men, and valiant: their comming was gratefull to the Emperour, and their entertainment was honourable: the Tartar Prince having brought with him his wives also, received of the Russe Emperour entertainment, and Princely welcome according to their estates.

Not long after, one thousand and two hundred Polish

Gentlemen, valiant Souldiers, and proper men came to Mosco, offering their service to the Emperour, who were all entertayned: and in like sort many Chirkasses, and people of other Nations came and offered service. And as soone as the report of this new created Emperour was spred over other Kingdomes of Europe, there were sent to him sundrie Ambassadors, to wish him joy and prosperitie in his Kingdome: thither came Ambassadors from the Turke, from the Persian, the Bogharian, the Crim, the Georgian, and many other Tartar Princes. There came also Ambassadors from the Emperour of Almaine, the Pole, the Swethen, the Dane, &c. And since his Coronation no enemie of his hath prevailed in his attempts.

It fell out not long after, that the Emperour was desirous to send a message to the most excellent Queene of England, for which service he thought no man fitter then Master Jerome Horsey, supposing that one of the Queenes owne men and subjects would bee the more acceptable to her. The summe of which message was, That the Emperor desired a continuance of that league, friendship, amitie and intercourse of traffique which was betweene his Father and the Queenes Majestie and her Subjects, with other private affaires besides, which are not to bee made common. *The new Emperor Pheodore Ivanowitch his Letters and Requests to the Queene.*

Master Horsey having received the Letters and Requests of the Emperour, provided for his journey over Land, and departed from Mosco the fift day of September, thence unto Otver, to Torshook, to great Novogrod, to Vobskie, and thence to Nyhouse in Livonia, to Wenden, and so to Riga: (where he was beset, and brought forthwith before a Cardinall, called Ragevil, but yet suffered to passe in the end:) From thence to Mito, to Golden, and Libou in Curland, to Memel, to Koningsburgh in Prussia, to Elbing, to Dantzike, to Stetine in Pomerland, to Rostock, to Lubeck, to Hamborough, to Breme, to Emden, and by Sea to London. Being arrived at her Majesties Royal Court, and having delivered the Emperours Letters with good favour, and gracious accept- *Master Horseys voyage from Mosco to England over land.*

ance, he was forthwith againe commanded to repasse into
Russia, with other Letters from her Majestie to the
Emperour, and Prince Boris Pheodorowich, answering
the Emperours Letters, and withall requesting the favour
and friendship, which his Father had yeelded to the
English Merchants : and hereunto was he earnestly also
solicited by the Merchants of London themselves of that
Companie, to deale in their behalfe. Being thus dispatched from London by Sea, he arrived in Mosco, the
twentieth of Aprill, 1586. and was very honourably welcommed, and for the Merchants behoofe, obtayned all his
Requests, being therein specially favoured by the Noble
Prince Boris Pheodorowich, who alwayes affected Master
Horsey with speciall liking. And having obtayned
priviledges for the Merchants, he was recommended from
the Emperour againe, to the Queene of England his
Mistresse, by whom the Prince Boris, in token of his
honourable and good opinion of the Queenes Majestie,
sent her Highnesse a Royall present of Sables, Luzarns,
cloth of Gold and other rich things. So that the Companie of English Merchants, next to their thankfulnesse
to her Majestie, are to account Master Horseys paines
their speciall benefit, who obtayned for them those priviledges, which in twentie yeeres before would not be
granted.

The manner of Master Horseys last dispatch from the
Emperour, because it was very honorable, I thought
good to record. Hee was freely allowed post-horses for
him and his servants, victuals and all other necessaries
for his long journey : at every Towne that he came unto
from Mosco to Vologda, which is by Land five hundred
miles, he received the like free and bountifull allowances,
at the Emperours charge. New victuall and provision
were given him upon the River Dwina at every Towne
by the Kings Officers, being one thousand miles in length.
When he came to the new Castle, called Archangel, he
was received of the Duke Knez Vasili Andrewich
Isvenogorodsky by the Emperours Commission into the

Castle, Gunners being set in rankes after their use, where he was sumptuously feasted: from thence he was dispatched with bountifull provision and allowance in the Dukes Boat, with one hundred men to rowe him, and one hundred Gunners in other Boats to conduct him, with a Gentleman Captaine of the Gunners. Comming to the Road where the English, Dutch, and French ships rode, the Gunners discharged, and the shippes shot in like manner fortie six pieces of their Ordnance, and so hee was brought to his lodging at the English house upon Rose Iland.

And, that which was the full and complete conclusion of the favour of the Emperour and Boris Pheodorowich toward Master Horsey, there were the next day sent him for his further provision upon the Sea by a Gentleman and a Captaine, the things following. Sixteene live Oxen, seventie Sheepe, six hundred Hens, five and twentie flitches of Bacon, eightie bushels of Meale, six hundred loaves of bread, two thousand Egges, ten Geese, two Cranes, two Swannes, sixtie five gallons of Meade, fortie gallons of Aquavitæ, sixtie gallons of Beere, three young Beares, foure Hawkes, store of Onions and Garleeke, ten fresh Salmons, a wilde Boare.

All these things were brought him downe by a Gentleman of the Emperours, and another of Prince Boris Pheodorowich, and were received in order by John Frese servant to Master Horsey, together with an honourable present and reward from the Prince Boris, sent him by Master Francis Cherry an English man: which present was a whole very rich piece of cloth of Gold, and a faire paire of Sables.

IVan Vasilowich is reported to have had seaven Wives, and of them to have left three children surviving, Theodore or Pheodore and Demetrius a yongling by his last wife, and a Daughter, which was the wife of L. Boris *Thuan. hist.* aforesaid, whose sister Pheodore had married in his *lib.* 120. Fathers life time, who would have caused her divorse for

her barrennesse (as he had caused Ivan his eldest sonne
divers times to doe and his refusing it at last, was the
occasion of that angry, last, and fatall blow, before mentioned) but being protracted by faire excuses for a time,
the divorse of soule and body in the Father prevented
that in the marriage bed of the Sonne. Yet by his
Testament he ordained, that if within two yeares she
proved not fruitfull, hee should marrie another. The
Divorce
urged.
executers urged this after that terme expired; but Gernia
or Irenia, so wrought with her husband, that their counsels
were frustrate: wherein she was assisted by the politicke
wisdome of her brother Boris, who was now become chiefe
Pilot, though not the Master in that Russian ship: and
is said formerly to have been no small doer in those cruel
designes of Ivan his deceassed Master; yet had he
cunningly cast the blame on him now dead, and wisely
insinuated into the peoples favour, by mitigating the
severitie of his Decrees. You have read before of his
great Revenues and wealth, recorded by eye witnesses.
D. Fl. &
S. I. H.
Thuanus saith, that three hundred of the Knazeys and
Boiarens, whereof the Senate of the Empire consisted,
Boris his plot.
by advise of the Executors, had subscribed. Boris made
the simpler Emperor beleeve, that it was a conspiracie
against him: whereupon they were all committed, ten of
which (whom he thought his most dangerous adversaries)
were suddainly and privly executed: to the rest, he
procured the Emperours pardon and favour, seeming very
sorrowfull that this clemency had beene so much fore-
slowed: and that the hastie execution had prevented his
officious indevors for their deliverance. And that he
Thuan. hist.
lib. 135. see.
Demetrius
slain some tell
that one pre-
tended his
coller stood
awry, in
mending it cut
his throate.
might seem serious, he got their goods to be restored to
their heires: so working himselfe into the good liking of
all degrees.
   But soone after, yong Demetrius the Emperours brother
was slaine, as hee was going to Church betwixt two
Boiarens, by a mad man (as he seemed) who was thereupon
suddenly slaine; but the author which set him on worke,
could not be found: whereupon Boris was suspected to

affect the soveraigntie. Thuanus elsewhere telleth, that hee corrupted those which were about Demetrius: and the great Bell being rung as is usuall in cases of fire to bring the people together, Demetrius at that noise running forth, some were set in that tumult to kil him, which accordingly was effected, as he was comming downe a Ladder: the rumour whereof, caused the tumultuous people (making no curious search for the doers) to kil those of the Family which they met in their furie, to put the suspition thereof from themselves: which notwithstanding, Boris exercised severer tortures and terrible executions upon them, and as one which hartily execrated the fact, burned the fort to expiate the parricide. This place being farre remote * from the Court, whither he was thought purposely to have sent him, could not admit so open evidence of manifold testimony; but that it gave occasion of other Tragedies, by another supposed Demetrius, as shall anon appeare. Meane while, Boris could not escape aspersion of the fact past, and suspition of like intended to the present Prince, and therefore was forced to conjure up his best wits to worke him into better reputation. He did hereof either take occasion, or make occasion by divers fires in * divers Cities of the Kingdome, the Houses being of wood, and easily consumed: which losse (made, as some deliver by his own incendiaries, he seemed much to commiserate, and by affected bountie, repaired those ruines out of the publique Treasure: others say, out of his private purse:) thus, not onely raising so many Phœnixes out of those ashes; but making devouring fire, become fuell to his magnificence, and raking reputation out of the flames and cinders: thence erecting a Theatricall scene whereon to acte in popular spectacles, his many parts of care, industry, alacrity, wisedome, power, bounty, and whatso-ever might fether his nest in the peoples hearts, thus easily stoln and entertained in affection to him, whiles Theodore lived, which was not long: he dying in the yeare 1598. on twelfe day, having lived thirty sixe yeares, and reigned neere fourteene. His impotency of body and

*It was in the Northern parts at Duglets. [III.iv. 745.]

*Some write that he caused divers places in Mosco to be fired, and then afterwards out of his owne cost repaired them.

minde, you have read before in part. Thuanus affirmeth, that Ivan Vasilowich his Father said, he was fitter to ring Bels in Churches, then to governe an Empire; aluding therein to his superexceeding devotion and most devout superstition. His death caused a new aspersion on Boris as procured, in some mens conceits (and reports) by poyson.

His dead body was buried with his ancestors, in Saint Michaels Temple in the Castle, and Souldiours were presently sent to the borders, to prohibite ingresse or egresse. Theodores will was read, and therein Gernia (or Irenia) his wife, and the Patriarch, entrusted with the administration of the State. Hereupon a generall State assembly was assembled at Mosco, and their oathes given to the Empresse. After this the Empresse went into a Nunnery, to passe there the fortie dayes destined to publique sorrow: in which time (whether of her owne or with her brothers accord) making shew of unspeakable sorrow for her deceased Lord, she renounced the world, and transferred the Imperiall government upon the Knazeys and Boiarens, which her Husband had bequeathed to her; that they, according to their wisdome, and love to their Countrie, might take care thereof. This was done by her brothers counsell, to try what the people would doe: who were so moved therewith, that they came thronging to the Nunnerie gates, lamentably imploring her care in so perillous a time, whom onely they were bound to serve. And when she bad them goe to the Knazeys and Boiarens; they protested against them, saying, they had sworne to her, and would be ordered by L. Boris, her brother. Hereupon Boris Pheodorowich goeth out to appease their tumult, and undertaketh for the fortie dayes of mourning, together with the Knazeys and Boiarens to administer the Empire. In which time, the Empresse renounced secular cares, and professed her selfe a Nunne; changing her name from Gernia to Alexandrina.

The time of mourning being past, the people were called into the Castle, and the Chancellour made an

Oration, perswading them to sweare obedience to the
Knazeys and Boiarens, which they with out-cryes dis-
claymed, offering to doe it to the Queene and L. Boris.
The Councell sitting to consider hereof, the Chancellor
came forth againe, and commanded them to sweare to the
Knazeys and Boiarens; the Queene having now become
a Nunne. Whereupon they all named Boris her Brother,
as one worthy of the State, to whom they were readie to
sweare. Hee being present, rose up and modestly excused
himselfe, protesting his unwillingnesse and unworthinesse, *Boris his will-*
and bidding them chuse some other more worthy. And *ing unwilling-*
going withall into the Church, they laid in manner force- *nesse.*
able hands on him, with loud cryes and lamentations,
beseeching him not to forsake them. Whereat he wept
and still refused, alleaging his insufficiencie: and to kindle
greater desire in the people and Nobles, absented and hid
himselfe with his Sister in the Nunnerie the space of a
moneth. In which space the people fearing his flight,
besieged the place, and with continuall clamours urged
the Queene, to perswade her Brother to accept of the
Empire which she had refused. Shee againe sends them
to the Knazeys and Boiarens, the mention of whose names
seemed to cast them into a fit of mutinie and sedition.
Boris then commeth forth and tels them, if they were no
quieter, he also would take Sack-cloth, and (as his Sister
had done) enter into a Monasterie. They made so much
greater stirres, casting out some desperate threats of
looking to themselves, where the Common-wealth was
desperately neglected. The Queene then wonne by their
importunitie perswadeth her brother no longer to resist
Gods will, which had put this constancie into the peoples
mindes, and to accept that which thus God seemed to
command, praying for his blessing therein.

Boris after new excuses, at last seeming overcome by
his Sisters intreaties, and to have held out sufficiently to
remove envie, assenteth to her, and shee signifieth as
much to the people, to whom she presents him, praying
them to be as loyall to him, as they had beene earnest for

Boris his
speech.

[III.iv.746.]

him. Boris also spake unto them: Forasmuch as it seemeth good to the Divine Grace and Providence, whereby all things are governed, that by common consent and continuall Prayers intreated, I take on mee the Princi-palitie over you, and all the Provinces of Russia, I will no longer resist, how heavie soever I conceive this burthen to my shoulders, but have determined to undertake your protection with greatest fidelitie, being readie to sway the Russian Scepter and Government, as farre as Gods grace shall enable mee. On the other side bee you faith-full to mee and to my command, as God may you helpe. I am your most gentle King.

Boris
Emperor.

Joyfull acclamations followed, with all protestation of their fidelitie and future obedience. He entring into the Monasterie, after Prayers, received the first Benediction. The people returned full of joy, and the Bels (of which are numbred in Mosco, three thousand) resounded the publike Festivitie. All the Magistrates and Officers, & such as received Salarie of the King, go presently to the Monasterie and carrie Gold, Silver, Precious Stones, Pearles, Bread, and Salt, (after the solemne custome) with wishes of long life & al happines, and desiring to accept in good worth their Presents. He with thankes rendred, accepts only the Bread and Salt, saying, these were his; the rest they should take to themselves. Then doth hee

His Wife, Son,
& Daughter.

bid them to a Feast, and presently with Mary his Wife, Theodore his Sonne of ten yeeres old, and Arsenica his Daughter being sixteene, he goeth out of the Monasterie with pompeous Procession to the Castle. Like Presents were offered to his Wife and Children, which accepted only the Bread and Salt, remitting the rest to the Pre-senters. When he was comne to the Castle, he chose his Sisters Lodging; for that of the Prince deceased, as offensive by his death, was destroyed and after new built.

After Festivall entertaynment of innumerable people, solemne Oath was taken of all the Governours; those things being in action till May. Then came newes that the Crim Tartars had entred the borders thinking to find

Tartars.

all things troubled with an interregne; whereupon he assembled an Armie of three hundred thousand, and went in person against them. But the Tartars hearing how things went, returned home and sent Embassadors to the Emperours Tents. Hee returned with them to Mosco, where the next September (which is the beginning of the Russian New yeere, which enters in other places with *Russian New* January following) hee was publikely blessed by the *yeere.* Patriarke, carrying a golden Crosse in his hand, and on the fourteenth of September, before the Knazeys, Boiarens, Bishops and other Orders, had the Crowne set on his head *Boris crowned.* by the Patriarke, and the Scepter put in his hand, with the Solemnitie in such cases accustomed.

Twelve dayes together all Orders were feasted in the Castle, and the Magistrates and Officers had a yeeres pay given them. Merchants also of other Countries had Immunities and Priviledges granted. The Rustickes had their payments to their Boiarens reasonably rated, and their persons made more free. Germane Merchants had moneyes lent them to repay seven yeeres after without Usurie. Widdowes, and Orphans, and poorer persons received much Almes. Pheodores Obsequies were solemnely performed, and the Priests richly rewarded; and that Empire which seemed dead with the death of the house of Beala, now was as it were revived, and received a glorious Resurrection.

Thus have we delivered you Thuanas his report touching Boris manner of acquiring the Empire without publike envie, and cunning wiping off the aspersions of Pheodore and Demetrius their deaths. And as every bodie is nourished by Aliments correspondent to the Principles of the Generation, so did hee seeke by politike wisdome to establish that which by wise Policies he had gotten. Wherein his care was not little to multiply Treasure, and *His policies.* as at first hee had seemed popularly prodigall, so after a small time of his Reigne, hee became providently penurious, the wonted allowances of the Court being much shortened from that which had beene in former times, as

I have received from eye-witnesses. Likewise he was carefull to hold good tearmes with his Neighbouring Princes, and aswell by plots at home, as by forreigne Aliance indevoured to settle on his Race this new gotten Empire. He is said for this end to have sought a Wife for his sonne out of England, and a Husband for his Daughter out of Denmarke. His Wife was a woman of haughtie spirit, who thought her too good for any Hollop (so they call a slave, and such she esteemed all the subjects) and on such tearmes she is said to have beene denied to a

P. Basman. great man his best Souldier and Commander of his Armie.

But while his Sunne shined now in the height of his course, and with brightest and warmest beames of prosperitie, there arose grosse vapours out of Demetrius his grave, which grew quickly into a blacke darke cloud, and not only eclipsed that Imperiall glorie, but soone engendred a bloudie storme, which with a floud swept away that whole Family, and over-whelmed also the whole Empire. Contraries set together cause the greater lustre;

*Where the for which cause I will bring on the stage a Gentleman,
censorious which attended Sir Thomas Smith employed in Honour-
bitternesse also able Embassage from his Majestie of Great Brittaine to
seemeth too the then flourishing Emperor Boris: and out of his large
much to insult Relations deliver you this which followeth in his owne
on Boris his words (omitting the most part * to our purpose not so
disasters. pertinent) in the Booke printed, Anno 1605.

[III.iv.747.]

§. II.

Occurrents of principall Note which happened in Russia, in the time while the Honourable Sir Thomas Smith remayned there Embassador from his Majestie.

Ir Thomas Smith Knight, accompanied with Sir T. Challenor and Sir W. Wray Knights, divers Gentlemen and his owne Attendants, repayred to the Court on the tenth of June 1604. then lying at Greenwich, where by the Right Honourable the Earle of

Salisburie he was brought to His Majestis presence, kissed his Hand, &c. The next day he tooke leave of the Prince, and on the twelfth being furnished with his Commission, he came to Gravesend, and next morning went aboord the John and Francis Admirall: and the two and twentieth of July anchored within a mile of the Archangell. The sixteenth of September, hee came to Vologda: the five and twentieth to Perislawe, and there staid three dayes, and then departed to Troites, (that faire and rich Monasterie) so to Brattesheen and Rostovekin, five versts from the great Citie of Musco. The fourth of October, the Prestave came and declared the Emperours pleasure that hee should come into the Mosco that forenoone: presently after came Master I. Mericke Agent, with some twentie Horses to attend his Lordship, which forth-with was performed. Then we did ride, til we came within a little mile of the many thousands of Noblemen and Gentlemen on both sides the way, attended on horsebacke to receive his Lordship. Where the Embassadour alighted from his Coach, and mounted on his foot-cloth Horse, and so rode on with his Trumpets sounding. A quarter of a mile farther, met him a proper and gallant Gentleman a-foot of the Emperours stable, who with Cap in hand, declared to the Embassadour, that the Emperour, the young Prince, and the Master of the Horse, had so farre favoured him, as to send him a Jennet, very gorgeously trapped with Gold, Pearle, and Precious Stone: and particularly, a great Chaine of plated Gold about his necke, to ride upon. Whereupon the Embassador alighted, imbraced the Gentleman, returned humble thankes to them all, and presently mounted. Then he declared that they likewise had sent horses for the Kings Gentlemen, which likewise were very richly adorned, then for all his followers: which Ceremonie or State performed, and all being horsed, he departed, we riding orderly forward, till wee were met by three great Noblemen, severed from the rest of the multitude, and the Emperours Tolmache or Interpreter with them.

They being within speech, thus began that Oration
they could never well conclude: Which was, That from
their Lord and Master the mightie Emperour of Russia,
&c. they had a message to deliver his Lordship. The
Embassadour then thinking they would be tedious and
troublesome with their usuall Ceremonies; prevented their
farther speech with this (to them a Spell) That it was
unfitting for Subjects to hold discourse in that kind of
complement, of two such mightie and renowmed Potentates on horsebacke. They (hereby not only put by
their Ceremonious Saddle-sitting, but out of their Paper
instructions) allighted suddenly, as men fearing they were
halfe unhorsed, and the Embassadour presently after them,
comming very courteously all three, saluting the Embassadour and the Kings Gentlemen, taking them by the hands.
Thus like a Scholer, too old to learne by rote (the Duke
named King Volladamur Evanywich Mawsolskoy) with
his Lesson before him, declared his message; which was,
that he with the other two Noblemen, were sent from the
Great Lord, Emperour and great Duke Boris Pheodorowich, selfe-upholder, great Lord Emperour, and great
Tedious Title. Duke of all Russia, Volademer, Moskoe and Novogrode,
King of Casan and Astracan, Lord of Vobskoe, great Duke
of Smolenskoe, Tuer, Huder, Ughory, Perme, Viatsky,
Bolgory, &c. Lord and great Duke of Novogrod in the
Low Countreyes, of Chernigo, Rezan, Polotskey, Rostove,
Geraslave, Bealozera, Leifland, Oudorskey, Obdorskey,
Condingskey. King of all Syberia and the North Coasts,
Commander of the Countreyes of Iversky, Grysinsky, and
Emperour of Kabardivskey, of Chirkasky, and of the
whole Countrey of Garskey, and of many other Countreyes
and Kingdomes Lord and Emperour, to know of his
Majesties health of England, the Queene and Princes.
The second, being a Captayne of Gunners (the Emperours
Guard) named Kazrine Davydowich Beaheetchove, pro-
nouncing the Emperour and Princes Title, said hee was
sent from them to know his Lordships health and usage,
with the Kings Gentlemen. The third, was one of the

Secretaries, named Pheodor Boulteene, observing the former order did deliver what he had in command from the Emperor, Prince and Empresse, to informe the Embassador of their much favour towards him, and the Kings Gentlemen, in providing for his Honourable entertayne and ease, a faire large house to lodge in: Also that they three were sent from the Emperour, Prince, and Empresse, to be his Prestaves, to supply the Emperours goodnesse toward him, to provide his necessaries, and deliver any sute it pleased the Ambassadour to make to the Emperour. To all which the Embassadour very wisely gave answere (as they made report unto the Emperour.)

So we all presently mounted againe, the Prestaves on either hand of the Ambassadour his Horse and Foot-cloth being led by his Page, some small distance, his Coach behind that, and some sixe thousand Gallants after behind [III.iv.748.] all: who at the Embassadors riding through the guard, that was made for him, very courteously bowed himselfe. Thus was he followed by thousands, and within the three wals of the Citie, many hundreds of young Noblemen, Gentlemen, and rich Merchants well mounted, begirt the wayes on every side: divers on foot also, even to the gate of the house where the Embassadour was to be lodged, which was some two miles. Whither being come, he was brought into his Bed-chamber by the Noblemen his Prestaves, where with many thankes for their honourable paines, they were dismist, betaking themselves to their further affaires. The next morning came three other Prestaves with the former, to know of his Lordships health, and how he had rested the night past: withall, that if his Lordship wanted any thing, they all, or any one of them, were as commanded, so readie to obey therein. These, with the Interpreter and sixe Gentlemen were most within the walls, lodged in a house over the gate, besides we had fiftie Gunners to attend, and guard us in our going abroad.

The eight of October being the fourth day after our

comming to Musco, the Prestaves came to his Lordship
to let him understand, they heard he should goe up the
next day : wherefore they desired his speech and Embassage to the Emperour : and the rather, that the Interpreter
might (as they pretended) translate it. To this purpose,
very earnestly at severall times they made demand. The
Embassadour answered, that he was sent from a mightie
Prince, to bee his Embassadour to their Emperour, and
being sent to their Master, he deemed it not only a dishonour to him, but a weaknesse in them, to require that
at his hands.

The eleventh of October, his Lordship being sent for
by his Prestaves there wayting, having excellent Jennets
for himselfe, the Kings Gentlemen, and good horses for
the rest : as likewise two gallant white Palfreis to carrie
or draw a rich Chariot, one parcell of the great Present,
with his followers and the Emperours guard, carrying the
rest : on each side the streets standing the Emperours
guard with Peeces in their hands well apparelled, to the
number of two thousand by esteeme, many Messengers
posting betwixt the Court and our Prestaves. Thus with
much state, softly riding, till we came unto the utmost
gate of the Court (having passed through the great Castle
before) there his Lordship dismounted. Then met him a
great Duke (named Knase Andriay Metowich Soome-
derove) with certayne Gentlemen, to bring him up. So
in order as we rode, we ascended the staires and a stone
Gallerie, where on each side stood many Nobles and
Courtiers, in faire Coates of Persian Stuffe, Velvet,
Damaske, &c. At the entry to the great Chamber, two
Counsellors encountred the Embassadour, to conduct him
through that Roome, round about which sat many grave
and richly apparrelled Personages. Then we entred the
Presence, whither being come, and making obeysance,
we staid to heare, but not understand, a very gallant
Nobleman, named Peter Basman, deliver the Emperours
Title : Then the particular of the Presents, and some
other Ceremonies : which performed, the Embassadour

having libertie, delivered so much of his Embassage, as the time and occasion then affoorded: After which the Emperour arising from his Throne, demanded of the King of Englands health, the Princes, and Queenes: then of the Embassadors and the Kings Gentlemen, and how they had beene used since they entred within his Dominions: to all which with obeysance wee answered as was meete. Then the young Prince demanded the very same.

The Embassador having taken the Kings Letter of his Gentleman Usher, went up after his obeysance to deliver it, which the Lord Chancellor would have intercepted. But the Embassadour gave it to the Emperours owne hands, and his Majestie afterwards delivered it to the Lord Chancellor: who tooke it, and shewing the superscription to the Emperour and Prince, held it in his hand openly with the Seale towards them. Then the Emperour called the Embassadour to kisse his hand, which he did, as likewise the Princes, and with his face towards them returned. Then did hee call for the Kings Gentlemen to kisse his hand, and the Princes, which they after obeysance made, did accordingly. Afterwards, his Majestie invited his Lordship, the Kings Gentlemen and the rest to dine with him, as likewise Master I. Mericke Agent by name, who gave his attendance there on the Embassadour, and was now (as divers times) very graciously used of the Emperour and Prince: no stranger (that I ever heard off) like him in all respects.

Being entred the Presence, we might behold the excellent Majestie of a mightie Emperour, seated in a *Emperours* Chaire of Gold, richly embroydered with Persian Stuffe: *glorie.* in his right hand hee held a golden Scepter, a Crowne of pure Gold upon his head, a Coller of rich stones and Pearles about his necke, his outward Garments of Crimson Velvet, embroydered very faire, with Pearles, Precious stones and Gold: On his right side, (on equall height to his Throne) standing a very faire Globe of beaten Gold, on a Pyramis, with a faire Crosse upon it, unto which before hee spake, he turned a little and crost himselfe.

Nigh that, stood a faire Bason and Ewer, which the Emperour often useth daily.

Princes splendour.

Close by him in another Throne sat the Prince, in an outward Garment like his Fathers, but not so rich, a high blacke Foxe Cap on his head, worth in those Countreyes five hundred pound, a Golden Staffe like a Friers, with the likenesse of a Crosse at the top. On the right hand of the Emperour, stood two gallant Noblemen in cloth of Silver Garments, high blacke Foxe Cappes, great and long chaines of Gold hanging to their feet, with Pollaxes

Pollaxes.

[III.iv.749.] on their shoulders of Gold. And on the left hand of the Prince two other such, but with Silver Pollaxes. Round

Counsell and Nobilitie.

about the benches sat the Councell and Nobilitie, in Golden and Persian Coats, and high blacke Foxe Caps, to the number of two hundred, the ground being covered with Cloth of Arrasse, or Tapistrie : The Presents standing all the while in the Roome, within little distance of his Majestie, where he and the Prince often viewed them. Being now by our Prestaves and others come for to Dinner, who led us through much presse and many Chambers to one very faire and rich Roome, where was infinite store

Plate.

of massie Plate of all sorts; Towards the other end stood the Emperours Uncle, named Stephean Vaselewich Godonove, Lord High Steward, being attended with many Noblemen and Gentlemen, whom my Lord in his passage saluted, which with an extraordinary countenance of aged Joy, he received, making one of their honourable Nods.

Dining roome.

The Embassador entred the dining Roome, where we againe viewed the Emperour and Prince, seated under two Chaires of State, readie to dine, each having a Scull of Pearle on their bare heads, but the Princes was but a

Change of Rayment.

Coronet. Also their Vestments were changed.

The former Duke, that for that day was the Embassadours Prestave, came, as commanded from the Emperor, and placed the Embassador at a Table, on the bench side, some twentie foot from the Emperour. Then the Kings Gentlemen, Master Mericke, Master Edward Cherrie, and all the rest were placed, so that our eyes were halfe opposite to the Emperour. Over against the Embassadour sat his Prestaves uppermost. Also in this large place sat the Privie Counsell, to the number of two hundred Nobles *Two hundred* at severall Tables. In the midst of this Hall might seeme *Nobles guests.* to stand a great Pillar, round about which, a great heigth stood wonderfull great pieces of Plate, very curiously wrought with all manner of Beasts, Fishes and Fowles, besides some other ordinarie pieces of serviceable Plate.

Being thus set (some quarter of an houre as it were, feeding our eyes with that faire Piller of Plate) we beheld the Emperours Table served by two hundred Noblemen, *Three hun-* all in Coats of cloth of Gold. The Princes Table served *dred noble* with one hundred young Dukes and Princes of Cassan, *Servitors.* Astrican, Syberia, Tartaria, Chercasses and Russes, none above twentie yeeres old.

Then the Emperour sent from his Table by his Noble Servitors, to my Lord and the Kings Gentlemen, thirtie Dishes of meate, and to each a loafe of extraordinary fine bread. Then followed a great number of strange and rare Dishes, some in Silver, but most of massie Gold; with boyled, baked, and rosted, being piled up on one another by halfe dozens. To make you a particular Relation, I should doe the entertaynment wrong, consisting almost of innumerable Dishes: Also, I should over-charge my memory, as then I did mine eyes and stomacke, little delighting the Reader, because Garlicke *Garlike and* and Onions, must besawce many of my words, as then *Onions.* it did the most part of their Dishes.

For our Drinkes, they consisted of many excellent kinds *Drinkes.* of Meades, besides all sorts of Wine and Beere. Divers *Meads.* times by name, the Emperor sent us Dishes: but in the midst of Dinner hee called the Embassadour up to him, and dranke our Kings health, where the Emperour held some discourse of our King and State. But at one time (striking his hand advisedly on his brest) Oh, said hee, my deere Sister Queene Elizabeth, whom I loved as mine *Memory of Q.* owne heart, expressing this his great affection almost in *Elizabeth.* a weeping passion. The Embassador receiving the Cup from his Princely hand, returned againe to his owne place, where all of us standing, dranke the same health out of the same Cup, being of faire Christall, as the Emperour had commanded, the Wine (as farre as my judgement gave leave) being Alligant.

Thus passing some foure houres in banquetting, and refreshing our selves too plentifully, all being taken away, we did arise. The Embassadour and the Kings Gentlemen beeing called by name to receive from his Emperiall hands, a Cup (or rather as they call it a Yendover) of excellent red Mead, a favour among them never observed before, which Cups for they were great and the Mead very strong, we often sipped at, but without hurting our memories, we could not say Amen unto: which the Emperour perceiving, commanded them to be taken away, saying, Hee was best pleased with what was most for our healths.

Thus after our low courtesies performed, wee departed from his presence, riding home with the same former guard and attendance to our Lodgings; where our Prestaves for that instant left us, but shortly after they came againe, to accompany a great and gallant Duke, one of them that held the Emperours golden Pollaxes, named Knes Romana Pheodorowich Troya Narove, who was sent from his Majestie to make the Embassadour and the Kings Gentlemen merrie: likewise having instructions to drinke their Emperours, our Kings, and both the Princes healths, and divers Princes else, which hee did himselfe very freely and some of us, as many of them as wee could with our owne healths, there being such plentie of Meades and other Drinkes, as might well have made fortie Russes have stumbled to sleepe. Thus light-headed, and well

Gifts. laded especially if you take knowledge of the thirtie yards of cloth of Gold, and the two standing Cups with covers, which the Embassadour rewarded him withall, before he departed.

But unwelcome newes within foure dayes after our audience so unhappily came, as not only our Affaires, but

any else, except counsell against present danger, was not
regarded. For this was held for currant, that one who named *Newes of*
himselfe Demetrie Evanowich Beala, as the Sonne of their *Demetrius.*
late Emperor Ivan Vasillowich; hee that in the reigne of [III.iv.750.]
Pheodor Evanowich his brother was in his infancie, as
was thought, murthered at Ougleets, is now revived
againe, and up in armes for his right and inheritance :
whereupon presently was sent an Armie of two hundred
thousand Souldiers, either to take or slay him. But he
was so strengthened with Poles, Cossacks, &c. that a
number of Russes yeelded to his obedience.

Upon the one and twentieth of November, the young
Prince of an ancient custome going to a Church within
Mosco, the Kings Gentlemen upon knowledge thereof
(the Ambassador being unwilling to be seene publike, as
also for that the Emperor himselfe did not goe as hee was
accustomed) went and attended where his Excellency
might see them, and they safely behold him, who rode in
a very faire and rich sled, having a gallant Palfrey lead by *Princes pomp.*
two Groomes to draw it, many hundreds running before
to sweepe the snowe away where he should passe, and were
said to bee slaves, which I verily beleeve, because certainly
they were his Subjects. Then came the Prince richly
apparelled with two Tartar Princes standing before on
his sled, and two young Dukes behind, with two hundred
sleds following him.

The eight of Februarie, the Emperor sent us sleds to
ride abroad, and this day the rather, that we might behold
a reported victorie, against the reputed Rebell Demetrie,
&c. So we the Kings Gentlemen did behold three
hundred poore Prisoners, seventeene Ensignes, and eleven
Drums brought in, with more glorie then victorie. About
this time returned Peter Basman, one of the Generals, *Peter Basman.*
who had performed very honourable service, and certainly,
he was the man of greatest hope and expectation in the
whole Empire, who was brought into the Mosco, with all
the Counsell, Nobles, Gentlemen, and Merchants, a grace
never performed before to any Subject. But not without

suspition of some extraordinarie secret herein, and besides
particular favours, bountifull rewards, and a promise he
should never goe againe untill the Emperor himselfe went,
he was, being but a young man, made a Privie Counsellor.
Forthwith one thing I will you shall observe the Emperors
favour, and his then noble Spirit, he making divers times
sute (as was thought) because they were in great danger,
to goe againe to the warres, once prostrated himselfe to
obtayne his desire, but falling down too humbly, hee could
not easily rise againe, whereby the Emperor understanding
of his many and great wounds, was said to weepe, rising
himselfe up to raise and helpe him up, but extraordinarie
Causes have the like Effects, as hereafter you shall understand.

We were lodged in the same house where the young
Prince John of Denmarke, brother to that King and our
now Queene of England, did lodge, (who would have
Oucsinia the married the young Princesse Oucksinia, the Emperors
Princesse. only daughter, but that he unhappily there died) but not
in any of those lodgings: for it is a custome there, that
where a Prince dyes (especially a stranger) not of long
time after to let any other lodge there.

Now the Ambassador understanding of the conveni-
ence of his passage downe by sled-way, also fearing (as
wise men had cause) what the issue of these warres would
be, knowing the state here used in any sutes, bethought
himselfe advisedly that it was high time, being the middest
of Februarie, to desire a second audience for his sooner
dispatch, which he forthwith requested, and wrote a letter
to that purpose unto the Lord Chancellor.

Second Upon the tenth of March, the Ambassador with the
audience. Kings Gentlemen all richly apparelled, and all his followers
decently attending, very honourably (as before) and with
the like recourse of beholders, and guard of Gunners (but
Citizens that they were said to bee Citizens by reason of their
Souldiers. warres, but in like apparell) was attended to the Court,
being received with the former grace, or more, he ascended
the Presence: the Emperour and Prince holding their

wonted state, onely changing their Vestments with the season, but for the riches nothing inferior.

So soone as the Ambassador and the Kings Gentlemen were come opposite to his Throne, hee commanded seates that they might sit downe: then with a Majestick countenance, representing rather constraint then former cheerfulnesse, he declared, that He, his Sonne and Councell, had considered his Majesties Letter, the Majestie of King James of England, as also on whatsoever else was desired, and in token of his joyfull received amitie with the renowmed King of England, as with his Predecessor, he had wrote his Princely Letters to that purpose. Herewith the Chancellor from the Emperour delivered the Ambassadors his Highnesse Letters to his excellent Majestie. Withall understanding by the Chancellor hee had some farther matter to intreat of, then in his Briefe to his Majestie was remembred: therefore hee had appointed foure principall Councellors to consult with him of his Requests, which was done. After, the Ambassador yeelding courteous thanks for his Majesties favour, his Lordship attended by many Nobles, proceeded to the Councell Chamber, whither presently after came foure Councellors, and the Emperours Tolmach: who after salutations, we withdrew to the next chamber, where wee passed away an houre in discourse, among many young Nobles, having the Ambassadors Interpreter. In the end, after three or foure goings and returnes of the Chancellor from the Emperour, wee went againe before him (where after hee had commanded us to sit downe as before) by the mouth of the Chancellor was openly delivered a Briefe of the whole Embassie (and that dayes particular desire, according to the Ambassadors request, confirmed.) Also in good and pleasing language, was declared the great [III.iv.751.] desire that the Emperour had, for the continuance of peace and amitie with the renowmed James King of England, as with the late Queene Elizabeth, withall that in due time (all accidents well ended) he would send an honourable Ambassador for further affaires, as likewise to congratulate with our King of his happinesse in so plausible comming to his Right and Inheritance. Likewise, a Grant of a new Priviledge for the Companie, which he said should be *Golden Seale.* under the golden Seale, &c.

Which ceremonious speech ended, the Emperor called for the Ambassador and the Kings Gentlemen to kisse his hand, and the Princes: which done, with the Emperors nod or bowing to us, as likewise the Princes, desiring the remembrance of his and the Princes commendations to his Majestie, the Prince, and Queene of England, we were dismissed, but not before the Emperor said he would send home to us. Thus we tooke our last leave of the Emperors Court, being more graciously and especially entertayned then before, or then ever any would take knowledge Ambassadors were used withall: we are honorably attended home, and a Duke of great account, named Knas Evan Evannowich Courletev, was attended with many of the Emperors servants within our Gates: follow-
Great dinner. ing him a dinner, sent from the Emperor by some two hundred persons, consisting of three hundred severall dishes of Fish (for it was now Lent) of such strangenesse, greatnesse, and goodnesse (for their number) as it were not to bee beleeved by any report, but by a mans owne eye-sight, with infinite store of Meades, and Beere, in massie plate, &c.

The eighteenth of March, the Emperor sent by Vassilly Gregorewich Telepnove, the Roll wherein was the Demands of the Ambassador, and the particulars of the whole negotiation, as there at large appeeres. The nine-teenth, his Majestie sent by Menshoy Buldecove, under Treasurer, a royall Present to the Ambassador of many particulars, also to each of the Kings Gentlemen, being rewarded, he departed.

The twentieth of March, being honourably accom-panyed with thousands of Gallants of each side the streets
Ambassadors all along as we passed, the Ambassador departed from the
departure. Citie of Mosco, with the whole numbers of horse-men still becking us, till we came a short mile on this side the

Citie where we made a stand, and after some complement betweene the Ambassador and his kinde and honourable Prestave, the Duke Vollagdemor, with almost weeping on his part, the Ambassador went from the Emperors sled to his coach set upon a sled, and wee alighted from the *Sled-passage.* Emperors horses, and betooke our selves to our easie and pleasant passage in sleds, such a passage as this part of the World would wonder at, in which a man though hee goe a Hackney pace, may as easily reade as sleepe.

Thus accompanyed with Master John Mericke, Master William Russel, sometimes Agent for the Dutch, and many other Merchants, we easily rode that night to Bratte-shin, thirtie miles from the Mosco. The next morrow taking leave of them all, we continued our journey fiftie and sixtie versts a day easily.

Within few dayes after wee heard newes certainly of the Emperors sudden and untimely death: which, con- *Emperor Boris* sidering neither the Prestave, the Governour, or Bishop, *his death.* had not or would not of ten dayes after take knowledge of, we might in the meane time have doubted of, but that his Lordship had it from Master John Mericke by Letter particularly. His death was very sudden, and it was in it selfe, very strange: for within some two houres after dinner, having (as hee usually had) his Doctors with him, who left him in their judgements in health, as the good meale he made could witnesse, for hee dined well, and fed plentifully, though presently after as may be thought, feeding over-much, hee felt himselfe not onely heavie, but also payned in his stomacke: presently went into his chamber, laid himselfe upon his bed, sent for his Doctors (which always speeded) yet before they came, hee was past, being speechlesse and soone after dying. Before his death (as speedie as it was) hee would bee shorne, and new *New* christned: what the cause was otherwise then the griefe, *christening.* inward sorrow, with divers distractions about the warres, and their bad successe, fearing the worst on his part, onely God knowes: yet who so remembers Gods judgements, or Princes policies for Kingdomes, with mans sinfulnesse, and considereth the one with the other, may bee satisfied, if not contented.

For the Emperours person, he was tall and well bodied, teaching out of his authoritie obedience, of an excellent presence, black and thin haired, well faced, round and close shaved, strong limmed. A Prince framed betweene Thought and Resolution, as being ever in labour, but never till death delivered : never acting (though ever plotting) but in his Closet or Councel Chamber. One rather obeyed then loved, being feared where hee was not served : doubtlesse, upholding a true Majestie and government in every part, but in his owne minde : that it is a question, whether he were more kinde to Strangers, or severe and just to his Subjects, or hatefull and terrible to his Enemies.

A father and a Prince, whose wordes, counsels, observations, policies, resolutions, and experiments, were but the life of his deare Sonne, never advising, entertayning, no not praying without him. In all Ambassies and Negotiations, remembring his sonnes name with his owne, loving him (being lovely) for that himselfe would bee loved, unwilling to spare his presence, desirous to have him at

all occasions before his eyes. I shall not doe amisse, to give a taste of the fruit sprung from so stately a Tree. Being by a learned and well travailed Gentleman divers times particularly advised, to let the Prince take some more (then no recreation) by which meanes he might aswell prolong his life, as instruct his judgement and delight his minde : Oh, would the Emperour answere, one sonne is no sonne : nay, I am perswaded, three sonnes to me is but halfe a sonne. But had I sixe sonnes, then I might safely say I had one, how then should I part with that at any time, I know not to bee mine for any time. This may give satisfaction to any understanding both of his feares

*Because he
had done more
for him, then
might law-
fully be
commanded.

and jelousies : his great love, and much care. It was an usuall speech with the Emperour upon good reason to say, hee was the Lord and father of his sonne, yet withall, That he was not onely his servant, but his very * slave.

Two policies of the said Emperour I shall willingly

acquaint you with, for divers reasons. One was, when hee caused fire to bee kindled in foure parts of Mosco; whereat himselfe was noted to be very diligent, with all his Nobles and Courtiers: and after it was quenched, he sent his bountie to them all, that builded anew their houses, and repaid all their losses. And this was but to stop the rumour, then so common, of his strange gayning the Empire: by which stratagem of his, when his people were readie to mutinie, they were created anew good Subjects; yet did admire his not onely care, but goodnesse towards them all.

A second, was at that time the Land was visited with a mightie famine, and as great a plague (some foure yeeres since) whereof a third of the whole Nation is rated to have died: and the murmuring multitude said the cause was, their electing of a murderer to the Empire; wherefore God did thus visit them: Whereupon, hee caused Galleries to bee builded round about the utmost wall of the great Citie of Mosco, and there appointed daily to bee given to the poore, twentie thousand pounds sterling: which was accordingly performed for one moneth; whereupon the common peoples mouthes and bellies were well stopped.

Here wee lodged till the sixt of May, being wearied with the inconstancie and ill-come newes of flying reports, whereupon the time of the yeere requiring, the Ambassador resolved to passe downe the River to Colmogro, as well that hee might the sooner have newes from England, as happily to bee out of feare of any disaster, the rumours being innumerable and uncertaine.

After the suspicious death of the old Emperour Boris Pheodorowich, &c. by the appointment of the Prince (then their expected Emperour) and the Counsell, Peter Basman (that noble Sparke) was speedily dispatched and sent as Generall unto their ill succeeding warres, as their last hope (indeed hee prooved so in a contrarie sense) and the onely refuge to the Commons: whither being come, hee with himselfe presented most of his command, as many as freely

Peter Basman sent against Demetrius, revolteth.

would offer themselves : Under which were all the English, Scots, French, Dutch and Flemmings, whatsoever :
and with him, or rather before him (as least suspected)
Ries Vasili Evanch Goleeche, the other Generall, a man
of great birth, and in the prioritie of place, to bee received
before Peter Basman. All which, the now well knowne
newly opinionated Emperour very graciously received,
happily not without some jelousie of many particulars.

Demetrius now sent Messengers with Letters which
entred the Suburbs, where the Commons in infinite
numbers brought them safe into the spacious Plaine before
the Castle gate : within which, as daily they did use, so
now were all the Counsellors in consultation ; but happily
not in a secret Counsaile ; also wherein was the Emperiall
Court.

Tumult of the
Commons.
There these Boyerens made demand for many of the
Counsellors, especially for the Godonoves, to come to
heare their right King Demetrius Evanowich speaking
unto them by Letters : Who yet after refusall (and I cannot
condemne all) many came ; the Commons being resolved,
else to fetch them out. Then, by the Boyerens aloud was
read the Emperours Letters, to this effect.

Demetrius his
Letter.
That hee much wondred at that time, wherein expedition was to bee accounted safest policie, having sent many
Letters and Messengers to them, concerning their
approoving him to bee their lawfull Prince, as being the
sonne of Evan Vasilowich their late Emperour, and the
onely brother of Pheodor Evanowich selfe-upholder, of
happy memorie, both with invincible Arguments and
direct Reasons to the manifesting thereof, they (notwithstanding his long patience and gracious remisnesse) were
not onely so proud as not to answere his Princely Letters,
but so presumptuous as to retayne his Messengers,
whereby they made themselves apparently to bee no lesse
Vipers to the State in obscuring him, then Traytors to
himselfe the true and right Emperour, by defrauding
them : yet giving him a strong Argument by their Silence,
of their guiltinesse ; also allowing thereby, time and oppor-

tunitie (if hee had not beene their true-borne Emperour, and with the naturall Mother, tendered the life of her deare Children) to have conquered and destroyed the whole Nation.

All which notwithstanding, hee (being confident in his owne conscience, of his just Title, made the Prince of patience and humilitie from his former many great miseries and dangers) had in his Princely wisedome and clemency againe wrote these (but certainly his last Peace-requiring, and Grace-offering Letters: yea, was content to desire them he might) and doubted not shortly but he should command, onely ayming at the good of the Commonwealth and State in generall; as he that without much shedding of his Subjects bloud, desired the Kingdome.

Also to this end hee had sent men of great birth, viz. [III.iv.753.] Rues Pheodor, Evanowich Methithsosky, and Rues Demetre, Evanowich Suskey; and given them Commission to displace his Enemies, and Prestave the Godonoves, and others, till his further pleasure were knowne, consuming those monstrous bloud suckers and Traytors, with returne of the Commons answere thereunto: Likewise to demand his Messengers, and they to bee brought before the Commons, whom hee had reason to beleeve were ill-intreated, if not murthered; withall, that if they did submit themselves now to him, as to their lawfull Prince and Soveraigne, (which hee was truely resolved their consciences were guiltie of) that yet they should finde him a gracious and mercifull Lord; if otherwise, a severe and just Revenger of them, and their many misdeedes towards him, as hee that had his Sword ever unsheathed to execute his vengeance on them all: and was easily perswaded they were not ignorant of the many Victories hee had obtayned formerly against them, when they would seeme able and willing to fight with his Souldiers: and how afflicted and troubled herewith they all were: But that now, he had their chiefe and strongest Heads and Armes in his owne hand, the whole World might not betroth him they durst once speake openly against him, as assured that all (excepting a very few, and they of the worst) in heart were his loyall Subjects, &c.

But before this Letter was halfe read, the Hearts and Hands of the multitude were strangely combined together, not one speaking, but all confusedly like fettered and chayned Horses stamping; being indeed without any feare, but of not doing mischiefe enough, all (as one) running violently into the Castle, where (meeting two of the pitifully tormented Messengers) they pawsed to heare them as sufficiently as their insufficiencie would permit them, deliver the vilde manner of their torturing, whipping, and roasting, which was in deede a Whip and Spurre to drive them, without wit or humanitie, as if they had beene fired like Gun-powder with the very sparkes of heate: Such barbarous crueltie, beastly actions, and inhumane spectacles, as without the great Devill had beene their Generall, no particular could have acted; laying violent hands on all they met: but not killing (the great mercy of God) any man of account.

Thus the whole Citie was in an uproare, all the Counsellors houses, sellers, and studies ransacked, beginning with the Godonoves; spoyling, renting, and stealing all they met with; but carrying little away but drinke, which they could not carry away.

The Commons (no doubt) would have made this day little inferiour to the massacre of Paris, so violent and devillish were their sudden resolutions; but that the Nobles (best beloved and obeyed) intreated, where none could command: others perswading, all wishing an end to this most miserable and never exampled mischiefe. But the multitude did what they would and could; especially on the greatest, which certainly were the worst: So as the Empresse flying to a safer lodging, had her coller of Pearle pluckt from her necke.

Then the Prince, Empresse, and Princesse, were prestaved (a second command being come from the Campe) with the Godonoves, and many others that were suspected most: The Nobles joyning in one counsell for the present ordering of these sudden accidents, and for answere to the Prince Demetrius Evanowich, who suddenly was by generall consent concluded (by the particular knowledge of Bodan Belskey a great Counsellor, that was privie to his departure, and some others) to bee their right and lawfull Emperour, onely a few excepted. So as the young Prince was by many (but particularly by his mother) counselled to leave the Kingdome utterly, before it forsooke him; to follow his Fathers example in murdering himselfe, and herein his mother (that Map of miseries, that Cradle of crueltie) and his onely deare sister would associate him.

Letters were devised, and Messengers framed to effect this desperate treacherie on his innocent life; so as in very few dayes (for Mischiefe hath the wings of Thought and Resolution) they three did consent (an unhappy conjunction) to destroy themselves; and rather to lay violent hands upon their hatefull lives, then make an Enemie seeme cruell in executing Justice on them: which * yet certainly this Emperour never dreamt of, but determined the Prince should be within himselfe, not lesse then Absolute, and in a very great Dukedome. The Princely Mother began the health of Death to her noble Sonne, who pledged her with a heartie draught, therein so much strength did hee adde to his vile wicked obedience, that hee prooved a banquerout presently, and hand in hand embracing each other, they fell, and died as one, the Mother counselling and acting, whilest the child bethought and suffered: yet see Providence and Commiseration, Constancy and Obedience: the Princesse dranke, but like a Virgin temperately: so as modestie (the want of which was the death of the Mother) now prooved the life of the Daughter.

Thus he: but others ascribe this murther to Demetrius his command, and this selfe-murther was pretended to avoid envy of the fact. Death of Mother & Sonne.

However it was with Boris for other things, I thought it not amisse to adde this testimonie of his respect to the English Nation and Merchants in Priviledges granted them, as followeth.

[One Almightie

[III.iv.754.]
*Emperor Boris
his Mosco
Patent trans-
lated whiles
Sir Th. Smith
was there.*

ONe Almightie God without and before the Beginning, the Father, the Sonne, and the Holy Ghost, whom we glorifie in the Trinitie, our onely God, Creator and Preserver of all things everywhere, by which Will and Working, he liveth and giveth life unto Man; Our onely God which inspireth every one of us his Children with his holy Word, through our Lord Jesus Christ, the Spirit of Life, now in this latter times, establish us to hold the right Scepter, and suffer us of our selves to reigne, for the good of the Land, and the happinesse of the People, together with our Enemies, and to the doing of good.

We the great Lord Emperour and great Duke Boris Pheodorowich of all Russia, sole Commander of Volodemer, Mosco, Novogrod, Emperour of Cazan, King of Astracan, Lord of Vobsko, and great Duke of Smolensko, of Twersko, Vhorskoy, Permskoy, Vatskoy, Bolharskay, and of others, Lord and great Duke of Novagrod in the low Country of Chernego, Rezan, Polotskay, Rostovskoy, Yeraslavskoy, Belozerskoy, Leeflanskoy, Owdorskoy, Obdorskoy, Condinskoy, and all Siberia, and the North parts; Lord and Commander of Everskoy Land, and Cabardinskoy Country, and of Cherces, and Igarskoy Land, as also of many others Lord and Commander, with our Sonne Prince Phedar Borisowich of all Russia. We have bestowed on the Merchants of England, viz. Sir John Hart, Knight; Sir William Webb, Knight; Richard Saltanstall, Alderman; Nicolas Moshley, Alderman; Robert Dove, William Garaway, John Harbey, Robert Chamberlin, Henrie Anderson, John Audwart, Francis Cherie, John Merick, Anthony Marlar; Wee have granted and licenced them to come with their ships into our Dominion the Country of Dwina, with all manner of Commodities, to trade freely from the Sea side and within our Dominions, to the Citie of our Empire of Mosco. Also there made sute unto us Sir John Hart, Knight, and his Companie, to gratifie them to trade to our Citie of Mosco, and to our Heritage of great Novogrod and

Vobsko, and to all parts of our Empire, with their Commodities, and to Trade freely without custome: upon
which Wee the great Lord Emperour and great Duke
Boris Pheodorowich of all Russia, with our Sonne Prince
Pheodor Borisowich of all Russia, have granted unto the
English Merchants, Sir John Hart, Knight, and his
fellowes, for our Sisters sake Queene Elizabeth, free
passage to come into our Kingdome of Mosco, and into
all the rest of our Dominions, with all manner of Commodities to trade and traffick freely at their pleasure. Also
we have commanded, not to take any kinde of Custome
for their goods, nor any other Customes whatsoever, viz.
for passing by any place by Land, nor for passing by any
place by Water; nor for Custome of their Boats or Head
money, nor for passing over Bridges and Ferries, nor for
any entrie of Wares: as also all manner of other Customes
or Duties whatsoever wee command shall not bee taken of
them: But they shall not bring other mens goods into our
Dominions, nor likewise recarry out of our Kingdome any
other mens goods as their owne: nor to sell or barter for
other men. Neither shall our Subjects buy and sell for
them or from them: neither shall they keepe any of our
peoples goods or pawnes by them to owne or colour them.
Likewise they shall not send any of our Subjects to any
Towne or Citie to buy Commodities. But what Citie
they come into themselves they shall sell their owne
Commodities, and buy our Commodities. And when they
shall come to our Heritage to great Vobsko and Novagrod,
or to any other Citie within our Dominions with their
Commodities, that then our Gentlemen and Governours,
and all other officers shall suffer and let them passe according to this our Letter, and to take no manner of Custome
of them whatsoever for any of their Commodities for
passing by, nor for passage over any Bridges: neither shall
they take any other Custom whatsoever in all our
Dominions. And wheresoever they happen to come, and
doe proceed to buy and sell; as also wheresoever they
shall passe through with goods not buying of any Com-

moditie nor selling their owne, then in those Cities they
shall take of them no manner of Custome whatsoever as
aforesaid: and wee have gratified and given them leave
to trade in all parts of our Dominions with their goods
freely without Custome. And likewise whensoever the
English Merchants shall bee desirous to buy or sell or
barter their wares with our Merchants wares for wares,
then shall they sell their wares whole sale and not by retaile,
Cloth by the pack and by Clothes and by remnants; and
Damasks and Velvets by the Piece and not by the Yard,
or askeene, and such Commodities as is to be sold by
waight, not to sell them by the small waights, that is to
say, by the Zolotnick. Also they shall sell Wines by the
Pipe and the Hogshead, but by the Gallon, Quart or Pot
or Charke they shall not sell: moreover, they shall buy,
sell and exchange their owne Commodities themselves,
and the Russe Merchants shall not sell or exchange for
them or from them their Commodities, neither shall they
carry any mans goods to no manner of place under colour
of their owne, and which of the English Merchants would
at any time sell his Commodities at Colmogro on the
Dwina, or at Vologda and at Yeraslavly they may, and of
all their Commodities throughout all our Cities and
Dominion, our Gentlemen, Governours, and all other
Officers shall take no manner of Custome according to this
our Imperiall Letter of favour. Also through all our
Dominions, Cities, and Townes they shall hire Carriers,
Boats, and men to labour or rowe in the said Boats at
their owne cost. Likewise when as the English Merchants shall desire to goe out of our Dominion into any
other Kingdome, or into their owne Land, and that we
thinke it good for them to take with them from our
Treasure any Commodities to sell or exchange them for
us, for such Commodities as shall be fitting to our Kingdome, and to deliver them to our Treasurer: and with
those their and our goods, our Gentlemen and Governours
shall suffer them to passe through all Cities and Townes
[III.iv.755.] within our Dominions without Custome as before. And

when they have ended their Market, and doe desire to goe
from the Mosko, then they shall appeare in the Chancerie
to the Keeper of our Seale, the Secretarie Vassily Yacolowich Schellcalov. Likewise, if there happen to the
English Merchants any extremitie by Sea, or that a ship
be broken, and that it be neere any place of our Kingdome, then we command that all those goods shall bee
brought out justly, and bee given to the English people
that shall at that time bee in our Land, or if they be not
here, then to lay them up all together in one place, and
when the Englishmen come into our Land, then to deliver
those goods to them. Also wee have bestowed on the
English Merchants the House of Yourya, in the Mosko
by a Church of Saint Maxims neere the Marget, to dwell
in it as in former time, keeping one House-keeper a Russe,
or one of their owne strangers: but other Russe folkes
they shall not keepe any. Likewise these Merchants have
Houses in divers our Cities as followeth: A House at
Yeres, a House at Vologda, a House at Colmogro, and a
House at Michael the Archangell, being the shipping
place: these said Houses they shall keepe as in former
time according to this our Imperiall Letter of favour, or
gratified without paying any manner of Rent or any other
duties whatsoever, either at Mosko, Yereslave, Vologda,
Colmogro, or at the Castle of the Archangell, neither shall
they pay any taxe. Also at those Houses at Yereslave,
Vologda, Colmogro, and at Archangell they shall have
House-keepers of their owne Countrey-men, or Russes of
a meane sort that are not Merchants, a man or two in a
House: to lay up their goods in those Houses, and to
make sale of their goods out of those Houses, to whom
they will according to this our Imperiall Letter of favour,
but their Russe House-keepers in their absence shall not
sell any of their Commodities. And the English Merchants shal come with their ship to their Port, as in former
times they have done to unlade their goods out of their
ships, and likewise to lade them againe with our Russia
Commodities, at their owne charges of Boates and hire of

men, and ferrying over the said goods from their ships to
their House at the Castle of Archangell. Likewise our
Officers, Customers, and Swornemen shall take a just note
of all such goods as they have both of Russia and English
Commodities, and the note to passe under the Merchants
Firma, because it may be knowne what goods passeth of
the strangers and of the Russes. But they shall not looke
over their goods, neither unbind any packs in any place,
and when they doe send their owne Englishmen from
Archangell to our Citie of Mosko, or doe send Russia
Commodities into their owne Land, Then all our Officers
and Customers shall let them passe without delay, according to this our Letter of favour. And whensoever the
Merchants shall be desirous to send any of their owne
Countreymen into their owne Land, or into any other
Kingdome over Land : they shall doe it freely with our
Imperiall Majesties order, without carrying any Commoditie over with them, and they shall have their Letters
of Passe given them in the Embassdours Office. And
concerning any matters of debate or controversie in Merchandize, or injurie, then they shall be judged by the
Keeper of the Seale, and Secretarie Vassily Yacolowich
Shelcolov, doing right and Justice to both parties with
equitie and truth, and what cannot be found out by Law,
Lot Law. or Inquisition, there shall be used Lots. His Lot that is
taken forth, shall have right done unto him. Likewise, in
what place else in all our Kingdome there doe happen any
matter of discord in Merchandize or by injurie, then our
men of authoritie, or Governours, and all manner of our
Officers shall doe true Justice betweene them : and what
cannot be sought out by Law shall be sought out by Lot :
his Lot that is taken out shall have right done unto him
as before mentioned, as also they shall not take any
custome or dutie of them for any Law matter, not in any
place in our Kingdome. Moreover, this our Imperiall
Letter in all our Realme and Dominion, our Officers, and
all manner of our subjects shall not disobey or breake it in
any point whatsoever, but if there bee any that doth dis-

obey this our Imperiall Letter of favour, that then those
people shall bee in our high displeasure, and executed to
death.   This our Imperiall Letter of gratitude, is given at
our Imperiall Palace and House in our Citie of Mosko,
from the yeere of the beginning of the World 7107. in
the month of November : being underwritten as followeth.

By the great Lord Emperour and great Duke Boris
Pheodorowich of all Russia, selfe-upholder : his Keeper
of the Seale, and Secretarie by name Vassily Yacolowich
Sheallcalove.

§. III.

One pretending himselfe to be Demetrius, with
the Popes and Poles helpes attayneth the
Russian Empire : his Arts, Acts, Marriage,
favour to the English, and miserable end.

Aving thus presented you Boris his Tragedie out of
that printed Author, and his Grant to the English
from a written Copie ; it shall not bee amisse to
take more leisurely and mature view of this Pretender,
against whom Boris his desire of secrecie (permitting none
guiltie of the murther to survive) had unfurnished him
of Arguments.   He produced a Purse given him by his
Mother ; with the Historie of his life after that sending
him away and acknowledging another whom she was more
willing to act that bloudy Scene then her own Son : with [III.iv. 756.]
other particulars which bred strong confidence in such as
(weary of Boris) were desirous it should be so.   But for
the death of the yong Emperor, & his mother, it is by
most ascribed to Demetrius, who seeing the people of
Musco his friends, and the Emperour and his Mother in
hold, pretended he could not come thither whiles his
enemies lived, whereupon they in a mutinie slue them ; to
avert the envie whereof, it is probable that it was made to
be their owne act, and their Keepers therefore by him
imprisoned.   Boris his daughter was thrust into a Nunnerie, and so made dead also to the succession.   But as I

157

have before delivered out of that diligent, learned and sincere Historian Thuanus, Boris his attayning the Scepter, I shall likewise intreat your patience out of him to receive these Relations of Demetrius.

Thu. li. 135. Thuanus writeth that after the murther of that (true or false) Demetrius, some yeeres after in the borders of Polonia and Muscovia, appeared one which called himselfe Demetrius, and in testimonie thereof, shewed a Wart in his face, and one arme shorter then the other (noted before in the true Demetrius) a man of sharpe wit, bold courage, liberall mind, gentle behaviour, and of parts composed to a Scepter-worthinesse. First, was he made *The Jesuites* knowne to the Jesuites of principall note in Poland, to *first authors,* whom he promised if he might receive helpe for the *or fautors at* recovery of his just Inheritance, his first care should be to *least of this* reduce the Russians to the Union of the Romish Church. *Demetrius.* This thing was commended to the Pope as conducing to the enlarging of the holy See, by his ayde, and furtherance with the Polish King and Nobilitie, to be promoted ; which also was done by the Jesuites themselves, who brought him to George Miecinsy Palatine of Sendomir a man potent in that Kingdome, with whom he covenanted also to marrie his Daughter if hee succeeded in his Russian Enterprize. He had lurked awhile in Liefland, casting off his Cowle, and had there learned to speake and write the Latine Tongue : and had written to Pope Clement the Eighth, with his owne hand not inelegantly. And being by the said Palatine, and Visnovitzi his Sonne in Law, brought *Sigismunds* before King Sigismund, he made a pithy and Masculine *father John* speech, that he should remember that himselfe had beene *was imprisoned* borne in Prison and Captivitie, whence Gods mercie had *by King Ericus* delivered him, to learne him to succour others afflicted with *1564.* like disastre.

Thus by the Kings favour, the Palatines money, the Jesuites industrie (not to mention the Popes Sanctitie) he procured an Armie of ten thousand Souldiers in Poland well furnished, and in his Russian March, winneth to his *Cossaks.* partie the Cossaks a kind of men which follow forreigne

Warres and prey, and leades with him tenne thousands of them. Passing Boristhenes hee first charged upon Zerniga, & summoned them to yeeld to the true heire *Zerniga.* Demetrius, which was done by Ivan Takmevy, who had before conceived dislike against Boris. Corelas commanded the Cossaks, a notorious Sorcerer. He was the Author of the siege of Putinna a populous Citie, which *Putinna* Michelowich Soltekovi held with eight thousand Cossaks, *yeelded.* whom also he wrought with, that hee admitted and followed Demetrius. Hereupon Boris sends an Army of an hundred thousand men against him. He also sends Ambassadors into Poland, to put them in minde of the league betwixt both Nations, and earnestly desired this counterfeit Demetrius, a Priests Bastard and notable Sorcerer, to bee delivered unto him alive or dead, adding threats if they persisted, and withall working under-hand with the Nobles to deterre the King from his ayde. But by the Popes and Jesuites prevayling power nothing was effected, the King and the Poles resolving to assist him, as thinking it the best course to accord both Nations.

Both Armies met at Novogrod, where Palatine *The Palatine* Sendomir the Generall, in the end of Januarie, 1605. *defeated.* thinking to find a revolt in the Russian Armie, gave a rash on-set, & was put to flight, and after returned to Poland. Demetrius retyred himselfe to Rilskie Castle (in the borders) with a few, and forsaken of others, he forsooke not himselfe. Hee had brought with him two Divines of the Cistercian Order which returned home: *Cistercians* two Jesuites also, Nicolas Cherracovi and Andrew Lovitizi, *and Jesuits.* which had beene Authors of the Expedition, and now encouraged him by their exhortations and examples of patience. He confident (as hee made shew) in the justice of his cause, when he was to begin battell or skirmish, used to call upon God, so as he might bee heard of all, with his hands stretched forth, and his eyes lifted up to heaven, in such like words. O most just Judge, kill me first with a *Demetrius his* Thunderbolt, destroy me first, and spare this Christian *confident* bloud, if unjustly, if covetously, if wickedly I goe about *Prayer.*

this Enterprize which thou seest. Thou seest mine innocencie, helpe the just cause. To thee O Queene of Heaven, I commend my selfe and these my Souldiers. Which if they be truly related, and he not the true Demetrius, he was either an impudent Jugler, or exceedingly gulled with fortunes daliance and prosperous successe, which concluded in a Tragicall period.

Part of Boris his Armie was now comne to Rilsky, where in a battle betwixt the horsemen of both parts, *Demetrius his* Demetrius got the better, and the lately conquered, and *victorie.* presently fewer, became Victors; at the first encounter a thousand being slaine, two hundred taken, and the rest put to flight, leaving their footmen to the slaughter, and the baggage to the spoyle. Hereupon five neighbouring Castles with their severall Territories, yeelded *Bialogrod.* to Demetrius, one of which, Bialogrod yeelded him a hundred and fiftie Peeces of Ordnance. The Captaynes *Leptina.* were delivered into his hands. Soone after Jaleka and Leptina yeelded, in which Hinsko Otiopelus, that famous *Severia yeelds.* Sorcerer was taken: after which all Severia, a large Principalitie, came in, and eight Castles; Demetrius using great modestie in this unexpected victorie. Boris meane- [III.iv.757.] while sent some with large promises to murther him, and the Patriarke excommunicated all which favoured him. Demetrius writ hereof modestly to the Patriarke, and to Boris also, offering faire conditions to his Family, if he would resigne his usurped Empire, which he with indignation rejected. That happened when the Embassadors of Denmarke and Sweden were in his Court to joyne league *Boris dyeth.* with him against the Pole. In that consultation Boris is *Some say, that* said to have beene in such a chase, that hee fell downe *hee had used* suddenly, much bloud passing from his mouth, nosthrils *with Aqua* *vitæ to poyson* and eares; and in the end of Aprill hee dyed; some say *others.* of an Apoplexie, others, of poyson which hee drunke: *Neque enim* after hee had reigned seven yeeres. His Wife with her *lex justior ulla* Sonne were advanced to the Throne after him, and the *est, quam necis* *artifices arte* Nobilitie sworne to them. The dead bodie was buried *perire sua.* without any pompe. Constantine Fidler a Lieflander of

Rie made an elegant Oration in his prayse, whose brother Gaspar served Boris.

Presently Peter Basman was sent away with an Armie.* Hodunius (a neere Kinsman of Boris) besieged Crom, to rayse whom, Demetrius used this policie. Hee sent a simple man thither, which being deceived himselfe might deceive others, with Letters that fortie thousand were comming to ayde the besieged. He being taken (sent by a way which he could not escape) and examined with tortures confesseth the same with his Letters: which caused a tumult in the Campe; and in the end, the besieged taking advantage of the rumour still increased by some sent purposely with reports that they had seen the new auxiliaries issued with a counterfeit shew of great numbers, and caused the Russians to consult of yeelding. Basman also the new Generall yeelded and cried out with a loud voyce, that Demetrius was the true heire, and therefore all true hearted Muscovites should follow his example; which the most followed. Hodunius was taken, and refusing to acknowledge Demetrius was cast in Prison. In the Tents were huge Ordnance found. After this Campe-alteration, followed the like in Mosco, the people resounding the name of Demetrius. The Empresse and her sonne were committed to ward, where some write that they poysoned themselves, some that Demetrius commanded it. The Germanes flying out of the Borissian Campe to Demetrius drew many with them.

From Crom doth Demetrius now march towards Mosco, the people all the way flocking to see their new Prince, who in twentie removes came thither on the 19. of June, and entred with pompous procession of Souldiers & Priests, the Russian Priests having Banners with the Pictures of the blessed Virgin and their Tutelare Saint Nicolas, in the end of al the Patriarch, and after him Demetrius by himselfe on a white Palfray with a gallant trayne of attendants. Thus hee goeth to the Temple of our Ladie, and after Prayers, from thence to Saint Michaels Church in which his Father lay buried, and hearing that

Some say of 60000. men.

Basman yeeldeth.

Demetrius commeth to Mosco, his pompous entrance.

Boris lay there interred, he presently commanded his body
to be taken up and to be removed to a meaner Chappell
without the Citie. Passing by Boris his peculiar House,
he could not endure the sight, but sent workemen presently to race the same; saying, they were infamous with
Sorceries, and that an image was said to be placed under
the ground, holding in the hand a burning Lampe, having
underneath store of Gunpouder buried; things so dis-
posed, that the Oyle failing, and the Lampe breaking the
fire should (had it not beene before spied and removed)
blow up that, and the houses adjoyning. Thus had Boris
impeached him, and he now Boris of Magicall arts, which
are usuall accusations in those parts.

Thence he went to the Imperiall Pallace, and beganne
Poles to governe the Empire, more inclining to the Poles and
advanced. forreiners, then to the Russes: which untimely expressing
himselfe, hastned his ruine. Seventie noble Families of
Boris his kindred or faction were exiled, that their Goods
might be shared amongst strangers, and new Colonies of
Clemencie to men planted, brought into Russia. His clemency was
Suiskey. remarkable to Suisky, who being condemned for not onely
refusing to acknowledge this Emperour, but uttering also
reproachfull speeches of him (as being of base Parentage,
and one which had conspired with the Poles to overthrow
the Russian Temples, & Nobility) and now his prayers
ended, and the fatall stroake on his knees expected, on the
seaventh of July, by unexpected mercy, even then received
his pardon. The last which yeelded to him were the
Plescovites. Some tell of exceeding Treasures also which
hee found laid up for other purposes, which through his
profusenesse soone vanished. The first of September, was
designed to his inauguration (being New yeeres day to the
Russes, as sometimes to the Jewes) but for other causes
it was hastned, and his Mother was sent for out of a
Monasterie (into which Boris had thrust her) farre from
the Court. An honorable Convoy was herein employed,
Respect to his and himselfe with great shew of Pietie went to meet her,
Mother. embraced her with teares, and bare-headed, on foot,

attended her Chariot to the Castle ; whence afterwards she removed with her women into a Monasterie where the Noblest Virgins and Widdowes of Russia use to sequester themselves from the World. His Mother was noted to answere with like affection to him, whether true or dissembled on both parts. At his entrance to the Kingdome, after Ceremonies ended, Nicolas Cnermacovius a Jesuite made him a goodly Oration : the like was done by the Senate. To the Jesuits was alotted a faire place of enter- *Jesuits.* taynment not far from the Castle, wherein to observe the Romish Rites and Holies : and even then by their meanes he had declared himselfe in that point, but for feare of Suiskie hee stayed till fitter oportunitie.

Having thus setled things, his care was to recompence the Poles, to enter league with that Nation, and to con- *Embassage to* summate the Marriage. For which purpose hee sent three *Poland.* hundred Horsemen with Athanasius the Treasurer, who [III.iv.758.] in November came to Cracovia, had audience of King Sigismund, where he with all thankfulnesse acknowledged the Kings forwardnesse with his Nobles to recover his right, whereto God had given answerable successe beyond expectation ; that he deplored the Turkish insolencies in Hungary and other parts : to vindicate which, he would willingly joyne with the Pole, and other Christian Princes : meane whiles hee was willing to make an everlasting league with him, and to that end entreated his good leave to take unto himselfe a Wife out of Poland, namely, Anna Maria, the Daughter of George Miecinsie the Palatine of Sendomir, to whom for money, men, and endangering of his owne life, hee was so much engaged. The eight day after, the Contract was solemnely made by the Cardinal, Bishop of Cracovia, and the Embassadour with her Parents feasted by the King. Demetrius had sent her and her Father, Jewels worth 200000. Crownes.

Thus farre have wee followed Thuanus, and hee Jacobus Margaretus a French Captayne of Demetrius guard of Partisans, which published a Booke hereof. Now let us present you a little English Intelligence touching this

Demetrius and his respect to men of our Nation in those parts, and first his Letter to Sir John Mericke.

The Copie of a Letter sent from the Emperor Demetry Evanowich, otherwise called Grishco Otreapyov : the which Letter was sent to Master John Merrick Agent, out of the Campe, as Master Merrick was taking his Journie to the Sea-side, the eighth of June, Anno 1605.

FRom the great Lord Emperour and great Duke Demetry Evanowich of all Russia. To the English Marchant John Merrick, wee give to understand, that by the just judgement of God and his strong power, we are raised to our Fathers throne of Vladedmer, Mosko, and of all the Empire of Russia ; as great Duke and sole commander : likewise we calling to memorie the love and amitie of our Father, the great Lord Emperour and great Duke Evan Vassilywich of all Russia, and our Brother Theodor Evanowich of all Russia, which was held, and kept by them and other great Christian Princes, in the same forme and manner doe we likewise intend, and purpose to hold and keepe Love and amitie : but especially, and above all others, doe we intend to send and to have love and friendship with your King James, and all you his English Merchants, we will favour more then before. Further, as soone as this our Letter doth come to your hand, and as soone as you have ended your Markets at the shipping place of Michael the Archangell, then to come up to Mosco to behold our Majesties presence. And for your poste Horse I have commanded shall be given you ; and at your comming to Mosco, then to make your appearance in our Chancery, to our Secretarie Ofanasy Vlassov. Written in our Majesties Campe at Tooly, in the yeare of the world Anno seaven thousand one hundred and thirteene.

The Copie of the translation of a Passe given to Master John Merrick, which was given him in the time of his being in the Campe at Molodove with the Emperour Demetry Evanowich, otherwise called Grishco Otreapyove.

FRom the great Lord Emperour and great Duke Demetry Evanowich of all Russia, from Mosco to our Cities and Castles, as also to the Castle of Archangell at the Shipping place and haven to our Generals, Secretaries, and all other our Officers, &c.

There did make suite unto us the English Marchant John Merricke and his Company, that we would gratifie them to be suffered to passe to the new Castle of Archangell, or to the shipping place or haven, in regard of trafficke of Merchandise.

Also, that if he doe send home any of his fellowes and servants from the shipping place, being of the English, that then they might be suffered to passe into England. Also that to whatsoever Citie of ours the English Marchant John Mericke, and his fellowes, doth or shall come unto; then all yee our Generals, Secretaries, and all other our Officers, shall suffer them to passe every where, without all delay. And as for our Customes, as for passing by or for head mony, our custome of goods, you shall not take any of them nor of their servants. Likewise, when the English Merchants John Merricke with his fellowes and servants, shall come to the Castle of Archangell, then Timophey Matphewich Lazarove, and our Secretary Rohmaneum Mocaryoved, Voronove, at the foresaid Castle of Archangell, shall suffer and permit the English Merchant, John and his companie to trade freely. Moreover, when at the shipping place they have ended and finished their Markets, and that then the said John Merricke shall desire to send into England any of his fellowes or servants with goods, then likewise they shall be suffered to passe. But Russe people, and other strangers of Mosco shall not be suffered to passe further: that if John Merricke with his fellowes and servants doe not goe for England: but after their Market is ended doe purpose to come backe againe to Mosco; that then at the Castle of [III.iv.759.] Archangell Timophey Matphewich Lazarove, and our Secretarie Rohmaneev Voronave; as also at all other our Castels and Cities, our Generals, Secretaries, and all other our Officers shall let passe the English Merchant John Merricke with his fellowes and servants, without all stay or hinderance, and as for custome of them, their goods, or their servants, there shall not be any taken.

And after the Reading of this our Letter and Passe, you shall keepe the Copie of it by you: but this you shall deliver backe againe to the said John, and his companie. Written at our Campe at Molodone, the yeare from the beginning of the World 7113. the eighteenth of June.

The last of July 1605. at Archangell.

The Copie of the translation of a Commission that was sent from the Mosko, from the Emperour Demetry Evanowich, alias Gryshca Otreapyove by a Courtier named Gavaryla Samoylowich Salmanove, who was sent downe to the Castle of Archangell, to Sir Thomas Smith, then Lord Embassadour: as followeth.

THe great Lord Emperour, and great Duke Demetry Evanowich of all Russia, hath commanded Gavareela Samoylowich Salmanove, to goe to Vologda, and from Vologda to the new Castle of Archangell, or wheresoever he shall overtake the English Ambassadour Sir Thomas Smith. Also when he hath overtooke the Ambassadour, then Gavareele shall send the Ambassadour his Interpreter Richard Finch, willing him to certifie unto the Ambassadour, that the great Lord Emperour and great Duke Demetry Evanowich, sole commander of Russia, hath sent unto him one of his Courtiers, in regard of his

Majesties affaires: and after some two houres respite, Gavareela himselfe shall ride to the Ambassadour, and deliver unto him his Majesties speeches, as followeth.

THe great Lord Emperour and great Duke Demetry Evanowich of all Russia, and of many Kingdomes Lord and commander, Hath commanded thee, Thomas the English Ambassadour, to certifie unto James, King of England, Scotland, France and Ireland, that by the just judgement of God, and his strange power, we are come and succeeded into the place of our Father and predecessours: as also we are come to the throne of the great and famous Kingdome of Vlodemer Mosco, and to the Empire of Cazan, Astaracan and Siberia, and of all the Kingdomes of the Empire of Russia; being an Empire belonging to the great Lords, Emperours, and great Dukes of all Russia. Moreover, we calling to memorie the sending, love and amitie betwixt our Father, the great Lord and Emperour, and great Duke Evan Vasilywich of all Russia, of famous memorie: as also our Brother, the great Lord and Emperour, and great Duke Feoder Evanowich of all Russia, sole commander, with their sister Elizabeth, Queene of England: in the like manner doe we purpose to have sendings, and to be in love with your Lord King James, and more then hath bin in former time. And in token of our said love and amitie, we doe intend to favour all his subjects in our Land, and to give unto them freer libertie then they have had heretofore; and you his Ambassadour, we have commanded to dispatch without all delay or hindrance. Therefore we would have you to make knowne unto your Lord King James, our Majesties love. And as soone as God shall grant the time of our Coronation to be finished, and that we are crowned with the Emperiall crowne of our predecessours, according to our manner and worthinesse; then we the great Lord Emperor, and great Duke Demeetry Evanowich of all Russia sole Commander, will send our messenger to salute each other, according to the former manner. And con-

cerning those Letters which were sent by you from Borris
Godenove, we would have you deliver them backe againe
to our Courtier Gavareela, and after the deliverie of our
speeches to returne him to the Emperour, under written
by the Chancellour Ofanasy Evanowich Vlaseov.

The Copie of the Translation of a new Priviledge that was given to the Company, by the Emperour Demeetry Evanowich, otherwise called Gryshca Otreapyove, the which Priviledge was sent into England over-land by Olyver Lysset Marchant, and servant to the foresaid Company.

GOd, the Trenitie before, and without the beginning,
the Father, the Sonne, and the holy Ghost, establish
us to hold and keepe our Scepter and Realme for the good
of our Land, and the happinesse of our people. Wee the
resplendant and manifest, and not the miserable upholder,
but sole commander, the great Duke Demetry Evanowich,
by the mercy of God, Cæsar and great Duke of Russia,
and of all the Empire of Tartaria, and many other Kingdomes; as also of the great Monarchie of Mosco, Lord
Emperour and Commander, Have bestowed, and gratified
[III.iv.760.] unto the English Merchants, viz. Sir Thomas Smith,
Knight, Sir John Spencer, Knight, Sir Humfrey Wild,
Knight, Robert Dove, Robert Chamberline, William Garaway, John Harvey, Richard Stapers, John Merricke,
Richard Wryght, Richard Cocks, Thomas Farrington,
Richard Wych, George Bowles, Bartholomew Barnes,
Richard Bowldra, John Casten, Edward Chery, Thomas,
the sonne of Alexander alias Hicks: we have given them
free liberty to come with their ships into our Realme and
Dominion, and to the Country of Dwina, & to the Castle
of Archangel, and to Colmogro, with all maner of commodities, and to trade freely, as also to come from the sea
side by land or by water, to our great dominion and
Cæsars City of Mosco, & great Novogrod and Vobsko,
and all other cities within our dominions, to trade with all

manner of commodities, in the same forme and manner, as heretofore was bestowed on the English Merchants, in the time of our father of famous memory, the great Lord and Cæsar, and great Duke Evan Vassilywich of all Russia, sole Commander, and as was granted unto them in the time of our Brother the great Duke Theodor Evanowich of all Russia sole Commander. And as for custome of their goods, or for passing by, as also for the custome of their boates, or for Head-money, or for going over bridges or Ferryes, or for entrie of goods, As also all manner of Custome whatsoever, we command shall not bee taken of them: Also the English Merchants shall not bring nor sell other mens goods in our Dominion, as their owne: neither shall our Subjects buy, or sell, or traffique for. Also our Subjects pawnes they shall not keep by them, nor send others about the Cities to buy goods: but what Cities they come into themselves they shall trafficke and sell their owne commodities, and buy Russe commodities freely: And when they come into our Dominion of great Novogrod and Vobsko, or to any other Cities within our Realme to trafficke with their goods, and that after the market is past, they shall bee desirous to passe for Mosco, or for England, then our Gentlemen and Governours, and all people shall according to this our Cæsars Letter, let them passe without delay, and as for Customes for them and their goods they shall not take any. And whithersoever they passe with their goods, without buying any commodities, or selling their owne; Then likewise in those Cities they shall passe, and not take of them any manner of Custome whatsoever as before: also the English Merchants shall trafficke as followeth; They shall barter their owne goods, by the whole Salecloth by the Packe, and by the Clothes: Damaske and Velvet not by the piece, but by the areshine and by retaile and retaile weights they shall not barter or sell. Also goods, which is sold by weight, by retaile, or by the zolotnicke they shall likewise not sell. And Claret wine they shall sell by the piece, but by retaile, as by the Veader stop, or Pot and Charck they shall not sell.

Likewise they shall buy and sell, and barter their goods
themselves: but the Russe Merchant shall not sell nor
barter their goods for them; neither shall they carry other
mens goods in colour of their owne, not to any place whatsoever. Also if the English Merchants bee minded to
make sale of their commodities at Colmogro, or on the
Dwina, or at Vologda, or at Yeraslave, then they shall doe
it freely. And for their said goods in all our Cities within
our Realme, our Gentlemen and Governors, and all
manner of our Officers shall not of them take any Tole
or custome, according to this our Cæsars Letter of Favour.
And in all our Cities within our dominion, they shall hyre
Carryers Boats, and men to row them freely as before.
And as the order is of the Merchants within our Realme:
so likewise if the English Merchants be desirous to goe
out of our Realme, into any other Kingdome, or into
their owne Countrey: as also if they bee desirous in our
Realme to buy any Staple commoditie, and to carry it into
their owne Land, then shall they likewise buy and trafficke
freely at pleasure, and those Staple commodities which are
fitting for our Cæsars Treasure, they shall likewise bring
it to our Treasure freely at pleasure, and for the said Staple
commodities in all our Cities, our Officers shall not take
any manner of Custome: but they shall suffer them to
passe without any staying of them. Also when the English Merchants have ended their market, and shall desire
to goe from the Mosco, then they shall appeare in the
Embassadours Office, to our Chancellour and Secretarie
Evan Cowrbatov Hramoteenop. Moreover, if that by the
providence of God, the English Merchants have any shipwracke, and that the said ship bee brought or driven to
any place within our Realme, then our Cæsars commandement to those places where the ship is brought in, that
our men in office doe seeke out the English Merchants
goods justly, and to give them to the English people that
shall bee at that time in our Land. But if at that time there
bee none of them in our Realme, then to gather them
together, and to lay them up in one place: and so when

the English Merchants doe come there, by our Cæsars
Order, to deliver those goods to the said Merchants.
And whereas the English Merchants according to their
former Letters of Favor had a house in the Mosco by the
Church of the holy Maxim by the market, which was
granted unto them by our predecessour the great Lord and
Cæsar of Russia, the said English Merchants shall dwell in
the said house as heretofore they have done : Keeping one
house-keeper a Russe, or one of their owne strangers, but
any other Russes they shall not keepe. Moreover the
said English Merchants have houses in other Cities, a
house at Yeraslave, a house at Vologda, a house at Colmogro, and a house at the shipping place at the Castle of
the Archangell : and those houses they shall keepe and
hold by them, according to our Cæsars Favour or Gratitude, as in former time they have done, and for any
subsidie, rent, dutie, or any custome whatsoever for the
said houses there shall not be any taken of them : and their
other houses, as at Yeraslave, Vologda, Colmogro and
Archangell, they shall have house-keepers of their owne
countrie-men or Russes, but the Russes shall bee meane
men, a man or two at a house : And they shall lay their
goods in those houses, and likewise shall make sale of their
goods out of their houses, to whom they will, according
to this our Cæsars Letter of Favour, and their house-
keepers being Russes shall not buy or sell any manner of
commodities in their absence. Also they shall come with
their ships to the shipping place, as before with their [III.iv.761.]
Commodities, and to unlade out of the shippe their goods,
and to lade their shippe with Russe goods, with their owne
hired labourers, as also to carry their owne goods over
in their owne Boats and Vessels, to their owne house at
the Castle of Archangell. And whatsoever goods they
have, our chiefe Customer, and Officers, and sworne men,
shall take a note of the goods under their owne firme, both
of goods they bring in, and also of goods they carry out.
But they shall not looke over, neither unpacke their packes
in any place; as also they shall suffer them to passe in all

places, without all stay or delay, according to this our
Cæsars priviledge and Letter of favour. Also whensoever
the English Merchants shall be desirous to send out of
our Realme into their owne Land any of their servants
overland, or into other Kingdomes, then they shall likewise
send their people overland with our Cæsars order freely,
but without carying any Commodities, and their passe shall
be given them in the Embassadours office. Further, concerning any matter of controversie that any man shall have
to doe with them either in bargaining, or in injury,
according to this our Cæsars order, they shall be judged
by our Counsellor and Secretary Evan Cowrbatov Hramo-
teev : Therefore, as before, wheresoever they, or any of
their servants, in all our Realme, in what Citie soever,
have any matter of controversie in Bargaining, or in
Injurie against any man, or that any man have any matter
against any of them, then in all our Cities, our Gentlemen,
and Governours, and all other our Officers, shall judge
them, doing justice betwixt either of them with equitie
and truth. This priviledge or letter of favour was given
at our Cæsars Pallace of Mosco. From the world Anno
7113. in the moneth of December.

The Copie of the Translation of a Contract, made
by the Emperour Demetry Evanowich, otherwise called Gryshca Otreapyove, and the
daughter of the Palatine Sendamersko, chiefe
Generall of Poland, in the time of Demetry his
being in Poland, the which was sent over by
Master John Merrick, and translated out of
Russe into English for the Kings Majestie, as
followeth.

A True Translation of a writing out of Polish into
Russe, given by a Monke who left his habit, called
by the name of Gryshca Ocreapyove, supposed to be the
Son of the Emperour Evan Vassiliwich, named Demeetry

Evanowich, who gave this assurance under his firme, to the Palatine Sendamersko, as also hath beene avouched by one Bewcheesko, principall Secretary unto the said Demetry, before all the Nobilitie of Russia, that this said writing was written by the Generall his owne hande, as followeth.

Wee Demetry Evanowich, by the mercy of God, Prince of all Russia, of Owgleets Demetryuskoy, and Lord of all the Empire of Mosco, and being of the stocke of Preatrove; Calling to memorie our former life, being not in that forme and manner, as is in other great Monarchies, as was in the time of our Predecessours, and other Christian people. Neverthelesse, by the providence of God almightie, from whom proceedeth a beginning and an end, and from whom commeth life and death; We have by him espied and made choise unto our selfe, with good liking, in the time of our being in the Kingdome of Poland, of a Companion, of great and honorable birth, and of godly education, and is such a companion, with whom we shall by the mercie of God, live peaceably: which is the resplendent and Noble Lady Marina, daughter to the great Palatine Sendemersko. And upon this occasion have taken him for our Father, and having requested of him to give unto us his Daughter, Maryna in mariage, and in regard that wee are not yet in our owne Kingdome, therefore doe we purpose hereafter to take order for her comming unto us with the Generall Sendamersko. Likewise, when I doe come to live in my owne Kingdome, then shall the Palatine Sendamersko remember his faithfull and true promise with his Daughter, the Lady Maryna her vow, my selfe remembring my owne vow, and so both of us to hold it faithfully with love and affection, and to that end doe we binde our selves by our writings. Likewise, first and principally, in the name of the holy Trinitie, I doe give my faithfull and true princely promise, that I will take in marriage the Lady Maryna. If on the contrary, I doe not, then, I wish that I might give this as a curse upon my selfe: also, so soone as I shall make entrance into our Kingdome, and heritage of Mosco, then will I give the Palatine, the Lord her Father, a reward of tenne thousand peeces of Polish gold. And to the Lady Maryna our wife, in consideration of her great and long Journey, as also for the providing and furnishing of her selfe, I will give out of my Treasure Velvets wrought with Silver and Gold. And the Messengers that shall be sent to me from the Lord her Father, or from the Lady her selfe, I shall not hold or keepe, but shall let them passe, and will reward them with gifts, which shall be a token of our Princely favour; and thereunto doe we give this our Princely promise. Secondly, as soone as we shall come to the Imperiall throne of our Father, then presently will we send our Embassadour to the resplendant King of Poland to certifie unto him, as also to intreate him to take knowledge of this businesse now passed betwixt us, and withall, that he would be pleased to suffer us to conclude and effect this our said businesse, without losse or hindrance. Also unto the forenamed Lady Maryna our [III.iv.762.] wife, we give two Lordships, viz. Novogrod the great, and Vobsko, with all the Provinces belonging to the same, with Counsellors, Gentlemen, and Yeoman, and Priests, fitting for a Congregation, to rule and governe freely with full authority in the same forme and manner, as if we ruled. And my selfe to have no more right or title nor authoritie in the said two Cities of Novogrod and Vobsko: and thereunto doe I binde my selfe with this writing, and doe wholly give and bestow all on the said Lady Maryna that is contained in this writing, as soone as by Gods helpe we shall be married together, and thereunto have given this our writing, sealed with our princely Seale. But if by chance our wife hath not by us any children, then in those two Lordships before specified, shee shall place men in authoritie of her owne, to governe and to doe Justice: and also it shall be free for the said men in authoritie, to give Lands and Inheritance to their owne Souldiers, and to trade freely at pleasure, as shall be best liking to them, and as though it were in

their owne true and lawfull dominion, and to build
Monasteries, and to set up the Romish Religion, and to
have Latine or Romish Priests and Schooles. But she
her selfe to abide and remaine with us. And concerning
her Priest, to have as many as shall be needefull to be kept
for her owne godly Romish Religion, without all let or
hindrance: and as wee our selfe by the mercy of God are
already inclined to the same, so will wee likewise with
earnest care, seeke by all meanes to bring all the Kingdome
of Mosco to the knowledge of the Romish Religion, and
to set up the Church of Rome. Also, if God should not
grant unto us good successe, whereby this be performed
within a yeare; then it shall be at the pleasure of our
Father to separate mee and his daughter Maryna. But if
it please him to forbeare till another yeare, then doe I passe
this my Bill, with my owne handwriting, and thereunto I
have sworne my selfe, and given a vow according to the
holy order, and all in this Bill to hold and keepe carefully:
as also that I shall bring all the Russe people to the Latine
Religion. Written at Sambore the five and twentieth of
May, in Anno 1604. Underneath was his firme, to all
this foresaid as appeareth: Prince Demetry of
Owglets.

Promise of Romish Religion.

NOw let us returne with Thuanus into Poland, where
with his Historical eies we see this glorious Spouse,
her Father, Uncle, & trayne of women accompanying the
Russian Embassador in his returne; whom many Merchants out of Italie and Germanie followed in hope of
gaine. In this lingring journey, they continued from the
end of January to the sixe and twentieth of Aprill, before
they entred Mosco. And the seventh day after, Peter
Basman with a great troupe of Courtiers and Nobles,
attended the Spouse to the Court, where shee was
solemnely entertayned by her Husband, and thence conveighed to the Monasterie where his Mother abode. The
fourth day after, all things being prepared, shee was
brought into the Palace, and the next day married to him

Demetrius his Marriage.

Both crowned.

Conspiracie.

by the Patriarch after Evening Prayer. Both of them also, solemnely crowned, returned with sound of Musick and Ordnance into the Castle, and the night passed with great Jubilee, Demetrius his mind being filled notwithstanding with cares. For a conspiracie which had beene hatching six moneths, now growing to ripeness, terrified him: against which hee had armed himselfe with forreigne aides. At first hee had brought a guard of Germanes out of Poland, which being without example of his Predecessors, and seeing it disliked of his subjects, hee dismissed, together with all forren Souldiers. They being thus sent away without pay, returned with the casheered Polanders to the borders, where they committed many outrages to the greater discontent of the Russes. Many of them found grievances notwithstanding, in his too much respect to the Poles: and many made question of his birth. Many were suspected of conspiracie, and divers tortured, which was but quenching fire with Oyle, the flame growing greater. And now beganne Demetrius to repent of his hastie dismissing his guards, and began a new Check-roll of Lieflanders and Germanes, to which hee added an hundred English Halberdiers and as many Scots (their Captaynes hee calleth Matthias Cnotsenius and * Albert Lant) and an hundred French under Jaques Margeret armed with Partisans. Then also he inlarged his pay, but too late.

*I suppose this should bee Gilbert: for one Captayne Gilbert I have often heard of in that place of service, which writ also commentaries of these affaires which I have much sought to little purpose in our Merchants hands.

Alexander Gosenskie Corvinus was sent Embassadour from Poland with rich Presents, and Letters from King Sigismund to Demetrius, which because they expressed not the Title of Emperour were not received nor opened. In excuse whereof the Embassadour used words unsufferable to Russian patience, that he should goe and deprive the great Turke of those Titles. Demetrius dissembled notwithstanding, in regard of his past experience, and hoped helpes from the Pole. The dayes following were spent in pastimes and sloth. Saturday was solemne to the Russians, a Feast then happening which they preferre before Easter. The Emperour and Empresse sate

crowned in the Hall, and made a great Feast to their
owne and to strangers; in which the Pole Embassadour
refused to be present, except he might sit at the Princes
Table, as the Russian Embassadour had beene honoured at
Cracovia. The Russes denied stiffely, but Demetrius at
length yeelded. Many peremptorie and licentious passages happened, the Poles carrying themselves domineer-
ingly to the Russes, as Victors to the conquered.
Demetrius at first over-bold, now beganne to feare, and
warned the Poles to bee warie, and sent for all his guards.
On Friday, the Russes preparing for offence, and the Poles
for their defence (for they and not the Prince, seemed to
bee then in danger) in the Evening the Nobles command
the people to arme against the next day. The Empresse
was this while secure, and made ready a magnificent Feast
against Sunday. But on Saturday (the sixteenth of the *Bloudie day.*
Kalends of June) the Conspirators assemble early, and a
great cry is raysed to kill the Poles and Demetrius. Some [III.iv.763.]
greedie of spoyle runne presently to the Poles Lodgings,
assault them and embroyle all with slaughters. Others
runne to the Castle. Few of the guard were there, delay
having bred securitie in Demetrius, nor were any of their
Captaynes seene. Margaret then lay sicke as he after told
me (Thuanus) which disease saved his life. Things were
done with such furie and celeritie, that many Russes in
Polish attire were slaine before they were knowne.

Peter Basman came running forth halfe naked, & was *P. Basman*
killed by one of his own servants. Suiskie their Leader, *slain.*
carrying a Sword in one hand, a Crosse in the other, caused
the great Bel to be rung in token of fire that Demetrius
might be raised & come forth of his Parlor. He awakned
with the noyse, now seeing a greater danger then fire,
taketh a Turkish Sword, and suddenly slips downe out of
a window, breaking his legge with the fall, whereby he
was easily taken by the people, and by Suiskoys command *Demetrius*
carried into the greater Hall, where Embassadours have *taken and*
audience. There some upbrayding his impostures, he *slaine.*
with his sword layd one on the ground : and then desired

the Nobilitie to permit him to speake to the people, which was denied. Some say that he obtayned of Suiskey, that he might be tryed by the testimonie of Vasilowich his Wife; which being brought out of the Nunnery, affirmed before the Nobles on her oath, that her Sonne Demetrius was many yeeres before murthered by Boris his perfidies, which she at first seeing the peoples favour, and just revenge on Boris, willingly dissembled, whereupon they ranne upon him, and with many wounds slue him. Thus writeth Peter Paterson of Upsal which then was in Russia.

Contumelious usage. When they had slaine him, they thrust a rope thorow his secret parts, and drew him thorow the myre into the Market place, where he remayned foure dayes lying all gorie and myrie on a boord, with Peter Basman under it, and an ugly Vizar over it, a Bag-pipe in his mouth, with other lascivious cruelties exercised on his dead body.

The Palatine Sendomir (or Sandamersko) was blocked up in his House, and other Poles Houses rifled, many of *Poles slaine.* which died not unrevenged, howsoever by numbers overcomne. Viteneskie after much slaughter of the assayling Russes, when he saw Ordnance brought, set forth a white flagge in token of yeeding, bidding his Servants cast abroad his money; which whiles the people were gathering, he and his made way with their Swords with great slaughter, & yeelded to the Boiarens which came from the *The Queene.* Castle. The miserable Bride was not only spoyled of inestimable Treasure, but of all her Apparell, and Jewels, carefull only of her Father and Uncle, and thinking it a happy purchase, if she might save her life and recover her Countrey. Meanewhile, without her Garment to cover her, without Bed to lye on, without securitie of life, shee expected in poore Weeds the issue of the peoples furie.

Merchants spoyled. Many Merchants endured like fates. Ambrose Cellar, besides the losse of thirtie thousand Crownes, lost his life. James Win was with his own Sword beheaded: Nathan lost one hundred and fiftie thousand Florens: Nicolas Limborough fiftie thousand. Two of Auspurg had lent two hundred thousand Crownes to Demetrius, which now was not to pay them. Marcellius lost an hundred thousand Florens. Twelve hundred Poles lost their lives; many were saved by the Boiarens. Foure hundred Russes were slayne. At night the tumult ceased. Scarsly would the people give leave to bury the bodies after three dayes wallowing in the durt, in the Germane Churchyard.

Russes slaine.

After this tempest was calmed, the Boiarens assembled in counsell about a new Election, where Suiskey made speech to them, professing himselfe sorrowfull for that had passed, in the execution of a just zeale to the Imperiall Family and his Countrey, and in hatred of a cruell Tyrant: that Ivan Vasilowich, how ever injuriously taxed by some, had left Kingdomes annexed to his Inheritance as Monuments of his great spirit; by whom he had beene sent to Stephen King of Poland to treate of peace, and ever since had so carried himselfe in the State, that none could justly blame him: that John being dead, Theodore succeeded, but another ruled, who murthered the yonger brother, and as was thought, after that poysoned the other; so attayning the Empire, which how miserable was it all his time? that Demetrius therefore (whosoever he was) found friends, himselfe amongst others, but when their Religion was endangered, Forreiners advanced, Lawes violated, Exotike fashions brought in, liberties suppressed, he withstood with the peril of his life; which it grieved him to have enjoyed, as a Theeves benefit, by his grant which had no right to take it: yet seeing their forwardnesse in a cause so just (would God it had not beene so bloudy) more regarding his Countreyes safety then rumours and reports, hee had beene their Captayne to doe that which God the disposer of Kingdomes by the successe had approved, so that now they were freed from a cruel Tyrant, nor had they any Sorcerer or Impostor to mock them: that it remayned now, seeing the Imperiall Family was extinct, they should now seeke one of noblest bloud, of wisest experience, of most religious zeale, who might esteeme his peoples hearts his strongest Forts, such an one as either is, or is thought to bee the best man to become

Suiskeys speech.

A.D.
1605.

He is chosen Emperour.

[III.iv.764.]

The Devill is often slandered: and by ill willers, bad is made worse. And so perhaps by Suiskeys faction was this Demetrius.

The former part of this intelligence I found in Master Hackluyts Papers; the latter by conference, &c. Son of Gregory Peupoly. See Suiskeys Letter following.

their Prince. Thus was himselfe chosen Emperour the thirteenth of the Kalends of June. A writing was published to justifie the killing of Demetrius, a runnagate Fryer called Grishka, or Gregorie Strepy, professed in the Monasterie in the Castle (which therefore hee would never enter lest hee should bee knowne) with other aspersions of Heresie, Sorcerie, affectation of inducing Popery (the Popes Letters also challenging his promise produced) to give the Jesuites Temples, Colledges, and other necessaries; with other over-tures to the Palatine Sandomersko, for Smolensko, and Novogrod; his bringing in Poles in Russian Roomes, his luxurie, riot, pompe, reserving Boris his Daughter in a Nunnerie with intent of incestuous lust, having Murthered her Mother and Brother; making a silver Throne with sixe Lions on each side, and other pride; abusing Nunneries to lust and lasciviousnesse, &c. But wee shall give you hereof more authenticke testimonie then this of Thuanus in Suiskeys Imperiall Letter to His Majestie. Meanewhile touching this Demetrius we will produce a few English Testimonies extracted out of their Letters and Relations: wherein if some circumstantial discrepance appeare (in things done both so farre and so foule in tumultuous furie, where men had rather hide themselves then become witnesses, lest whiles they would bee Spectators, they should bee forced to bee Actors, and have their parts acted in that bloudie Tragedy) it is no marvell. I produce all Witnesses I can, in a cause of so remarkeable consequence, and choose rather to bee prolixe then negligent, that the Reader out of so much evidence may better weigh and examine the truth.

THe late Emperour of Russia called by the name of Demetry Evanowich, is now credibly said (as some of them say) to have beene the Sonne of a Russe Gentleman, named Gregorie Peupoloy, and that in his younger yeeres he was shorne a Frier into a Monasterie: from whence hee afterwards privily got away, travelled into Germanie and other Countreyes, but had his most abiding in Poland, in which time he attayned to good perfection in Armes and Military knowledge; with other abilities of sufficiencie; Afterwards finding a conceit taken by the Russes of a secret conveying away of Demetry Evanowich, brother and heire to Pheodore Evanowich Emperour; and that some other should be made away in his steed: And finding also the generall distaste of the Government of Boris then Emperour, who after a faire beginning, did in his latter yeeres uphold himselfe, and his house with oppression and crueltie: And having also many circumstances and oportunities of time and age, and such other likelihoods, to advantage and second his pretence, began first to broach his Title (as before) and by degrees found such a generall acceptation of all sorts of people, that it so daunted Boris, that (as it was then rumoured about) hee, first, and afterwards his Wife, and his Sonne succeeding him, made themselves away by Poyson. Though now it goeth for certayne, that the poysoning of them was procured by the Pretender, to make the easier way to the Empire, which thereby he obtayned, entring and continuing the same with all the State, and greatnesse that such a place required: Untill at length the Russes moved rather by other certainties, then by any thing discovered by himselfe, the sixt day after his marriage (which was kept with very great pompe and solemnitie) being the seventeenth of May last past, taking a time when the Poles stood least on Guard; came to the Court with one consent of Nobilitie and Commons about three of the clocke in the morning, and mastring the Guards, drew the Emperour out of his bed from the Empresse, and charging him that hee was not the true Demetry Evanowich, but a false Pretender, he confessed the Deceit, and was forthwith hewed in pieces by the multitude: Peter Basman resisting was likewise slaine; and both brought into the Market place, where their bodies lay for a time to bee viewed of every man. The old Queene denied him to bee her Sonne, excusing her former acknowledgement to have proceeded from feare and the generall acceptance which he

Occasion of ambition.

Boris ill government.

Demetrius Emperour.

He is slaine.

found amongst the people. As many Poles as made resistance, were slaine to the number of seventeene hundred. The new Empresse, her Father, his brother with the other Poles were committed to safe keeping, to the number of eight or nine thousand.

And then proceeding to a new Election they chose *Suiskey Emperour* Vassiloe Evanowich Shoskey, who not long before was at the Blocke to have beene beheaded, for reporting that hee had seene the true Demetry Evanowich after he was dead, and did helpe to burie him. But the Emperour did recall him, and afterwards advanced him to the chiefest place of dignitie about his person. He is the next of bloud * living, descended of the Race of the old Emperour Ivan Vasilowich, of the age of fiftie yeeres or thereabouts, never married, but kept under during Boris time, a Prince of great wisdome, and a great favourer of our Nation, as did specially appeare by the care hee had to guard the English House from rifling, when the late Demetry was brought in by the Poles.

The late Pretender was of stature low, but well set, hard favoured and of no presence; howsoever otherwise of a Princely disposition, executing Justice without partialities; And not remitting the insolencie even of the Poles; well seene in martiall practises, and trayning his Nobilitie to the Discipline of warre, to make them the readier against the Tartar, not given either to women or drinke, but very liberall and bountifull, which occasioned some grievous Exactions to maintayne the same. And to conclude, a man in the opinion of such as knew him, not unworthy of a better gotten, and longer continued Empire, which hee lost chiefly through the greatnesse of his minde, supposing that none of his Subjects durst attempt any such matter against his person, when as in the meane time the practice went on with such a generall Conjuration, that the Russes were summoned by the ringing of a Bell to bee readie to enter the Court. And to shake off that Government which would have made them a more noble Nation then formerly they beene.

Suiskey Emperour

*This might be rumoured: Others say hee was not of that but of very noble bloud. See sup. in Fletcher and Thuanus. Demetrius his person described. Some say that he was not like Demetrius and that he seemed a dozen yeeres elder: but perhaps they mistake this for an other after Pretender, calling himselfe the same Demetrius, &c., as after shall appeare, a deformed man. [III.iv.765.]

IT is reported by some of Ours, that hee the rather was inclinable to our Nation in the respect he bare to his Majestie, having read that his worthy Worke dedicated to Prince Henrie. Hee is said also to have beene a resolute man of his hands, to have delighted in fighting with the Beare; active and strong. I have likewise heard that hee gave the command of his Guard consisting of strangers to Captayne Gilbert a Scot; to have made one *Captayne* Buchenskoy (a Learned and Religious Protestant) his *Gilbert.* Secretarie; and otherwise to have beene so alienated from *Buchenskoy.* Russian manners, and so well affected to Strangers, that they conspired as aforesaid. The people are said to have entred the Castle (which was a quadrant, having a high bricke wall of seven stories, and another of stone, and a *Stones rare* Market place) with stones in their pockets (which are rare *about Mosco.* thereabouts) and some with weapons.

Some report from Captayne Gilberts Relation, that lying *Captaine* on his bed not long before his death (as hee thought, *Gilberts report* awake) an aged man came to him, which sight caused him *of a Vision.* to arise and come to Captayne Gilbert, and his guard that watched, but none of them had seene any thing. Here-upon he returned to his Bed, but within an houre after he againe troubled with like apparition called, and sent for Buchinskie: telling him that he had now twice seene an aged man, who at the second comming told him, that though for his owne person he was a good Prince, yet the injustice and oppressions of his inferiour Ministers must bee punished, and his Empire should bee taken from him. In this perplexitie his Secretarie gave him good and holy counsell, saying till true Religion were there planted, his Officers would bee lewd, the people oppressed, and God Almightie offended, who perhaps by that Dreame or Vision had admonished him of his dutie. The Emperour seemed much moved, and to intend that good which that Countrey was not so happy to receive. For a few dayes after (as that Relation averreth) his Russe Secretarie came to him with a Sword, at which the Emperour jested, and hee suddenly after sawcie speeches assaulted him, with many other Grandes of that Conspiracie, and like another Cæsar slue him, crying Libertie, before his guards could apprehend the danger; of which some were slaine, but the most with Gilbert their Captayne, got to a place called *Coluga.* Coluga, which with the helpe of some Russes they forti-fied and held for their defence. Buchinskie the Secretarie was taken and imprisoned, the strangers murthered, the English except, who have in all changes been well beloved of the Russians; as indeed they deserve, having alway done good service to the Emperours. And their interest saved the life of that worthy man Buchinskey, which they requited with much observance to the succeeding Em-perour Suiskey, who comes next to be spoken of; and first you shall have his Letter to our Gracious Sovereigne.

§. IIII.

Suiskey the Successour his Letter to our King, des-cribing the former Demetrius his Acts and Tragedie.

The Copie of the Translation of a Letter sent from the new Emperour Vassily Evanowich Shoskey to the Kings Majestie by Master John Mericke.

The love and mercie of God that guideth us in the wayes of peace, we glorifie with the Trinitie.

Rom the great Lord Emperour and great Duke Vassily Evanowich of all Russia, sole Commander of Voladomer, Mosko, Novogrod, King of Cazan and Astracan, of Syberia, Lord of Vobsko, and great Duke of Smolensko, Twerskoy, Yavharskoy, Pearmskoy, Vats-koy, Bollharskoy, and of other: Lord and great Duke of Novogroda of the Low Countrey of Cherneego, Rezanskoy, Polotskoy, Rostovskoy, Yereslaveskoy, Bealo-zerskoy, Leeflanskoy, Owdorskoy, Obdorskoy, Condin-skoy, and Commander of all the North parts: also Lord

of the Land of Eeverskoy, Cartalinskoy, and over the
Empire of the Gorgians of the Land of Cabardinskoy,
and Eeharskoy Land, likewise of many other Lordships
Lord and Commander.

To our beloved Brother James King of England, Scotland, France, and Ireland, Wee give to understand that
Sigismund King of Poland, and great Duke of Letto, in
Anno 7109. did send unto the late Emperour Boris, his
Embassadour named Lewis Sapeago, being Chancelor of
the great Dukedome of Poland, requesting the said
Emperour Boris, that the former league and peace
made and concluded upon by the great Lord Emperour and great Duke Theodore Evanowich of all
Russia, and him Sigismond King of Poland, might be
stedfastly holden and continued till the time of that league
were expired. As also that the Emperour Boris would
inlarge the said league for thirtie yeeres more, whereupon
the Emperour Boris yeelded thus farre unto the request
of the King of Poland, that hee would continue the old
league till the full time were expired, and assent to a new
league for twentie yeeres more; and to that effect he
tooke an Oath, to hold and keepe all the contents faithfully, mentioned in the said Writing, touching the same
league: and instead of the King of Poland, his Embassadour Lewis Sapeagoe was sworne in the presence of the
Emperour Boris. And after the Polish Embassadour was
departed from the Mosko, the Emperour Boris sent unto
Sigismund King of Poland his Embassadour, being one
of the Privie Councell, called Michailo Zleabowich
Sallteecove, with some others to end and finish the aforesaid league, to the which league the King of Poland
himselfe was sworne in the presence of the Emperour's
Embassadour to hold and keepe the said league faithfully,
according to the tenour of their Writing.

But not long after Sigismund King of Poland, with one
Pavarade, entred into such a practise, as he therein falsified
his Oath, and made way to the shedding of much Christian
bloud: First, by retayning and upholding one Gryshca

[III.iv.766.]

*League with
the Pole.*

*He taxeth the
King of
Poland.
Allegations
against the
pretending
Demetrius.*

Otreapyove, a Runnagate, a Conjurer, and one that left
his profession being a Monke, and ran away out of Russia
into Poland; and being come thither, tooke upon him
to be the Son of the great Emperour Evan Vassilawich
of famous memorie, and by name Demetry Evanowich:
when as it was well knowne in our Kingdome, that
before he was shorne a Monke, he was commonly
called Yowshco, Son to one Bowghdan Otreapyove,
dwelling at a place called Galitts: and when hee had
committed much villanie, to save his life he shoare

A Frier. himselfe a Frier, and so runne from one Monasterie
to another; and lastly, came into a Monasterie called
Chowdo, where hee was made one of the Clearkes;

A Clearke. being so placed there by the Patriarke of Mosko himselfe: But he did not leave off his former life; for he
continued still in his most Devillish actions, as he did
before he was shorne, committing villany, forsaking God

Magician. and falling to the studie of the Blacke Arte, and to many
such like evils he was inclined. Also there was found
by him a Writing which shewed how he was falne from
God, and the same was made well knowne to the holy
Patriarch of Mosko, and of all Russia, and to the Metropolitanes, Archbishops, and Bishops, and to all the holy
Cleargie: whereupon the said Rulers of our true Christian

Greeke Faith, which is from the Grecian Law, for these his most
Church. ungodly works, consulted to send him to perpetuall Prison,
there to end his life. Whereupon this notorious Instrument of Satan, perceiving this his overthrow, and that his
vile practises were discovered, ran away out of the King-

Flight to Letto. dome of Mosko, beyond the borders, and into Letto to a
place called Keeyeve: thus according to the Devils
instructing of him, as one forsaken of God, he made this
his doing manifestly known to all people, leaving off his
Monks Habit, and withall by the counsell and advice of
our Enemie the Polish King, and one of his Palatines

ᵐ George. named Sandamersko Yourya,ᵐ with Duke Constantine,
and Duke Veshnevetskoy and his Brethren with other
Polish Lords that were of his Councell, began to call him

the Son of the great Lord, Emperour and great Duke
Evan Vassilywich, by name Prince Demetry of Owglitts.

As also by his villanous treacherie and the Devills perswading of him, he made much trouble in our Land, by
sending abroad many of his intising and provoking
Letters, to divers places upon the borders of our
Countrey: that is, to a place called Done, and to the
Volgoe, to our Cossacks and Souldiers, naming himselfe to
be the Prince Demetry of Owglitts. Moreover, there
came to our Kingdome of Mosko many Polish Spies,
which brought and dispersed Libels both in Citie and
Townes, and in the high-wayes, practising to rayse dissention in the Kingdome of Mosko. Also it is well
knowne, not only to them in the Empire of Mosko, but
likewise in other Kingdomes, that the great Lord
Emperour, and great Duke Evan Vassilywich of famous
memory, had a Sonne called by the name of Prince
Demetry, and after his Fathers decease, there was given *Demetry of*
unto him and his Mother the Citie of Owglitts. But in *Owglits.*
the yeere 7095. being in the Reigne of the great Lord, *His murther.*
Emperour and great Duke Theodore Evanowich of all
Russia, this foresaid Demetry was murthered by the order
and appointment of Boris Godenove. And at his Funerall
was his Mother now called the Empresse Martha, with
her owne Brethren by name Michaila and Greegory the
Sonnes of Theodore Nahovo. Likewise to his burying,
there was sent from the Mosko Metropolitanes, and
Archimandreets, and Abbots: and the great Lord
Emperour, and great Duke Theodore Evanowich sent
to his Funerall many Nobles and Courtiers of the Land *Buriall.*
which saw him buried in the chiefest and principall Church
of Owglitts. Moreover, Martha the Dutches and
Empresse his Mother is yet living, and many of her
Brothers and Unckles, which doe at this present time
serve us the great Lord Emperour, and great Duke Vassily
Evanowich, of all Russia sole Commander: Likewise in
these last yeeres past, as in Anno 7111. and in Anno 7112.
and 7113. concerning that foresaid Traytour and Here-

ticke, the forsaken of God Gryshca Otreapyove, many of
our Gentlemen, Captaynes and others our Officers did
many times write from the North parts of the borders of
our Kingdome into Poland and Letto, and to others their
inferiour Cities, to the Rulers and Governours of the
same; as also our spirituall people: the Patriarke, the
Metropolitans, Archbishops, and Bishops wrote unto the
Letters to spirituall people of Poland, declaring unto them what that
Poland. Heretick and Traytor was, likewise from whence he came
and what manner of person he was; as also of his
demeanour, and likewise of the occasion why hee runne
away to them out of the Land, as also the manner of the
making away of the Prince Demetry, and withall
requested the Rulers and Spirituall people of Poland, that
they knowing what Runnagate this was, would not give
credit unto him, nor to make a breach of the late league
concluded upon.

[III.iv.767.]   But the Governours of the Dukedome of Poland and
Letto, as also the spirituall men, according to the King of
Poland his commandment, gave no credit unto our writings, but began, more then before to intice and perswade
men to uphold the Traitor, and to aide him.   Moreover,
to make trouble and dissention in our Land, they tooke
this forsaken of God, Greeshca unto them, and cald him
by the name of Prince Demetry of Owglits: likewise the
King gave unto him a chaine of gold, with many thousand
Polish aides. peeces of Polish gold, to the defraying of his charges; as
also sent in armes to our borders with one of his Lords,
the Palatine Sendamersko, and another of his chiefest
Lords, with many troopes of Poles.   But when the
Emperour Boris understood how that this Gryshca
Otreapyove was called, by the name of Prince Demetry
Evanowich of Owglits, and withall, that they did aide and
helpe him against the Kingdome of Russia: he caused his
Counsell to send a messenger, as from themselves, to the
Polish Lord Panameerada, which Messenger was named
Smeernoy sent. Smeernay Otreapyove, being Unckle to the said Gryshca
Otreopyove being the Son of one Jamateen Otrepayov,

onely to declare unto them what this Gryshca was; but that Polish Lord Panameerada would not suffer him, and his Unckle to be brought face to face. But he made answer to the said Messenger Smeernay, that they did not aide him, neither did they stand for him in any sort.

So after he had sent away the Messenger Smeernay, the King of Poland, and the Lord Panameerada did aide Gryshca Otreapyove with men and treasure more liberally then before, purposing to make great strife and trouble, and to shed much bloud in the Kingdome of Mosco. Also at the same time Sigismund, King of Poland, requested the aide of one of the Princes of Crim in *Crim Tartar.* Tartaria, named Cazateera; and to that end he should aide Gryshca with his forces, against the Kingdome of Mosko; and he in consideration, did promise to give unto the foresaid Crim, Prince, what hee would demand. Then the Emperour Boris understanding what practises were in hand, being altogether contrary to the league; thereupon purposely he sent to Sigismund King of Poland, another speciall Messenger, one named Posnicke Agareove; like-wise at the same time, the holy Patriarke of Mosco, and all Russia, with the Metropolitans, Archbishops, and Bishops, with all the rest of the holy Clergie, sent their Messengers with Letters to the State of Poland, and so *Another* the great Dukedome of Letto, to the Archbishops, and *Messenger.* Bishops, and to all the Spiritualtie. Moreover, in the said Letters, the Emperour Boris with the Patriarke, and all the holy assembly, wrote unto the Lord Panameerada concerning Gryshca, making it knowne unto them what he was, and wherefore he ranne away into Poland, and likewise that the Sonne of the great Lord Emperour, and great Duke Evan Vasiliwich, the Prince Demetry was dead: And to that intent, that the King Sigismund should not give credit to the said Gryshca, and that they should not spill Christian bloud, nor violate the league.

Hereupon Sigismund King of Poland writ unto the Emperour Boris, and further, by word of mouth, both he and Panameerada delivered to the said messenger in his

message, that hee did hold and keepe their League, and
moreover, did not violate or breake his oath no manner of
way : and likewise did write, that he did not ayde that
foresaid Gryshca, neither did give credit unto him : withall
denying that he was with him in his Kingdome : and
further he did write, that if there were any out of Poland
or Letto that did aide or assist him, that then they should
be executed. But after he had dispatched away the
messenger of Boris, not regarding his oath, still more and
more did aide and helpe this Gryshca Otreapyove. Also
the Palatine Sendamersko, and Myhala Ratanisko came
into the Kingdome of Mosco, to a place called the Land
of Seeversko, putting the people of that Land in feare,
and perswading them there, this Gryshca was the true
Prince, and that the King of Poland and Panameerada,
had found out the certaintie thereof : and therefore they
will have Poland and Letto stand for him. Also from out
of many other Kingdomes they goe to aide and assist
him : likewise other inferiour Kingdomes are willing to
stand for him : moreover, that Gryshca in the foresaid
Land of Seeversko, and in other places of our Borders,
by the meanes of his divellish practises and conjurations
did intise and tempt him to fall to him : likewise the people
of those foresaid places of the Land of Seeversko, and on
the Borders, being simple people, and resorting seldome to
the Citie of Mosco, and being intised by Gryshca, and the
rest of the Governours, could not withstand, but yeelded
them unto them. Whereupon against those Polonians
and Lettoes, and other enemies that were already entred
the Kingdome of Mosco, the Emperour sent his Nobles
with a great Armie : but by the appointment of God, the
Emperour Boris deceased ; upon whose death, the chiefest
of the Nobles departed the Campe. And after their
departure, the Armie hearing of the death of the
Emperour, and being drawne thereto by feare and otherwise, at last yeelded themselves over unto Gryshca, as the
Borderers had done before.

Also the foresaid Gryshca, by the helpe of the Divell,

and King Sigismund, and Panameerada, came into the Citie and Kingdome of Mosco, to the great disquietnesse and trouble of the whole Land; by whom the Religion was corrupted, and by him were many true Christians put to exile, for denying his right and interest to the Kingdome of Mosco. And shortly after he was setled in the Kingdome, and he tooke to wife the daughter of one Sandamersko, as was appointed by the King of Poland and Panameerada: the which wife of his was in Mosco with her Father and Brother Senatskoy, and with one Veshnevetskoy, with their Polish and Letto Lords, and other people, by whom Religion was prophaned: as also we were *Mutation of* forced and driven to receive many wrongs and injuries, *Religion.* which the people of the Kingdome of Mosco could not indure. Also, at last this Greeshca, by the counsell of the Palatine Sandamersko his Father in Law, and by the counsell of Veshnevetskoy, and other Polish and Letto people, which he brought in with him, was purposed, by a [III.iv.768.] secret politicke devise to have put to death the Metropolitans, Archbishops, and Bishops, and all the holy and spirituall assembly, with the Nobles, and Courtiers, and divers others which were of the better people, and so to have sent others into Poland and Letto; withall to have changed the Religion, and to have established the Romish *Romish* Religion, for which purpose he brought with him many *Religion and* Jesuites. *Jesuites.*

The which we the great Lord and great Duke Vasily Evanowich, of all Russia, with the Metropolitans, Archbishops, and Bishops, and with all the holy spirituall assembly, and with the Nobles, Courtiers, and Commons of the Kingdome of Mosco, well considering, and perceiving what an alteration this would be to our Christian faith, with the overthrow and utter undoing to our whole Kingdome: we then earnestly bewail'd and lamented, and withall hartily prayed to the almightie Trinitie our onely Lord God, that liveth and defendeth mankinde, that it would please him to deliver us, and the Common-wealth from those vile, cruell, divellish attempts, and devises of theirs. Thus desiring the mercy of God, we all returned and stood stedfast to our former unspotted and true Christian faith, against that usurper and counterfeit Gryshca and his Counsell, with a resolution to stand in the same manfully, and even to the death, hoping and longing for the time that all people, and warlik men and Souldiors and many others of the Empire of Mosco might come to gather themselves together, & that they might likewise perceive and discern this usurping Heretick, and his divellish courses, by which he did decline from the true *Large Empire* Christian faith of our Religion. The largenesse of the *of Russia.* Kingdome of Mosco cannot be unknowne unto you our loving Brother, how farre it extendeth it selfe both to the South, and to the West, as also to other places, that in halfe a yeares space they could not gather themselves together. But when as the power and warlike Souldiours, and all other people were gathered together, then through the mercie and favour of God, this enemy of Gods Commonwealth was discovered to all what he was. And the Empresse Martha, being Mother of the true Prince Demetry Evonowich, did certifie unto us before the Metropolitans, Archbishoppes, and Bishoppes, and before all the holy assembly, as also to the Nobles and Courtiers, and other Officers, and men of worth within our Empire, did shee deliver, that her Sonne the Prince Demetri was murthered beyond reason, at a place called Owglits, by appointment of Boris Godenove, and that he dyed in her armes; yet did this Gryshca falsely call himselfe by the name of him that was murthered.

Also we found in the custody of this Gryshca, the Copie of a writing, which was the contract and agreement that he made betwixt him and the Palatine, before his comming *See before.* out of Poland; in which was written, that as soone as he did come to the Kingdome of Mosco, that then he would take to wife the daughter of the Palatine, and would give her two Provinces, called great Novogrod and Vobsko, with counsell, Courtiers, Gentlemen, and Priests, fitting to a Congregation, with inferior Castles and Lands, freely in those foresaid, to build and set up Monasteries, and also to set up the Romish Religion; And when he came to the Kingdome of Mosco, that then he should give unto the Palatine tenne thousand pieces of Polish Gold, which is by our Russia account, three hundred thousand Markes: and to his wife, in consideration of her long Journey, he promised to give cloth of Gold, and cloth of Silver, and of all the best things that was in the Treasurie of the Kingdome of Mosco. Likewise, that hee the said Gryshca at his comming to Mosco, would take order to bring these things to passe with all diligence, whereby he might draw all the Dominion of Mosco from our true Grecian Religion, and so to have turned us into the Romish Religion, and to have destroyed the holy Church over all the Empire of Mosco, and so to have built up the Religion of the Church of Rome: and for the performing of all this, the said Gryshca was sworne to the Palentine Sandamersko, in the presence of the Teachers of the Land, as beforesaid; that he according to his owne handwriting, would hold all the said covenants with all diligence, as likewise to bring all the Empire of Mosco to the Romish Religion. The which covenants and agreements the Generall Sandamersko himselfe hath confessed to our Majestie, and Nobles, that the foresaid agreements and covenants betwixt him and the foresaid Gryshca were true, and how that they trusted one to another: moreover, the Palatine did certifie unto our Nobles, how Gryshca sent him a Letter under his owne hand and Seale, in which he promised to give him Smolensko, with all the Provinces belonging thereto, and another place called Seeverow, as also gave him liberty to set up Monasteries, and the Religion of the Church of Rome. Further, there was found by him Letters which were sent to him from the *Popes Letter.* Pope of Rome, and the Cardinals, and Priests, to that effect, that he should remember and withall be mindefull to take in hand speedily those matters and businesse upon which he had given to Sigismund, and the Cardinals his troth and vow, the which was, as beforesaid, to be himselfe

of the Romish Religion, as also to bring all the people of
the Kingdome of Russia into the same Romish Religion,
not onely them that of themselves were willing thereto,
but also others by compulsion, and to put them to death
that sought to contrary the same. And not onely them
of the Kingdome of Russia, but likewise other godly
people of severall Religion: and that doe serve in the
Kingdome of Mosco, as the Catholicks, and the Calvinists,
them likewise he should seeke to bring into the Romish
Religion with all perswasions. Moreover, Gryshca himselfe, before us, and our Nobles, and Courtiers, and before
our Commons, did acknowledge as much, and thereupon
yeelded himselfe to be in fault: as also that he did all with
helpe of the Divell, having forsaken God.

For which these his vile actions, this Gryshca, according
to the true justice, received an end to his life, and was by
abundance of people slain in the Mosco, where he lay
three dayes in the midst of the Citie, to the view
of all such like usurpers, and disturbers. And because his
body was loathsome unto us, we caused it to be carried out
of the Citie, and there to be burnt.

This Enemie thus having ended his life, then the Kings
sonnes of divers Countries, now dwelling within our Kingdome, with the Patriarke, Metropolitanes, Archbishops,
and Bishops, with the Nobles, Courtiers, and the Commons, made entreaty unto us Vasili Evanowich, to raigne
and governe over them and over all the Kingdome of
Mosco, as their Lord, Emperour, and great Duke of all
Russia. According to which entreatie made unto us by
the said Kings sons of divers Countries, as likewise by our
Nobles, Courtiers, Merchants, and all the rest of the
Commons of all the Kingdome of Mosco, Wee are come
to the great Kingdomes of Volodemar, Mosco, Novogrod,
and as also of the Kingdomes of Cazan, Astracan, and
Siberia, and over all the Provinces of the Empire of
Mosco: as also wee the great Lord Emperour, and
great Duke of all Russia, are crowned with our Imperiall
Crown: and for the said Kings sonnes of divers

[III.iv.769.]

*Slaine &
burnt.*

*Election of
Swisky.*

Religions, and our Nobles, Courtiers, and Souldiers, and
all manner of People, doe serve our Imperiall Majesty
with desire and good liking voluntarily, and not by
delusions and conjurations, as the Poles and Lettoes were
bewitched by Grishca. But we the great Lord Emperour
and great Duke Vasili Evanowich, with great care stayed
and restrayned our People from the spoyle of the Poles
and the Lettoes, defending them from death; and withall
have commanded to let goe many of them into Poland and
Letto: but the chiefest of them that were of the Councell,
and that practised to bring trouble and dissention in the
Kingdome of Mosco, are now taken. And we to doe an
honour unto the dead body of the true Demetrie, have
(upon conference with our Metropolitanes, Archbishops,
and Bishops, and all the holy Assembly, our Nobles and
Courtiers, and all the Kingdome of Mosco) sent to the
Citie of Owglets a Metropolitan, named Filareta, of
Rostove and Yeraslave, who was called before he was made
Metropolitan, Theodor Neekete, which being one of the
Nobles in times past, and with him the Archbishops of
Astracan, called Feodosia, and our Nobles the Duke Evan
Michalowich Vorotinskoy, with the rest of his fellowes,
commanding them to bring up with them the body of the
Prince Demetrie Evanowich, who was murthered by the
appointment of Boris Godonove, and to bring it up to our
Citie of Mosco with great honour, which body shall be
buried in the principall Church of Mosco, called Michael
the Archangel, neare to his father the great Lord
Emperour and great Duke Evan Vasilowich of famous
memorie, and by Gods power his body shall not be touched
or abused any manner of way. Likewise will we, by the
favour of God, honour the Funerall of Demetrie Evanowich with speciall solemnitie, which body performeth many
cures, and worketh miraculously unto them, that come to *Miracles.*
him with Faith to be cured of their diseases.

And now most loving and deare brother, wee calling
well to minde the great amitie and friendship that was
betwixt the great Lord Emperour, and great Duke Evan

Vasilywich, and his Sonne Theodor Evanowich, the Emperour Boris, and the great Lady Queene Elizabeth: the like brotherly love doe we desire to have with you, most loving and deare brother, to be established and continued betwixt us, as it was with them, during our lives. Therefore may it please you, our loving brother James, King of England, after the hearing of these great and strange dangers past, to rejoyce with us, that he hath delivered from such a vile enemy, and that he, our mercifull God, hath divided and scattered that wicked counsell, and that he hath turned their cruelty upon their owne head, to their shame and confusion. And concerning your Merchants that were in our Kingdome, John Merricke with his fellowes, we have graced them with our Emperiall presence; as also have given unto the said John Merricke and his fellowes, a new privilege, and Letters of favour, by which they shall come into our Kingdome, and to traficke with all manner of goods freely, without paying any Custome whatsoever, and as to them was granted in former time, and this favour we have given them to manifest unto you our loving Brother, our Brotherly love. And the reason that we have not sent to you, loving brother, our Embassadour, is, because we had not time, in regard of many our Emperiall affaires, but hereafter doe purpose to send, to visite you in your Kingdome. Written at our Emperiall palace and Citie of Mosco, from the beginning of the World Anno 7114. the fourth day of June.

Thus is Demetrius painted out by his Enemies, which perhaps were not altogether led with simplicitie of truth, but in many things made him worse, that they might make their owne cause (bad enough) to appeare better. They tell also of great outrages committed by the Poles, (like those sometimes here in England by the Danes) their proud insulting over the men, ravishments of women, fetching them out of their houses and husbands bosomes to serve their lusts: neither did Demetrius, as they say, punish them; one onely being sentenced, and hee violently rescued from execution by the Poles. They say also that

Demetrius his body was plucked out of the grave and burnt, the ashes throwne into the aire, the seeds, as the sequele seemed to shew, of many Demetrii after.

Suiskey is also by some reported to have beene chosen by lot in this manner. The Nobles cast lots foure times to receive a Successor, as it were, by divine sentence in lot-oracle: in every of which times the lot fell upon Suiskey (for as some say, there were three or foure neerer then hee) he modestly refusing and enforced by constancy of the various lot to accept that Scepter; whereof others thinke him as ambitious, as was modest Boris before him. However, he hath left his name and memorie written in as blacke inke as either Boris or Demetrius, if Reports bee true, which say that he proved a wicked Prince, partly by poison, partly by the Tartars, making away all, whose bloud might by Nobilitie threaten a probabilitie of their proving his Corrivals. Yea, he is said to have sent for Witches and Sorcerers, Laps, Samoeds, Tartars, or whatsoever other Nation yeelded such Hell-hags, incarnate Fiends, the Devils blacke guard, to consult about his Empire and succession; and (the Devill is a murtherer) to have sealed their predictions with bloud. Thus being told that one Michalowich should succeed, he is said presently to have plotted the death of three Grandes of that name, his best servants: yet the superstitious people observe (after much chopping and changing) that in little time the State was settled on one of that Name, which still swaieth the Scepter; Who then being a youth of no State-terror, was his attendant in Court and bare an Axe (after their custome) before him.

One of his first Acts, was to send into Poland an Embassage, which could not bee admitted audience till Januarie. Hee thereby complayned of Sandomerskos artes which obtruded that Changeling on Russia, whereby above two hundred of principall Nobilitie had lost their lives: demanding restitution of the moneys which that Impostor had caused to bee transported into Poland, and restitution of goods; otherwise hee would with Charles

Choosing by lot.

[III. iv. 770.]

Suiskeys vices. The like is told of K. Edward the fourth that upon prediction of one to succeed, whose name began with G, he put to death George Duke of Clarence his brother, and yet Gloster succeeded. A printed book 1614. tels of a great man, named Tragus, which betraied by one Glasco was arrayned, and to prevent the furie of Suiskey stabbed himselfe, &c.

of Sweden Duke of Suderman, enter Poland with an
Armie to bee revenged for the league (which they had
sworne) broken, &c. Sigismund answered modestly, with
excuse of their helping the right Heire in their conceits,
and that his desire was that peace should continue (being
loth in times then tumultuous at home, to provoke a
forreine enemie, so neere in dwelling, so remote in
affection) Sandomersko still remayned prisoner in Russia.
But things being better setled in Poland, and growing
worse in Russia, by the dislike conceived against Suiskey,
a double danger grew to him both from another revived
Demetrius (yea many pretending that Name and Title did
after arise, as out of his dispersed ashes) within Russia;
and from the Poles without, willing both to assist him
under colour of Revenge, and with hope of Conquest also,
to invade and fish for themselves in troubled waters.

As for that Demetrius new risen from the dead (not to
mention the others of inferiour note) I shall relate Captaine
Gilberts reports which knew him and was by him entertayned, as I received them of a judicious friend of mine,
which had them from his owne mouth. Hee being at
Coluga (as before is said) received a Letter from this new
Demetrius *, so written that it appeared to bee of the
former Demetrius his owne hand : and thus also he used to
doe to others being able to counterfeit his writing, and to
relate such other particulars as seemed impossible to any
but Demetrius to doe. Hereupon Captaine Gilbert went
with his Guard of Souldiers to meete him and the Polake
Generall which came with him. And whiles he was yet a
good distance off, Ah (this Demetrius called to him) my
true servant, where were you and my Guard, when the
villaines hurt me? but if I had followed the counsell which
you gave me such a time in such a place (relating the
particulars) I had prevented them. This circumstance had
moved him to beleeve this to be the former Demetrius,
had not he differed from this in person, as night from day.
Thus also he said he affirmed to the Pole Generall, asking
him how he liked this Demetrius, that This and That were

Cap. Gilbert.

*Thuan tels
that fourteene
horses were
missing in the
Kings stable
on the massacre
day, and
hence was
occasioned a
suspicion of
escape, &c.

A strange
Juggler.

as like as Night and Day (for the former was of goodly personage, and this a very deformed wretch.) The Pole replyed, It is no matter, Captaine, this Demetrius shall serve our turne to bee revenged of the perfidious and bloudie Russe. And this Demetrius acted the other so neerly, and could so cunningly and confidently relate particular passages of past occurrents, that the Lady of Demetrius was by him bedded. Thus was miserable Russia ground betwixt these two Mill-stones, the pretending Demetrius and the super-intending Pole. Suiskey is helped not a little by the English, which *English aide.* brought him strangely and adventurously powder and munition to his Castle to Mosco, which yet at last by revolt of the Citizens delivers up it selfe and him to the Poles. And as for that pretending Demetrius, he was afterwards murthered in his Campe by a Tartar. But it is meet to take hereof larger view.

Sigismund King of Poland layeth claim to Sweden, as *Sweden Title.* sonne to King John (who is said to have unjustly deprived Ericus of his life and Kingdome) whose yonger brother Duke Charles first received his Nephew King Sigismund (then also elected and still continuing King of Poland) but upon warres which after arose betwixt them, the issue was, that the Pole holds the Title; but Charles obtayned both Regall Title and Power, wherein his Sonne hath succeeded. Suiskey takes hold of this difference, and Charles assists him with an Armie sent under the command of Pontus de la Gard a French Coronell, consisting of English, French, *Forraine aides* and Scots. These march to Mosco, which the new *to the Russes.* Demetrius and Poles held besieged, and put Demetrius into such feare, that not trusting the Pole, and fearing his Adversaries on both sides, he stole away by night with a small retinue: and the Poles obtayned Articles of composition and departed. But miserable were the distresses by famine, fire, sword, rapes, and other outrages in other parts of Russia, caused by other Poles; and yet these but as a beginning and prelude to other following. For the King of Poland entred with a huge Armie (some say of an hundred thousand men) invaded the Muscovite, and especially laid siege to Smolensko. He is reported thence to have sent twentie thousand to besiege Mosco.

Suiskey had sent to King Charles for more aide, which he procured out of England, and other Countries, of which I had rather let you heare an eye-witnesse speake of this, as elsewhere other English men have related their owne voyages. This indeed deserveth relation, as a tragedie of meaner persons with manifold vicissitudes of miseries (attending voluntarie Souldiers) as before you have seene tragedies of Princes and Grandes. And first you may reade King Charles his compact and promised stipend to such voluntaries, which for the more understanding Readers delight I have here inserted.

NOs Carolus Nonus, Dei gratia Suecorum, Gothorum, Wandalorum, Finnonum, Coreliorum, Lapporum, Conanorum, Esthonumque in Livonia, &c. Rex. Notum facimus quod illustrem & generosum nobis syncere dilectum Dominum Jacobum Spentzium, Baronem Wolmerschonium in ministrorum nostrorum numerum clementer receptum, omnium qui nostris nunc militant, aut in posterum militaturi sunt auspiciis, Anglorum, Scotorumque ducem & præfectum constituimus, ea conditione ut in nostrum, Regnique nostri usum, pedites mille, & equites quingentos, spectatæ virtutis milites conscribat, adductosque ineunte vere ad 12. scilicet Maii sequentis Anni 1609. in Regno sistat. Cui nos ad dictos milites tam colligendos quàm in regnum traducendos, in pedites quidem novem, in equites vero quatuor thalerorum imperialium millia & quingintos assignavimus. Cum autem in regnum præfatus militum numerus appulerit, illis si equos & arma subministraverimus, ea peditum quidem singulorum dimidii equitum vero duorum de cujusque stipendio menstruo thalerorum singulis mensibus donec pro armis & equis nobis satisfiat, detractione solventur. Ipsi duci primario Peditum vero singulis cohortibus (quarum quævis ducentis Capitaneo cæterisque officiariis una comprehensis constabat) mille septingentos thaleros in mensem dabimus. Equidem autem cohors quælibet centum equites continebit. Quod si pauciores fuerint, quot personæ in prima lustratione defecerint, totidem thalero menstruo Capitaneorum, Equicumque Magistrorum stipendio detrahentur: In sequentibus vero lustrationibus quæ singulis mensibus semel institui debent, si qui forte interea ex hac vita decesserint, aut alio quocunque modo, militum numerus fuerit ita diminutus, ut pedites cujusque cohortis ducentis pauciores sint (non tamen in eam paucitatem redactus ut ad tuendum, ornandumque vexillum modo militari pedites impares inveniantur) Capitanee nihilominus stipendium integrum ad sex menses persolvetur, quod si postea defectum non suppleverit, ipse officio Capitanei carebit & pedites ipsius per cæteras cohortes, ad earum supplementum distribuentur. Equites vero cohortis cujusque, si centum pauciores fuerint, Magister equitum nihilominus donec numerus sexagenario major fuerit stipendium integrum consequetur, idque ad sex menses duntaxat. His autem exactis, nisi præstitutum, centum equitum numerum suppleverit, ipse munere suo privabitur, & equites per cæteras cohortes distribuentur. Magistro equitum centum, Vicario seu locum tenenti quadraginta, Signifero triginta, Decurioni viginti, singulis ductoribus viginti, cuique buccinatori sex, Equitibus vero singulis duodecem thaleri, in singulos menses munerabuntur. Dicto autem duci generali, ut sequentes officiarios sibi adjungeret clementer permisimus: Vicarium generalem, cui quadringintos, præfectum vigiliarum, cui nonaginta, Secretarium cui octoginta, Prætorem cui sexaginta, Præfectum annonæ cui sexaginta, Pastorem cui sexaginta, Chirurgum cui quadraginta, Archicustodem cui quadraginta, Inspectorem armorum cui quadraginta, Tympanistam cui sedecim florenos in singulos menses promissimus. Primus autem stipendii mensis intra decimum quintum diem à militum in regnum adventu inchoabitur. Liberam quoque habebit præfatus dux Primarius plenamque justitiæ exercendæ potestatem in omnes suo imperio subjectos, idque in omni criminis genere excepto crimine lasæ Majestatis ; Peditum cuique subsidii loco thalerum unum ; Capitaneis autem & reliquis officiariis stipendii singulis designati dimidium ; Magistro militum duodecim ; Ejus Vicario octo ; signifero sex, cuique Decurioni quatuor singulis ex tribus ordinum ductoribus tres, Buccinatori unum cum dimidio, singulis vero equitibus duos in septimanam thaleros dabimus ; Semestri quolibet exacto habitaque accurata supputatione, quod de menstruo stipendio reliquum est, eis persolvetur, habita tamen ratione numeri quem in singulis delectibus seu militum lustrationibus Capitanei equitumque Magistri exhibuerint. Quod si dux militibus suis secundum aliquod prælium fecerit, aut arcem urbemque aliquam vi expugnaverit, eo ipso die quo id contigerit priore finito novus mensis inchoabitur. Liberum quoque erit Ducibus singulis, quoties necesse erit ad cohortium supplementum adducendum aliquem mittere, qui dum absens erit stipendium suum nihilominus consequetur, pro singulis autem qui in supplementum adducti fuerint decem thaleri numerabuntur. Quod si in præliis, velitationibus, excubiis aut alio quovis casu quenquam ducum, aut militum in hostium potestatem venire contigerit, idque non spontanea deditione aut alia ratione subdola & fraudulenta accidisse compertum fuerit, is alius suæ conditionis statusque captivi permutatione liberabitur. Hostium vero aliquis si captivus ad nos nostrive exercitus Ducem à quoquam eorum perductus fuerit, quod pro sui liberatione captivus prætium spoponderit, id ei, qui captivum duxerit, numerabitur. Quod si quisquam horum militum pila ictus tormentaria, aut alio quovis modo mutilus, aut mancus evadat, ita ut ipse se alere victumque quærere nequeat, illi à nobis pro ut cujusque requirit status & conditio, honestum stipendium per omnem vitam suppeditabitur : sin vero diutius in hoc Regno nostro commorari noluerit, tum unius mensis accepto stipendio integrum ei erit, quo libuerit commigrare. Cum cohortes, sive simul, sive seperatim exauctorabuntur, singulis officiariis & militibus mensis unius numerabitur stipendium. Si aut præfatus primarius aut alius inferiorum Ducum vel Officiariorum à S. R. M. Britanniæ accersetur, persoluto quod tunc forte restabit stipendio, ipsoque duce remunerato, libera dabitur discedendi facultas. In quorum evidentiorem fidem manus propria subscriptione Regiæque [III.iv.772.] nostri sigilli appensione præsentes munivimus. Ex Regia nostra Stocholmensi die 7. Octobris, Anni Millesimi sexcentesimi octavi.

Subscript. CAROLUS.

ABout a fortnight before Midsummer, which was A. 1609. a companie of Voluntaries, to the number of a thousand and two hundred Souldiers, were at severall times shipped from England to passe into Sweden, to aide the King of that Countrie in his warres against the King of Poland. To which aide divers other Nations did likewise resort, as French, high Dutch, &c. Of the English Companies that went thither, the first was commanded by one Calvine a Scot; who by appointment was made Lieutenant Colonell, and chiefe of the other Captaines over the footmen.

1200. Souldiers shipped from England.

Colonel Calvine.

After the first Companie was gone, a second number of three hundred men (of which I the Relator of this, was one) were put into one ship belonging to Sweden, and came from thence for us. We were assaulted with a great tempest, and were tossed so long, that all our victuals were almost spent: the miserie of which, threw us into more desperate feares: now were wee assaulted by double deaths (Famine and Shipwrack) what course to take for our reliefe no man presently knew. Continue without foode it was impossible, and as impossible was it for us to recover the Land in any short time, without the assured destruction of us all. At this season, our Commanders were these; Lieutenant Benson, Lieutenant Walton, who was Provost Martiall of the field; and an Ancient of the Colonels companie. The common Souldiers vowed and resolved to compell the Mariners (seeing the present

A tempest.

miseries, and no hopes promising better) to set us all on shoare upon the first Land that could be discovered. Our Commanders did what they could by disswasion to alter this generall resolution, because they feared it would bee the losse of the greatest part of our Companies, if they came once to bee scattered: and besides, they knew that it would redound to their dishonour and shame, if they should not discharge the trust imposed upon them by our Captaines, which trust was to conduct us and land us before, whilest our Chieftanes remayned a while behinde in England, to take up the rest of our Companies. Yet all this notwithstanding, Land being discovered, there was no eloquence in the world able to keep us aboord our *Another* ship, but every man swore if the Master of the ship would *tempest of the* not set us on the shoare, the sailes should be taken into *mutinous* our owne hands, and what was resolved upon (touching *vulgar.* present landing) should in despite of danger be effected. Upon this the Master of the ship and the Mariners told us, that if we put to land in that place, we should all either perish for want of victuals, which were not to bee had in that Countrie, or else should have our throats cut by the people. Wee resolved rather to trie our bad fortunes on the land, and to famish there (if that kind of death must needes attend upon us) then to perish on the Seas, which we knew could affoord us no such mercy: and on shoare wee went, as fast as possibly we could. When our Officers saw, that there was no remedie, nor force to detayne us aboord, they then disheartned us no longer, but to our great comforts told it, that the Master of the ship (which thing hee himselfe likewise openly confessed) knew both the Land and Governour thereof (as indeed we proved afterwards he did:) and therefore desired they all our companies not to misse-behave themselves toward the people, *They land in* for that it was an Iland called Juthland, under the *Jutland.* Dominion of the King of Denmarke, but subject to the command of a Lord, who under the King (as his Substitute) was the Governour.

And that we might be the better drawne to a civill

behaviour towards the Inhabitants, our Officers further told us, that they would repaire to the Lord Governour of the Countrie, and acquaint him with the cause of our unexpected landing there; upon which we all promised to offer no violence to the people; neither was that promise violated, because we found the Inhabitants tractable, and as quiet towards us, as we to them: yet the greater numbers of them ran away with feare, at the first sight of us, because (as afterward they reported) it could not bee remembred by any of them, that they ever either beheld themselves, or ever heard any of their ancestors report, that any strange people had landed in those places and parts of the Iland: for they thought it impossible (as they told us) that any ship should ride so neere the shoare, as ours did, by reason of the dangerous Sands.

Our Officers so soone as they were at land, went to the Governour of the Iland, whilest the Souldiers (who stayed behind them) ran to the houses of the Ilanders, of purpose to talke with the people, and at their hands to buy victuals for a present reliefe: but when wee came among them, they could neither understand us nor we them; so that the Market was spoiled, and wee could get nothing for our money, yet by such signes as wee could make, they understood our wants pitied them, and bestowed upon us, freely, a little of such things as they had. In the end, a happy meanes of our reliefe was found out by a Souldier amongst us who was a Dane by birth, but his education having beene in England, no man knew him to be other then an English man.

This Dane made use of his owne native language, to the good both of himselfe and us, certifying the people [III.iv.773.] (who the rather beleeved him because he spake in their knowne tongue) of the cause that compelled us to land upon their Coast, and that we intended no mischiefe, violence, or money: to which report of his they giving credit, stood in lesse feare of us then before, and thereupon furnished us with all such necessaries, as the Countrie affoorded to sustaine our wants. The foode which wee

Fish cheape. bought of them was onely fish, and a kinde of course bread, exceeding cheape. Of which foode there was such plentie, that for the value of three pence wee had as much fish as twentie men could eate at a meale, and yet none of the worst sorts of fish, but even of the very best and daintiest, as Mackrels and Lobsters, and such like. In which our trading with the poore simple people, we found *Ignorant* them so ignorant, that many, yea most of them regarded *Bores.* not whether you gave them a Counter, or a Shilling: for the bigger the piece was, the more fish they would give for it: but besides fish wee could get no other sustenance from them, or at least, could not understand that they had any other. But observe what happened in the meane time that we were thus in traffique with the Ilanders for victuals, our Officers (as before is said) being gone to the Lord Governour, who lay about twelve English miles from the Sea side, the Master of our ship on a sudden hoysed up sailes, and away he went, leaving one of his owne men at shoare, who accompanied our Officers as their guide, through the Iland. The cause of the ships departure, did so much the more amaze us, by reason it was so unexpected, and the reason thereof unknowne to us: But wee imagined the Master of the ship and Mariners feared to receive us into the Vessell againe, because some of our men at their being at Sea, threatned the Saylers, and offered them abuses before they could be brought to set us on land.

On the next day following, the Lord Governour of the Iland came to us, bringing our Officers along with him, yet not being so confident of us, but that (for avoyding of any dangers that might happen) he came strongly guarded with a troupe of Horse-men well armed. And (upon his first approch) demanding where our ship was, it was told him in what strange manner it stole away and forsooke us: he then asked what we intended to doe, to which we all answered, that we would be ruled by our Officers: hereupon hee inquired of them, what they would have him to doe in their behalfes: they requested nothing else at his hands, but onely his favourable Passe through the Countrie, and a ship to carry us forward into Sweden : to which request hee made answere, that he could grant no such licence untill he had made the King of Denmarke acquainted with our being there, for the Iland belonged to the King, he said, and he was no more but an Officer or Substitute under him. Yet in consideration that our ship had so left us in a strange Land, he promised to doe all that lay in his power to effect our good : but withall told us, that the people had inward feares, and were possest with suspitions, that our intents of landing upon such a Coast, were not, as we our selves affirmed, only to get foode, but rather to make spoile of the poore Inhabitants. And therefore, to remoove all such feares and jealousies out of the peoples hearts, he held it most convenient for the generall safeties of both parties, to separate our numbers, and to spreade us abroad in the Countrie, one and one in a house, where it was agreed that we should receive both a lodging, and meate, and drinke, untill hee had sent to the King of Denmarke some of his owne men with our Officers, to understand his Majesties pleasure, and what should become of us.

To this we all agreed, and accordingly for that purpose, were by the Lord Governour, safely by these armed horse-men which were his guard, conducted to his owne house. To that place were al the people of the Iland summoned together, they came at the appointed day to the number of five or six hundred, circling us round with Bils, Holbards, two-hand Swords, and divers other weapons : And at the first sight of us grew into such rage, that presently they would have cut all our throats, and hewed us to pieces, but that the authoritie of the Governor kept them from offering violence, yet was hee faine to use the fairest meanes of perswasion to allay their furie. For they would not beleeve but that our arrivall there was to destroy them. Yet the Governour shewed unto them all our number, which was but three hundred men, and those all unweaponed, and so consequently, neither likely nor able to undertake any mischiefe against them: Charging the unruly multitude, upon paine of death, not to touch the least finger of us, but to divide us equally into severall Villages, as it should seeme best unto them, and so bestow kinde and loving entertainment upon us till they heard further from him, which command of his they accordingly performed.

Immediately upon this setling of them and us in quietnesse, one of our Officers with two of the Governours men, were sent away to the King of Denmarke, to understand his Highnesse pleasure, which Messengers were no sooner dispatched about the businesse, but the Ilanders growing *Jealousie of* more and more suspitious, came againe to the Governour, *the people.* and never would cease or give over troubling him, untill they had gotten him to make Proclamation (in hearing of us all.) That if any of us would freely discover the true cause of our landing upon that Coast, and reveale the plots of any dangerous enterprise intended against them, he should not onely be rewarded with great store of money, and have new apparell to his backe, but also should without tortures, imprisonment, or death be set free, and sent backe againe into his owne Countrie. This [III.iv.774.] Proclamation strucke us all with feare and astonishment, because albeit we to our selves were not guiltie of any plot, or villany intended to the place or people, yet wee knew this might be a meanes to endanger all our lives, how innocent soever. Our suspition of danger fell out *Griffin a base* according to our feares: for one Thomas Griffyn a Welch *coward and* man, one of our owne company, went and kneeled before *traitor to his* the Governour, and with a face counterfeiting a guiltinesse *fellowes.* and fearefull destruction, told him that we came thither onely, and for no other purpose, then to surprise the Iland, kill the Inhabitants, make spoile of their wives and goods, and having set fire of their Townes and Villages, to flye to Sea againe. Yet for all this would not the *A wise* Governour beleeve him, telling him it was a matter very *Governour.* unlikely, that so small a number, so distressed for want of foode, so weather-beaten and so disarmed, should

venture upon an enterprise so full of dangerous events:
but the villaine replyed, that all those complaints of want,
were but songs to beguile the people, for that upon the
least Allarum given, other ships that lay hovering at Sea,
and furnished both with men and armour, would on the
sudaine, and that very shortly land for the same desire
of spoyle, as these their fellowes had done, and therefore
counselled the Governour to prevent such imminent
mischiefes betimes.

The Governour being thus farre urged, presently called
before him Lieutenant Walton, whose lodging was
appointed in his house, and having related to him all that
Griffin had discovered, and withall, demanding of Lieutenant Walton what he could say to this matter of treason
and conspiracie: the Lieutenant at the first stood amazed,
and utterly denied any such intended villany, protesting
by the faith of a Souldiour, that this report of the Welch-
man proceeded from the rancour of a vile traitors heart,
and therefore on his knees intreated the Governour, not
to give credit to so base a villaine, who for the greedinesse
of a little money, went about to sell all their lives, and to
make all the inhabitants of the Iland become murderers:
The rest lay scattered about and knew nothing of the
matter. Now soone after, just as the traitor had told
the Governour, that more ships were not farre off, but
were ready to second us upon our arrivall, it chanced that
in the very heat of this businesse, and their feares of danger
where none was, two other shippes full of armed Souldiers *Two Ships.*
came to the same place of the Iland where our shippe
put in: These two ships had brought Souldiours out of
the low Countries (a cessation of warres being there) and
were going into Swethland, as we were, but by crosse
windes and fowle weather, lay so long at Sea, that wanting
victuals, they were driven in hither for succour. Whose
sudaine approach and arivall being signified to the Lord
Governor, the Welch-mans words were then thought true;
all the Iland was presently up in Armes to resist the
strength and furie of a most dangerous supposed enemy:

and so secretly did the Inhabitants put on Armes, that we who were kept like prisoners amongst them, knew not of these uproares. But night approaching, the Generall gave speciall charge that secret watch should be set and kept over every Souldior that lodged in any mans house: which by the common people was as narrowly performed, for they did not onely watch us as the Governor commanded, but amongst themselves a secret conspiracie was made, that in the dead of night, when wee should be fast asleepe, they should come and take us in our beds,

Hard usage. and there to binde us with cords: it being an easie thing to doe so, when our company were divided one from another over the whole Iland. At the houre agreed upon, the plot was put in force, for they entred our Chambers, and bound every Souldier as he lay, making them all ready like so many sheepe marked out for the slaughter. For mine owne part, I had five men and three women to binde me, who so cunningly tyed me fast with cords, whilst I slept, and felt nothing, nor dreampt of any such matter, that with a twitch onely I was plucked starke naked out of my bed, and laid upon the cold earth underneath a Table, with my armes bound behinde me, so extreamely hard, as foure men could draw them together, my feete tyed to the foote of the Table, and my necke bound to the upper part or bord of the Table.

In these miserable tortures lay I, and all the rest (in severall houses) all that night, and the most part of the next day, our armes and legges being pinched and wrung together in such pittilesse manner, that the very bloud gushed out at the fingers ends of many. The enduring of which torments was so much the more grievous, because none knew what we had done that could incense them to this so strange and spitefull cruelty, neither could we, albeit we inquired, learne of our tormenters the cause, because we understood not their language.

Whilest thus the whole Iland was full of the cries of wretched men, and that every house seemed a shambles, ready to have Innocents there butchered the next day,

and that every Ilander had the office of a common cut-
throate or executioner; Gods wonderfull working turned
the streame of all their cruelty: For the two ships that
came out of the low Countries, and whose arrivall drave
so many miserable soules almost upon the rocks of
destruction, having in that dolefull and ruinous night,
gotten some provision aboord, weighed Anchor, and
departed towards Swethland. Which happy newes being
served up at breakfast to the Lord Governour betimes
in the morning, and that the Shippes had offerd no violence
to the Countrey, but had paid for what they tooke: About
eleaven of the clocke the very same day at noone, wee
were all like unto so many dead men cut downe, and
bidden to stand upon our legges, although very few had
scarce legges that could stand.

Of one accident more that befell, I thinke it not amisse
to take note, which began merrily, but ended tragically, [III.iv.775.]
and in bloud; and that was this: Foure of our company
being lodged in one Village, and they being bound to
the peace, as you may perceive the rest were; it happened
that an Hoast, where one of them lay, had tipled hard,
and gotten a Horses disease, called the Staggers: In comes *Effects of*
he stumbling, to the roome where the poore Englishman *drunkennesse.*
was bound to the Table hand and foote: which thing
the drunken Sot beholding, drew his Hatchet, which he
wore at his girdle, according to the fashion of the Country,
and because hee would be sure his prisoner should not
escape, with his Hatchet he cleft his head. And thinking
in that drunken murderous humour, he had done a
glorious act, away he reeles out of his owne house to that
house where the other three Souldiours lay bound, where
beating at the doores and windowes, and the Hoast asking
what he meant to make such a damnable noyse; he told
him so well as he could stammer it out, that the Lord
Governour had sent him thither to put the three Englishmen to death. Upon this, the divell and he (hand in
hand) were let in, the one standing so close at the others
elbow, that he never left him till he had cleft two of their

heads, that lay bound : and being then weary (it should seeme) with playing the butcher, he never ceased swearing and staring, and flourishing with his bloudy Axe about their heads, till the people of the house had hung the third man upon a beame in the roome. But they having lesse cunning in the Hang-mans trade, then will to practise it, tyed not the halter so fast about his necke, as to strangle him : so that after hee had hung an houre, hee was cut downe, revived againe, was well, and afterwards was slaine in Russia.

This bloudy feast being thus ended, and all stormes as we well hoped, being now blowne over to our freedome, and sitting at liberty from our tormentors ; on the necke of these former miseries fell a mischiefe more dangerous to us then all the rest : for tidings were brought to the Governour, that our Auncient, who travailed with the Governours two men to the King, had trayterously murdered those his guides, and then ranne away himselfe : upon this rumour, nothing but thundring and lightning flew from the common peoples mouthes : there was no way now with us but one, and that one was, to have all *Cruell* our throats cut, or our heads cleft with their Axes. But *cowardise and* the Governor pittying our misfortunes, laboured both by *base jealousie.* his authority & by faire speeches, to keepe that many-headed dogge (the multitude) from barking. And in the end, when he saw nothing but the bloud of us poore Englishmen would satisfie their thirst, because they still held us in suspition and feare ; he most nobly, and like a vertuous Magistrate, pawned to the inhumane Rascals (to my knowledge) his honour, all that ever he was worth, yea, his very life unto them, that within three dayes the messengers sent to the King, should returne home, and that during those three dayes we should be of good behaviour to the Ilanders : and besides that, if they did not returne in such a time, that then he would deliver us up into their hands. Our Auncient with the Governours *King of Den-* two men, came home upon the third day, to the Gover-*marks bounty.* nours house, and brought from the King of Denmarke

his licence, to carry us not onely through the Country,
but commanding that we should be allowed shipping also
at convenient place, to carry us to Sweveland, whither
we were to goe: And according to this Licence the
Governour caused us to be called all together the very
next day; at which time, Thomas Griffin the Welch Judas,
who had all this while lyen feasting in the house of the
Lord Governour, began to tremble and repent him of his
villanie, begging most base forgivenesse on his knees,
both from the Governour, and us his Countrimen and
fellow Souldiours, protesting that what he did, came out
of his feare to save his owne life.   But our Officers (upon
hearing him speake thus) had much adoe to keepe the
companies from pulling downe the house where Griffin
lay, because they would in that rage have hewed the
villaine in peeces.

But leaving him and all such betrayers of mens bloud
to the hell of their owne consciences, let us set forward
out of this infortunate Iland, and not stay in any place
else, till in small Boates wee come by water to Elzinore *Elzinore.*
in Denmarke, where wee joyfully got aboard once more;
and are hoysing up sailes for Sweveland.   Yet even in
this sun-shine day a storme fals upon us too: for our
Officers not having sufficient money to furnish us with
victuals, wee were enforced to pawne our Auncient and
Lieutenant Walton, for the safe returne of the Shippe,
with condition, that they should not be released untill a
sufficient summe of money was sent to defray all charges.
So that we left our Officers behinde us; but the King
of Sweveland did afterwards release them, and then they
came to us.   But before their comming, wee having a
good winde, landed at a place called Newleas in Sweve:
and from thence were carried to Stockholme (the Kings *Stockholme.*
seate) and there was the King at the same time; betweene
which two places, it was a daies march on horsebacke.

Upon this our arrivall at Stockholme, wee met with the
rest that had gone before us, and with divers others of
our Countrimen, that came out of the Low-countries, as

before is related.   In this place we lay so long, and had
such poore meanes, that wanting money to buy foode, wee
wanted foode to maintaine life, and so a number of us
Misery after were readie to starve : till in the end, our miseries making
misery. us desperate, we fell together by the eares with the Burgers
of the Towne : in which scambling confusion and mutinie,
every man got one thing or other, of which he made
present money to relieve his body withall : yet lay wee
[III.iv.776.] at the walles of the Citie, crying out continually for money,
money, till our throates grew hoarse with bauling, but
the stones of the walles gave more confort to us, then
the Inhabitants.   One day (above all the rest) wee heard,
that the King was to ride a Hunting ; and wee imagining
that all the abuses, wrongs, and miseries, which wee
endured, proceeded from some under-hand hard dealing,
and packing of our Captaines and Officers, resolved to
gather about the King at his comming forth, and to cry
out for money : but the King being angry (as wee supposed) came riding amongst us, drawing his Pistoll from
the Saddle-bow, as if hee purposed to have shot some
of us : but seeing none of us to shrinke from him, nor
to be dismayed, hee rode backe againe, wee following him,
and desiring, hee would either give us money, or else to
kill us out-right ; one amongst the rest (whose name was
William Attane) spake to the King aloud, thus : I hold
it honour to dye by the hands of a King, but basely to
starve to death, I will never suffer it.   Upon these our
clamours, the King looking better upon our necessities,
sent money the next day, and immediately after gave us
a moneths meanes in money, and two moneths meanes in
cloath, to make us apparrell.

Of the cloath wee received some part, but the money
Captaines being payed, was by our Captaines sent into England to
cozenage. their wives ; no part of it ever comming to the poore
common Souldiours hands : for presently upon this, wee
were commanded aboord the Ships, with promise that
when wee were aboord, wee should have our money.   But
being in the Shippes under hatches, away were wee carried

with provision onely of one moneths victuals: when by
reason of the weather, wee were forced to lye eight weekes
at Sea: in all which time, wee had nothing but pickelled
Herrings, and salt Stremlings, with some small quantitie
of hard dryed meates: by which ill dyet, many of our
men fell sicke, and dyed. In the Shippe wherein I was,
wee lived fourteene dayes without bread, all our best foode
being salt Herrings, which wee were glad to eate raw;
the best of us all having no better sustenance.

At the last, it pleased God to send us to a place called
Ufrasound in Fynland, where wee landed, (Fynland being *Finland.*
subject to the King of Sweveland.) From Ufrasound wee
were to goe to Weyborough, a chiefe Towne in the
Countrie of Fynland: where wee no sooner arrived, but
our Souldiors ranne some one way, and some another, so
long that the Captaines were left alone with the Shippes:
This running away of them, being done onely to seeke
foode, so great was their hunger.

By this carelesse dispersing themselves, they lost the *Dispersing.*
command of the whole Countrey, which they might easily
have had, if they had beene united together: and not
onely were deprived of that benefit, but of Horses also,
which were allowed by the King for them to ride upon.
So that, what by the reason of the tedious Journey (which
wee were to travell, being fourescore leagues) and what
by reason of the extreame cold, being a moneth before
Christmas, at which time the Snow fell, and never went off
the ground untill Whitsontide following; but all the
Raine, and all the Snow that fell, freezing continually,
divers of our men were starved to death with the Frost. *Distresse by*
Some lost their fingers, some their toes, some their noses, *Frost.*
many their lives: insomuch, that when wee all met at
Weyborough, wee could make no more but one thousand
and foure hundred able men; and yet when we were
landed at Ufrasound, wee were two thousand strong; the
extremity of the cold Countrey having killed so many
of our Souldiours in so little time.

At our landing at Weyborough wee had good hopes

to receive better comforts, both of money and victuals:
for the Inhabitants told us, the King had allowed it us,
and in that report they spake truth: yet contrary to our
expectation, wee lay there about fourteene dayes, and
had nothing but a little Rice, of which we made bread,
and a little butter, which was our best reliefe. Drinke
had we none, nor money: our Captaines gave us certaine
letherne pelches, onely made of Sheeps skins, to keepe us
from the cold.

At this place we received armes to defend us against
the enemy, and six Companies that were allowed by the
King for Horsemen, received Horses there. From thence
Their miser- wee were to march into Russia, where our enemies con-
able march tinued. But the journey was long and uncomfortable:
into Russia. for wee marched from Newyeares day untill Whitsontide,
continually in Snow, having no rest, but onely a little in
the nights. So that the miseries and misfortunes which
wee endured upon the borders of Fynland, were almost
insufferable, by reason the number of them seemed
infinite. For all the people had forsaken their houses
long before wee came, because they were evermore
oppressed by Souldiours: by which meanes we could
get neither meate nor drinke, but were glad to hunt
Cats, and to kill them, or any beasts wee could lay
hold on, and this wee baked, and made them serve for
daily sustenance. The greatest calamitie of all was, wee
Want of meate could get no Water to drinke, it had beene so long frozen
and of Water. up, and the Snow so deepe, that it was hard to say, whether
wee marched over Water, or upon Land. So that wee
were compelled to digge up Snow, and with stones redde
hot, to melt in tubbes, and then to drinke it.

[III.iv.777.] This affection continued about twelve or fourteene
dayes, till we came into Russia. Upon our very first
entrance into which Kingdome, we marched over an arme
of the Sea, that was eight leagues over, many of us
starving to death in that passage, by the cold freezing
windes that blew the same day. In which frosty journey,
I saw so much bread as a man might buy for twelve pence,

sold away in little bits, for the value of fortie shillings.
But this misery ended the next day, at our setting foot
into Russia, where we found plenty both of corne and
cattle; onely the people of the Countrey ranne away, *Russians*
leaving all their goods behinde them, but so cunningly *runne away.*
hidden, that the best pollicie of ours could hardly finde
them out. By this meanes of the peoples running away,
we were glad to play the Millers, and to grinde all our
corne our selves, to bake our bread, and to dresse our
owne victuals. Then marched wee up to Novogrod (a *Novogrod.*
chiefe Citie in Russia) where wee were to receive all our
meanes that rested behinde unpayed: but our Captaines
beguiled us, and kept it for themselves: yet to stoppe
our mouthes, they told us wee should goe into Muscovy,
and there all reckonings should be made even.

We had scarce marched above three dayes towards
Muscovy, but that newes came, how a certaine number
of our enemies lay in a sconce by the way; the strength *Polake*
of them was not perfectly knowne, but it was thought *enemies.*
they were not above seven hundred, and that we must
use some stratagem to expell them from thence: upon
which relation, our Captaines drew forth to the number
of three hundred English horsemen, and two hundred
French horsemen: so that in all we were about five
hundred that were appointed to set upon the supposed
seven hundred Polanders, (our enemies) that so lay
insconsed: upon whom we went. Our chiefe Commander
in that service was Monsier la Veile, a French man, who
so valiantly led us on, that the enemy hearing of our
comming, fled over a water that was by the sconce; yet *They fled.*
not with such speede, but that wee slue to the number of
foure hundred of their side, and lost onely three men
of our owne: but we tooke the sconce. About the sconce *Sconce taken*
stood a faire Towne called Ariova, with a river called the *with store of*
Volga, running through the middle, but no bridge over *Armes.*
it; onely a few Boates and Sloates (made and cut out of
trees) were there, to carry the people over from the one
halfe of the Towne to the other. This sconce furnished

us not onely with great store of riches, but also with a
number of Polish Horses, and as many armes as served
to arme five hundred men; our want of that commoditie
being as much as of any thing besides: for of those five
hundred men that went upon the service, there were not
three hundred fixed armes; yet through the hand of him
that deales victories, or overthrowes, as it pleaseth him
best, the day was ours.

Over this river Volga the enemies were never driven
before, either by the Emperor of Russia, or by the King
of Swethland: for which cause (as afterward wee heard)
the next day when they departed from the other side of
the River, they burnt that halfe of the Towne on which
side they were themselves, and in most bloudy, barbarous,
Poles cruelties and cruell manner, made havocke both of men, women and
most execrable. children, albeit (not above halfe a yeare before) the Inhabitants on that side had revolted from their owne Emperour,
and turned to them. In which tyrannicall uprore, their
custome was, to fill a house full of people, and then (the
doores being locked upon them, that none might issue
forth) the house was fired about their eares: and oftentimes were yong children taken by the heeles, and cast
into the middest of the flames: This inhumane tyrannie
being practised not onely by the Poles, that were our
enemies, but even by those Russes that were traitors to
their owne Emperour, and served under the Poles, and
were called Cossakes, whose cruelty farre exceeded the
Polish.

The Towne being thus burnt to the earth, all the sixe
thousand (which as I said before, fled over the River,
out of the sconce, and were by us supposed to be but
seven hundred) came downe in full battalion to the Rivers
side with such fiercenesse, as if presently they and their
horses would have swom over, to fight with us, which
being perceived, our poore five hundred stood ready to
resist them. But whether they feared our numbers to be
greater then they were, and that wee had some other secret
forces, I know not: but away they marched, the selfe same

day in which they came downe in that bravery, not doing
any thing: of which, wee for our parts, were not much
sorry; because if the battailes had joyned, wee knew our
selves farre unable to withstand them. And this was the
service of the most noate, that wee went upon.

Two or three other sconces and Townes we tooke from
our enemies, they not once daring to resist us, because
they knew nothing of our numbers and force. But the
dishonest dealings of our Captaines, made the whole Armie *Caytiffe*
discontent; insomuch, that our Souldiors would often- *Captaines.*
times deny to goe forth upon service, because they had
beene almost a yeare in the Land and had received no
more but one Rubble (amounting to the value of ten
shillings English.) So that upon these discontents, fiftie
of our men ranne away to the enemy at one time, and *Fugitives.*
discovered to them our strength. After which, we durst
not be so bold as before we had beene. The fire of a
new conspiracie was likewise kindling, but it was perceived, and quenched with the bloud of the conspirators,
of which, the chiefe were hanged. On therefore we went:
when we came within fortie leagues of Muscovie, newes [III.iv.778.]
was brought, that the enemy had beleaguard seven
thousand Russes that were our friends, and that unlesse
wee forced the siedge to breake up, the seven thousand
Russes would every man be starved where they lay. This
sad report, (albeit we had resolved never to goe upon
any more service, untill wee had our pay) so wrought in
our hearts, that wee much pittied the miseries of others,
because wee our selves had tasted of the like.

Our Generall (whose name was Everhorne) was a
Fynlander, and with a company of Fynland blades (as they
tearme them) well appointed on Horsebacke, was by the
King of Sweveland, sent after us, as our Convoy, untill
wee should come to Pontus le Guard, who was chiefe *Pontus le*
Generall over the whole armie of strangers that came into *Guard.*
the Land: so that according as he was sent and charged
by the King, hee overtooke us before we came to Ariova.
By the intreatie therefore of this Fynlander, and the

flattering promises of our owne Captaines, we were contented to goe upon this service, and to deliver the Russes, or to dye our selves in the action. Yet with condition, that (as they promised to us) we should by the way meete our chiefe Generall, Pontus le Guard, who with certaine numbers of English, French and Dutch (which the yeare before were come into the Land) was upon a march out of Muscovy, not onely to meete us, but to joyne with us, and pay us all our money which remained good to us; provided likewise, that so soone as ever wee should release the seven thousand Russes, our money should be payed downe. On these conditions (I say) wee yeelded to goe upon the businesse.

They meet.   At length Pontus le Guard met us (according to the promise) and with him was money brought to pay us, and his word given that presently wee should receive it. But the lamentable estate, in which the poore besiedged Russes were (within the sconce) being at the point of death for want of foode, required rather speedy execution, then deliberation: so that the necessities of their hard fortunes craving haste, on wee went, having about ninteene or [III.iv.779.] twenty thousand Russes, that were people of the same Countrey, joyned to our Armie, to aide them in this enterprize. But as we all were upon a march, the enemy having received intelligence of our approaching, set forward, to the number of eight thousand Lanciers and more, to intercept us by the way: and being within one dayes march of the place to which wee were likewise going, they set fire upon three or foure Villages hard by the place where we lay at Grasse with our Horses, for a token that *An.* 1610.   they were comming. And this was done upon Midsummer day last in the morning, by breake of day. Then came they thundring with shouts and cries to set upon us: but no sooner was the Alarum given, when the greatest part of those nineteene or twenty thousand *Base Russe*   Russes, that were joyned to us as our aide, fled most basely *flight.*   before any blow was given. This sudden cowardize of theirs somewhat amazed us: but the houre being now come, wherein we were not to talke of dangers, but to goe meete them, with our sixe companies of English horse, we bravely resisted the Polanders, and with great hurt to them, but with little losse upon our part, charged them three severall times.

At last Pontus le Guard (our chiefe Generall) tooke his heeles and fled too, leaving us utterly destitute of all direction: which much astonished us, as not well understanding what to doe: for our greatest strength (being by their flight) taken from us, none but wee strangers were left in the field, and of us there was not in all, above two thousand, and of that number there were above six hundred French horsemen, who seeing both the Generall gone, and the Russes fled, turned their backs upon us, and ranne away too most valiantly, yet not out of the field, but to the enemy. *P. le Guard fleeth.* *French flee.*

Then were wee not above twelve or fourteene hundred at the most left to resist eight thousand at the least: upon whom notwithstanding, our six companies of English horsemen, charged three severall times, without any great losse, but with much honor: And at the fourth time, for want of powers to second them (which the French should have done) all our six companies were scattered and over-throwne with the losse of few of our colours. The Captaines over these sixe Companies of Horse, were these: *English honour.*

Captaine Crale, of whose company I was. Captaine Kendricke, Captaine Benson, Captaine Carre, Captaine Colbron, Captaine Creyton.

Which six Captaines had not in all their companies above five hundred men. In this battaile, Captaine Creyton was slaine in the field; Captaine Crale was shot in the knee, and within a short time after dyed of that wound; not above twelve of his companie escaping. Captaine Kendrick was wounded in divers places of the head, and dyed. Captaine Benson was shot in the hand, and wounded in the head, and yet escaped, and lived: onely Captaine Carre and his Cornet escaped, but all his companie scattered and lost. Divers other Officers were slaine, whose names I cannot remember.

Thus were all our English horse-men dispersed and overthrowne, to the number of five hundred and upwards. Our Generall Everhorne with his companies of Finland, or Finsco blades, were also put to retrait: so that there was not left in the field above sixe or seven hundred, which were foot-men. And of these, one halfe was English, one halfe Dutch, who kept onely a certaine place by a wood side, barricadoed about with wagons, having with them foure field pieces, with which they did great spoile to the Enemie. But their number being but few, neither durst they venture on the Enemie, nor durst the Enemie enter upon them, but kept them still (as it were besieged) in that place onely, because they could no wayes escape. The inconvenience of which cooping up in so narrow a roome, being looked into, and the dangers on every side well considered, it was held fittest for safetie, to summon the Enemie to a parley. In which parley, the Enemie offered, that if they would yeeld, and fall to their sides, they should have good quarter. And if any man had desire to goe for his owne Countrie, hee should have libertie to goe with a Pasport from the King of Poland. Or if any would serve the King of Poland, hee should have the allowance of very good meanes duly paid him. Upon these compositions they all yeelded, and went to the Enemie; onely Captaine Yorke and his Officers, with some few of their Souldiers, went backe into the Countrie, and came not to the Enemie, as the rest had done: who from thence marched up to the Polish Leaguer, being ten miles distant from the place, and there they continued. But such as desired to travell to their owne Countries, were sent to the King of Polands Leaguer, which lay at that time at a place called Smolensko, and there accordingly had their Passe, to the number of one hundred, of which number I my selfe was one. What became of the rest I know not: but I with five more held together in travell, untill we came to Dantzicke, a great Towne in

Prussia, being distant from Smolensko one hundred leagues.

To make an end of this Storie of the Foxe and the Beare, the pretending Demetrius and contending Suiskey; it is reported, that Demetrius seeing these perplexities of Suiskey, raysed a great Armie of such Russes as voluntarily * fell to him (the Pole having now rejected him, except some Voluntaries) and againe laid siege to Mosco; Zolkiewsky for Sigismund, beleagred another part thereof with fortie thousand men, whereof one thousand and five hundred were English, Scottish, and French. Suiskey seeing no hope to withstand them, his Empire renouncing him, hee would seeme to renounce the Empire first, betaking himselfe to a Monasterie. But not the sanctitie of the place, nor sacred name of an Emperour might protect or secure him. The Muscovites yeelded up their Citie and his Person to the Pole, and the Castle was manned for Sigismund. All joyne against Demetrius, who betaketh him to his heeles, and by a Tartar (as before is said) was slaine in his campe. Charles King of Sweden dyed Octob. 30. 1611. and Gustavus his sonne succeeded. Sigismund obtayneth Smolensko also after two yeeres siege and more: in which time the Defendants had held out so resolutely, that the Polish Peeres and States (which in that Kingdom beare great sway) had called the King to their Parliament, the rather in regard of the King of Denmarke warring upon Sweden (in which warre divers thousands of our English voluntaries * assisted the Dane) but he first desiring to trie his fortune, carried the Citie with two hundred pieces of Ordnance and other rich spoile. Many were slaine, and divers great persons taken, of which was the Archbishop. Many were blowne up (as was thought) by their owne voluntarie act, by fire cast into the storehouse, in which is said to have beene (if our Author mistake not) fifteene thousand vessels of poulder: whereupon seemed to returne the very Chaos, or in stead thereof a Hell into the World. It is accounted one of the strongest Forts in Christendome, the walls able to beare

*Some say he had 100000. which is scarsely credible.

[III.iv.780.]

Mosco yeelded.

Second Demetrius slaine.

*Under the Lord Willoughby Gen. Sir John Poole, &c.

A. Jansonius, quindecies mille vasorum pul. sul.

two Carts meeting in the breadth. It was taken the twelfth of July, 1610.

Suiskeys
imprisonment
and death.

Suiskey was carried into Poland and there imprisoned in Waringborough Castle, and after the losse of libertie and his Empire, exposed to scorne and manifold miseries, hee dyed in a forraine countrie. But before that Tragedie, the Poles are said to have more then acted others. For when they held him prisoner before his departure from Moscovia, they sent for many Grandes in Suiskeys name, as if he had much desired to see them before his fatall farewell, to take a friendly and honourable leave of them.

Polish crueltie. They come, are entertayned, and in a private place knocked on the head and throwne into the River: and thus was most of the chiefe remayning Nobilitie destroyed. The Poles fortified two of the Forts at Mosco, and burnt two others, as not able to man them. But the Muscovite also there held them besieged till famine forced them to yeeld:

Their reward. the Russians finding there sixtie barrels of pouldred mans flesh (it seemeth of such as had dyed, or were slaine, that

Eaters of mans flesh forced to eate mans flesh. their death might give life to the Survivers) a just, but miserable and tragicall spectacle. We shall conclude this Discourse with giving you two Letters, the one taken out of a Letter written from Colmogro Sept. 7. (the yeere is not dated) amidst these broiles; the other from Captaine Margaret before mentioned by Thuanus: and after them, for further illustration and profitable use of this storie, is added part of a Letter of Doctor Halls.

*The Polish Vaivud whose daughter married Demetrie that was slaine; who now had recovered libertie.

ON Thursday morning came George Brighouse from Mosco, he hath beene three weekes on the way, but by reason of his small staying here, I can learne but small occurrents, which is, still Mosco holdeth out, of late some of the Nobilitie issued out and gave the Enemie a small skirmish, slue neere foure thousand of them, tooke prisoners one hundred and seventie, whereof eleven Polish Gentlemen gallant men, are almost starved in prison. Sandomirsky * is entred the borders with a new supply

HONDIUS HIS MAP OF MUSCOVIA

of Souldiers, the which Demetrie his sonne in Law hath
long since expected.

The Crim Tartar is returned from thence into his owne *Russia spoyled*
Country, hath taken more then twentie thousand prisoners *by Tartars.*
captives out of Resan and thereabouts: Knez Scopin *
is two nineties from Yeraslave, he meanes to march from
thence to Mosco, but by Georges speeches he makes no
great haste.

Bouginsky that was Secretarie to Demetrie, is still under
prestave with an Officer, was almost starved with hunger,
but Master Brewster doth daily releeve him to his great
comfort.

George Brighouse came Poste by Volodemer: the
Princesse, wife to Evan Evanowich, that was eldest sonne
to the ᵃ old Emperour (shee to whom you gave the good *ᵃ Generall of*
intertainment to) is there at his going up and comming *the forces of*
backe, made very much of him; he dined in her Presence: *Suiskey in the*
field.
after dinner sent him a great Present of many dishes and *A Dane*
drinkes for your sake, and often remembred you and your *borne, see*
great kindnesse to her and hers; still remembring T. La. *Doct. Halls*
and kept him so a long time in her owne Cell. *Epistles.*
Evan
There is a great conspiracy still in the Mosco against *Vasilowich.*
the Emperour Vasili Evanowich, onely the Muscovites *Suiskey now*
stand with him, and very few of the Nobilitie. Daily *raigning.*
there issueth out by force or stealth divers of the Gentrie, *Those of the*
Citie onely.
most of the Dutch ᶜ, specially the Women are gone out *ᶜ Lieflanders*
of the Mosco to the Tartar. It is supposed that the *that inhabit*
Emperour cannot long hold out, and * Demetrie Evano- *there.*
wich is reported to bee a very wise Prince. *＊The second*
Demetrius,
which was
Captain Margarets Letter to Master Merick from *soone after*
slaine by a
Hamborough, Jan. 29. *1612. *Tartar.*
＊1611. in
Right worshipfull Sir, I could not omit this commoditie *English*
without commending my service to your Worship, *account.*
and also briefly to advertise you of the State of Mosco,
which is not as I could wish. Also I left Master Brewster
in good health at my departure; but three dayes after the

*The Poles in
Mosco besieged
by the Russes.*
[III.iv.781.]
*English house
burnt.*

Towne within the red wall was burnt with certaine fire
Bals shot in by the Russes, so that there is but three houses
left whole, the English house also being burnt. Master
Brewster is constrained to have his dwelling in a Seller
under the Palace, without great friends except Misslofsqui.
The Generall Cotquevilsh is arrived there, and left a
sufficient number of men to keepe the Castle, and the
red Wall, hee himselfe with his Armie is gone towards
Resan, and he hath sent with much to doe, and upon
certaine conditions, to the River of Sagia towards the
Volga, to bring victuals to maintayne them that are in the
Castle besieged of the Muscovites. The King of Poland
is altogether resolved to goe there in person this summer,
and if the Russes have no forraine helpe, as there is no
appearance, no question it will come to passe as I writ
last to your Worship, that they will be forced to yeeld.
I write briefly to your Worship, because I hope to take
my voyage to France through England, and there to meet
with your Worship; intreating your Worship to accept
these few lines as a testimony of the service I have vowed
to your Worship, &c. and so I end in haste.

Thus have we finished foure Acts of this Tragedie:
the first, ending with the end of Bealas family; the second,
with the ruine of that of Boris; the third, with that (whatsoever) Demetrius; the fourth, with this Suiskey, attended
with that shadow or ghost of another Demetrius. Now
as I have seene sometimes the Spectators of Tragedies
whiled with discourse of a Chorus, or (as in our vulgar)
entertayned with musicke, to remit for a time those bloudie
impressions fixed in attentive mindes; so have we repre-
sented Pheodores Coronation added to the first; Boris his
Charter to the English to conclude the second; that of
Demetrius to the third, and for this fourth I have here
made bold with a Letter of my worthy friend (so am I
bold to call that good Man, zealous Protestant, elegant
Writer, industrious Preacher, learned Doctor, and
Reverend Deane, Doctor Hall, a Hall adorned with so

rich Arras, and with all the ground, light, life, the All
of these, Christian humilitie) which may serve as a Letter
of commendation to my intent, as it was intended to another
worke, which had it beene publike, might have prevented
the greatest part of this : A worke of Master Samuel   *Master Sa.*
Southeby, in Sir Th. Smiths Voyage mentioned, touching *Southeby.*
those Russian occurrents which he in part saw. As a
Traveller he deserveth place here. And howsoever I have
neither beene so happy to see the Worke nor the Work-
man, yet this Epistle tells what we have lost, and my
worke easily proclaimes the defect of such a Wardrobe,
being (as you see) like a Beggars cloke, all of diversifyed
patches ; so much more labour to mee, in both getting
and stitching them, though so much lesse satisfaction to
thee. Once, as I have placed this long Russian storie in
the midst of Marine Discoveries, to refresh the Reader
a while on Land : so amidst these tragicall, harsh Relations,
I thus seeke to recreate thy wearie spirits with this chat
of mine, and after these Minda gates, more really, with
this Letter so usefull to the present subject, so pleasing
in the stile. The whole, and the next following to
Buchinski, the Reader may finde in his so oft published
Decades of Epistles.

TRavell perfiteth wisedome ; and observation gives
perfection to travell : without which, a man may
please his eyes, not feede his braine ; and after much earth
measured, shall returne with a weary body, and an empty
minde. Home is more safe, more pleasant, but lesse
fruitfull of experience : But, to a minde not working and
discursive, all heavens, all earths are alike. And, as the
end of travell is observation ; so, the end of observation
is the informing of others : for, what is our knowledge
if smothered in our selves, so as it is not knowne to more ?
Such secret delight can content none but an envious nature.
You have breathed many and cold aires, gone farre, seene
much, heard more, observed all. These two yeares you
have spent in imitation of Nabuchadnezzars seven ; con-

versing with such creatures as Paul fought with at
Ephesus. Alas! what a face, yea what a backe of a Church
have you seene? what manners? what people? Amongst
whom, ignorant Superstition strives with close Atheisme,
Treachery with Cruelty, one Devill with another; while
Truth and Vertue doe not so much as give any challenge
of resistance. Returning once to our England after this
experience, I imagine you doubted whether you were on
Earth, or in Heaven. Now then (if you will heare mee,
whom you were wont) as you have observed what you
have seene, and written what you have observed; so,
publish what you have written: it shall be a gratefull
labour, to us, to Posteritie. I am deceived, if the fickle-
nesse of the Russian State, have not yeelded more memorable matter of Historie then any other in our Age, or
perhaps many Centuries of our Predecessors. How shall
I thinke, but that God sent you thither before these broiles,
to bee the witnesse, the Register of so famous mutations?
He loves to have those just evils which hee doth in one
part of the World, knowne to the whole, and those evils,
which men doe in the night of their secresie, brought
forth into the Theater of the World; that the evill of
mens sinne being compared with the evill of his punishment, may justifie his proceedings, and condemne theirs.
Your worke shall thus honour him; besides your second
service, in the benefit of the Church. For, whiles you
discourse of the open Tyrannie of that Russian Nero, John
Basilius; the more secret, no lesse bloudy plots of Boris;
the ill successe of a stolne Crowne, though set upon the
head of an harmelesse Sonne; the bold attempts and
miserable end of a false, yet aspiring challenge; the per-
fidiousnesse of a servile people, unworthy of better
Governours; the misse-carriage of wicked Governours,
unworthy of better Subjects; the unjust usurpations of
men, just (though late) revenges of God; crueltie rewarded
with bloud, wrong claimes with overthrow, treachery with
bondage; the Reader, with some secret horror, shall draw
in delight, and with delight instruction: Neither know

I any Relation whence hee shall take out a more easie Lesson of Justice, of Loyaltie, of Thankefulnesse.

But above all, let the World see and commiserate the [III.iv.782.] hard estate of that worthy and noble Secretarie, Buchinsky. Poore Gentleman! his distresse recalls ever to my thoughts Æsops Storke, taken amongst the Cranes: He now nourishes his haire, under the displeasure of a forreigne Prince; At once in durance, and banishment. He served an ill Master; but, with an honest heart, with cleane hands. The Masters injustice doth no more infect a good Servant, than the truth of the Servant can justifie his ill Master. A bad Worke-man may use a good Instrument: and oft-times a cleane Napkin wipeth a foule mouth. It joyes me yet to thinke, that his pietie, as it ever held friendship in Heaven, so now it winnes him friends in this our other World: Lo, even from our Iland unexpected deliverance takes a long flight, and blesseth him beyond hope; yea rather, from Heaven, by us. That God, whom hee serves, will bee knowne to those rude and scarce humane Christians, for a protector of innocence, a favourer of truth, a rewarder of pietie. The mercy of our gracious King, the compassion of an honourable Counsellour, the love of a true friend, and (which wrought all, and set all on worke) the grace of our good God, shall now lose those bonds, and give a glad welcome to his libertie, and a willing farell to his distresse. He shall (I hope) live to acknowledge this; in the meane time, I doe for him, Those Russian Affaires are not more worthy of your Records, than your love to this friend is worthy of mine. For neither could this large Sea drowne or quench it, nor time and absence (which are wont to breed a lingring consumption of friendship) abate the heate of that affection, which his kindnesse bred, religion nourished. Both rarenesse, and worth shall commend this true love; which (to say true) hath beene now long out of fashion. Never times yeelded more love; but, not more subtle. For every man loves himselfe in another, loves the estate in the person: Hope of advantage is the Load-stone that drawes the yron hearts of men; not vertue, not desert. No Age affoorded more Parasites, fewer friends: The most are friendly in sight, serviceable in expectation, hollow in love, trustlesse in experience. Yet now, Buchinsky, see and confesse thou hast found one friend, which hath made thee many, &c.

§. V.

Of the miserable estate of Russia after Swiskeys deportation, their election of the King of Polands Sonne, their Interregnum and popular estate, and chusing at last of the present Emperour, with some remarkable accidents in his time.

THus have we seene the Russian sinnes utterly rooting up so many Russian Imperiall Families and persons: the whole Family of Ivan extirpate, that of Boris succeeding, annihilate; two pretending Demetrii and Suiskie extinct: and yet have wee greater abhominations to shew you. No Tyrant, no Serpent, no Dragon is so exorbitant and prodigious as that which hath many heads: and therefore in divine Visions Monarchies (how ever excessive and tyrannical) have beene resembled by simpler and more uniforme beasts, but the Devill in a great red Dragon with seven heads and ten hornes, and the Beast likewise to which hee gave his power and his seat and great authoritie, which opened his mouth in blasphemie against God, &c. On which sate the great Whore, the Antichristian Babylon. There was no King in Israel, is both Alpha and Omega, Preface and Conclusion Divine Writ to some misery in Israel; as if all Kings and no King, were the Circumference of all the lines proceeding from Mischiefes Centre. And now was Russia a Monster of many heads, that is, a bodie fallen into many pieces. One man possessed of the Wife of that double Demetrius, got to Astracan, there

Dan. 2. & 7. & 8. *Ap.* 12. 3. & 13. 1, 2. & 17. 1. *Jud.* 17. 6. & 18. 1. & 19. 1. & 21. 25.

seating himselfe to set up an usurped shop of Rule; the Southerne parts chose Prince Vladislaus, Son of K. Sigismund of Poland; those of the North thought of other Princes; and at last when neither the Fig-trees *Jud. 9.* sweetnesse nor Olives fatnesse, nor cheering Wine from the Vine could take place in their inconstancie, the Brambles conceived a fire which devoured the Cedars of Libanus: a popular government happened, or if you will, *Popular* a Confusion of the multitude bare sway, which killed and *government in* murthered every Great Man, whom any Rascall would *Russia.* accuse to be a friend to the Poles, or to any of the dead Emperours, whom those popular injudicious Judges fancied not. And now Russia blushed with impudencie, that is with shamelesse sight of the daily effusion and profusion of her best bloud; now every man was an Actor: and oh had they beene but Actors! too really did they present (not represent) bloudie Tragedies, of which their whole Countrey was becomne the Theatre; the Devill the Choragus (a Murtherer from the beginning) and the whole World Spectator, stupid with admiration, quaking with horrour of so uncouth a sight!

Now for the overtures betwixt the Muscovites, and Stanislaus Stanislawich Zolkiewskie, Generall of the Polakes, touching their Election of Vladislaus Sonne of King Sigismund, and the Articles propounded: also the answere of Prince Vladislaus to the same Articles, Anno 1612. I have here expressed in Latine as I found them; fearing I should be over-tedious to translate them, especially seeing the businesse came not to effect: and the English Articles following of the Russian Embassage to [III.iv.783.] the King of Poland, doth lay open that and other passages of the Russian Confusions.

Pactainter Primarium Ducem Exercituum Regni Poloniæ, & inter Heroes Moscoviæ.

SErenissimi Potentissimique Imperatoris Sigismundi tertii Dei gratia Regis Poloniæ, Magnique Ducis Lithuaniæ, Russiæ, Prussiæ, Samogitiæ, Kieviæ, Volhoniæ,

Podoliæ, Podlachiæ, Suecorum, Oestonorum, aliorumque
nec non hæreditarii Regis Suecorum, Gottorum, Van-
dalorum, Finlandiæque Principis. Palatinus Kijeviensis,
Primarius Dux Exercituum Regni Poloniæ Capitaneus
Rohativensis, Camænacensis, Kalusciensis. Ego Stanislaus Stanislaides Zolkiewsky de Zolkwia, Manifestum
facio præsentibus pactis, & confirmatis meis literis. Quòd
Omnipotentis in Trinitate adorandi Dei gratia, & volun-
tate, tum & benedictione venerabilis Hermogenis, Moscovitarum, totiusque Russiæ Patriarchæ, Metropolitarum,
Archiepiscoporum, Episcoporum, Archimandrytarum,
Humænorum totiusque venerabilis Cleri. Et post
pacta omnium Heroum, Comitum, Capitaneorum,
Primariorum Dapiferorum, Aulicorum, Tenutariorum,
Aulicorum arcibus Præfectorum, & Decurionum Sclo-
petariorum, necnon quorumvis Moscoviæ hæredum,
Heroumque liberorum, Advenarum, Mercaturam exer-
centium, Jaculatorum, velitum, Fabrorum tormentariorum,
& reliquorum incolarum magni Imperii Moscovitarum.
Heroes, utpotè Comes Albertus Ivanoviz Mscislawskii,
Dux Venceslaus Venceslaides Galicziin, Albertus Ivanoviz
Seremetii, Dux Venceslaus Mieliechii, & Primarii Deputati
Venceslaus Telepnievii, & Thomas Lugowskii, & universi
totius Moscoviæ Primates, Egerunt, deliberaveruntque
mecum, de eligendo Imperatore, in Wlodiimiriense
universumque Moscovitarum Imperium, ac tradiderunt
mihi suam confirmatam sigillatamque obligationem &
sacrosanctum vivificum baptisma sacræ Regiæ Majestatis
exosculati sunt non tantum Primarii Comites, sed etiam
Heroes, incolentes Aulici, Capitanei, Primarii Dapiferi,
Aulici, Cubicularii, Structores, Tenutarii, & Decuriones
Sclopetariorum, omnisque dignitatis homines, Jaculatores,
velites, Fabri Tormentarii, variisque status serviles, &
liberi homines Imperii Moscovitici, Hunc in modum:
Quod venerabilis Hermogenes Moscoviæ, & universæ
Russiæ Patriarcha, Metropolitæ, Archiepiscopi, Episcopi,
Archimandrytæ, Humæni singuli & universi venerabiles
Heroes, Capitanei, Primarii Dapiferi, Aulici, Cubicularii,

Structores, & Decuriones Sclopetariorum, Tenutarii,
hæredes Heroum, Advenæ, homines Mercaturam exer-
centes, Jaculatores, Velites, Fabri tormentarii, omnis sortis
serviles, & hæreditarii Imperii Moscovitici, constituunt
Legatos mittere, atque supplicare magno Imperatori,
Serenissimo Sigismundo Regi Poloniæ, & Serenissimo
sacræ ejus Majestatis Regiæ filio Vladislao Sigismundi, ut
Serenissimus Imperator Sigismundus Rex, commisereri
eorum velit, constituatque Vlodiimiriensis totiusque
Imperii Moscovitici Imperatorem Vladislaum Sigismundi
sacræ suæ Regiæ Majestatis filium. Quod ut fiat,
venerabilis Hermogenes totius Moscoviæ Patriarcha,
Metropolitæ, Archiepiscopi, Episcopi, Archimandrytæ,
Humæni, totus denique venerabilis Clerus, Deum ter
optimum maximum rogat, & Imperatorem Serenissimum
Vladislaum Sigismundi filium sacræ Regiæ Majestatis
Imperio totius Moscoviæ constitui læto exoptant animo.
Omnes etiam Heroes, Aulici Imperatorii, Capitanei,
Primarii Dapiferi, Equites, Cubicularii, Structores,
Decuriones Sclopetariorum, Tenutarii, in arcibus Præfecti,
Dispensatores, liberi Heroum, Advenæ, Mercaturam exer-
centes, Jaculatores, velites, Fabri tormentarii, omnisque
conditionis serviles, & liberi incolæ Imperii Moscoviæ,
Serenissimi Imperatoris, filii Serenissimi Regis Poloniæ
Vladislai Sigismuntoviz, & posteritatis (si quæ ipsius
futura) exosculati sunt sacrosanctum vivificum baptisma,
hoc signo indicantes, se cùm ipsi Imperatori, tùm omni
ipsius posteritati æternis temporibus servituros, omniaque
prosperima exoptantes, in omnibus non secus ut superiori-
bus hæreditariis magnis Imperatoribus, & Cæsaribus,
Magnis item Ducibus universi Imperii Moscovitici, nec
ullum malum ipsi, & ejus posteritati ominaturos, machina-
turos, cogitaturos, aut alium quempiam ex Moscovito
Imperio, viciniisque Imperiis, in Imperatorem Moscoviæ,
præter Serenissimum Vladislaum Sigmuntoviz filium
Serenissimi Regis Poloniæ introductores, adoptaturosve.
Quibus verò cum conditionibus in Imperatorem Moscovitici Imperii eum sint suscepturi, hac de re Heroes

Dux Albertus Ivanoviz Mscislawskii cum Collegis suis
tradidere mihi obligatorium pactum. Ego verò Primarius
dux Regni Poloniæ, post pactum istud in scriptis mihi
traditum, de omnibus punctis cum Heroibus certam con-
clusionem constituimus, & approbavimus. Harumque
conditionum approbandarum gratia tradidi Heroibus Duci
Alberto Ivanoviz cum Collegis ejus obligationem, & con-
firmavi meæ manus subscriptione, & sigilli appositione, &
sacrosanctum vivificum Baptisma exosculatus sum ego
Primarius Dux exercituum Regni Poloniæ & omnes
Primipili, Centuriones sese obligando, pro Magno Imperatore nostro Serenissimo Sigismundo Rege Poloniæ,
ipsiusque filio Serenissimo Vladislao, Sigmuntoviz, & pro
magnis Imperiis, universoque magno Regno Poloniæ,
Magnoque Ducatu Lithuaniæ, & pro nobismetipsis,
totoque exercitu, qui est penes sacrosanctam Regiam
Majestatem, & penes me Primarium suum. Eum in
modum. Quòd benedictione castissimæ Deiparæ, &
Sanctorum, qui magna miracula in Moscovia præstitere,
utpotè Sancti Petri Alexii & Anthonii, omniumque
Sanctorum, Serenissimus Sigismundu Rex noster Poloniæ
miserebitur Imperii Moscovitici, & creabit Imperatorem
Wlodiimiriensem, omniumque magnorum Imperiorum,
totius Muscoviæ, filium sacræ suæ Regiæ Majestatis
[III.iv.784.] Vladislaum Sigmuntoviz. Cum verò jam Serenissimus
Vladislaus Sigmuntoviz filius Serenissimi Regis Poloniæ
advenerit ad Arcem Sedis Imperatoriæ Moscoviticæ, tùm
coronabitur in Imperatorem Wlodiimiriensem, omniumque
totius Moscoviæ Imperiorum, ipsique Imperatoria Corona,
& Diadema imponetur à venerabili Hermogene Patriarcha
totius Moscoviæ, & ab universo venerabili Clero Græcæ
Religionis, secundum pristinum morem & dignitatem.
Factus verò Serenissimus S.R. Majestatis filius Vladislaus
Sigmuntoviz Imperator Moscoviæ, Templa Dei in Mos-
covia per omnes Arces, Vicos, universumque Imperium
Moscoviæ repurgabit, & augebit in omnibus ad pristinam
consuetudinem, & ab omni incommodo tutabitur, tum
Sanctis Dei, & Divorum imaginibus, & castissimæ

Deiparæ, omnibus ossibus Sanctorum, quæ magna prodigia in Moscovia faciunt, debitum cultum flexis genibus præstare, illaque adorare tenebitur. Et Politicæ, nec non Spirituali utriusque sexus Christianitati, omnibusque verè Christianis, ut sint veræ Christianæ legis Græcæ Religionis non prohibebit. Romanæ Religionis aliarumque diversarum Sectarum Religionis Templa, aut Synagogas, in Moscovitici Imperii Arcibus, & pagis, nullibi ædificare debet ut nihilominus in Arce Moscovia præfata, unum Romanum Templum esse possit, propter homines Polonos, & Lithuanos, qui penes Imperatorem filium Serenissimi R. Polo. sunt futuri, ea de re cum sacra R. Majestate, & venerabili Hermogene Patriarcha Moscoviæ, omnibus spiritualibus, tum Heroibus, & Capitaneis collatio instituenda.

Religio autem sacrosancta Græca nullo in puncto violanda, aut perturbanda, vel alia quæpiam inusitata introducenda est, in idque danda opera, ut sancta, vera, Christiana Græca Religio, suam integritatem, & cultum retineat, juxta morem antiquum, nec Imperium Moscoviticum, ejusque incolæ, veri Christiani, à Græca Religione ad Romanam, aut aliam quampiam, vi, seu robore, & servitute, aliisque his similibus modis abducantur.

Judæi in universum Moscoviæ Imperium causa Mercaturæ, aut alterius cujuspiam rei proficisci ne permittantur. Venerabilia & ossa Sanctorum, ab Imperatore filio Serenissimi R. Pol. Vladislao Sigmuntoviz sancta cum veneratione debent venerari. Et venerabilem Hermogenem Patriarcham Moscoviæ, Metropolitas, Archiepiscopos, Episcopos, Archimandrytas, Humænos, Præsbyteros, Diaconos, & præsentes spirituales, universumque Clerum Christianæ sacrosanctæ Religionis Græcæ, debito afficere honore, in omnibusque tutari, spiritualibus negotiis sese immiscendo, alienas sectas præter Græcam religionem introducere nullas debet. Quod autem Templis, Monasteriisve non Patrum dicatur, de variis proventibus, & qui dabantur antiquorum tempore Imperatorum Moscoviæ, utpotè sacrati panes, legumina, summæ pecuniales, & his de variis reditibus similia : hos proventus Ecclesiæ dicatos, & omnium Imperatorum antiquorum Moscoviæ, nec Herorum, aut aliorum hominum donationes, si quas Templis, aut Monasteriis Dei dicaverunt, aut dicaturi sunt, adimere debet, nulla secundum antiquum morem constituta violando. Spirituales, & Regulares status nullo modo infringendo, Dimensariis omnia pensa spiritualia, & Regularia, quibus antiquitus dabantur, ex fisco Imperatorio omnia reddendo, ut solitum fuit, & ex Imperatorio Thesauro in Templa & Monasteria, stipem variorum redituum augendo. Heroes, Imperatorii Aulici, Capitanei, Primarii Dapiferi, Cubicularii, & cujusvis generis Tenutarii, in omnibus negotiis, in omnibus Imperialibus, Castrensibus, & terrestribus causis, in Arcibus Palatini, Capitanei, sive Tenutarii & Telonarii, aut alii cujusmodi Præfecti, & omnis conditionis homines, ut antiqua retineant Privilegia prout constitutum est in Moscovitico Imperio, ab antiquis magnis Imperatoribus, in id Serenissimus Imperator incumbet seriò.

Poloni verò & Lithuani, in Moscovia nullis in terrestribus, forensibus negotiis, aut Arcibus Palatinorum, Capitaneorumve esse debent, nec successiones Præfecturæ, aut dignitatis in Arcibus illis tribuendæ sunt.

Quia autem Poloni, & Lithuani ex utroque Imperio videtur consultum, ut præficiantur confinibus Arcibus ad absolutum levamen hujus Imperii, ea de re Serenissimus Imperator cum Heroibus collationem instituet suo tempore.

Jam vero universa Respublica supplex Serenissimum Imperatorem precatur, ne ad executionem perducat hanc conditionem, antequam fuerit hac in parte utrinque deliberatum.

Qui verò Poloni & Lithuani penes Serenissimum Imperatorem Vladislaum Sigmuntoviz sunt futuri, eos non solum honoraturi, sed etiam contentaturi pecuniali numeratione, & promoturi secundum uniuscujusque merita sumus.

Moscovitici Imperii Heroes, Aulicos, Imperatorios, Capitaneos, Primarios Dapiferos, Cubicularios, Præfectos, Structores, Tenutarios, Arcium Præfectos Sclopetariorum, omnesque ad Aulam Imperatoriam pertinentes homines, & liberos Heroum, Advenas, Mercatores, Jaculatores, velites, Fabros tormentarios, & omnis conditionis bellicosos homines, aliosque hæredes Imperii Moscovitici, Serenissimus Imperator debet habere in dignitate, honore, gratia, & amore, ut fuit antiquitus apud primos magnos Moscoviæ Imperatores; Nec antiquos mores & status qui erant in Imperio Moscoviæ immutare, vel Moscoviæ Ducum, Heroumque viduas Advenis in patria, vel Tenutis elocare, aut deprimere.

Tributa pecunialia, stipendia reddere, & hæreditates quas aliquis possidebat ad hæc usque tempora, is etiamnum, & in posterum possidere debet.

Hæreditaria bona à nemine abalienare, sed semper omnibus hominibus Moscovitici Imperii providere perpendendo servitia eorum, prout aliquis de Republica meritus est.

Advenis omnibus qui vocati fuerant ex variis Nationibus, à primis Imperatoribus Moscoviæ, necessariis [III.iv.785.] providere, prout antea solitum fuit: nec stipendia, Tenutas, & possessiones eorum ab iis abalienare.

Heroibus, Aulicis, Cubiculariis, Dapiferis, & liberis Heroum, omnibusque Aulæ Imperatoriæ inservientibus, Imperatoriam benevolentiam commonstrare, & salaria debita, secundum antiquum morem reddere, Serenissimus Imperator tenebitur.

Quod si verò alicui salaria multiplicabuntur, possessionesque aut tenutæ, supra ejus dignitatem, vel contra alicui minuentur, præter culpam ipsius, ea de re Serenissimus Imperator conferre, & consultare debet cum Heroibus Primariis: & prout unanimes decreverint, idque secundum æquitatem, ita sit facturus.

Qui vero Aulici, aut liberi Heroum sumunt beneficio Imperatoris, ex Arcibus omnibus stipendiariis, quibus beneficia tempore præteritorum Magnorum Imperatorum

Moscoviæ ob merita ipsorum dabantur, illis quoque jam
& stipendia pecunialia, & alimentaria, ex Mandato Imperatoris danda sunt.

In Arce dicta Moscovia, aliisque Arcibus, Judicia
exequi debent, & observari ut solitum, secundum statuta
Moscovitici Imperii. Quod si verò aliqua essent corri-
genda, ad corroborationem Judiciorum, conceditur Serenissimo Imperatori, sed cum consensu omnium Heroum
Universitatis Moscoviæ, ita tamen, ut respondeant
æquitati.

Magnus autem Imperator Serenissimus Rex Poloniæ,
Magnus Dux Lithuaniæ, cujusque totius Regni Poloniæ,
Imperia, necnon Magnus Ducatus Lithuaniæ, cum Magno
Imperatore filio Regis Poloniæ Vladislao, Sigmuntoviz, cum
omnibus Imperiis Moscoviæ, in amicitia, societate, amore,
æternis temporibus inviolabiliter, nec contra se invicem
exercitus colligere, & bella concitare nullis modis debent.

Quod si autem aliquis hostium tentarit impetus facere in
Imperium Moscoviæ, sive etiam in Regnum Poloniæ, &
Magnum Ducatum Lithuaniæ : contra istiusmodi omnes
hostes junctis viribus insurgere utrumque Imperium
tenebitur.

Cæterum, in Tartarorum finibus quod si necessum
fuerit servare utriusque Imperii milites, cum jam
coronatus fuerit filius Serenissimi Regis Poloniæ, Imperator Imperii Moscovitarum : hac de re collatio cum
Heroibus instituenda, & cum magno Imperatore Serenissimo Sigismundo Rege Poloniæ, idque decenter, animo
sincero, absque ulla machinatione damni alicujus, aut
Tyrannidis illationis in homines Moscovitici Imperii :
honorem, vitam, aut aliud quippiam istiusmodi nemini
adimendo, cujuscunque conditionis ille fuerit : Aut si in
Poloniam, vel Lithuaniam, aliaque Imperia Moscovitici
Imperii homines transmittendo, aut ex Lithuania in locum
eorum alicujus alterius generis homines supponendo :
Uxores, aut liberos alicujus dolose corrumpendo, vel
sobolis procreandæ gratia sumendo, & ad exteras Nationes
parentes cum liberis transmittendo.

Qui autem ex quocunque Imperio istiusmodi facinoris reus, & pœna dignus inveniretur : Is in Imperatoriis & terrestribus judicibus prout meruit, puniendus est : & decretum per Imperatorem aut Heroes, vel Capitaneos de illo ferendum.

Uxores autem eorum & liberi, fratres, & qui istud facinus nec perpetrarunt, nec ipsis fuit cognitum, aut illud perpetrandum consentiêre. Illi nedum puniendi, sed secundum æquitatem Privilegiorum suorum, patrimonia, tenutas, vitam, aulas, retinere debent.

Sin verò reus non possit explorari, nemo tum Judicio Imperatoris, at Heroum judicari, puniri, proscribi, vel incarcerari, aut ad alienos transmitti debet : sed unusquisque in suis Tenutis & Aulis conservari.

Steriles autem, quia ex hac decesserint vita, bona ab illis relicta, vel consanguineis ipsorum, sive cuicunque ipsi legaverint, tradenda : id tamen non absque mutua collatione, & consilio esse debet.

Porro quoniam tempore præsentis seditionis multi perire, & multos ex Moscovitis prostratos constat à Polonis, & Lithuanis, & contra Polonos & Lithuanos à Moscovitis : istud factum, & nunc, & imposterum, nec commemorandum, nec ulla vindicta utrinque pensandum esse debet.

Qui autem Poloni, & Lithuani Primipoli, Centuriones, aliique diversæ sortis homines duxêre captivitatem in Imperio Moscoviæ, quorum aliqui adhuc in vinculis tenentur, illi ex Moscoviæ Imperio reddendi, sine ulla pecuniali liberatione. Tum quoque vice versa Aulici, liberi Heroum, Jaculatores, Velites, Fabri tormentarii, omnesque serviles & liberi homines, Aulicorum liberi, Jaculatorum, Fabrorum tormentariorum, Sclopetariorum, & horum similium. Item Matres, Uxores, Liberi, & his similes, ex Imperio Moscovitarum, virilis aut muliebris sexus, in præsentem servitutem præsente primo Moscovitarum, virilis aut muliebris sexus, in præsentem servitutem præsente primo Moscovitarum Imperatore Venceslao accepti in Poloniam vel Lithuaniam, illi ab Imperatore Serenissimo Rege Poloniæ, restituendi à

minimis ad maximos usque absque pecuniali redemptione.
Proventus Imperatorios ex Arcibus, aliisque possessioni-
bus, tum ex tenutis & arendis census, omnesque reditus,
debet Serenissimus Imperator exigere, ut antea fecere
Primi Imperatores, & prioris Magistratus mores, & statuta
absque consensu in nullis immutare.

Arces, aut Civitates, quæ bello vastatæ, ad eas mittere
debet Serenissimus Imperator, & præcipere, ut con-
scribantur Registra eorum, quæ per vastationem periere:
ut vicissim sumptis proventibus aliunde, secundum con-
scripta registra, possint resarciri.

Quorum verò Hæreditates, Possessiones, vel Tenutæ
[III.iv.786.] spoliatæ, iis levamen dandum, sed non absque consensu
Heroum. Et quæ recens vastatæ Arces, illas quam-
primum restaurare, consilio inito cum Heroibus, &
Nobilibus.

Mercatores Moscovitici Imperii omnium Civitatum, in
Polonia & Lithuania, sic Poloni, Lithuani, in Moscovia,
Polonia, Lithuania, merces coemere debent more usitato,
ut antea: Istud tamen cavendum, ne invicem sibi facessent
negotia Mercatores, & alii Christiani in Lithuaniam ex
Russia, & ex Lithuania in Russiam, sese transportando
cum mercibus Heroes, & Aulici omnes, mancipia debent
in servitute detinere, prout solitum.

In Volda, Dona, & Tekier Arcibus, velites, si illis opus
fuerit, servari debent: de quibus Serenissimus Imperator
conferre debet cum Heroibus, & Nobilibus, postquam
coronabitur.

Arces Moscovitici Imperii, ad Imperatorem pertinentes,
tum illæ, quæ in tenutas Polonis, & Lithuanis traditæ sunt,
vel quas jam Vor præfatus sub potestatem suam subjecit:
Ego Primarius Dux exercituum Regni Poloniæ, constitui
cum Heroibus Moscoviæ, quod Serenissimus Rex Poloniæ,
Filio sacræ suæ Regiæ Majestatis Serenissimo Vladislao
Sigmuntoviz, has arces, cum omnibus quæ sunt vastatæ,
Moscovitico Imperio restituere debet. Illustres vero
Legati Moscovienses, hoc in negotio tractaturi sunt cum
sacra Regia Majestate de sumptibus, & expensis sacræ

Regiæ Majestatis in milites expositis, & de persolvendis
Polonis, & Lithuanis, sunt quoque consultaturi, quomodo
absolvi possint.

Vor autem præfatus, qui sese Cæsaridem Moscovitici *Demetrius*
Imperii, Demetrium Evanoviz appellat: de illo, mihi *supposititius*
Primo Duci Regni Poloniæ consilium ineundum, & omnis *secundus.*
cura habenda, ut capi, vel penitus è vita tolli possit.

Qui postquam captus, vel occisus fuerit, Ego Primarius
Dux Exercituum Regni Poloniæ, cum exercitu sacræ
Majestatis à primaria Arce, sedis Imperatoriæ, Moscovia
præfata discedere ad Arcem Mozaisko, vel ubi fuerit opus,
post collationem cum Heroibus institutam, ibique Legatos
Moscoviæ, & mandatum sacræ Regiæ Majestatis, præ-
stolari tenebor. Quod si nihilominus Vor præfatus contra
Imperatoriam arcem Moscoviam sic dictam tentaverit
insidiari, aut seditiones aliquas excitare; Ego Primarius
Dux Regni Poloniæ, illum profligare, & armis persequi
tenebor.

Dominum vero Sapieza, qui se Vor præfato adjunxit, ab
illo & exercitum Polonicum, & Lithuanicum abducere;
Quod si idem Vor præfatus, ex Moscovia cum Ruthenis
discesserit, militum autem Polonorum, & Lithuanorum
quosdam apud se detinuerit; Ego Primarius Dux Regni
Poloniæ, cum exercitu sacræ Regiæ Majestatis, una cum
Heroibus Moscoviæ, ne sanguicidium imposterum ex-
ordiatur, sed Imperium pace publica assecuratum
stabiliatur, dabimus operam.

Mulier verò, quæ cum eodem Vor præfato per *Demetrii*
Moscoviticum Imperium, cum exercitu passim grassatur, *primi sup.*
Imperatricem Moscoviæ sese ventilando; Illi prohibendum *uxor. Pala-*
ne eandem se imposterum cognominare, vel quippiam *timfilia.*
istiusmodi, aut aliquas difficultates, contra Imperium
Moscoviticum moliri audeat: sed, quamprimum in
Poloniam reducenda est. Imperator verò Serenissimus,
filius Regis Poloniæ Vladislaus Sigmuntoviz in omnibus
antiquitus, jura sancita, & pacta Magnorum Legatorum
Moscoviæ, cum Serenissimo Sigismundo Rege Poloniæ, &
confirmata privilegia imitari debet.

Civitatem & Arcem Smolinsk præfatum quod attinet;
Ego Dux Primarius exercituum regni Poloniæ supplicabo
apud S. R. Majestatem, ut prohibeat, ne milites in
Civitate tanta homicidia exerceant, & Arcem spolient.

De Baptismo
repetendo.
De baptismate verò, ut illud Imperator Vladislaus
Sigmuntoviz, filius sacræ Regiæ Majestatis suscipiat, &
baptizetur in illorum Sacrosancta legis Græcæ religione, in
illaque perseveret, ut & de aliis nondum contractis actis, &
conditionibus, & reliquis circumstantiis antiquitus in
Imperio Moscovitico, ad præsentem usque expeditionem
bellicam observatis : Inter Serenissimos Imperatores &
Imperia omnium, consilium & collatio institui debet, ut
amor, & amicitia, utrinque augeri, & conservari possit.
Qua de re, Ego Primarius Dux militiæ, cum jam à S. R.
Majestate commissa, & mandata nulla habeam, contuli cum
Heroibus, quid ipsis responsi sum daturus : sed primùm
cum sacra Regia Majestate hoc in negotio, tum etiam cum
Serenissimo Imperatore Vladislao Sigmuntoviz filio sacræ
Regiæ Majestatis, conferam.

Insuper, Ego Primarius Dux exercituum regni Poloniæ,
in Arcem Moscoviam præfatam, Polonos, Lithuanos, Ger-
manos, & omnis generis bellicosos, qui sunt mecum, &
cum Domino Sapieza, absque permissu Heroum, vel ipsa
necessitate, intromittere non debeo. In Arcem Moscoviam præfatam, Mercatorum Polonorum, & Lithuanorum, mercium coemendarum gratia, ex omnibus
Provinciis regni Poloniæ, cum meis Imperialibus testimonialibus literis, non ultra viginti, vel paulo plures sunt
intromittendi : absque literis à me datis testimonialibus, in
Arcem Moscoviam præfatam, aut alibi, nemo proficisci
debet.

Ob majus verò robur, & confirmationem Pactorum
istorum, Ego Primarius regni Poloniæ Dux exercituum,
Stanislaus Stanislaides, Zolkiewsky de Zolkwia sigillum
meum apposui, & manum propriam subscripsi. Sic etiam
Domini Primipoli, & Centuriones exercitus, qui tum
temporis mihi aderant, ad hæc mea scripta nomina sua sub-
scripsere. Datum in Castris, apud Arcem, sedis Impera-

toriæ Moscovitici Imperatoris. Anno 1610. Augusti 27. die.

Responsum ad Pacta inter Primarium Ducem [III.iv.787.] Exercituum Regni Poloniæ, & Heroes Moscoviæ, Serenissimi Regis Poloniæ, & Serenissimi Vladislai Sigmuntoviz Filii Sacræ Regiæ Majestatis.

MAgnus Dei gratia Imperator Vladislaus Sigmuntoviz, Filius Serenissimi Regis Poloniæ, Sueciæ, &c. Amplissimi Moscovitarum Imperii universo venerabili Clero, Ministris Dei vigilantissimis, Heroibus, Capitaneis, Liberis Heroum, Advocatis velitum, Jaculatoribus, & Velitibus, Advenis, Mercatoribus, omnibus servilibus, & liberis hominibus significamus. Nos quandoquidem vobis Imperatorem totius Imperii Moscovitici, Cæsarem, & Magnum Principem Wlodymiriensem, necnon universarum Moscovitici Imperii Provinciarum coronari petiistis : Nos quoque post Legatorum vestrorum supplicationem, pro vobis intercessimus apud Serenissimum Tertium Regem Poloniæ, Magnumque Ducem Lithuaniæ, Dominum parentem nostrum, ut secundum suæ sacræ Regiæ Majestatis misericordiam, consuetudinem, vestræ subveniat calamitati, & prout cæpit, ad finem usque vos, & totum Moscoviticum Imperium restauret, & pace confirmet : & sanguinem Christianum qui per malos quosdam pacis publicæ violatores, & perjuros effunditur, coerceat : Serenissimus itaque Rex Poloniæ, Dominus Parens noster, post vestrûm Legatorum supplicationem, & nostram filii sui intercessionem, Decrevit nobiscum filio suo, in Moscoviticum Imperium, iter quamprimum suscipere : ut confirmetur Imperium, & sanguicidium sanguinis vestri cohibeatur, vobis verò pax, & Patria, ex integro restituatur. Et vobis venerabili Clero, Heroibus, Incolis, Capitaneis, & universis cujuscunque sortis hominibus, Spiritualibus, & Politicis, istud necessariò sciendum est. Vos autem, qui Serenissimo Regi Poloniæ, Domino Parenti nostro, &

nobis, ad hoc usque tempus fidem inviolatam conservastis,
jam quoque nobis Magnis Imperatoribus vestris officia
vestra, & promptitudinem animi conservabitis, advent-
umque nostrum in Imperium Moscoviticum, cum gaudio
in pace expectabitis. Qui verò malâ de nobis opinione,
contumacia, & seductione Vor præfati, repulsam fecere, iis
ne ampliùs tergiversentur, promittendo illis nostram
benevolentiam, & amorem, persuadere debetis, & ad nos
Imperatores convertere, ut sint quoque vobiscum unanimes, Et supremi Cancellarii Exercitus, Serenissimique
Regis Poloniæ, Domini Parentis nostri, nostrisque sese
adjungant: Et cum supremo Cancellario, de nostris
Imperatoriis, & terrestribus negotiis consultent, com-
modaque Patriæ curent, ut quamprimum possit Imperium
Moscoviticum, ad pristinum statum reduci, & paci, ac
tranquillitati antiquæ restitui: ac nos, donec venerimus,
læti præstolentur. Seditiosis, ac malè de nobis opinanti-
bus, nullam fidem habeant, nec ullis obediant, qui
secundum animi sui præsumptionem falsam, se suamque
posteritatem Imperatoribus Moscoviticis successuram
arbitrantur. Et qui de sacra Regia Majestate, Domino
Parente nostro, nobisque metipsis, rumores nefarios,
scriptis ad Arcium Præfectos literis sparsêre, & dissemi-
narunt, verbaque dolosè excogitata, inter homines dimisêre,
& jam disseminant: atque hac tyrannide, & malitia sua,
recentes seditiones in Moscovia concitaverunt, quibus
multam copiam sanguinis Christiani frustra effundi passi
sunt, & totum Imperium diviserunt, & hac pertinacia, atque
malitia sua, Dei ter Opt. Max. castissimæque Deiparæ
voluntati, necnon Serenissimi Sigismundi Dei gratia Regis
Poloniæ misericordiæ, & ipsius benevolo erga se animo
adversantur, Nobisque Serenissimo Imperatori juramen-
tum exosculatione vivifici Baptismatis præstitum violant.
Quare quosdam eorum jam etiam propterea Deus Omnipotens, justo suo judicio, ex hac vita sustulit, & puniit:
quosdam verò, ejus atrocissima vindicta expectat, nisi à
sua contumacia conversi, apud nos, Magnos Imperatores
suos, culpam quamprimum supplices deprecentur. Insuper,

omnibus vobis in universum sciendum est, quod ii, qui ad nos Magnos Imperatores suos, & nostram misericordiam, asylumque confugerint, iis secundum magnum affectum nostrum Imperatorium, miserebimur : pænis remissis condonabimus omnia, & in tutelam eosdem nostrum recipiemus.

Sacrosanctam quoque Religionem vestram Legis Græcæ permittimus, earumque secundum constitutiones Patrum Sanctorum, tuebimur, in nullo puncto violandam, & immutandam. Et universam venerabilium Patrum, Ministrorum Dei Confessariorum vestrorum Coronam, debito in honore sumus habituri. Heroes, Aulicos, & cujuscunque sortis alios diligere, promovere, patriam possessionem, pecunialem, aliamque omnem provisionem, à nemine abalienando : sed suum unicuique attribuere promittimus, secundum antiquam consuetudinem : & insuper nostra Imperatoria provisione, unumquemque secundum ipsius dignitatem, & merita promovere. Qui autem in malitia, & contumacia sua perseverare non cessabunt, ii, Deum Opt. Max. & castissimam ejus Genitricem, strictissimo illos gladio punituros certo sciant : & nostrum Imperatorium benevolum animum, in iram, & vindictam mutatum experientur. Non vult enim Deus Omnipotens, ut, ob malitiam, & contumaciam Rebellium, innocentium ulterius sanguis effundatur, Templa Dei spolientur, & gloria sancti Nominis ejus, magis, ac magis deprimatur. Vos omnes, apud animum vestrum diligentius perpendite, & his, qui adhuc nobis tergiversantur renunciate, ut animo mutato, ad veritatis agnitionem redeant, & seditiosos, & pacis publicæ diremptores relinquant.

Jam vero, ad quas Arces, & Civitates, hæ literæ nostræ pervenerint, Mandamus, ut eorum Capitanei, & Tenutarii, omnia ad victum necessaria, & pecuniam colligant, in paratisque habeant, ad nostrum adventum. Interea Exercitus sacræ Regiæ Majestatis, Domini Parentis nostri, nostrique proprii, ne ullum detrimentum patiantur, sed una in fraterno amore, quoad venerimus, vinatis : Et donec

[III.iv.788.] Opt. Max. ex mera gratia sua, nostraque Imperatorium cura, & diligentia, toto Imperio Moscovitico firmato, & restaurato, vobis potiri concesserit. Dabantur Varsoviæ, Anno Domini 1612. 9. die Martii.

The points of the Embassage of the Russian Messenger sent to his sacred Majesty, briefly collected.

Rureck.

BY what manner their naturall Lords ruled over them, they alleaged, to wit, beginning from Borik, who was of the bloud of Augustus Cæsar, Emperour of Rome, even unto the last Lord and Emperour Pheodor Evanowich, in whom their Race ceased.

Pheodor Evanowich.

Boris Godonove.

That Boris Godonove abiding with Pheodor Evanowich, was created (by his owne force and power) Emperour or Lord: but after a little time, the pleasure of God so working, being thrust out of the Imperiall seate, departed this life shamefully, and by violent death, together with his Wife and Children.

Gregorii Eutropio, Rostrige. Demetrii Evanowich.

That Christophorus Otropitii the Rostrige, being of base descent, under the Name which he did beare of Emperour, otherwise Demetrii Evanowich, slaine at Owglets, did fraudulently and by deceit (wherewith he deceived the common people, and others that beleeved them) obtaine the Imperiall Seate by force, without the consent of the Spiritualtie, and all the chiefe Bishops and Lords, and great men of the Kingdome, who durst not withstand the same, seeing the Commons to yeeld thereunto.

Primates.

Lord Palatin of Sandomire.

How the excellent Lord Palatin of Sandomire, gave his daughter in marriage to the Rostrige, and himselfe (many Gentlemen both of the Kingdome of Poland, and great Duchy of Litow, accompanying him) came into Moscovia.

Vasili Evanowich Suiskey.

Then, that Vasili Evanowich Suiskey, with his brethren, and many others associated to this attempt, and stirring up other great men of the Land, did kill the Rostrige,

with many Gentlemen of Poland, and the great Duchy
of Litow, and put the rest into divers Castles.   And himselfe was made Emperour, although he were not elected
by all the States.   Whereupon many of our sort did not
willingly acknowledge him Emperour, and many would
not obey him.

How another named the Wor, did rise up at Kalusia, *The Wor.*
and caused himselfe to bee named Demetrii, and so *Coluga.*
accounted.   Whereof when many (both Russes and Poles)
heard, they assembled unto him, thinking him to be the
true Demetrii: and the Russes did so much the more
willingly draw unto him, because of the murtherers.

How others called Wors, did name and call themselves *Other Wors,*
sonnes of the slaine Emperour, as Ivan, Peter, Pheodor, *or pretenders,*
and by many and divers other names : and under the same *Ivan, Peter,*
names, did consume the State, and shead much bloud. *Pheodor.*

How the Kings sacred Majestie, comming to Smol- *The King of*
ensko, sent his Messengers the Lord of Præmislave, and *Poland.*
other noble men, who comming unto the Campe, the *The Lord of*
forenamed Wors fled away : but divers of the Russes came *Præmislave.*
unto his Majestie.   And taking counsell with the Boiarins,
at that time remayning with Suiskey in the chiefe Citie,
we sent our Messengers to his Majestie at that time, being
at Smolensko, viz. Michael Salticove, and others, request- *Michael*
ing that his Majestie would grant us his Sonne to be our *Salticove.*
Lord.

How they were dispatched away, and what answere they
brought from his Majestie, with conditions engrossed, and
signed with his hand and seale.

How that after the deposing of Suiskey, the noble *The Articles*
Lord Generall of the Kingdome, comming into Moscovia, *are before in*
concluded all the said businesses and treaties : and con- *Latin.*
firmed them with the oath of himselfe, and his fellow
Souldiers.   And that they after that oath, likewise made
their oath for the same.   Then, that for the greater defence
of the said principall Citie from the Wors, they sent
Souldiers into the Citie, and sent also their Messengers
from the whole Countrie Fidareta, the Metropolitan and

*Vasili
Galichin.*

Vasili Galichin, with others, unto the Kings Majestie, and required an oath in his Majesties behalfe, of all the severall Provinces.

How that his Majesties Souldiers dwelled and behaved themselves in this capitall Citie of Mosco, before the troubles began, without injuring any man, punishing the evill according to their deserts.

How the Boiarins handled other Gentlemen, and principall persons of the Russe Religion, although more inclined unto them: but especially the Officers and Servants of the Wors, as also such as had fled over.

It followeth, how they often sent word unto the Citie of Smolensko, and willed them to deliver up the Citie unto his Majestie, to bee under his prosperous government and power. As for the secret plots of their Messengers,

Galechin.
*Halusin a Wor
or Pretender.*

Galechin and others, they said, they were ignorant, as also of some unknowne practises, handled with the Wor called Halusin. But they said, that they had written very often to the Citie of Smolensko, and commanded them to doe whatsoever stood with his Majesties pleasure, and liked him, without further effusion of bloud.

[III.iv.789.]
*Lepun.
Saruski.*

How also it befell in the chiefe Citie to Lepun, and Sarusky, and the other Rebels, when they violated their fidelitie.

That they certified his Majesties Souldiers thereof, and that they, with them, did rise against the Rebels, and that even to this present, they doe keepe, and will keepe their oath once made, and their due obedience unto their Lord.

And, in that Lepun was punished of God for his treacherie, and departed this life with so shamefull a death, wee thinke it to bee for the good example of others, to reduce them into their former estate, to revoke others unto their fidelitie, and for keeping their oath alreadie given.

Therefore, after many circumstances, they inferred, that they would presently send their Messengers to the generall Parliament: but mooved with the perswasion of the honourable Lord Generall, to wit, that his Majestie would bee contented with their fidelitie once made, and performed under oath, and with their griefe for the same cause, and will cheerefully forgive them : and doth not refuse to give his Sonne to raigne over them. Adding withall, that many Kingdomes, to wit, the Kingdome of Hungarie, the Kingdome of Bohemia, and a great part of Russia, doe earnestly request, that he would receive them under the happy government of his Majestie : that they might enjoy the priviledges of Poland, and Litow, to which, none in the whole world can be compared.

But, because his Excellent Majestie, as a Christian Lord, rejecting all other Kingdomes, and Dominions, will graciously receive under his Rule and government the said Dominions, and that he is sorry for their destruction : he therefore now admonisheth them, if they will bee under his prosperous Rule, and enter into an union together with the Kingdome of Poland, and the great Duchy of Litow, and live friendly with them : if they will performe, and consent thereunto, His Excellent Majestie promiseth to remit their offence, and to receive them under his happy government and authoritie, and refuseth, and by no meanes will alter or change their faith and conscience, or places dedicated unto God, or builded for devotion : neither will impose on them any other Religion, or alter their ancient Manners, or Customes, but will bestow on them priviledges and offices : and that the Rights and Priviledges, which the Poles, with the great Duchy of Litow doe enjoy, shall be conferred on them : and that they shall be equalled with the Kingdome and great Duchy of Litow, &c. which jurisdictions and priviledges, in former times, their Predecessors wanted. *The King assents.*

For this perswasion therefore of the honourable Lord Generall, which he had in charge from his Majestie to make, they yeeld all thankes : but notwithstanding they propound, and plainly adde, that their oath shall be so, that his Majesties sonne shall succeed in their government, with certaine additions, to wit, that they will have none

other over them but onely his Majesties sonne, and that
the whole Land doth make it knowne, and propound their
judgement and sentence, by way of denunciation, that by
no meanes, but by offering his Majesties sonne, these
troubles of Moscovia can be extinguished. Adding
withall, that at that time, in the first troubles, when the
honourable Lord Generall came into the Country of Moscovia, and required the oath for the Kings Majesties
sonne: if his Majestie had made any mention thereof,
it is certaine, that the Commons and all the Nobilitie,
would not have consented thereunto by any meanes, and
that greater effusion of bloud had risen thereupon: And
Klutzinsky a that they had taken for their Prince Klutzinsky, called the
Wor or Wor, to whom all were not assembled, who also at that
Pretender, time had a great power of men, as well of Poles, as Russes
acknowledged and Litowes. They therefore seeing the great discord
Emperour. amongst the people, taking counsell, did freely choose for
their Lord and Emperour his Excellent Majesties sonne,
unto whom they had a great affection, and who had a
long time before layen in their hearts: assuring themselves also, that by this election of his Majesties sonne,
many troubles and dissentions would be pacified, and so
rejected the aforesaid Wor Klutzinsky: As also they
received into their chiefe Citie the chiefe Generall. But,
when it was heard that his Excellent Majestie, would by
no meanes give unto them his sonne for their Lord, and
to rule over them, they fell into such effusion of bloud
and insurrections, As also the same time, the whole
Country of Moscovia looked and expected nothing else
then his Majesties sonne. Calling to memorie, for their
better advice, that it was to be feared, least whilest his
Majestie came too late with his sonne, divers parts of
the Land should choose unto themselves severall Lords.
As to the Southward the Castles Strachen and others, to
Astracan. the King of Persia; part of Pomerland and Siberia, to
Lapland. the Kings of Denmarke and England; Novogrod, Plesco,
Ivanogrod, and others, to the King of Sweden: and that
the other Cities would choose to themselves other Lords

separate from the rest. In the meane season, they desire
his Excellent Majestie, to make a speedy end of these
warres, according to his Obligation and promise ratified
by the oath of the honorable Lord Generall, and the
whole Armie: and that his Majestie himselfe, with his
sonne, would come into Moscovia. They request also,
that his Excellent Majestie would retayne with himselfe
and his Sonne, Counsellors, and Messengers of their
Commonwealth, for the ordayning and concluding of perpetuall Conditions. They request also, that his Majestie,
in the name of his Sonne, would send unto all the Inhabitants of the Townes, and write unto the severall Cities,
signifying his comming into their Dominions, and willing, [III.iv.790.]
that out of the severall Provinces, all sorts of men send
their Messengers, to treate and conclude of the affaires
of all sorts of People, and of perpetuall tranquillitie.
Promising after the said Charge and Letters to all people
in generall, and notifying from their said Lord, that (by
Gods grace) there may bee throughout the whole Land
of Moscovia, tranquillitie, peace, and securitie.

To conclude, they pray heartily unto the Lord God, to
grant unto his Majestie in this businesse begun, a prosperous and speedy end.

Thus have wee seene dissolute resolutions, or resolute
dissolutenesse, men onely constant in inconstancy, resolved *Russian*
upon irresolution. As we often see sicke persons turning *inconstancy.*
every way, and no way eased; in the night time longing
for day, and in the day for night; such was now the Russian
sicknesse, they would and they would not, and yet would
againe, and againe would not, they scarsly knew what or
why; fluctuating in an inward storme of diversifyed hopes,
feares, desires, distracted affections, no lesse then in that
outward broile of State. For it was not long that they
looked toward Poland, whether for breach of conditions
of that part, or out of inveterate hate to the Pole, or their
Nationall jealousie and distrust of Strangers, or a naturall
inconstancy; they fell off from that Prince: and their
Chancellor (Father to the now raigning Emperour)

employed there with others in Embassage) were detayned thereupon prisoners. It is also reported that they made secret overtures to His Majestie of Great Britaine, and that Sir John Merick and Sir William Russel were therein employed: but the strong convulsions and sharpe agues and agonies of that State could not, or would not endure the lingring of such remote phisicke; the wheele of Things being whirled about before such a Treatie might admit a passage of Messengers to and fro. Once that Russian Head grew so heady and giddy, that at last it bred *Many-headed* innumerable Heads, yea the whole Body became Heads *body.* in the worst of tyrannies, a popular (government shall I say? or) confusion. Neither were Hydras heads (monstrously multiplying two for each cut off) like this: for besides so many Wor's after the first and second Demetrius (which might make up that comparison) each limbe, nay almost each haire of this Hydra (not the Nobles alone, but the basest which had nothing but themselves, and were nothing but Numbers) became so many prodigious Heads; they also like Pharaohs leane kine devouring the fat, and upon light pretences beheading themselves in cutting off the heads and nobler Persons amongst them.

Janson. A. When they had thus made away almost all the Grandes, *1612.* and left the South parts to the spoile of the Poles, which once againe were drawing neere to Mosco to besiege it; the Poles also suffered some disaster, their Souldiers mutinying for want of pay, and banding themselves to returne into Poland, there invaded the Mints and Custome-houses, and some governments, detayning them for their pay; sending also threatning Letters to divers Cities and Townes, forced divers Nobles and Plebeians to composition. The Turkes and Tartars brake likewise into Walachia, Moldavia, and Polonia, so that Zolkiewsky or Sulcosky the Generall was forced to goe against them, of whom he made so great a slaughter, that the Great Turke committed the Polake Embassadour at Constantinople to Ward, and threatned the Poles with invasion. These mutinous Souldiers continued meane while that and the next yeere to spoile Poland, doing much damage to the King and the Bishops, challenging many millions due, as they said, for pay. Yea they passed further into Prussia, and made spoile in every place, on the eight of November 1613. passing with a great prey to Thorn, being parted into three Bands, the Sapians, the Sborovians, and Smolenskians. Another companie of them terrified Silesia. The Tartars likewise made impression and committed great spoile in Podolia.

Thus an Armie divided could not conquer, nor so utterly exterminate Russia as otherwise opportunity was offered: the Pole Souldiers being herein like angry Elephants which sometime recoyle upon their owne troupes and doe more spoyle then the enemy could either have effected or expected. But whiles the Invaders were thus invaded, the Russes were forward to worke those executions on themselves, which their enemies could have wished to them; till at last awakened with the horrour of their owne evils, some began to thinke of a better course. In the North about the Dwina, a bold fellow, a Butcher, rayling at the Nobilities basenesse, and the Officers corruptions, said, if they would choose a good Treasurer and pay Souldiers well, they might have those which would fight and expell the Poles their Enemies: provided, that they would first choose a worthy Generall, for which place he recommended to them a poore maymed Gentleman, called Pozarsky, who had done good service, but being neglected, now had retyred himselfe not farre off. The multitude approved the Butchers counsell, and chose Pozarsky for their Leader, and that Butcher for a Treasurer, delivering into his hands what money they had, which he so faithfully disbursed, Pozarsky also discharging so well the trust reposed, that a great Army was gathered, and the siege of Musco thereby raysed. And joyning with Knes Demetry Mastroukswich (a kind of Tartar which commanded an Army of Cossaks in service of the Russe) they fell in consultation with Boris Liciu, the third Great Souldier of that Countrey, upon choice of an Emperour.

Gods providence permits the utter ruine of Russia.

Strange alteration of affaires by a Butcher.

Pozarsky chosen Generall, and a Butcher Treasurer.

Boris Liciu.

Their mindes herein disagreeing (some naming one, some another) some named Mastroukswich himselfe, other for
[III.iv.791.] further securitie against the Poles, and to recompence the sufferings and imprisonment of the Russian Chancellor in

Micalowich Son to the Chancellor chosen. Poland, named his young Sonne Micallowich, under whose Empire (having a good Councell appointed) they might live happily. This was first approved by the Cossaks, and then by the other Armies, the Butcher also was taken to become a Counsellor, and those three Leaders aforesaid were made Militarie Commanders for the present Emperour against the Poles. Embassadours also were sent to divers Princes to mediate betwixt them and the Pole, and betwixt them and the Sweden; and by his Majestie of Great Brittaine (whom God long preserve to reigne over us) his countenance and intercession, there hath beene some agreement, and the young Emperour hath

Our Kings mediation. setled his Dominions in peace, making at last a truce for fourteene yeeres with the Poles, obtayning also in that
His Fathers returne and Patriarkship. Treatie his Father the Chancellour his libertie and returne out of Poland, who since is consecrated Patriarke of Russia.

His Embassadour to the Emperour came to Lintz in December 1613. and thence was conveighed by the Emperours Officers to the Court, where hee had solemne audience, where after rich presents of Furres and his
Janson. Letters, he delivered his speech, that Michael Phedorowich was now by unanimous consent advanced to the Russian Empire, and willing to entertayne and continue the ancient confederacie betwixt both Empires: desiring the Imperiall Majestie to dehort the Pole from his unjust attempts, to deliver the Russe Captives, and not againe to infest the recovered Musco, but to enter into peace, and abstayne from Christian bloudshed. Likewise to send an Embassadour to his Court, &c. This mediation Cæsar promised, and gave the Embassadour liberall entertainment, and gentle dispatch.

Not long after in May 1614. the Russian Embassadour had audience with the States of the United Provinces at

Hage; and before that in England. I was present both at his arrivall at Gravesend, and his honourable entertaynment into London, and saw him also presently after the running at Tilt at White-hall, the foure and twentieth of March, admitted to his Majesties presence, performing that Russian Rite of bowing with his face downe to or neere the ground, &c.

Anno 1615. The Turkish Embassador treated with the Cæsarean Majestie about the mediation betwixt the Pole and the Muscovite, who employed to that purpose Erasmus Heidel and the Baron of Dohn. The Pole notwithstanding sent an Army in his Sonnes challenge (who was shortly to follow to Smolensko) into Muscovia; Pontus Tellagard the Sweden Commander infesting also the Russians at the same time. But the next yeere 1616. Sir John Merike Knight, a man of great experience in those Northerne parts, was employed his Majesties Embassadour to negotiate betwixt those two Great Princes, the Moscovite and the Sweden, the Articles of whose composition I obtayned by the mediation of Sir Thomas Smith (my ancient Benefactor in this kind) and have here communicated to thee, but in another Chapiter as being now past our Tragicke Thunders: as also the following Russe-China Newes, that you may see not only the face of Russia washed from her bloudy pollutions, but her hands further then ever extended (fortunate in treaty of Commerce) as far as China: likewise the Russe Patent to the English. Sweet is the name of Peace, and the thing it selfe a Heaven upon Earth. Blessed are the Peacemakers (His Majesties word else-where, here his deed) for they shall be called (said the only begotten Son) the Children of God; even the God of peace will make them his heires of Heaven, which (models of Deity) seeke to establish the peace of God upon Earth. And let it not seeme tedious here to present these His Majesties Travels, amongst our other Travellers, but in a more glorious manner (liker to God unmoveable which moveth all things) who hath not only been our Sunne, and with

Sir J. Merikes negotiation. Sir Dudley Digs was also sent Embassador in a troublesome time, when he could not with safetie passe up to Mosco for the enemie, in the first times of Micalowich.

lightsome heate and influence filled our Brittish Hemisphere, but hath dispersed his bright rayes of Light, and
warmed with sweet quickning beames of heat, those
remoter frozen Climates of Sweden ,and Russia, (not to
mention, or but to mention the quarrels of Denmarke and
Sweden) and after their long frostie Night (such is the
nature, such was the state of those States) to reduce the
faire day-light of Peace, the warmth whereof hath thawed
the Icie hardned hearts of Enmity, and filled all things with
sweets, and cheere of a returning Spring. Nulla salus
bello, pacem te poscimus omnes.

[III.iv.792.]

Chap. X.

A briefe Copie of the points of the Contracts
betweene the Emperours Majestie, and the
Kings Majestie of Sweden: at Stolboua the
seven and twentieth of February, 1616.

*Oblivion of
former
quarrels.*

INprimis, and especially that all matters
be set aside, forgotten, pacified, and
renounced, which passed these former
yeeres since the conclusion of peace at
Taffina in the yeere 7003. betweene the
former great Lords, Emperours, and great
Dukes of all Russia, and afterwards our

*Michaelo
Pheodorowich
Emperor of
Russia.*

great Lord, Emperour and great Duke Michaelo Phedorowich of all Russia Sam. his Imperiall Majestie, and Empire
of Russia; and betweene their late high, mightie Lord
King Charles the Ninth of Sweden, the above named
Kings Majesties highly honored and beloved Father,

*Gustavus
Adolphus
King of
Sweden.*

especially their high mighty Lord King Gustavus Adolphus
of Sweden, his Kingly Majesty and the Crowne of
Sweden: As also both the Princes their Dominions, Lands,
Cities, and people, chance or hap of the Subjects, which
happened or was done by robbery, burning, killing, or
other enmities whatsoever might bee, or by whom it was
done, that all those griefes and troubles in all matters shall

256

be set aside, and hereafter not be revenged or remembred of neither party, for ever and by this present strong conclusion of peace betwixt our great Lord Emperour and great Duke Michaelo Pheodorowich of all Russia, Sam. and betwixt their great mightie Lord, King Gustavus Adolphus of Sweden, &c. and of other Dominions, Lands, Castles, aswell those of old, as those which by this conclusion of peace are given and yeelded up, and betwixt all the Subjects and people to bee renewed, established, confirmed and held unremoveable in the manner of a peace for ever and ever; and sure friendship perpetually: Also that the Emperours Majesty, and the Kings Majesty shall desire one anothers best in all matters, and neyther seeke a better friend, but to deale faithfully and truly in all matters reciprocally.

2. Item, is given unto our great Lord Emperour and great Duke Michaelo Pheodorowich of all Russia, Sam. his heires, successors and hereafter comming great Lords, Emperors, and great Dukes of all Russia, and the Empire thereof, by their great Lord King Gustavus Adolphus of Sweden; for himselfe, his successors, and hereafter being Kings of Sweden, and for the whole Crowne of Sweden, doth deliver and cleere by the power of this conclusion of peace, these Castles of the Empire in Russia with the Townes and Suburbs which were taken in these yeeres, namely, great Novogrod, Stararousse, Porcove, Lodiga, *Great Novo-* Odo, with their Territories, Somerskey, Volost, with the *grod, &c.* Villages belonging to the Emperors Houshold, to Metro- *returned to the* polie, Monasteries, Gentlemens Lands, Inheritances, *Russe.* Farmes, with all their profits and revenues according to former Borders and Limits, except those Castles which the Emperours Majestie doth yeeld by power of this Contract of peace, as hereafter more certainly shall be exprest.

3. Item, The Kings Majestie of Sweden doth give unto the Emperours Majestie, with the aforesaid Castles and Townes, all manner of Church ornaments which are in the *Churches* Church of Sophia, The Sapience of God, and within all *restored with* Churches and Monasteries in Novogrod, and in other *&c.* *their goods,*

Castles and Townes which the Kings Majesty hath given
to the Emperours Majesty without carrying any thing
away. Also the Kings Majesty doth give the Metropolite
and all the Spiritualtie, with all their goods, as also all
manner of Russe people what calling soever they be, which
are in those Townes, Castles, and Territories, dwelling
now or planting themselves there with their Wives,
Children, and all their goods whatsoever any hath. As
also the Kings Majesty shall give all manner of Writings
and Bookes, which are in those Castles and Townes to be
found in Roserades judgement houses, or elsewhere with
all Russe Ordnance, Munition, and Provisions there
belonging, and the Bells in those aforesaid Castles and
Townes, in such manner as they were the twentieth of
November last past, according to agreement made with
the Kings most excellent Majesty of Great Britaines
Sir J. Merike Ambassadour Sir John Merick, except those Bells which
Ambassador. the people of Novogrod themselves did sell after that
agreement, for the payment of Souldiers, and were carried
away from Novogrod, but those Bells which the Kings
servants and people did take perforce without buying, shall
be in right manner sought out and brought backe againe
to Novogrod and restored there. Also which Bells the
Kings Majesties people bought at Novogrod, it shall bee
free for the Novogrod men to redeeme them backe againe
at the same price they sold them for, and the Kings people
hereafter shall not buy any more Bells of the people of
Novogrod by no meanes whatsoever.

4. Item, the Kings Majesties people of Sweden, at
their departure out of the Emperours Majesties Castles
and Towns aforesaid, namely, great Novogrod, Stararouse,
Porcove, Lodiga, Somersko, Volosco, &c. shall use no
Libertie of violence to the Emperors Majesties people by burning,
persons. robbing, or killing, neyther carry any Russe people with
them to the Kings Majesties side, neither men, nor women,
nor children, nor any of their goods: and if any goods
remayne of the Swethish people, at their going out of the
aforesaid Towne, which at that time they cannot take all

258

with them, such goods shall be kept in safetie by those
with whom they are left, till such time as every one of
them shall come thither for his owne goods, or send some
bodie for them, and these people shall have free libertie to
goe without all molestation or let, to come for their goods,
and to returne againe at their owne convenient time.

5. Item, the Kings Majesties Governours and Officers [III. iv. 793.]
shall deliver unto the Emperours Majesties Voyavodes
and Commanders the above named Townes and Castles,
to say great Novogrod, Stararouse, Porcove, with their
Territories, and Somerskey, Volost in presence of the great
Gentlemen, the which the above said great Ambassadour
Sir John Merike Knight, &c. or the said Kings Majesties
Gentlemen, the which the above said great Ambassadour
shall send to that end clensing and giving over the said
Castles and Townes, two weekes after this contract is con-   *Time of*
firmed betweene us both, great Commissionors by   *deliverie.*
Writings, Hand, Seale, and Kissing of the Crosse of our
side, and on their part, by oath upon the holy Evangelists.

6. And after that the Castle of Lodiga and Territories,
shall bee delivered to the Emperours Majesties Messengers
by the Kings Majesties Governour, three weekes after the
confirmation of this contract, in presence of the abovesaid
great Lords, James King, &c. his Gentlemen, which to
that purpose the great Ambassadour shall send, then the
said Castle and Province to be redeemed and given up,
with all the Russe Ordinance, people thereto belonging,
none to be carried away, nor no violence to bee offered
them by robbing, or otherwise spoyling of them; nor no
Russe Ordnance to bee carried away. But the Castle of
Odow, and Province, and people is to remayne on the   *Odow to*
Kings Majesty Gustavus Adolphus of Sweden, for a time,   *remayne*
till this contract of peace be confirmed by both the   *cautionary.*
Potentates, by their Writings, by the Emperours Majesty
with the Seale of the Empire, and by the Kings Majesties
hand and Seale of the Kingdome of Sweden, as also by
the Emperours Majesties kissing of the Crosse, and the
Kings Majesties Oath upon the holy Evangelists con-

firmed, and the borders divided and measured out justly. And the Ambassadour which both the Princes shall send to that effect having beene with both the Princes shall returne againe to the borders, having well concluded the busines, as then two weeks after that time the Emperors Majesties Voyavodes and Commanders, which his Majestie shall send for the receiving of the said Castle and Province of Odow from Vlasquo shall receive the said from the Kings Majesties Governours, with all the Russe people and Ordnance with all their goods, and what they have, and as long as the Castle of Odow is on the Kings Majesties side, all the people of Odow and the Province thereof shall give unto the Kings Majesty their former Corne, and doe service as before for the mayntayning of those Souldiers that remayne there, the Kings Majesties people in the meane time shall do to those people of Odow no violence nor robbery, neyther carry any Russe people, or Ordnance from thence, nor cause any to be conveighed away.

Charles Philip Prince of Sweden not to lay clayme.   7. Item, the Kings Majestie G. A. &c. best beloved brother Prince Charles Phillip, Prince hereditarie of S. &c. shall hereafter lay no claime or challenge to these Castles, and Townes, namely great Novogrod, Porcove, Stararouse, Somerskey, Volost, Odow, Ladogo, and all their confines, borders and Provinces; nor come upon them with no manner of Warre, to seeke to attaine them: nor remember any more that oath which formerly the people of those places made to the Prince C. Ph. Also the Kings Majestie G.A. shall promise not to give any aide of men or money to his abovesaid Brother C.Ph. against the aforesaid Castles and Townes in no wise.

Zar or Czar, is a Title of the great Duke.   8. And against or in lew of the above said our great Lord Emperor, and great D.M.F. of all Russia, Sam. &c. for himselfe, his successours, and hereafter being great Lords, Zares, and great Dukes of all Russia, &c. and for the whole Empire of all Russia, &c. especially, for the dominion of Novogrod the great, hath given and yeelded unto their high mighty Lord King G.A. of S. &c. from the dominion of Novogrod, from himselfe and the whole *Places yeelded* Empire of Russia, especially in respect of love and friend- *by the* ship, these Castles, Forts, and Land, following, which here- *Muscovite to the Sweden.* tofore did adjoyne to the Dominions of Novogrod, as namely Evanogrod, Yam, Coporea, Orieseke, with all unto them adjoyning, Townes, Lands, and Provinces, with all Townes, and Villages in the Countrey to them belonging, and due unto them, according to their former, just, and auncient borders, with the people that dwell, and plant themselves there, with all other profits, revenewes; and paiments, with the shoares of Rivers, with Lakes, nothing exempted, the Emperours Majestie hath yeelded, and given to their Kings Majestie, G.A. of Sweden &c. as proper and owne to him and his Majesties successours, and hereafter being Kings of Sweden, and to the Crowne of Sweden for an everlasting propertie for them to hold, without cavillation or any contradiction, by the Emperours Majestie, or his Majesties Successours, or hereafter being Emperours, and great Dukes of all Russia, as also by the whole Empire of Russia, and from the Dominion of Novogrod, for everlasting times, in all points, as former great Lords, and great Dukes of all Russia, held and kept the same ; namely the late, of blessed memory, great Lord Emperour, and great Duke Evan Vasiliwich, of all Russia, Sam. and the great Lord Emperour, and great Duke, Pheodor Evanowich of all Russia, Sam. and the spiritualty, as Monkes, and all others in those Castles and Townes, as well Gentlemen, as other inhabitants of the said places, two weekes after the conclusion of this contract, when it shall be revealed unto them, they shall have free libertie, all such as desire to goe to the Emperours Majesties side, with their wives, children, families, all goods and chattels, which way soever they will into the Emperours Majesties Lands and Townes. And that all Russe people, in the said Castles, Forts, and Townes, might know the same : it is here agreed and concluded, that as soone as the con-clusion of this peace shall be effected and confirmed betwixt us both, the great Potentates great Commissioners

shall send their Posts and Messengers into all the afore-
named Townes and Castles, which they in presence of the
Lord King James his great Ambassadours, Messengers,
shall openly reveale and proclaime, that all spiritualty, with
their goods, Courtiers, Gentlemen, Burgesses, and Townes-
[III.iv.794.] men, which are desirous to goe from thence within two
weeks after to the Emperors Majesties side, they shall
have libertie to go from thence with their wives, children,
families, all their goods, and chattles, and none of them
to leave any thing behinde them against their wil, neither
to be staied nor violated by the Kings Majesties people;
but moreover, to have convoys and prestaves, to bring
them without all feare or wrong to the Emperours
Majesties next borders, in such manner that they be
neither robbed nor killed, but especially and certainely, it
is concluded and agreed on betweene us both sides great
Commissioners, that all Russe Countrie Priests, and
Husbandmen in the said Townes and Countries which are
given and yeelded by the Emperours Majestie, shall by
no manner of meanes be inticed or carried from thence, but
shall remaine there with their wives, children, and familie,
under the Sweths Crowne, as also all Courtiers, Gentlemen, and Burgesses, which doe not remove from thence,
in the foresaid two weekes.

9. As also from the Emperours Majestie, great Lord
and great Duke M. F. of all Russia, Sam. &c. the Kings
Money to be given to the Sweden. Majestie, &c. shall have 20000. rubbles, in ready good
current unchangeable Silver deynings, and those monies
immediately as soone as this contract of peace shall be
concluded and confirmed betweene us, shall be given to
the Kings Majestie of Sweden great Commissioners by the
great Embassadour of the Kings most excellent Majestie
of great Brittaine his great Ambassadour Sir John Merricke, Knight.

Ordnance and Munition to remaine. 10. And as for the Russe Ordnance in these Castles
which shall be given to our Lord Emperour, and great
Duke, &c. from the Kings Majestie G.A. &c. which
Ordnance shall remaine there, shall be given to his

Majesties Officers, and what munition of Artillerie, as provision for Warres, and Bels, and other matters, which their Kings Majestie hath taken in the Land of Russia out of those Castles, before the contract which the Kings Majesties great Commissioners, and the great Lord King James &c. great Ambassadour Sir John Merricke, Knight, did erect, as the twentieth of November, such Ordnance and provisions shall remaine to the Kings Majesties use, and Crowne of Sweden, without all contradiction or cavilation.

11. And because the late great Lord Emperour, and great Duke Vasilly Evanowich of all Russia, Sam. did give and confirme by writings, unto their high, mighty, late Lord, King Charles the ninth of S. &c. and to the Crowne of Sweden the Castle Corela, and the Province thereof, for that faithfull and good willing aide which was done unto him, against the Polish people : in like manner doth confirme, and establish the same by this contract of our great Lord Emperour, and great Duke M.F. &c. the same yeelding and donation of the great Lord Zare, and great Duke Vasily Evanowich, &c., for himselfe, his successours, and hereafter being Emperours, and great Dukes of all Russia, and for the whole Empire of all Russia, that the said Castle of Coreila, with all profits, revenewes, and rents, by Land and by Water, according to their former auncient, and now being borderers, nothing exempted in all, accordingly as it was by former Emperours, and great Dukes of all Russia, as they possest and held it, so hereafter it shall remaine to their Kings Majestie, G.A. of S. &c. and to his Majesties Successours, and hereafter following Kings of Sweden, and the Crown of Sweden, without all cavillation or contradiction for everlasting times. *The contract of V. E. for Corelia and the Territories, confirmed to Sweden.*

12. And that hereafter there be no more difficulty or variance concerning the borderers of the Land, it is concluded and agreed upon, that in this yeare 7125. upon the first of June, our great Lord Emperour, and great Duke M.F. &c. and their high, mighty King G.A. &c.

shall send on both sides, speciall good Courtiers, and
Notaries, to meete between Lodiga and Oreseke, at the
mouth of the River Lava, whence it doth fall into the
Lake of Lodiga, so that they shall meete upon the said
River, on the midst of the Bridge, which of both sides
their people shall make upon that River, and when there
the one shall have shewed the other their ample Commis-
sions, and shall appeare that they are worthy to measure
out the borders thereby, betweene the Emperours
Majestie, and the Kings Majesties Lands : so that from
the borders of Novogrod, Lodiga, and Odow, with their
Provinces, and also from Somerskey, Volost, be devided
from the auncient and former precincts, and borders of
Oreseeke, Copora, Yam and Evanogorod, in just manner
as it ought to be, at the same time next ensuing the first
day of June, then the said Courtiers and Notaries, three
in presence in the said manner on both sides, shall meete
together upon the borders of Novogrod, betweene the
Province of Olimets and Corela at Salomensky Towne, by
the Lake of Lodiga ; which Courtiers also shall view the
same Provinces according to the former borders, and as the
former are exprest, how they have bin, and confirme the
same, and if they so chance, that they cannot happen upon
the former auncient borders, then shall they, by just
inquisition, make new borders and Land-markes, in such
manner, that hereafter there be no further controversie
concerning those borders, and those Courtiers or Gentlemen shall not part asunder of neither side, till they have
sufficiently and friendly ended that businesse in all manner,
and what those Courtiers shall finish and effect in this
manner, the same according as befitteth there shall expresse
by writing upon parchment on both sides, and confirme
the same by their subscription, Seales, kissing of the
Crosse, and oath interchangeable : and as concerning the
deviding of borders, and the Gentlemen shall doe it, as
namely of Novogrod, Lodiga, Odo, Somerskey, Volost, of
one part, and also betweene Oreseke, Copora, Yam, and
Evanogorod, on the other side, and also betweene the

borders of Novogrod and Corela, shall be set downe and written, the same shall be inremoveable and fast for ever-lasting times, by our great Lord Emperour, and great Duke Michall Fedorowich of all Russia, &c. and the Kings Majestie Gustavus Adolphus, &c. and their successours, and hereafter being on both sides, for everlasting times, according to this contract of an everlasting peace: and for [III.iv.795.] more firme confirmation of the same, that it shall be held and kept; it shall be declared further in the Letters of contract, which shall be hereafter given betweene both Princes, from the Emperours Majestie, by kissing the Crosse, and confirmation of his said Letters by his great Seale, and by the Kings Majesties oath upon the holy Evangelists.

13. As also the former, of blessed and most famous memory, great Lord Emperour, and great Duke Fedor Evanowich of all Russia, Sam. our great Lord Emperour, and great Duke Michall Fedorowich, of all Russia, Sam. &c. Unckle in conclusion of peace made at Tavsin, in the yeare 7103. did yeelde and give over all his pretention and claime to the Countrey of Leifland, as also the great Lord Emperour, and great Duke Vasily Evanowich, of all Russia, Sam. in a conclusion of peace made at Wyburgh, in the yeare 7117, did renounce the same; so it is now here concluded and agreed, that our great Lord Emperour, and great Duke M.F. &c. and his successours, and here-after being Emperours and great Dukes, shall at no time for ever challenge unto themselves any right, or pretence to the Countrey of Leifland; neither shall our great Lord Emperour and great Duke M.F. of all Russia, Sam. nor his successours, great Lords, Emperours, and great Dukes of all Russia, hereafter write unto their great Lord, King Gustavus Adolphus, nor his successours hereafter, being Kings of Sweden, nor to the Crowne of Sweden, with the title of Leifland, or those Castles which the Emperours Majestie hath now renounced to the Kings Majestie for ever, neither by Letters of confirmation to write them-selves, or name themselves in them, nor suffer his

The title of Leifland resigned by V. E. at Wiburgh, Anno 7117. now confirmed.

Voyavodes, Servants and Commanders, to write themselves with the title of Leifland, or the Townes aforesaid, neither in writing nor speeches, to name themselves. As also our great Lord Emperour, and great Duke M.F. of all Russia, Sam. his successours, and hereafter being great Lord Emperour, and great Duke of all Russia, in their writings and speeches, shall give to their Kings Majestie, and hereafter being Kings of Sweden, their accustomed title of Leifland, and Corella. Item, on both sides, the great Commissioners have agreed, since at this Treatie we could not accord upon the full title of both the great Potentates; As to intitle the Emperours Majestie, and of many other Dominions, Lord and Conquerour, and the Kings Majestie, with the title of Ingermanland, wee have of both sides great Commissioners, referred the same to both great Potentates liking therein; and if that either *Title to be given.* Potentate will be pleased to write the other with the full title, as to the Emperours Majestie, the Kings Majestie doth write the full title with the word Conquerour; and that the Emperours Majestie also doe write to the Kings Majestie his full title with Ingermanland, then both the Potentates are to send those titles by their Ambassadours, and nominate the same full title in one of their Letters of confirmation, and the other Letter to be written according to this our present agreement: and if in both the Letters, the titles be written to the full as the Emperours Majesties full title, with Conquerour, and the Kings Majestie with Ingermanland, then both sides Ambassadours shall shew one the other the said Letters, and having shewen them, shall goe to each Prince with the same; if then on either side the Potentate shall not like thereof, and shall send the said Letters of confirmation with the short title, according to this our present agreement: the Ambassadours of both sides shall in like manner make knowne the same one to the other, and so proceede therewith to both Potentates.

Commerce of Trade. 14. Also it is agreed and concluded, that there shall be free commerce of Trade betweene both the great King-

domes, the Empire of Russia, and the Kingdome of
Swethen, and both Kingdomes subjects: so that all the
subjects of our great Lord Emperour, and great Duke
Michael Fedorowich, of all Russia, Sam. Merchants of
the Dominions of Russia, from Novogrod, Plesco, and
other Cities and Townes, paying their due custome, shall
have free liberty without let to trafficke at Stockholme,
Wiburgh, Revell, Narve, and other Townes in the Countries of Swethland, Fynland, and Leifland, and they that
dwell and plant themselves at Ivangrod, Yam, Copora,
Nettingburgh, and Coreilla, what Nation soever, either
Russe or other people, shall have free liberty without let
to trafficke, and to trade, paying their due custome, in the
right Custome houses, at Mosco, Novogrod, Plesco,
Lodiga, and other Townes of Russia, with the Emperours
Majesties subjects, and also have libertie to travell through
the Dominions of our great Lord Emperor, and great
Duke M.F. &c. for their trade of Merchandize within the
Dominions of Russia.

15. And by reason heretofore our great Lord Emperour
and great Duke Michall Phedorowich, of all Russia, &c.
his Majesties subjects Merchants, had their free house of *Merchants of*
merchandize at Revell, also now by contract of Tavsin and *both Kingdoms*
Wiburgh, it is concluded they should have a good place *to have houses*
for a house, appointed them in Revell, as also in other the *in each others*
Kings Majesties Townes, as at Stockholme, and Wyburgh, *Countries.*
they shall have house and Divine Service, according to
their Religion, in the said houses, without let or hinderance, but at Revell in their Church, as formerly they have
done; yet to set up no Church, according to their Religion.
And as heretofore their Kings Majesties his Subjects have
had a free house of trade at Novogrod, now also according
to the contract of Tavsina, and Wyburgh, they are to
have a good place for a house, prepared them at Novogrod,
and the Emperours Majesties other Cities, at Mosco and
Plesco, house for the said purpose, and use their Divine
Service according to their Religion, in the house; but to
build no Churches for that use any where.

For brevitie, I have omitted the following Articles to
the 29. the substance whereof is as followeth. The 16.
determineth what debts shall be recoverable. The 17.
Free passage of Subjects thorow each others Territories.
18. Freedome of Prisoners, on both sides. 19. Liberty of
Inhabitants to stay in the places surrendred. 20. Fugi-
[III.iv.796.] tives to be redelivered. 21. Borderers to be restrained
from robberies. 22. For ending of quarrels, if any
happen. 23. 24. Confirmation of former contracts, of
Tawsina and Wiburge. 25. No private or publike practise
to be made against each other. 26. Shewing of Letters
of confirmation at the meeting of Ambassadours of both
sides. 27. Honorable convoy for Ambassadours on either
part. 28. And also for Interpreters free passage.

29. Item, It is agreed and concluded, that if by the
permission and pleasure of God, there happen an alteration
of government in Sweden or Russia, then that Prince
which shall newly come to his government first, shall
New Ambas- reveale by his Ambassador to the other Prince from him-
sadors in case selfe, and after that the other shall visit him by his
of new Ambassadour.
successors.

30. Item, If it so fall out at any time, that of both sides
the Princes, as our great Lord, &c. & their great Lord
King Gustavus Adolphus shall send one to the other their
great Ambassadours, to confer of good matters, then those
said great Ambassadours upon the borders shall meet with-
Place of out all controversie or strife, either betweene Odow and
Ambassadors Evangorod; or betweene Lodiga and Oreseke, where they
meeting. shall thinke most fitting for them on both sides, in the
midst of the division of the borders, and there to conferre
of these good matters in friendly and loving sort, eyther
by the Princes Commission or other commandement, as
they shall have.

31. Item, If it happen that the Emperours Majesties
Subjects and Merchants, their Boates, Lodies, and Merchants Vessels shall go to Revell, Wybourgh, or other
Townes and Castles of Swethen, Fynland or Liefland, or
ships and other Vessels, whereupon the Emperours

Majesties Ambassadours and Messengers shall be going to the Emperors Majestie, to the Pope, into England, or any other Kingdome, by the Kingdome of Swethen, or comming backe againe bee cast away and brought to the Swethish shoare, eyther upon the Salt Sea or the Lake of Lodiga, by tempests or other meanes, such people shall have free libertie without hinderance to goe from thence with all the goods they can save or shall get saved, and the Kings Majesties people shall helpe them to save their goods. In like manner if it happen with the Kings Majestie Gustavus Adolphus of Swethen, &c. Subjects, and Merchants Boats, and Merchants Vessels with Commodities, or otherwise be cast away and brought to the Emperors Majesties shoare upon the Ladigo or Plesco Lake, then these people shall have free liberty to goe away with all their goods which they can save or get to be saved without let or hinderance, and the Emperors Majesties people shall helpe them to save their goods.

Case of Shipwracke.

32. Item, It is concluded and agreed on, that our great Lord, &c. shall not ayde or assist against the Kings Majesty of Sweden Gustavus Adolphus, and the Crowne of Swethland, the Kingdome of Poland and Lettow, nor his Sonne Ladislaus and the Crowne of Poland, and the Dukedome of Lettow, nor all the Dominions of Poland and Lettow, nor shall helpe him with men or treasure, nor stand for him as one himselfe, nor any other Prince for him shall not practise or seeke any thing against the King of Sweden. Those Lands and Castles which belongeth to the Kingdome of Sweden of old, or those which now the Emperours Majesty hath yeelded to the Kings Majesty by this conclusion of peace, he shall not seeke to get them under him, or have possession of them. In like manner the Kings Majesty of Sweden shall not stand against the Emperours Majesty &c. to assist the King of Poland and Lettow, and all the Dominions of Poland and Lettow, neyther with men nor treasure, and not to be with him as one. Neyther shall the Kings Majesty by himselfe or other Princes and Governours seeke any practise against

Neither party to aide the Pole, &c.

the Emperours Majestie and his Lands and Castles which belong to the Emperour of Russia, hee shall by no meanes seeke to get under him or possesse the same. It is also agreed and concluded betweene us, that those Ambassadours which the Emperours Majesty shall send to the Kings Majesty, and the Kings Majesty to the Emperours Majesty for the confirmation of this conclusion of peace, shall have full authority to conferre betweene the Emperours Majesty and the Kings Majesty of Swethland for a union and joynt assistance against Sigismond King of Poland, and the Crowne of Poland, and the great Dukedome of Lettow in such manner as shall be thought fit and requisite by both the Princes.

Confirmation. 33. And for more certaine and firme assurance, that all this here hath bin concluded, and agreed on betweene us the above said Emperours Majestie, and Kings Majesties great, ample, and powerfull Ambassadours, by the mediation and intercession of the great Lord King James his Majesties great Ambassadour, in his presence, this conclusion is made, established, and finished, and shall by our great Lord, and great Duke M.F. of all Russia, Sam. and by his successours, and hereafter being great Lords, Emperours, and great Dukes, be kept faithfully, firmely, and unmoveable, and shall be followed in all points, and finished without all falshood or deceipt: and our great Lords, Emperours, and great Dukes, &c. by his command-
Names of the ment, wee his great Commissioners, Ocholvech and
Commis- Namestincke of Susdall Knese Dannyll Evanowich
sioners. Mezetskey. I the Emperours Majesties Dwarenni and Namestincke of Shatskey Olexsey Evanowich Zuzen. I the Emperours Majesties Duke, Michcola, Meketesin Novokseno. I the Emperours Majesties Duke, Dobrenia Semenov, have confirmed this conclusion of peace, with the kissing of the Crosse, and thereunto set our hands and Seales: also the Kings Majesties of great Brittaines great Ambassadour, Sir John Merricke Knight, Gentleman of his Majesties privie Chamber, for the more witnessing of the same, that this is also concluded here betweene us,

hath firmed with his owne hand and Seale, both these obligations, and a confirmation, which wee the Emperours Majesties ample Ambassadours, have given to the Kings Majesties great Commissioners; and against that we have taken the like writing of confirmation, from the Kings Majesties great Ambassadours. Written at Stalbo, in [III.iv.797.] the yeare from the creation of the World 7125. the seven and twentieth day of February.

HAving here presented the fruits of his Majesties mediation betwixt the Muscovite and Sweden: I thought good also to adde this other testimonie of Beati Pacifici, in the peaceable fruits of his endevours betwixt the said King of Sweden, and the King of Denmarke, after bloudy warres betwixt them, in which the English voluntaries were so great a part: of whom (if I mistake not) foure thousand served the Dane, under the command of the right honorable the Lord Willoughby. The Articles of agreement betwixt them are these six, concluded January 16. 1613. translated out of the Dutch Copie, Printed at Copenhagen first, and after at Hamburge.

1. That the King of Sweden shall have againe the Citie of Calmar, with all that belongeth unto it, excepting Artillery, which shall be restored to the King of Denmarke, or to be sold for his profit.

2. That the King of Denmarke shall have Elsborch and Orland, with all the forces and strength of Arensborch, in pawne, for the space of twelve yeares ensuing, for the sum of fifteene Ton of Gold; the which sum of money the King of Sweden shall pay unto the King of Denmark within the foresaid twelve yeares, at certaine times, in consideration of his charges during the said warres.

3. That the Navigation and passages by Seas and Land to Norway shall be used free without any hinderance of those of Sweden.

4. That Lapland shall be free without giving of any contribution.

5. That the King of Denmarke shall have Grone-land free, without paying of any contribution unto the King of Sweden.

6. That the King of Denmarke shall beare the three Crownes without any gaine-saying or contradiction of the King of Sweden (which was the first and principall cause of these aforesaid bloudy and unneighbourly warres, and continuall irruptions.) Both Kings subscribing hereto.

Chap. XI.

A relation of two Russe Cossacks travailes, out of Siberia to Catay, and other Countries adjoyning thereunto. Also a Copie of the last Patent from the Muscovite. A Copie of a Letter written to the Emperour from his Governours out of Siberia.

O our Lord Emperour and great Duke Michailo Fedrowich of all Russia, your Majesties Vassals, Evan Koorakin, and Evan Koboolitin, doe knocke their heads, &c. Lord this present 7127. yeere (or 1619) we writ unto your Majestie by a Cozack of Tobolsko, Clement Oboshkin, that there were come to Tobolsko Ambassadours out of the Dominions of Catay, and from the King of Altine, with the people of Tobolsko. Evashko Petlin, and Andrashko Madiegene: And with them together doe go to you great Lord Ambassadours, out of the Dominions of Labin, and the Altine Char, from Skiugia with presents, the which we dispatcht to your Majestie, with Burnash Nikonove, the sixt of July, and before them wee dispatcht to your Majestie Evashko Pettlin and Patoy Kizall, by whom we sent unto your Majestie a Letter from Tambur, King of Cathay, and a Copie of the King Altines Letter translated, with a Card and description of the places, which way Evashko Petlin, & Andrushko Madigene, passed

Ambassadour from Catay and from the King of Altine. See sup. pag. 527. *& 552.*

from the Castle of Tomao, into the Dominions of Catay, as also in what other Dominions they were. The Letter it selfe which came from Altine Char, Labatharshan doth carrie to your Majestie: but as for the Letter out of Catay, there is none in Tobolsko to translate it.

None able to translate the China Characters.

The Copie of the Altine Chars, or golden Kings Letter to the Emperour of Russia.

TO the Lord Emperour and great Duke: The golden King received your Letter. In former times (Lord) it came to my hearing, that your Princely good Ambassadours, did seeke a way or passage to come to me, since which time it is now thirteene yeeres, but then the people of Iskirgi, Tubents, Mattara, & black Kolmaks did not suffer your Princely good Ambassadors to come to me, but did rob and spoile them. Now since ten of your Majesties people are come to me, and I have sent to you Ichkmen Kichenga, to do obeysance unto your Majesty, and see your Princely eyes, whom your Majestie vouchsafed to doe their obeysance and see your Princely eyes. And to me you sent of your Grace three Cups of Silver, a Bow, a Sword, two Gunnes, and two Garment Clothes, all which your Princely favours I have received, and what shall bee behovefull for your Majesty from hence, I will furnish you withall: As also I am to request your Majestie in respect the Ambassadours doe passe betweene us very miserably, and poore, by reason there are now some small warres betwixt us and the blacke Kolmacks, and there are but small forces in Tobolsko Castle, and in the Castles of Tomuo, Tarko, and from the Barban people. Now if so be your Majestie will favour me, and defend me with these people from Karakula; and will bee pleased to proceed on warre on your owne side, and I on mine, that matter will bee done betweene us; and all good matters continue betwixt us. And so by your Princely favour, Ambassadors may continually passe betweene us. Ivan Tarchan Varchies and Andrei Tarchan Varchies, did

[III. iv. 798.]
Easterne Tartar Nations.

Russian Presents.

conduct two of your Majesties Messengers into the Dominions of Catay, according to your Majesties commandement, and they are returned to me againe out of Catay. Also (Lord) there is come unto me the Tarchan *Tarchan of* of Labaia, and I have sent unto you with my Presents the *Labaia.* said Tarchan Labar and Kitibacshii Anchaii, and with them ten men, and two men of Sirgos; in their Letter is written *Sirgos.* that there is sent unto your Majestie three Leopards with *Three* their clawes, an Irbish with his clawes, three Lizernes with *Leopards, &c.* their clawes, a red and a yellow Damaske upon a gold *for a Present.* ground, a piece of Velvet, and an ambling Horse. And I am humbly to request your Majestie, if it bee your *His requests.* Majesties favour to grace mee for your owne honour with a garment of cloth of Gold, and of divers colours, five Garments of fine Cloth, a Head-piece, a shirt of Male, a Sword, a Bow, twentie Gunnes, a Flaggon of Gold, a Kettle of Silver, and five sorts of Precious Stones, of each one, a Jennet, a Dwarfe, and Workmen to make Guns and Powder, and two thousand pence. Your Majesties name is growne renowmed and famous every where, therefore I doe reverence unto your Majestie, because many Kings of many Countreyes have spread abroad the fame of your Majesties name every-where. And I request that Ambassadours may speedily passe betwixt us, and now if it be your Majesties favour, I desire you to dispatch these my Ambassadours with speed to me backe againe.

Relation of Anno 7128. the three and twentieth of September in *two Russe* the Emperours Dominions at Soldota, a Cazacke of *travellers of* Siberia, called Evashko Pettlin, did report, beeing *their Voyage* examined of his Travels. The last yeere past 7127. hee *to Catay.* said that the Boiaren and Voyavod Knez Evan Simonowich *Tomo a new* Koorockin, sent him from the Castle of Tomo, and his *Castle beyond* fellow Andrashko, to conduct the Kings Altines Ambassa- *Ob. See sup.* dours, as also to inquire or search the Kingdomes of Catay. *pag. 527.* They went from the Castle of Tomo, about the ninth of May, and travelled from Tomo to Kirgis, with much *Kirgis.* expedition tenne dayes, and in Kirgis is a Duke subject to the Emperours Majestie, his name is Nemi, who gave them victuals and post. Through this Land of Kirgis they went halfe a day, and came to the Dominion of Mutalla, to the Altine King, who gave them provisions *Mutalla.* and post, and dispatched them thence: so they passed through his Land five weekes to the Country of Shere- *Sheremugala.* mugaly; where raigneth a Queene called Manchika, who *Q. Manchika.* caused to have provision and post given them. In this Countrey of Sheromogula they travelled foure dayes, and came into the Dominions of Catay; called Crim, where is a wall made of stone fifteene fathomes high, alongst the *Wall of* side of which wall they went ten dayes, where they saw *Catay.* pettie Townes and Villages belonging to the Queene Manchika; but in those ten dayes they saw no people upon the wall at all. At the end of these ten dayes, they came to the gate, wherein lye very great Peeces of *The gate and* Ordnance, shooting shot as bigge as a mans head, and *guard.* in the said gate standeth in watch three thousand men, and they come with their Merchandizes to traffique at the gate. The Altine men also come to the gate, with their Horses to sell to the Catay men; but are not permitted to come within the walls, except very few at once. Thus their whole travell from Tomo Castle to this gate, was *See for better* twelve weekes, besides some dayes that they stood still, *understanding* and from the gate to the great Empire of Catay tenne *hereof, Goes* dayes, and came to the Citie or Castle of Catay about the *& other* *Jesuites* beginning of September, and were lodged in the great *Relations in* Embassadors house: and having beene there in Catay *the second* foure dayes, there used to come unto them a Secretary *Booke.* with two hundred men upon Asses very well apparelled, and did entertayne and feast them with Sacke and other Drinkes made of Grapes, and told them that the Emperour, or King Tambur had sent him to aske them wherefore they were come into the Dominions of Catay. Whereupon they answered that our great Lord and Emperour had sent them to discover the Dominions of Catay, and see the King thereof; but hee answered them againe, that without presents they could not see the King, and withall gave them a Letter, which Letter they brought with them to Tolbosko, and from thence is sent to the Emperours Majestie by them. Out of Catay they went about the twelfth of October, and came to the Castle of Tobolsko about Whitsontyde the same yeere 1619.

[III.iv.799.] A Description of the Empires of Catay and Labin, and other Dominions aswell inhabited, as

Such are the Tartars dwellings or fleetings, rather with their beasts. Their Journal, or daily journeyes from place to place. Huge Lake.

places of Pasture* called Ulusses and Hords, and of the great River Ob, And other Rivers and Land passages.

FRom Kirgis to the River Bakanna is sixe dayes travell, and from Bakanna to Kinchike, is nine dayes travell, from Kinchike to the great Lake, (in which Lake Rubies or Saphires grow) is three dayes travell, and the compasse of that Lake is twelve dayes travell on horsebacke. There falleth also into the said Lake foure Rivers, to wit from the East, South, West and North, yet the water doth not increase in the Lake, nor decrease. There falleth yet another River into the said Lake, which commeth from betweene the East and the North, and is called Kitta, upon which we went fifteen dayes to the head of it, where we found the King Altine in progresse; the way is very stony.

King Altine. Ulusses, or Tartarian Hords.

And from the King Altine to an Ulusses five dayes travell; the Ulusses is called Algunat, and the Duke in it is called Tormoshine; from him to another Ulusses five dayes, the Ulusses is called Chikursha, and the Duke in it is called Carakula; from thence to an Ulusses five dayes called Suldussa, wherein is a King called Chaksata, from him to an Ulusses called Bisut, five dayes, the Dukes name is Chichim; from him to an Ulusses called Iglethin, five dayes, the Duke is Taschils Cherekta, from him to an Ulusses called Beskutæ, five dayes, the Duke is called Cherkar, from him to an Ulusses called Girut, foure daies without water, the Duke is called Chichevoas. From him to an Ulusses called Isut five dayes, the Duke of it is called Chechen. From him to an Ulusses called Tulent

Unient foure dayes, the Duke is called Tayku, Katin.
From him to the Ulusses Yogorsin three dayes, there is a
King called Bakshuta. From thence to an Ulusses of
the yellow Mugalls called Mugolchin, wherein is a *Yellow*
Dutchesse called Manchika, with her Sonne Ouchai *Mugals, or*
Taichie, it is within two dayes journey of the Land of *Moal-Tartars.*
Mugalla, a very dangerous passage through the cliffes of
the Rockes, which being past they came into the Land of
Mugalla, wherein are two Castles or Cities built of stone, *Mugalla, or*
they are called with them Bashum, in one of them is a *Tartaria*
Duke called Talaii Taishen; and in the other the Duke *Orientalis*
is called Egidon Taishen; there is also a third Citie in *from Bughar*
in Bactria to
it called Lobin, wherein doth governe a woman called *the Sea.*
Dutchesse Manchika with her Sonne, the said Dutchesse
doth command all the Cities of Mugalla, and her command
extendeth into Catay. If any man be to travell over the
borders, and into Catay, he must have a Passe under her
Seale; which if they have not, they may not passe through
Catay. The Land of Mugalla is great and large from
Bughar to the Sea; all the Castles are built with stone *Their*
foure square: at the corners, Towers, the ground or *buildings.*
foundation is layd of rough, grey stone, and are covered
with Tiles, the gates with counterwards as our Russe
gates are, and upon the gates alarum Bels or Watch-bels
of twentie poode weight of metall, the Towers are covered
with glazed Tiles; the houses are built with stone foure
cornerd high, within their Courts they have low Vaults,
also of stone, the seelings whereof, and of their houses are
cunningly painted with all sorts of colours, and very well
set forth with flowres for shew. In the said Countrey
of Mugalla are two Churches of Friers, or Lobaes, built *Friers.*
of square stone, and stand betweene the East and the
South; upon the tops of them are made beasts of stone,
and within the Church just against the doore are set three
great Idols or Images, in the forme of women of two *Idols.*
and an halfe fathome long, gilt all over from the heads
to the feet, and sit a fathome high from the ground upon
beasts made of stone, which beasts are painted with all

Candles.

manner of brave colours. Those Idols have each in their hand a Vessell, and there burne before them three tallow Candles; on the right side of them are erected eight Idols more in the forme of men, and on the left side eight Idols more in the forme of Maydens, gilt all over from the head to the foote, their armes stretched out after the manner as the Mugall people, or Religious men use to pray. And a little way from these Idols stand two Idols more made naked as a man is in all parts, not to be discerned, even as though he were alive, having before

Candles burning without flame.

them Candles burning, as small as a straw, and burne without a flame only in an Ember or Corall.

Rites of Religion.

Their service or singing in these Churches is thus. They have two Trumpets of a great length, about two fathomes and an halfe long, and when they sound on these Trumpets, and beate upon Drummes, the people fall downe upon their knees and clap their hands againe, casting their armes asunder, they fall to the ground and lye so halfe an houre. Their Churches are covered with glazed Titles. As for bread in the Land of Mugalla there groweth

Corne.

all manner of Graine, as Prosso, or Russe Rice, Wheate, Oates, Barley, and all sorts of other Graine in abundance, and their Wheate bread is as white as Snow. As for

Fruits.

Fruit in Mugalla they have of all sorts, as Apples, Melons, Arbuses, Pompeons, Cheries, Lemons, Cucumbers, Onions,

People and attyre.

Garlicke. The men are not faire, but the women exceeding faire, and weare for their Apparell, Velvets and Damasks, the Capes of their Garments both of the men and women hang downe to their shoulders. They distill

Distilled wine.

Aquavitæ out of all sorts of Graine, without Hops. As for Precious Stones and Gold they have none, but for Silver they have great store out of Catay. Their Boots

[III.iv.800.]

they weare of their owne fashion. They have no Horses, only Mules & Asses in abundance; they till and plough their ground with great and small Ploughes, as we doe in Siberia at Tobolsko. Their Cuttuffs are in our Language

Cutuffs, or Patriarkes.

Patriarkes, and both in Mugalla and Catay are but two Cuttuffs; the one was about twentie, and the other thirtie yeeres of age. Within the Churches are made for them high places with seats whereupon they sit : the King doth honour them with bowing downe before them. Their Lobaes are in our Language Friers, which are shorne about *Lobas, or* twentie yeeres of age, and know no women from their *Friers* Mothers wombe, they eate flesh continually every day, *Continencie,* and shave both Beards and Mustachoes: their Garments *shaving.* are of Damaske of all sorts and colours, and their Hoods yellow, they say that their Religion and ours are all one, only the Russe Monkes are blacke, and theirs white.

Beyond the Land of Mugalla are three other Countreyes *Three* or Dominions, stretching towards Bughar, the one called *Kingdomes.* Ortus, the Kings name there is Evakan, the Citie is of *Ortus.* stone, and the Kingdome rich.

The other is called Dominions of Talguth, the Kings *Talguth.* name is Savelanche, his Cities are also of stone, and his Kingdome rich.

The third Countrey where the chiefe Citie is, is called Shar, and the King thereof is called Zellezney, or Iron *Shar.* King, his Kingdome is rich, and not farre from Bughar. From this Iron King come Diamonds, and all these three Kingdomes are under the South, and on the other side of the blacke Mugalls are the yellow Mugalls, stretching all *Blacke* alongst the Sea, aswel Townes as walking people, with *Mugols, or* their Families and Herds. *Cara Catay.*

From the Countrey of Mugalla, where the Dutchesse Manchika dwelleth, to the Citie of Shrokalga in Catay, *Shrokalga in* is two dayes travell on horsebacke: and the bordering *Catay.* or frontier wals stand under the South towards Bughar, *Walls of* two moneths travell, all made of Bricke of fifteene fathome *Catay.* high, whereupon they told about a hundred Towres in sight, on both sides of them, but towards Bughar, and towards the Sea, the Towres are not to bee numbred, and every Towre standeth from another about a flight shot distant. The said wall stretcheth downe towards the Sea foure moneths travell. The people of Catay say, that this wall stretcheth alongst from Bughar to the Sea, and the Towres upon it stand very thicke; it was made, as they say, to be a border betweene Mugalla and Catay. The Towres upon it are to the end, that when any enemy appeareth, to kindle fires upon them, to give the people warning to come to their places where they are appointed upon the wall. At the entring without the wall dwell the blacke Mugalls; and within is the Countrey and Cities of Catay. In the wall to Catay are five gates, both low, and straight or narrow, a man cannot ride into them upright on horse-backe, and except these five gates there is no more in all the wall; there all manner of people passe into the Citie of Shrokalga.

*Cara Catay.
But five gates
in the wall.*

Within the borders or wall is a Citie or Castle of Catay, called Shirokalga, built of stone, the Governour thereof is called Duke Shubin, who is sent thither for a time from Tambur King of Catay, the Castle is very high walled and artificially built; the Towres are high after the manner of Mosco Castle, in the Loope-holes or Windowes are Ordnance planted, as also upon the Gates or Towres; their Ordnance is but short, they have also great store of small shot, and the Watchmen every-where upon the Gates, Towres, and Wals, well appointed; and assoone as they perceive the Sunne going downe, the Watch dischargeth their Peeces of Ordnance thrice, as also at the breake of day in the morning, they shoot out of their Pieces thrice, and doe not open the Castle Gates till the sixt houre of the day. Within the Castle are shops built of stone, and painted cunningly with divers colours, wherein they have all manner of Merchandizes, as Velvets, Damaskes, Dorogoes, Taffataes, Cloth of Gold, and Tissue of divers colours, sundry sorts of Sugars, Cloves, &c. in the Governours house is a strong Watch of Partisans and Halberds, and their Drummes made like great Barrels. When the Governour goeth abroad, they carry a Canopie over him, and make way before him with Rods, as before our Emperour in Mosco.

And from Shirokalga to the Citie Yara is three dayes travell: this Citie is large, built of stone, and the circuit of it is two dayes travell, with many Towres, and foure

Gates to come in at, the Markets in the Citie are well
and richly accommodated, with Jewels, Merchandizes,
Grocerie, or Spices, the Citie well inhabited having no
place void or waste in it. The houses and shops are
built with stone, with streets betweene; the Governours
here are called Duke Bym and Duke Juchake, heere they
have Post Stages as wee, their Markets have a very
odoriferous smell with Spices.

And from this Citie, to a Citie called Tayth, is three *Tayth.*
dayes journey, it is built of stone, large, and high walled,
& is in compasse two daies travel about, at the first
comming to it are five gates barred and bolted with Iron,
very thicke and close, fastned with Nailes; the houses and
shops, or Ware-houses are all built of stone, wherein are
all manner of Merchandizes, Spices, or Grocerie, and
precious things more abundant then in the aforesaid Cities,
they have Tavernes or Drinking houses stored with all
manner of Drinkes, as Aquavitæ, Meade, and Wines
from beyond Seas in abundance, there they have also their
Watch, Ordnance, and Munition in great store; the
Governours of this place are one Duke Tuga, and the
other Duke Zumia, there wee saw Sinamon, Anniseeds,
Apples, Arbuzes, Melons, Cucumbers, Onions, Gar-
licke, Radish, Carrets, Parsenips, Turnops, Cabbage, [III.iv.801.]
Limons, Poppiseeds, Nutmegs, Rice, Almonds, Pepper,
Rubarbe, & many other Fruits, which we know not, so
that they want nothing whatsoever groweth in the World;
the shops are within the Citie, stored of all manner of
Commoditie as is said, as also victualling and drinking
Houses, stored with all manner of Drinkes, where they
have also Dicers and Whores, as with us. Their Prisons
in the Citie are of stone, for theft they hang the theeves,
and for Robberie or Murther they stake the Murtherers,
or else head them.

And from Shirokalga to a Citie of Catay, called Shirooan *Shirooan.*
is a dayes journey: this Citie is built of stone high walled,
and large in compasse, it is a dayes travell, it hath twelve
Towres; whereupon, as also on the Citie Gates is planted

Ordnance and small shot great store, with a continuall Watch or Guard, night and day, at the first comming are five Gates well furnished with Ordnance and Warlike Munition; and from one Gate to the other through the Citie is halfe a dayes going. The Governour of this place is called Duke Sanchik. For Victuals and Merchandizes, here is more then in the Cities mentioned, all their shops very full, and the Citie so populous, that one can hardly passe the streets for the throng of people. The Ambassadors Houses are also faire built of stone, their Wels covered with Brasse, so that this Citie is adorned more with precious things then the former mentioned, and much more populous.

White Castle. Now from the Citie of Tayth, to a Citie called White Castle, is two dayes travell: this Citie is built of white stone, and thereof hath his name, it is high walled and large, being in compasse or circuit three dayes travell, at the first entry it hath three Gates under one Towre, the Gates are high and wide with strong Iron barres: and the Gates fastened with Iron Nayles whited with Tinne, it hath great Ordnance in the Gates and Towres: some Peeces carrying shot of two Poode waight, the shops within the Citie reach from Gate to Gate, and betweene them are streets paved with stone, all their shops and houses are built of stone before their shops. They have grates painted cunningly, with all manner of colours, flowres and such like, and upon the shops are the houses painted cunningly with Pictures and flowres in divers colours, and the painting within is upon Pastboord adorned with Damaske and Velvets; heere is more abundance of Riches and Commodities then in any of the Cities afore mentioned. The Governours names here were Duke Toyvan, and Duke Sulan.

From this white Citie, or Castle, to the greatest Citie of all Cataya, called Catay,* is two dayes journey, where

---

*Catay greatest Citie of Catay. If Catay be the same with China (as before in Goes and the Jesuites is observed) many difficulties arise. But this Russian Relation and that of Chaggi Memet seeme to agree to place

the King himselfe dwelleth, it is a very great Citie, built of white stone foure square, and in compasse it is foure dayes journey, upon every corner thereof are very great Towres high built, and white, and alongst the wall are very faire and high Towres, likewise white and inter-mingled with Blue or Azure, upon the Gates, Wall, and Towres, the Loop-holes or Windowes are well furnished with Ordnance, and a strong Watch. In the midst of this white Citie standeth a Castle built of Magnet, or Load-stone, wherin the King himselfe dwelleth, called Tambun; this Castle standeth so in the midst of this Citie, that every way you have halfe a dayes going to it from the Gates, through the streets which hath stone shoppes on both sides with all manner of Merchandizes; upon their shops they have their houses built of stone, cunningly painted more then the former Cities. The Castle of Magnet is curiously set forth with all manner of artificiall and precious devices, in the middest whereof standeth the Kings Palace, the top whereof is all gilt over with Gold. And they would not admit us to come before their King without Presents, saying, it was not the manner of Catay, to come before their King without some Present, and though (said they) your white Emperour had but sent with his first Ambassadours to our King some thing of no great value, our King would have sent him many precious things, and dismissed you his Ambassadours honourably, and have sent his Ambassadours with you:

some Catay, North from China, if this did not speake of the wall. The Tartar names so differ from those of the Portugalls, that it is hard to reconcile them. And the Jesuits make foure moneths travell from the wall to Pequin, which is here but a few daies: except we say the Russes entred the wall at the North East part of it: which the shortnesse of their journey admits not. Perhaps this chiefe Citie was but the chiefe of that Province where the Vice-roy resided, and they were willing to make the most of their travells Russica fide. Yet the neerenesse of the Sea, there also causeth scruple. I suppose rather that these Russes entred China but a little way, and received the Vice-royes Letter only (there observed with Regall Rites) and had much by Relation of that little which they tell. How ever I have here offered this to thy view at more leisure to use thy more judgement.

but now hee only endeth his Letter to your Emperour. The Citie of Catay, where the King dwelleth, is built upon an even plaine ground, and is incompassed round about with a River called Youga, which falleth into the blacke Sea, which is from the Citie Catay seven dayes travell, so that there come no ships neerer the Citie Catay, then seven dayes travell off, but all things are transported in small Vessels and ship-boats. The Merchandizes the King doth send into all parts of his Dominions of Catay, and from thence are carried over the borders, into the Land of Mugalla, to the King Altine, to the blacke Kollmakes, to the Iron King, into Boghar and other Dominions, their Patriarkes and Friers, travell with the Commodities, as Velvets, Sattens, Damaskes, Silver, Leopard Skinnes, Turkesses, and blacke Zenders, for which they buy Horses, and bring them into Catay, for in Catay are but few horses, only Mules and Asses, and Cloth they have none, their Horses and Silver goeth into strange Countreyes, or as they say, Nemtsii, the Silver is made in Brickes, which they call Kritsii, valued each Kritsii at fiftie two Rubles, their Apparell they weare with long broad hanging sleeves, like the Gentlewomens Summer-coats or Lettniks in Russia, the people are very faire but not warlike, timorous & most their endevour is in great and rich traffick. They told us that not long before our comming, the people of Mugalla had taken two Castles

[III.iv.802.] from them by deceit, also they told us that their King hath a stone which lighteth as the Sunne both day and night, called in their Language Sarra, and in our Tongue Jachant, or Rubie; another stone they say hee hath, which driveth away water from it, it is also called a Rubie.

Merchants. There come to them Strangers, or Nemtsii every yeere, with all manner of Merchandizes, and barter for Deere Skinnes, and Loshids, Sables, Bevers, Velvets, Taffataes, and Zendews, or Calico; these strangers, they say, come to them out of the blacke Sea, from the East and the South, also, they say, there is a River called Kartalla: which falleth into the great River Ob; but they know

*Kartalla
River.
Ob.*

284

neyther the head, nor the fall of it, they imagine it commeth out of the blacke Sea, and falleth into it againe, upon this River dwell many people with walking Herds.

For a triple testimony of Sir John Merikes honourable courtesie, I have added this succeeding Patent, which howsoever in some things it concurre with the former of Boris and Demetrius; Yet those being obscurely translated or written, this may illustrate them; and it also presenteth both larger Priviledges, the Patriarkes name joyned with the Emperours, and the Golden Seale.

WE the great Lord Emperour and great Duke Michaell Pheodorowich of all Russia, sole Commander of Volodemer, Mosco, and Novogrod, Emperour of Cazan, Emperour of Astracan, Emperour of Siberia, Lord of Plesco, and great Duke of Smolensky, Twensky, Ugorsky, Psermesky, Vatsky, Bolgorsky, and others; Lord and great Duke of Novogrod, in the lower Countreyes, Cheringosky, Rahansky, Rostovskey, Yaraslavsky, Belozersky, Udorskey, Obdorsky, Condinsky, and of all the Northerne parts Commander, and Lord over the Country of Iversky, and Caberdynland, Cherkaskey, and of the Dukedomes of Igorskey, and of many other Kingdomes, Lord and Conquerour. Together with the great Lord Philleret Neketich, the holy Patriarke and Head of the Reverend Clergie of the Imperiall Citie of Mosco, and of all Russia by the flesh our naturall Father, and by the power of the Holy Ghost our Spirituall Pastor and Ghostly Father.

Whereas there was sent unto us the great Lord Emperour, and great Duke Michaell Pheodorowich of all Russia, and to our Father, the great Lord, the holy Patriarke of Mosco, and of all Russia, From our loving Brother James, by the grace of God, King of England, Scotland, France, and Ireland; and of many others his Majesties Ambassadour Sir John Merike, Knight and

Gentleman of his Majesties Privie Chamber, upon both
our Princely Affaires.

The said Sir John Merike, in the name of our said
loving Brother King James requested our Imperiall
Majestie, and our Father the great Lord, the holy
Patriarke, to bee pleased graciously to favour the English
Merchants, to grant them leave to come with their shippes
unto our Port and Havens of Archangell, with all kind
of Commodities, and freely to traffique from the Sea side,
to our Imperiall Citie of Mosco, and to our Patrimonie
of great Novogrod and Plesco, and unto all other our
Cities, Townes, and Countreyes of our Empire, with all
sorts of Commodities, without paying of Custome in as
ample manner as formerly hath beene granted to the
English Merchants, and that our Imperiall Majestie,
together with our deere Father the holy Patriarke, would
be pleased to grant anew our gracious Priviledges
under our Princely Seale, according as our Predecessors
Emperours, and great Dukes of all Russia, have heretofore granted unto them.

We therefore the great Lord Emperour, and great Duke
Michaell Pheodorowich of all Russia, sole Commander;
together with our deere Father the holy Patriarke of
Mosco, and of all Russia; for the love we beare to our
most loving Brother the great Lord King James, with
whom wee are willing and desirous ever to remayne in
the strongest bonds of brotherly love and friendship, have
graciously granted to his Kingly Majesties Subjects the
English Merchants, Sir Thomas Smith Knight, Sir John
Merike Knight, Sir Richard Smith Knight, Sir William
Russell Knight, Sir George Bowles Knight, Hugh
Hamersley Alderman, Ralph Freeman, Richard Wytch,
Morris Abbot, Robert Bateman, William Stone, Rowland
Healing, Job Hanby, Richard Ironside, Edward James,
John Caslen, Benjamin Deicrow, Fabyan Smith, and their
fellowes free leave to come with their shippes into our
Kingdomes, into our Countreyes of Dweena, unto the
Port of Archangell, and from thence to our Imperiall

Citie of Mosco, and of Novogrod the Great, and unto
Plesco, and into all other the Cities of our Empire, to
trade and traffique with all kind of Merchandizes, free
of all Customes, as well the great Customes as Tole:
unlading of Vessels or Boats, passages through any place
by water or Land entries, Head-money, Bridge-money,
Ferryings, or any manner of Customes, or Duties whatsoever can bee named.

The English Merchants being thus licensed to trade
in our Kingdomes, free of all customes for their owne
commodities, shall neither colour nor sell strangers wares,
as their owne; neither shall our people sell for them any
of their goods, nor yet shall they keepe any of our people
under their protection: and into what Cities the English
Merchants themselves, or their Factors, or Servants shall
come with their goods, it shall be lawfull for them freely
to trafficke and sell their owne commodities, in barter,
or otherwise against Commodities of our Countrey.

And whensoever the said Merchants shall come into
our Patrimony of great Novogrod and Plesco, or into
any other the Cities of our Empire; Wee straightly
command our Nobles in generall, and all other our [III.iv.803.]
authorized people, that according to this our Imperiall
letters of priviledge, they suffer the foresaid Merchants
to passe without all manner of hindrance or lets, & without taking any manner of custome of them for themselves,
or for their goods; and into what place soever they shall
come, or passe with their Merchandize, and shall not
desire to buy nor sell with our people; those our authorized
people shall freely let them passe without taking any
manner of customes, according to this our Imperiall
gracious priviledge.

And wheresoever the English Merchants shall happen
to sell or barter any of their commodities with our
Merchants, they are to barter and sell them in their owne
house by grosse sale, and not by retaile, in small measure *This doth*
and weight, as by the yard, pound and ounce; that is to *cleer the*
say, their Cloath by whole Cloathes and Packs: Damaske *doubtfull pass-*
ages, pag. 760.

and Velvets by the Peece; and all other wares that are to be sold by weight accordingly. Also the Wines by the great, viz. by the Butt, the Pipe, the Hogshead, and by the Aume, and not by small measure, as Veders or Pots.

And the said English Merchants are to sell and barter their owne Commodities themselves in our Empire. But the Russe Merchants shall neither sell nor barter for them, neither shall the English carry or transport to or from any place, any Wares belonging to other Strangers, by way of their owne goods.

And if the said English Merchants shall be desirous to sell any of their commodities, at Colmogro, or upon the River of Dwina, or at Vologda or Yereslave, or other the Townes and Cities of our Empire, they may sell at their pleasures; as likewise at their owne choise and pleasure, they may transport their goods into all or any part of our Dominions, and hire Carriers, Boats, and men at such price as they themselves can agree.

Also when the English Merchants themselves, or any of their Factors, doe travell out of our Dominions into their owne, or other forraigne Kingdomes, and that wee shall be pleased to deliver them of our Treasure, they shall take it with them, and sell, and barter it for such commodities as wee shall thinke fit and necessarie for our use, and Treasury: our Governours, and all other our Officers, in all our Cities and Dominions, shall suffer them and their people freely to passe without taking any custome of them: but when the English Merchants have done their trafficke, and are going from our Citie of Mosco, they shall give notice thereof unto the Chancellour of our Office of Ambassadours.

Further, when any English Merchants shall come with their Shippes and Vessels by Sea, into our Dominions, and that any misfortune happen unto them by shipwracke on any of our shoares or coasts, our Governours and Officers shall cause search to be made for their goods, and shall aide and helpe them faithfully therein, and the goods gathered together shall be restored to the English

Merchants, who shall be at that time in our Kingdomes;
and if there shall be at that time none of the English
Merchants, or people in our Kingdomes, the said goods
shall be taken and laid up in safety, and delivered without
delay to the English Merchants when they shall come into
our Countrey, and shall challenge the same.

Further, of our gracious goodnesse, we gave free leave
to the English Merchants, and Company, to keepe the
house in Mosco by Saint Maxsime behinde the Market
place, and shall remaine after their old manner, and therein
shall have one housekeeper a Russe, or else one of their
owne Servants, but no other Russe people: the houses
which the English Merchants have in other places of our
Dominions, as at Yereslave, Vologda, Collm. and at Saint
Michaell Archangell, they shall keepe and use at their
pleasure, according to our former gracious favour, without
paying any duetie, rent, taxe, or any manner of custome
whatsoever: neither shall the people of the said Townes
take any thing of them, or theirs, for any duetie whatsoever belonging to their houses: and the said English
Merchants shall enjoy their said houses peaceably to themselves, without the annoyance of any Stranger or other
to lodge in them, whether in time of their being there,
or in their absence.

And in their houses at Yereslave, Vologda, Collmogro,
and Archangell, they shall likewise have a housekeeper of
their owne people, or of our Subjects, a man or two of
the meaner sort; but so, that those our people be no
merchants.

Their Housekeeper being a Russe shall not undertake
to meddle or sell any of their wares without themselves
be present, and they the English· Merchants, by vertue
of this our gracious Letters of priviledge, shall lay their
wares and commodities in their owne houses, and sell
them to whom they please.

And it shall be lawfull for the said Merchants, when
they shall arrive at our Sea Port, to lade and unlade their
Merchandizes, as in times past, at their pleasures: and

when they lade or unlade their Shippes, it shall be lawfull
for them to hire any of our Subjects to helpe them, and
shall have leave to carry their goods to and fro with their
owne Vessels, and howse them in their owne Ware-houses:
onely they shall give a note under their hand to our
Governours, Customers, or sworne men, what goods they
bring in, and Shippe out; Whereby it may be knowne
what goods commeth in, and goeth out of our Kingdomes:
but in no wise our Officers shall open or unpacke any
of their Wares or Merchandize in any place wheresoever.

Also when the English Merchants shall Shippe or
transport any of their Countrie Commodities from Saint
Michaell Archangell, to our royall Citie of Mosco, or
Russe Commodities, into their owne Countrie: our
authorised Officers and Customers, by vertue of this our
[III.iv.804.] Imperiall Letters of priviledge, shall suffer them to passe
with their goods in and out, without doing them any
manner of hindrance.

And whensoever any of the said English Merchants
or Factors shall have occasion to send overland, out of
our Dominions, any of their people, or Servants, into their
owne Countrie overland, they shall freely passe by this
our speciall command, onely they are to take a passe letter
from our Chancellour of the Office of Embassie.

And whosoever in any of our Cities, shall have any
matter against the English Merchants by way of con-
tention, we command that none of our Governours, nor
other of our Officers, doe judge the English Merchants,
their Factors or people: neither shall they send Officers
for them, except for matter of murther or theft, and that
also not to be done, but by manifest token thereof: but
the English Merchants, their Factors and people, shall
onely have triall, and be judged in our Imperiall Citie of
Mosco, by vertue of this our gracious Letters of priviledge, before our Chancellour in this Office of Embassie,
and in no other place or Towne, and he to heare their
causes, and to give justice betweene both parties, according
to equitie and right; and where the truth cannot be found

out by Law, it shall be referred to oath and lot, and on whom soever the lot fals, to him shall the right be adjudged.

And if any of the English Merchants, in any of our Cities within our Kingdomes, doe complaine of any wrong offered them by our people, for debts growing by trade or otherwise: we command our Governours, and all other our authorised people, that they presently minister true justice unto them. And for any wrong or other matter of controversie that the English Merchant shall have against any of our Subjects, our Governours and other our authorised people upon their complaint for all controversies (matters of debt excepted) shall give our Subjects so offending upon suretie, setting them time to appeare at Mosco, to answere the same with the English Merchants, face to face, before our Chancellour, in the Office of Embassy: and in these matters our Chancellour shall truely examine the businesse, and minister true justice: and what by examination cannot be found, shall be referred, as before, to oath and lot: the Judges and Justices through our Dominions shall take no kinde of duetie of the English Merchants for their matters of Law.

We will and command, that these our Imperiall gracious Letters of priviledge, be strictly observed in all points, in all parts of our Dominions, and by all our Subjects, Governours, Secretaries, and other Officers, without disobeying in any thing.

And whosoever shall not obey this our Princely and gracious Letters of priviledge, but shall offer wrong to the English Merchants, those our Subjects shall be with us in our high displeasure.

These our gracious Letters of priviledges, are sealed with our Imperiall Seale of Gold, in our Princely Pallace *Sealed with* of our Imperiall Citie of Mosco, in the yeare from the *the Golden* Worlds creation 7129. in the moneth of May, the eleventh *Seale.* day.

Subscribed by our Imperiall Majesties Chancellour of

our Office of Embassy, and our privie Chancellour Evan
Corbatovesin Gramotin.

BUt it is now high time to leave Russia, and all that
Barbarous shoare, of Samotees and Tartars: onely
we will borrow helpe of some Barbarians to shippe us
thence to Sea. And although Finch, Gourdon, and others
have in the former Booke inserted so great light: yet
seeing Master Marsh hath entertained other guides, we
will take Sea by Ob, and thence set forth on further discoveries.

Chap. XII.

Notes concerning the discovery of the River of
Ob, taken out of a Roll, written in the Russian
tongue, which was attempted by the meanes of
Antonie Marsh, a chiefe Factor for the Moscovie Company of England, 1584. with other
notes of the North-east.

Irst he wrote a Letter from the Citie of
Mosco, in the yeare 7092. after the Russe
accompt, which after our accompt was in
the yeare 1584. unto foure Russes that
used to trade from Colmogro to Pechora,
and other parts Eastward: whose answere
was:

By writings received from thee, as also by reports, wee
understand thou wouldest have us seeke out the mouth
How to finde of the River Ob; which we are content to doe; and thou
out Ob from must give therefore fiftie rubbles: it is requisite to goe
Pechora. to seeke it out with two Cochimaes, or companies; and
each Cochima must have ten men: and wee must goe by
the River Pechora upwards in the Spring, by the side of
the Ice, as the Ice swimmeth in the River, which will aske
Ouson River. a fortnights time; and then we must fall into Ouson

River, and fall downe with the streame before we come to Ob, a day and a night in the spring. Then it will hold us eight dayes to swimme downe the River Ob, before we come to the mouth: therefore send us a man that can write; and assure thy selfe the mouth of Ob is deepe. On the Russe side of Ob sojourne Samoeds, called Ugorskai & Sibierskie, Samoeds; and on the other side dwel another kinde of Samoeds, called Monganei, or Mongaseisky, Samoeds. We must passe by five Castles that stand on the River of Ob. The name of the first is Tesvoi Gorodok, which standeth upon the mouth of the River Padou. The second small Castle is Nosoro-gorodock, and it standeth hard upon the side of Ob. The third is called Necheiour-goskoy. The fourth is Chared-mada. The fift is Nadesneàa, that is to say, The Castle of comfort, or trust; and it standeth upon the River Ob, lowermost of all the former Castles toward the Sea.

Heretofore your people have bin at the said River of Obs mouth with a Ship, and there was made shipwracke, and your people were slaine by the Samoeds, which thought that they came to rob and subdue them. The Trees that grow by the River are Firres, and a kinde of white, soft and light Firre, which we call Yell. The bankes on both sides are very high, and the water not swift, but still and deepe. Fish there are in it as Sturgeons, and Cheri, and Pidle, and Nelma, a dainty fish like white Salmons, and Moucoun, and Sigi, and Sterlidi: but Salmons there are none. Not farre distant from the maine, at the mouth of Ob, there is an Island, whereon resort many wilde beasts, as white Beares, and the Morses, and such like. And the Samoeds tell us, that in the winter season, they oftentimes finde there Morses teeth. If you would have us travell to seeke out the mouth of Ob by Sea, we must goe by the Isles of Vaygats, and Nova Zembla, and by the Land of Matpheove, that is, by Matthewes Land. And assure thy selfe that from Vaygats, to the mouth of Ob, by Sea, is but a small matter to sayle. Written at Pechora, the yeare 7092. the twenty one of February.

[III.iv.805.]

Ugorskai and Sibierskie.

A shipwracke at the mouth of Ob.

An Island neere the mouth of Ob.

The way to discover Ob by Sea.

Mattpheove or Matthewes land.

After our stile 1584.

Master Marsh also learned these distances of places and Ports, from Caninos to Ob by Sea.

FRom Caninos to the Bay of Medemske (which is somewhat to the East of the River Pechora) is seven dayes sayling. The Bay of Medemsky is over a day and a halfe sayling. From Medemske Savorost to Carareca, is sixe dayes sayling. From Carska Bay to the farthest side of the River Ob, is nine dayes sayling. The Bay of Carska is from side to side, a day and a nights sayling.

He learned another way by Nova Zembla and Matthuschan Yar to Ob, more North-eastward. From Caninos to the Iland of Colgoieve, is a day & a nights sayling. From Colgoieve to Nova Zembla are two dayes sayling. There is a great Osera or Lake upon Nova Zembla, where wonderfull store of Geese and Swannes doe breede, and in moulting time cast their feathers, which is about Saint Peters day: and the Russes of Colmogro repaire thither yearely, and our English men venter thither with them severall shares in money: they bring home great quantitie of Doune-Feathers, dried Swannes, and Geese, Beares skinnes, and Fish, &c. From Naromske Reca or River to Mattuschan Yar, is sixe dayes sayling. From Mattuschan Yar to the Perovologli Teupla, that is to say, To the warme passage over-land, compassing or sayling round about the Sands, is thirteene dayes sayling: And there is upon the Sands at a full Sea, seven fathomes water, and two fathomes at a low water. The occasion of this highing of the water, is the falling into the Sea of the three Rivers, and the meeting of the two Seas, to wit, The North Sea, and The East Sea, which make both high water and great Sands. And you must beware that you come not with your Shippe neere unto the Iland by the River Ob. From Mattuschan Yar to this Iland, is five dayes sayling. Mattushan Yar is in some parts fortie Versts over, and in some parts not past six Versts over.

Naromske.
Mattuschan
Yar.
The Sands.
The two Seas:
that is, the
North and the
East Sea.
The bignes of
the Cliffe or
Isle of
Mattuschan.
Anthonie
Marsh sent
two of his men
upon the dis-
covery of Ob
by land with
foure Russes.
Bodan Master
Marsh his
man brought
to Mosco.

The aforesaid Anthonie Marsh sent one Bodan his man,

a Russe borne, with the aforesaid foure Russes, and a yong youth, a Samoed, which was likewise his Servant, upon the discovery of the River of Ob, by Land, through the Countrie of the Samoeds, with good store of commodities to trafficke with the people. And these his Servants made a rich Voyage of it, and had bartered with the people about the River of Ob, for the valew of a thousand rubles in sables, and other fine Furres. But the Emperour having intelligence of this Discovery, and of the way that Bodan returned home by, by one of his chiefe Officers lay in waite for him, apprehended him, and tooke from him the aforesaid thousand Markes worth of Sables, and other Merchandises, and delivered them into the Emperours Treasurie, being sealed up, and brought the poore fellow Bodan to the Citie of Mosco, where he was committed to prison, and whipped, and there detained a long while after, but in the end released. Moreover, the Emperours Officers asked Anthonie Marsh, how he durst presume to deale in any such enterprise? To whom he answered, that by the priviledges granted to the English Nation, no part of the Emperours Dominions were exempted from the English to trade and trafficke in : with which answere, they were not so satisfied, but that they gave him a great checke, and forfeited all the aforesaid thousand Markes worth of goods, charging him not to proceede any further in that action : whereby it seemeth they are very jealous that any Christian should grow acquainted with their Neighbours that border to the North-east of their Dominions, for that there is some great secret that way, which they would reserve to themselves onely. Thus much I understood by Master Christopher Holmes.

[III.iv.806.]
Russian jealousie of discovery.

[The report

The report of Master Francis Cherry a Moscovie
Merchant, and Master Thomas Lyndes touch-
ing a warme Sea to the South-east of the River
Ob, and a Note of Francis Gaulle.

Master Francis Cherry, one of the chiefe Merchants
of the Moscovy Companie, which was the Emperour
Ivan Basiliwich his Interpreter, and hath travailed in
person into Permia farre to the East in Russia, saith,
That he hath eaten of the Sturgeon that came out of the
River of Ob. And that in those parts it is a common
received speech of the Russes that are great travailers,
that beyond Ob to the South-east there is a warme Sea.
Which they expresse in these words in the Russe tongue;
Za Oby reca moria Teupla, that is to say, Beyond the
River Ob is a warme Sea. Furthermore, Master Thomas
Lynde an honest and discreet English Merchant, which
hath likewise lived many yeeres in those parts of Moscovy,
saith, That this Sea beyond Ob, is by the report of the
Russes, that are travailers, so warme, that all kinde of
Sea fowles live there as well in the Winter as in the
Summer, which report argueth, that this Sea pierseth farre
into the South parts of Asia.

A warme Sea
beyond Ob.
Master
Thomas Linde.

Third Volume
of English
voyages, pag.
446.

FRancis Gaulle that passed the Ocean betweene Japan
and Nova Hispania, in the Latitude of 37. degrees
and a halfe, writeth thus. Proving a great Sea to come
from the North-east parts of Tartarie; running thus East
and East and by North about three hundred leagues from
Japan, we found a very hollow water, with the streame
running out of the North and North-west, with a full
and very broad Sea, without any trouble or hinderance
in the way that we past. And what winde soever blue,
the Sea continued all in one sort with the same hollow
water and streame, untill we had passed seven hundred
leagues. About two hundred leagues from the Coast of
New Spaine we began to lose the said hollow Sea, whereby

I perswade my selfe that there you shall finde a Channell or strait passage betweene the firme Land of New Spaine and the Countrie of Asia and Tartaria. We found all this way Whales, Tunnies, Bonitos, which are fishes that keepe in Channels, Straits, and running Waters, there to disperse their seede, which further confirmeth me in that opinion.

But seeing thus we are shipped from Russia, and have againe taken Sea, that which Ice permitted not to Stephen Burrough, Pet and Jackman, nor others, English and Dutch, which have attempted that North-east passage; and that which Master Baffin said to me, that if he might have imployment, he would adventure to discover from the Coast of China and Japan on the North of Asia hitherward; all this shall be suddenly pervious to our swifter and unstayable thoughts, to set us in a new discovery by Danish and English assistance for a North-west passage, so often, not so fortunately attempted, as by Reason it seemeth probable and almost certaine, especially that way where Sir Th. Button and Nelson left. But we will discover these Discoveries more methodically and historically to you, that you may see the English ancient right, as I may say, to those parts of the new World. *See of these voyages. Hak. Tom. 1.*

Chap. XIII.

Discoveries made by English-men to the Northwest: Voyages of Sir Sebastian Cabot, Master Thorne, and other Ancients: and of Master Weymouth.

E have before given some light of the North-west, in Hudsons and other mens Voyages. The desire of Riches in some, of Knowledge in others, hath long wheted mens industries, to finde out a more compendious way to the East Indies, by a shorter cut then the usuall passage, which in going to the places of principall Trade there, and

the returning thence by enforced compassings, is made
no lesse a Voyage for time, cost, danger and labour, then
the immediate compassing of the whole Globe, as in
Master Candishes circumnavigation (not to mention
others) is evident. But if either by the North-east, or
North-west, or North, a passage be open, the sight of the
Globe (the Image of the site of the World) easily sheweth
with how much ease, in how little time and expense the
same might be effected, the large Lines or Meridians
[III. iv. 807.] under the Line contayning six hundred miles, contracting
themselves proportionably as they grow neerer the Pole,
where that vast Line and Circumference it selfe becomes
(as the whole Earth to Heaven, and all earthly things
to heavenly) no Line any more, but a Point, but Nothing,
but Vanitie. Hence such laborious searches from
Columbus his first discoverie (that also occasioned by a
conceit of finding the East by the West, whereupon he
named Hispaniola Ophir, thinking he had then arrived
at the East Indies) especially the English, seated commodiously for that discoverie, and to reigne over the
Northerne and Westerne Ocean, have herein beene more
then industrious.

Doctor Powell in his historie of Wales saith, that
Madoc sonne of Owen Guyneth left the Land in conten-
tion betwixt his brethren, and prepared certaine ships with
men and munition, and sought adventures by Sea, sayling
West, and leaving the Coast of Ireland so farre North,
that hee came unto a Land unknowne, where he saw
many strange things. There hee left many of his people
An. 1170, and returned for more of his owne Nation and
Some thinke Friends to inhabite that large Countrie, going the second
that the time thither with ten sailes. This westerne Land is like
Mexican to be some part of the West Indies, though the
Kings (Mute- universavagenesse of those parts make it questionable
zuma the last, where. But he which seeth how some of our English in
professed that small time have growne wilde in Ireland, and become in
they were language and qualities Irish, few of whom doe in exchange
strangers) become civilized and English (even as healthfull men are
were hence
derived.

easier infected in a contagious aire, then sicke men
recovered in that which is wholesome and sound) will
not wonder that in so many Ages the halfe civilized Welsh
amongst Barbarians, without succession of Priests and
entercourse of these parts might wholly put on feritie.
Meredith ap Rise a Welsh Poet, which lived before
Columbus, had begun his discoverie, hath these verses.

> Madoc wyf, myedic wedd, Jawn Genau, Owyn
>   Guynedd
> Ni finnum dir, fy enaid oedd Na da Mawr, ond y
>   moroedd.   that is.

> Madoc I am the sonne of Owen Gwynedd, with stature
>   large and comely grace adorned,
> No lands at home nor store of wealth me please, My
>   mind was whole to search the Ocean seas.

Columbus also sent his brother Bartholomew to King
Henrie the seventh, to make offer of his service in the
New-Worlds discoverie, which fell by the way into the
hands of Pirats, whereupon povertie assaulted him with
sicknesse in a forraine Countrie, so that hee was forced *D. F. Colon*
to get somewhat about him by making of Maps: one *de vita patris*
whereof had this more ancient then elegant inscription. *Christoph.*
Col. c. 13.

> Janua cui patria est, nomen cui Bartholomæus
> Columbus de Terra Rubra, opus edidit istud
> Londoniis An. Domini 1480. atque insuper anno
> Octavo decimaque die cum tertia mensis.
> Februarii. Laudes Christo cantentur abunde.

Whose Countrie Genua is, whose name Bartholomæus
Colon de Terra Rubra, this worke set forth new
At London, A thousand foure hundred eightie
Februarie thirteenth, sing praise to Christ on height.

One of these Maps hee presented to King Henrie with

the said offer, who cheerfully accepted the same, and sent to call his brother into England, who before he could effect it, was imployed by the King of Castile.

Columbus his fortunes awakned others industrie, amongst the rest John Cabota a Venetian, and his three sonnes Lewis, Sebastian, and Sancius, who obtayned a Patent of King Henrie the seventh for discoverie with five ships with English Masters, Mariners, and Colours also, the same to erect in whatsoever Lands unknowne before to Christian, to hold the same to them and their Heires as Vassals and Lieutenants to the Crowne of England, paying the fifth part of their gaine at Bristoll, &c.

See Hak. tom. 3. pag. 5.

In the yeere 1497. John Cabot a Venetian, and Sebastian his sonne (these are the wordes of the great Map in his Majesties privie Gallerie, of which Sebastian Cabot is often therein called the Authour, and his Picture is therein drawne, with this Title, Effigies Sebast. Caboti Angli filii Io. Ca. Venetiani Militis Aurati, &c.) discovered that Land which no man before had attempted Jun. 24. about five in the morning. This Land he called Prima vista (primum visam, or first seene) because that was first descried from Sea. That Iland which lyeth out before the land, he called Saint Johns Iland, because on that feast day it was discovered. The Inhabitants weare beasts skins and as much esteeme them, as we doe garments most precious. In their warres, they use Bowes, Arrowes, Pikes, Darts, Clubs of wood and Slings. The soile is barren in some places and yeeldeth little fruit, but it is full of white Beares and Stags of unusuall greatnesse. It aboundeth with Fishes and those great, as Seales and Salmons; Soles also an elle long. Especially there is great store of those fishes which they call commonly Bacallaos. There breede also Hawkes as blacke as Ravens, Partridges and blacke Eagles.

This Map, some say, was taken out of Sir Seb. Cabots Map by Clem. Adams 1549.

Thus wee see New-found Land discovered by English Ships, Mariners and jurisdiction. Sir Sebastian Cabot, for his English breeding, conditions, affection and advance-

Ramus. Tom. 2.

ment, termed an English man, thus reported of this
voyage; That upon occasion of the admiration of Columbus his voyage into the East, where Spices grew, by the
West, so rife then in the Court of King Henrie the
seventh, there arose in his heart a great desire to attempt
some notable thing. And understanding by the Sphere
(saith he) that if I should saile by the North-west, I should
by a shorter Tract come into India; I thereupon caused
the King to be advertised of my devise; who immediately
commanded two Carvels to bee furnished with all things
appertayning to the Voyage; which was, as farre as I
remember, in the yeere 1496. in the beginning of Summer.
I beganne therefore to saile toward the North-west, not
thinking to find any other Land then that of Cathay, and
from thence to turne toward India. But after certaine
dayes I found that the Land turned toward the North,
which was to me a great displeasure. Neverthelesse,
sayling along by the Coast to see if I could finde any
Gulfe that turned, I found the Land still continent to the
56. degree under our Pole. And seeing that there the
Coast turned toward the East, despayring to finde the
passage, I turned backe againe, and sayled downe by the
Coast of that Land toward the Equinoctiall (ever with
intent to finde the said passage to India) and came to that
part of this firme land, which is now called Florida; where
my victuals fayling I returned towards England; the
tumults and preparations of warres against Scotland caused
that then no more consideration was had to this voyage.
Whereupon I went into Spaine, &c. By the King and
Queene there he was set forth and discovered the River
of Plate, and sayled into it more then six score leagues.
After this he made many other voyages, &c. Sir Seb.
Cabot was after by King Edward the sixt constituted
grand Pilot of England with the annuall stipend of one
hundred and sixtie six pounds thirteene shillings and foure
pence, and was Author of the Russian and North-easterne
discoveries. Fabian in his Chronicle A. R. Hen. 7. 14.
hath this testimonie. This yeere also were brought unto

See Hak.
Tom.3.pag.7.
[III.iv.808.]

*All the Coast
to Florida dis-
covered by the
English: from
67. deg. 30.
min. as he
writ to
Ramusio. R.
præfat. Tom.
3. as likewise
he was the
cause of the
Russian and
Greenland
discoveries.*

See sup. l. 2.
c. 1.

the King three men taken in the New-found Land, in William Purchas time being Major. These were clothed in beasts skins, and did eate raw flesh, and spake such speech that none could understand them, and in their demeanour like to bruit beasts, whom the King kept a long time after. Two yeeres after I saw two of them at Westminster, apparelled like English, &c.

Master Robert Thorne writes, that his Father and Master Hugh Eliot a Merchant of Bristoll, were the first discoverers of New-found Land: and if the Mariners would have beene ruled and followed their Pilots minde, the West Indies had beene ours: so that it seemeth this Discoverie was before that of Columbus. Master Hakluyt hath published the particulars of these things more fully, as also divers Treatises touching the Northwest of Sir Humphrey Gilbert and others: to which I referre the Reader; and no lesse for the Voyages made by divers English into those parts: three by Sir Martin Frobisher, in the yeeres 1576, 77, and 78. Two of Captaine John Davies, in 86, and 87. that of Master Hore, An. 1536. that of Sir Humphrey Gilbert, 1583. that of Master Charles Leigh to Ramea, An. 1597. and before in 1593. that of George Drake; with those of Jaques Cartier, and divers others. My purpose is not to steale Master Hakluyts labours out of the World, by culling and fleecing them for our purpose, but by this Index to instruct men where they may have festivall store in this kinde. I had rather give you new things. Such are to the World, these that you had before in Hudsons voyages set together, as also those of Greenland: and such are those of Waymouth, Knight, Hall, Baffin, &c. And first, as Foreman of our Quest, we will give you Sir Humphrey Gilberts Letter, written with his owne hand from New-found Land, whereof he tooke formall possession to the Crowne of England, and was as a Martyr of those Discoveries. It was written to Sir George Peckham (a great Adventurer in that voyage, and a greater in one of longer life, his written Treatise of Westerne planting, extant in

Master Hakluyts third Tome) and I have here inserted,
it being hitherto unprinted, as a memorial of both their
worths; and after it (though in time before) wee will
recreate you with a plaine Mariners Letter endorsed in
homely phrase, To the Honourable Kings Grace of England, here (as I thinke) given you from the Originall. I
have also another written to Cardinall Wolsey touching the
same voyage in Latin, by Albertus de Prato; for the
antiquitie, rather then any remarkable raritie, worthy here
to be mentioned.

SIr George, I departed from Plymouth on the eleventh
of June with five sailes, and on the thirteenth the
Barke Rawley ran from me in faire and cleere weather,
having a large winde. I pray you solicite my brother
Rawley to make them an example of all Knaves. On
the third of August wee arrived at a Port called Saint
Johns, and will put to the Seas from thence (God willing)
so soone as our ships will be ready. Of the New-found
Land I will say nothing, untill my next Letters. Be of
good cheare, for if there were no better expectation, it
were a very rich demaynes, the Country being very good
and full of all sorts of victuall, as fish both of the fresh
water and Sea-fish, Deere, Pheasants, Patridges, Swannes,
and divers Fowles else. I am in haste, you shall by every
Messenger heare more at large. On the fifth of August,
I entred here in the right of the Crowne of England; and
have engraven the Armes of England, divers Spaniards,
Portugals, and other strangers, witnessing the same. I
can stay no longer; fare you well with my good Lady:
and be of good cheare, for I have comforted my selfe,
answerable to all my hopes. From Saint Johns in the
New-found Land, the 8. of August, 1583.

    Yours wholly to command, no man more,
                HUM. GILBART.

I mentioned before Master Thornes fathers finding [III.iv.809.]
New-found Land, with Master Eliot. These animated

King Henrie the eight to set forth two ships for discoverie, one of which perished in the North parts of New-found Land. The Master of the other, John Rut, writ this Letter to King Henrie, in bad English and worse Writing. Over it was this superscription.

Master Grubes two ships departed from Plymouth the 10. day of June, and arrived in the New-found Land in a good Harbour, called Cape de Bas, the 21. day of July: and after we had left the sight of Selle, we had never sight of any Land, till we had sight of Cape de Bas.

PLeasing your Honorable Grace to heare of your servant John Rut, with all his Company here, in good health, thanks be to God, and your Graces ship. The Mary of Gilford, with all her   thanks be to God: And if it please your honorable Grace, we ranne in our course to the Northward, till we came into 53. degrees, and there we found many great Ilands of Ice and deepe water, we found no sounding, and then we durst not goe no further to the Northward for feare of more Ice, and then we cast about to the Southward, and within foure dayes after we had one hundred and sixtie fathom, and then wee came into 52. degrees and fell with the mayne Land, and within ten leagues of the mayne Land we met with a great Iland of Ice, and came hard by her, for it was standing in deepe water, and so went in with Cape de Bas, a good Harbor, and many small Ilands, and a great fresh River going up farre into the mayne Land, and the mayne Land all wildernesse and mountaines and woods, and no naturall ground but all mosse, and no inhabitation nor no people in these parts: and in the woods wee found footing of divers great beasts, but we saw none not in ten leagues. And please your Grace, the Samson and wee kept company all the way till within two dayes before wee met with all the Ilands of Ice, that was the first day of July at night, and there rose a great and a marvailous great storme, and much foule weather;

I trust in Almightie Jesu to heare good newes of her.
And please your Grace, we were considering and a writing
of all our order, how we would wash us and what course
wee would draw and when God doe send foule weather,
that with the Cape de Sper shee should goe, and he that
came first should tarry the space of sixe weeks one for
another, and watered at Cape de Bas ten dayes, ordering
of your Graces ship and fishing, and so departed toward
the Southward to seeke our fellow: the third day of
August we entered into a good Haven, called Saint John,
and there we found eleven saile of Normans, and one
Brittaine, and two Portugall Barkes, and all a fishing, and
so we are readie to depart toward Cape de Bas, and that
is twentie five leagues, as shortly as we have fished, and
so along the coast till we may meete with our fellow, and
so with all diligence that lyes in me toward parts to that
Ilands that we are commanded by the grace of God, as
we were commanded at our departing: And thus Jesu
save and keepe your honorable Grace, and all your honourable Rever. in the Haven of Saint John, the third day of
August, written in haste. 1527.

By your servant John Rut, to his uttermost
of his power.

I have by me also Albert de Prato's originall Letter,
in Latin stile, almost as harsh as the former English, and
bearing the same date, and was indorsed, Reverend. in
Christo Patri Domino Domino Cardinali & Domino Legato
Angliæ: and began, Reverendissime in Christo Pater
salutem. Reverendissime Pater, placeat Reverendissimæ
paternitati vestræ, scire, Deo favente postquam exivimus
à Plemut quæ fuit x. Junii &c. (the substance is the same
with the former, and therefore omitted) Datum apud le
Baya Saint Johan in Terris Novis, die x. Augusti, 1527.
Rever. Patr. vest. humilis servus, Albertus de Prato. (the
name written in the lowest corner of the sheet.)

[The voyage

The voyage of Captaine George Weymouth, intended for the discoverie of the North-west Passage toward China, with two flye Boates.

ON Sunday the second day of May, 1602. in the after-noone, I weighed anchor and set saile from Redcliffe with two Fly-boates, the one called the Discovery, of seventie Tunnes; and the other called the God speed, of sixtie Tunnes, to discover the North-west passage, having in my ships five and thirtie men and boyes, throughly victualled and abundantly furnished with all necessaries for a yeere and an halfe, by the right Worshipfull Merchants of the Moscovie and Turkie Companies: who for the better successe of the voyage provided mee of a great travailer and learned Minister one Master John Cartwright. The Master under mee in the Discoverie was one William Cobreth, a skilfull man in his profession; and in the God speed, one John Drewe, and Mate in the said ship one John Lane.

The first of June, we descried Buquhamnes in the Latitude of 57. degrees. The second day we saw the Point of Buquhamnes North-west from us, being a very smooth land; and the land by it to the Southward riseth with many Homocks. There lyeth a ledge of Rockes hard by the Nesse, in a sandie Bay faire by the shore. When we came neer the land, we met with a fisher Boat, and I agreed with one of the fisher men to carry me betweene the Isles of Orkney, because I was not acquainted with the coast. The fourth day, at ten of the clocke, wee descried the Isles of Orkney. Some of those Southerne Ilands are prettie high land; but the Northerne Iland, which is called the Start, is very low land. There is no danger, giving the shore a good birth, unlesse it be by the Norther point of the Start: there doth a ledge of Rockes lye a mile from the shoare. At noone I found my selfe to be in the latitude of 59. degrees and 30. minutes, the point of the Start bearing West: and at one

Mosc. and
Turkie
Companies.
Master Cart-
wright had bin
in Persia and
Turkie. See
the former
Tome.
Buquhamnes.

[III. iv. 810.]

Orkney.

The Start.

59. *degrees*
30. *minutes.*

of the clocke in the afternoone, we saw a faire Ile, which *Faire Ile.*
bare North-east and by North from us: and at eight of
the clocke at night, wee were North of the Start: Then
I directed my course West and by North. The fifth day
about ten of the clocke in the morning, we ranne some
tenne leagues, and then we saw two small Ilands, some *Two small*
two leagues off: and at eight and nine of the clocke we *Ilands.*
saw foure or five Boats of Fisher-men, and spake with
one of them, and they were Scottish-men. The sixt, in
the morning fell much raine, and lasted till nine of the
clocke: and at ten of the clocke it cleared up, and became
very faire weather, and very temperate and warme, and
our course was West. The seaventh, the winde was at
East and by North, faire weather, and our course West.
The eight, at noone I observed the Sunne, and found
us to be in 59. degrees and fortie seven minutes, and we
ran West South-west.

The twelfth day we held our course West, the winde
at East North-east, with fogge in the morning: at noone
I observed the Sunne, and found my selfe in 57. degrees, *57. degrees*
and 55. minutes. the variation here was nothing at all. *55. min. no*
The thirteenth at noone, our course was West and by *variation.*
North, the winde at North-east, with fogge some three
or foure houres, and then cleare againe: the ayre very
warme, as in England in the moneth of May. The foureteenth was faire weather, and the winde at East North-
east, and our course West and by North. The fifteenth
much raine all the forenoone, our course West, the winde
at East and by North. The sixteenth, the winde was at
North North-east, with much raine, winde and fogge.
In the forenoone, being very cold, and at noone, I observed
the Sun, and found us to be in 57. degrees and 35.
minutes: we found the variation to be eleven degrees *Variation*
Westward; and by that meane I found my selfe to be *eleven degrees*
one degree more to the Southward, then we should have *Westward.*
bin by our course; for we could not see the Sunne in
96. houres before this day at noone, and at our last observation before this, which was the twelfth day, we could

No variation. not finde any variation at all. Then we stood close by a winde to the Westward, the winde being at North North-east. The seaventeenth wee ranne North and by West, the winde at North North-east, faire weather. This *Guls and* day we saw many gray Gulles, and some Pigions. The *Pigions.* eighteenth at noone I observed the Sunne, and found our *59. deg. 51.* selves to be in the latitude of 59. degrees, and 51. minutes. *min.* And then we first descried a great Iland of Ice, which *A great Iland* lay North from us, as farre as we could ken it from the *of Ice.* head of our maine topmast: and about two of the clocke *Groneland.* in the afternoone, we saw the South part of Groneland, North from us some ten leagues. As we coasted this Ice *A maine bank* to the Northward, we found it to be a maine banke of *of Ice.* Ice; for we saw the other end of it to beare West North-west from us; the winde being at South South-west, little winde: Then we ranne West South-west, to cleere us of the Ice. The nineteenth, the winde was at East South-east, with some small raine. The twentieth, our course was West North-west, the winde being at North and by East, little winde. This day sometimes we came into *Black water* blacke water as thicke as puddle, and in sailing a little *as thick as* space the water would be cleare againe. Seeing this *puddle.* change of water, so often to be thick, and cleare againe so suddenly, we imagined it had beene shallow water: then we sounded, and could fetch no ground in one hundred and twenty fathomes: and the Sea was so smooth, that we could discerne no current at all. At this time *The Cape of* I reckoned the Cape of desolation to beare North North-*desolation.* east twentie foure leagues from us. The one and twentieth, the winde was variable. The two and *60. deg. 37.* twentieth, we were in the latitude of 60. degrees and *min.* 37. minutes: the winde being at West, wee ranne North and by West. The seaven and twentieth, the winde was at West South-west: then our course was North-west and by North, the weather faire and warme, as in England, in the moneth of May. This day we saw great store of *Store of Guls.* Gulles, which followed our Ship sundry dayes.

The eight and twentieth, the winde being at North

and by West, wee directed our course to the Westward; and about twelve of the clocke the same night, we descried the land of America, in the latitude of 62. degrees and 30. minutes; which we made to be Warwicks foreland. This Headland rose like an Iland. And when we came neere the Foreland, we saw foure small Ilands to the Northwards, and three small Ilands to the Southward of the same Foreland. The Foreland was high land: all the tops of the hils were covered with Snow. The three small Ilands to the Southward were also white, that we could not discerne them from Ilands of Ice: also there was great store of drift Ice upon the Eastside of this Foreland: but the Sea was altogether voide of Ice: the Land did lye North and by East, and South and by West, being six leagues of length.

The nine and twentieth, at sixe of the clocke in the morning, wee were within three leagues of this Foreland: then the winde came up at North-east and by East, a good stiffe gale with fogge: and wee were forced to stand to the Southward, because wee could not wether the Land to the Northward: and as wee stood to the Southward along by Warwicks Foreland, we could discerne none otherwise, but that it was an Iland. Which if it fall out to be so, then Lumleys Inlet, and the next Southerly Inlet, where the great Current setteth to the West, must of necessitie be one Sea; which will be the greatest hope of the passage that way. The thirtieth, the winde was at North-east, with fogge and Snow. This day wee came into a great whirling of a Current, being in the latitude of 61. degrees, and about twelve leagues from the coast of America.

The first day of July, the winde was at West, with fogge and Snow; the ayre being very cold. This day wee came into many Overfals, which seemed to runne a great current; but which way it did set, wee could not well discerne. The greatest likelihood was, that it should set to the West. But having contrary windes some sixteene or seventeene dayes, we alwayes lay in traverse

[III.iv.811.]

*Warwicks Foreland supposed to be an Iland.
The greatest hope of the North-west passage.
A current Westward in sixtie one degrees.*

among these overfals; but could never finde any great current by our courses: wee sounded sometimes, but could get no ground in one hundred and twentie fathomes.

A maine bank of Ice in 60 degrees. The second day, wee descried a maine Banke of Ice in the latitude of 60. degrees: the winde was at North North-west, and very faire weather. Wee wanting fresh water did sayle close to this Land of Ice, and hoysed out our Boate, and loaded her twice with Ice, which made us very good fresh water. Within twenty leagues of the *The North coast of America seemeth to be broken land.* coast of America, wee should oftentimes come into many great overfals. Which doth manifestly shew, that all the coast of America is broken Land.

The third, the winde was at South-west, very foggie: and as wee stood toward the coast of America, wee met with another maine Banke of Ice. The fogge was so thicke, that we were hard by the Ice, before wee could see it. But it pleased God that the winde was faire to put us cleare from this Ice againe; and presently it began to cleare up, so that wee could see two or three leagues off; but we could see no end of the Ice. Wee judged this Ice to be some tenne leagues from the coast of *Blacke puddle water.* America. We found the water to be very blackish and thicke, like puddle water.

The eight, the winde was at North North-west, very faire weather; wee standing to the Westwards met with a mighty maine Banke of Ice, which was a great length and breadth, and it did rest close to the shoare. And at eleven of the clocke in the forenoone, wee descried againe the *America againe discried in 63. deg. 53. min.* Land of America, in the latitude of 63. degrees and 53. minutes, being very high Land: and it did rise as Ilands, the toppes being covered with Snow. This Land was South-west and by West, some five leagues off us: we could come no neerer it for the great quantitie of Ice, which rested by the shoare side.

The ninth, the winde being at North-east and by East, blew so extreamely, that we were forced to stand to the Southward, both to cleare our selves of the Land, and of the Ice: for the day before we passed a great banke

of Ice, which was some foureteene leagues to the Eastward
of us, when the storme began; but thankes be to God,
we cleared our selves both of the Land and of the Ice.
This day in the afternoone the storme grew so extreame,
that we were forced to stand along with our forecourse
to the Southward.

The seventeenth was very foggie, the winde being at
East: and about two of the clocke in the afternoone, wee
saw foure great Ilands of Ice, of a huge bignesse: and
about foure of the clocke we came among some small
scattered Ice, and supposed our selves to be neere some
great Banke. The fogge was very thicke, but the winde
large to stand backe the same way wee came in; or else
it would have indangered our lives very much. And at
nine of the clocke at night we heard a great noyse, as *The loathsome*
though it had bin the breach of some shoare. Being *noyse of Ice.*
desirous to see what it was, we stood with it, and found
it to be the noyse of a great quantity of Ice, which was
very loathsome to be heard. Then wee stood North
North-west, and the fogge continued so thicke, that wee
could not see two Shippes length from us: whereupon
we thought good to take in some of our sayles; and when
our men came to hand them, they found our sayles, ropes, *Sayles, ropes*
and tacklings, so hard frozen, that it did seeme very strange *and tackling*
unto us, being in the chiefest time of Summer. *frozen.*

The eighteenth day, the winde was at North-east and
by North, the ayre being very cleere and extreame cold,
with an exceeding great frost; and our course was North-
west. This day in the forenoone, when we did set our
sayles, we found our ropes and tacklings harder frozen
then they were the day before: which frost did annoy
us so much in the using of our ropes and sayles, that wee
were enforced to breake off the Ice from our ropes, that
they might runne through the blockes. And at two of the
clocke in the afternoone, the winde began to blow very
hard, with thicke fogge, which freezed so fast as it did fall *Thick fogge*
upon our sayles, ropes, and tackling, that we could not *freezing as*
almost hoyse or strike our sayles, to have any use of them. *fast as it fell.*

This extreame frost and long continuance thereof, was a maine barre to our proceedings to the Northward, and the discouraging of all our men.

The nineteenth day, the winde was at North and by East, and our course to the Eastwards. The same night following, all our men conspired secretly together, to beare up the helme for England, while I was asleepe in my Cabin, and there to have kept mee by force, untill I had sworn unto them that I would not offer any violence unto them for so doing. And indeede they had drawn in writing, the causes of their bearing up of the helme, and thereunto set their hands, and would have left them in my Cabin: but by good chance I understood their pretence, and prevented them for that time.

The twentieth day, I called the chiefest of my Company into my Cabin, before Master John Cartwright our Preacher, and our Master, William Cobreth, to heare what reasons they could alleadge for the bearing up of the Helme, which might be an overthrow to the Voyage, seeing the Merchants had bin at so great a charge with it. After much conference, they delivered mee their reasons in writing:

Concluding, that although it were granted, that we might winter betweene 60. and 70. degrees of latitude, with safetie of our lives and Vessels, yet it will be May next before wee can dismore them, to lanch out into the Sea. And therefore if the Merchants should have purpose to proceede on the discoverie of these North-west parts of America; the next yeare you may be in the aforesaid latitudes for England, by the first of May, and so be furnished better with men and victuals, to passe and proceede in the aforesaid action.

Seeing then that you cannot assure us of a safe harbour to the Northward, wee purpose to beare up the Helme for England, yet with this limitation, that if in your wisedome, you shall thinke good to make any discovery, either in 60. or 57. degrees, with this faire Northerly winde, we yeelde our lives with your selfe, to encounter any danger. Thus much we thought needefull to signifie, as a matter builded upon reason, and not proceeding upon feare or cowardise.

Then, wee being in the latitude of 68. degrees and 53. minutes: the next following, about eleven of the clocke, they bare up the Helme, being all so bent, that there was no meanes to perswade them to the contrary. At last understanding of it, I came forth of my Cabin, and demanded of them, who bare up the Helme? They answered me, One and All. So they hoysed up all the sayle they could, and directed their course South and by West.

68. deg. 53. min.

They return from the North.

The two and twentieth, I sent for the chiefest of those, which were the cause of the bearing up of the Helme, and punished them severely, that this punishment might be a warning to them afterward for falling into the like mutinie. In the end, upon the intreatie of Master Cartwright our Preacher, and the Master, William Cobreath, upon their submission, I remitted some part of their punishment. At twelve of the clocke at noone, wee came hard by a great Iland of Ice: the Sea being very smooth and almost calme, wee hoysed out the Boates of both our Shippes: being in want of fresh water, and went to this Iland to get some Ice to make us fresh water. And as wee were breaking off some of this Ice (which was verie painefull for us to doe; for it was almost as hard as a Rocke:) the great Iland of Ice gave a mightie cracke two or three times, as though it had bin a thunder-clappe; and presently the Iland began to overthrow, which was like to have sunke both our Boates, if wee had not made good haste from it. But thankes be to God, we escaped this danger very happily, and came aboord with both our Boates, the one halfe laden with Ice. There was great store of Sea Foule upon this Iland of Ice.

Mutiners punished.

A great Iland of Ice cracked like a thunder-clap, and was overthrowne.

Great store of Sea Foule upon the Ice.

The five and twentieth and six and twentieth, the winde being at East, did blow a hard gale, and our course was West and by South, with fogge. This day in the afternoone I did reckon my selfe to be in the entering of an

A.D.
1602.

An Inlet in 61. degrees & 40. minutes.

Inlet, which standeth in the latitude of 61. degrees and 40. minutes.

The seven and twentieth, the winde was at South Southeast, and blew very hard, our course was West. The eight and twentieth and nine and twentieth, our course was West and by South, the winde blowing very hard at East South-east, with fogge and raine. The thirtieth, the winde came up in a showre by the West North-west, blowing so hard, that wee were forced to put a fore the Sea. Now because the time of the yeare was farre spent, and many of our men in both Shippes sicke, wee thought *The return out* it good to returne with great hope of this Inlet, to bee *of the Inlet.* a passage of more possibilitie, then through the Straight of Davis: because I found it not much pestered with Ice, and to be a straight of fortie leagues broad. Also I sayled an hundred leagues West and by South, within this *The variation* Inlet; and there I found the variation to be 35. degrees *35. degrees* to the Westward, and the needle to decline, or rather *Westward.* incline 83. degrees and an halfe.

The fifth of August (the winde all that while Westerly) wee were cleare of this Inlet againe. The sixth the winde was at East South-east with fogge. The seaventh, eight, and ninth, we passed by many great Ilands of Ice. The *An Iland on* ninth day at night, we descried the land of America, in *the coast of* the latitude of 55. degrees, and 30. minutes. This Land *America in* was an Iland, being but low land and very smooth: then *55. deg. &* the night approaching, and the weather being something *30. min.* foggie and darke, we were forced to stand to the Northward againe. This night we passed by some great Ilands of Ice, and some bigge peeces which did breake from the [III.iv.813.] great Ilands: and we were like to strike some of them two or three times: which if we had done, it might have *The God-* endangered our Shippes and lives. Our consort, the God- *speede stroke* speede, strooke a little piece of Ice, which they thought *upon a piece of* had foundred their Shippe; but thankes be to God they *Ice.* received no great hurt, for our Shippes were very strong.

The tenth day, the winde was at North-east and by North, with fogge and raine; and our course was to the

314

South-eastward: for we could by no meanes put with the shoare, by reason of the thicknesse of the fogge, and that the winde blew right upon the shoare, so that we were forced to beare saile to keepe our selves from the land, untill it pleased God to send us a cleare, which God knoweth we long wanted. At sixe of the clocke in the afternoone, it was calme; and then I judged my selfe, by mine account, to be neere the Land: so I sounded, and had ground in 160. fathomes, and fine grey Osie Sand: and there was a great Iland of Ice, a ground within a league of us, where we sounded, and within one houre it pleased God to send us a cleere. Then we saw the land some foure leagues South-west and by South from us. This land lyeth East and by South, and West and by North, being good high land, but all Ilands, as farre as *Many Ilands.* wee could discerne. This calme continued untill foure of the clocke in the afternoone of the eleventh day: the weather being very cleere, we could not discerne any Current to goe at all by this Land. This day the Sea did set us in about a league neerer the Land, so that wee judged our selves three leagues off. Here we sounded againe, and had but eightie fathoms.

The variation of the Compasse we found to be 22. *The variation* degrees and 10. minutes Westward. At five of the clocke *22. degrees to* there sprung up a fine gale of winde, at East South-east, *West.* and being so neere night, wee stood to the Southward, thinking the next day to seeke some harbour. But it pleased God, the next day, being the twelfth, to send us a storme of foule weather, the winde being at East *A Storme.* and by South, with fogge: so that we could by no meanes get the shoare. Thus wee were forced to beate up and downe at Sea, untill it should please God to send us better weather.

The foureteenth, I thought good to stand to the Westward to search an Inlet, in the latitude of 56. degrees. I have good hope of a passage that way, by many great and probable reasons.

The fifteenth the winde continued at the South, with

exceeding faire weather, and our course was West. We

55. deg. 31.
min.
Variation 17.
degr. 15. min.
They discrie
the land again.

were this day at noone in the latitude of 55. degrees and 31. minutes: and I found the variation to be 17. degrees and 15. minutes, to the Westward. And about seven of the clocke at night, we descried the Land againe, being tenne leagues to the Eastward of this Inlet. This Land did beare from us South-west, some eight leagues off: and about nine of the clocke the same night, the winde came to the West; which blew right against us for our entring into this Inlet.

The sixteenth, the winde was at West North-west, and was very faire weather, and our course South-west: about nine of the clocke in the forenoone, we came by a great Iland of Ice; and by this Iland we found some peeces of Ice broken off from the said Iland: And being in great want of fresh water, wee hoysed out our Boates of both Shippes, and loaded them twice with Ice, which made us very good fresh water. This day at noone wee

55. deg. 20.
min.

found our selves to be in the latitude of 55. degrees and twentie minutes: when we had taken in our Ice and Boates, the weather being very faire and cleare, and the winde at West North-west, we bent our course for the Land, and about three of the clocke in the afternoone, we were within three leagues of the shoare. It is a very

A pleasant
low land, being
all Ilands.
55. degrees.
The variation
18. deg. and
12. min.
Westward.

Temperate
ayre.
Great hope of
a passage in
three places.

pleasant low Land; but all Ilands, and goodly sounds going betweene them, toward the South-west. This Land doth stand in the latitude of 55. degrees; and I found the variation to be to the West 18. degrees and 12. minutes. This coast is voide of Ice, unlesse it be some great Ilands of Ice, that come from the North, and so by windes may be driven upon this coast. Also we did finde the ayre in this place to be very temperate. Truely there is in three severall places great hope of a passage, betweene the latitude of 62. and 54. degrees; if the fogge doe not hinder it, which is all the feare I have. At sixe of the clocke, wee being becalmed by the shoare, there appeared unto us a great ledge of rockes, betweene us and the shoare, as though the Sea did flye

over it with a great height. As we all beheld it, within
one houre, upon a sudden it vanished cleane away; which
seemed very strange unto us all. And to the Eastward
of us, some two leagues, we saw a great Rocke, lying
some three leagues off the Land: we then supposing it
to be shoald water, by this broken ground, sounded, but
could get no ground in one hundred and sixtie fathoms.
About seven of the clocke, there sprung up a gale of
winde, by the South South-east, which was a very good
winde to coast this Land.

But the seventeenth in the morning, the winde being
at the South, it began to blow so extreamely, that we
durst not stay by the shoare, for it was like to be a great
storme: then our course was East North-east, to get us
Sea roome. This storme still increasing, our flye-boates
did receive in much water; for they wanted a Sparre-decke,
which wee found very dangerous for the Sea. About
twelve of the clocke at noone, this day there rose up a
great showre in the West, and presently the winde came
out of that quarter with a whirle, and taking up the Sea
into the ayre, and blew so extreamely, that we were forced
alwayes to runne before the Sea, howsoever the winde did
blow. And within twelve houres after this storme
beganne, the Sea was so much growen, that we thought
our flye Boates would not have beene able to have endured
it.

The eighteenth, the winde was at North-west, and the
storme increased more extreame, and lasted untill eight
of the clocke in the morning of the nineteenth day, so
furious, that to my remembrance, I never felt a greater:
yet when we were in our greatest extremities, the Lord
delivered us his unworthy servants. And if the winde,
with so great a storme, had bin either Northerly, or
Southerly, or Easterly but one day, we had all perished
against the Rocks, or the Ice: for wee were entred thirty
leagues within a Head-land of an Inlet, in the latitude
of 56. degrees. But it pleased God to send us the winde
so faire, as we could desire, both to cleare our selves of

*A great ledg of
Rocks strangly
vanishing.
A great Rocke.*

*A Whirl-
winde taking
up the Sea.*

[III.iv.814.]

*They were
entered 30.
leagues into an
Inlet in 56.
degrees.*

317

the Land and Ice. Which opportunitie caused us for this

time to take our leaves of the coast of America, and to shape our course for England.

The fourth, in the morning, wee descried the Iland of Silly North-east and by East, some foure leagues off us. Then wee directed our course East and by North: and at tenne of the clocke in the forenoone, wee descried the

Lands end, and next day were forced to put into Dartmouth.

Chap. XIV.

James Hall his Voyage forth of Denmarke for the discovery of Greeneland, in the yeare 1605. abbreviated.

IN the name of God Amen, we set sayle from Copeman-haven in Denmarke, the second day of May, in the yeare of our redemption 1605. with two Shippes and a Pinnace: The Admirall, called the Frost, a shippe of the burthen of thirty or fortie lasts, wherein was Captaine, and

chiefe commander of the whole Fleet, Captaine John Cunningham, a Scottish Gentleman, servant unto the Kings Majestie of Denmarke, my selfe being principall Pilot. The Lyon Viceadmirall, being about the foresaid burthen, wherein was Captaine, one Godscaio Lindenose, a Danish Gentleman, and Steereman of the same, one Peter Kilson of Copeman-haven. The Pinnace, a Barke of the burthen of twelve Lasts, or thereabouts: wherein

was Steereman or commander, one John Knight, my Countrie-man. So setting sayle from Copeman-haven, with a faire gale of winde Easterly, wee came unto Elsonure, where we anchored, to take in our water.

The third day we tooke in our water, at which time, the Captaines, my selfe, with the Lieutenants, and the other Steeremen, did thinke it convenient to set downe certaine Articles, for the better keeping of company one

with another, to which Articles or covenants wee were
all severally sworne, setting thereunto our hands.

The sixt we came to Flecorie, into which harbour, by *Flecorie.*
Gods helpe, we came at two a clocke in the afternoone.
The seaventh day we supplied our wants of wood and
water. The eight day, about two a clocke in the afternoone, we set sayle forth of the harbour of Flecorie, about
six a clock it fell calme, till about eight, about which
time, the Nase of Norway, by the Danish men, called
Lyndis-nose, bare next hand North-west of us, sixe leagues
off; at which time I directed my course West North-
west, finding the compasse varied 7. degrees 10. minutes,
to the Eastwards of the true North.

The thirteenth, we had sight of the Iland of Faire Ile,
and also of the South-head of Shotland, called Swimborne
head, which are high Lands: at noone, the Iland of Faire
Ile bearing West halfe a point Northerly: foure leagues
off I made observation, and found us in the latitude of *Variation*
59. degrees 20. minutes. This night about seven a clocke, *observed.*
wee came about an English league to the Northwards
of the North-west end of Faire Ile, wee met with a great
race of a tyde, as though it had beene the race of Portland, *A race of a*
it setting North North-west. Being out of the said race, *tide.*
I directed my course West and by North, having the
winde North-east and by North: this evening Faire Ile
bearing East South-east foure leagues; Swimborne head,
North-east and by North eight leagues: the Iland of
Foole, North-east and by East, seven leagues. I found
by exact observation, the compasse to be varied to the *Variation*
East-ward of the true North 60. degrees 10. minutes. *observed.*

The fourteenth in the morning, the winde came to the
East South-east, wee steering West and by North away:
this morning the Iland of Faire Ile did shew in my sight
to bee about ten leagues off, at which time we did descrie
two of the Westermost Ilands of Orkney, which did beare
South-west and by South.

The eighteenth, the winde at North-west and by West,
wee laid it away South-west and by West, and sometimes

South-west. This day at noone wee were in the Latitude of 58. degrees 40. minutes. The nineteenth day, the winde at South-west and South-west and by West, wee lying as the night before, being at noone in the Latitude of 59. degrees and a halfe. The foure and twentieth day, the winde at North-east and by East, we steering still with a fresh gale West South-west, this evening we looked *Busse Iland* to have seene Busse Iland, but I doe verily suppose the *wrong placed.* same to be placed in a wrong Latitude in the Marine Charts. The sixe and twentieth at noone, wee were in the latitude of 57. degrees 45. minutes. The thirtieth day in the morning betweene seven and eight, the weather began to cleere, and the Sea and winde to waxe lesse, wee looking for the Lion and the Pinnasse, could have no sight of them, we supposing them to bee asterne off us, we standing still under our courses. This day the winde came to the North-east and by East, being very cold weather, we lying North North-west away. Making my observation at noone, I found us in the latitude of 59. degrees 15. minutes, our way North North-west fortie leagues. This afternoon between one and two a clock *First sight of* we descried Land, it bearing North North-east off us *Groenland.* about ten leagues off North-east & by North off us about ten leagues, it being a very high ragged land, lying in the latitude of 59. degrees 50. minutes, lying alongst South-east and by South, and North-west and by North.

Cape This Head-land wee named after the Kings Majesties *Christian.* of Denmarke, because it was the first part of Groenland, which we did see. This afternoone about one a clock, bearing in for the shoare we saw an Iland of Ice, which bore West South-west of us three leagues off, so having the wind at East South-east, we bore in for the shoare, *The shoare* where wee found so much Ice that it was impossible either *full of Ice.* for us or any other ship to come into the shoare without great danger: yet wee put our selves into the Ice as wee thought convenient, being incumbred and compassed about with the same in such sort, as the Captaine, my selfe, the Boatswaine with another of our companie, were forced

to goe overboord upon an Iland of Ice, to defend it from
the ship, at which time I thought it convenient to stand
off into the Sea againe, and so being cleere of the Ice,
to double Cape Desolation, to the North-westwards of *Cape*
which I doubted not but to find a cleer coast, so standing *Desolation.*
away all this night West South-west, to cleere us of the
Ice, which lay farre from the shoare, being very thicke
towards the Land with great Ilands of Ice that it is
wonderfull. This evening, the Cape Christian bearing
North-east and by East five leagues, I found the Compasse *Compasse*
varied 12. degrees 15. minutes to the North-westwards. *varied.*
Moreover, standing to Seaward from the foresaid Cape,
we came in blacke water, as thicke as though it had beene *Black water.*
puddle water, we sayling in the same for the space of
three houres.

The one and thirtieth in the morning faire weather,
with the winde somewhat variable, wee steering away
North-west and by West, betweene foure and five in the
morning we had sight of the Lion againe, but not of the *Sight of the*
Pinnasse. They being a Sea-boord off and having espied *Lion.*
us, they stood with us, at which time the Captaine, Lieutenant, and Steereman came aboord us, earnestly intreating
mee to bestow a Sea Chart of the Steerman, and to give
him directions if by tempestuous weather they should
lose us, they protesting and swearing that they would
never leave us as long as winde and weather would permit
them to keepe companie with us. By whose speeches
I being perswaded did give them a Sea Chart for those
Coasts, telling them that if they would follow me, that
by Gods assistance I would bring them to a part of the
Land void without pester of Ice, and also harbour the
ships in good Harbour, by Gods helpe; they swearing
and protesting, that they would follow mee so long as
possibly they could, with which oathes and faire speeches
I rested satisfied, thinking they had thought as they had
sworne, but it fell out otherwise. So having made an
end with us about noone, they went aboord againe, wee
being this day in the latitude of 59. degrees 45. minutes,

having stood all the night before, and this forenoone also, so nigh the shoare as wee could for Ice, the Cape Christian South South-east and North North-west, and from the Cape to Cape Desolation, the Land lyeth East and by South, and West and by North about fiftie leagues. This day betweene one and two a clocke, the Vice-admirals Boat, being newly gone aboord, it fell very hasie and thicke, so that wee could not see one another by reason of the fog, therefore our Captaine caused to shoote off certaine Muskets with a great peece of Ordnance, to the intent the Lion might heare us, which heard of them they presently stood with us, at which time the fogge began somewhat to cleere, wee having sight one of another and so stood alongst the shoare, as nigh as we could for Ice.

The first of June, wee had a fresh gale of winde at South-west, wee steering North-east and by North into the shoare, about three in the morning there fell a mightie fogge, so that we were forced to lye by the lee, for the Lion playing upon our Drum to the intent for them to heare us, and to keepe companie with us, they answering us againe with the shooting of a Musket, wee trimming our sailes, did the like to them, and so stood away North-east and by East: larboord tackt aboord halfe a glasse,

Ilands of Ice.
Mightie
incumbrance of
Ice.
A mightie
current setting
North North-
west. when we were hard incumbred amongst mightie Ilands of Ice, being very high like huge Mountaines, so I caused to cast about and stand to the Westwards North-west and by West. About twelve of the clocke this night it being still calme, wee found our selves suddenly compast round about with great Ilands of Ice, which made such a hideous noyse as was most wonderfull, so that by no meanes wee could double the same to the Westward: wherefore wee were forced to stand it away to the Southwards, South

South-West, stemming the Current, for by the same Current wee were violently brought into this Ice, so being incumbred and much to doe to keepe cleere of the mightie Ilands of Ice, there being as both I and others did plainly see upon one of them a huge rocke stone, of the weight of three hundred pounds or thereabouts, as wee did suppose. Thus being troubled in the Ice for the space of two or three houres, it pleased God that we got thorow the same.

The second day in the morning about three a clocke, I came forth of my Cabin, where I found that the Shipper whose name was Arnold had altered my course which I had set, going contrarie to my directions North North-west away, whereupon hee and I grew to some speeches, both for at this time and other times hee had done the like. The Captaine likewise seeing his bad dealing with me, did likewise roundly speake his minde to him, for at this instant wee were nigh unto a great banke of Ice, which wee might have doubled if my course had not beene altered, so that we were forced to cast about to the South-wards, South and by East and South South-east, with the winde at South-west and by South or South-west till ten a clocke, when we stood againe to the Westwards, lying West North-west and North-west and by West, being at noone in the latitude of 60. degrees 18. minutes, Cape Desolation is, I did suppose, bearing North and by West three or foure leagues off, the weather being so thicke and hasie that wee could never see the Land.

The fourth day betweene one and two a clocke in the morning, it began to blow a fresh gale Easterly, we steering away North and North and by West, we being at noone in the latitude of 59. degrees 50. minutes, having made a West and by North way foure and twentie leagues. This evening about seven a clocke we had very thicke water, and continued so about halfe an houre: about nine a clocke we did see a very high Iland of Ice to the windward of us, and about halfe an houre after with some drift Ice, they in the Lion thorow the fearefull-nesse of their Commanders presently cast about standing away larboord tackt, till they did perceive that I stood still away as I did before, without impediment of the Ice, they cast about againe and followed us.

The fift in the morning, being very faire weather with

the winde at East South-east, our course North North-west, some of our people supposed they had seene the Land: our Captaine and I went aboord the Pinnasse, when after an houre of our being there wee did see the supposed Land to be an hasie fogge, which came on us so fast that wee could scarce see one another. But the Lion being very nigh unto us, and it being very calme, wee laid the Pinnasse aboord of her, and so the Captaine and I went aboord of them.

The ninth day about foure a clocke, it began to blow an easie gale at South-east and by South, I directing my course still North North-west, when some of our people would not be perswaded but they did see Land, and therefore I stood in North and by East and North North-east, till about three a clocke in the afternoone, when wee met *A huge high* with a huge and high Iland of Ice, wee steering hard to *Iland of Ice.* board the same, and being shot a little to Northwards of it, there fell from the top thereof some quantitie of Ice, *Noyse by the* which in the fall did make such a noyse as though it had *fall.* beene the report of five Cannons. This evening wee came amongst much drift Ice, being both windwards and to leewards of us, yet by Gods helpe we got very well through the same, when being cleere I directed my course againe North North-west.

The tenth day the winde at South-west and by West, I steering still North-west and by North. This forenoone also wee met with great Ilands of Ice, it being very hasie and thicke weather, the which did drive them in the Lion into great feare, and calling to us very fearfully perswaded me to alter my course and to returne homeward, saying that it was impossible for us by any working, and course keeping to sease upon the Land, which did drive all our *Our people* companie into such a feare, that they were determined, *determined to* whether I would or not, to have returned home, had not *returne backe* the Captaine as an honest and resolute Gentleman stood *againe.* by mee, protesting to stand by me so long as his blood was warme, for the good of the Kings Majestie, who had set us forth, and also to the performing of the Voyage.

Which resolution of his did mitigate the stubbornenesse
of the people: yet nothing would perswade those fearfull
persons in the Lion, especially the Steerman, who had
rather long before this time have returned home, then
to have proceeded on the action, as before the said Steerman had done when he was imployed eight yeeres before *Former*
in the said action or discoverie. Therefore our Captaine *discoveries.*
and my selfe seeing their backwardnesse now, as before
we had done, went our selves the same evening into the
Pinnasse, having a mightie banke of Ice of our larboord *A mightie*
side, and spake to them very friendly, giving order both *banke of Ice.*
to our owne ship and to them, that they should keepe a
Seaboord of us (for I did suppose this banke of Ice to
lye in the narrowest of the Streight, betweene America
and Groenland, as indeed by experience I found the same
to be) therefore I determined to coast the Ice alongst till
I found it to bee driven and fall away, by reason of the
swift current that setteth very forcibly through the said
Strait, and then by the grace of God to set over for a
cleere part of the coast of Groenland, so all this night
we coasted the Ice as close aboord as we could East North-
east and North-east and by East, till about midnight,
when we found the said banke to fall away.

The eleventh day, being cleere of the Ice, I stood away
North North-east till sixe a clocke, when we met with [III.iv.817.]
another great banke of Ice, at which time the Commanders *Another banke*
of the Lion being now againe very fearfull as before, *of Ice.*
came up to our ship, perswading the Shipper and Companie to leave us, and to stand to Seaboord with them.
But the Shipper who was also Lieftenant of the ship,
being more honestly minded, said, that he would follow
us so long as he could: with which answere they departed,
using many spitefull wordes, both of the Captaine and
mee, saying we were determined to betray the Kings
ships, at which time they shot off a peece of Ordnance, *The Lions*
and so stood away from us. I seeing their perverse *departing*
dealing let them goe, wee coasting alongst the Ice North *from us.*
North-east with a fresh gale, it being extreme cold with

PURCHAS HIS PILGRIMES

snow and hayse, the Sea also going very high by reason
of a mightie current, the which I found to set very force-
ably through this Strait, which being nigh unto America
side, setteth to the Northwards, and on the other side
to the contrarie, as by proofe I found. So coasting alongst
this mayne banke of Ice, which seemed as it had beene
a firme Continent till about eleven a clocke, when wee
espyed the Ice to stretch to windward, on our weather
bow wee setting our starboord takes aboord, stood away
East and by South with the winde at South and by East,
till wee had doubled a Seaboord the Ice, at which time
I directed my course directly over for the cleere coast of
Groineland, East and by North, which course I directed
all the Frost to goe, wee standing away our course all
this night, it being very much snow and sleete.

Sight of Land. The twelfth day in the morning about foure a clocke,
we espyed the Land of Groenland, being a very high
ragged Land, the tops of the Mountaines being all covered
with snow, yet wee found all this coast utterly without
Ice, wee standing into the Land espyed a certaine Mount
above all the rest, which Mount is the best marke on
Mount all this Coast, the which I named Mount Cunningham
Cunningham. after the name of my Captaine. We comming into the
shoare betweene two Capes or Head-lands, the Land lying
betweene them North and by East, and South and by
Queene Annes West, the Southmost of which Forelands I named Queene
Cape. Annes Cape, after the name of the Queenes Majestie
of Denmarke, and the Northermost of the two I called
Queene Queene Sophias Cape, after the name of the Queene
Sophias Cape. Mother.

So standing into the Land, we came amongst certaine
Ilands, where sayling in still amongst the same unto the
Southermost foot of the foresaid Mount, wee came into
a goodly Bay, which wee did suppose to be a River, being
on both sides of the same very high and steepe Moun-
Christians taines, wee named the same King Christianus Foord, after
Foord. the name of the Kings Majestie of Denmarke. So sayling
up this Bay, which wee supposed to bee a River, the space

of sixe or seven English leagues, finding in all that space no anchoring, being marvellous deepe water, till at the length we had sayled up the Bay the foresaid distance, at length I brought the Ship and Pinnasse to an anchor *Our* in sixteene fathom shelly ground, at which time our *Anchoring.* Captaine and I went aland, giving thankes unto God for his unspeakable benefits, who had thus dealt with us as to bring us to this desired Land into so good an Harbour; which done, the Captaine and I walked up *Our first* the Hills, to see if wee could see any of the people, *landing in* having our Boat to row alongst with us. Having gone *Groinland.* alongst the River side upon the tops of the Hills the space of three or foure English miles; at length looking towards our Boat, wee saw upon the River side foure of the people standing by their Houses or rather Tents, *Our first sight* covered over with Seale-skins. Wee comming downe the *of the people.* Hills towards them (they having espyed us) three of them ranne away upon the Land, and the other tooke his Boat and rowed away leaving their Tents. Wee being come downe the Hills called to our men in the Boat, and entring into her rowed towards the Savage who was in his Boat *Boat of Seale* made of Seale-skins. Hee holding up his hands towards *skins.* the Sunne, cryed Yota; wee doing the like, and shewing to him a knife, hee presently came unto us and tooke the same of the Captaine. When hee had presently rowed away from us, wee rowed a little after him, and seeing it was but in vaine wee rowed aland againe and went *Our entring* into their Tents, which wee found covered (as is aforesaid) *into their* with Seale-skins. Wee finding by the houses two Dogs *Tents.* being very rough and fat, like in shape to a Foxe, with very great abundance of Seale fish, lying round about their Tents a drying, with innumerable quantities of a little fish unto a Smelt (which fish are commonly called Sardeenes) of which fish in all the Rivers are wonderfull skuls, these fishes also lay a drying round about their Tents in the Sunne in great heapes, with other sundrie kindes. Then entring into their Tents, wee found certaine Seale skins and Foxe skins very well drest; also certaine Coates of Seale skins and Fowle skins with the feather side inward: also certaine Vessels boyling upon a little Lampe, the Vessell being made after the manner of a little Pan, the bottome whereof is made of stone, and the sides of Whales finnes; in which Vessell was some little quantitie of Seale fish boyling in Seale oyle; and searching further, wee did finde in another of their Vessels a Dogs head boyled, so that I perswaded my selfe that they eate Dogs flesh. Moreover, by their houses there did lye two great Boates, being covered under with Seales skins, but aloft open after the forme of our Boates, being about twentie foote in length, having in each of them eight or ten tosts or seates for men to sit on, which Boates, as afterwards I did perceive, is for the transporting of their Tents and baggage from place to place, and for a saile they have the guts of some beast, which they dresse very fine and thin, which they sow together.

Eaters of Dogs.

Also the other sorts of their Boats are such as Captaine Frobisher, and Master John Davis brought into England, which is but for one man, being cleane covered over with Seale skins artificially dressed except one place to sit in, being within set out with certaine little ribs of Timber, wherin they use to row with one Oare more swiftly, then our men can doe with ten, in which Boates they fish being disguised in their Coates of Seale skinnes, whereby they deceive the Seales, who take them rather for Seales then men; which Seales or other fish they kill in this manner. They shoot at the Seales or other great fish with their Darts, unto which they use to tye a bladder, which doth boy up the fish in such manner that by the said means they catch them. So comming aboord our ships having left certaine trifles behind us in their Tents, and taking nothing away with us, within halfe an houre after our comming aboord, the Savage to whom wee had given the Knife with three others, which we did suppose to be them which we saw first, came rowing to our ships in their Boats, holding up their hands to the Sunne, and striking of their brests, crying Yota. We doing the like,

[III.iv.818.]
Of the other sort of Boats. There is one of these Boats in Sir T. Smiths Hall.

The manner of killing of their great fish or Seales.

Their comming to our ships.

they came to our shippe or Captaine: giving them bread
and Wine, which, as it did seeme, they made little account
of; yet they gave us some of their dryed fishes, at which
time there came foure more, who with the other bartered
their Coats, and some Seale skinnes, with our folke for
old Iron Nailes, and other trifles as Pinnes and Needles,
with which they seemed to be wonderfully pleased, and
having so done, holding their hands towards the Sunne
they departed.

The thirteenth, there came fourteene of them to our
ship, bringing with them Seale skinnes, Whale Finnes,
with certayne of their Darts and Weapons, which they
bartered with our people, as before. This day I made
observation of the latitude, and found this Roadsted in *Observation of*
the latitude of 66. degrees 25. minutes, and the mouth *the latitude.*
of this Bay or Sound, lyeth in the latitude of 66. degrees
30. minutes. Also here I made observation of the tydes, *Observation of*
and found an East and West Moone to make a full Sea, *the tides.*
upon the Full and Change, more it floweth, three fathome
and an halfe water, right up and downe.

The fourteenth and fifteenth dayes we rode still, the
people comming to us, and bartering with us for pieces
of old Iron, or Nailes, Whale Finnes, Seales Skinnes,
Morse Teeth, and a kind of Horne which we doe suppose
to be Unicornes Horne, at which time the Captaine went
with our Boat, to the place where we had seene their
Tents, but found them removed; and the other fish and
the Seale fish lying still a drying: the Captaine taking
a quantitie of the Sea fish into the Boat, caused some of
the Mariners to boyle it ashoare, the Savages helping
our men to doe the same, the Captaine using them very
friendly, they having made about a barrell and an halfe
of Oyle, leaving it aland all night, thinking to bring
the same aboord in the morning. But the Savages the
same night let the same forth. Yet notwithstanding, the
Captaine shewed no manner of discontent towards them. *Our departing*

The sixteenth day, I went into the Pinnasse, to discover *in the Pinnasse*
certaine Harbours to the Northwards, the wind being *from the ship.*

at East South-east, I loosed and set saile, but instantly it fell calme, and so continued about an houre. When the wind came opposite at the West North-west a stiffe gale, we spending the tide till the floud being come, I put roome againe, and came to an Anchor a little from the Frost in twelve fathomes sandie ground. About one in the afternoone, the Frost departed from us further up the Bay, which we did suppose to be a River, promising to abide our returne two and twentie dayes.

The seventeenth day, the wind continuing at the West North-west blowing very hard, wee rode still, the people comming and bartering with us.

The eighteenth day, the winde and weather as before, wee riding still. This forenoone there came to the number of thirtie of them, and bartered with us as they had done before, which done, they went ashoare at a certaine point about a flight-shot off us, and there upon a sudden began *The Savages* to throw stones with certaine Slings which they had with-*begin to sling* out any injury offered at all; yea, they did sling so *stones at us.* fiercely, that we could scarce stand on the hatches. I seeing their brutish dealing, caused the Gunner to shoot a Falcon at them, which lighted a little over them, at which time they went to their Boates, and rowed away. About one a clocke in the afternoone, they came againe to us crying in their accustomed manner, Yliont, they being sixtie three in number, the shipper inquired of me whether they should come to us or not, I willed him to have all things in a readinesse, they comming in the meane time nigh to the Pinnasse, I did perceive certaine of them to have great bagges full of stones, they whispered one *They sling* with another began to sling stones unto us. I presently *stones againe.* shot off a little Pistol which I had for the Gunner, and the rest of the folke to discharge, which indeed they did, but whether they did hurt or kill any of them or not, I cannot certainly tell, but they rowed all away making a howling and hideous noise: going to the same point, whereas in the forenoone they had beene, being no sooner come on Land, but from the Hils they did so assaile us with stones, with their slings, that it is incredible to report, in such sort that no man could stand upon the Hatches, till such time as I commanded for to lose sailes and bonnets two mens height, to shield us from the force of the stones, and also did hide us from their sight; so that we did ply our Muskets and other Peeces such as wee had at them: but their subtiltie was such, that as soone as they did see fire given to the Peeces, they would suddenly ducke downe behind the Cliffes, and when they were [III.iv.819.] discharged, then sling their stones fiercely at us againe. Thus having continued there till foure a clocke, they departed away.

The nineteenth day in the morning, about foure a clocke it beeing calme, I departed from this Roadsted, so causing our men to row alongst the shoare, till the tide of the ebbe was bent, at which time it began to blow a fresh gale at North-west and by West, we turning downe till about two a clocke, when the tide of floud being come: when I came to an Anchor in an excellent Haven, on the South side of Cunninghams Mount, which for the goodnesse thereof, I named Denmarkes Haven.

Denmarks Haven.

The twentieth day, in the morning the weather beeing very rainie with a little aire of wind, I loosed and caused to row forth of the foresaid Harbour, and comming forth betweene the Ilands and the maine, the people being as it seemed looking for us espied us: making a hideous noise, at which time at an instant were gathered together about seventie-three Boats with men rowing to us. I seeing them, thought it best to prevent the worst, because we were to come hither againe: therefore to dissemble the matter, I thought it best to enter into barter with them for some of their Darts, Bowes and Arrowes, wee finding every one of them to bee extraordinarily furnished therwith: so rowing forth to Sea amongst the Ilands, there stil came more Boats to the number of one hundred and thirtie persons, they still rowing by us, made signes to us to goe to anchor amongst some of the Ilands: but I preventing their devices, made certaine Skonces with

The people come againe.

our sailes, to defend us from their Stones, Arrowes and
Darts. They seeing this, went certaine of them from
us rowing to certaine Ilands, to which they did thinke
wee would come: leaving no more but about ten men
and Boates about us, who rowed alongst the space of
an houre with us, making signes of friendship to us. At
length perceiving, that wee were not minded to goe forth
amongst these Ilands, upon which the rest of their folke
were, they threw certaine shels and trifles into the Boat,
making signes and tokens to fetch them, the which my
Boy called William Huntries did. He being in the Boat,
*My Boy shot
with a Dart.* they presently shot him through both the buttockes with
a Dart, at which time they rowed from us, they mustering
upon the Ilands to the number of three hundred persons,
keeping themselves farre enough from our danger.
About sixe a clocke this Evening it began to blow a faire
gale Easterly, we getting off to Sea, stood all this night
North and by East alongst the Land.

A Topographicall Description of the Land as I did discover the same.

NOw having proceeded for the discoverie of the Coast
and Harbours so farre, and so long time as the time
limited to me, therefore I thinke it convenient, to make
a briefe description of the same, according as by my short
experience I found the same to be.

*The descrip-
tion of the land
of Groenland.* The Land of Groenland is a very high, ragged and
mountainous Countrey, being all alongst the Coast broken
Ilands, making very goodly Sounds and Harbours, having
also in the Land very many good Rivers and Bayes, into
some of which I entred sayling up the same the space
of ten or twelve English leagues, finding the same very
navigable, with great abundance of fish of sundrie sorts.

*Of the fer-
tility of the
Countrey.* The Land also in all places wheresoever I came, seemed
to be very fertile, according to the Climate wherein it
lyeth: for betweene the Mountaynes was most pleasant

Plaines and Valleyes, in such sort as if I had not seene
the same, I could not have beleeved, that such a fertile
Land in shew could bee in these Northerne Regions.
There is also in the same great store of Fowle, as Ravens, *Store of fowle.*
Crowes, Partridges, Pheasants, Sea-mewes, Gulles, with
other sundry sorts. Of Beasts I have not seene any,
except blacke Foxes, of which there are very many. Also *Blacke Foxes.*
as I doe suppose there are many Deere, because that
comming to certaine places where the people had had
their Tents, we found very many Harts Hornes, with
the bones of other beasts round about the same. Also
going up into the Land wee saw the footing and dunging
of divers beasts, which we did suppose to be deere, and
other beasts also, the footing of one which wee found
to be eight inches over, yet, notwithstanding we did see
none of them: for going some two or three miles from
the Pinnasse we returned againe to goe aboord. Moreover, in the Rivers we found sundry sorts of Fishes, as *Fishes.*
Seales, Whales, Salmons, with other sorts of fishes in great
abundance. As concerning the Coast, all alongst it is *Of the Coast.*
a very good and faire Land, having very faire shoalding
of the same: for being three English leagues off the
same, I found very faire shoalding in fifteene fathomes,
and comming neerer the same fourteene, twelve, and tenne
fathomes very faire sandie ground. As concerning the
people, they are (as I doe suppose) a kinde of Samoites, *Of the people.*
or wandring Nation travelling in the Summer time in
Companies together, first to one place, and having stayed
in that place a certayne time in hunting and fishing for
Deere and Seales with other fish, streight they remove
themselves with their Tents and baggage to another. *The colour of*
They are men of a reasonable stature, being browne of *the people.*
colour, very like to the people of the East and West *The people*
Indies. They be very active and warlike, as we did per- *very active.*
ceive in their Skirmishes with us, in using their Slings *They eat their*
and Darts very nimbly. They eat their meate raw, or *meat most part*
a little perboyled either with bloud, Oyle, or a little water, *raw.*
which they doe drinke. They apparell themselves in the [III. iv. 820.]

skinnes of such beasts as they kill, but especially with Seales skins and fowle skins, dressing the skins very soft and smooth, with the haire and feathers on, wearing in Winter the haire and feather sides inwards, and in Summer

outwards. Their Weapons are Slings, Darts, Arrowes, having their Bowes fast tyed together with sinewes; their Arrowes have but two feathers, the head of the same being for the most part of bone, made in manner and forme of a Harping Iron. As concerning their Darts, they are of sundry sorts and fashions. What knowledge they have of God I cannot certainly say, but I suppose them to bee Idolaters, worshipping the Sunne. The Countrey (as is aforesaid) seemeth to be very fertile, yet

could I perceive or see no wood to grow thereon. Wee met all alongst this Coast much Drift-wood, but whence it commeth I know not. For coasting all this Coast alongst from the latitude of 66. degrees and an halfe, untill the latitude of 69. degrees, I found many goodly Sounds, Bayes, and Rivers: giving names unto divers of them, and purposing to proceed further, the folke in the Pinnasse with me did earnestly intreate me to returne to the ship againe, alleaging this, that if we came not in convenient time, the people in the ship would mutinie: and so returne home before we came: the which indeed had fallen forth, if the Captaine as an honest Gentleman had not by severe meanes withstood their attempts, who would needes contrarie to their promises have beene gone home within eight dayes after my departure from them. But the Captaine respecting his promise to mee, would by no meanes consent, but withstood them both by faire meanes and other wayes. So that upon the seventh day of July, I returned again into the Kings Foord, which they in the ship had found to be a Bay, and comming to the place where wee had left the ship hoping to have found them there, I saw upon a certaine point a Warlocke of stones, whereby I did perceive that they were gone downe the Ford. So the tide of ebbe being come, it being calme we rowed downe the Foord, finding in the mouth of the same amongst the Ilands, many good Sounds and Harbours.

The tenth day of July the wind being at North North- *July 1605.* west, I beeing in a certaine Sound amongst the Ilands, it being high water I weighed, stood West forth of the Foord going to Sea on the South side between a little Iland and the Maine, which Iland at our first comming, we called Frost Iland, after the name of the ship: we *Frost Iland.* espied on the South sides certaine Warlockes set up, whereupon I suspected that the Frost might be there, commanded the Gunner to shoot off a Peece of Ordnance, they presently answered us againe with two other. We seeing the smoake (but heard no report) bore in to them, *Our meeting* comming to an Anchor in a very good Sound by them, *againe with* and found them all in health: the Captaine being very *the ship.* glad of our comming, forasmuch as hee had very much trouble with the company for the cause aforesaid. Also in the time of our absence the people did very much villanie to them in the ship, so that the Captaine tooke three of them; other of them also he slew, but the three *Three of the* which he tooke he used with all kindnesse, giving them *people taken.* Mandillions and Breeches of very good cloth, also Hose, Shoes, and Shirts off his own backe. This afternoone, I with my Boy came againe aboord the ship, taking in this Evening all our provision of water.

The eleventh day, the wind being at North North-east, we set saile forth of the Sound which we named Frost Sound, but before our comming forth of the same our Captaine commanded a young man whose name was Simon, by the expresse commandement of the State-holder of Denmarke to bee set aland, wee also in the Pinnasse *Two men set* set another aland, they both being Malefactors, the which *aland.* was done before our comming away, we giving to them things necessarie, as victuall and other things also. Thus having committed both the one and the other to God, wee set saile homewards, we standing forth to Sea South-west, and South-west and by West till noone, when making observation, Queene Annes Cape bearing South and by

East halfe Easterly some ten leagues, I found my selfe in the latitude of 66. degrees 10. minutes, when I directed my course South South-west till sixe aclocke when wee were amongst much Drift Ice, being to leeward two points upon our lee-bow, so that I was forst to lie off West North-west till we were cleere of the same, at which time I directed my course South-west and by South, wee sayling so all the night following.

The twelfth day, the wind at North North-east, wee went away South-west and by South till ten a clocke, when we were amongst more Drift Ice, wee being againe to lie West North-west, to get cleere of the same, which we did about noone, we having this day and the Evening before a mightie hollow Sea, which I thought to be a *A great* current, the which setteth thorow Fretum Davis to the *current setting* Southwards, as by experience I proved: for making obser-*to the South-* vation this day at noone, we found our selves in the *wards.* latitude of 62. degrees 40. minutes, whereas the day before we were but in the latitude of 66. degrees 10. minutes, having made by account a South and by West way about ten leagues. This afternoone I directed my course South South-west.

The thirteenth day, the wind as before, we steered still South and by West, being at noone in the latitude of 60. degrees 17. minutes, going at the same time away South and by East. This foresaid current I did find to set alongst the Coast of Gronland South and by East. The fourteenth day, close weather, being an easie gale we steering South-east and by East. The fifteenth day, [III.iv.821.] stil close weather til noone, we steering as before, being in the latitude of 59. degrees. This day at noone I went away East South-east; this afternoone it was hasie and *Drift Ice.* still weather, when we had sight of some Drift Ice. The 16. day, close weather with the wind at North-west and by West, our course East South-east til about ten aclock, *A mighty bank* when we met with a mightie bank of Ice to windward *of Ice.* of us, being by supposition seven or eight leagues long, wee steering South South-east to get cleere of the same.

336

We met all alongst this Ice a mightie scull of Whales. *A great scul of*
Moreover, wee light with a great current, which as nigh *Whales.*
as we could suppose, set West North-west over for *A great*
America. This day at noone, the weather being very *current.*
thicke, I could have no observation, this Evening by
reason of the Ice, wee were forced to lye South and by
West, and South South-west, to get cleere of the same,
amongst which we came by divers huge Ilands of Ice.

The seventeenth day, being cleere of the Ice, about
foure in the morning, I directed my course South-east by
South till noone, at which time I went away East and by
South, the weather being very haysie and thicke: about
midnight it fell calme, the wind comming up Easterly.

The eighteenth day, the wind still Easterly, we lying
East South-east, away under a couple of courses larboord
tackt. This day in the forenoone, we saw certayne Ilands
of Ice. The nineteenth day, the wind still Easterly with
the weather very hasie.

The first day of August also it was very thicke weather,
with a faire gale at South-west and by West. This forenoone wee met with a scull of Herrings, so that I knew
wee were not farre from the Iles of Orkney, so having
a shrinke at noone, I found us in the latitude of 58.
degrees 40. minutes, at which time I sounded with the
deepest Lead, finding 42. fathomes redde sandie ground,
with some blacke dents. This Evening betweene five
and sixe a clocke wee sounded againe, when we had no
more but twentie fathomes dent ground, whereby I knew
that we were faire by the shoare, when some of our men
looking forth presently, espied one of the Ilands of *We fell with*
Orkeney, it being very thicke, wee cast about, and stood *Orkney.*
with a small sayle to Seaboord againe, we lying West
North-west off all this night.

The tenth day, about five in the morning, we came
thwart of the Castle of Elsonvere, where we discharged
certaine of our Ordnance, and comming to an Anchor in
the Road, the Captaine with my selfe went ashoare, and
hearing of his Majesties being at Copeman-Haven, wee

presently went aboord againe, and set sayle comming thither about two a clocke. The Pinnasse also which he had lost at Sea, in which my Countreyman John Knight was Commander, came also the same night about foure a clocke, both they and we being all in good health, praised bee Almightie God. Amen.

Chap. XV.

The second Voyage of Master James Hall, forth of Denmarke into Groenland, in the yeere 1606. contracted.

E departed from Copeman-Haven, the seven and twentieth of May, in the yeere of our Redemption 1606. with foure ships and a Pinnasse. The Frost beeing Admirall, wherein went for principall Captaine of the Fleet Captaine Godske Lindeno a Danish Gentleman with my selfe, being under God Pilot Major of the Fleet. In the Lyon which was Vice-Admirall, went for Captaine and Commander, Captaine John Cunningham a Scottish Gentleman, who was with me the yeere before. In the Yewren went Hans Browne, a Gentleman of Norway. In the smal ship called The Gilleflowre, went one Castine Rickerson a Dane. In the Pinnasse called the Cat, went one shipper Andres Nell, of Bergen in Norway. So by the providence of God, wee weighed and set saile about sixe a clocke in the Evening, with a faire gale at South South-west, comming to an Anchor in Elsonoure Road to take in our water.

Godske Lindeno.

Captaine Cunningham.

Hans Browne a Gentleman of Norway. Rickerson a Dane. Andres Nell of Bergen.

The nine and twentieth in the morning, we shot off a Peece of Ordnance, for all the Captaines and Commanders to come aboord of us, who being come, our Captaine commanded the Kings Orders to bee read, which done, they returned aboord, at which time wee weighed with a faire gale at East North-east, standing away North

and by West till I had brought the Cole North-east and
by East off, when I steered away North North-west, and
North-west and by North. This Evening about five a
clocke, I set the Annold, it bearing West halfe Northerly,
three leagues and an halfe. All this Evening wee stood
away North-west and by North.

The thirtieth day, the wind at East South-east, wee
steering as before, this morning about sixe a clocke, the
Lesold bore West and by North of us sixe leagues off.
At five this Evening, the Scaw bearing West South-west
five leagues, I directed my course West North-west, with
the wind at North-east and by East.

The one and thirtieth in the morning, very hasie weather
with a stiffe gale at East North-east, we steering West [III.iv.822.]
North-west away, till about nine a clocke, when we had
a shrinke of the Land which was the wester gate of
Mardo, we steering alongst the Land. Wee came to an
anchor in Flecorie, where we were to make and take in *Our comming*
wood and water.   *to Flecorie.*

The second of June we weighed, and came forth of *Our*
the Harbour of Flecorie about sixe in the morning, having *departure.*
a fresh gale at East North-east. About eleven at noone,
I set the Nase of Norway, it bearing North North-west
foure leagues off. The fourth day in the morning about
two a clock, we were faire by the high Land of the Yeddoe,
I causing to cast about stood to the Southwards, West
and by South and sometimes West. This day at noone,
I found my selfe in the latitude of 57. degrees 45. minutes,
the Nase of Norway bearing East North-east two and
twentie leagues off. This day at noone also I cast about
and stood to the Northwards, lying North with the
stemme, having the winde at North North-west. This
afternoone dyed one of our Groinlanders called Oxo. All *One of our*
this evening, and the night following, the winde as before, *Groenlanders*
we lying also North with little winde.   *dyed.*
                                                    The fift and
The seventh day, the winde at South-west and by *sixt mostwhat*
South and South South-west, we steering West and West *calme.*
and by North. This day at noone we were in the latitude

of 58. degrees 40. minutes. The tenth day about foure in the morning, it began to blow a fresh gale at East and by South, at which time we stood alongst the Land to the Southward, till I had brought the South Head of Shotland, called Swinborne Head, North-west and by North about three leagues off; and Faire Ile next hand South-west and by South eight leagues off, at which time I directed my course away West with a fresh gale at East South-east about halfe an houre to three. I set the

Shotland.

South head of Shotland it bearing North-east eight leagues off, Faire Ile next hand South-east seven leagues off, foule next hand North foure leagues, wee still steering away West with a fresh gale at East South-east. All this afternoone and the night following it was very thicke and raynie weather, the winde continuing as before. This

*Our Groen-
lander dyed.*

night at midnight dyed the Groenlander which we had aboord us, named Omeg.

The fourteenth day, the winde as the night before a faire gale, we steering as we did before, with haysie weather having a shrinke, at noone I found us in the latitude of 58. degrees 40. minutes, having made a West and by South way Southerly two and thirtie leagues, differing to the Westward from the Meridian of the Nase 19. degrees 45. minutes. This afternoone we had a faire gale at South-east with thicke weather, we steering away West.

The fifteenth day, the winde as before, we steering away West, being by my imagination in the latitude of 58. degrees 40. minutes. The three and twentieth day, the winde at the North-east a faire gale, we steering betweene the West North-west, and the West and by North, being at noone in the latitude of 56. degrees 10. minutes, having by reason of a Northerly current contrarie to my expectation, made a West way Southerly two and twentie leagues. The Compasse also as I doe suppose, being varied more then a Point to the westwards.

*Sight of Land
with Ice.*

The first of July wee saw Land being eight leagues off, with a great banke of Ice lying off South-west, wee setting our tacks aboord laid off East and by South and East South-east, to double the same, about two a clocke having doubled the same, wee went away West and by South all this evening and night following. This Land I did suppose to be Busse Iland; it lying more to the Westwards then it is placed in the Marine Charts.

The second day thicke weather with the winde at North North-west, we steering West and by North. This after-noone we were in a great Current setting South South-west. The which I did suppose to set betweene Busse Iland and Freseland over with America; wee steering West North-west with a faire gale at North. This night about nine a clocke, the Pinnasse came foule of the Vice-admirall, where with her anchor shee tore out about a foot of a planke a little above water, and broke downe the beakes head.

A current.

The Pinnasse came foule of the Lion.

The sixth making observation, I found us in the latitude of 58. degrees 50. minutes, contrarie to my expectation, whereby I did see the Southerly Current to bee the princi-pall cause. The seventh day, the winde at North and by East, we lying West North-west, being at noone in the latitude of 59. degrees 40. minutes, our way North-west two and twentie leagues. This evening I found the North Point of the Compasse to be varied 12. degrees 5. minutes, to the Westward of the true North.

South current.

Variation observed.

The eight day, the winde came up more Southerly betweene the South-west, and the South-west and by West with an easie gale, we steering away North-west and by West; being at noone in the latitude of 59. degrees 30. minutes, having by reason of the Current and Varia-tion made a West way Southerly about ten leagues.

The ninth day close weather, it being calme all the forenoone, wee perceiving by our ships which lay becalmed, a violent Current setting South-west. This day at noone, we were in the latitude of 59. degrees 40. minutes. The tenth about foure in the morning, the winde came up to the North North-west. I casting about stood to the Westwards, lying West with the stemme, being in the

A current setting South-west.

A.D.
1606.

Sight of America in 58. degrees and 30. minutes.

[III.iv.823.]

A Current.

latitude of 60. degrees 16. minutes. We saw the coast of America about nine leagues off, at which time I made observation of the variation, and found the Needle varie 24. degrees to the Westwards of the true North. The Hill tops were covered with snow, and the shoare to the Northwards full with Ice, but to the Southwards it seemed cleere. Here I found a great Current to set West into the shoare, which about midnight did bring us to bee incumbred with very many Ilands of Ice, having much to doe to get cleere off the same without danger: but by Gods helpe it being faire weather with a fresh gale at South-west, wee got cleere off the same, standing East South-east and South-east and by East.

The fourteenth in the morning being cleere of the Ice, I went away East North-east and North-east and by East till eight a clocke, when I directed my course North-east and by North, being at noone in the latitude of 59. degrees, the Cape or Head land which wee saw that night bearing West South-west sixteene leagues off. All this afternoone and night following it was for the most part *Variation observed.* still weather: this evening I found the variation 23. degrees 55. minutes.

The sixteenth faire weather with a fresh gale at East South-east, our course as before, being in the latitude of 60. degrees 20. minutes, the ships way North and by East northerly twentie leagues. This afternoone and the night following the wind as before, we steering still North-east and by North.

The eighteenth also thicke weather, being forced to stand away North North-west to double a great banke with great Mountaines of Ice almost incredible to be reported, yet by the helpe of God wee passed the same, sayling all this day by great and huge mountainous Ilands of Ice, with the winde at South-west and by South, being at noone in the latitude of 63. degrees 45. minutes. Wee *Compassed about with Ice.* did see our selves beset round about with mightie bankes of Ice, being forced to make more saile, and to lye to and againe all this night to keepe us cleere of great and

small Ilands of Ice, where many times we were in such
danger, that we did looke for no other thing then present
death, if God had not beene mercifull unto us and sent
us cleere weather, where by his assistance we kept our
selves very hardly and with great difficultie cleere of the
Ice.

The nineteenth day in the morning cleere weather with
a fresh gale at South-west, wee plying amongst the Ice
to see if wee could get a gut to get cleere of the same,
at which time wee saw the Land of America about the *Land of*
latitude of 64. degrees, it lying next hand South and *America.*
North, being high ragged Land covered with snow, the
shoare being all beset with Ice. So lying off and on
amongst the Ice in great perill till about noone, when
God of his goodnesse sent us to espie a little gut where
wee went through, and stood South South-east away,
comming still by many Ilands of Ice. Heere I did finde
both by my course and reckoning (the variation also of
the Compasse respected) that wee were carried with a
mightie Current to the Westwards, as both now and *A mighty cur-*
afterwards wee did probably proove and see the same. *rent setting to*
For I setting my course from the coast of America in the *the westward.*
latitude of 58. degrees and a halfe for the coast of Groenland North North-east with a compasse, whose wyers were
placed more then two third parts of a Point to the Eastwards of the North, the variation being 23. degrees 30.
minutes Northwesting and 24. degrees, as by observation
I found betweene the latitude of 58. and a halfe and 54. *Note.*
degrees, yet I did finde my selfe contrarie either to mine
owne, or to any of their expectations which was in the
Fleet with mee, carried almost foure Points with the
Current to the westwards over our judgements.

The twentieth, wee still sayled to the Eastwards by *Here I did*
many great Bankes and Ilands of Ice, being still compassed *give direction*
in, wee being forced to stand to the Southwards to get *to the other*
cleere, where being sometimes becalmed, wee did plainly *steerman to*
direct their
see and perceive our selves carried into the Ice to the *course for*
westward very violently. This Current setteth West *Groenland.*

Variation observed.

North-west. The twentieth in the evening I found the Compasse varied 23. degrees.

The one and twentieth day in the morning faire weather, wee espyed a gut through the Ice, it seeming cleere to the southwards of the same, where bearing into the same about noone, wee were cleere of all the Ice by the mercifull providence of God. Here I observed the latitude, it being 63. degrees 33. minutes. Now having the one and twentieth day at afternoone caused the Admirall to call the other Captaines and Steermen aboord, with whom wee might conferre, and having shewed briefly my reckoning with the other events, which contrarie to my expectation had happened, the cause whereof at that instant they did plainly see and perceive: They confessing, the

The Current. Current as they did now plainly see, to bee the cause of the same. So having done, I gave to the other Steermen directions, that being cleere of the Ice they should goe betweene the East and the East and by North over for the coast of Groenland and not to the Northwards of the East and by North, because of the former events. And now at this instant, by Gods helpe, being cleere I called to them, giving the same directions. This afternoone and the night following it was calme. This evening I found

Variation observed. the Compasse varied 23. degrees 25. minutes.

The two and twentieth day at noone I found us in the latitude of 63. degrees 20. minutes. The three and twentieth faire weather, the ayre very cold, as with us in the moneth of Januarie, the winde variable betweene the East North-east, and the South-east and by East, being at noone in the latitude of 63. degrees, having made

[III.iv.824.] a South-east and by South way eleven leagues. This day at noone I cast about to the Westwards, the other ships doing the like, lying North-east and by North with the

Variation observed. stemme, finding this evening the Needle varied to the Westwards 23. degrees 30. minutes.

The foure and twentieth, the winde variable betweene the South South-east and the South-east and by South with raine and fogge. This day about eleven a clocke

wee did see much Ice to leeward, wherefore I cast about
to the Southwards, the winde comming to the East North-
east, wee lying South-east with the stemme, supposing
the ship to have made a North and by West way halfe
Northerly two and twentie leagues.   This afternoone, by
reason of the fogge, we lost sight of the Lion and the *Wee lost the*
Gilliflowre, wee looking earnestly forth for them, and *Lion and*
shooting both we and the Urin divers pieces of Ord- *Gilliflowre.*
nance, but wee could neither see nor heare them, at
which time the winde came up Southerly, we standing
away our course betweene the East and East and by
North.

The five and twentieth, wee had sight of Groenland,
being about ten leagues to the Southward of Queene
Annes Cape.   Wee standing away East South-east in
with the Land with the winde at South.   All this night
it did blow very much, wee steering North by West and
North North-west.

The seven and twentieth day in the morning was reasonable cleere weather with a fresh gale at South South-west.
This morning betweene foure and five of the clocke, I
espyed Queene Annes Cape to beare East by South next
hand of mee, and King Christians Foord South South-
east of me, being thwart of Rumels Foord, Queene Sophias
Cape bearing North halfe westerly, about five leagues off.
Therefore I thought it convenient to put into Cunninghams Foord where the silver was, both in regard that I *The silver*
had sworne to his Majestie as concerning the same ; and *Myne.*
also because wee were expressely commanded to bring
home of the same.   So having a faire gale at West South-
west, wee came into the aforesaid River, anchoring in a
very good Sound, hard by the Ure, in sixteene fathoms,
at the mouth of Cunninghams Foord, about five of the *The place of*
clocke.   There came presently foure of the Countrie *the silver*
people unto us after their old accustomed manner.   This *Myne.*
evening about six of the clocke the Urin anchored by
us.   This night the Admirall, my selfe, and Captaine
Browne went on Land to see the Myne of silver : where

it was decreed, that we should take in as much thereof as we could.

On Sunday the third of August, the Savages seeing our curtesie toward them, bartered Seales skinnes and Whales finnes with us: which being done, wee went to our Boat, and rowing away, three of them taking their Boats, rowed with us up the Foord, calling to other of the people, telling them and making signes to us, of our dealing towards them. Then they also came to us and bartered with us for old Iron and Knives, for Seales skinnes and coates made of Seales skinnes, and Whales finnes, and rowed still all with us. In the end, having rowed five or sixe leagues up the Foord, and seeing it to bee but a Bay, wee returned alongst many greene and pleasant Ilands, where wee found good anchoring: the people still followed us to the number of five and twentie persons till about sixe of the clocke; when it fell thicke with some raine, and the winde being Southerly, wee rowed in among the Sounds, at which time they went from us: wee rowing our Boat to one of the Ilands went to supper. And having supped, wee rowed some three leagues up an other Foord, where we found very shallow water, in which place we stayed with our Boat all that night.

The fourth day in the morning about three of the clocke, wee returned to our ship againe with a gale of winde Southerly, being somewhat thicke and raynie weather, sayling by the Land among the Ilands, till we came three leagues to the Northwards of Queene Sophias Cape, when going without the Ilands, wee met with a very high Sea, so that wee had much to doe, but by the providence of Almightie God, the Boat was preserved from being swallowed up of the Sea. In the end, wee got againe among the Ilands, and so about noone wee came to our ships. The fift day, some of our men went on Land among the Mountaines, where they did see reine Deere.

The sixt day, I casting about, stood into the shoare South-east, till wee had brought Ramels Foord East and by North off us, bearing roome for the same Foord.

Barter for Seales skinnes and Whales finnes.

Many greene Ilands.

Another foord.

Queene Sophias Cape.

Reine Deere.

Ramels Foord.

There goeth a very hollow Sea betweene the Ilands of *A hollow Sea.*
the Kings Foord and Ramels Foord. The winde being
somewhat still, wee towed on head with our Boats till
wee came thwart of a Bay, in which I was in the Urins
Boat, which I named Fos Bay, after the name of Philip *Fos Bay.*
de Fos, Pilot of the Urin. But the Admirals wilfulnesse
was such, that I could by no meanes counsaile him therein
though night were at hand, but hee would goe up the
Foord, till wee came on the starboord side of the Foord
to sixe and twentie fathomes sandie ground. The Urin
let fall anchor by us, but the winde comming off the
Land (our Captaine and Companie being so obstinate and
willfull, that I could by no meanes get them to worke
after my will) the ship drave into the mid-foord, where *No ground at*
wee could have no ground at an hundred fathoms, till *100. fathoms*
the Tyde of flood came, when the flood set the ship to *in the middest*
the shoare : but I laying out a Cage-anchor got the ship *of Fos Bay.*
off ; and setting our foresaile, stood for another roade up
the River.

The eight day about foure in the morning, wee came
to an anchor in twentie fathomes sandie ground, having *[III.iv.825.]*
very faire shoalding within us. About noone the Urin
came and anchored by us. It floweth in this River South- *Fos River in*
east and North-west, and it standeth in the latitude of *66. degrees*
66. degrees and 25. minutes. *25. minutes.*

The ninth in the morning, our Captaine with the *A Town found*
Captaine of the Urin, went with their Boates up the *ten leagues up*
River, where they did come to see their winter houses, *the River.*
which were builded with Whales bones, the balkes being
of Whales ribbes, and the tops were covered with earth,
and they had certaine Vaults or Sellers under the earth
foure square, about two yards deepe in the ground. These
houses were in number about some fortie. They found
also certaine Graves made up of stones over the dead
bodies of their people, the carkasses being wrapped in
Seales skins, and the stones laid in manner of a Coffin
over them. *A man left on*
This day, in this place we set a man on Land, which *Land.*

had served our Captaine the yeere before, which for a
certaine fault committed by him our Captaine left behinde
in the Countrie. About noone our men came aboord
againe; and after Dinner some of the people came unto
us, of whom wee caught five with their Boates and stowed
them in our ships, to bring them into Denmarke, to
enforme our selves better by their meanes of the state of
their Countrie of Groineland, which in their owne
language they call Secanunga, and say, that up within
the Land they have a great King, which is carried upon
mens shoulders.

The tenth of August in the morning, the winde being
at East South-east, we weighed and came forth of Rombes
Foord, but being come forth to Sea amongst the Ilands,
the winde came up to the South-west and by South, the
Sea going marvellous high, we lying West and West and
by North to Sea, doubling certaine Ilands and Rockes.
Where the Sea going so wonderfull high had set us upon
the Rockes, where we had all dyed, if God of his mercy
at that instant, when wee saw nothing before our eyes
but present death, had not sent us a great gale of winde
at South South-west, whereby wee lay West North-west
away with a flawne sheat, wee doubling of the Ilands and
Rocks, were forced to goe between certaine little Ilands,
which lye off Queene Sophias Cape foure leagues into
the Sea. The which Ilands I named the yeere before,
Knights Ilands, after the name of John Knight. So
having passed these Ilands not without great danger, wee
found betweene them many blinde Rocks, and being cleere
in the Sea. The thirteenth at noone, we were in the
latitude of 66. degrees 50. minutes, being off Cape Sophia
West and by North halfe westerly about sixteene leagues.

The eighteenth about foure in the morning, we got
cleere off the Ice, steering South and by West away, it
being very thicke weather till noone, when it cleered up:
at which time wee saw the shoare rising like Ilands, being
very high and stretching South and by East, and North
and by West about foure and twentie leagues, the shoare

Five of the people taken againe.

Groenland called by the Inhabitants Secanunga.

Knights Ilands.

being beset all full with Ice, so that in that place it is impossible for any ship to come into the shoare. Also of the Southermost of these two Capes, lay such a great banke of Ice stretching into the Sea, that wee were forced to lye West and by North to double the same.

All this afternoone, wee were almost compast with Ice, we bearing to the same, the winde comming up to the East South-east, we standing South to the Ice were forced to loose for one Iland, and to beare roome for another till about foure a clocke, when by Gods helpe wee got cleere off the same, the winde comming up to the South-east and by South, wee lay South-west and by South off all this night.

The two and twentieth thicke weather, the winde as before. This morning about seven a clocke we saw a saile West and by South of us, we standing to him, for it was our Vice-admirall the Lion, who had beene greatly troubled with the Ice, wee being glad to meete one another againe. *We met againe with the Lion.*

The eight and twentieth about foure in the morning, the storme ceased, the winde comming up to the West South-west. About three a clocke wee set our sailes standing South-east away. But being under saile, we spyed great bankes and Ilands of Ice to leeward of us, lying off East and by South, which Ice I did judge to lye off Cape Desolation about eight leagues off : the which by reason of the fogge we could not see.

The nine and twentieth about six in the morning, the winde came up to the North-east and by North, we making saile went South South-east away till noone with a stiffe gale, wee seeing in the morning pieces of drift Ice to windward of us ; having at noone a shrinke of the same I found us in the latitude of 59. degrees 46. minutes, having from noone to noone made a South-east and by South way eight leagues.

The one and thirtieth, the winde continuing, wee holding still our course with the winde still at North North-west, with faire and cleere weather it blowing very much, so that wee stood away under a couple of courses low set, the Sea very much growne, being in the latitude of 59. degrees 10. minutes, having made an East South-east way somewhat Easterly foure and thirtie leagues. This afternoone after my observation, wee saw some Ilands of Ice with some drift Ice, I something marvelling of the same, knowing both by my account and my noones observation, that we were shot too farre from any part of [III.iv.826.] Groinland, that was described in the Marine Chart. For the furthermost part described therein is not in the latitude of 60. degrees, and we being now in the latitude of 59. degrees ten minutes, Cape Desolation bearing West North-west halfe Northerly about sixtie foure leagues, and Cape Christian which was the next known part of Groenland North-west and by West westerly eight and thirtie leagues, so holding our course East South-east *Sight of Land.* away, about foure a clocke we had sight of Land, being very high Land, it lying alongst East South-east about sixteene leagues, the westermost part seemed either to fall away East North-east, and the southermost point bearing East northerly, fell away East and by North. This Land is very high, having the Hills covered with snow, the shoare being very thicke with Ice: this place because I knew not whether it was of the Mayne or *Frost Iland.* an Iland, I named Frost Iland, after the name of the ship.

The first of September, at noone, I made observation, and found us in the latitude of 58. degrees, having made a South-east and by South way southerly sixe and twentie leagues. This day at noone I directed my course East and by South. This afternoone about sixe a clock it fell calme, and so continued all the night following. This *Variation* evening I found the variation 10. degrees 50. minutes *observed.* Northwesting.

The fourth day the winde at East and by South, we lying South and by East, having a shrinke of the sunne about noone, I did suppose us in the latitude of 57. degrees 20. minutes, having made a South-east and by

South way southerly about ten leagues; all this day and the night following we lay as before.

The eight day faire weather, the winde as before, it being almost calme, wee going away as before, being at noone in the latitude of 58. degrees 36. minutes, having made an East North-east way northerly twentie leagues, by reason of the great southerly Sea. All this afternoone and the night following it was for the most part calme. This evening I found the Compasse varied about two degrees 45. minutes northwesting. *A great Southerne Sea. Variation observed.*

The ninth day also faire weather, the winde southerly a fresh gale, our course still East, being at noone in the latitude of 58. degrees 40. minutes, our way East and by North easterly twelve leagues. This afternoone the winde came up to the South or South and by East with raine. This night about midnight thicke weather with raine, the winde comming to the South-east, we lying East North-east and North-east and by East with the stemme.

The tenth day about two in the morning, the winde came up to the South South-west, wee steering our course East, being at noone in the latitude of 59. degrees 10. minutes, having made an East and by North way easterly foure and fortie leagues, wee having a fresh gale westerly. This day wee saw one of the Fowle the which are on the Iland of Bas in Scotland, called Bas Geese. This evening I found the variation 1. degree 4. minutes north-easting. *A Bas Goose. Variation observed to the North-east.*

The eighteenth, this forenoone about nine a clocke, wee espyed land, rising somewhat ragged, the Eastermost point of the same bearing South-east and by South, and the Westermost part South and by West about eight leagues. These Ilands by my account and observation, I found to be the Ilands of Ferris, being at noone in the observation of 62. degrees 5. minutes. *Sight of Ferris.*

The nineteenth I set a little Rocke, called the Monke; which lyeth off to the South-east end, it being about five a clocke, East South-east of us three leagues off. This night about ten a clocke it fell calme.

The twentieth, wee did see the streame had set us to the Northwards. This streame setteth under the Ilands of Farre next hand East and West. So casting about wee stood to the westwards, lying West South-west and sometimes West and by South, and sometimes South-west, it being very raynie weather, about midnight it fell calme and so continued all night unto the morning.

The first of October in the afternoone about foure of the clocke, we had sight of The Holmes. The second day, wee steered away South-east and by South and South South-east for The Col. And about eight of the clocke

this night wee came into Turco, where wee rode all the day following. The third day at night the winde came to the North-east; so wee weighed and came into Elsenor Road. The fourth day, by the providence of God, we arrived in our desired Port of Copen Haven, 1606.

The severall burthens and numbers of men employed in the ships of the Fleet aforesaid, were as followeth.

THe Trust being Admirall, was of sixtie tunnes, had eight and fortie men. The Lion Vice-admirall, was of seventie tunnes, had eight and fortie men. The Urin or Eagle Reare-admirall, of one hundred tunnes, had fiftie men. The Gilliflowre was of fortie tunnes, had six-teene men. The Pinnasse called the Cat, was of twentie tunnes, had twelve men. Bredaransies Foord is most Northerly. Cunninghams Foord is next in sixtie seven degrees and odde minutes. The Foord wherein they saw the Towne ten leagues up the same, is two leagues to the South of Cunninghams Foord. The Kings Foord is in sixtie sixe degrees and an halfe.

[III. iv. 827.] William Huntris of Stowborow in Yorke-shire, is Master Hall his man, and is allowed thirtie pound by the yeere of the King of Denmarke, for his skill in Navigation.

I have also Master Halls Voyage of the next yeere
1607. to Groenland from Denmarke, written, and with
representations of Land-sights curiously delineated by
Josias Hubert of Hull, but the Danes (envious perhaps
that the glory of the Discovery would be attributed to
the English Pilot) after the Land saluted, mutinied, and
in fine forced the ship to returne for Island. For which
cause I have here omitted the whole.

Chap. XVI.

The Voyage of Master John Knight, (which had beene at Groenland once before 1605. Captaine of a Pinnasse of the King of Denmarke) for the Discovery of the North-west Passage, begun the eighteenth of Aprill 1606.

Set sayle from Gravesend in a Barke of *April* 18.
fortie tunnes, called the Hope-well, well 1606.
victualled and manned at the cost of the
Worshipfull Companies of Moscovie, and
the East Indie Merchants, for the Discoverie of the North-west Passage the
eighteenth of Aprill 1606. and arrived
the sixe and twentieth of the same moneth in the Ile of
Orkney, in a Sound called Pentlefrith. Heere wee were *Pentlefrith, in*
stayed with contrary winds at West and North-west, and *Orkney.*
with much storme and foule weather above a fortnight.
In which meane space, I entertained two men of this
Countrey, which are both lustie fellowes at Sea and Land,
and are well acquainted with all the Harbours of these
North parts of Scotland. These men brought us into a
very good Harbour, called Saint Margarites Hope, where *Saint Marga-*
we had the Sea open to us for all winds that are good for *rites Sound.*
us to proceed on our Voyage. In this Countrey we found
little worthy of Relation. For it is poore, and hath no
wood growing upon it. Their Corne is Barley and Oates.

Their fire is Turffe, their houses are low and unseemely without, and as homely within.

Upon Munday the twelfth of May, I set sayle from Saint Margarites Sound or Hope in Orkney, at nine of the clocke in the morning, our course being West and by South: and at eight of the clocke at night, the Hill called Hoyce, did beare West Southerly eleven or twelve leagues, and the Stacke South and by East Easterly three leagues and an halfe, the winde beeing at East Southeast.

This day was for the most part calme, and sometimes wee had a fresh gale of winde: our course was West and by South, halfe a point Southerly. This day I passed by *Two small Ilands.* two small Ilands. The one of them is called, the Clete, and the other the Run. They are distant foure leagues the one from the other. The course betweene them is South-west and North-east. The Southermost is called the Clete, and is the lesser of the twaine: it is distant from the North-east part of Lewis, called the Bling-head, seven leagues: and the course betwixt them is North-west *The Bling-head the North-east part of Lewis.* and South-east. Also this Bling-head is distant from the Farro Head, of the Hieland of Scotland West and by North halfe a point Westerly, and is distant seventeene leagues. Also the course betweene Bling-head and the North-west part of Lewis, is West and by South halfe a point Westerly, and faire low Land without Wood. There is good riding all along the shoare, the winde beeing off the Land, and in some places are very good Harbours for all winds. From eight to twelve at night, we ran sixe leagues West South-west.

This morning we had a fresh gale of wind at East North-east: our course was South-west and by West two houres five leagues. From two to ten South-west, and by South 20. leagues. From ten to twelve West South-*Fifty-eight degrees 27. min.* west sixe leagues. The latitude at noone was 58. degrees 27. minutes.

From Wednesday at noone till Thursday at noone, was for the most part raine and fogge, the wind at North-east

and by East: our course was West halfe a point Southerly:
our latitude at noone being Thursday, 58. degrees 23.
minutes. From Thursday at noone till Friday at noone,
being the sixteenth, our way was West Southerly about
twentie leagues: the latitude at noone was 58. degrees
19. minutes. This night the wind was sometimes variable
betweene the South and by West and South-east, with
faire weather, the Magneticall Declination 18. degrees: *Eighteene*
the height of the Pole was 58. degrees 10. minutes. Also *degrees of*
in the morning the Sunne beeing tenne degrees above the *variation.*
Horizon, was distant from the East to the North-wards
of the East twentie two degrees.

From Friday at noone untill midnight was little wind
Southerly, and sometimes calme, and from midnight till
twelve at noone the next day a stiffe gale of wind at
East North-east. This foure and twentie houres I judged
our way to be made good West, something Southerly
thirtie leagues. The latitude at noone was 58. degrees [III.iv.828.]
10. minutes. Also the sunne did rise fiftie degrees to
the Northward of the East.

From Saturday at noone being the seventeenth, till
Sunday at noone being the eighteenth, our course was
West and by South a stiffe gale of wind fiftie leagues,
being close weather, we made no observation of latitude.

From Sunday at noone till Munday at noone I steered
away West and West and by South, having a storme at
East and by North: our course was West and Southerly
fiftie leagues.

From Munday at noone till midnight, our course was
West and Southerly: and from that time till noone West
and by North and West among. I judged wee sayled
fortie leagues these foure and twentie houres, being for
the most part foggie. The latitude at noone was 57.
degrees 50. minutes.

From Tuesday at noone till noone on Wednesday, our
course was West and by North fortie five leagues, being *A current to*
foggie weather without observation. Here wee had a *the North-*
current, which I judge setteth to the Northwards. *ward.*

From Wednesday at noone till Thursday at noone, being the two and twentieth, our course was West and by North fiftie leagues with much fogge and close weather, and much winde at North-east and by East.

From Thursday at noone till midnight, our course was West and by North. Then the winde came to the North: wee tooke in our mayne course, and I spooned away with our fore-saile till Friday, the winde being at North North-east, I judged our way West South-west, the twelve houres that I spooned about fifteene leagues, the other twelve houres West Northerly five and twentie leagues. This *Many Gulles* three and twentieth day, wee saw many Gulles and much *and much* Rock-weed. *Rock-weed.*

From Friday at noone till Saturday at noone, I judged our way to bee made South-west and by West, but it proved West and by South, rather Westerly, twentie *A current to* leagues by reason of a current, that I judge setteth to *the North-east* the North-eastward. The latitude at noone was 57. *ward.* degrees 53. minutes. The variation of the Compasse was about a point to the Westward. This forenoone and all night the wind was at North a very hard gale; wee spooned with our fore-sayle. Also this forenoone, we saw much Sea Tange and Rock-weed.

From Saturday at noone till Sunday at noone, our course was Southward about twentie leagues, the wind being Northerly. This day we saw much Rock-weed and Drift-wood. The latitude was fiftie seven degrees. The *The variation* variation was to the Westward thirteene degrees or there-*13. degrees* about. The sunne being five degrees high in the *Westward.* morning, was twentie foure degrees to the Northward of the East.

From Sunday at noone till two of the clocke the next day in the morning, beeing Munday, our course was West North-west, we made our way West and by North twentie leagues, having a fresh gale at South-east and by East: it fell calme till foure of the clocke: then it blew an easie gale at West South-west, wee stemming North-west, &c. betweene that and North North-east the wind being variable. The wind freshed toward noone. This morning we saw an Owle.

The latitude at noone the eight and twentieth, was 57. degrees 57. minutes. The variation of the Compasse was fourteene degrees and an halfe to the West. This day wee had blacke water, and many over-falls, streame leeches, and sets of currents, as it seemed to the Northward, and some to the Westward.

The variation 14. degrees and an halfe to the West.

The thirtieth, we found our latitude to be fiftie eight degrees. Heere it seemed that we were in a tyde gate, which I judged to set North and South, or that it was the Eddie of the currents, which we saw the other day. Also wee saw white Fowles, which cheeped like Sparhawkes. Also we saw driving many dead Cowes.

Fiftie eight degrees of latitude.

White fowles.

Dead Cowes.

The one and thirtieth, the sunne being fiftie degrees above the Horizon, I found it to bee twentie seven degrees to the Eastward of the South : againe in the afternoone, the sunne beeing fiftie degrees high, it was distant from the South to the Westward fiftie one degrees : at noone it was 55. degrees 6. minutes, the height of the Pole was 58. degrees 3. minutes. The variation of the Compasse was twentie foure degrees toward the North-west. Our way made these twentie foure houres was not above sixe leagues West, being little wind for the most part.

The variation of the Compasse 24. degrees North-westward.

From Saturday at noone till two of the clocke it was calme : then it began to blow an easie gale at North. At night I observed the sunne setting, and found it to set twentie one degrees to the Westward of the North, the winde continuing variable betweene the North and the West North-west till noone, being the first of June. Then I found my selfe by observation to be in the latitude of 57. degrees 35. minutes. I judged our way from noone to noone West and by South or thereabout thirteene leagues.

June 1.

From Sunday at noone till ten of the clocke the same Evening, it was calme. Then it began to blow a stiffe gale of wind at South South-east. Our course was West till noone, the next day being Munday, twentie three

Many blacke
wild fowles.

Latitude 56.
degrees.
[III. iv. 829.]
Variation 24.
degrees
Westward.

Fifty eight
degrees.

A small
current to the
South-west.

Sight of Land
like Ilands.

leagues. This day wee saw many blacke Fowles like Willockes flying in flockes together.

The fourth my latitude at noone, was 56. degrees 40. minutes. The latitude next day at noone was fiftie sixe degrees. The variation of the Compasse by the Scale was twentie degrees, and by my other Instrument twentie foure degrees to the West. The sunne was twentie two degrees and an halfe high, and to the North of the West thirtie degrees by the Instrument, and twentie sixe degrees by the Scale.

Our latitude at noone the eleventh, was fiftie eight degrees. And at night the sunne did set fourteene degrees to the Westward of the North, and did rise fiftie degrees to the Eastward of the North.

The thirteenth, the Ice seemed to be dispersed thinner with the wind, or some other accident: then I set sayle with our two courses, but was forced to take them in againe, and moored to another great Iland of Ice, about a mile to the Westward of the other. Here setteth some smal current to the South-westward. For the great flakes of Ice that were somewhat deep, drave to the Southward, and the other small Ice which was flotie drave with the wind, which was variable betwixt the North-west and the North. Here we were in sight of Land, which bore West South-west from us, shewing in some parts like Ilands. Our latitude at noone was 57. degrees 25. minutes.

From Friday at noone till eight of the clocke at night, wee continued moored to the aforesaid Ice: then it fell calme, and I loosed and rowed to the West-ward with our Oares, hoping to get thorough, till twelve of the clocke, then the Ice grew very thicke. I moored againe till foure of the clocke the next morning. Then we rowed and sayled with an easie gale of wind till eight of the clocke the next morning being Saturday. Then it began to blow a fresh gale Easterly, and we cunned the ship among the Ice with our Oares till noone. Our latitude was fiftie eight degrees. From Saturday at noone till midnight wee guided our shippe to the Westward

among the Ice with our Oares, hoping to get thorough:
but wee were suddenly compassed about with many great
Ilands of Ice, and continued so distressed with a sore
storme of wind at South-east, being foggie and thicke
weather: we were so bruised betweene mightie great
Ilands of Ice, that we were in danger every minute to
be crushed in pieces with force of the heaving and setting
of the said Ice with the great Sea that the wind made,
had not God of his mercie provided for us: for our owne
endevours did little availe to our helpe, though wee
employed all our industries to the uttermost of our
powres.

The nineteenth, we descryed the Land of America, *The Land of*
which riseth like eight Ilands: the Northermost part of *America*
it did beare North and by West about fifteene leagues *descryed in*
56. degrees
from us. I observed the latitude, and found my selfe *48. minutes.*
to be in 56. degrees and 48. minutes. The variation of *America here*
the Compasse was twentie five degrees to the Westward. *sheweth like*
All this Coast sheweth like broken Land or Ilands; and *broken Ilands.*
the tyde of floud commeth from the Northward.

Tuesday the foure and twentieth all the morning, there
blew a storme Northerly, and such a suffe of the Sea,
and so much Ice came in, that our fasts brake that were
fast on shoare, and our Rudder was driven from our
sterne with the force of mightie Ilands of Ice; so that
we were forced to hale close into the bottome of the Cove
to save our clothes, furniture and victuals: wee did our
best, but before we had done, our ship was halfe full of
water: the night comming upon us being wearie, we
tooke a little rest.

On Wednesday, we went hard to worke when the ship
was on ground, to get the water out of her, and to stop
so many of her leakes as we could come by, and to save
so much of our bread as we could; and some went to
building our shallop. Also I caused our Boate to be
lanched over the Iland; and sent my Mate Edward Gorrell, *Edward*
Gorrell the
with three others, to seeke for a better place where to *Masters*
bring our ship on ground, if it were possible, to mend *Mate.*

A.D.
1606.

PURCHAS HIS PILGRIMES

her againe. But they returned without any certaintie by reason of the abundance of Ice, which choked every place. They found wood growing on the shoare.

M. John Knight with five more passeth over to a great Iland, where he and three of his company seem to have bin intercepted by the Savages.

Thursday being faire weather.] Here Master John Knight ended writing in this Journall. On this Thursday the sixe and twentieth of June in the morning, our Master caused some of our men to goe aboord our ship, to save what things they could. And hee and Edward Gorrell his Mate, and his brother, and three more of our Company tooke the Boate, carrying with them foure Pistols, three Muskets, five Swords, and two halfe Pikes for to goe over to a great Iland, which was not above a mile from our ship, to looke if they could find any Harbour or any Cove, to get our ship into for to mend her. Also he carried an Equinoctiall Diall with him, and paper to make a Draught of the Land. When they were passed over to the other side, our Master, his Mate, and his brother, and one more went on shoare, leaving two of us in the Boate with one Musket, one Sword, and an halfe Pike to keepe it: which two stayed in the Boate from ten of the clocke in the morning, untill eleven of the clocke at night, but could heare no newes of them after their departure up into the top of the Hill. Then did the

Their Trumpettor.

Trumpettor sound two or three times, and the other did discharge his Musket two or three times, and so they came away to the other side to the West of the Company, where the ship was: where they were watching for our comming; who seeing us two comming and no more, they marvelled where the rest of the company were. When wee came on shoare, they enquired for our Master and the rest of our company. But we could tell them no newes of them after their departure out of the Boat, but that we did see them goe up to the top of the Iland.

[III. iv. 830.]

Which report did strike all our men into a great feare to thinke in what extremitie we were, because we did want our Master and three of our best men, and our

Their Shallop not finished.

Ship lay sunke, and we had nothing to trust to but our Shallop, which was not at that time halfe finished. This

night lying on shoare in our Tent, which was betweene
two Rockes, we kept very good watch, for feare of any
peoples sudden assaulting of us: or if our Master and
his company had travailed so farre, that they could not
come againe that night, and would shoote a Musket, that
wee might heare them. But they came not at all.

The next day being Friday, and the seven and twentieth
of June, wee consulted to goe over seven of us with our
Boate, to try if we could see or learne any news of our
Master, or any of our men; for we were afraid that they
were either surprised by the Savages of the Countrie, or
else devoured by the wilde Beasts. So we tooke with us
seven Muskets, and Swords, and Targets, and such provision as we had in the Ship, and went downe to the
Sea-side, but wee could not get over for Ice. At length *They could not*
we returned, with much adoe to get on shoare, and went *passe to the*
to our Ship, to save what things we could all that day. *great Iland*
for Ice.
On Saturday, the eight and twentieth, we did likewise
save what things we could, and gat all our things out of
our Ship, and made her cleane in hold, having faire
weather, hoping in God to save her, and to mend all
things, as well as we could; for she lay upon hard rocks:
wherefore we kept her as light as we could, for beating
and bruising of her hull. That night about nine of the
clocke, it began to raine very sore, and so continued all
night: and about one of the clocke at night, our Boate-
Swaine and our Steward being at watch, and their watch
almost out, the Steward went aboord the Ship to pumpe,
leaving the Boate-Swaine at watch some Musket shot
length from our Tent: while he was in pumping, there
came over the rocks a great sort of the Countrey people
toward the place where the Boate-Swaine was: who when
they saw him, they shot their arrowes at him, running *The Savages of*
toward him as fast as they could. Whereupon hee dis- *the Countrie*
charged his Musket at them, and fled to our Tent as *assault our*
fast as hee could, thinking they had beset us, they were *men at one of*
so many of them in sight. The Steward hearing his *the clocke at*
Musket goe off, came out of the Ship, and as he was *night.*

comming, saw the Savages running to our Shallop, and cryed out to us that were asleepe in our Tent, to come to rescue the Boate-Swaine, and the Shallop. We made what haste we could; when we came towards them, and saw so many of them in our Shallop, we were afraid we were betraid. At this time it rained very sore; yet calling our wits together, we sent two of our men backe unto our Tent, the rest of us made toward them, and shot at them some three or foure Muskets: who when they saw us shoote, they stood in our Shallop, and held up their hands unto us, calling one to another. Then thought we with our selves, that we were better to dye in our defence in pursuing of them, then they us, being but eight Men and a great Dogge. When they saw us marching toward them so fiercely, our Dogge being formost, they ranne away: but we durst not pursue them any further, for it was in the night, and they were in sight above fiftie men. Thus we recovered our Shallop. Then we sent some more of our men to our Tent to keepe it; and the rest followed toward the place whither they fled. But before we could overtake them, they were gotten into their Boates, and were rowing away through the Ice; which was so thicke, that they could not passe away, but stucke fast; for their Boates were very great: wee seeing them sticke fast in the Ice, some setting with Oares, and some rowing, came so neere them, as we could, and shot at them some dozen shot, before they could get cleere: which shot caused them to cry out very sore one to another; for their Boates were full of men. As farre as we could judge, they be very little people, tawnie coloured, thin or no beards, and flat nosed, and Man-eaters.

On Sunday, the nine and twentieth, all day long we gat such things as we could aboord our Shippe, for feare they should come over with more men, and beset us, our Ship lying betweene two great Rocks, and all without so full of Ice, that we could not passe any way to Sea, no not with a Boate. That day, two of our men kept watch upon the Rocks, to give us warning, if they did come over with Boats. Then did our Carpenter make what shift hee could with our Shallop, and did tench her in some places, but neither calked her, nor pitched her. Then did wee take her, and bring her downe close to the Shippe, and there shee did stand all night.

On Munday, the thirtieth day in the morning we went to worke to cut the Ice with Axes and Pick-axes, to get our Shippe; for all about the Iland was nothing but Ice, and no place to ride free neither with Shippe nor Boate. That night it pleased God, that wee got her out, and came away rowing with our Oares; but she was exceeding leake, and our Shallop too: and, which was worse, we had never a Rudder to stirre our Ship withall. Wee rowed all that night among the Ice.

The first and second dayes of July, we continued also rowing up and downe among the floting and driving Ice, with little hope of recovering our Countrey.

The third of July, we had a gale of winde at North, and a great current setting to the Southward: Then made we fast our Ship to an Iland of Ice, and went to worke, and to stow her things within boord, to make her stiffe; for wee had never a whit of balast in her. Then did our Carpenter make what shift he could, to hang our Rudder, having nothing convenient in our Ship to make Gudgins, nor Pintels. Then were we forced to breake open our Masters Chest, and to take all the Iron bands off it, to make fast two Pick-axes, for two Pintels, and to binde our Rudder withall. So, as it pleased God, that night we hanged our Rudder, having but two Pintels and a Cable through the middle of it, to keepe it to with two tacks. Then were we in good hope to get cleare of the Ice, because wee had some steerage, though it was but bad: for before, we durst beare but little sayle, our Ship being so leake, and her stemme so sore beaten with the rocks and Ice, and having no steerage, but were forced to rowe with our Oares, till wee were all sore and weary.

The next day about tenne of the clocke in the morning,

A great Current setting to South.

[III. iv. 831.]

Pintels are small Iron pins mode fast to the Rudder, and hung the Rudder to the Stern-post, &c.

the winde came to the West North-west, and was faire
weather: so we steered away East and by North, to get

us out of the Bay: And at noone, the watch being out,
which was the third watch that we had after we came
out of the Countrey (for before, continually we did watch
all, to keepe our Shippe cleare of the Ice, as neere as we
could) we began to Pumpe our Shippe, but could not
make her sucke in a thousand stroakes, if she had stood
but one halfe houre unpumped. Then were wee forced
to unromage our Ship, to see if we could finde our leakes.
We soone found a great many of leakes, but not that
which caused us to Pumpe so sore. At the last, we found

it close abaft our forefoot, where her keele was splintred
in two or three places, where the Sea came running in
so fast, that it was not possible to keepe her free with
both our Pumps, and wee could not come to it to stop
it; for it was under the timbers. Then did wee take
our maine Bonnet, and basted it with Occom, and put
it overboord, right against our leake, which eased us some
foure or five hundred strokes in an houre. Then upon

*They consult to
touch at New-
found Land.* consultation had among our selves, wee resolved to shape
our course towards Newfound Land, to see if we could
get any place to mend our Ship, hoping there to meete
with some English or French men. At this time we had
one of our men very sicke, and another had his hand
very sore splitted; and most of us all were so sore with
rowing and pumping, that we were scarce able to stirre,
but that we must perforce.

The fift of Julie, wee shaped our course for New found
Land, with the winde at West South-west.

The one and twentieth, the winde was at South South-
west; and we fell with the Land, being nothing but broken

Ilands. Then we stood to the Westward, being in the
latitude of 49. degrees and an halfe.

The two and twentieth was faire weather, and the winde
very variable: and about sixe of the clocke at night, the
winde came to the West North-west. Then we steered
in among the Ilands, to see if we could finde any harbour

to mend our Shippe; for she was very leake. When we were come in among them, we found nothing but broken Ilands, and a great current, which did set from Iland to Iland, and had no ground at an hundred fathoms. That night we were very sore intangled with sunken Rocks, and in great danger of casting away our Ship, having very thicke weather : wherefore we kept to and fro all that night.

Many broken Ilands which were the Isles de Foga. Sunken Rocks.

The foure and twentieth of July, in the morning, we spied some dozen Shallops, which were fishing some two leagues from us. Then wee made what way wee could toward them, &c. We remained in this Bay of Fogo, in repairing our Shippe, and refreshing of our selves untill the two and twentieth of August. Then taking our leaves of our kinde and loving friends, with giving them most heartie thankes for their goodnesse towards us, we put forth to the Sea, and with an indifferent and reasonable good passage we arrived safely in Dartmouth in Devonshire, and sent word to London unto our owners, of the losse of our Master and his three companions, and of the dolefull successe of our Voyage, the foure and twentieth day of September, 1606.

Twelve Shallops of Fishermen.

The rest of this Journall, from the death of Master John Knight, was written by Oliver Browne, one of the Company.

Chap. XVII.

The fourth Voyage of James Hall to Groeneland, wherein he was set forth by English Adventurers, Anno 1612. and slaine by a Greenelander. Written by William Baffin.

Ednesday, the eight of July, 1612. in the morning I perceived the Sunne and the Moone, both very faire above the horizon, as I had done divers times before. At which time I purposed to finde out the longitude of that place, by the Moones comming to the Meridian. Most part of this day I spent about finding of the Meridian line;

which I did upon an Iland neere the Sea, hanging at the extreames of my Meridian line two threeds with Plummets at them, instead of an index and sights.

[III.iv.832.] Thursday, the ninth day very early in the morning I went on shoare the Iland, being a faire morning, and observed till the Moone came just upon the Meridian. At which very instant, I observed the Sunnes height, and found it 8. degrees, 53. minutes, North: in the elevation of the Pole 65. degrees 20. minutes. By the which, working by the doctrine of sphericall triangles, having the three sides given, to wit, the complement of the Poles elevation; the complement of the Almecanter; and the complement of the Sunnes declination, to finde out the quantitie of the angle at the Pole: I say, by this working, I found it to be foure of the clocke, 17. minutes, and 24. seconds. Which when I had done, I found by mine Ephemerides, that the Moone came to the Meridian at London that morning at foure of the clocke, 25. minutes, 34. seconds: which 17. minutes, 24. seconds, substracted from 25. 34. leaveth 8. 10. of time, for the difference of longitude betwixt the Meridian of London (for which the Ephemerides was made) and the Meridian passing by this place in Groenland. Now the Moones motion that day, was 12. degrees 7. minutes: which converted into minutes of time, were 48. minutes, 29. seconds: which working by the rule of proportion, the worke is thus: if 48. minutes, 29. seconds; the time that the Moone commeth to the Meridian sooner that day, then she did the day before, give 360. the whole circumference of the earth, what shall 8. minutes 10.

60. degrees 30. minutes difference of longitude betweene the meridian of London and Cockins Sound in Groenland. seconds give, to wit, 60. degrees, 30. minutes, or neere there about: which is the difference of longitude betweene the Meridian of London, and this place in Groenland, called Cockins Sound, lying to the Westward of London.

This finding of the longitude, I confesse is somewhat difficult and troublesome, and there may be some small errour. But if it be carefully looked unto, and exactly wrought, there will be no great errour, if your Ephe-

merides be true. But some will say, that this kinde of
working is not for Marriners; because they are not
acquainted to worke propositions by the table of signes,
and an instrument is not precise enough to finde out the
houre, minute, and second. For the losse of one minute
of time, is the losse of 7. degrees of longitude. I answere,
that although the most part are not used to this worke,
yet I know some of the better sort, which are able to
worke this and the like propositions exactly. And·those
which yet cannot, and are desirous to learne, may in short
space attaine to such knowledge as shall be sufficient for
such things. And how necessary it is, that the longitude
of places should be knowne, I leave to the judgement of
all skilfull Marriners, and others that are learned in the
Mathematicks.

This afternoone it was agreed by the chiefe of our
Company, that our Master, James Hall, should goe in
the smaller Ship, farther to the Northward.

The foresaid Thursday in the evening, he departed
out of the Patience into the Harts-ease, to get forth of
the Harbor, which our Master called Cockins-ford, in
remembrance of Alderman Cockin one of the Adventurers: which place, is in the latitude of 65. degrees, 20.
minutes. And the variation of the compasse is 23.
degrees, 58. minutes, to the Westward. That evening
was very calme, and we towed our Shippe forth with
the Shallops and Ships Boat. But within an houre or
two after we were got into the Offin; the winde being
at North, it blew a great storme, which continued all
that night.

The foureteenth, our Master turned the Ship up to the
River againe, toward the River where the supposed mine
should be. But the tyde was so farre spent, that we
could not get to Sea, but were constrained to Anker in
a roade at the South side of the River, some three leagues
from the Patience, in which place are many good Rode-
steeds to be found.

Thursday, the sixteenth day, the winde was at North-west, and blew so stiffe a gale, that we could not get to Sea that day. That night, eighteene of us went into the Ilands to looke for some Deere, but found none. But *Great footing.* we perceived the foote-steps of some great Beast, which wee supposed to be of some great Elke: the foote was as bigge as any Oxe foote.

Tuesday, the twentie one, the weather still continued in such sort, that wee could not by any meanes get to the River, where the supposed Myne should bee. Where- *Ramels River.* fore our Master bare roome for Ramelsford, being a River Southward of another, called Cunninghams ford, some twelve leagues. And we came to an Anchor at the entrance on the Southside of the Ford, about seven of the clocke.

Wednesday, the two and twentieth day, about nine or ten of the clocke, the Savages came to barter with us, being about fortie of them, and continued about an houre *James Hall* and an halfe: At which time our Master James Hall, *deadly* being in the Boate, a Savage with his Dart strooke him *wounded by a* a deadly wound upon the right side, which our Surgean *Savage.* did thinke did pierce his liver. We all mused that he should strike him, and offer no harme to any of the rest: unlesse it were, that they knew him since he was there with the Danes; for out of that River they carried away five of the people, whereof never any returned againe: and in the next River, they killed a great number. And it should seeme that he which killed him, was either brother, or some neere kinsman to some of them that were carried away: for he did it very resolutely, and came within foure yards of him. And, for ought we could see, the people are very kinde one to another, and ready to revenge any wrong offred to them. All that day he lay very sore pained, looking for death every houre, and resigned all his charge to Master Andrew Barker, Master of the Harts-ease, willing him to place *[III.iv.833.]* another in his roome Master of the small Ship. *The death of* Thursday, the three and twentieth, about eight of the *James Hall.* clocke in the morning he dyed, being very penitent for all his former offences. And after we had shrowded him, wee carried him in the Shallop, to burie him in some out Iland, according to his owne request while he was living. After we had buried him, we went in the Shallop to seeke for the mine, which we had expected so long. All that day we rowed along toward the North, passing by a Cape called, Queene Sophias Cape. That night we staied at an Iland, some three leagues short of the River.

Friday, the foure and twentieth, in the morning, wee rowed along, and came to the place, which is on the South-side of the entrance of Cunninghams River: And we found divers places, where the Danes had digged; it was a kinde of shining stone, which when our Goldsmith, James Carlile, had tried, it was found of no value, and had no mettall at all in it: but was like unto Moscovie sludde, and of a glittering colour. That day after we had dyned, wee rowed up that River some foure leagues, where divers of our company went up into the Moun-taines, and found a Valley more pleasant, then they had seene in the Countrey. That evening we returned, and came to the place where the Danes had digged their supposed Mine, and tooke some of it in our Boate to carry with us, and returned toward our Ship. That night we rowed and sailed, and the next morning about nine of the clocke, we came to our Ship.

Saturday, the five and twentieth, being Saint James his day, in the forenoone, we came to our Shippe, lying on the South side of the River, called Ramels River. And as soone as our Master found, that the people came no more to trade with us, he determined to depart with the Shippe into the Kings Ford to the Patience: and rowing about the harbour, where we lay to finde some neerer way out to the Sea, we found among the Ilands, where many of their winter houses had bin, and some of their Tents were but lately carried away. In which place wee also found one of their long Boates, made of wood, and bound together for the most part, with shivers of Whales fins, and covered with Seales skinnes, being some two and thirtie foote in length, and some five foote broad, having tenne thoughts or seates in it. That day about twelve of the clocke we weighed anchor, and *Ramels Ford* departed out of Ramels Ford, which lieth in the latitude *in the latitude* of 67. degrees, and the variation of the compasse is 24. *of 67. degrees.* degrees 16. minutes, being a very faire River, and one *The variation* of the most principall, which wee saw in that Countrey, *is 24. degrees.* stretching in East and East and by South. This night, *16. minutes.* about one of the clocke, we came to the Patience, lying in the Kings Ford.

Sunday, the sixe and twentieth, Master Andrew Barker, and our Merchant, Master Wilkinson, with other of the Company, were in conference about returning home, because that since our Master was slaine, none of the Savages would trade with us, as they were wont.

Wednesday, the nine and twentieth, we were likewise occupied about taking in of ballast; for our Shippe was very light: and that evening it was agreed, that Andrew Barker, Master of the Harts-ease, should goe Master of the Patience, which was sore against the minde of William *William* Gourdon: and William Huntrice was appointed Master *Huntrice* of the Harts-ease, and John Gartenby, one of the quarter *Master of the* Masters of the Patience, was Masters mate of the Harts-*Hearts-ease.* ease.

Tuesday, the fourth of August, in the morning the *They come out* winde being Northerly, a very small gale we got to Sea, *of harbour.* where the winde came to the Southward, and we tacked sometime on the one boord, and sometime on the other, making small way on our course.

Munday the tenth, was raine and foule weather, as it had continued every day since wee came from harbour, saving the seventh day, which was somewhat faire: For *Thick and* commonly while the winde is South, it is very thick and *foggie* foule weather. We tacked sometimes on one boord, and *weather, the* sometimes on the other, making a South by West way, *winde being* at noone sixe leagues. *South.*

Wednesday, the twelfth, it waxed calme, we being some-*Burnils Cape.* what Southward of a Cape, called Burnils Cape: and about three or foure of the clocke in the afternoone, the winde came to the North and by West, an easie gale, with faire weather.

The eighteenth, at noone we were in 58. deg. 50. min. The seventeenth day, I tooke the variation of the compasse, finding it to be 13. degrees 22. minutes, contrary to the observations of others in this place. And if any doe doubt of the truth thereof, they may with a little paines prove it. The eighteenth of August, the declination of the Sunne was 9. degrees 58. minutes, for the Meridian of London. But we being almost foure houres of time to the Westward thereof, there are three minutes to be abated from the rest: and so the declination was 9. degrees 55. minutes; and his height above the horizon was 24. degrees 40. minutes in the latitude of 59. degrees 0. min. and his distance from the South to the Westward, by the compasse, was 81. degrees. And for truth of the first observation, I tooke another shortly after, finding them not to differ above 4. minutes.

Variation 13. *degr.* 22. *min.*

Wednesday the nineteenth, the winde still continued with thicke and hasie weather, we being at noone in the latitude of 58. degrees 30. minutes, or thereabout, making a South South-east way, about ten leagues.

Thursday the twentieth, was faire weather, the winde at East North-east, wee steered away South-east and South-east and by East, making at noone a South-east and by South way, about thirtie leagues, being at noone in the latitude of 57. degrees 20. minutes. This day in the afternoone, I tooke the variation of the compasse, and found it about 11. degrees 10. minutes.

Variation 11. *degr.* 10. *min.*

Friday the one and twentieth, faire weather, with the winde at North and North by East, and we made an East South-east way, halfe Southerly twentie foure leagues, being at noone by observation, in the latitude of 56. degrees 50. minutes.

[III.iv.834.]

Saturday the two and twentieth, faire weather, the wind at North and North by East, wee made an East way halfe

Southerly, some twentie two leagues, being at noone in the latitude of 56. degrees 47. minutes.

Sunday the three and twentieth, faire weather, the wind at West North-west, we making an East and East by North way about twentie foure leagues. This day I tooke the variation of the Compasse, and found it to be 7. degrees 23. minutes, being at noone in the latitude of 57. degrees 26. minutes.

Variation 7. degrees 23. minutes.

Munday the foure and twentieth, being S. Bartholomewes day, faire weather with a North North-west wind wee making an East North-east way, halfe Northerly about twentie seven leagues, and were at noone by observation in the latitude of 58. degrees 4. minutes. This day I observed and found the Compasse to be varied 7. degrees 20. minutes.

Variation 7. degrees 20. minutes.

Tuesday the five and twentieth, faire weather and calme: the winde at North, wee made a North-east and by East way seventeene leagues, being at noone in the latitude of 58. degrees 30. minutes. This day I found the common Compasse to be varied one point, and the true variation to bee 6. degrees 4. minutes.

The true variation 6. deg. 4. minutes.

Wednesday the sixe and twentieth faire weather also, with the wind North North-west, we made a North-east and by East way halfe about twentie two leagues, being in the height of 59. degrees 10. minutes.

Thursday the seven and twentieth indifferent faire weather, with a stiffe gale of wind at the North Northwest, we making a North-east way about thirtie one leagues, being at noone in the latitude of 60. degrees 10. minutes.

Friday the eight and twentieth, the wind at South-east with a stiffe gale, wee made good about noone a Northeast and by East way about twentie nine leagues. This day in the afternoone it blew so great a storme, that wee were in great distresse, the winde at East South-east. But about eleven of the clocke it came to the North-west, and North-west by North. And we ranne some twentie leagues.

Saturday the nine and twentieth, it blew so stiffe, that wee could beare none but our fore-saile, making an East and by South way halfe Southerly, about thirtie leagues.

Sunday the thirtieth, all the forenoone it blew a very stiffe gale, and about noone the winde came Southerly; and it blew a very great storme, which continued all that day and that night in such sort, that we could not saile at all, but all that night lay at hull.

Munday the one and thirtieth, in the morning about foure of the clocke, the winde came to the South-west a very stiffe gale. At which time we set our fore-saile. The wind continued all this day and night, we steered away East and by South, making at noone an East North-east way about thirtie foure leagues.

Tuesday the first of September, the wind still continued at South-west, blowing a very stiffe gale, we steered away East and by South, making an East way about fiftie leagues. This day at noone we were in the latitude of 60. degrees 45. minutes.

Wednesday the second faire weather with the wind at South-west, wee made an East and by South way halfe a point Southerly about fortie two leagues, being at noone in the latitude of 60. degrees 10. minutes. This day I observed, and found the Compasse to be varied three degrees to the Westward.

Thursday the third day faire weather, the wind at South-west: wee made an East by North way at noone about twentie leagues. This day in the after-noone, the winde being at North North-west, it blew a very stiffe gale for two Watches; and toward seven or eight of the clocke the storme so increased, that our shippe was not able to beare any saile. And all that night wee lay at hull.

Friday the fourth, the storme still continued, and we could beare no saile all that day till about foure of the clocke in the afternoone, at which time we set our fore course, and our maine course. The night before in the storme, we lost The Harts-ease. This day wee made

They lose company of their consort, The Hartsease.

some twelve leagues East and by North.   And we fell to lee-ward lying at hull some five leagues South by West.

Saturday the fift calme weather, but very thicke and close all the forenoone : the wind continued still at North North-west, we making from the time wee set our courses the day before, about twentie leagues East halfe Southerly ; beeing at noone in the latitude of 59. degrees 53. minutes.

Sunday the sixt, faire weather, the wind at North North-west, we steering away East North-east, and East and by North, made an East by North way, halfe Northerly some 29. leagues, being at noone in 60. degrees 10. minutes.

Variation 6. degrees to the East. Ground found.

This day the Compasse was varied to the East sixe degrees. This afternoone it was almost calme : and wee sounded, and found ground at sixtie eight fathomes.   This Evening about ten of the clocke the wind came to the South-east.

[III. iv. 835.]

Munday the seventh, very faire weather, the wind South-east and South-east by East, wee tacked in the morning to the North-ward, and ranne East North-east and East by North untill seven or eight in the afternoone : at which time we tacked up to the Southward, and went away South-west till toward twelve a clocke that night twentie leagues.

Tuesday the eight, in our morning Watch I found our selves to be in 59. degrees 20. minutes : And about five

Land descryed. The Iles of Orkney.

of the clocke I espied Land, which we supposed to bee the Iles of Orkney, as afterward we found them to be the same.   And toward three of the clocke, we came to an Anchor in a Channell running betweene the Ilands ; where the people came to us, and brought us Hennes, Geese, and Sheepe, and sold them to us for old clothes and shooes, desiring rather them then money.   There are about eighteene of these Ilands, which are called by the name of the Orkeneis.

Wednesday the ninth, it was thicke weather, and the winde so Easterly that wee could not weigh Anchor.

Thursday the tenth, faire weather, and the wind came to the North-west, and about noone we weighed Anchor ; and toward five of the clocke we were cleere off the Iles.

WILLIAM BAFFIN

The Channell for the most part lyeth North-west and
South-east. All that night we stood away South-east.
Friday the eleventh, faire weather, with the wind at
North North-west. And about nine of the clocke in the
morning, we steered away South South-east. At which
time wee had sight of Buquham-nesse: And about two *Buquham-*
of the clocke we were thwart of it. The seventeenth, *ness.*
we came to an Anchor in Hull Road, for which the Lord *They arrive*
bee praysed. *at Hull.*

Here I thinke it not amisse briefly to relate the state
and manners of the people of Groenland, forasmuch as I
could learne: As also what likelihood there is of a passe
into the Sea, which lyeth upon Tartarie and China.

The North-west part of Gronland is an exceeding high
Land to the Sea-ward, and almost nothing but Moun- *High Moun-*
taynes; which are wonderfull high all within the Land, *taynes of stone*
as farre as wee could perceive: and they are all of stone, *very pure.*
some of one colour, and some of another, and all glistering,
as though they were of rich value; but indeed they are
not worth any thing. For our Gold-smith James Carlile
tryed very much of the Ure, and found it to bee nothing *No profitable*
worth. If there bee any Mettall, it lyeth so low in the *Ure.*
Mountaynes, that it cannot bee well come by. There
are some Rocks in these Mountaynes, which are exceeding
pure Stone, finer, and whiter then Alabaster. The sides
of these Mountaynes continually are covered with Snow *Continuall*
for the most part, and especially the North sides, and the *Snow.*
North sides of the Valleyes, having a kind of Mosse, and
in some places Grasse with a little branch running all along *Grasse.*
the ground, bearing a little blacke Berrie, it runneth along
the ground like Three-leafed Grasse heere in England.
There are few or no Trees growing, as farre as wee could *No Trees.*
perceive, but in one place some fortie miles within the
Land, in a River, which wee called Balls River. There *Balls River.*
I saw on the South-side of an high Mountayne, which
we went up, and found (as it were) a yong Grove of small *A Grove of*
Wood, some of it sixe or seven foot high like a Coppice *small wood.*
in England, that had beene some two or three yeeres

cut. And this was the most Wood that wee saw growing in this Countrey; being some of it a kind of Willow, Juniper, and such like.

We found in many places much Angelica. We suppose the people eate the Roots thereof, for some causes. For we have seene them have many of them in their Boats.

Foxes.

There are great store of Foxes in the Ilands, and in the Mayne, of sundry colours: And there are a kind of

White Hares. Hares as white as Snow, with their furre or haire very long.

Deere.

Also there be Deere, but they are most commonly up within the Mayne very farre; because the people doe so much hunt them, that come neere the Sea. I saw at one time seven of them together, which were all that wee did see in the Countrey: But our men have bought divers Coates of the people made of Deeres skinnes, and have

These seeme bought of their Hornes also. Besides, we have divers
to be Elkes, or times seene the footsteps of some beast, whose foote was
Losshes. bigger then the foot of a great Oxe. Furthermore, the
Dogges like Inhabitants have a kinde of Dogges, which they keepe
Wolves. at their Houses, and Tents, which Dogges are almost like unto Wolves, living by fish, as the Foxes doe. But
The pizzels of one thing is very strange, as I thought: for the Pizzels
Dogges and of both Dogges and Foxes are bone.
Foxes are
bone: so also The people all the Summer time use nothing but fishing,
is the Morses drying their fish, and Seales flesh upon the Rockes for
pizzle, of their Winter Provision. Every one both man and woman
which I have have each of them a Boate made with long small pieces
by me one of of Firre-wood, covered with Seales skinnes very well drest,
stone. and sewed so well with sinewes or guts, that no water can pierce them through, beeing some of them above twentie foot long, and not past two foot, or two foot and an halfe broad, in forme of a Weavers shittle, and so
The great light, that a man may carrie many of them at once for
swiftnesse of the weight. In these Boates they will row so swiftly,
their Boats. that it is almost incredible: for no ship in the World is able to keepe way with them, although shee have never so good a gale of wind: and yet they use but one Oare,

who sitting in the middle of their Boate, and holding their Oare in the middle, being broad at each end like our Oares, will at an instant goe backward and forward, as they please.

In these Boates they catch the most part of their food, being Seales and Salmons, Morses, and other kinds of fishes. Some they kill with their Darts, and other some with Angles, having a Line made of small shivers of Whales Finnes, and an Hooke of some fishes bones: with which Line and Hookes, we also have caught very much fish.

Also they have another kinde of Boate, which is very long. For wee have seene one of them thirtie two foot in length, open in the toppe like our Boates; having tenne seates in it. In which when they remoove their Dwellings, they carrie their Goods or House-hold-stuffe: for they remoove their Dwellings very often, as their fishing doth serve, living in the Summer time, in Tents made of Seales skinnes, and in Winter in Houses some-what in the ground.

Wee could not particularly learne their Rites or Ceremonies: but generally they worship the Sunne, as chiefe Authour of their Felicitie. At their first approach unto us they used with their hands to point up to the Sunne, and to strike their hands upon their brests, crying Ilyont; as who would say, I meane no harme: which they will doe very often, and will not come neere you, untill you doe the like; and then they will come without any feare at all.

They burie their dead in the Out-Ilands neere the Sea side. Their manner of Buriall is this. Upon the tops of the Hils they gather a company of stones together, and make thereof an hollow Cave or Grave, of the length and breadth of the bodie, which they intend to burie, laying the stones somewhat close like a wall, that neyther Foxes, nor other such beasts may devoure the bodies, covering them with broad stones, shewing afarre off like a pile of stones. And neere unto this Grave where the bodie lyeth, is another, wherein they burie his Bow and

Their Oares broad at both ends.

[III.iv.836.] *Salmons and Morses, &c.*

Angles and Lines.

Their great Boats 32. foot long.

They worship the Sunne. Their salutation.

Their burials.

They burne the weapons and all other Furniture of the dead.

Arrowes, with his Darts and all his other Provision, which hee used while hee was living. Hee is buried in all his Apparell: and the coldnesse of the Climate doth keepe the bodie from smelling and stinking, although it lye above the Ground.

They eate all their Food raw, and use no fire to dresse their Victuals, as farre as wee could perceive. Also wee have seene them drinke the Salt-water at our shippes side: But whether it bee usuall or no, I cannot tell. Although *They use fire.* they dresse not their meate with fire, yet they use fire for other things, as to warme them, &c.

Divers of our men were of opinion, that they were Man-eaters, and would have devoured us, if they could *They are not* have caught us. But I doe not thinke they would. For *Man-eaters.* if they had bin so minded, they might at one time have caught our Cooke, and two other with him, as they were filling of water at an Iland, a great way from our ship. These three I say were in the ships Boate without eyther Musket, or any other Weapon, when as a great company of the Savages came rowing unto them with their Darts, and other Furniture, which they never goe without, and *Nailes & old* stood looking into the Boate for Nayles, or any old Iron, *Iron greatly* which they so greatly desire, while our men were in such *desired of the* a feare, that they knew not what to doe. At length our *Savages.* Cooke remembred that hee had some old Iron in his pocket, and gave each of them some, as farre as it would goe, *Men are not* with his Key of his Chest. And presently they all *to goe among* departed without offering any harme at all. But this I *Savages* speake not, that I would have men to trust them, or to *without their* goe among them unprovided of Weapons. *weapons.*

Chap. XVIII.

A true Relation of such things as happened in the fourth Voyage for the Discoverie of the Northwest Passage, performed in the yeere 1615. Written by William Baffin.

Fter three sundry Voyages towards the *The first by* North-west, to the great charge of the *Hudson, in* Adventurers: the last being under the *which hee* command of Captaine Gibbins (in which *perished; the* was little or nothing performed.) Yet *second by Sir* the Right Worshipfull Sir Dudley Digges *Thomas* Knight, Master Wostenholme Esquire, *Button, the third by Cap-taine Gibbins.* Master Alderman Jones, with others being not therewith discouraged, This yeere 1615. againe set forth the Discovery, a ship of fiftie five tunnes or thereabouts, which ship had beene the three former Voyages on the action. The Master was Robert Bileth, a man well acquainted that way: having beene employed in the three former Voyages: my selfe being his Mate and Associate, with fourteene others and two Boyes.

The sixteenth, we weighed Anchor at Saint Katharines, and that tyde came to Blackwall, the winde being at South South-west. The seventeenth, wee went downe to Gravesend, and the eighteenth to Lee, where we anchored that night.

Upon the sixt of May, we saw Land on the Coast of *[III.iv.837.]* Groenland, on the East side of Cape Farewell: and that *Groenland.* night we had a great storme: so wee kept a Southerly *Cape* course to get about the Ice which lay on that shoare, and *Farewell.* then kept our course untill the seventeenth day of May, all which forenoone we sayled by many great Ilands of *High Icie* Ice, some of which were above two hundred foot high *Ilands.* above water (as I proved by one shortly after) which I found to be two hundred and fortie foot high, and if report of some men be true, which affirme, that there is but one seventh part of the Ice above water, then the height of that piece of Ice, which I observed was one hundred and fortie fathomes, or one thousand sixe hundred and eightie foote from the toppe to the bottome: this proportion I know doth hold in much Ice, but whether it doe so in all, I know not.

This seventeenth of May, about noone we were come to the firme Ice, as one would suppose, being in the latitude of 61. degrees 26. minutes or thereabout, being the latitude of the South part of the Ile of Resolution: we comming to this Ice, our Master asked my opinion concerning the putting into the Ice. My judgement was it would be best for us to stand, and ply it up to the Northwards. Hee answered, we were on the North side of the South Channell, and much Ice we must passe through, and if that we could get some two or three leagues within the Ice, it would every tide open, and we should get some thing onward of our way, having all the Channell to the South-wards of us. So with this resolution we put within the Ice, the wind being at East North-east: this first entrance I liked not very well, scarce finding any place to put in our ships head, and being neere thirtie leagues from the shoare, towards Evening wee were fast amongst the Ice.

But sometimes each day the Ice would a little open, we making what way we could towards the North-west in for the shoare till the two and twentieth day, having had the wind all Southerly. Yet we plainly saw that we set to the Southwards, for all that wee could doe.

The two and twentieth day, the wind came up at North North-west: then our Master determined to stand forth againe. For if the wind should have come to the North-east, it would be unpossible for us to fetch any part of the Channell, seeing wee drove so fast to the Southwards, with Southerly winds, and having so farre into the shoare, not having seene the Land.

Our Master was also determined to spend some twentie, or foure and twentie dayes in Fretum Davis, to see what hopes would be that wayes, supposing there would be little good to be done in Hudsons Streights for this time limited: then we plying to get to Sea-ward, and so by eight a clock at night, the three and twentieth day, we were cleere of the thick Ice: againe, the Lord make us thankfull, the wind at North-west and by North faire weather: but no sooner were we forth of the Ice, but that our Master changed his opinion: and beeing cleere of this thicke Ice wee stood to the Northward as much as the Ice and winde would give us leave, running some thirteene leagues true North-east by North, being in the latitude of 61. degrees 50. minutes. The foure and twentieth day faire weather: the five and twentieth day, also faire weather, the wind at North and by West, till sixe a clocke, we having made a North-east by North way about twelve leagues and an halfe, our latitude at noone 62. degrees 20. minutes, at sixe a clocke the wind was at the North North-east. The sixe and twentieth day, all the forenoone faire weather and cold: but in the afternoone it blew very hard, being close hasie weather, that about two a clocke this afternoone wee tooke in our sailes and hulled with our ship till the next morning at foure a clocke, all the time that we sayled this day we past through many ledges of Ice having great quantitie to the Northward of us, and having runne about twentie one leagues true upon a West course. And note where I put this word true, I meane the true course, the variation of the Compasse, and other accidents allowed.

The seven and twentieth day close foggy weather with much snow freezing on our shrowds and tackling: the like we had not all this yeare before: but towards foure a clocke in the afternoone it began to cleere up, and about five a clocke we saw Land, being the Iland of Resolution, and bearing West from us about thirteene or fourteene leagues. This morning we set sayle, and stood to and fro as the Ice would suffer us, and at ten at night, wee moored our ship to a piece of Ice, the wind being at West.

The eight and twentieth day being Whitsunday, it was faire weather, but the winde was at the West, and West by North: al this day we were fast to the piece of Ice. Yet we plainly perceived that we set a great deale more into the Streights with the floud. Then we set forth with the ebbe the nine and twentieth day, the wind was variable, and faire weather: about eleven a clock we set saile and tacked to and fro along by the Iland. And about two a clocke the next morning, the wind came to the South South-east, but we had so much Ice that we could doe but little good with a faire wind, the wind continued

No night. all this day and night a stiffe gale: this night (or rather Evening, because it was not darke at all) we were set within the point of the Iland: so that now we were within the Streights.

The one & thirtieth day also faire weather, the wind for the most part at North North-west, the afternoone being cleere wee saw the point of the South shoare, called Buttons Iles, to beare from us due South by the Compasse, which is indeed South South-east, somewhat Eastward,

Variation 24. *degrees.* because here the Compasse is varied to the Westwards twentie foure degrees.

[III. iv. 838.] The first of June, wee had some snow in the forenoone, but very faire weather in the afternoone, the wind at West North-west. We perceiving the Ice to be more open close aboord the shoare, made the best way we could to get in, and to come to Anchor, if the place were convenient; and by seven a clocke we were in a good Harbour, on the North-west side of the Iland of Resolution, where an East South-east Moone maketh full Sea, or halfe an houre past seven on the change day, as Sea-men account the water doth rise and fall, neere foure fathomes; the Compasse doth vary to the West 24. degrees 6. minutes, and is in longitude West from London 66. degrees 35. minutes. The breadth of the South Channell, or the distance betweene the Iland and the South shoare, is six-teene leagues, and the North Channell is eight miles wide in the narrowest place.

Upon this Iland we went on shoare, but found no certaine signe of Inhabitants, but the tract of Beares and Foxes, Rockes and stonie ground, hardly any thing growing thereon: it is indifferent high Land to the Northward, having one high Hill or Hummocke on the North-east side, but to the Southward is falleth away very low.

The second of June in the morning the wind came up at East South-east, with much snow and fowle weather: about noone wee weighed Anchor, and stood up along by the Iland, so well as the Ice would give us leave to get to the North shoare. Wee continuing our courses so neere the North shoare, as conveniently we could, with much variable weather and windes, but stedfast in continuance among Ice, till the eight day, having the wind full contrary to us, and being somewhat neere a point of Land, or rather a company of Ilands, which after wee called Savage Iles, having a great Sound or In-draught, *Savage Iles.* betweene the North shoare and them. At sixe a clocke we came to Anchor neere one of them, being the Easter-most saving one. But whiles wee were furling our sailes, we heard and saw a great company of Dogges running up *Dogges.* and downe, with such howling and barking, that it seemed very strange. Shortly after we had moored our ship, we sent our Boat somewhat neerer the shoare, to see if they could perceive any people; who returning, told us that there were Tents and Boats, or Canowes, with a great many Dogges, but people they saw none. After Prayer, when our men had supt, wee fitted our Boate and our selves with things convenient: then my selfe with seven others landed, and went to their Tents, where finding no people, we marched up to the top of a Hill (being about a flight shot off) where we saw one great Canow or Boat, *Great Boat* which had about fourteene men in it, being on the furthest, *with 14. men.* or North-west point of the Iland, and from us somewhat more then a Musket shot. Then I called unto them, using some words of Groenlandish speech, making signes of friendship. They did the like to us; but seeing them so fearefull of us, and we not willing to trust them, I made another signe to them, shewing them a Knife and other Trifles, which I left on the top of the Hill, and returned downe to their Tents againe. There wee found some Whales Finnes to the number of fortie or fiftie, with a few Seale skinnes which I tooke aboord, leaving Knives, Beades, and Counters instead thereof; and amongst their houses I found a little bagge, in which *Bagge of* was a company of little Images of men; one the Image *Images.* of a woman with a child at her backe, all the which I brought away.

Among these Tents being five in number, all covered with Seales skinnes, were running up and downe, about *Their Dogges* thirtie five or fortie Dogges; most of them muzled. They *described.* were of our mungrell Mastiffes, being of a brinded blacke colour, looking almost like Wolves. These Dogges they use in stead of Horses, or rather as the Lappians doe their Deere, to draw their sleds from place to place over the Ice: their sleds are shod or lined with great bones of fishes to keepe them from wearing, and their Dogges have Collars and Furniture very fitting.

The people These people have their Apparell, Boots, Tents, and *described.* other necessaries much like to the Inhabitants in Groine-land, saving that they are not so neate and artificiall, seeming to bee more rude and uncivill, ranging up and downe as their fishing is in season. For in most places where wee came ashoare, we saw where people had beene, although not this yeere; but where their Habitation or their abode in Winter is, I cannot well conjecture.

Situation. This Iland lyeth in the latitude of 62. degrees 30. minutes, and in longitude West from London, 72. degrees or neere thereabouts, being sixtie leagues from the entrance of the Streights: here the Compasse doth varie 27. degrees 30. minutes, and a South-east Moone foure degrees East maketh a full Sea: it doth ebbe and flow almost as much water, as it doth at the Resolution, and here the floud commeth from the Eastward, although our Master was of opinion to the contrarie.

The tenth day in the morning, at sixe a clocke we set sayle, the winde at North, which continued not, but was very variable till noone, and then it came to North-west, we having sayled along by the shoare, about some nine leagues and an halfe North North-west, the Ice lying so thicke in the offen, that wee could not well get out of it: then perceiving a good Harbour betweene two small Ilands and the Mayne, wee went in with our ship, where wee moored her, and stayed till the twelfth day at Evening.

In this place it is high water on the change day, at nine of the clocke, or a South-east Moone maketh a full Sea: the latitude of this place is 62. degrees 40. minutes; and the floud doth come from the Eastward, although our [III.iv.839.] Master was perswaded otherwise, as well in this place, as at Salvage Ilands: for being among Ilands, every point hath his severall set and eddie. But I going to the top of the Iland, plainely perceived the Ice to come from the South-east, and from the North-west on the ebbe. In this place is no signe of people, as we could perceive.

The sixteenth day, lying still in the Ice, the weather being very close and hasey, as it hath beene these six dayes: and being neere a great company of Ilands, in the afternoone, the winde being at West North-west, wee stood in amongst these Ilands, and in the evening we moared our Shippe to one of them in a small cove, the better to defend her from the Ice. In this place wee stayed all the seventeenth day: and upon the eighteenth, being Sunday, about eleven a clocke we set sayle, being almost calme, making the best way wee could to get forth. Here are a great company of Ilands, each hath his severall *Many Ilands* set and eddy, that the Ice doth so runne to and fro, and *and severall* with such violence, that our Shippe was in more safetie *tyde Sets.* further off then in this place: the latitude of the Ile we rode by is 63. degrees 26. minutes, and longitude West from London, neere 72. degrees 25. minutes: the Compasse hath variation 27. degrees 46. minutes; and at a quarter of an houre after nine on the Change day, doth make a full Sea. This Evening, and the next morning,

wee had a faire steering gale of winde at South-east, wee
standing along by the Land, it beeing all small broken
Ilands, to a point of Land about twelve leagues in distance
from the Ile wee put last from: which Point, I called
Broken Point. Broken Point, it being indeede a point of broken Iles.

On the nineteenth day, by twelve a clocke at noone,
wee were about foure miles from the Point before named,
fast inclosed with Ice, very faire weather; and well we
might have called this Point Fairenesse or Faire Point,
for from this day till the thirtieth day, the weather was
so faire, and almost, or altogether calme, that in few places
elsewhere, finer weather could not be; and till the seven
and twentieth at night, wee were so fast inclosed up with
Ice, that at some times one could not well dippe a paile
of water by the Ship sides: while wee were thus fast in
the Ice, upon the one and twentieth day, I saw both the
Sunne and Moone at one time, as indeede it is usuall in
faire weather.

This one and twentieth, being faire weather, as afore
is said, and I seeing both the Sunne and Moone so faire:
Observations I thought it a fit time to make an observation for the
of longitude. longitude.

But the two and twentieth day being very faire and
cleare, and also calme, being almost as steedy as on shoare:
it was no neede to bid me fit my Instrument of variation
to take the time of the Moones comming to the Meridian,
having also my quadrant ready to take the Sunnes almicanter, it being indifferent large, as of foure foote
semideamiter: have taken the variation of my needle as
precisely as possible I could, which was 28. degrees 20.
minutes West, and if any be desirous to worke the same,
they may, but my worke was as followeth.

The Sunnes almicanter, at the instant when the Moone
was on the Meridian, was 26. degrees 40. minutes: and
the Sunnes declination for that time 23. degrees 6.
minutes. By which three things given, I found the houre
to be five a clocke 4. minutes 52. seconds, 1. third 4.
fourths, or 76. degrees, 13. minutes, 16. seconds, of the

equinoctiall afternoone: and according to Searles Ephemerides, the Moone came to the Meridian at London at foure a clocke 54. minutes, 30. seconds: and after Origanus the Moone came to the Meridian at foure a clocke 52. minutes, 5. seconds, at Wittenberge the same day. Now having this knowne, it is no hard matter to finde the longitude of this place sought. For according to the Moones meane motion, which is 12. degrees a day, that is in time 48. minutes: and to this account, if she be on the Meridian at twelve a clock this day, to morrow it will be 48. min. past 12. So I having the time found by observation at this place, viz. 5. houres, 4. minutes, 52. seconds, 1. third 4. fourths: but in this I neede not come so precise: and at London, at 4. houres, 54. minutes, 30. seconds: which substracted from the former, leaveth 10. minutes, 22. seconds, 1. third, 4. fourths, now the Moones motion the foure and twentie houres, was 22. degrees, 38. minutes: which converted into time, is 50. minutes 25. seconds 20. thirds: then the proportion standeth thus; If 50. minutes, 25. seconds, 20. thirds, give 360. degrees, what shall 10. minutes, 22. seconds, 1. third, 4. fourths give? the fourth proportionall, will be 74. degrees 5. minutes, which is West of London; because the Moone came later by 10. minutes, 22. seconds, and by the same working by Origanus Ephemerides, the distance is 91. degrees, 35. minutes, West of West. But whether be the truer, I leave to others to judge: in these workings may some errour be committed, if it be not carefully looked unto: as in the observation, and also in finding what time the Moone commeth to the Meridian, at the place where the Ephemerides is supputated for, and perchance in the Ephemerides themselves: in all which, the best judicious may erre: yet if observations of this kinde, or some other, at places farre remote, as at the Cape Bonasperanze, Bantam, Japan, Nova Albion, and Magellan Straits, I suppose wee should have a truer Geography then we have. And seeing I am entred to speake of celestiall observations, I will note

another which I made the twenty sixt of April, being
outward bound at Sea, by the Moones comming in a
right line, with two fixed Starres; the one was the Lyons
heart, a Starre of the first magnitude; the other a Starre
in the Lyons rumpe, of the second magnitude, as
followeth: The circumference or outward edge of the

[III.iv. 840.] Moone, being in a right or straight line, with those two
Starres before named: at the instant I tooke the altitude
of the South ballance, which was 2. degrees 38. minutes,
because I would have the time: but in this it is good
to waite a fit time, as to have her in a right line, with
two Stars not farre distant, and those not to be much
different in longitude, because the Moon will soone alter
the angle or position, and such a time would be taken
when the Moone is in the nintieth degree of the eclipticke
above the horizon, for then there is no paralell of longitude,
but onely in latitude: but who so is painefull in these
businesses, shall soone see what is needefull, and what is
not: my observations were as followeth:

Lyons heart
$\begin{cases} \text{Right assention} & 46. \text{ deg. } 28. \text{ min. } 30. \text{ sec.} \\ \text{Declination} - - & 13. \text{ deg. } 57. \text{ min. } 30. \text{ sec.} \\ \text{Longitude} - - - & 24. \text{ deg. } 29. \text{ min. } 45. \text{ sec.} \\ \text{Latitude} - - - - & 00. \text{ deg. } 26. \text{ min. } 30. \text{ sec.} \\ \text{Almicanter} - - & 33. \text{ deg. } 40. \text{ min. } 00. \text{ sec.} \end{cases}$

Lyons rumpe
$\begin{cases} \text{Right assention} & 163. \text{ deg. } 23. \text{ min. } 00. \text{ sec.} \\ \text{Declination} - - & 22. \text{ deg. } 38. \text{ min. } 00. \text{ sec.} \\ \text{Longitude} - - & 5. \text{ deg. } 53. \text{ min. } 45. \text{ sec.} \\ \text{Latitude} - - - - & 14. \text{ deg. } 20. \text{ min. } 00. \text{ sec.} \end{cases}$

Moones
$\begin{cases} \text{Paralax} - - - & 00. \text{ deg. } 47. \text{ min. } 46. \text{ sec.} \\ \text{Latitude} - - - & 03. \text{ deg. } 20. \text{ min. } 00. \text{ sec.} \\ \text{Almicanter} - - & 37. \text{ deg. } 00. \text{ min. } 00. \text{ sec.} \end{cases}$ North.

Latitude of the place - - 56. deg. 43. min.

These notes I have set downe, that if any other be
desirous to trie, they may spend a little time therein;
my selfe have spent some therein, and more I would have
spent, if leisure would have permitted: but finding it

not to my minde, I have not here set downe my particular worke: the working of this observation I received from Master Rudston.

Master Rudston.

But if it had pleased God, we had performed the action we were bound for, I would not feare but to have brought so good contentment to the Adventurers, concerning the true scituation of notable places, that small doubt should have beene thereof: but seeing so small hopes are in this place, I have not set downe so many observations as otherwise I would.

We lying here inclosed with the Ice with faire & calme weather (as before is said) till the seven and twentieth day at evening, at which time we set sayle; the winde at South-east, an easie gale: all the eight and twentieth and nine and twentieth dayes, we made the best way through the Ice we could, but the nine and twentieth day, the Ice was more open then it had beene these ten dayes before, and at noone we saw Salisbury Iland, it bearing due West from us.

The first of July close foggie weather, with much raine, the winde at South South-east: by noone this day we were some three leagues from the Land: but having much Ice by the shoare, we stood along the Iland to the Northward: and the next morning wee were faire by another small Ile, or rather a company of small Ilands, which after we called Mill Iland, by reason of grinding the Ice, as this night we made proofe thereof: at noone, being close to this Ile, wee took the latitude thereof, which is neere 64. degrees. Here driving to and fro with the Ice all this day, till seven or eight a clocke, at what time the Ice began to open and separate; The Ice, as is said, beginning to open: we had not stood along by the Ile, on the East side thereof, an houre; but the Ice came driving with the tide of floud from the South-east, with such swiftnesse, that it over went our Shippe having all our sayles abroad with a reasonable gale of winde, and put her out of the streame, into the eddy of these Iles.

Mill Iland.

This Iland or Iles, lying in the middle of the channell,

having many sounds running through them, with many
points or headlands, encountering the force of the tide,
caused such a rebound of water & Ice (which ran one
way, and the streame another) our ship having met the
Ice with the first of the floud, which put her so neere the
shoare, that she was in the partition betweene the Ice,
which the eddy caused to runne one way, and the streame
the other, where shee endured great distresse; but God,
which is still stronger then either Ice or streame, preserved
us and our Shippe from any harme at all. This continued
till towards a high water, which was about one a clocke;
then with no small trouble we got into the channell, and
stood away to the North-west ward. After we had past
some distance from this Iland, wee had the Sea more open
then it was since we put first into the Straits; and sailed
all the next day through an indifferent cleare Sea, with
the winde at South-west: but towards eight a clocke at
night, wee were come againe into much Ice; this Ice
being more thicker and bigger then any wee had beene
among: this place where we began to be inclosed againe,
is six and twenty leagues distant from the small Iland
we were at last: and our true course North-west by West:
after wee were fast in the Ice, we made but small way,
yet we perceived a great tyde to set to and fro. The next
day, wee sounded, and had ground at one hundred &
twentie fathoms, soft Osey ground: standing more
Northerly: the next morning we had ground at eightie
fathoms, then the winde came to the North, and we
setting somewhat Southward, had ground at a hundred
and ten fathoms. Thus seeing this great abundance of
Ice in this place, and the more we got to the North-west
ward, the shoalder it was, the Ice also being foule and
durtie, as not bred farre from shoare: our Master determined to stand to the Eastward, to be certainely informed
of the tide.

The sixt day in the morning, we brake in a planke
and two timbers in our Ships bow, which after we had
mended, we proceeded for to get to the East side, which

we called the North shoare, because it is the Land stretching from the Resolution, on the North side of the Straits.

The seventh day we saw the land, it being but low land, [III.iv.841.] and the Sea is shoald, in respect of other places, having ten or twelve fathom about a league off from shoare, some thirty fathoms five or six leagues off shore, but further off some twenty or eighteene leagues, there is a hundred or a hundred and five fathoms; having very good channell ground, as small stones & shels, some twelve or fourteene leagues from shoare, but the further off the more Osey: and also here is a very great tide runneth to the Northward, which this evening we found to be the tyde of ebbe, for comming with our Shippe neere the shoare, about seven a clocke, we hoysed out our Boate, then I with five other went on shoare, and found it to ebbe: we staied on shoare about an houre and a halfe, in which time the water fell about three foote and a halfe, and a South-south East Moone maketh a full Sea, or halfe an houre past tenne, as Sea men account: we saw no signe of people to be here this yeare, but in yeares heretofore they have beene, as we might well see by divers places, where their tents had stood: and perchance their time of fishing was not yet come, there being such great abundance of Ice as yet.

The eight day the winde was at West, and the ninth almost calme: wee reeking neere to this shoare the tenth day, our Master determined to stand for Nottinggams *Nottinggams* Iland, to make triall of the tide there; yet the winde was *Iland.* at South-west so that we were forced to turne, but towards night it came to the North North-west, so that then we stood away to the West wards, leaving the search of Nottinggams Ile, having a great swelling Sea, come out of the West with the winde which had blowne, which put us in some hope: the eleventh day in the morning, we saw Land West from us, but had no ground at one hundred & thirty fathoms: so standing along by the Land which here lay about North-west by North, the next morne we were thwart of a Bay: then standing over to the

Northwards towards a faire Cape or head land which we saw, in the after-noone it was almost calme, and being about a league from shoare, we hoysed out our Boat, and sent some of our men in her, to see what tide it was by the shoare, and from whence it came; they went from the Ship at five a clock, and came aboord againe at eight, who brought us word, that it was falling water, and that it had eb'd while they were on shoare somewhat above two foot: also they affirmed, that the floud came from the Northward in this place, the which we also perceived by the setting of our Ship, she setting a pace to the Northward, although no whit of winde: also we might see by the rocks, that the water was now falne: this put us in great comfort and hope of a passage in this place.

Cape Comfort. Then our Master called this Cape or head land, Cape Comfort, for the reasons beforesaid; also we had one hundred and fortie fathoms in depth, not a league from the shoare: and here a South by East Moone maketh a full Sea: the latitude of this Cape is 65. degrees 00. min. and 85. degrees 20. minutes West from London. But this our sudaine comfort was as soone quailed, for the next day having doubled the Cape, and proceeded not past ten or twelve leagues, but we saw the land trending from the Cape to the Westward, till it bare from us North-east by East, and very thicke pestered with Ice, and the further we proceeded, the more Ice, and the more Northerly, the shoulder water and small shew of any tide. At six a clocke this afternoone, we sounded, & had ground in one hundred and thirty fathoms, soft Osey, having had at noone one hundred & fiftie fathoms.

This was the farthest of our Voyage, being in the latitude of 65. degrees 26. minutes, and longitude West from London 86. degrees 10. minutes: for seeing the land North-east by East, from us about nine or ten leagues off, and the Ice so thicke: our Master was fully perswaded, that this was nought else but a Bay, and so tacked and turned the Shippes head homewards, without any farther search.

The fourteenth day, the winde was for the most part at South-east, that we could make but small way backe againe: and the next morning very foule weather, we comming to an Anchor in a small Inlet, neere the Cape Comfort, on the North-west side thereof; here wee found, as on the other side, a South by East Moone, to make a full Sea; but from whence the floud came, we could not well see, it being so foule weather at Sea: in the afternoone the winde came to North by West: then we waied, and stood along to the Southwards by the shoare, with a stiffe gale of winde, and very hasey. By the sixteenth day at noone we met with a great quantitie of Ice, lying some few leagues within the point of the Land: among this Ice we saw a great number of Sea Morse, not seeing any more in all the Straits but here, and these very fearefull, not suffering a Ship or Boat to come neere them: by eight a clock we were come to this Southern point, which I called Sea Horse point, where we came to anchor *Sea Horse* open in the Sea, the better to try the tide: here most *point.* apparently we found to all our companies sight, that in this place the tide of floud doth come from the Southeast, and the ebbe from the Northwest. We weighed, and stood over with a stiffe gale of winde, which continued all this day, and toward night very foule weather & a sore storme: by tenne a clocke we were come to Anchor on the North-west side of Nottinghams Ile, where are two or three smal Iles, lyeth off from the greater, which make very good Sounds & Harbors: about this Ile we had store of Ice, but nothing as we had heretofore in other places. We staied about this Iland til the seven and twentieth day, having much foule weather, many stormes, often fogs, and uncertaine windes, many times we weighed anchor to goe to that side of the Ile, where this Ship road when Captaine Button was in her: finding in other places of this Ile the tyde of floud to come from [III.iv.842.] the South-east ward, and the time of high water on the change day, to be at halfe an houre past ten, and not at halfe an houre past seven, as they supposed. In these ten dayes we staied about this Ile, we fitted our Ship with ballast, and other necessaries, as we had neede of.

Then proceeded as followeth the sixe and twentieth day, being indifferent faire weather, we passed betweene *Salisburie Ile.* Salisburies Ile and Nottinghams Ile at the South Point thereof, I meane of Nottinghams Ile, where are many small low Iles, without the which had beene a fit place for us to have anchored, to have found out the true set of the Tyde. But our Master being desirous to come to the same place where they had rode before, stood along by this Ile to the Westward, and came to an anchor in the eddy of these broken grounds, where the ship rode at no certaintie of Tyde.

The seven and twentieth, the next morning the weather proved very foule with much raine and winde, so that our Reger anchor would not hold the ship at eightie fathoms scope, but was driven into deepe water, that wee were forced to set saile, the winde being at East, and then come to the East North-east and about noone at North-east, still foule weather, being under saile, we stood away towards Sea horse Point: our Master (as I suppose) was perswaded that there might bee some passage betweene *Swan Iland.* that Point of Land and that Land which they called Swan Iland: so this afternoone we saw both Sea horse Point and Nottinghams Iland, the distance betweene them is not past fifteene or sixteen leagues, bearing the one from the other North-west and South-east.

The eight and twentieth day in the morning, wee were neere to Sea horse Point, the Land trending away West South-west so farre as wee saw, and very much pestred with Ice. At seven a clocke our Master caused us to tacke about, and stood away South-east and by South.

The nine and twentieth the next day at eleven a clocke, *Digges Ile.* we came to anchor at Digges Ile, having very foule weather. At this place where we rode it lyeth open to the West, having two of the greatest Iles, breake off the force of the Flood, till the Tyde be well bent; for after the water were risen an houre and a halfe by the

shoare, then would the ship ride truly on the Tyde of
Flood all the Tyde after. Now the time of high water
on the change day, is halfe an houre past ten or neere
thereabout.

The thirtieth day, being faire weather, wee weighed and
stood along close by Digges Ile, where we presently perceived the Salvages to bee close on the top of the Rocks : *Salvages.*
but when they saw we had espyed them, divers of them
came running downe to the water side, calling to us to
come to anchor, which we would have done if conveniently
we could. But in this place the water is so deepe, that
it is hard to finde a place to ride in, which we seeing lay
to and fro with our ship, while some of our men in the
Boat killed about some seventie fowles, for in this place
is the greatest number of fowles (whom we call Willocks) *Willocks.*
that in few places else the like are not seene, for if neede
were we might have killed many thousands, almost
incredible to those which have not seene it. Here also
as we lay to and fro with our ship, wee had sufficient
proofe of the set of the Tyde : but when our men were
come aboord againe, we set all our sailes for homewards,
making the best expedition we could ; but on the third
of August, wee were forced to come to anchor about
thirtie leagues within the Resolution Ile on the North
shoare. The next day wee weighed anchor : And the fifth
day in the forenoone, we past by the Resolution Iland,
but saw it not : Thus continuing our courses (as in the
briefe Journall may be seene) with much contrarie windes
and foule weather.

Wee had sight of Cape Cleere in Ireland the sixt of
September : the next morning by day light, we were faire
by Seely, and that night at two a clocke the next morne,
we came to anchor in Plymouth Sound with all our men
living, having onely three or foure sicke, which soone
recovered.

The next yeere being againe employed in discoverie,
amongst other instructions they received this. For your

course you must make all possible haste to the Cape Desolation, and from thence, you William Baffin as Pilot, keepe along the Coast of Groenland and up Fretum Davis, untill you come toward the height of eightie degrees, if the Land will give you leave. Then for feare of inbaying, by keeping too Northerly a course, shape your course West and Southerly, so farre as you shall thinke it convenient, till you come to the latitude of sixtie degrees: then direct your course to fall with the Land of Yedzo about that height, leaving your farther sayling Southward to your owne discretion, according as the time of the yeere and windes will give you leave, although our desires be, if your voyage prove so prosperous that you may have the yeere before you, that you goe so farre Southerly as that you may touch the North part of Japan, from whence or from Yedzo, if you can so compasse it without danger, we would have you to bring home one of the men of the Countrey, and so God blessing you with all expedition to make your returne home againe.

[III. iv. 843.]

Chap. XIX.

To the Right Worshipfull Master John Wosten-holme Esquire, one of the chiefe Adventurers for the discoverie of a passage to the North-west.

Orthy Sir; there neede no filling a Journall or short Discourse with preamble, complement, or circumstance, and therefore I will onely tell you, I am proud of any Remembrance, when I expose your Worth to my Conceit, and glad of any good fortune, when I can avoid the imputation of ingratitude, by acknowledging your many favours: and seeing it is not unknowne (to your Worship) in what estate the businesse concerning the North-west hath beene heretofore, and how the onely hope was in searching of

Fretum Davis, which if your selfe had not beene the more
forward, the action had well nigh beene left off : Now it
remayneth for your Worship to know, what hath beene
performed this yeere : wherefore I entreat you to admit
of my custome, and pardon me if I take the plaine highway
in relating the particulars, without using any refined
phrases and eloquent speeches.

Therefore briefly, and as it were in the forefront, I
intend to shew you the whole proceeding of the voyage
in a word : as namely, there is no passage, nor hope of
passage in the North of Davis Streigths, wee having
coasted all or neere all the Circumference thereof, and
finde it to be no other then a great Bay, as the Map here
placed doth truly shew : wherefore I cannot but much
admire the worke of the Almightie, when I consider how
vaine the best and chiefest hopes of man are in things
uncertaine.   And to speake of no other matter, then of
the hopefull passage to the North-west ; How many of
the best sort of men have set their whole indevours to
prove a passage that wayes, and not onely in Conference,
but also in Writing and publishing to the World, yea
what great summes of money hath beene spent about that
action, as your Worship hath costly experience off.
Neither would the vaine-glorious Spaniard have scattered
abroad so many false Maps and Journals, if they had not
beene confident of a passage this way, that if it had pleased
God, a passage had beene found, they might have eclipsed
the worthy praise of the Adventurers and true Discoverers ; and for my owne part, I would hardly have
beleeved the contrarie, untill mine eyes became witnesse
of that I desired not to have found, still taking occasion
of hope on every little likelihood, till such time as we had
almost coasted the Circumference of this great Bay.
Neither was Master Davis to be blamed in his report and
great hopes, if he had anchored about Hope Sanderson, to
have taken notice of the Tydes : for to that place which is
in 72. degrees 12. minutes the Sea is open, of an unsearch-
able depth, and of a good colour, onely the Tydes keepe no

*Howsoever the
passage this
way was
embayed ; yet
that former
discoverie of
Sir Tho.
Button (then
by him kept
secret for some
intent of his)
is both more
probable and
to the most
judicious more
then probable ;
and that by
that Tyde
argument from
the West, as in
Master Brigs
his Map
and notes
appeareth.*

certaine course, nor rise but a small height, as eight or nine
foote, and the flood commeth from the Southward, and in
all the Bay beyond that place the Tyde is so small, and not
much to be regarded, yet by reason of snow melting on the
Land, the Ebbe is stronger then the Flood, by meanes
whereof, and the windes holding Northerly the fore-part
of the yeere, the great Iles of Ice are set to the Southward,
some into Fretum Hudson, and others towards New found
land, for in all the Channell where the Sea is open are great
quantities of them driving up and downe, and till this
yeere not well knowne where they were bred.

Now that the worst is knowne (concerning the passage)
it is necessarie and requisite, your Worship should understand what probabilitie or hope of profit might here be
made hereafter, if the voyage bee attempted by fitting
men. And first for the killing of Whales, certaine it is
that in this Bay are great numbers of them, which the
Biscainers call the Grand Baye Whales, of the same kinde
which are killed at Greenland, and as it seemeth to me
easie to be strooke, because they are not used to bee chased
or beaten, for we being but one day in Whale Sound (so
called for the number of Whales that wee saw there)
sleeping and lying aloft on the water, not fearing our ship
or ought else; that if wee had beene fitted with men and
things necessarie, it had beene no hard matter to have
strooke more then would have made three ships a saving
voyage, and that it is of that sort of Whale there is no
feare. I being twise at Greenland, tooke sufficient notice
to know them againe; beside a dead Whale wee found at
Sea, having all her finnes (or rather all the rough of her
mouth) of which with much labour, we got one hundred
and sixtie the same evening we found her; and if that
foule weather, and a storme the next day had not followed,
wee had no doubt, but to have had all or the most part of
them, but the winde and Sea arising shee broke from us,
and we were forced to leave her. Neither are they onely
to be looked for in Whale Sound, but also in Sir Tho.
Smiths Sound, Wostenholme Sound, and divers other places.

*Store of Grand
Bay Whales.*

*Baffin twice at
Greenland.*

Morses.

For the killing of Sea Morse, I can give no certaintie, but onely this, that our Boat being but once ashoare in all the North part of this Bay, which was in the entrance of Alderman Jones Sound, at the returne, our men told us, they saw many Morses along by the shoare on the Ice; but our ship being under saile, and the winde comming faire, they presently came aboord without further search, besides the people inhabiting about 74. degrees, told us by divers signes, that toward the North were many of those beasts, having two long teeth, and shewed us divers pieces of the same.

*Sea Unicorne.
The horne is
still kept in
the Robes at
Windsore
(where I have
seene it) neere
seven foot long
and cressed,
&c.*

As for the Sea Unicorne, it being a great fish, having a long horne or bone, growing forth of his forehead or nostril (such as Sir Martin Frobisher in his second voyage found one) in divers places we saw of them, which if the horne be of any good value, no doubt but many of them may be killed.

[III.iv.844.]

And concerning what the Shoare will yeeld, as Beach finnes, Morse teeth, and such like, I can little say, because we came not on shoare in any of the places where hope was of finding them.

But here some may object and aske, why we sought that Coast no better: to this I answere, that while we were thereabout, the weather was so exceeding foule wee could not, for first wee anchored in Wostenholme Sound, where presently our ship drove with two anchors a head, then were we forced to stand forth with a low saile. The next day in Whale Sound, we lost an Anchor and Cable, and could fetch the place no more; then we came to anchor neere a small Iland, lying between Sir Tho. Smiths Sound, and Whale Sound, but the winde came more outward, that we were forced to weigh againe; neverthelesse if wee had beene in a good harbour, having but our Ships Boat, we durst not send her farre from the ship, having so few men (as seventeene in all) and some of them very weake; but the chiefe cause wee spent so little time to seek a Harbour, was our great desire to performe the Discoverie, having the Sea open in all that part, and still likelihood of a

passage; but when we had coasted the Land so farre to
the Southward, that hope of passage was none, then the
yeere was too farre spent, and many of our men very
weake, and withall we having some beliefe that ships the
next yeere would be sent for the killing of Whales, which
might better doe it then wee.

And seeing I have briefly set downe, what hope there is
of making a profitable voyage, it is not unfit your Worship
should know what let or hinderance might be to the same.
The chiefest and greatest cause is, that some yeere it may
happen by reason of the Ice, lying betweene 72. degrees
and a halfe, and 76. degrees no minutes, that the ships
cannot come into those places, till toward the middest of
July, so that want of time to stay in the Countrey may
bee some let: yet they may well tarry till the last of
August, in which space much businesse may be done, and
good store of Oile made: neverthelesse if store of Whales
come in (as no feare to the contrarie) what cannot bee made
in Oile may bee brought home in Blubber, and the Finnes
will arise to good profit. Another hinderance may bee,
because the bottome of the Sounds will not be so soone
cleere as would be wished, by meanes thereof now and
then a Whale may be lost (the same case sometime
chanceth in Greenland) yet I am perswaded those Sounds
before named, will all be cleere before the twentieth of
July: for we this yeere were in Whale Sound the fourth
day among many Whales, and might have strooke them
without let of Ice. Furthermore, there is little wood to
bee expected, either for fire or other necessaries, therefore
Coles and other such things must bee provided at home,
they will bee so much the readier there.

Thus much I thought good to certifie your Worship,
wherein I trust you will conceive, that much time hath not
beene spent in vaine, or the businesse over carelesly
neglected, and although wee have not performed what we
desired (that is, to have found the passage) yet what wee
promised (as to bring certaintie and a true description)
truth will make manifest, that I have not much erred.

And I dare boldly say (without boasting) that more good discoverie hath not in shorter time (to my remembrance) beene done, since the action was attempted, considering how much Ice we have passed, and the difficultie of sayling so neere the Pole (upon a traverse) and above all, the variation of the Compasse, whose wonderfull operation is *Variation of* such in this Bay, increasing and decreasing so suddenly *the Compasse* and swift, being in some part (as in Wostenholme Sound, *admirable.* and in Sir Tho. Smiths Sound) varied above five Points or 56. degrees, a thing almost incredible and matchlesse in all the world beside, so that without great care, and good observations, a true description could not have beene had. In fine, whatsoever my labours are or shall be, I esteeme them too little, to expresse my thankefull minde for your many favours, wherein I shall be ever studious, to supply my other wants by my best endevours, and ever rest at
Your Worships command,
WILLIAM BAFFIN.

A briefe and true Relation or Journall, contayning such accidents as happened in the fift voyage, for the discoverie of a passage to the North-west, set forth at the charges of the right Worshipfull Sir Tho. Smith Knight, Sir Dudly Digges Knight, Master John Wostenholme Esquire, Master Alderman Jones, with others, in the good ship called the Discoverie of London ; Robert Bileth Master, and my selfe Pilot, performed in the yeere of our Lord 1616.

IN the Name of God, Amen. The forenamed ship *March 26.* being in full readinesse upon the twentie sixe of March, we set saile at Gravesend, being in number seventeene persons, having very faire weather, which continued till the second of April: by that time we were off Portland, then the winde comming Westward with foule weather, we kept Sea till the fourth day, then being not able to fetch Plimouth, bore roome for Dartmouth, where wee stayed eleven dayes, in which time was much foule weather and westerly windes.

[III. iv. 845.] The fifteenth day of Aprill, being cleere of Dartmouth, we were forced the next day to put into Plimouth. The nineteenth day we set saile from thence, and the twentieth in the morning we past betweene the Lands end and Silly with a faire winde. Continuing our course, as in the briefe Table or Journall is set downe, with every particular from noone to noone, that here I need not make a tedious repetition, nothing worthy of note hapning, but that we had a good passage, and the first Land we saw was in *Groinland.* Fretum Davis, on the coast of Groinland in the latitude of 65. degrees 20. minutes. On the fourteenth of May in the forenoone, then sixe of the people being a fishing came to us, to whom we gave small pieces of Iron, they keeping us companie being very joyfull, supposing wee had intended to come to anchor: but when they saw us stand off from shoare they followed us a while, and then went away discontented, to our seeming.

We prosecuting our Voyage, were loth to come to anchor as yet, although the winde was contrarie, but still plyed to the Northward, untill we came into 70. degrees 20. minutes: then wee came to anchor in a faire Sound (neere the place Master Davis called London Coast.) The twentieth of May at evening, the people espying us fled away in their Boates, getting on Rocks wondring and gasing at us, but after this night we saw them no more, *Men and dogs.* leaving many Dogs running to and fro on the Iland.

At this place we stayed two dayes, in which time wee tooke in fresh water and other necessaries: here we had some dislike of the passage, because the Tydes are so small as not arising above eight or nine foot, and keepe no certaine course, but the neerest time of high water on the change day is at a quarter of an houre past nine, and the Flood commeth from the South.

The two and twentieth day at a North Sunne, wee set

saile and plyed still Northward, the winde being right against us as we stood off and on. Upon the sixe and twentieth day in the afternoone, we found a dead Whale, about sixe and twentie leagues from shoare, having all her finnes. Then making our ship fast, wee used the best meanes wee could to get them, and with much toile got a hundred and sixtie that evening. The next morning the Sea went very high and the winde arising, the Whale broke from us, and we were forced to leave her and set saile, and having not stood past three or foure leagues North-westward, came to the Ice, then wee tacked and stood to the shoare-ward, a sore storme ensued.

Dead Whale.

By the thirtieth day in the afternoone, wee came faire by Hope Sanderson, the farthest Land Master Davis was at, lying betweene 72. and 73. degrees; and that evening by a North Sunne we came to much Ice, which we put into, plying all the next day to get through it.

Hope Sanderson.

The first of June, we were cleere of the Ice before named, and not farre from shoare, the winde blowing very hard at North North-east, then we put in among divers Ilands, the people seeing us fled away in all haste leaving their Tents behinde, and upon a small Rocke they hid two young Maides or Women. Our ship riding not farre off, we espyed them, to whom our Master with some other of our companie went in the Boate, they making signes to be carried to the Iland where their Tents were close adjoyning. When they came thither, they found two old women more, the one very old, to our esteemation little lesse then fourescore, the other not so old. The next time we went on shoare, there was another Woman with a child at her back, who had hid her selfe among the Rocks, till the other had told her how well wee had used them, in giving them pieces of Iron and such like, which they highly esteeme, in change thereof they give us Seales skinnes, other riches they had none, save dead Seales, and fat of Seales, some of which fat or blubber afterward we carried aboord, the poore women were very diligent to carry it to the water side to put into our caske, making

Tents, Men and Women.

shew that the men were over at the Mayne, and at an other small Iland something more Eastward. Then making signes to them that wee would shew them our ship and set them where the men were: the foure youngest came into our Boate; when they were aboord they much wondred to see our ship and furniture: we gave them of our meat, which they tasting would not eate. Then two of them wee set on the Iland, where they supposed the men to be; the other two were carried to their Tents againe. Those that went to seeke the men could not finde them, but came as neere the ship as they could, and at evening wee set them over to the other.

*Womens
Ilands.*

This place wee called Womens Ilands; it lyeth in the latitude of 72. degrees 45. minutes: here the Flood commeth from the Southward, at nep Tydes the water ariseth but sixe or seven foote, and a South South-east Moone maketh a full Sea. The Inhabitants very poore, living chiefly on the flesh of Seales, dryed, which they eate raw, with the skinnes they cloathe themselves, and also make coverings for their Tents and Boats which they dresse very well. The Women in their apparell are different from the men, and are marked in the face with divers blacke strokes or lines, the skin being rased with some sharpe instrument when they are young, and blacke colour put therein, that by no meanes it will be gotten forth.

*The people
described.*

Women.

Religion.

Concerning their Religion, I can little say: onely they have a kinde of worship or adoration to the Sunne, which continually they will point unto and strike their hand on their breast, crying Ilyont; their dead they burie on the side of the Hils, where they live (which is commonly on small Ilands) making a pile of stones over them, yet not so close but that wee might see the dead body, the aire being so piersing that it keepeth them from much stinking savour. So likewise I have seene their Dogs buried in the same manner.

*Buriall of
Men and
Dogs.*

[III. iv. 846.] Upon the fourth day we set sayle from thence, having very faire weather, although the winde were contrary, and

plyed to and fro betweene the Ice and the Land, being as
it were a channell of seven or eight leagues broad : then on
the ninth day, being in the latitude of 74. degree 4.
minutes, and much pestered with Ice, neere unto three
small Ilands, lying eight miles from the shore, we came to
anchor neere one of them.

These Ilands are used to be frequented with people in
the latter part of the yeare, as it seemed by the houses and
places where the tents had stood : but this yeare as yet
they were not come : here the tides are very small,
especially the floud, which ariseth not above five or six
foot, yet the ebbe runneth with an indifferent streame,
the cause thereof (in mine opinion) is the great abundance
of Snow, melting on the Land all this part of the yeare.

The tenth day wee set sayle from thence, and stood
through much Ice to the Westward, to try if that further
from the shoare, wee might proceede; but this attempt
was soone quailed, for the more Ice we went through, the
thicker it was, till wee could see no place to put in the
Ships head.

Seeing, that as yet we could not proceede, we determined to stand in for the shoare, there to abide some few
dayes, till such time as the Ice were more wasted and gone
(for we plainely saw that it consumed very fast) with this
resolution we stood in, and came to anchor among many
Ilands, in the latitude of 73. degrees 45. minutes. On
the twelfth day at night here wee continued two dayes
without shew or signe of any people, till on the fifteenth
day in the morning, about one a clocke, then came two and
fortie of the Inhabitants in their Boates or Canoas, and
gave us Seale skinnes, and many peeces of the bone or
horne of the Sea Unicorne, and shewed us divers peeces
of Sea Mors teeth ; making signes that to the Northward
were many of them : in exchange thereof, we gave them
small peeces of Iron, Glasse Beads, and such like : at foure
severall times the people came to us, and at each time
brought us of the aforesaid commodities, by reason thereof
we called this place Horne Sound.

*42. Inhabi-
tants.*

*Unicornes
hornes.*

Horne Sound.

Here we stayed six dayes, and on the eighteenth day at night, we set sayle, having very little winde; and being at Sea, made the best way we could to the Northward, although the winde had beene contrary for the most part this moneth, but it was strange to see the Ice so much consumed in so little space, for now we might come to the three Ilands before named, and stand off to the Westward almost twenty leagues, without let of Ice, untill we were more North (as to 74. degrees 30. minutes) then we put among much scattered Ice, and plyed to and fro all this month, still in the sight of shoare, and many times fast in the Ice, yet every day we got something on our way, nothing worthy of note happening, but that at divers times we saw of the fishes with long hornes, many and *They see many* often, which we call the Sea Unicorne: and here to write *Sea Unicornes.* particularly of the weather, it would be superfluous or needlesse, because it was so variable, few dayes without *Sharp frost on* Snow, and often freezing, in so much, that on Midsummer *Midsummer* day, our shrowds roapes and sailes were so frozen, that we *day.* could scarce handle them; yet the cold is not so extreame, but it may well be endured.

The first of July we were come into an open Sea, in the latitude of 75. degrees 40. minutes, which a new revived our hope of a passage, and because the winde was contrary, wee stood off twenty leagues from the shoare, before we met the Ice: then standing in againe; when we were neere the Land, we let fall an anchor to see what tyde went, but in that we found small comfort. Shortly after the winde came to the South-east, and blew very hard, with foule weather, thicke, and foggie: then we set sayle, and ran along by the Land: this was on the second day at night. The next morning we past by a faire Cape, or head land, *Sir Dudly* which wee called Sir Dudley Digges Cape, it is in the *Digs his Cape.* latitude of 76. degrees 35. minutes, and hath a small Iland close adjoyning to it, the winde still increasing, we past by a faire Sound twelve leagues distant from the former Cape, having an Iland in the midst, which maketh two entrances. Under this Iland we came to anchor; and

had not rid past two houres, but our Ship drove, although
we had two anchors at the ground, then were we forced
to set sayle, and stand forth : this Sound wee called Wosten-   *Wostenholme*
holme Sound; it hath many Inlets or smaller Sounds in it,   *Sound.*
and is a fit place for the killing of Whales.

The fourth day at one a clocke in the morning, the
storme began againe at West and by South, so vehement,
that it blew away our forecourse, and being not able to
beare any sayle, wee lay a drift till about eight a clocke,
then it cleared up a little, and we saw our selves imbayed
in a great Sound : then we set sayle and stood over to the
South-east side, where in a little Cove or Bay we let fall
an anchor, which we lost with cable and all, the winde
blowing so extreamely from the tops of the hils, that we
could get no place to anchor in, but were forced to stand to
and fro in the Sound, the bottome being all frozen over ;
toward two a clocke it began to be lesse winde, then we
stood forth.

In this Sound we saw great numbers of Whales, there-
fore we called it Whale Sound, and doubtlesse if we had   *Whale Sound.*
beene provided for killing of them, we might have strooke
very many. It lyeth in the latitude of 77. degrees 30.
minutes. All the fift day it was very faire weather, and
wee kept along by the Land till eight a clock in the
evening, by which time we were come to a great banke
of Ice, it being backed with Land, which we seeing, determined to stand backe some eight leagues, to an Iland we   [III.iv.847.]
called Hackluits Ile, it lyeth betweene two great Sounds,
the one Whale Sound, and the other Sir Thomas Smiths   *Sir Thomas*
Sound : this last runneth to the North of seventy eight   *Smiths Sound*
degrees, and is admirable in one respect, because in it is   *in 78. deg.*
the greatest variation of the Compasse of any part of the   *Variation of*
World known : for by divers good Observations I found it   *the compasse*
to be above five points or fifty six degrees varied to the   *56. degrees to*
                                                            the West.
Which may make questionable D. Gilberts rule. Tom. 1. l. 2. c. 1. that where more earth is,
more attraction of the compasse happeneth by variation toward it. Now the known continents
of Asia, &c. must be unspeakably more then here there can be, and yet here is more variation
then about Japan, or Brazil, Peru, &c.

Westward, so that a North-east and by East, is true North,
and so of the rest. Also this Sound seemeth to bee good
for the killing of Whales, it being the greatest and largest
in all this Bay. The cause wherefore we minded to stand
to this Iland, was to see if we could find any finnes or
such like on the shore, and so indeed this night wee came
to anchor, but with such foule weather, that our Boat
could not land. The next day wee were forced to set
sayle, the Sea was growne so high, and the wind came more
outward. Two dayes wee spent and could get no good
place to anchor in: then on the eight day it cleered up,
and wee seeing a company of Ilands lye off from the shoare
twelve or thirteene Leagues, wee minded to goe to them,
to see if there we could Anchor. When wee were something neere, the winde tooke us short; and being loth to
spend more time, we tooke opportunitie of the wind, and

Caries Ilands. left the searching of these Ilands, which wee called Careyes
*This Map of Ilands, all which Sounds and Ilands the Map * doth truly
the authour for describe.
this and the
former Voyage So we stood to the Westward in an open Sea, with a
with the stiffe gale of wind, all the next day and till the tenth day
Tables of his at one or two a clocke in the morning, at which time it fell
journall and calme and very foggie, and wee neere the Land in the
sayling, were entrance of a faire Sound, which wee called Alderman
somewhat Jones Sound. This afternoone being faire and cleere, we
troublesome sent our Boat to the Shoare, the ship being under sayle,
and too costly and assoone as they were on shoare, the wind began to
to insert. blow; then they returned againe, declaring that they saw
Alderman many Sea Morses by the shoare among the Ice, and as
Jones Sound. farre as they were, they saw no signe of people, nor any
good place to anchor in along the shoare. Then having
an easie gale of wind at East North-east, we ranne along
by the shoare, which now trendeth much South, and
beginneth to shew like a Bay.

On the twelfth day we were open of another great
Sound, lying in the Latitude of 74. degrees 20. minutes,
and we called it Sir James Lankasters Sound: here our
hope of passage began to be lesse every day then other,

for from this Sound to the Southward, wee had a ledge of
Ice betweene the Shoare and us, but cleare to the Sea
ward, we kept close by this ledge of Ice till the foureteenth
day in the afternoone, by which time wee were in the
latitude of 71. degrees 16. minutes, and plainely perceived
the Land to the Southward of 70. degrees 30. minutes, *They see Land*
then wee having so much Ice round about us, were forced *and find them-*
to stand more Eastward, supposing to have beene soone *selves embaied.*
cleare, and to have kept on the off side of the Ice, untill
we had come into 70. degrees, then to have stood in againe.
But this proved quite contrary to our expectation : for wee
were forced to runne above threescore leagues through
very much Ice, and many times so fast, that wee could goe
no wayes, although we kept our course due East; and
when wee had gotten into the open Sea, wee kept so neere
the Ice, that many times we had much adoe to get cleare,
yet could not come neere the Land, till we came about 68.
degrees, where indeede we saw the shoare, but could not
come to it by eight or nine leagues, for the great abundance
of Ice.   This was on the foure and twentieth day of July :
then spent we three dayes more to see if conveniently
wee could come to anchor, to make trial of the tides,
but the Ice led us into the latitude of 65. degrees 40.
minutes.   Then wee left off seeking to the West shoare,
because wee were in the indraft of Cumberlands Iles, and *Cumberlands*
should know no certaintie, and hope of passage could *Iles.*
be none.
   Now seeing that we had made an end of our discovery,
and the yeare being too farre spent to goe for the bottome
of the Bay, to search for drest Finnes; therefore wee
determined to goe for the Coast of Groineland, to see if
we could get some refreshing for our men : Master Hubert
and two more, having kept their Cabins above eight dayes
(besides our Cooke, Richard Waynam, which died the day
before, being the twenty six of July) and divers more of
our company so weake, that they could doe but little
labour.   So the winde favouring us, we came to anchor in
the latitude of 65. degrees 45. minutes, at six a clocke in

Cockin Sound.

the evening, the eight and twentieth day, in a place called Caukin Sound.

Scurvy Grasse.

The next day going on shoare, on a little Iland we found great abundance of the herbe called Scurvie Grasse, which we boyled in Beere, and so dranke thereof, using it also in Sallets, with Sorrell and Orpen, which here groweth in abundance; by meanes hereof, and the blessing of God all our men within eight or nine dayes space were in perfect health, and so continued till our arrivall in England.

Six men.

Wee rode in this place three dayes before any of the people came to us; then on the first of August, six of the Inhabitants in their Canoas, brought us Salmon Peale, and such like, which was a great refreshment to our men: the next day following, the same six came againe, but after that we saw them no more untill the sixt day, when we had wayed anchor, and were almost cleere of the harbour; then the same six and one more, brought us of the like commodities, for which we gave them Glasse Beads, Counters and small peeces of Iron, which they doe as much esteeme, as we Christians doe Gold and Silver.

[III. iv. 848.]
Plenty of Salmon.

In this Sound we saw such great Scales of Salmon swimming to and fro, that it is much to be admired: here it floweth about eighteene foote water, and is at the highest on the change day at seven a clocke: it is a very good harbour, and easie to be knowne, having three high round hils like Piramides close adjoyning to the mouth of it, and that in the middest is lowest, and along all this coast are many good harbours to be found, by reason that so many Ilands lye off from the maine.

The sixt of August, by three a clocke in the afternoone, wee were cleere of this place, having a North Northwest winde, and faire weather, and the Lord sent us a speedy and good passage homeward as could be wished: for in nineteene dayes after, wee saw Land on the coast of Ireland, it being on the five and twentieth day: the seven and twentieth at noone we were two leagues from Silly, and the thirtieth day, in the morning wee anchored at Dover in the roade, for the which and all other his blessings the Lord make us thankfull.

Chap. XX.

A briefe Discourse of the probabilitie of a passage to the Westerne or South Sea, illustrated with testimonies : and a briefe Treatise and Mappe by Master Brigges.

Thought good to adde somewhat to this Relation of Master Baffin, that learned-unlearned Mariner and Mathematician; who wanting art of words, so really employed himselfe to those industries, whereof here you see so evident fruits. His Mappes and Tables would have much illustrated his Voyages, if trouble, and cost, and his owne despaire of passage that way, had not made us willing to content our selves with that Mappe following of that thrice learned (and in this argument three times thrice industrious) Mathematician, Master Brigges, famous for his readings in both Universities, and this honourable Citie, that I make no further Voyage of Discovery to finde and follow the remote Passage and extent of his name. Master Baffin told mee, that they supposed the tyde from the North-west, about Digges Iland was misreported, by mistaking the houre, eight for eleven : and that hee would, if hee might get employment, search the passage from Japan, by the coast of Asia, or (qua data porta) any way hee could. But in the Indies he dyed, in the late Ormus businesse, slaine in fight with a shot, as hee was trying his *Baffins death.* Mathematical projects and conclusions.

Now for that discovery of Sir Thomas Button, I have solicited him for his Noates, and received of him gentle entertainment and kinde promises : but being then forced to stay in the Citie upon necessary and urgent affaires, he would at his returne home, seeke and impart them. Since

I heare that weightie occasions have detained him out of England, and I cannot communicate that which I could not receive: which if I doe receive, I purpose rather to give thee out of due place, then not at all. Once he was very confident in conference with me of a passage that way, and said that he had therein satisfied his Majestie, who from his discourse in private, inferred the necessitie thereof. And the maine argument was the course of the tyde: for wintering in Port Nelson (see the following Mappe) hee found the tyde rising every twelve houres fifteene foote (whereas in the bottome of Hudsons Bay it was but two foote, and in the bottome of Fretum Davis discovered by Baffin, but one) yea and a West winde equalled the nep tydes to the spring tydes; plainely arguing the neighbourhood of the Sea, which is on the West side of America. The Summer following he found about the latitude of 60. degrees a strong race of a tide, running sometimes Eastward, sometimes Westward; whereupon Josias Hubbard in his plat, called that place Hubbarts Hope, as in the Map appeareth. Now if any make scruple, because this discovery was not pursued by Sir Thomas Button, let him consider, that being Prince Henries Servant, and partly by him employed (whence I thinke he named the Country New Wales) the untimely death of that Prince put all out of joint; nor was hee so open, that others should have the glory of his discoverie.

And if any man thinke that the passage is so farre, as the Maps use to expresse America, running out into the West: it is easily answered, that either of negligence, or over-busie diligence, Maps by Portugals in the East, and Spaniards in the West, have beene falsely projected. Hence that fabulous strait of Anian, as before by Francis Gaules testimonie and navigation is evident: And hence the Portugals to bring in the Moluccas, to that moity of the world agreed upon betwixt the Spaniards and them, are thought to have much curtalled Asia, and the longitude of those Ilands, giving fewer degrees to them then in just longitude is requisite. So the older Maps of America

412

make the Land from the Magelane Straits to the South
Sea, runne much West, when as they rather are contracted
somewhat Easterly from the North. The like is justly
supposed of their false placing, Quivira, and I know not
(nor they neither) what Countries they make in America,
to run so farre North-westward, which Sir Francis Drakes
Voyage in that Sea (his Nova * Albion, being little further
Westward then Aquatulco) plainely evince to be otherwise.
Yea the late Map of California found to be an Iland, the
Savages discourses in all the Countries Northwards and
Westwards from Virginia: fame whereof filled my friend
Master Dermer with so much confidence, that hearing of
strange Ships which came thither for a kinde of Ure or
earth, the men using forkes in their diet, with Caldrons
to dresse their meate, &c. things nothing sutable to any
parts of America, hee supposed them to come from the
East, neere to China or Japan, and therefore he made a
Voyage purposely to discover: but crossed with divers
disasters, hee returned to Virginia, frustrate of accomplishment that yeare, but fuller of confidence, as in a Letter
from Virginia he signified to me, where death ended that
his designe soone after. But how often are the usuall
Charts rejected by experience in these Navigations, in this
worke recorded? Painters and Poets are not alwayes the
best Oracles.

    For further proofes of a passage about those parts into
the West Sea (or South, as it is called from the first
discovery thereof to the South, from the parts of New
Spaine, whence it was first descried by the Spaniards) there
is mention of a Portugall (and taken in a Carricke in
Queene Elizabeths dayes, of glorious memory) confirming
this opinion; Sir Martin Frobisher also from a Portugall
in Guinie, received intelligence of such a passage, he
saying he had past it. The Pilots of Lisbone are said
generally to acknowledge such a thing; and the Admirall
of D. Garcia Geoffroy Loaisa of Cite-Real, in the time of
Charles the fifth, is reported by the Coast of Baccalaos and
Labrador, to have gone to the Moluccas. Vasco de

*This easily
appeareth in
observing his
Voiage, &
comparing that
before of
Fr. Gaul
therewith.

Coronado writ to the Emperour, that at Cibola he was one
hundred and fiftie leagues from the South Sea, and a little
more from the North. Antonio de Herera, the Kings
Coronista Major (part of whose worke followeth) maketh
with us also, in the distances of places by him described.
But to produce some authority more full, I have here
presented Thomas Cowles a Marriner, and Master Michael
Locke Merchant, and after them, a little Treatise ascribed
to Master Brigges, together with his Map. And if any
thinke that the Spaniard or Portugall would soone have
discovered such a passage: these will answere, that it was
not for their profit to expose their East or West Indies to
English, Dutch, or others, whom they would not have
sharers in those remote treasures by so neere a passage.
First, Thomas Cowles averreth thus much.

*Some of our
Merchants are
said not to be
so willing for
like causes
with this
discoverie.*

I Thomas Cowles of Bedmester, in the Countie of
Somerset, Marriner, doe acknowledge, that six yeares
past, at my being at Lisbon, in the Kingdome of Portugall, I did heare one Martin Chacke, a Portugall of
Lisbon, reade a Booke of his owne making, which he had
set out six yeares before that time, in Print, in the Portu-
gale tongue, declaring that the said Martin Chacke had
found, twelve yeares now past, a way from the Portugall
Indies, through a gulfe of the New found land, which he
thought to be in 59. degrees of the elevation of the North
Pole. By meanes that hee being in the said Indies, with
foure other Shippes of great burden, and he himselfe in a
small Shippe of fourescore tunnes, was driven from the
company of the other foure Shippes, with a Westerly
winde: after which, hee past alongst by a great number
of Ilands which were in the gulfe of the said New found
Land. And after hee overshot the gulfe, he set no more
sight of any other Land, untill he fell with the Northwest
part of Ireland; and from thence he tooke his course
homewards, and by that meanes hee came to Lisbone foure
or five weekes before the other foure Ships of his company
that he was separated from, as before said. And since the

same time, I could never see any of those Books, because
the King commanded them to be called in, and no more
of them to be printed, lest in time it would be to their
hindrance. In witnesse whereof I set to my hand and
marke, the ninth of Aprill. Anno 1579.

A Note made by me Michael Lok the elder, touching the Strait of Sea, commonly called Fretum Anian, in the South Sea, through the North-west passage of Meta incognita.

WHen I was at Venice, in Aprill 1596. happily arrived
there an old man, about threescore yeares of age,
called commonly Juan de Fuca, but named properly
Apostolos Valerianos, of Nation a Greeke, borne in the
Iland Cefalonia, of profession a Mariner, and an ancient
Pilot of Shippes. This man being come lately out of
Spaine, arrived first at Ligorno, and went thence to
Florence in Italie, where he found one John Dowglas, an
Englishman, a famous Mariner, ready comming for
Venice, to be Pilot of a Venetian Ship, named Ragasona
for England, in whose company they came both together
to Venice. And John Dowglas being well acquainted with
me before, he gave me knowledge of this Greeke Pilot,
and brought him to my speech: and in long talke and   [III. iv. 850.]
conference betweene us, in presence of John Dowglas: this
Greeke Pilot declared in the Italian and Spanish languages,
thus much in effect as followeth.

First he said, that he had bin in the West Indies of
Spaine by the space of fortie yeeres, and had sailed to and
from many places thereof, as Mariner and Pilot, in the
service of the Spaniards.

Also he said, that he was in the Spanish Shippe, which in
returning from the Ilands, Philippinas and China, towards
Nova Spania, was robbed and taken at the Cape California,
by Captaine Candish Englishman, whereby he lost sixtie   *Captaine*
thousand Duckets, of his owne goods.   *Candish.*

Also he said, that he was Pilot of three small Ships

which the Vizeroy of Mexico sent from Mexico, armed
with one hundred men, Souldiers, under a Captain,
Spaniards, to discover the Straits of Anian, along the coast
of the South-Sea, and to fortifie in that Strait, to resist the
passage and proceedings of the English Nation, which
were feared to passe through those Straits into the South
Sea. And that by reason of a mutinie which happened
among the Souldiers, for the Sodomie of their Captaine,
that Voyage was overthrowne, and the Ships returned
backe from California coast to Nova Spania, without any
effect of thing done in that Voyage. And that after their
returné, the Captaine was at Mexico punished by justice.

Also he said, that shortly after the said Voyage was so
ill ended, the said Viceroy of Mexico, sent him out againe
Anno 1592. with a small Caravela, and a Pinnace, armed
with Mariners onely, to follow the said Voyage, for discovery of the same Straits of Anian, and the passage
thereof, into the Sea which they call the North Sea, which
is our North-west Sea. And that he followed his course
in that Voyage West and North-west in the South Sea,
all alongst the coast of Nova Spania, and California, and
the Indies, now called North America (all which Voyage
hee signified to me in a great Map, and a Sea-card of mine
owne, which I laied before him) untill hee came to the
Latitude of fortie seven degrees, and that there finding
Land trending that the Land trended North and North-east, with a broad
in 47. Inlet of Sea, betweene 47. and 48. degrees of Latitude :
degrees. hee entred thereinto, sayling therein more then twentie
dayes, and found that Land trending still sometime North-
west and North-east, and North, and also East and
South-eastward, and very much broader Sea then was at
the said entrance, and that hee passed by divers Ilands in
that sayling. And that at the entrance of this said Strait,
there is on the North-west coast thereof, a great Hedland
or Iland, with an exceeding high Pinacle, or spired Rocke,
like a piller thereupon.

Also he said, that he went on Land in divers places, and
that he saw some people on Land, clad in Beasts skins :

and that the Land is very fruitfull, and rich of gold, Silver, Pearle, and other things, like Nova Spania.

And also he said, that he being entred thus farre into the said Strait, and being come into the North Sea already, and finding the Sea wide enough every where, and to be about thirtie or fortie leagues wide in the mouth of the Straits, where hee entred; hee thought he had now well discharged his office, and done the thing which he was sent to doe : and that hee not being armed to resist the force of the Salvage people that might happen, hee therefore set sayle and returned homewards againe towards Nova Spania, where hee arrived at Acapulco, Anno 1592. hoping to be rewarded greatly of the Viceroy, for this service done in this said Voyage. *The mouth of the Straight where he entred* 30. *or* 40. *leagues broad.*

Also he said, that after his comming to Mexico, hee was greatly welcommed by the Viceroy, and had great promises of great reward, but that having sued there two yeares time, and obtained nothing to his content, the Viceroy told him, that he should be rewarded in Spaine of the King himselfe very greatly, and willed him therefore to goe into Spaine, which Voyage hee did performe.

Also he said, that when he was come into Spaine, he was greatly welcommed there at the Kings Court, in wordes after the Spanish manner, but after long time of suite there also, hee could not get any reward there neither to his content. And that therefore at the length he stole away out of Spaine, and came into Italie, to goe home againe and live among his owne Kindred and Countrimen, he being very old.

Also he said, that hee thought the cause of his ill reward had of the Spaniards, to bee for that they did understand very well, that the English Nation had now given over all their voyages for discoverie of the North-west passage, wherefore they need not feare them any more to come that way into the South Sea, and therefore they needed not his service therein any more.

Also he said, that in regard of this ill reward had of the Spaniards, and understanding of the noble minde of the

Queene of England, and of her warres maintayned so valiantly against the Spaniards, and hoping that her Majestie would doe him justice for his goods lost by Captaine Candish, he would bee content to goe into England, and serve her Majestie in that voyage for the discoverie perfectly of the North-west passage into the South Sea, and would put his life into her Majesties hands to performe the same, if shee would furnish him with onely one ship of fortie tunnes burden and a Pinnasse, *The straight to be discovered in 30. dayes.* and that he would performe it in thirtie dayes time, from one end to the other of the Streights. And he willed me so to write into England.

[III.iv.851.] And upon this conference had twise with the said Greeke Pilot, I did write thereof accordingly into England unto the right honourable the old Lord Treasurer Cecill, and to Sir Walter Raleigh, and to Master Richard Hakluyt that famous Cosmographer, certifying them hereof by my Letters. And in the behalfe of the said Greeke Pilot, I prayed them to disburse one hundred pounds of money, to bring him into England with my selfe, for that my owne purse would not stretch so wide at that time. And I had answere hereof by Letters of friends, that this action was very well liked, and greatly desired in England to bee effected; but the money was not readie, and therefore this action dyed at that time, though the said Greeke Pilot perchance liveth still this day at home in his owne Countrie in Cefalonia, towards the which place he went from me within a fortnight after this conference had at Venice.

And in the meane time, while I followed my owne businesse in Venice, being in Law suit against the Companie of Merchants of Turkie, and Sir John Spencer their Governour in London, to recover my pension due for my office of being their Consull at Aleppo in Turkie, which they held from me wrongfully. And when I was (as I thought) in a readinesse to returne home into England, for that it pleased the Lords of her Majesties honourable Privie Counsell in England, to looke into this Cause of my Law suit for my reliefe; I thought that I should be able of my owne purse to take with me into England the said Greeke Pilot. And therefore I wrote unto him from Venice a Letter, dated in July 1596. which is copied hereunder.

Al Mag^{co.} Sig^{or.} Capitan Juan De Fuca Piloto de Indias, amigo mio char^{mo..} en Zefalonia.

MUy honrado Sennor, siendo yo para buelverme en Inglatierra dentre de pocas mezes, y accuerdandome de lo trattado entre my y V. M. en Venesia, sobre el viagio de las Indias, me ha parescido bien de scrivir esta carta à V. M. paraque si tengais animo de andar con migo, puedais escribirme presto, en que maniera quereis consertaros. Y puedais embiarmi vuestra carta, con esta nao Ingles que sta al Zante (sino hallais otra coientura meier) con el sobrescritto que diga, en casa del Sennor Eleazar Hycman Mercader Ingles, al tragetto, de San Thomas en Venisia. Y Dios guarde la persona de V. M. Fecha en Venesia al primer dia de Julio, 1596. annos.

Amigo de V. M. Michael Lok Ingles.

And I sent the said Letter from Venice to Zante, in the ship Cherubin. And shortly after I sent a copie thereof in the ship Mynyon. And also a third copie thereof by Manea Orlando Patron de Nave Venetian. And unto my said Letters he wrote mee answere to Venice by one Letter which came not to my hands. And also by another Letter which came to my hands, which is copied here-under.

Al Illmo. Sig^{or.} Michal Loch Ingles, in casa del Sig^{or.} Lasaro Merca. der Ingles, al tragetto de San Thomas en Venesia.

MUy Illustre Seg^{or.} lo carta de V. M. recevi à 20. dias del Mese di Settembre, por loqual veo Loche V. M. me manda, io tengho animo de complir Loche tengo

promettido à V. M. y no solo yo, mas tengo vinte hombres
para lievar con migo, por che son hombres vaglientes; y
assi estoi esperando, por otra carta che avise à V. M.
parache me embiais los dinieros che tengo escritto à V. M.
Porche bien save V. M. como io vine pover, porche me
glievo Capitan Candis mas de sessanta mille ducados, come
V. M. bien save: embiandome lo dicho, ire à servir à
V. M. con todos mis compagneros. I no spero otra cossa
mas de la voluntad è carta de V. M. I con tanto nostro
Sig$^{or.}$ Dios guarda la Illustre persona de V. M. muchos
annos. De Ceffalonia à 24. de Settembre del 1596.

Amigo & servitor de V. M.

Juan Fuca.

And the said Letter came to my hands in Venice, the
16. day of November, 1596. but my Law suite with the
Companie of Turkie was not yet ended, by reason of
Sir John Spencers suite made in England at the Queenes
Court to the contrarie, seeking onely to have his money
discharged which I had attached in Venice for my said
pension, and thereby my owne purse was not yet readie
for the Greeke Pilot.

And neverthelesse, hoping that my said suite would
have shortly a good end; I wrote another Letter to this
Greeke Pilot from Venice, dated the 20. of November,
1596. which came not to his hands. And also another
Letter, dated the 24. of Januarie 1596. which came
to his hands. And thereof he wrote me answere,
dated the 28. of May, 1597. which I received the
first of August 1597. by Thomas Norden an English
Merchant yet living in London, wherein he promised still
to goe with me into England, to performe the said voyage
for discoverie of the North-west passage into the South
Sea, if I would send him money for his charges according
to his former writing, without the which money, he said
he could not goe, for that he said he was undone utterly,
when he was in the ship Santa Anna, which came from
China, and was robbed at California. And yet againe

[III.iv.852.]

*The Ship
Santa Anna.*

420

afterward I wrote him another Letter from Venice, where-unto he wrote me answere, by a Letter written in his Greeke language, dated the 20. of October, 1598. the which I have still by me, wherein he promiseth still to goe with me into England, and performe the said voyage of discoverie of the North-west passage into the South Sea by the said streights, which he calleth the Streight of Nova Spania, which he saith is but thirtie daies voyage in the streights, if I will send him the money formerly written for his charges. The which money I could not yet send him, for that I had not yet recovered my pension owing mee by the Companie of Turkie aforesaid. And so of long time I stayed from any furder proceeding with him in this matter.

The Streight of Nova Spania thirtie dayes journey in the Streight.

And yet lastly, when I my selfe was at Zante, in the moneth of June 1602. minding to passe from thence for England by Sea, for that I had then recovered a little money from the Companie of Turkie, by an order of the Lords of the Privie Counsell of England, I wrote another Letter to this Greeke Pilot to Cefalonia, and required him to come to me to Zante, and goe with mee into England, but I had none answere thereof from him, for that as I heard afterward at Zante, he was then dead, or very likely to die of great sicknesse. Whereupon I returned my selfe by Sea from Zante to Venice, and from thence I went by land through France into England, where I arrived at Christmas, An. 1602. safely, I thanke God, after my absence from thence ten yeeres time; with great troubles had for the Company of Turkies businesse, which hath cost me a great summe of money, for the which I am not yet satisfied of them.

[A Treatise

A Treatise of the North-west passage to the South
Sea, through the Continent of Virginia, and by
Fretum Hudson.

THe noble plantation of Virginia hath some very
excellent prerogatives above many other famous
Kingdomes, namely, the temperature of the aire, the
fruitfulnesse of the soile, and the commodiousnesse of
situation.

The aire is healthfull and free both from immoderate
heate, and from extreme cold; so that both the Inhabitants
and their Cattell doe prosper exceedingly in stature and
strength, and all Plants brought from any other remote
climate, doe there grow and fructifie in as good or better
manner, then in the soile from whence they came. Which
though it doe manifestly proove the fruitfulnesse of the
soile, yeelding all kindes of Graine or Plants committed
unto it, with a rich and plentifull increase; yet cannot the
fatnesse of the earth alone produce such excellent effects,
unlesse the temperature of the aire be likewise so favourable, that those tender sprouts which the earth doth
abundantly bring forth, may bee cherished with moderate
heate and seasonable moisture, and freed both from
scorching drought, and nipping frost.

These blessings are so much the more to be esteemed,
because they are bestowed upon a place situated so conveniently, and at so good a distance both from Europe, and the
West Indies, that for the mutuall commerce betwixt these
great and most rich parts of the habitable world, there
cannot bee devised any place more convenient for the
succour and refreshing of those that trade from hence
thither: whether they be of our owne Nation, or of our
Neighbours and Friends, the multitude of great and
navigable Rivers, and of safe and spacious Harbours, as it
were inviting all Nations to entertaine mutuall friendship,
and to participate of those blessings which God out of the
abundance of his rich Treasures, hath so graciously

bestowed some upon these parts of Europe, and others no lesse desired upon those poore people: which might still have remayned in their old barbarous ignorance, without knowledge of their owne miserie, or of Gods infinite goodnesse and mercy; if it had not pleased God thus graciously both to draw us thither with desire of such wealth as those fruitfull Countries afford, and also to grant us so easie, certaine, and safe a meanes to goe unto them: which passage is in mine opinion made much more secure and easie by the commodious Harbours and refreshing which Virginia doth reach out unto us. The coasts of Florida to the West, being not so barberous; and of New England to the East, somewhat more out of the way, amongst so many Flats and small Ilands not so safe. Neither is the commodiousnesse of Virginia's situation onely in respect of this West Atlanticke Ocean, but also in respect of the Indian Ocean, which we commonly call the South Sea, which lyeth on the West and North-west side of Virginia, on the other side of the Mountaines beyond our Falls, and openeth a free and faire passage, not onely to China, Japan, and the Moluccaes; but also to New Spaine, Peru, Chili, and those rich Countries of Terra Australis, not as yet fully discovered. For the Sea wherein Master Hudson did winter, which was first discovered by him, and is therefore now called Fretum Hudson, doth stretch so farre towards the West, that it lyeth as farre Westward [III.iv.853.] as the Cape of Florida: So that from the Falls above Henrico Citie, if we shape our journey towards the North-west, following the Rivers towards the head, wee shall undoubtedly come to the Mountaines, which as they send divers great Rivers Southward into our Bay of Chesepiock, so likewise doe they send others from their further side North-westward into that Bay where Hudson did winter. For so wee see in our owne Countrie, from the ridge of Mountaines continued from Derbishire into Scotland, doe issue many great Rivers on both sides into the East Germane Ocean, and into the Westerne Irish Seas: in like sort from the Alpes of Switzerland and the Grizons, doe runne the Danubie Eastward into Pontus Euxinus, the Rhene into the North Germane Ocean, the Rhosne West into the Mediterrane Sea, and the Po South into the Adriatike Sea. This Bay where Hudson did winter, stretcheth it selfe Southward into 49. degrees, and cannot be in probabilitie so farre distant from the Falls as two hundred leagues; part of the way lying by the Rivers side towards the Mountaines from whence it springeth: and the other part on the other side cannot want Rivers likewise, which will conduct us all the way, and I hope carry us and our provisions a good part of it. Besides that Bay, it is not unlikely that the Westerne Sea in some other Creeke or River commeth much neerer then that place: For the place where Sir Thomas Button did winter, lying more Westerly then Master Hudsons Bay by one hundred and ninetie leagues in the same Sea, doth extend it selfe very neere as farre towards the west as the Cape of California, which is now found to bee an Iland stretching it selfe from 22. degrees to 42. and lying almost directly North and South; as may appeare in a Map of that Iland which I have seene here in London, brought out of Holland; where the Sea upon the North-west part may very probably come much neerer then some doe imagine: who giving too much credit to our usuall Globes and Maps, doe dreame of a large Continent extending it selfe farre Westward to the imagined Streight of Anian, where are seated (as they fable) the large Kingdomes of Cebola and Quivira, having great and populous Cities of civill people; whose houses are said to bee five stories high, and to have some pillars of Turguesses. Which relations are cunningly set downe by some upon set purpose to put us out of the right way, and to discourage such as otherwise might be desirous to search a passage by the way aforesaid into those Seas.

Gerardus Mercator, a very industrious and excellent Geographer, was abused by a Map sent unto him, of foure Euripi meeting about the North Pole; which now are found to bee all turned into a mayne Icie Sea. One

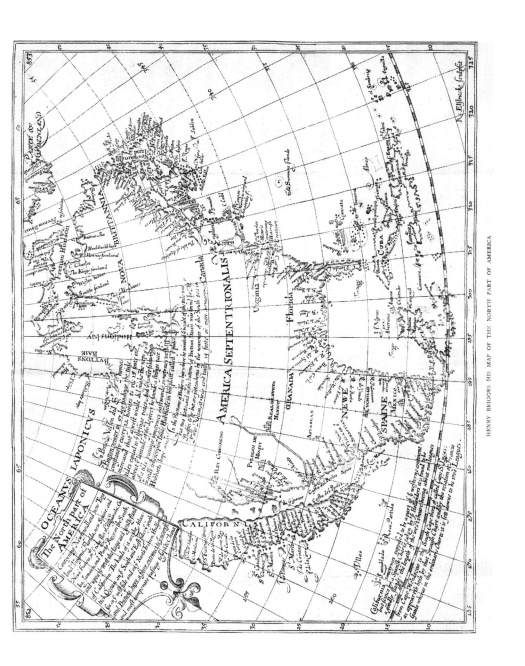

The material originally positioned here is too large for reproduction in this reissue. A PDF can be downloaded from the web address given on page iv of this book, by clicking on 'Resources Available'.

demonstration of the craftie falshood of these usuall Maps
is this, that Cape Mendocino is set in them West North-
west, distant from the South Cape of California, about
seventeene hundred leagues, whereas Francis Gaule that
was imployed in those discoveries by the Vice-roy of New
Spaine, doth in Hugo Linschotten his booke set downe
their distance to be onely five hundred leagues.

Besides this, in the place where Sir Thomas Button did
winter in 57. degrees of latitude, the constant great Tydes
every twelve houres, and the increase of those Tydes
whensoever any strong Westerne winde did blow, doe
strongly perswade us that the mayne Westerne Ocean is
not farre from thence; which was much confirmed unto
them the Summer following; when sayling directly North
from that place where they wintered, about the latitude of
60. degrees, they were crossed by a strong Current running
sometimes Eastward, sometimes Westward: So that if
we finde either Hudsons Bay, or any Sea more neere unto
the West, wee may assure our selves that from thence we
may with great ease passe to any part of the East Indies:
And that as the World is very much beholding to that
famous Columbus for that hee first discovered unto us the
West Indies; and to the Portugal for the finding out the
ordinarie and as yet the best way that is knowne to the
East Indies, by Cape Bona Speranza: So may they and
all the world be in this beholding to us in opening a new
and large passage, both much neerer, safer, and farre more
wholesome and temperate through the Continent of
Virginia, and by Fretum Hudson, to all those rich Countries bordering upon the South Sea, in the East and West
Indies. And this hope that the South Sea may easily from
Virginia be discovered over Land, is much confirmed by
the constant report of the Savages, not onely of Virginia,
but also of Florida and Canada; which dwelling so remote
one from another, and all agreeing in the report of a large
Sea to the Westwards, where they describe great ships not
unlike to ours, with other circumstances, doe give us very
great probabilitie (if not full assurance) that our endevours

this way shall by Gods blessing have a prosperous and happy successe, to the encrease of his Kingdome and Glorie amongst these poore ignorant Heathen people, the publique good of all the Christian world, the never-dying honour of our most gracious Soveraigne, the inestimable benefit of our Nation, and the admirable and speedie increase and advancement of that most noble and hopefull Plantation of Virginia; for the good successe whereof all good men with mee, I doubt not, will powre out their prayers to Almightie God.

H. B.

Voyages, and Travels

to and in the New World, called America : Relations of their Pagan Antiquities and of the Regions and Plantations in the North and South parts thereof, and of the Seas and Ilands adjacent.

THE FIFTH BOOKE.

Chap. I.

A Description of the West Indies, by Antonio De Herrera* his Majesties Chiefe Chronicler of the Indies, and his Chronicler of Castile.

To the Licentiate Paul of Laguna, President of the Royall and Supreme Councell of the Indies.

He Licentiate John of Obando, Predecessor of your Lordship (in whose time the Office of chiefe Chronicler of the Indies was instituted, for writing with greater authoritie, foundation, and truth, the Acts of the Castilians, in the New World, and to see and examine that which the other Chroniclers should write (for I finde that almost to

*I found this Worke translated in M. Hakluyt's Papers; but I can scarsely call it English, it had so much of the Spanish garbe, in litterall

427

all that is written no credit could be given, for over-much licence, wherewith untill then it was done) hee used great diligence in gathering the most certaine Relations that were found as well in the Indies, as in Spaine, of that which happened in the Discoveries of those Regions, the foundations of those Townes and Customes of the people. And many yeers being past after his death, without making any beginning of this History, your Lordship being provided for President of the Royall and Supreme Councell of the Indies, knowing how much it behoved, [III. v. 856.] that deeds so worthy of memorie should no longer be buried, and that they should be written by a Royall Chronicler (seeing so much fruit is gotten of Historie, that it exceedeth so much the Picture, as the soule, the bodie, against the opinion of a moderne Writer.) Providing all the meanes necessarie with liberalitie and diligence, have beene the meere and onely Instrument; following the opinion of S. Augustine, that this Historie, and the Description that followeth hath come to the present estate. And because it hath not beene of least importance to honour the Author, animating him to goe forward with so great a labour, conforming your selfe with the universall opinion of the much that is due to the watchings, and labours of the Writers; placing this Office of Chiefe

and verball affectation and obscuritie. I have examined it with the Spanish Originall, and compared it also with the Latine Translation, with great paines for thy greater pleasure & profit, correcting and illustrating the phrase and sence, being before very rude, obscure and in very many places utterly sencelesse. But having none to write for mee but my owne hands, I rather chose to amend this as I could, then to translate it anew. I have seene it also in French. The Latine is exceeding false in some numbers, as 2000. for 20000. divers times, &c. which I note for their sakes which reade that and have not the Spanish. I have not contracted this (as I have done divers other Relations) because it is a briefe contraction of the Spanish-Indian Contractation, presenting the Spanish Proceedings, Colonies, Townes, Officers and Government Spirituall and Temporall in the Indies. This Author hath written eight Decades of the Spanish Acts in the West Indies, which give great light to those parts, but would be too long for this Worke.

Chronicler in that point and reputation that so noble an Exercise deserveth, (as the most famous men of the World have judged it, and it is esteemed and talked of among all Nations be they never so barbarous) your Lordship shall be praysed eternally, and thanked of all that are interested in it; by which is procured the making mention of their Fathers, and Predecessors with their Names and Countrey, all that hath beene possible, against the barbarous and most unjust opinion of John Baptista Ramusio, in his Proeme in the third Volume of the Navigations, where hee saith to bee a vaine thing, and ridiculous, that the Spanish Authors should take paines in writing the names and Countrey of those which served in the matters of the Indies. Wherein he sheweth the venime of the envie conceived of the glorious deeds of these Catholike Kings, and of the Castillian Nation, seeing the Chronicles doe serve to honour the good, and to reproch the evill, for an example of those to come; which could not be obtayned with the opinion of this Ramusius, whom the saying of Cato against the Grecians doth fit. But the opinion of your Lordship hath beene according to your prudence and valour, of the which as it is just, there will be a perpetuall memorie, and for that which this Nation is indebted unto you for the same, you shall bee reknowledged of it eternally. God keepe your Lordship, from Vallyadolyeede the fifteenth of October 1601.

Ramusio uncharitably taxed: for he doth but blame the folly of Spanish Authors which are more curious to set downe the names, &c. of those which have there done any thing though but rebellions, then the description of the beasts, fishes, fowles, plants, Earth, Heaven, &c. in the Indies: for which hee there commends Oviedo.

THe compasse of the Earth is 360. degrees, which being reduced to leagues of Castile are 6300. and by the compasse of the Earth is understood the Sea together with it, which two Elements make the Globe; whose upper face in part is Earth, and in part is Sea: The Ancients divided the Earth in three parts, and gave to every one his name. The first they called Europe, more celebrated then any of the other. The second Asia, which is greater then the rest, and contayneth the great King-dome of China. The third Africa. And men being in a supposition that the World contayned no more then was

Chap. 1. Of the bounds and division of the West Indies.

rehearsed, not contenting themselves with it, entred in the
Art of Navigating, and in the invention of ships of high
building, fitting them in such order that they might abide
the force of the waves of the Sea, & in this Art[1] the
Spaniards have surpassed all the Nations of the World.
For whiles there reigned Ferdinand in Castile and in Lyon,
the famous Kings Catholike Ferdinando the Fift, and
Isabella a most wise, prudent, and most puissant Queene;
and Don John the Second, called the Pellican, raigned in
Portugall, (hee that ever will be worthy of memory) Don
Christopher Colon, first Admirall of the Indies, having
lived many yeeres married in Spaine; with the counsell
of Martin of Bohemia, a Portugall borne in the Iland of
Fayall, a famous Astrologian; and especially a Judiciarie,
and of others with whom he communicated it, gave a
beginning to the Discovery of that which at this day is
counted the fourth part of the World, and the greatest of
them all, and taking his course toward the Sunne setting,
going from Pallos a Village of the Earle of Miranda, in
the Coast of Andaluzia, he sayled so much by the Ocean,
that hee found this great Land, which the Equinoctiall
Line cutteth in the middest, and it goeth so farre toward
the South, that it reacheth to fiftie two degrees and an
halfe, and goeth so high to the North, that it hides it selfe
under the Pole Articke, without[m] knowing any end.

The greatnesse of this fourth part hath set the people
in great admiration, whose description shall here be
handled, under the name of Ilands, and firme Land of the
Ocean Sea, because they are compassed with this Sea, and
placed to the West, and are commonly called, the West
Indies, and the New World, and comprehended within the
limits of the Kings of Castile and of Lyon. Which is an
Hemisphere, and halfe of the World, of 180. degrees,
beginning to reckon from a Meridian Circle, which passeth
by thirtie nine, or by fortie degrees of longitude,
Occidentall from the Meridian of Toledo, through the
mouth of the River Maranyon, and to the Orientall,
through the Citie of Mallaca, in sort, that at twentie

leagues sayling for a degree, these bounds have from the one part to the other 3900. Castillan leagues, every one of 3000. paces, of five foot of a Castillan yard, which men say are sixtie Italian miles, from the Orient to the Occident, which the Sea-men doe call East and West. And this account of twentie leagues to a degree, is according to Ptolomie, and to the opinion of many curious men. It hath seemed to others that the miles of every degree are seventie, and that they make no more then seventeene leagues and an halfe of Castile, which is held for the truest account.

The degrees of longitude, which are those that are reckoned by the ⁿEquinoctiall, which goeth from East to West, through the middest of the Orbe, and Globe of the Earth, have not beene able to bee taken well, because there is no fixed signe in the Heaven. Degrees of altitude are those which are taken, and reckoned from the Pole which fall out certayne, because it is a fixed point, which is the marke that is taken, by the which it shall be shewed in this description.

ⁿ *How the degrees of longitude are reckoned.*

[III. v. 857.]

There is discovered, and navigated from the North to the South, from 60. degrees of Septentrional altitude, unto fiftie three Austral, which are 1977. leagues of ground, which hath in breadth, at the broadest 1300. and thence downewards unto eighteene, which is the narowest by Nombre de Dios, or Portobelo, unto Panama, whereby Nature divided this Land, leaving almost the halfe of it to the North, and the rest to the South, which are the two parts of these bounds. The third, is the Ilands and firme land, that lye to the East of Mallaca, where through passeth the Line of the partition, betweene the two Crownes of Castile and Portugall, the which although they are part of the East India, they are named of the West in respect of Castile, as shall bee seene in the generall Map that followeth.

What is discovered and navigated. The English have discovered far more: From 81. in Greenland, and from 78. in Groinland to 57. of South latitude.

And because the Discoverie of all these Regions, from whence so great Riches have beene brought to these Kingdomes, is due unto the Load-stone, I will set downe

A marvellous effect of the Loadstone.

431

*Don Antonie
Ossorio, dis-
covereth a
great secret of
the Loadstone.*

heere a wonderfull effect of his, discovered by Don
Antonie Ossorio, a Gentleman of Valladolid, and it is,
that it doth communicate to the Iron, more attractive
vertue then naturally it hath of it selfe, seeing that apply-
ing an Iron to the part of the stone that hath most force,
much more weight will bee raysed with the Iron, then
with the stone it selfe, so it bee joyned with it, in sort that
to a Load-stone, that weigheth no more then two pound one
quarter, and hath no naturall vertue for to lift more then
sixe ounces weight, it made the Iron in my presence to lift
fourteene pound of Iron, and this vertue hath not the
Load-stone of Spaine, a thing that causeth the Philosophers to muse much upon.

The Author had here inserted a Table or Generall Map
of America; the defect of which wee have supplyed with
this farre more complete of Hondius.

[III. v. 858.]
*Chap. 2.
Of the
Navigation of
the Indies.*

THe Ocean that is toward the East, is called the North
Sea, and that which falleth to the West, Mar del Sur,
or the South Sea: this washeth Nova Hispania and Peru:
that washeth those Regions which are situated on the
South coast of Brasile toward the Magellan Streight: and
especially the North coast from Brasile toward Castile, and
other Septentrional parts. These two vast Seas are
divided into other lesser Seas and Gulfes, and are sayled by

*How many
Navigations
there bee to
these Indies.*

foure principall Navigations. The first and most ancient,
from Castile to Terra firme, and to Nova Hispania. The
second, from Castile to the River of Plate, and the Streight
of Magellan. The third, from the coast of Nova
Hispania to Guatimala, and Panama, to Peru, Chile, and
the Streight. And the last, and newest, from Nova
Hispania to the Ilands of the West, and trafficke of China,
as it is seene in the Table preceding.

The first Navigation, because it is most used, called
Carrera de las Indias, The course of the Indies, is divided
in two, one to the port of Saint John of Ulua in Nova
Hispania, whitherto from Sivil is sayled about one
thousand and seven hundred leagues in two moneths and

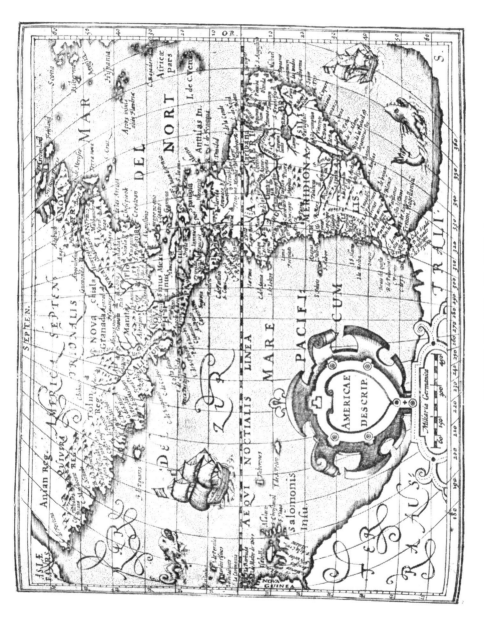

HONDIUS HIS MAP OF AMERICA

an halfe: and another to Nombre de Dios, and now to
Porte bellò, which is in the Kingdome which they call
Terra firme, of one thousand and foure hundred leagues,
in two moneths large, and both goe by one course, till they
come to the Ilands of the North Sea, from Saint Lucar of *Difficultie in*
Barrameda, whence yee cannot take Sea without a Pilot *going out of the*
skilfull in the Channell, a fit winde and spring Tydes, and *Barre of Saint*
light of the .day, or lights, for to see the markes of the *Lucar.*
Barre.

The Times for to begin these Navigations, are divers. *In what times*
For Nova Hispania, the winter being past, from the *these Naviga-*
beginning of April unto the end of May, and not after, *tions are to be*
that they may not come to the Ilands of the North Sea *made.*
after August, when the North windes begin to reigne, and
the Uracanes doe begin, which are stormes and great gusts *Monsons.*
arising of contrarie windes. And to Terra firme, the
Navigation is before the entring of the Winter, in all
August and September, that they may come to Porte bello
from November forward, when by the beginning of the
North windes that Coast is alreadie least diseased, and
more healthfull.

From Saint Lucar they goe to the Canaries, whither *The voyage of*
there is about two hundred and fiftie leagues of Naviga- *the Fleets till*
tion, of eight or ten dayes, through the Gulfe de las *they come to*
Yeguas; which in winter is very dangerous for stormes: *the place where*
and in the Port of Canarie they cast anker when they *they goe.*
thinke it good, or else in the Port of Gomera, which is
the best of those Ilands. From the Canaries they saile
to Desseada, which stands in 15. degrees and little more;
and to Dominica, whither they make seven hundred
leagues, through the great Ocean, and they stay five and
twentie dayes, whereby they cannot returne, because the
Brises are ordinarie, and contrarie at their returne. The
Brises are windes which comprehend all the Easterne *What thing*
windes with all their quarters, and are so ordinarie and *the Brises are.*
firme, because the swift motion of the First Moover, doth
carry after him the Element of the Aire, as the other
superior Orbes: and so the Aire followeth alwaies the

motion of the Day, going from East to West, never
varying, and the effectuall motion of the Aire carrieth
after him also the vapours and exhalations that doe arise
from the Sea, and therefore the Brise winde which runneth
from the East, is so continuall in those parts. This voyage
from the Canaries to Dominica, Peter Arios of Avila,
which was called Gentill and the Juster, made the first, the
yeere of 1514. when hee went with an Armie for
Governour and Captaine generall of the Kingdome of
Golden Castile, now called Terra firme, since which the
Navigation hath beene ordered, that untill then went out
of order.

Because it is now ordered that fresh water and wood be
not taken in the Iland of Desseada, and in Dominica, the
Fleet of Nova Espanna goe hence to Occoa, a Port of the
Iland Hispan-yola, to take refreshing, and they stay long
because the stormes from Cuba doe overtake it. And
*They take
water alreadie
in the Ile of
Guadalupe,
where the
Courses are
divided.*
they that goe for Nova Espanna, doe water in the Iland
of Guadalupe, and there they divide the courses. The
fleet of Nova Espanna goeth in demand of the Cape of
Saint Antonie, which is in the furthest part and most
Occidentall of the Iland of Cuba, to which place they saile
about five hundred leagues in twentie dayes ordinarily, in
sight of Saint John of Porto Rico and of Espannola, two
leagues off the Port of Saint Domingo, running along the
coast by the Point of Nizao, and betweene the Ilands of
Cuba and Jamayca, they goe with great heede of the
shoales, which are called the Jardines, neere to the middest
of the coast of Cuba where many ships have beene lost,
passing afterward in sight of the Iland of Pinos and Cape
Correntes twelve leagues short of the Cape of Saint
Antonie. From whence there are two courses to the Port
of Veracruz, both of ten or twelve dayes; one which
they call Within Land, of two hundred and fiftie leagues,
for the Summer time from May to September, when there
bee no North windes which are crosse windes on the coast
of Yucatan, whereby they passe; and another which they
call Without, for the time of Winter, of about two

hundred and eightie leagues somewhat higher in altitude : and the best Navigation, for to goe to the Port of Saint John de Ulua, is to leane to the coast of Florida, and the Playnes of Almeria, that no contrarie wind stay him from seasonable attayning the Port of Saint John de Ulua.

Which is the best Naviga- tion from that Cape of S. Antonie, to S. John de Ulua.

The fleets that went from Dominica, and now goe from Guadalupe to Terra firme (whither is about foure hundred leagues voyage of fifteene dayes) they goe in demand of Cartagena, farre off the coast of Terra firme, where the Brises are almost perpetuall, and contrarie to the returne, and the Southerne windes continuall in Summer, and the Northerne in Winter, which are crosse windes. They doe reknowledge by the way the Cape de Vella, between Santa Martha and ᵃVenezuela, and the Cape ᵇ del Aguja neere Cartagena, where they unlade the merchandise that are to goe to New Kingdome; and those which are to passe to Peru, are carried to Porte bello, whitherto from Carta- gena are ninetie leagues, foure or sixe dayes sayling, reknowledging the Point of Captina, and from the Canaries to Cartagena is five and thirtie dayes sayling.

[III. v. 859.]

ᵃ*Or little Venice.*
ᵇ*Or of the Needle.*

Those that goe to Hunduras and Guatemala, goe in companie with them of Nova Espanna, unto Cape Tiburon, the utmost Westerne part of Espannola, from whence running along by the Iland of Jamayca on the North side, unto the Point of the ᶜNegrillo, the uttermost of it, they put to Sea in demand of the Cape of the Camaron, the beginning of the Gulfe and Province of Hunduras, from whence they goe to anker to Truxillo fifteene leagues to the West from the Cape, where the merchandize are unladen that are to remaine there, and the rest doe passe to the Port of Cavallos, and to Golfo Dulce, along the coast by the Gulfe of Hunduras, to transport them to Guatemala.

The voyage of Hunduras and Guatemala.

ᶜ*Or little black Moore.*

THe returne from the Indies to Spaine, cannot be made by the course which they take in going thither, and therefore they must come to a greater height, going out of the Tropicks to seeke fresh windes which doe blow from

Chap. 3. Wherein hee prosecuteth the Naviga- tions of the Indies.

PURCHAS HIS PILGRIMES

The Fleets doe
returne to
Castile by
another way.
When the
fleets ought to
depart to come
for Castile.
Whither the
Fleets doe goe
from
Cartagena.

towards the North; all the Fleetes doe meete in the Port of Havana, about the moneth of June, to come to Spaine before Winter; for the East winde is against them, and is traverse in the Channell, and the South also is traverse in the Coast from the Cape Saint Vincent to Saint Lucar. The fleet of Terra firme, departeth from May forward from Porte bello, when the North windes doe alreadie cease; and returneth to Cartagena to take the freight of Silver and Gold from the new Kingdom of Granada: and also for to avoid the Coast of Veragua, and the streame of Nicaragua, whence they can hardly get out if they ingulfe themselves by reason of the Brises, and contrarie and dangerous Currents that are in the way. From Cartagena they goe for Cape Saint Antonie, the furthest West of Cuba about two hundred leagues, voyage of ten dayes, with care of the shoales that are in the way of Serrana and Serranilla, and ^dQuitasveno, and from the Cape of Saint Antonie to the Avana, are neere fiftie leagues: and the ships that come from Hunduras, doe come also to reknowledge the Cape of Saint Antonie.

^d Or take
away sleepe.
The ships of
Hunduras re-
knowledge the
Cape of Saint
Antonie.
When the
Fleets of Nova
Espanna doe
depart thence.

The fleetes of Nova Espanna doe depart in the beginning of May, while the North windes doe last, which doe serve for the returne to the Avana, ascending a little in altitude unto the Sound, which they call las Tortugas, unto which place they saile about three hundred leagues in fifteene dayes.

The voyage of
them of Santa
Martha and
Venezuela.

The ships of Santa Martha and Venezuela, to come to Castile, came out betweene Cuba and Hispaniola, to reknowledge the Cape of Saint Nicholas in the Western part of it, from whence through the middest of the Iles of the Lucayos, they goe take the course of the fleets, and when they come in sight of the Cape of Saint Antonie, they goe to the Avana for feare of Pirates.

From the Avana to Castile, having past the Channell of Bahama (which the Pilot Antonie of Alaminos sayled first of all, the yeere 1519.) they doe saile through the Gulfe which is called of the North, or of the Sagarzo, about nine hundred or a thousand leagues or more (a sayling of five

and twentie or thirtie dayes with ordinarie windes) by two
wayes, one for Summer, in a greater height, till they come
to thirtie eight or thirtie nine degrees, in the which stand
the Ilands of Azores; and another for Winter, by a lesser
height, because of the stormes and showres which doe come
alwayes neere unto it, whereby they goe unto thirtie nine
degrees no more, wherein standeth the Iland of Santa
Maria, one of the Iles of Azores, and they ascend one
degree more for to touch in the Tercera, where the fleets
doe always come to take refreshing, without permitting
any one to goe ashoare. And from the Ilands of Azores
unto Saint Lucar of Barrameda, the Mariners make three
hundred leagues of Navigation in fifteene dayes, others in
thirtie for the many Brises that doe reigne in this Gulfe
of the Azores, whereby they saile till they come upon the
Coast of Portugal, and the doubling of the Cape Saint
Vincent; and after in sight of the Coast unto the Port of
Saint Lucar.

Navigation from the Ilands of Azores unto Saint Lucar.

The Navigation from Castile to the River of Plata
(whitherto there is one thousand and six hundred leagues,
and to the Streight of Magelanes neere two thousand)
hath beene much longer in the time then in the distance
of the way, because being necessarie to come to those
Provinces in their Summer, which is from September
forward, they cannot depart from Castile at such time as
not to passe the Equinoctiall by June or August, when in
it the Calmes are many and very great, and therefore they
stay five moneths in the Voyage, which might bee made
in two or three, if from Sivil they did depart by August
or before: and touching in the Canaries they goe North
and South, to eight or nine degrees on the other side of
the Equinoctiall, from whence some doe saile East and
West, to reknowledge the Cape of Saint Augustine in
Brasile, and afterward in sight of the Land unto the River
of Plate and the Streight. Others from the eight degrees
have gone straight through the South Sea to the Streight,
although few have come to passe it, before the Summer bee
ended, which is very short and full of stormes, because it

Navigation to the River of Plata.

[III. v. 860.]

437

stands in so great a height, whereby this Navigation is
very difficult.

*Navigation of
the South Sea.* The Navigation of the South Sea hath alwayes beene
along the Coast, and because the South windes are very
continuall, and the Current of the Streight ordinarie to
*Navigation of
Panama to the
Citie de los
Reyes.* the North; The Navigation of Panama to the Citie of
The Kings, is wont to continue two moneths, and the
returne lesse then thirtie dayes, and the same from the
Kings to Chile, from whence to Panama are sayled nine
hundred leagues in lesse then two moneths, eight being
needfull for the going, which is alreadie shorter then it
was: for putting to the Sea they finde better windes to
performe it.

*Navigation of
the West
Indies.* The Navigation to the Westerne Ilands, Malucas and
Philippinas, from Castile to the Streight of Magellane
passeth foure thousand leagues, and so for being so long
as for the difficultie of passing the Streight of Magellanes,
it is held for difficult to use it, and from Nova Espanna
through the Westerne Gulfe, which is in the South Sea.
This Navigation was made from the Port of the Nativitie
in the Coast of Nova Espanna; at this time it is made
from the Port of Acapulco,₁ from whence to the Malucas
and Philippinas, they doe make a voyage of one thousand
six hundred, or a thousand and seven hundred leagues,
which is sayled in two moneths, or two and a halfe, departing in November which is the time most free from calmes.
And the returne to Nova Espanna is longer, because not
being able to returne the way they went, it is necessarie
to ascend to 39. degrees, and depart in May and June,
when the Brises bee less, and they stay foure moneths
in sayling two thousand leagues that may bee in the
journey.

Chap. 4.
*Of the Indies
of the North.* NAture having divided these western Indies in two
parts, by the Isthmos or narrownesse from Porte bello
to Panama, placed the one to the North, and the other to
the South; wherefore wee will call them the Indies of the
North, and of the South. The Kings of Castile and Lion,

with the advice of the supreme Councell of the Indies, have ordayned, that in each place there bee a Vice-roy, Courts, and Governments, and Bishopricks, as hereafter shall bee shewed. And first shall be entreated of the Northerne Indies, which commonly they call Nova Hispania, because the first discoverers (which were John Grijalva and his Companions) having not seene in the Ilands houses of stone, nor other things as in Spaine, which here they found with people apparelled, and more civill; They named it New Spaine: which exceedeth the other part of the Indies in pastures, and therefore they have innumerable Cattle of all sorts: and it exceedeth also in husbandrie and fruits: it hath no wine, because generally the grapes doe not ripen with perfection, the raines of July and August not suffering them to ripen. The * upper Ilands have also great Pastures, and a pleasant prospect: for all the yeere they are greene and flourishing, with great pleasantnesse, and great Arcabucos, which are very thick Groves and Inclosures, and in the Playnes are great Lakes and Quagmires. Neither Bread nor Wine grow in them; for the great ranknesse of the ground doth not suffer it to ripen nor eare: the Rivers for the most part have gold. Florida, Nicaragua, and Guatimala are almost in this manner, as of all more particularly wee will rehearse in their place, and in the Table following shall the bounds of these Northern Indies bee seene.

THe Court of the Iland Hispaniola, which in time and place is the first, being neerest unto Castile, it hath of bounds East and West five hundred and fiftie leagues, and North and South more then three hundred, wherein are included the Ilands and Governments of Hispaniola, Cuba, Saint John, Jamayca, Margarita, and the fishing of the Pearle: the Province and Government of Venezuella, and for neernesse the Provinces of new Andaluzia, Guayana, and Florida, with all the Ilands of the North Sea, which doe passe a hundred which are named, and are above six hundred great and small: and those which doe leane toward the Coast of Terra firme, the Mariners doe call of the Leeward, and the other to the Weatherward. The temperature of them all is commonly moist and exceeding hot, and although they be plentifull in Pastures and Trees, they are not so of the Seedes of Castile, nor of Wheat, Barly, Vines, nor Olives: but there is great store of great Cattell and small, as Kine, Mares, Swine, and Sheepe, and therefore their principall trafficke is Hides and Sugar, for there is great store; and although in the most of them there is gold; it is not sought for.

Chap. 6. Of the Iland Hispaniola and of Cuba.

THe Countrie-men called the Iland of Hispaniola, Ayti and Quisqueya, which signifieth Roughnesse, and a great Countrie. The figure of it is like a Chesnut leafe: it stands in nineteene degrees and a halfe of elevation of the Pole, it compasseth about foure hundred leagues and somewhat more, and hath in length East and West an hundred and fiftie, and North and South from thirtie to sixtie where it is broadest, it is very plentifull of Sugar, and Cattell, and of Yuca, the roote whereof maketh the *Cazabi bread.* Cazabi, the bread of the Countrimen. They have no Millet nor Wheat, although they begin to reape some in the inward parts and coldest. It is rich of Copper mynes and other metals, and some veine of Gold though but *Ten Spanish Townes.* little is gotten, for want of workemen: it hath ten Spanish Townes.

[III. v. 861.] The Citie of Saint Dominga.   The Citie of Saint Dominicke or Domingo neere the Coast of the South, on the River of Ozama, stands in the said 19. degrees and a halfe, and 60. of Occidentall longitude from the Meridian of Toledo, from whence unto it there may bee by direct line one thousand two hundred fortie seven leagues, it hath above sixe hundred housholds. There is resident in it the Audience or Councell, the Officers of the Goods and Royall Treasure; a Mint house, and the Cathedrall Church. And the Archbishoprick hath for Suffraganes the Bishopricks of the Conception de la Vega (which is united with that of Saint Dominicke) those of Saint John, Cuba, Venezuela, and the Abbotship of

Jamayca; and in the Citie are Monasteries of Dominicans, Franciscans, Mercenaries, and other two of Nunnes, a Grammar Schoole, with foure thousand * Pesos of Rent, and an Hospitall with twentie thousand. The Haven which is great, and capable of many ships, is in the mouth of the River Ozama, and hath the Citie on the West, which the Deputie Don Bartholomew Collon did build the yeere 1494. on the East side, better and wholsomer in situation, and the chiefe Knight of Alcantara, Nicholas of Ovando being Governour of Hispaniola, An. 1502. removed it where now it is, from the other side the River to the East, upon occasion that the Citie had fallen by a great Earthquake. The Village of Salvalyon of Yguey, eight and twentie leagues from Saint Dominicke to the East, of the Archbishoprick; the Captaine, John of Esquivel, did people it. The Village of the Zeybo, twentie leagues from Saint Dominicke to the East, toward the Iland of Saona: the Captaine also planted it in the time of Nicholas of Ovando. The Village of Cotuy sixteene leagues from Saint Dominicke to the North, and very close in his circuit, Roderick Mexia of Trillo, founded it. The Village of Azua in Compostella, in the coast of the South, foure and twentie leagues from Saint Dominicke to the West, in his borders are many sugar Mills; it was peopled by the President James Vellazques, it was called Compostella by a Gallizian Knight, which held an Heritage in that situation, and Azua is the name of the place which the Indians had there. The first that carried sugar Canes to the Indies, and began to make triall of them there, was one Atiença, and the Bachellor Velosa. The Village of Yaguana, which they call Santa Marie of the Port, seated on the Westerne coast of the Iland, is fiftie or sixtie leagues from Saint Dominicke, as betweene the North and the West; the chiefe Knight Nicholas of Ovando did people it.

The Citie of the Conception of the Valley, is in the Kingdome of Guarinoex, which the first Admirall Don Christopher Collon built, neere to the which he obtayned

*Peso is foure shillings English.

Salvalyon of Yguey.

The Village of Zeybo.

El Cotuy.

Azua.

Who carried to the Indies the sugar Canes.
La Yaguana.
[III. v. 862.]

Concecion de la Vega.

441

the victorie in the great battaile of the Valley Royall: it is twentie leagues from Saint Dominicke to the North-east, where is a Cathedrall Church (although there is no Prelate, for it is united to the Church of Saint Dominicke) it hath one Monasterie of religious Franciscans, where is *The wood of* the wood of the Crosse which the Indians could not burne, *the Crosse of* cut, nor overthrow, which hath done many miracles.

the Valley. Saint Jago de los Cavalleros is ten leagues from the *Saint Jago de* Citie de la Vega directly to the North-east; it was first *los Cavalleros.* a Fortresse which the first Admirall made in the Countries of the Cacique Guanacovel, for the securitie of the Valley, and the Fort Magdalene which was foure leagues off.

The chiefe Knight of Alcantara, Nichòlas of Ovando, *Puerto de* An. 1502. did people the Port of Plate in the North *Plata.* coasts, five and thirtie or about fortie leagues from Saint Dominicke, because the ships of Castile might more commodiously trafficke, and because it was no more then ten leagues from the great Valley, where in other ten leagues stood the Village of Saint James, and the Conception within sixteen, and within twelve the Mynes of Cibao, and it was of the Bishoprick of the Valley, the Port of Plate stands in little more then twentie degrees. *Monte* The Village of Monte-Christe, is in the coast of the *Christe.* North fourteene leagues, to the West of Port of Plate, and fortie from Saint Dominicke, is of the Bishoprick of the Valley; it hath a good Haven, and certaine salt Pits in it; Nicholas of Ovando did build it.

La Isabella. There was in old times in this Iland the Citie of Isabella, now disinhabited, which the first Admirall built the yeere *La Verapaz.* 1493. the Village of Verapaz in Xaragua, which James Velazques built in the yeere 1503. and the same yeere *Salvatierra.* peopled also Salvatierra of the Zabana, which signifieth Playnes and Pastures, in the Indian language: and that Province is plaine and faire. Hee also peopled (betweene the two mightie Rivers Neyba and Yaqui) the Village of *The* Saint John of the Maguana, in the middest of the Iland, *Maguana.* where the Church continueth yet; and heere reigned Coanabo, who tooke Alfonso de Oieda. Hee also planted

Villanueva de Yaquime upon the Haven, where Oieda *Villanueva.*
cast himselfe to swim, being prisoner in a ship, with two
paire of fetters; and it stands in the South coast, which
the Admirall did call the Coast and Haven of Brasile.
The Village of Bonao is neere unto Cotvy, which the *El Bonao.*
first Admirall also built, where hee made a Fort for the
securitie of the Mynes, which were the first that were
found in this Iland. The Village of Bonaventure is eight *La Buenaven-*
leagues from Saint Dominicke to the North, and Lares *tura.*
de Guahaba, which Nicholas of Ovando peopled, being
Comendador Lares.

This Iland flourished so much, that there were in it
fourteene thousand Castillanes, many of them Noble *14000.*
people, and the Plantations of other parts which happened *Spaniards*
afterward, caused it to be disinhabited; for from it, and *there were in*
from the Iland of Cuba, went all the substance for the *at her*
new Countreyes that were found. *beginning.*

The Ports, Roades, Capes, and Points most famous, *Ports &*
and the Ilands pertayning to the Coast of this Iland, are *Points most*
in the South Coast, the Point of Nizao, ten leagues from *notable.*
Saint Dominicke to the West. The Port of Ocoa, eighteene, which is a Bay where the Fleets which goe for
Nova Espania doe anchor and take refreshing, when they
doe not anchor in the nooke of Zepezepin, which is neere
unto it, or in another which they call the Faire Haven, *Puerta*
two leagues before they come to Ocoa. Azua a Port and *Hermoso.*
Towne twentie foure leagues beyond Ocoa la Calongia, a
large Point thirtie leagues, right against the Ilands of
Boata and Altobelo, five leagues from the Coast, and the
Beatados. Yaquimo about thirtie foure more to the West,
and Abaque, an Iland neere the Cape of Tiburon, the
furthest West of Hispaniola: la Nabaza ten leagues to
the Sea East and West from the Cape, and Cape Rojo
twelve leagues from it to the North: the Rookes, or
Hermanos Trees, Isle Oucillos neere the Coast that turneth
to the East: Caymito another little Iland betweene these,
and Guanabo another Iland of eight leagues in length,
in the nooke of Yaguana. The Port and Cape of Saint

Nicholas, the furthest West on the North side of the Iland. A little further the Port of * Mosquitos, in the North Coast, and twentie leagues forward the Port of Valparayso, or of the Conception, North and South, with the Tortuga an Iland neere the Coast of five leagues in length: Port Royall twelve leagues to the West from Monte-Christe, which is as much, or a little more before Isabela, and this from the Port of Plate, other twelve leagues: Cabo Frances, and Cabo del Cabron, in the turning, which the Coast maketh to the East, before the Gulfe of Samana, which entreth five or sixe leagues the Land inward, unto the place where the Towne of Sancta Cruz stood. And in the River of Samana, was the first time that Armes were taken against the men of the Indies; because they would have done violence to the first Admirall. The Cape of Deceit, (Cabo del Enganno) is the furthest West of the Iland where the Coast returneth by the South to the West, at the beginning of the which stands the Saona, an Iland which the fleets doe reknowledge, when they goe, and somewhat more towards Saint Dominicke is another little Iland, which is called Saint Katherine; and all the names rehearsed were given by the first Admirall.

The Iland of Cuba which first was called Juana, or Joane, by the Father Don Juan, and after it was commanded to be called Fernandina by his Father. The Captaine Sebastian of Ocampo, made an end of compassing the yeere of our Lord 1508. by order of Nicholas of Ovando: for untill then it was not wholly believed that it was Land, and the yeere 1511. the President James Velazques went over with three hundred Spaniards, by order of the second Admirall to pacifie it. It hath two hundred and thirty leagues from the Cape of Saint Antonie, unto the Point of Mayzi, going by Land, although by the Sunne, and by water there are not so many. It hath in breadth from the Cape of Crosses, to the Port of Manati, fortie five leagues, and then it beginneth to streighten, and goeth to the last Cape, or

Occidentall Point, where it is narrow, of twelve leagues, little more or lesse, from Matamano to the Avana. Her situation is within the Tropicke of Cancer, from twentie to twentie one degrees, the Countrey is almost all plaine, with many Forrests, and thicke Woods : from the Easterne Point of Mayci, for thirtie leagues it hath most high Mountaynes, and likewise in the middest it hath some, and there runne from them to the North, and to the South, very pleasant Rivers, with great store of fish. On the South side it hath the little Ilands, which the first Admirall called the Queenes Garden, and the other on the North side, which James Velazquez called the Kings Garden, the trees are of many differences, and wild Vines as bigge as a man : they gather no Wheate nor other Seedes of Spaine, but great abundance of Cattle : it hath great Copper Mynes, and of Gold, and it is found in the Rivers, though it be base in the touch.

James Velazquez peopled first the Citie of Saint James *S. Jago.* in the South Coast, fortie leagues from the Cape of Tiburon, which is in Hispaniola, and two leagues from the Sea, neere to a Port, one of the best in the World, for securitie and greatnesse. The Citie came to have two thousand Inhabitants; now it hath few with a Governours Deputie : the Cathedrall Suffragane to Saint Domingo, is resident in it, and a Monastery of Franciscan Friers. The Village of Baracoa, is a Towne furthest East of the *Baracoa.* Iland of Cuba, at the beginning of the North Coast 60. leagues from the Citie of S. James toward the East North-east, which was also an inhabiting of the President James Velazquez. The Village of Bayamo, which *Bayamo.* James Velazquez also built, is 20. leagues from S. James to the North-west, it is the soundest Town of the Iland, of a more open soyle, and of a good disposition. The Village and Port of the Prince, in the Coast of the North, *Puerta del* is about fortie leagues from Saint James to the North- *Principe.* west. The Village of Sancti Spiritus, is a Port on the *Sancti* South side, betweene the Trinidad, and the Cayo de Basco *Spiritus.*

Porcallo, of Figueroa, about fiftie leagues from Saint James, a Colonie of James Velazquez.

El Albana, or
the Havana. The Village and Port of Saint Christopher of the Abana, is in the North Coast, almost opposite to Florida, in twentie two degrees and an halfe in height, of more then sixe hundred Housholds; where the Governour resides and the Officers Royall. The Port is marvellous in greatnesse and securitie, especially since that King Philip the Second, the prudent, sent the Campe-master John of Texeda, and Baptista Antonelli, to fortifie it: in it all the Fleetes of the Indies doe meete for to come for Spaine Puerto de
Carennas. in company. It was first called the Port of Carennas: and James Velazquez built this Village, and all the rest of the Iland, with the assistance of the Father Bartolome de las Casas, which afterward became a Dominicke Frier, and Bishop of Chiapa.

The Ports and Capes, and point of the Coast of Cuba, and the Ilands belonging to it besides those which are rehearsed are in the South Coast, the Port of the Citie of Saint James in twentie degrees, and twentie five leagues to the West: the Port of Sancti Spiritus, Cape of the Crosse twelve leagues forward, and the Queenes Gardens, which is a great shelfe of Ilands and shoales: the Port of Trinitie in twentie one degrees, about thirtie leagues from the Cape of the Crosse, and ten more to the West, the Gulfe of Xagua, a great defence with some Ilands, in the middest, and forward the Two Sisters, two Ilands at the beginning of the great shelfe, and Ilands, and shoales, which they call Camarco, betweene the Coast and the Ilands, which is of ten leagues in length, and seven in breadth twelve leagues from the Cape of Correntes, which is as many from the Cape of Saint Antonie, the furthest West of this Iland. In the North Coast standeth Wherefore it
was called the
Slaughters. the Port of Abana, and thirtie leagues to the East is the Port of Slaughters where was a Towne, and was called de Matanças, of the Slaughters, because the Indians killed certaine Spaniards, which they carried in their Canoose under securitie to the other side, only one escaping, and

two women whom they kept sometime with them. From
the * Matanças to the Port of Yucanaca, are fiftie leagues   *Or
to the Kings Garden, which is a great shelfe of little   Slaughters.
Illets and shoales, and at the end of the Iland Obahava,
eight leagues before the Port of the Prince, foure or six
from the Port of Fernando Alanso, and six to the East
of this, Cubana which is a point. The Port of Varocoa
is about twentie leagues before the point of Maizi, the
farthest West of Cuba, and the hidden Port and Gulfe
neere to Cape ᶠ Roio, in the South-coast, about twentie   ᶠ Or Red.
leagues from the Port of Pidgeons, which is about ten
leagues from the Port of Saint James.

THe Iland of Jamayca was so abundant of victuals,   [III. v. 864.]
and breedings, that it gave great provision of Cotton,   Chap. 7.
Horses, Swine, and Cozabi, for the new Discoveries, and   Of the Ilands
the first Admirall called it Saint James, when hee discovered   of Jamayca,
it: and the first that passed to inhabit it, was the Captayne   S. John, the
John Esquivell, the yeere 1509. by order of the second   Lucayos, &
Admirall Don Diego Colon. It stands in seventeene   the Caniballs.
degrees and an halfe of altitude in the middest of it, and
twentie leagues from Cuba to the South, and as many
from Hispaniola, direct to the West. It hath in compasse
one hundred and fiftie leagues, it hath East and West
fiftie, and twentie in breadth. There are in it three
Villages, Sivill in which is the Seat of the Colledge, toward
the North Coast somewhat Westerly; John Squivell a   Sivill, Melilla,
Gentleman of Sivill peopled it: Melilla, which stands in   & Oriston,
the North Coast, fourteene leagues from Sivill to the   inhabitings of
East: Oristan in the South Coast towards the West four-   Jamayca.
teene leagues from Sivill, and are Plantations of the
President Francisco de Garay, which governed in it. But
of the Towne de la Vega, whence the Admirals Lords
of this Iland tooke the Title of Dukes, nor of other two
Plantations painted in some Maps, there is no notice.
There is in the Coast of this Iland, the Point of   Cape of
Morauta the uttermost West of it, by the North Coast   Morauta.
ten leagues to the West, the Port of Jauta, and tenne

leagues forward the Port of Melilla, where they say the
first Admirall arrived, and called it Santa Gloria, when
hee returned lost from Veragua; and heere happened to
him the mutiny of the Porras of Sivill: and it was the
The first civill first Civill Warre of the Indies. Other ten leagues thence
warre among standeth the Port of Sivill, before the Point Negrillo,
the Spaniards, from whence the Coast windeth, unto the Cabo de Falcon,
was in neere to Oristan, and goeth by the South to the Port of
Jamayca. Guayano. And five leagues from this Coast, are the
Harmingas, a dangerous shoale, and seven leagues further
las Vivoras, small Ilands compassed with shoales, and to
the South of them the Serrana, and a little Iland compassed
with shoales, with other foure or five neere unto it, and
to the North-west of it, the Serranilla, and to the West
of it the Roncador, another Rocke, and to the South-west
of it, Saint Andrewes, an Iland compassed with shoales
North and South, with Nombre de Dios, about fortie
leagues from it, and neere from thence another called
[n] *Or Lizards.* Sancta Catilina; the [n] Caymanes directly West from
[o] *Or Negrillo.* Jamayca, twentie five leagues from the little [o] Blackmoore,
which are two little Ilands six leagues the one from the
other, and the great Cayman another Iland of seven
leagues in length, fifteene leagues from the Caymanes to
the West, and to the North Coast, betweene Cuba and
[p] *Or open the* Hispaniola, another shoale which is called [p] Abre-ojo.
eye. The Iland of Saint John of Port Rico, which the Indians
S. Juan de called Barriquen, lyeth betwixt twelve and fifteene leagues
puerto Rico. from Hispaniola, to the East, of fortie five leagues in
length, East and West, and from North to South, betwixt
twentie and thirtie, very plentifull of all that Hispaniola
hath, and of Millet, Yuca, and of Mynes of Gold. The
temperature is good, and almost one all the yeere, except
in December and January. There is in it three Spanish
Townes with a Government, and a Bishoppricke: the
President John Ponce of Lion passed to discover this
Iland the yeere 1508. being Governour in the Province
of Yguey, for Nicholas of Ovando in Hispaniola, and
returned the yeere 1510. by order of the King to people

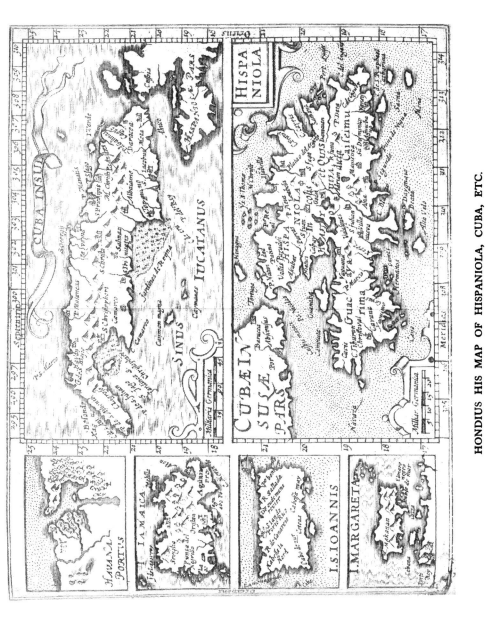

HONDIUS HIS MAP OF HISPANIOLA, CUBA, ETC.

it. The Citie of Saint John, is in the beginning of the *S. John.*
North Coast, on the East side in eighteene degrees of
height, and they call it of Port Rico, for the excellencie
of the Haven. The Bishop and the Governour are
resident in it, and the Officers of the Kings Revenues:
and it is Suffragane to Saint Domingo. Arrecibo stands *The Arrecibo.*
thirtie leagues to the West from Port Rico: the Towne
of Guadianilla, or Saint German the New, in the Westerne *Guadianilla.*
Coast three and thirtie leagues from Port Rico to the *S. German.*
South-west.

There was in old time in this Iland another Towne
which was called Guanica, in the South Coast, at the end
of it where now is the Port of Mosquitos, which is very
good, from whence it was removed to another situation
of the Westerne Coast, which they call Aguada, or the
Watering, with name of Soto-Mayor: there is in this
Iland a row of Mountaynes, that divide it in the middest
East and West unto the Sea, and Borders of Saint German,
and heere is found the Tree called Tabernaculo, which *The tree*
yeeldeth white Rozen, like Gumme-Anime, and it serveth *Tabernacle.*
for Pitch for the ships, and for fire or light, and it is
medicinable to take out the colde or numnesse, and to
cure wounds.

There are few Ports in this Iland, for all the Coast of
the North is very foule with shoales, and Rockes: those
that are, are to the East from the Port of Saint John. The
River of Luysa, and that which they call Canoba, and la *The havens of*
Cabeça; the farthest East point of the Iland, neere to *this Iland.*
the Hill of the Loquillos, and in it a Port which they
call Saint James; three leagues further is another called
Yabucoa, and three leagues from the Coast, on this side
of the passage, is a little Illet, and at the beginning of
the South passage, another which they call Boyqui, and
forward the Iland of Saint Anne, Guayama a Port, and
afterward the Rivers Neabon, and Xavia, six leagues
before the Port of Guadianilla, two leagues to the East
of the River of Mosquitos, in whose mouth is the River
called Guanica, and six leagues from it, the Cape Roio,

the furthest West of the South Coast: and to the West of it, toward Hispaniola is the Iland of Mona, and to the North of it the Manico, and Zecheo, other two little Ilands: the Port of Pines, and the Port of Mayaguez, and the Bay of Saint German the old, and the mouth of the River Guanabo, or the Watering, and that of Guahataca more forward, and afterward in the North Coast, that of Camay, and of Cibuco, and Toa, neere to Port Rico, and in the middest of the Coast of the South Sea, leaning unto it the Haberianas, foure or five little *Who carried* Ilands. There is also much Ginger gathered in this Iland, *the Ginger to* which is a Root like unto Madder, or Saffron, which *the Ilands of* the Portugals brought from the East, to this Iland of *Barlovento.* Barlovento.

The Ilands which are to the North of Saint John, Hispaniola, and Cuba, of which none is inhabited with *The Ilands of* Spaniards, are called the Lucayos. One the most Septen- *the Lucayos.* trionall, is above twentie seven degrees of altitude, which is called Lucayoneque, or Yucayoneque, which hath almost to the West Bahama another Iland in twentie six degrees and an halfe, of thirteene leagues in length, and eight *Where the* in breadth, from whence the Channell of Bahama betweene *Channell of* Florida and the shoales Delos Mimbres taketh the name, *Bahama is.* whereby the Currents of the Sea doe goe so swift to the *Admirable* North, that although the wind be prosperous the ships *Current.* cannot enter it, and although they be contrary they goe with the Currents.

Baxos de The shelves of Bimini, are so called of an Iland in the *Bimini.* middest of them, of five leagues in length, which the first Admirall gave the name the first time he came to Cuba, and it is that which John Paul of Lyon did agree to inhabit. Abacoa, is another in the middest of the said shelfe of twelve leagues in length: Cigateo of twentie five. Curateo, another small Iland in twentie sixe degrees: and Guanima fifteene leagues of length, and ten *Guanahani the* in breadth, and neere unto it Guanahani, the first Land *first Land that* of the Indes, which the first Admirall discovered, which *was discovered* he called Saint Saviour; Yuma of twentie leagues, and *in the Indes.*

eight in breadth, in twentie foure degrees and an halfe, which the Admirall named Isabella, in honour of the famous Queene Donna Isabella his particular Protectresse, and that gave him this Discoverie. Jumeto in twentie three degrees and an halfe, fifteene leagues in length, to the North of Hispaniola. Samana seven leagues over, betweene Jumeto and Guanima, three square of eight leagues in length, in twentie foure degrees, Yabaque of ten leagues, in twentie two degrees and an halfe. Mira-par-vos, are three little Ilands in triangle, compassed with shelves, to the South of Jumeto. Mayaguava, twentie leagues in length and ten in breadth, in twentie three degrees. Yuagua of ten leagues, in twentie degrees and an halfe. The Caycos, an Iland of five leagues, in twentie one degrees, and to the North of it is another, called Hamava, and another Conciva. Maçarey stands in twentie degrees compassed with shelves. Abreojo is a great shelfe of fifteene leagues, the middest of it in twentie degrees, and among these Ilands are many little ones without name.

The Ilands that are from the Iland of Saint John of Porte-Rico, to the East of it, toward the coast of Terra firme, were called the Canibals, by the many * Caribes, eaters of humaine flesh that were in them: and in their language, Canibal, is to say Valiant man; for they were held for such of the other Indians. All these Ilands are dangerous for shelves, and the nearest to Saint John, are Sancta Cruz, to the South-west from it, in 16. degrees, and a halfe of sixteene leagues, and Saba las Virgines, two little illets compassed with shelves, and other eight or ten Ilands, the greatest of ten leagues: Virgen gorda, and the Blancos or White Ilands, Westward from Virgen gorda, La Ane gada, or seven leagues in length, in 18. degrees and a halfe compassed with shelves, as Sambrero is, a little Iland neere unto it: and these Ilands which are called the Weather Ilands or Barlovento, the first Admirall discovered: and in particular, the men of Sancta Cruz, and others, had a custome to goe and hunt for

The Canibals.
Or Indian Canibals.
What a Caniball signifieth.

Men hunters. men to the Iland of Saint John, for to eate, and at this
day they of Dominica doe it. They did eate no women,
but kept them for slaves. Now they say, that within this
Frier unwhol- little while, they of Dominica did eate a Fryer, and that
some food. all they which did eate his flesh, had such a fluxe, that
some dyed, and that therefore they have left eating humane
flesh: and it may be, because instead of men, with lesse
danger, they steale Kine and Mares, for the great quantitie
there is of them, and with this they satisfie their raging
appetite.

Anguilla hath ten leagues of length, it standeth in 18.
degrees. Saint Martin in 17. degrees and a halfe, it is
of sixteene leagues, compassed with little Illets: and neere
unto it Saint Eustace, Saint Bartholomew, and Saint
Christopher, every one of tenne leagues. The Barbada
in 17. degrees and a halfe, compassed with shelves, neere
to the Redouda and the Snowes or Nieves, and of
Mouserrate, of five leagues every one, in 15. degrees
and a halfe. The Antigua, Guadalupe, and Todos Santos,
from 14. to 15. degrees. The Desseada to the East of
Guadalupe, about six leagues, the first which the Admirall
Don Christopher discovered, in the second Voyage that
he made to the Indies, in 14. degrees and a halfe, for
which the fleete goe alwayes from the Canaries. Mari-
galaute, the name of the Shippe the Admirall had, five
leagues to the South-west from the Desired, and from
the Dominica, in 13. degrees, twelve leagues in length,
where the Fleetes take in water and wood, for it hath good
roades, although with danger of the Canibals. Neere
unto Dominica to the South, stands Matinino, Sancta
Lucie, and the Barbudos, the which because they fall on
the left hand of the Fleetes, when they goe, they call
them already of the Ilands of the Leeward (de Sotavento)
which appertaine to the coast of Terra firme: and of them
the greatest, the first, and the most Orientall is the
[III. v. 866.] Trinidad, neere two hundred leagues from Hispaniola,
North and South with the Dominica, about sixtie leagues
from it. It hath fiftie leagues in length East and West,

and almost thirty in breadth. The Admirall discovered it the yeare 1498. the third Voyage that he made to the Indies, and called it the Trinitie, because having great trouble in the Voyage, he had promised to God to give such a name to the first Land that he should finde, and presently the Mariner that was in the top, saw three points of Land, whereby the name fitted every way to his vowe: then hee discovered also the mouthes of the Dragon, and of the Serpent, the gulfe of Paria, and all the firme Land unto Cumana, which injustly Americus Vesputio claimes to himselfe, whose name unworthily is given to the port which they call Peninsula Australis or Indies of the South. This Iland of Trinidad is knowne that it is no good Countrie, though it hath many Indians; it hath thirtie five leagues of longitude, and others say more, and twentie five of latitude, it stands in 8. degrees: the most orientall part of it, is a point on the North side, which is called de la Galera: and to the North of it a small Iland, compassed with little Iles, which they call Tabago: and in the South coast a Cape which they call the Round Point: at the East, the point of Anguilla, at the West in the gulfe of Paria, which is that that is from the Iland to Terra firme, which may be eight leagues of distance, because the firme Land maketh an oblique semicircle, as a Diadem; and in the entrance of the East is the distance recited; in the entrance of the West, the straightnes is much, and with great depth, and two little Ilands at the end of the North coast; by the West, which is called the Dragons mouth: and to the North S. Vincent, and Granada, other two little Ilands.

The Iland of Margarita, so named by Christopher Colon, the first Admirall (as also all the rest, a most sufficient proofe of the Finder, to the confusion of those which deprived him of the glory of the discoverie of the firme Land, attributing it to themselves, although changing the times) it is twentie leagues from Trinidad Westward, and one hundred and seventy from Hispaniola: it hath sixteen leagues in length East and West, and yet some say twenty, and the halfe in breadth; it hath no store of water, although it is very plentifull of Pastures for Cattle. There is in it two Townes, one neare the Sea, which reacheth to a fortresse where the Governour is resident, and another two leagues within the Land, which is called the Valley of Sancta Lucie: there is in his coast a good port, and a nooke, and many beds of Pearles, whither the fishing of them is removed, which before was in Cubagua, and they say it went away from thence, for the rumour of the ordnance of the many Shippes that *Wherefore* resorted to this Iland, to the trafficke of the Pearles, which *men do say* was very great. Cubagua stands one league from Mar-*that the fishing* garita to the East, there is no water in it, and yet the new *of the Pearles* Cadiz was built there, and they carried their water seven *passed from the* leagues, from the River of Cumana. To the East of *Iland of* Cubagua are foure little Illets, close by the shoare, which *Cubagua.* the first Admirall called Los * Frayles: and to the East **Or the* between them and Granada, other foure or five, which he *Friers.* called (Los Testigos) the Witnesses, and to the West after Cubagua, another little Iland which he named (Tortuga) the Tortoyse, neere to the point of Araya: and from hence the discovery being made from below Paria, he went to Hispaniola, with a purpose to finish the discovery of Terra firme: and as here after shall be seene, hee went after to discover, and found the Ilands of the Guanaios, and from before Veragua, untill he passed Nombre de Dios. The Officers and Royall treasure are in Margarita: and it, and the Iland of Cubagua, are in *Chap. 8.* eleven degrees, a little more.

Of Venezuela,
river of
Hacha, new THe Government of Venezuela parteth the bounds *Florida, and* in the coast of Terra firme, to the East, with the *Gulfe of Nova* new Andaluzia, from whence to the River of Hacha, and *Hispania,* Government of Sancta Martha, with which it joyneth *which is the* by the West, is an hundred and thirty leagues, and within *rest that* the Land about eightie, unto the bounds of the new King-*remaineth of* dome of Granada. In this Countrie are vaines of Gold *the limits of* of more then two and twentie carracts and a halfe: it is *this Counsell.*

plentifull of Wheate, because there is two harvests in the yeare, and most abundance of all kinde of Cattle, great and small. There goeth from this Province great store of Meale, Bisket, Cheese, Bacon, and much Cotten-linnen: and in the port of Guayra, in the Province of Caracas, are laden many Cowe-Hides, and Sarsaparilla. There is in it eight Spanish Townes: and the name Venezuela was given it, because when the Belzares, Almaines, went to governe in this Province the yeare 1528. by a covenant which they made with the Emperour, they thought to inhabit in a Rocke and hils that are in the mouth of the *Wherefore it* Lake of Maracaybo, where it falleth in the Sea, a Towne *was called* which they named Venezuela. It stands in 8. degrees, *Venezuela, or* a little more, and from hence the Government tooke the *little Venice.* name. His first Towne is the Citie of Coro, which the *The Citie of* Indians call Coriana, which commonly they call now *Coro.* Venezuela, it stands in 11. degrees of altitude, and 79. degrees one third part from the Meridian of Toledo, one thousand and five hundred leagues from it: here the Governor is wont to be resident, and there is the Cathedrall Church suffragane to the Archbishop of S. Dominicke. John of Ampues built first this Citie, and then those that went for the Belzares made their abode in it, the first was Ambrose Alsinger: it is so healthfull, and of so good an ayre, that there is no neede of Physitians.

The second place is our Lady of Carvalleda, in the *Our Lady of* Province of Caracas, neere to the Sea, East from Coro *Carvalleda.* eightie leagues, and with a bad Haven: Don Francisco Faiardo built it the yeare 1560. which went for that [III. v. 867.] purpose from the Margarita. S. James of Lyon in the same Province, seven leagues within the Land, and three from Carvalleda to the South, and sixtie from Coro, where at this time the Governour is most resident. The new Valencia sixtie leagues from Coro, and twentie five from S. James of Lyon, seven from the port of Burburata, The *S. Jago de* Captaine Villacinda peopled it. The new Xerez about *Leon.* fifteene leagues, almost South from the new Valencia, and *Xerez.* twentie from the new Segovia, and sixtie from Coro to the *Segovia.*

South-east, a new Towne. The new Segovias, in the Province of Bariquizimito, twentie leagues from Xerez to the South, and tenne from Tucuyo, and eightie from Coro to the South-east, where the Officers royall, the Governour, and the Lieutenant are resident at times: John of Villegas peopled it in the yeare 1552. The Citie of Tucuyo is famous, because in it they slew the tyrant Lope of Aguirre, it stands tenne leagues from Segovia, to the South-west, eightie five from Coro; it is the habi-

tation of the Captaine Carvajal. Truxillo, or our Ladie of Peace, in the Province of Cuycas, about eightie leagues almost to the South, direct from Coro, somewhat to the East, and twentie five from Tucuyo, directly to the West.

The Auditor Vallejo discovered this the yeare 1549, the Bacheller Tollosa being Governour in it: and the yeare 1559. the Captaine James Garcia of Paredes inhabited Truxillo: and there may be in this Government more then 100000. Indies tributaries, and in them are not comprehended from eighteene under, nor above fiftie yeares, because the supreme Counsell of the Indies hath provided, that in no place of this Orbe, these doe pay tribute: and because daily they increase and diminish in number, it cannot be said precisely and perfectly how many there are.

The Lake of Maracaybo, which the Castilanes call of our Lady, is of fresh water, it entreth fortie leagues within the Land, from the Sea, and hath more then tenne in breadth, and eighty in compasse, with many Townes upon his Borders: in the end of it entreth a River that descendeth from the new Kingdome of Granada, by the which, and the Lake, Marchandise are transported which came to the new Kingdome of Castile, and to other places; some of the men of this Lake doe live in Boates, their houses being made in the Trees within the water, and at the Border, whence it tooke also at the first, the name of Venezuela; sayling by some parts of this Lake, ye can see no Land: there enter into it other great Rivers, it runneth to the Sea, it hath about halfe a league of mouth, and in it the shoale and rocks abovesaid.

The Ports, Capes, and Points of the coast of this Government, and those annexed unto it, are to the West, Marcapava, the Urchila, an Iland against the River Oynare, neere to another called Rocke of the Ilets, and afterward the Cape of the Codera, and Puerto Flechardo, and the haven of Sardinas or Pilchers: and opposite the Ile of Aves or Birds, before Burburata, a marvellous haven, which the Bachiler Tolosa peopled, and is a Scale or Port for the new Kingdome (Nuevo Reyno) & Provinces of Peru, and after that is Gulfo triste, and to the North of the Bonayre, an Iland of ten leagues in length, and eight in breadth, and afterward Punta seca, and right against it Curacao, and a little forward Curacaute, foureteene leagues in length, right against the Cape of S. Roman to the South of the Iland of Aruba. S. Roman entreth twentie leagues into the Sea, it standeth twelve from Coro, the Indians doe call it Paraguana, it lacketh a little to be an Iland: it may have in compasse twenty five leagues and more of plaine ground, with a Mountaine almost in the middest: it is discovered a great way into the Sea. There is at the beginning of the Gulfe of Venezuela, the entrance and channell of the Lake of Maracaybo, and at the entrance of it the River Mitare, and to the West the Monkes, three little Ilets close by the Point and Cape of Coquibocoa, where onely in all the Indies was found waight and touch for the Gold, and afterwards the deepe Baye (Balna Honda) and the Portete, the Cape de Vela, which the Captaine Alfonsus of Ojeda named, when Americo Vespucio went with him the first time, much after that the Admirall discovered this coast, which stands in 12. degrees, somewhat more. And there is from the Cape de Vela, to the River of Hache eighteene leagues, without any stone in them, nor water, but raine water. This Government remained destroyed, since the time of the Almaines, because they would not inhabit, onely seeke to make slaves, and to waste the Countrie.

They called first the River of Hache, our Ladie of the Snowes, and after of the Remedies, neere unto the Sea, betweene Venezuela, and Sancta Marta to the East, thirtie leagues from it, and sixtie from Coro to the West, North and South with the Cape de Vela, with eight leagues of bounds betweene Venezuela and Sancta Marta, without showes of Gold. It is governed by Alcaldes immediate to the Counsell of Hispaniola, and the Spiritualtie is of the Bishopricke of Sancta Marta. The Towne is 1000. paces from the Sea, on a little hill: the Haven hath the North for travers, it is a most fertile Countrie, and yeeldeth whatsoever is in Castile: there are many Tigers, Beares, Ants, and Lizards in the Rivers, much Gold, and Stones of divers vertues, for the Spleene, the Kidneys, for the Milt, and Flux, and they have good Salt-pits. Nicolas Federman for the Belzares, was he that began to inhabit this Towne. The government of Serpai, which they call the new Andaluzia, and in the Indian Language Guayana, extends the limits. From the Iland of Margarita unto the river Marauyon, three hundred leagues to the East, and as many North and South within the Land, wherein [III. v. 868.] the Indians Omagues are included, and the Omygas, with the Provinces of Dorodo, to the south of this Government, wherein falleth by the Coast the Province of Maracapana, in the bounds of Veneculela, where the mouths of Sancta Fe were inhabited, in whose Borders is the knob of Unare, and neere unto it a great Lake with great store of fish and salt, and the Indians which are called of Perito, twentie leagues within the Land, and the Indians Paleuques, so called for the Poles wherewith they fortified themselves, and the Province of Cumana, North and South with the Margarita, where is a Towne of Spaniards, which is called new Cordova, which the Captayne Gonçalo of Ocampo built, when he went to chastise the Indians of Cumana, for the destruction of the Monastery of the Religious Franciscans. And to the East of the Iland of Trinidad, and the River of Saint John of the Amazones, is the Province of the Indians Arvacas, part

of the Caniballs, and all Warlike, that never are quiet
or peaceable.

After the point of Paria, which stands in seven degrees,
and the Dragons Mouth neere unto Trinidad stands the
point Del Gallo, or Anegada, to the South of the Trinitie,
and the River of Paria, or Orivico, which some call
Yuyapari; and others will have that these two, and
the River of Saint John, and of Orellana be all one
thing, and also the Marauyon; but in this they are
deceived. There be other Rivers in the Province of the
Arvacas that are well knowne, the River of Saint John,
or of Orellana springeth in the Andes of Peru, right
against Cuzco, from whence it runneth fifteene hundred
leagues, or more, winding under the Equinoctiall, by
Countreyes well inhabited, though not well discovered,
till it came to run into the North Sea, whose mouth hath
in breadth fiftie leagues; and in the first five hundred from
the mouth upward, many Ilands inhabited; and eightie
or a hundred leagues more to the West, stands the River *River*
of Morauyon, almost in the bounds whereby passeth the *Morauion.*
Line of the Division betweene Castile and Portugall, and
is great and terrible, having fifteene leagues of mouth,
and the streame commeth from the parts of the South, and
the Provinces of Brasill, and they say that the spring is
under Popayau, and the bounds of the new Kingdome of
Granada.

Seven leagues from Cumana stands the Iland of *The Iland of*
Cubagua, where stood as was said, the new Cadiz which *Cubagua.*
was disinhabited because the fishing for Pearles fayled:
this Iland had no water that could be drunke, nor trees,
nor beasts; for all is brackish, except those Hogges that *Strange Hogs.*
have the Navell in their backe-bone, and some small
Conies, and having so great inhabiting, they went seven
leagues to the river of Cumana for water, although there *An earthquake*
was an opinion that it bred webbes in the eyes. In this *in the coast of*
River and coast, hapned in the yeare 1530. the first of *Terra firme,*
the yeare
September, the haven being cleare, the Sea did rise foure *1530. very*
fadomes from his ordinary course, and entring into the *admirable.*

earth it began to shake, and the fortresse which the Captaine Jacome of Castellon had built by order of the Counsell of Hispaniola, fell, and the earth did open in many places, whereout sprang much salt water as blacke as inke, and did stinke of brimstone, and the mountaine of the gulfe of Cariaco remained open with a great rift: many houses fell, many people died drowned, and with

Margarita. feare, and taken with the earth quake. Margarita one league from Cubagua a more pleasant Iland, the Bachiller Marcelo of Villalobos did people it.

Florida. The Province and Government of Florida, bordering on the Counsell of Hispaniola, according to the Government of Peter Melendez, is all that which lyeth from the River of Palmes, which doth confine with the Government of Panuco in new Spaine, limits of the Counsell of Mexico, which is neere the tropicke in 22. degrees, unto the point of Bacallaos, which falleth in 48. degrees, and a halfe, in the which are 1258. leagues of Coast, and from thence to 73. degrees of altitude to the North by the Coast, and within the Land all that which hee discovereth. Of this hath beene coasted and discovered, from the River of Palmes unto the Point of Sancta Helena, and the River Jordan, which are about 600. leagues, it is a firme Land of a good climate, plentifull, and well inhabited in many places, as those that went through it with Hernando of Soto did know it, the yeare 1536. and 1537. John Pardo borne in Cuenca, went by Land from Florida to new Spaine, in lesse then two yeares, and it is the neerest Europe of any part of the Indies, & from the Bay of S. Joseph, which is eightie leagues from Panuco. There is also discovered unto New found Land, but that which is particularly taken for Florida, is the point that goeth into the Sea North and South, with the Iland of Cuba, of a hundred leagues in length, and twentie five

The spring in breadth East and West, and (when it is most) thirtie.
which John John Ponce of Lyon discovered it Anno 1512. on Easter
Ponce did seeke day, and for this cause he called it Florida: and after-
that renued the ward returned the yeere 1521. and retired wounded to
old men.

Cuba, where he dyed, leaving a report that he sought the Fountaine or River which the Indians said that old men washing themselves therin, became yong. This Province is according to the temperature of Castile, and many fruits were found there like the fruits of Spain, and it seemeth fit for Cattle and Corne. There is no Gould, neither seemeth that the Indians did know it, nor Silver; for it hath beene seene that they have found the Chests with bars of it and money in their coasts, and made no account of it: yet Hernando de Soto, within the inward parts of the great River, found great abundance of Pearles.

They of Florida knew neither Gold, Silver, nor Monie.

There are but two Fortresses in this Province with men in Garison, both in the Coast that looketh to the East: the one is called Saint Marke, in the point of Saint Helena, about one hundred leagues from the Havana, and another of Saint Augustin, which is the principall, because the haven is good, and is neere the channell of Baliama. It stands about fiftie leagues from los Martyres, which are many little Ilands inhabited, which are neare the point of Florida, whereby it joyneth most with the Iland of Cuba, a league and a halfe, and lesse, the one from the other, with a ranke of shelves with mouthes, in twentie three or twentie foure leagues, which these Martyres have in length; whose beginning on the West side, is called the Point of the Martyres, and to the East, the Head of the Martyres; and there is an Iland of foureteene leagues in length, and very narrow, the Point of it is the first of Terra firme to the East, in 24. degrees and a halfe, where a Towne of Spaniards was built, which continued not, and to the North, almost direct the River Ays, and more Northward in 28. degrees, the Point of the Caves, and forward the River of * Gnats, before the River of Matanca, which is so called by that which Peter Melendez did to the Captaine Ribao, and his Frenchmen: and the Point of S. Augustin in 29. degrees three quarters, and ten leagues from thence the River of S. Mathew, from whence the Coast turneth to the North

[III. v. 869.]

Ports, Capes, and Points of Florida.

*Or Mosquitos. Slaughter of the French in Florida. See Hak. 103.

North-east, all with the Ilands and Bays leaning unto it
unto the Cape, or Point of Saint Hellen, which stands in
32. degrees and a halfe, which was discovered by chance
the yeare 1520.

In all the rest of the Coast that is betweene the point
of Sancta Helena, by New found Land and the Bacallaos,
unto the Land of Labrador, which reacheth and passeth
the height of England, there is no Towne nor Government of Spaniards, although by divers times and Nations,
it hath beene discovered and Navigated, and it is knowne
there is above one thousand leagues journey of Land
without gold, and the more in height the worse, and lesse
habitable. There be many Rivers, and Ports, that because
they are not well knowne nor frequented, there is no
mention made but of the River of the * Stagges, by
another name of Sancta Marie, which is a very great and
maine River, almost in the midst of the Coast betweene
the Baccallaos, from whence the great River Ochelago
entreth within the Land toward the West, which divers
times the strangers have navigated, beleeving to have
found that way passage to new Spaine. And in the Coast
of Florida, which looketh to the West, are the * Tortoyses,
seven or eight Ilands together: and to the North of the
point of los Martyres, the Muspa in terra firme. And
thirteene leagues to the North, the Bay of Charles, by
another name of John Ponce of Lyon, and as much more
forward, the Bay of Tampa, thirtie three leagues from
the Bay of Tocobaga, by another name, of the Holy
Ghost, or de Mervelo, in twentie nine degrees and an
halfe of height, where beginneth that which properly is
called Florida. Many have thought, that by this side
of Florida, toward the land of Labrador, there might a
streit be found to communicate the North & the South
Seas together, saying that as it had beene found to the
South, there should be one to the North: but experience
doth shew, that the South passage is no streight, at the
least it is alreadie in doubt, and by the North untill now,
though it hath beene much sought for it hath not beene

found, and hee that went neerest to it was the President
Peter Melendez, by some conjectures.

All the Coast on the West side, unto the Government
of Panuco, which is above 300. leagues, is called The
Gulfe of New Spaine, wherein is no Towne of Spaniards, *The Gulfe of*
though it was given for a government to Pamphilo of *nova Espania.*
Narvaez, and to Hernando of Soto, and first to Francisco
de Garay, and of his people in particular. The Country
is very poore of victuals, and the people miserable, and
although in it are many Rivers and Ports, no mention is
made of them, because they are not well knowne. This
Gulfe hath two entrances: by the one the currents doe
enter furiously, betweene Yucatan and Cuba, and goe out
with a greater force betweene the same Iland of Cuba, and
the point of Florida, and running doe make the channell *The Channell*
of Bahama, which taketh his name of the Iland rehearsed. *of Bahama.*

THe second Audience which was setled in the Indies, *Chap. 9.*
is that of New Spaine, and Nunyo de Guzonau *Of the limits*
Cavallero de Guadalajara was the first President, till a *of the Councell*
Governour were provided, and because he gave no satis- *of Mexico.*
faction, there was another new Councell quickly sent,
and for President of it Don Sebastian Ramirez of Fuen- *Don Sebastian*
leal, which of a Judge of the Chancerie of Granada, went *Ramirez*
for President of the Councell of Saint Dominicke, and *Judge of*
Bishop of the Citie of the Conception of the Valley, a *Granada goeth*
person of great Learning, Vertue, and Valour. Hee had *of S.*
the charge of the Government, Justice, and disposition *Dominicke.*
of the goods Royall, the Warre remayning at the charge *Great*
of the Marquesse of the Valley, with order to communi- *conformity*
cate with the President, that which appertayned thereto; *betweene Don*
and betweene them was alwayes great conformitie. The *Ramirez and*
bounds of this Councell, on the one side doth not com- *Don Hernando*
prehend that which commonly is called New Spaine, and *Cortes.*
on the other it comprehendeth more, because the new
Gallicia, which is a Councell by it selfe, is part of New
Spaine.

The Province of Yucatan, falleth within the bounds

of it, which as now it is, may have in length about foure hundred leagues, from the furthest East of Yucatan, unto where it parteth bounds with the Councell of new Gallozia, and North and South, about two hundred from the end of the Government of Panuco unto the South Sea, his bounds remayning open on the North side, whose principall Provinces are the Archbishopricke of Mexico, the Bishoprickes of Mechoacan, and that of los Angelos, or Tlascala, and of Guaxaca, and of Chiapa, and the Governments of Panuco and Yucatan, with that of Tobosco, and for circuit or commerce, the Ilands Phillipinas, and the dispatch of the Navigation of China.

New Spaine. New Spaine is one of the best Provinces of the new World, and the most habitable in a good temper, having abundance and plentie of Corne, Millet, and Cattle, and all other necessaries for humane life, except Oyle and Wine, and although in many places of it there is Gold, Silver is most generall, whereof there are many good Mynes.

The Archbishopricke of Mexico, falleth betweene the Bishopricke of los Angelos, and that of Mechoacan, it hath in length North and South, one hundred and thirtie leagues, and in breadth eighteene, which it hath by the Coast of the South Sea, unto sixtie within the Land, wherein are included the Provinces of Mexico, and to the North-east of it Lateotlalpa, Meztitlau, Xilotepeque, and Panuco the most distant: and to the West, Matalzingo neere to Mexico, and Cultepeque the furthest off: and to the East, Tezcuco neere to Mexico: and to the South-east, Chalco, neere to that of Mexico: and to the South of it Suchimilco, the first, and after Tlaluc, and betweene South and South-west Coyxca, and Acapulco, the furthest to the South. There are no more in all but foure Townes of Spaniards, although in the Province of Mexico are *Tenoxtitlan.* many Spaniards dwelling in the Townes of the Indians. *Mexico described, it is* They called Mexico in old time, Tenoxtitlan; it stands *from Toledo* in nineteene degrees and an halfe of altitude, and one *1740. leagues.* hundred and three degrees of longitude from the Meridian

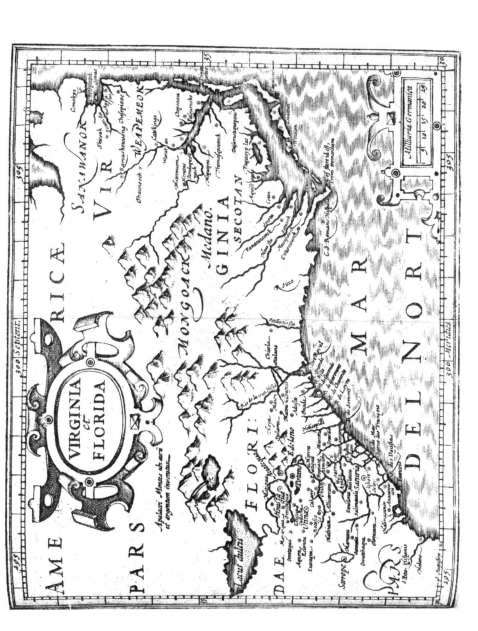

HONDIUS HIS MAP OF FLORIDA

of Toledo, from whence it may be distant by a direct Line, one thousand seven hundred and fortie leagues, which are eight houres of * Sunne: it stands in the middest of two great Lakes that doe compasse it, the one of salt water, because his bottome is Salt-petrish; the other fresh having fish, and voydeth into the Salt one; each is of five leagues in breadth, and eight in length, and both doe compasse thirtie three leagues. They goe into the Citie by three causies of halfe a league in length, and there are in it foure thousand Spaniards, and thirtie thousand Houses of Indians or more. In the foure ancient streets wherein the Citie was divided, in the time of their Paganisme, which at this day is called of Saint John, Saint Mary the Round, Saint Paul, and Saint Sebastian; and the Tlatelulco is the principall street which they call Saint James.

[III. v. 871.]

The Councell is Resident in Mexico, and the Vice-roy governeth in it, and three Judges, the Officers of the Revenue and Royall Treasure, a Founding House, and a Mint House, and the Archiepiscopall Metropolitane, that hath for Suffraganes the Bishoprickes of Tlascala, Guaxaca, Mechoacan, new Gallicia, Chiapa, Yucatan, Guatemala, Verapaz, and the Phillipinas. And Don Fernando Cortes was he that built this great Church, and set for Bases of the Pillars certayne Idols of stone which are seene to this day, and the Bishop, President and Governour of New Spaine, Don Sebastian Ramirez of Fuenleal, continued the building with great speed. The first Bishop of Mexico was Frier John de Zumarraga of the Order of Saint Francis, of great vertue and example, borne in Durango, in the Lordship of Biskeye, which also was the first Archbishop.

There are in Mexico Monasteries of Dominican, Franciscan, and Austine Friers, the company of Jesus, El Carmen, la Merced, the Bare-foot, and Trinitarie Friers; ten Monasteries of Nunnes, one Colledge of Indian children, and another of Arrepentidas, the Repentantes[m] and [n]Recogidas, or Retyred, and the Universitie, where

*That is, the Sunne riseth eight houres sooner at Toledo, then at Mexico: which seemes not justly calculated.

Suffraganes of the Arch-bishopricke of Mexico.

[m] Sc. of the life they led in the Stewes.
[n] From the World.

curious and learnedly the Sciences are read with other Colledges and Hospitals. And the Spaniards which

*Los ciento y cinco cabeceras de doctrina. I thinke he meaneth some Parishionall division, in each of which the Indians had their peculiar Priests and Schooles of priests to teach them religion. After in cap. 28 he cals them beneficios curados. Benefices, with Cure, as Personages.
[III. v. 872.]

inhabit the bordering Townes of the Indians, and Granges, are about three thousand, and there are reckoned about two hundred and fiftie Townes of Indians, in which the chiefe places of *Doctrine are one hundred and five : and in them and thereabouts are six thousand Granges, more then five hundred thousand tributarie Indians, and more then one hundred and fiftie Monasteries of Franciscan, Dominican, and Austine Friers. And the Doctrines (or Schooles) of Priests and Friers, to teach the Faith Catholike to the Indians, are without number, besides the Fathers of the Company, and Mercenarie Friers: there is also Resident in Mexico, the holy Office of the Inquisition, whereof we will intreat hereafter.

In the Coast bounding on this Archbishopricke towards the South Sea, and the Province of Acapulco, is the good Port of Acapulco, in seventeene degrees height, sixe leagues from the River Yopes, whereby the Archbishopricke is joyned with the Bishopricke of Tlascala. And other eight more to the West, the River of Citala, and other foure, the River of Mitla. In the Coast of the North, it hath that which falleth in the Government of Tanuco. In the limits of this Councell are the Mynes of Puchuca, fourteene leagues from Mexico, and the Mynes of Tasco twentie two, those of Ysmiquilpo, which are of Lead, twentie two, the Mynes of Talpuiana twentie foure, the Mynes of Temazcaltepeque eighteene, those of Cultepeque 22. those of Zacualpa twentie, those of Zupanguo 40. those of Guanaxato sixtie, those of Commaia, seven. From Guanaxuato: those of Achichica, eighteene from the Citie of los Angelos, and those of Gantla, or Zumatlan, and Saint Lewes of the Peace, and in them all there may bee above foure thousand Spaniards, which with industrie and labour doe attend these Mynes, all of Silver except one, which as hath beene said, is of Lead, and procuring that the Indians taking example of them, may live politickly : and the first that with marvellous cunning and wisdome, brought in the breedings of cattell and tillages, which have beene the mightiest meanes for the preservation of the Mynes, was the above said President Don Sebastian Ramirez of Fuenleal, originall and the foundation of all the good of those Realmes.

The Province of Panuco to the North of Mexico, Nunno of Guzman had in government: it hath fiftie leagues in breadth, and in length, and after it was incorporate with the limits of the Councell or Audience of Mexico.

The Countrey that looketh toward New Spaine is the best, plentifull of victuals, and hath some Gold. That which runneth toward Florida is miserable, from whence till yee come to his bounds, are more then five hundred leagues. This government hath three Spanish Townes, Panuco, in somewhat more then twentie three degrees, and by another name the Village of Saint Stephen of the Haven, which Gonçalo of Sandovall built, by order of the Marquesse Don Fernando Cortes, when they went to resist Francisco Garay, and to pacifie the Indians of Chila, the yeere 1520. and it standeth sixtie five leagues from Mexico to the North North-east, eight leagues from the Sea, neere to a River whose entry is a Haven: it is a chiefe Alcaldia, or Justiceship, provided by the Vice-roy of New Spaine. The Village of Saint James of the Valleyes, twentie five leagues from Panuco to the West.

The Village of Sant Luys de Tampico, eight leagues from Panuco to the North-east, neere to the Sea: and although in the Coast of this government are many Rivers, & some rode unto the River of Palmas, they are not knowne in the Gulfe of New Spain, but the River of Panuco, & his haven, which is not very good.

The Bishopricke of Tlascala, which by another name is called de los Angelos, betweene the Archbishopricke of Mexico, and the Bishopricke of Guaxaca, is of 100. leagues, and more in length, from the Coast of the South to that of the North, and betwixt the confines of the Archbishopricke, and of Guaxaca 80. and as many in breadth, by the Coast of the North Sea, and no more then

18. or 20. by that of the South. There is not in it all more then three Spanish Towns, which is the City or Towne of the Angels 22. leagues from Mexico to the East, somewhat inclining to the South, of 1500. housholds in foure streets: it is a Chiefe Justice-ship where the Cathedral Suffragane to the Archbishoprick of Mexico is Resident, with Monasteries of Dominicks, Franciscan, and Austine Friers, one of Nuns, & one Colledge of more then 500. Indian children, to be instructed, with 10000.

*The Bishop
Don Sebastian
Ramirez built
the Citie of
the Angels.*

Pezos rent, which the Bishop Don Sebastian Ramirez built, which sent the Batchelor Salmeron Auditor of the Councell to build this City, and although he had determined to have made it in Tlascala, he left it because he would not endamage the Indians, nor touch their Lands; for he had a great regard in generall to the good of the Indians, and in particular for those of Tlascala, being so well deserving of the Crowne Royall.

The Citie was built in the bounds of Cholula, from whence went 25000. men to warre, and it was seated in a Plaine called Cuetlaxcoapa, neere to a Valley called Atlisco, on the border of a small River that commeth out of the

ᵈ*Vulcan or
Bolcan, is a
place whence
fire issueth, as
Etna, Hecla,
&c.*

ᵈVulcan, where they gather Wheate, Wine, and all the Fruits of Castile, Sugar and Flaxe, and all manner of Herbs. For it is a temperate Countrey, more hot then cold, although the Corne of the grounds neerest the Citie, are somewhat blasted: and a little space from Tlascala, spring Fountaynes whence groweth a River that when it commeth betweene the Citie of the Angels and Cholula, it goeth very great and without fish, it passeth through the Provinces of Mechoacan, and entreth into the South Sea by Zacatula, and there bee in it so many Caymanes, or Crocodiles, that they have dispeopled some places.

Tlascala.

In Tlascala to the North of the Angels, which stands in more then twenty degrees in height, where the Cathedrall Church was till the yeere 1550. when it was remooved to

*The Valley of
Atlisco
famous.*

the Citie: the first Bishop was Frier Julian Garces, the Valley of Atlisco, which may have in breadth about one league and an halfe, where the Corne is never blasted, and there is gathered in it above 100000. Haveges, and there are more then 1000. Spaniards that do traffick in it, and 7. leagues from the Citie to the East, is the Valley of Ocumba : and in the Province of Tepeaca, the Marquesse of the Valley built a Spanish Towne, which he called Segura : and in the Valley of S. Paul, may be other 1300. housholds of Spaniards, in Farmes and Grangeries of cattle, that multiply so much, that there were men that with two shag-haird sheepe came to have above 40000.

The Citie of Veracruz, one way stands sixtie leagues *La Veracruz.* from Mexico, and by another sixtie five, it stands one quarter of a league from the Sea, it is of more then two hundred Spanish housholds. There is in it Treasurie Royall, and House of Contractation. The Port is called *San Juan de* Saint John of Ulua, a name which the Captayne John *Ulua.* Grijalva, which discovered it the yeere 1518. and the frame [III. v. 873.] of the Key that it hath, the Vice-roy Don Antonie of Mendoça began. It is five leagues from the mouth of the River of Veracruz, between the Coast and the little Iland, which is about one league in compasse, compassed with shelves, and so low that the tydes doe cover it right against the mouth of the River of Saint John of Ulua. They goe into this Haven by two Channels : the most frequented is that of the Flat, the other is called the Gallisian Channell, which is very deepe, and there the ships doe fasten themselves to a great wall of more then foure hundred foot with Rings of Iron and Brasse, and when the North winds are very strong, they are not very sure. The Veracruz stands in eighteene degrees, somewhat more, and there was wont to be the unloading of the Fleets, and they stayed foure or five monethes in unloading, because it stands five leagues from Saint Juan of Ulua, therefore it is now made in the Port of Buytron, which is from the Port of Saint John of Ulua about eight hundred paces, and it is finished in one moneth and an halfe, and it is called Buytron, by a House that was there of one called Buytron, and they begin to make a Towne there in that situation.

There are in this Bishopricke two hundred chiefe

Townes of the Indians, and one thousand subject, although there may be two hundred fiftie five thousand Tributarie Indians, in thirtie six charges of * Doctrine of Priests, and thirtie Monasteries of Dominicke, Franciscan, and Austine Friers: and in the Coast of this Bishopricke on the North Sea, is the River of Alvarado, where the bounds of the Bishopricke of Guaxaca, and the River of Almeria doe joyne neere to the River of Saint John of Ulua, where the Towne of Medellin was built by Andrew of Tapia, the yeere 1522. when the Marquesse Don Fernando Cortes sent the said Andrew of Tapia, and Gonçalo of Sandevall, to conferre with Christopher of Tapia, which had Warrants to take away the Government of New Spaine from the Marquesse, and the Factor Salazar, and the Over-seer Peralmindez dispeopled. The River of Almeria springeth in the long Rowe, in the Provinces of Totonaques, and Micantle, and betweene Mountaynes it goeth into the North Sea, and against this River is the Iland of Sacrifices, which the Captayne Grijalva gave the name unto, and the River of Zempoala to the North from Veracruz, and upward the River of Saint Peter and Saint Paul, which springeth in the same Rowe, and the River of the Cazones, Tuspa, and Tamiagua, neere the Government of Panuco.

A kinde of Parish or Schoole division. Spa. partidos de doctrina.

Chap. 10. Of the Bishoprickes of Guaxaca, Mechoacan and Yucatan: & of the Province of Tabasco, which is the rest of the bounds described.

THe Bishopricke of Guaxaca (so called by the Province wherein it is, and Antequera by the Citie where the Cathedrall is resident betweene the Bishopricke of the Angels, and the Bishoprickes of the Councell of Guatemala) is of one hundred and twentie leagues, from the one Sea to the other, by the Confines of the Bishopricke of Tlascala, and sixtie by the Confines of Chiapa, and one hundred in breadth by the Coast of the South Sea, and fiftie by the North Sea, wherein are included the Provinces of la Misteca, high and low; the high fortie leagues from Antequera to the West, & the low more to the South Sea. John Nunnez Sedenno, and Fernando of Badajoz inhabited first the Citie of Antequera: and after the first Councell of Mexico inhabited it againe; the only Judges therein were Batchelour John Ortiz of Matienzo, and Delgadillo, which was the first, that as a man of Granada, began to breed Silke in Mexico. The President and Governour, the Bishop Don Sebastian Ramirez, began the Cathedrall Church, the beginning of the good of those Kingdomes: the Church hath all the Pillers of Marble of one piece, very great and bigge, and the Citie hath about foure hundred Spanish Housholds.

This Valley of Guaxaca, from whence the Marquesse of the Valley taketh his Title, beginneth from the Mountayne of Cocola, in the bound of Guaxoloticlan. In it is gathered much Silke, Corne, and Millet; it hath the Zapoteca Tongue. There hath beene in it good Mynes of Gold. The situation of the Citie of Antequera (which as hath beene said) they call Guaxaca, was inhabited with people of Mexico, which lay in Garrison by order of the second Motezuma, and the many Garrisons that the Kings of Mexico had through their Empire made general in it the Mexican Tongue. The River of this Citie doth sinke under the ground, against Cimatlan, and riseth two leagues off, at the Mountaynes of Coatlan, other two from Guaxaca; and at a halfe a league from the Citie right against a Hill that stands to the North, is a point of a little Hill, and there goeth a glade of a Valley all plaine, for the space of eight leagues, which is the abovesaid faire Valley of Guaxaca, pleasant, and temperate, and of a most healthfull Ayre, where plentifully are gathered all kind of things, and especially fruits of Castile, most pleasant. To the South-west stands the Province of Tutepeque, which hath many Townes by the Sea-coast, and is of more then sixtie leagues: and that of the River of Alvarado, betweene the North and North-east: and that of the Zapotecas to the North-east from Antequera, and Guazacoaloco in the Confines of Tabasco, all rough Countrey, & notwithstanding the rich Mynes of Gold, little is gotten because of the roughnesse. There are foure Spanish Townes. The said Citie of Antequera is eightie leagues from Mexico, to the South-east in the high way of Chiapa, and Guatemala:

Guaxaca Title of the Marquesse of the Valley.

Sinking River.

Tutepeque.

and the first that entred to pacifie this Province, was John
Nunnez of Mercado, the yeere 1522. by Commission of
Don Fernando Cortes, and from thence were men of War
sent to serve the King Quantimoc, in the defence of
Mexico, when Don Fernando Cortes subdued it.

[III. v. 874.]
S. Alifonso of
the Zapotecas.

The Treasurer Alfonso of Estrada, when he did governe
in Mexico, inhabited the Village of Saint Alifonso de los
Sapotecas, twentie leagues from Antequera, toward the
North-east. They live in it by Gold, Cotton-wooll, and
Millet, there are above thirtie thousand Indians tributaries.

S. James of
Nexapa.
El Espirito
Santo.

It stands betweene most high Hils. Saint Jago de Nexapa
in the Valley of Nexapa, twentie leagues from Antequera
to the East, in the way of Chiapa, and Guatemala. The
Village of the Holy Ghost in the Province of Guazacoalco,
at the Coast of the North Sea, in the Confines of Tabasco,
is ninetie leagues from Antequera. Gonçalo of Sandovall
inhabited it in the yeere 1522. It hath about fiftie Townes
of Indians, it stands on the border of the River, on the
side of Chiapa: this River springeth in the Mountaynes
of the Mixes, and Choutales, neere to Tecoantepeque, and
with the waters of the Neighbour Provinces of Chiapa,
and the Choutales, it goeth into the North Sea, there enter
into it ships of one hundred tun.

Golden
Rivers.

Cocao-money
and Wine.

In all this Bishopricke there is no River that doth not
yeeld Gold, and the Indians doe live without want if they
will worke, for they lacke nothing for backe nor belly: and
they have the Cacao, a Fruit like Almonds, which serveth
for Money, and they make Wine of it, and it is eaten
tosted, and is held for a great sustenance. They are wholsome Countreyes, and pleasant. The silke was before
nourished by the Castilians, with the Mulberie Trees of
the Countrey, wherewith the Indians served themselves,
for to make Paper of the second barke: and the Spaniards
have planted so many of Castile, that they grow infinitely:

The Indians
should pay no
Tithes.

and if the Indians did pay tithe of it, and of other things,
five Bishoprickes might be made; but none doe pay tithe
but the Castilians onely.

This Bishopricke hath three hundred and fiftie Head

HONDIUS HIS MAP OF NEW SPAINE

townes of Indians, and in them, and in three hundred Granges of more then an hundred & fifty thousand tributary Indians, & one hundred and twentie Monasteries of Dominicke Friers, and the rest Schooles of Priests for Doctrine. The Coast of the North Sea of this Bishopricke, beginneth in the River of Alvarado, that commeth *River of* from the Mountaynes of the Zapotecas, and betweene *Alvarado.* many other it goeth to the Province of Chinautla, and crossing overthwart the Mountaynes whence it sprung, goeth out into the North Sea, betweene the River of Guazacoalco, and Saint John of Ulua, and there is also the River called Agualulco, whose mouth may serve for a Haven; and the divided Rocke, a point of the Land that commeth from the Mountaynes of Saint Martine, named by ships that have bin lost upon a shoale full of Rockes under water, which lye along the Coast right against them in the Coast of the South Sea. This Bishoprick hath the Haven of Guatulco in fifteene degrees and an halfe, great, *Guatulco.* good, and frequented. The President Don Peter of Alvarado set this Province of Guatulco in obedience, and the Port of Tecoantepeque is neere, which also is reasonable; and the Towne is great, and there is in it a great fishing for Shrimps, and other fish which they carrie to Guaxaca, and in the high way of Cuyztata is a Myne of Christall-borill. Tecoantepeque is fortie five leagues from Antequera, they passe by the Mountaynes of the Choutales, Nixapa, and Mexalpeque, whitherto this Bishopricke extendeth, and hath many Townes subject by the Coast of the Sea.

The Bishopricke of Mechoacan (which is a Province *The Bishop-* betweene the Archbishopricke of Mexico, and the new *ricke of* Galicia) hath in breadth by the Coast of the South Sea, *Mechoacan.* about eightie leagues, and sixtie within the Land, with open bounds, by the Septentrionall parts: in it are included the Provinces of Zacatula, and of Colima, both in the Coast of the South Sea. The Citie of Mechoacan, or Pazcuaro, in little more then nineteene degrees, and fortie *Pazcuaro.* seven leagues from Mexico, of plaine way. In Guayan-

gareo called Vallodolid, is Resident the Cathedrall
Suffragane to Mexico, with two Monasteries of Francis-
cans, and Austine Friers. The Master of the field
Christopher of Olid built Mechoacan, the Cathedrall was
Zinzonza. first Resident in Zinzonza, unto the yeere 1544. that he
removed it to Pazcuaro. The Bishop was Don Basco de
Quiroga ; and it hath one Monasterie of Franciscan,
another of Austine Friers, and it stands seven leagues from
Mechoacan, to the East.

Guauaxnato. The Mynes of Guauaxnato, are twentie eight leagues
from Mechoacan, to the North, toward the Zacatecas,
wherein there are about sixe hundred Castilians, in two
*Reales. Campes * which they have with their chiefe Alcade or
Commissioner, and the seate and dwelling of those that
follow the Mynes is a Reall or Campe. The Village of
Village of S. Saint Michaell, in the Province of Mechoacan, is thirtie
Michaell. five leagues from Pazcuaro, to the North-east, in a rough
The Concep- Countrey. And the Village of the Conception of Salaya,
tion of Salaya. which was built by commandement of the Vice-roy, Don
Martin Enriquez, the yeere 1570. for to assure the way
The Village of of the Chichimecas. The Village of Saint Philip fiftie
S. Phillip. leagues off Mechoacan, toward the North, and sixtie two
from Mexico to the North-west, with one Monasterie of
Austine Friers, in a barren soyle and cold ; it was built for
the securitie of the way of the Zacatecas.

Zacatula. The Province and Village of Zacatula, in the Coast of
the South Sea, stands in more then 18. degrees, and fortie
leagues from Mechoacan, to the South-west, neere the Sea ;
John Rodriguez of Villavorte, and Sinon of Cuenca, built
it the yeare 1523. it stands ninetie leagues from Mexico,
Colima. and the Province and Village of Colima, in little more then
18. degrees, in the Coast of the South Sea, and in the
confines of new Galicia, fiftie leagues from Mechoacan, to
[III. v. 875.] the South-west, with a chiefe Commissioner, in a hot soyle,
and plentifull of Cacao, and Cassia Fistola, with Gould,
and well conditioned people. Gonçalo of Sandonal built
it in the yeare 1522. All the Countrie of Mechoacan is
most plentifull of Wheate, Millet, and all kinde of Spanish

Fruites, and Cattle, stored of Fish: it hath Graine, Cochinilla, and Cotten wooll, and the people is industrious, and given to labour.

There are in this Bishopricke one hundred and thirtie Townes, the nintie foure head Townes with Schooles of Doctrine: this Bishopricke reacheth no Coast of the Sea of the North, in the South Sea are many Rivers, and in the furthest West of the Province, almost in the border of the new Galicia, is the port of Navidad, in the height of 19. degrees, good and frequented, from whence the Navigation is made to the Phillipinas; and more to the East, neere the Port of Saint James: there are very good Copper Mines in these bounds, of the which the Indians make very curious Vessels, for it is pleasant, and other so hard that they digge the ground with it instead of Iron, which they could never doe till the Spaniards taught it.

Yucatan.

The Province and Government of Yucatan (which tooke this name when the Captaine Franciscus Fernandez discovered it, and our Ladie of the Remedies, when John of Grijalva discovered Cozumel) was at the first held for an Iland, because it was almost compassed with Sea, in sort that it may be called Peninsula, and it compasseth more then two hundred and fiftie leagues: it is in length where it extends it selfe East and West, about one hundred leagues, and as many North and South, from the Coast that looketh to the North, unto the part that doth confine with the Provinces of Guatemala, whereby it hath overthwart about five and twentie leagues. The temperature is hot, and very moist, and though there be no River, nor running water in it all, the water is so neare for Wels, and they finde so many shels of Sea-fish under the stones, that this, and the Coast being so low, hath given occasion to suspect that it hath beene Sea in other times: it is much compassed with Wood: they gather no Corne, nor seedes of Castile, there is no Gould, nor any other kinde of Mettall, whence is knowne the invention (or deceit) of those which said that there were found in this Province, *It was a devise of those which said the Crosses were found of Latten in Yucatan, whereas there never was Crosse in the Indies before the Spaniards.*

when the Spaniard entred in it, Crosses of Latten, which was never found in any Province of the Indies: it is very plentifull of game, especially wilde Boares and Deere, they breede up in it great store of Poultrie: they gather much Cotten wooll, and Azure, the people multiplieth and liveth *A Man of* long; a man there was which attained to three hundred *300. yeares* yeares: it hath all the kinde of Cattle of Spaine, and good *old.* Horses.

There are in this Government without that of Tabasco, which goeth joyntly with it, foure Spanish Townes, and one Bishopricke: and the Townes are buildings of the first Governour, the President Don Francisco of Monteio. *Merida.* The Citie of Merida is in twentie degrees height, almost in the middest of the Province, neerer to the coast of the North Sea, twelve leagues within the Land. In it are resident the Governour, the Officers of Revenues, and treasure Royall, and the Cathedrall suffragane to Mexico, with a Monasterie of Franciscane Fryers, they called it Merida, for the great and auncient buildings that it hath like Merida in Castile, and it causeth admiration, that having no kinde of Mettall in this Province, so great Stones could be wrought, in the which were found engraven naked men, with eare-rings, whereof is inferred that they were Temples, and that it was a very famous *Valladolid.* Countrie. The Village of Valladolid is thirtie one leagues from Merida, toward the South-east with a most sumptuous Monasterie of Franciscan Fryers, and 15000. tributarie Indians in the limits. The Village and port of *Campeche.* Saint Franciscus of Campeche, in 20. degrees, in the Coast that looketh to new Spaine, about fiftie leagues from Merida to the West, declining to the South, it hath a reasonable Haven, though little depth for being a Bay. Don Franciscus of Monteio gave it the name. The *Salamanca.* Village of Salamanca the President called so by his owne Countrie. In the Provinces of Bacalar, and Chetemal, seventie leagues from Merida, North and South, leaning to the West, and other seventie from Valladolid, neere to the Coast of the gulfe of Honduras: there are in this

Province Monasteries of Franciscanes, and six Schooles of Priests for Doctrine.

The Coast of all this Province is so shallow, that in few parts ye can ride at anker at lesse then foure or five leagues from the Land, and so there is no Port but for small Shippes, and it floweth and ebbeth more in this Coast then in any other place of these Provinces of new Spaine. The Ports that are, be these: Ciclo, and Telichaque, Cical and Cauquil: the River with two mouthes, Campeche in the Coast that looketh to new Spaine, and in it the small Cape from whence the Coast beginneth to winde to the East, and neere to the Point a little Iland which is called la Desconocida or the Unthankefull, compassed with shelves: and to the West from this, about eighteene leagues, another which they call the Zarza, and the Triangle, which are three small Ilands, close by another little Iland compassed with shelves, other sixteene leagues from ᵃ Cabo Delgado, Ilands de Arenas (of Sandes) and the Redde (la Bermeia) and another Iland thirtie leagues from the said Cape to the North, and los Negrillos, three little Ilets compassed with shelves, to the East from the ᵇ Redde, about thirtie five leagues, and the ᶜ Scorpiones twentie leagues of the coast North and South, with Merida, and the Cape of Coutoche, the Point most to the East of Yucatan, from whence goe foure little Ilands, which are called de Mugeres of Women, leaning to the Coast in the which is the Iland of Cozumel, named by the famous Idoll Place in it, whither all the people of the Province went in Pilgrimage; it stands foure leagues to the Sea, at the beginning of the Gulfe of Honduras, almost North and South with Valladolid, more inward to the Gulfe, other three little Ilets with shelves, almost over against the Lake of Bacalal, which is within the Land thirtie leagues from the Lake of Chetemall, in the Coast that goeth painted with Ilands unto Salamanca, which is the first Pantoia, neere one shelfe called *Quitasnenno, and another Zaratan, and another Lamanay, and the last Ylbob.

The Province of Tabasco, which goeth with the

Shallow Coasting. Tides.

The Ports and points of this Government.

ᵃ *Or Sharpe.*

ᵇ *Or Bermeia.*

ᶜ *Or Alacranes.*

[III. v. 876.]

A famous worshipping place of the Gentiles in Cozumel.

* *Or take away sleepe.*

Tabasco.

Government of Yucatan, and falleth upon the Coast of the
North Sea in the gulfe of new Spaine, hath in length East
and West, about fortie leagues, from the confines of
Yucatan, unto the confines of Goazacoalco, wherewith it
joyneth on the East, and as much North and South from
the North Sea, unto the confines of Chiapa. It is all
plaine ground of Marshes, Lakes and Quagmires, and so
they goe over it in Boates, and Canoes; it is very moist,
and hot, and therefore very plentifull of Pastures for Kine,
and of Millet and Cacao, which is the greatest stocke or
substance of this Province, wherein is onely one Town,
which is Tabasco, and by another name, the Village of our
Lady of the Victorie, so called for the Victory that Don
Hernando Cortez had there of the Indians, when hee went
to new Spaine, the yeare 1519. The tribute which the
Indians doe pay in this Province, is two thousand
Xiquipiles of Cacao, and every Xiquipill are eight
thousand Almonds, and one load maketh three Xiquipiles

Rivers of this
Province.
Lake of
Xicalango.

or Terces. In the Coast of this Province besides other
Rivers and Marshes, is found the Lake of Xicalango, or
Port Royall, great and capable, with two little Ilands at the
mouth, and it was the Captaine Lewis Martin, that by
order of Don Fernando Cortes, made an end of pacifying
this Province.

Chap. 11.
Of the bounds
of the Counsel
of Guada-
lajara.

THe bounds of the Counsell of new Gallicia or of
Xalisco (which Nunno of Guzman said hee had discovered, and Don Fernando Cortes, that the Captaine
Goncalo of Sandovall, did it in his name, when hee sent
him to pacifie the Colimas) it parteth bounds with the
Counsell of new Spaine, neere by the Port of the Nativitie,
and the Lake of Chiapala, going toward the North-east,
whereby (and by the North, and somewhat of the West,
for it is not all discovered) it hath the bounds open, for
the rest to the West is all Sea: that which is inhabited
on the one side, and the other, may come to one hundred
leagues, wherein are comprehended the Provinces of
Guadalajara, Xalisco, the Zacatecas, Chiametla, Culiacan,

the new Bizkey, and Cinoloa; and for Circuit the discoverie of the Provinces of Cibola, and of Quibira.

The temperature of the Province, and borders of Guadalajara, is good, and the Countrie plentifull of Corne, *Guadalajara.* and Millet, and other Seedes of Spaine, and many Vaines of Silver: there are in it Spanish Townes. Nunno of Guzman peopled the Citie of Guadalajara, the head of this Kingdome, the yeare 1531. and gave it the name of his Countrie: it stands in 106. degrees and a halfe of longitude from the Meridian of Toledo, 1780. leagues by a direct Voyage, & in 20. degrees one third part in height, eightie seven leagues from Mexico, betweene the North and the West, more toward the West: in it is resident the Counsell, the Officers of the revenues, & Royall treasurie, and the Cathedrall suffragan to Mexico, since the yeare 1570. for before it was commanded to be built in Compostella: it hath one Monasterie of Franciscan, another of Austine Friers. Nunno of Guzman built also the Village of the Holy Ghost in Tepique: and the Village of Sancta *The Holy* Marie of the Lakes, stands thirtie leagues from Guadalajara *Ghost.* to the South-east, with the chiefe Commissioner. It was *Sancta Marie* built for to be sure of the Chichimecan Indies, that are in *The Chichime-* Countries between the North and the East, a barbarous *cas Savages.* people, which live scattered in the field, without any taste of humanitie or policie, living in Caves, & in the Groves like savage beasts; they live upon wilde chase and fruits, they know no riches, nor pleasure; they goe naked, and some covered with Beasts skins: their Weapons are Bowes and Arrowes, they are well bodied, great eaters, they make wine of certaine rootes wherewith they drinke themselves drunke.

In the Province of Xalisco, which is plentifull of Millet, *Xalisco.* more then of Sheepe, or Horses, there is onely the Citie of Compostella neere the Sea, three and thirtie leagues from Guadalaxara, to the West, where the Counsell was at the first, and commanded to build the Cathedrall, untill the yeare 1560. that they removed to Guadalajara to be more in the borders: there is in it a Monasterie of Fran-

ciscan Friers; and it was also inhabited by Nunno
Guzman, the yeare 1531. which travelled two yeares in
these Countries, which they called the greater Spaine, in
emulation of Don Fernando Cortes, in all that time
nothing being knowne of him in Mexico. The Village
of the Purification, to the South-west, from Guadalajara,
and thirtie leagues from it, neere the port of the Nativitie,
in the confines of the bounds of this Counsell, and of that
of Mexico, in a very hot and sickly Countrie: and unto
the end of the yeare 1531. Nunno of Guzman discovered
one hundred and fiftie leagues of Land by the Coast of
Xalisco, which stand in somewhat more then 22. degrees.

The Zacatecas. In the Province of the Zacatecas, are rich mines of
Silver, and want of Water, Corne and Millet: there are
three Townes of Spaniards, and foure Camps appointed of
mines: those which they call of the Zacatecas are the
principall, fortie leagues from Guadalaxara to the North,
[III. v. 877.] and eightie from Mexico, wherein are ordinarie more then
five hundred Spaniards, five hundred Slaves, one thousand
Horses and Mules, and one Monasterie of Franciscane
Fryers; and there is resident alwayes one of the Officers
Royall of Guadalajara. In this Province also are the
Mines of Avinyo, in the confines of the Zacatecas, and
those of Saint Martin seven and twentie leagues from the
Zacatecas, to the North-west, wherein are wont to be about
foure hundred Spaniards, and Xerez of the Frontier, thirtie
leagues from Guadalaxara, to the North, and tenne from
the mines of the Zacatecas, in the way to them. There are
besides these other Reales or Campes, whereof no mention
is made, because they are so famous. The Village of the
The Erena. Erena, & the Mines called of the little * Hat, are five and
Or twenty leagues from Zacatecas to the North-west, neere to
Sombrerece. those of Saint Martin, and others that are in the limits. The
The Name of Village of * Nombre de Dios, is sixtie eight leagues from
God. the Citie of Guadalajara, and tenne from the Mines of
Saint Martin to the North, with a Monasterie of Francis-
can Friers, aboundant in Corne, and Millet, and good
Mines in his Borders. The Village of Durango, in the

Borders of the Mines of Saint Martin, and the Valley of Saint Salvador, eight leagues from Nombre de Dios, a wholesome Countrie, & many Rivers, with whose watering they gathered great store of Corne, and Millet, and of other Provisions, and in the Borders are the Mines of Saint Luke, and a very good Salt-pit. And the Indians of this Kingdome in many places were in armes, and the Chichimecas, and Guachachiles did great hurt in the way of Guadalajara to the Zacatecas, and this warre was very costly, and tedious, and was ended, the Marquesse of Villamanrique being Viceroy. The Indians are divided in this precinct in one hundred and foure partitions or tribes.

The Province of new Bizkie, is North-westward from *Nueva* the Zacatecas fiftie leagues from them; a Countrie of *Vizcaya.* Provisions, and much Cattell, and of good Silver Mines, the Mines of Hindehe are in it, of Sancta Barbola, and of Saint John, and in it is the Province of Topia; and in this discovery, and inhabiting, Franciscus Ybarra did many services. The Province of Chiametla, twenty leagues *Chiametla.* broad and long, in the Coast of the South Sea, about fortie leagues from Xalisco, hath Mines of Silver, and in it stands Saint Sebastian, a Village of Spaniards, which was first of the Counsell of Mexico, and it stands in more then 22. degrees. Culiacan is a government in the South Sea, more to the East, and West from Chiametla; it is a plentifull Countrie of Victuals, and showes of Silver Mines, whereof there is a Campe peopled, which they call of the Virgins. The Village of Saint Michael, eightie *S. Michael.* leagues from Compostella, and one hundred and three from Guadalajara, Nunno of Guzman inhabited it the yeare 1531.

The Province of Civaloa, the last, and most Septen- *Civaloa.* trionall of the new Kingdome of Galicia, two and fortie leagues from Culiacan, one hundred and fiftie from Guadalajara to the North, was a Towne built in it that was called Saint John of Civaloa, of Spaniards, and could not be kept. This Province was discovered, Don Antonie of Mendoca being Viceroy in new Spaine, and they said there

was a Citie seene wrought with stone, which they called
Granada, and that those Indians were warriers, and that
in the Countrie was great store of Victuals. Quibira,
stands in fortie degrees, of a temperate and fruitfull soyle,
Cibola, stands thirtie leagues from Culiacan, toward the
North, and Quibira two hundred from Cibola to the East;
it is all of poore people; for that they have no Cotten, they
weare Deere skinnes, and of the Countrie Kine, which
have a lumpe on the ridge of the backe, and long haire in
the fore parts, the hornes lesser then ours; and in them
consisteth the greatest part of the sustenance of the people,
for of the skinne they cloathe, and make Shooes, and
Cords; they eate the flesh, and make tooles of the bones:
they have sundry languages in this Province, because they
communicate little the one with the other.

California is a great point of the Land that putteth out
to the Sea in the uttermost West of new Spaine in two
and twentie degrees height, from whence it extendeth to
the North-west, neere about two hundred leagues,
although of it there is no certaine notice, nor of the Ports,
and Ilands of the Gulfe California, which is made betweene
the said point, and Gulfe of new Spaine, which goeth along
that way, as to the North-west; in the which although
there be many Rivers, Capes, and Points, and landing-
places, there is no particular notice had of them, because
they are not much frequented. At the beginning, and
entrance of this Gulfe are very long and narrow Ilands
along the Coast, and very close with it, which is called the
Guayavall, that reacheth from the River of our Ladie, or
of Sebastian of Bora, unto the River of Christmas in
Culiacan. The River of the Village of Saint Michael is
called Ciguatlan; and neerer to new Spaine is the River
of Pastla, and against it the Desart Iland, and afterward
the River of the Holy Ghost, and the port of Xalisco, and
to the South of the point of California, is Annublada or the
Cloudie Iland, and the Iland of Saint Thomas, and the
Iland of Flores, and another which is called Las Monias.

IT was first called the Counsell of Guatemala of the confines, because it was commanded first to be built in the confines of the Provinces of Nicaragua, and Guatemala, without assigning any certaine Towne. It hath in length East and West two hundred and fortie leagues, and from the Meridian from 84. to 98. of longitude, and North and South, in breadth one hundred and eightie, from 9. to 10. degrees of height, unto eighteene or nineteene, in the which are comprehended the Provinces of Guatemala, Soconusco, Chiapa, Suchitepeque, the ᵃVerapaz, Honduras and Cacos, Saint Saviour, and Saint Michael, Nicaragua, Chuluteca, Taguzgalpa, and ᵇCostarica, and in every one of these Provinces they alter in speech: and according to the opinion of Religious men, it was the worke of the Divell, for to plant dissentions and discord betweene these Nations which were bloody and revengefull. The Government and Province of Guatemala on the South Sea coast, in length of it may be about seventie leagues, and in breadth North and South thirtie: it is a Countrie of a good temperature, plentifull of Millet, Cotten wooll, Corne and other fruits, though they preserve not the Seede of one yeare for the other: the waters are few, but when it raineth they are very violent from Aprill to October, the windes are North and South, and the North lasteth but fifteene or twentie dayes, and it is very cold, and furious. There are in it five Spanish Townes, buildings of the President Don Pedro of Álvarado, in the yeare 1524. and 25. The Citie of Saint James of Guatemala, whose situation was called Cachequill, which signifieth an Eagle, because the Generall of this Nation, when hee went to warre, did beare an Eagle for his Plume: it is the head of the Government, where the Counsell is resident, in 24. degrees and a halfe of height, and 93. degr. from the Meridian of Toledo, from whence it may bee 'distant by a greater circle of one thousand six hundred and sixtie leagues, and it is twelve from the Sea, and a towne of six hundred Spanish housholds: the Officers of the goods and Royall Treasure, are resident there, the melting house,

Chap. 12.
*Of the Bounds
of the Counsel
of S. James of
Guatemala.*

ᵃ *Or true
Peace.*

ᵇ *Or Rich
coast.*

Guatemala.

Saint James.

and the Cathedrall Suffragane to Mexico, with one Monasterie of Dominicans, and another of Mercenarie Friars, and one Hospitall, and in the bounds five and twentie thousand tributarie Indians. This Citie is seated in a very pleasant Valley, with fruits of divers sorts, and all kinde of provision and dainties.

Saint Salvador. The Citie of Saint Saviour, which in the Indian language is called Cuzcatlan, is fortie leagues from Saint James to the South-east, with one Monasterie of Domini-*The Trinitie.* cans. The Village of the Trinitie, which in the Indian tongue was called Conzonate, sixe and twentie leagues from Saint James to the South-west, foure leagues from the Port of Axacutla. It is a chiefe Commissionership with title of his Majestie, with one Monasterie of Dominicans, in a plentifull soile of Cacao, and the Indians of it are of the jurisdiction of Saint James, it is a place of great trafficke, and the Port a touch for the ships of Peru, *Saint Michael.* and of New Spaine. The Village of Saint Michael sixtie two leagues from Saint James, and two and twentie from Saint Saviour to the South-west, two leagues from the Sea and Bay of Fonseca, which serveth it for Haven, and in the bounds are eightie Townes of Indians. The *Xerez.* Village of Xerez of the frontier, in the Indian speech called Chuluteca, in the confines of Guatemala and Nicaragua, eightie leagues from Saint James, and twentie from Saint Michael to the South-east, both plentifull of Cotton wooll and Millet. Neere the Citie of Saint James **Or fierie* is that * Volcan so famous of Guatemala, and in all the *mouthes like* Indies are many of these Volcanes (but the most famous *Ætna.* are those of Guatemala, which hath burst out divers times, casting fire, stones, and ashes, with great hurt of the Countrie.) That of Arequipa, of Tlascala, Quito, and others. In this Countrie are many springs of water, hot, and of sundrie properties and colours; there is much and good Balme, which the Spaniards knew without learning it of the Indians, against the which some Author speaketh, and also liquid Amber, Gumme-anime, Copall, and Suchi-copall, and other Gummes, and Liquoris most perfect, and beasts that breed the Bezar stone, they gather great store of Cacao, which is great riches: it is a meane Tree, the *Cacao* leaves like a Chesnut though bigger, it giveth flower and *described.* fruit every Moone, and the same doe in that Countrie the Orange trees. The Cacao is a tree that loveth moisture better then the Sunne, and therefore they plant neere him another tree to shadow him.

The Ports of this Government in the South Sea, beside *Ports of this* the rehearsed, are the Bay of Fonseca neere to Saint *Government.* Michael, in twelve degrees and a halfe of height, Gil Gonçales of Avila gave it the name in the yeere 1522. for the Bishop John Rodrigues of Fonseca, President of the Councell of the Indies. And within the Bay is an Iland which he named Petronilla, by a Neece of the Bishop. The Port of Acaxutla, neere to the Trinitie, in twelve degrees height, is the best of this Government for New Spaine and Peru, and the Bay of Guatemala twelve leagues from it, and the River of Xicalapa seven leagues from the Bay to the West. On the North side this Province hath no coast, for it commeth not to the Sea by fortie leagues, unto a landing place which they call the Port of the fresh Gulfe, from whence the merchandize that goe from Spaine, are conveighed by the Gulfe of Honduras, into the Land with carriages unto Guatemala, Saint Saviour, and the Trinitie, and twelve leagues before Guatemala, in the high way of Mexico, is the great Lake of Atitlau, of ten *Bottomlesse* leagues in compasse, and foure in breadth, without bottom. *Lake.*

The Province and Government of Soconusco is the *Soconusco.* furthest West from Guatemala upon the coast of the South Sea, of length and breadth about foure and thirtie leagues, plentifull of Cacao (the greatest trafficke of it, and of all that in it is sowne except Wheat) there is no more then one Spanish towne, which is called Guevetlan, founded by Don Pedro de Alvarado, where the Governour is resident; her coast which is in the South Sea, beginneth seven leagues from the River of Ayutla to the West, and presently the Rivers Coatlan, Capanercalte, Colatl, Haztatlan, Amituc, and Quizatatlan.

The Province and Bishoprick of Chiapa is Mediterranean, betweene Soconusco by the South, and the
uttermost of New Spaine by the West, and by the North
and the East, betweene Tabasco and *Verapaz, in length
East and West about fortie leagues, and some lesse in
breadth, some lesse fertile of Wheat and Millet, and other
Seedes, and of Cattell, except Sheepe that are not many.
It hath one Towne of Castilians, which is called Citie
Royall, seventie leagues from Saint James of Guatemala
toward the North-east, which by a particular priviledge is
governed by ordinarie Justices. The Cathedrall is resident
here with one Monasterie of Dominicke Friars, and many
Indian Townes in her limits: Chiapa is the principallest
Towne of them, from whence the Province tooke the
name. The Countrie-men have skill in breeding of
Horses, that those of this Countrie become the best that
are in New Spaine: they are Musicians and Painters, and
learne any Trade that doth consist in arte: they were in
old time of Nicaragua, and the Captaine James of Maza-
riegos, the yeere 1531. built this Citie in a Valley where
now it stands, round, of a marvellous situation in 18.
degrees and a halfe, sixtie leagues from the North Sea,
and as many from the South.

The Province of Verapaz (a name which the Dominicke
Friars gave it, because they pacified it with preaching) is
also Mediterranean betweene the bounds of Soconusco,
Chiapa, Yucatan, Honduras, and Guatemala, of thirtie
leagues over, and as many from Saint James of Guatemala;
a moist Countrie, and therefore the better for the Millet
that in it is gathered twice a yeere, and for Wheat. There
is Cotton wooll, and some Cacao, and much Fowle of those

that give the coloured feathers for the pictures which the
Indians doe make, which is a merchandize of this Province, and the Kings of Mexico carried them from this
Province, which was the most esteemed thing they had,
and it was judged for a great sinne to kill these Fowles,
but to plucke them and to let them flie. There is in this
Countrie but one Monasterie of Dominicke Friars, with

one Indian Towne of seventeene Indian children that are
there, by order of the religious men for to instruct them
the better; for before they lived scattered and like savages,
and now they live like Christians, and in temporall things
politikely.

In this Province there is no Governour, but a chiefe
Justice, provided by the Councell. The River of Zacatula
divideth this Province from the Province of Guatemala,
from the which it extendeth unto the fresh Gulfe, whither
all the Rivers of it doe runne, whereby and by the many falls
of waters that descend from most high Hils, the Countrie
was so moist, that the Millet rotted; but it is bettered
in the temperature, since the cutting downe of the Woods:
it hath many Lions, Tigres, and Buffes, whose flesh the
Indians doe eate although it be luscious and soft; it is
called the Fresh Gulfe, for the multitude of the Rivers *Golfo dolce.*
which on that side doe enter into the Sea. The water is
fresh, and there are exceeding great Fishes, and specially
the Manati, which is the Sea calfe, which swimmeth so *Manati a fish*
delicately, that being very great he maketh no noyse; when *described.*
hee fleeth he goeth to the Deepe, and waxeth angrie and
fierce against them that seeke him, and giveth great
strokes; his flesh is very fat like unto fat beefe.

THe Province and Government of Honduras hath in *Chap. 13.*
length East and West, by the coast of the North Sea, *Of Honduras,*
more then one hundred and fiftie leagues, and in bredth *Nicaragua,*
from the Sea unto the bounds of Costa Rica and Guate- *and Costa*
mala, in parts eightie: it hath many Hills, and is plentifull *Rica, or the*
Rich Coast.
of Millet, Wheat, and all sorts of Cattell, and some Mynes *Honduras.*
of gold and silver: there is in it sixe Spanish Townes in
one Bishopricke, and the first Bishop was Friar John of
Talavera, Prior of Prado, of the Order of Saint Jerome of
Spaine.

The Citie of Valladolid, in the Indian language, is called
Comayagua, in more then sixteene degrees, stands sixtie
leagues from Saint James of Guatemala to the East, and
about fortie from the North Sea: in it is the Governour

resident, and the Cathedrall, since the yeere 1558. when it
went from Truxillo, whereat first it was; and one Monasterie de la Merced.* The Captaine Alonso of Caceres
pacified this Countrie, by order of Don Peter of Alvarado:
it stands in the middest of the two Seas, and from the one
to the other are three and fiftie leagues, from the Port de
Cavallos or of Horses in the North Sea, unto the Bay of
Fonseca in the South Sea, and the Inginer Baptista
Antoneli visited this way, by order from the King; because
many thought that by it the trafficke of the North Sea
was more easie to the South Sea, and hee found that it had
many inconveniences.

The Citie of * Gracias à Dios, is thirtie leagues from
Valladolid almost to the West; the Captaine Gabriel of
Rojas peopled it 1530. for the benefit of the Mynes of
gold that were thereabouts, and had great encounters with
the Indians, which assaulted him many times in a Fort that
he had. But the Governours of Honduras and Nicaragua,
not succouring him by reason of grudges betweene them,
hee was forced to forsake it. And in the yeere 1536.
Captaine Gonçalo of Alvarado, inhabited this Citie againe.
The Village of Saint Petro is thirtie leagues from Comayagua to the North, somewhat aside to the West, and
eleven from the Port of Cavallos, where the Officers Royall
are resident, because the Port of Cavallos is sickly, whither
the dispatches of the ships doe come. The President
Don Peter Alvarado built it 1536.

The Village of Saint John of the Port de Cavallos is
in 15. degrees of altitude, eleven leagues from Saint Peter,
foure from Comayagua, it is inhabited with Factors of the
Merchants, and with Black-moores, because it is an
unwholesome Port; for although it be a Bay, it is a good
one, it was called the Port of The Horses, because some
were cast in the Sea by a storme. The Citie of Truxillo
is sixtie leagues from Comayagua to the North-east, and
fortie from the Port of Horses to the East, and one from
the North Sea: the Cathedrall was here, the Haven is
called Saint Gil, it is good, though it be a Bay dead and

*Or of our
Lady of the
Favour.*

*Visitation of
the Inginer
Baptista
Antoneli of
the way of the
Port of
Cavallos or
Horses, to the
Bay of
Fonseca.
*Thankes bee
to God.*

Saint Peter.

Saint John.
[III. v. 880.]

Truxillo.

sheltered, where the ships that goe for Guatemala doe touch first. Francisco de las Casas, began to inhabit this Citie 1524. and because they were all people of Estremadura, he called it Truxillo, and Don Hernando Cortes ended the inhabiting of it when he went to the Ybueras. The Village of Saint George of Olancho, is fortie leagues *Saint George.* from Comayagua to the East, of fortie housholds, and in her borders sixteene thousand tributarie Indians, and much gold, chiefly in the River of Guayape, ten leagues from this Towne. This Valley of Olancho is very pleasant and *Valley of* profitable, and in it was much gold gotten, and the *Olancho.* Governours of Honduras and Nicaragua, had in other times great differences: for every one would have it in his jurisdiction, and therefore here it was where Gil Gonçales Davila tooke one hundred and twentie thousand Pesos of gold of Hernando of Soto, and dismissed the people which Pedrarias Davila had for his defence; and here Gabriel of Rojas defended the entrance of Gonçalo of Sandoval, for Don Hernando Cortes did send him from Truxillo, and here the Indians killed John Grijalva, a very famous Captaine, and others.

The coast of this Province is all in the North Sea, in the *Points and* Gulfe which they call de Honduras, which is all the Sea *Ports of this* coast betweene this Province and Yucatan, to the place *Government.* where it joyneth with it by Verapaz, where it was called the Gulfe of Guanajos, the first Point is of the Ybueras, so called, because they first found many pompions on the Sea, which they call Ybueras in the language of Hispaniola; it stands in sixteene degrees of height. Neere to the Fresh Gulfe a Port for Guatemala, where Saint Gil of Bonavista was built, neere to the Cape of Three Points to the East from the Fresh Gulfe, and Gil Gonçales Davila peopled it 1524. And more to the East is the River Piche, and Rio Baxo, and the River of Ulva, by another name Balahama before the Port of Horses, which stands in fifteene degrees. And afterward the River and Point de la Sal, and Triumpho de la Cruz, a Cape of three points, where the yeere 1524. the Master of the field

Christopher of Olid planted; and the River Hulma or of Xagua, and to the North of his mouth the Iland of Utila; and to the North-east, Guayana, Helen, and Guanaja, and Saint Francise North and South with the Point of Truxillo, which are the Ilands of the Guanajos. The said Point is called by another name, Cabo Delgado, the Small Cape, *Or Shrimpe.* or of Honduras, from whence to the Cape of *Camaron, in search whereof they goe from Jamayca, are thirteene Rivers, and at the Point of the Cape a plazell or great shelfe of more then twentie leagues into the Sea, and in the middest of it neere to the Coast a great Iland, which is called the Iland de los Baxos (of the shelves) and another to the North, neere the shelfe called Saint Millan, and having passed the shelfe, the Bay of Cartago, and the *Bahia honda.* Deepe Bay, before the Cape of thanks be to God, which *Cabo de* stands in fourteene degrees one third part, and to the North *Gracias a* of it three Ilands, which they call the Viciosas, and Quita *Dios.* suenno or Take away sleepe, and Roncador, the Suorter, two dangerous shelves, and having passed the Cape, the Gulfe of Nicuesa, where hee was lost in the yeere 1510. and the River of Yare in thirteene degrees, where the Governments of Honduras and Nicaragua are joyned.

The Ilands of the Guanajos, which are the rehearsed, the first Admirall Don Christopher Colon discovered 1502. in the last voyage he made to the Indies, when he discovered Terra firme in the coast of Veragua, where his ill lucke appeared; for if as he went to Veragua, hee had gone to the other side, he had discovered New Spaine.

Nicaragua. The Province and Government of Nicaragua, which the Governour James Lopez of Salzedo, called the New Kingdome of Lion, on the West joyneth with Guatemala, and *Or rich* on the North with Honduras, and on the South with *Costa *Coast.* Rica. It is of one hundred and fiftie leagues East and West, and eightie North and South, a plentifull Countrie of Millet, Cacao, Cotton wooll, store of Cattell, without Corne or Sheepe, it hath five Spanish Townes, Lion of Nicaragua is one hundred and foure leagues from Saint James of Guatemala about the South-east, and twelve from

the South Sea, neere to the great Lake of Nicaragua, where
the Governour is resident, the Royall Officers, and the
Cathedrall, and James Alvarez Ossorio was the first Bishop.
It hath five Monasteries of Mercenaries, and in her bounds
one hundred and twentie thousand tributarie Indians.
The Citie of Granada is sixteene leagues from Lion, which *Granada.*
and Lion were built by the Captaine Franciscus Hernandez
1523. and Granada stands by the border of the great Lake,
and foure and twentie leagues from the Port of Realejo,
besides the great Lake, stands the Lake of Lindiri, and
the famous Vulcan or Fierie mouth of Massayatan. The *Lake of*
great Lake ebbeth and floweth, it hath many Ilands, it *Nicaragua.*
runneth into the North Sea, by the River which is called *Volcan of Massayatan and*
El Desaguadero, or The Voyding, it hath great store of *Mombacho.*
Fish and many Lizards. At two leagues from it, and
seven from Granada is the great fierie mouth of Mombacho, very high with many Groves of divers fruits, of
which much refresh the Countrie. A Friar perswading
himselfe that that masse of fire that in so many yeeres
burned without consuming within the mouth of Massaya
was gold, having made by a certaine arte certaine
Cauldrons with their chaines to draw it, they scarcely came
at the fire, when the Cauldron and the Chaine were melted
like Lead.

The new Segovia which was the beginning of Peter [III. v. 881.]
Arias his plantation, is thirtie leagues from Lion to the *Segovia.*
North, and as many from Granada, somewhat Northward
also, in which limits much gold is gotten. And Jaen a *Jaen.*
Citie is thirtie leagues from the North Sea, in the end of
the great Lake, whereby the River which they call the
Voyding, and the merchandize which are carried from
Nombre de Dios, and now from Porte bello, are convayed
in it. The Village of Realejo one league from the Port of
the Possession, which commonly is called of the Realejo, *Realejo.*
stands in eleven degrees and a halfe, and is one of the
best Ports and surest in all that Coast, wherein are made
good ships by reason of the good provision of Timber
there.

There are in this Government many Townes of Indians,
and in them store of tributaries, and in the Confines of
this Government, and of Costa Rica, and of Nicoya eight
and fortie leagues from Granada, in the South coast, is a
Corregidorship; in which, and in the Iland of Chyra,
which is of the jurisdiction thereof eight leagues to the
Sea, are many tributarie Indians of the Crowne Royall,
subject in other times to the Councell of Panama, unto the
yere 1573. at which time it was incorporated in Costa
Rica; whose Governour placeth a Deputie, and the Bishop
of Nicaragua a Vicar. There is in it a reasonable Port,
in the coast of this Province on the North Sea. After
this is the River Yare that divideth it from that of Honduras, the River of Yairepa, before the River and Port
of Saint John, which is called the Voyding or Desaguadero,
with a great Iland at the mouth, and after, some other
Rivers common to Costa Rica. In the South Sea, it hath
besides the Realejo, the Port of Saint James, before the
Chira, and the Port of Paro right against Nicoya, in the
Gulfe called of the * Salt-pits, before the Point of Saint
Lazarus, and the Cape of Borrica, at the East side whereof
are the Ilands of Saint Marie, Saint Martha, Cobaya, and
Sebaco, neere to the bounds of Veragua, common to Costa
Rica.

*Ports and
Rivers of this
coast.*

*De Salinas.

In the Coast of Nicaragua, on the South side, the Village
of Bruxelles was peopled 1529. and James Lopes of
Salcedo disinhabited it, because they had received in it
Pedro de los Rios, Governour of Castilla del Oro, which
went to take the Government of Nicaragua, where Salcedo
had thrust himselfe, and had gone from Honduras his
owne Government unto it. Captaine Franciscus Hernandez,
planted it 1524. in the doubtfull Streight, in the seate of
Uritina, and on the one side it had the Sea, on the other the
Playnes, and on the third side the Mountaine of the
Mynes, and in all this Orbe there are no Indians more
expert in the Castillan tongue then those of Nicaragua.

Bruxelles.

The Province and Government of Costa Rica, the
furthest East of the Northerne Indies, and Councell of

Costa Rica.

ANTONIO DE HERRERA

Guatemala, hath in length East and West ninetie leagues from the Confines of Veragua unto those of Nicaragua, with which it joyneth by the North, and by the West. In it are two Townes, it is a good Countrie, with many showes of Gold, and some of Silver. The one Towne is the Village of Aranjues five leagues from Chomes *Aranjuez.* Indianes, a Towne of the jurisdiction of Nicoya. The Citie of Cartago, fortie leagues from Nicoya, and twentie *Cartago.* from the Sea almost in the middest of the Province, hath a Port and landing place in the Coast of the South Sea, and the North Sea, wherein there is some Rivers betweene Nicaragua and Veragua, common to this Government, and the Bayes of Saint Jerome and of Caribaco, neere the limits of Veragua.

THe part of the Indies of the South is unjustly called *Chap. 14.* America, it is all that is discovered from Nombre de *Of the Indies* Dios and Panama to the South, wherein is included Terra *of the South.* firme, the Kingdomes of Piru, the Piru Chile, which the Indians call Chille; The Provinces of the Streight, the River of Plate and Brasile, where are five Councels of Panama, new Kingdome of Granada, Saint Francise of Quito, Lima, the Charcas, and the eleven Governments: part of their Coast toucheth in the North Sea, and part in the South: in the which for the most part reigneth the South and the South-west, which contrarie to his nature is there pleasant, and doth mitigate the great heate, whereby that Countrie may bee inhabited, although it never rayneth nor hayleth in it, but in a very little distance. And the two rowes of Mountaines that runne equally *A great* through all these Indies, have a great difference, though *difference of* they are in one altitude of the Pole: for the one is well *temperature in* replenished with Trees and it alwayes rayneth in it, and *the two rowes* it is hot: the other is all bare, and cold in Summer and *of Piru.* Winter. These rowes are called Andes, and Sierra or the Mountayne; they have most high Hils, and goe in sight *The two rowes* the one of the other one thousand leagues, almost equally. *doe runne* In the Hill are bred sundrie beasts, and in the parts where *almost 1000. leagues equall.*

493

they open they make Valleys, which is excellent dwelling, as that of Xanxa, and Guaylas, and Yucay. In the Andes also are bred sundrie beasts, and past the Citie of Cuzco, these rowes doe divide themselves, leaving in the middest *Qualities of* a great champaine Countrie, which is the Province of *the Province* Collao, where are infinite Rivers, Lakes, and Pastures, *of Callao.* without Trees or Wood, for the distemperature of the Countrie, though wholesome and much inhabited. There followeth after it the Province of the Charcas, hot and of great plentie, with very rough Hills of great riches of Mynes: and the figure of these Indies is seene in the Table before going.

[III. v. 882.] THe limits of the Counsell of Panama, which was first called Castilla del Oro, and afterwards Terra Firme, are very small, for the Counsell is principally resident there, for the dispatch of the Fleetes, and Merchants, *Quantities of* which goe and come to Piru: it hath in length East and *the Countrie of* West, about nintie leagues, from the confines of the *Panama, and* government of Cartagena, and Popayan, unto the Castle *her bounds.* of Veragua, and in breadth from the South Sea to the North sixtie leagues, and thence downeward unto eighteene by Nombre de Dios, or Porto bello to Panama: it is a ground generally very rough with Mountaines, full of quagmires, the ayre close with vapours, moist, hot, and for this cause very sickly from May unto November, a barren soyle, and destitute of many things: for there groweth nothing but Millet, and very little, though there be good Pastures for Kine, and breeding of Cattle. The government of Veragua stands in the bounds of this Counsell, and in it, and in that of Panama these Townes following.

Panama. The Citie of Panama is in the coast of the South Sea, neere unto it, in 9. degrees of latitude, and 82. of longitude from the Meridian of Toledo, from whence it is distant by direct way one thousand five hundred and sixtie leagues. It is a Towne of six hundred housholds, the most are Merchants and dealers. And with the Counsell are resident the Kings Officers, and Royall treasurie, which doe goe already to Portobello, when there is any Fleete to the dispatching of it, and likewise the Cathedrall suffragan to the Archbishopricke of the Kings (delos res) is here resident with three Monasteries, of Dominicke, Franciscane and Merced Friers. The Port of this Citie is reasonable, although at low water the Ships remaine dry, and therefore in Summer they ride in the strand, and in winter in the haven of Perico, two leagues from the citie. Pedrarias Davila peopled it, being Governour of Castillo, del Oro, or of the Gold, against the will of the dwellers of Sancta Marie, the auncient of Darien, the yeare 1519. and a little after the Cathedrall Church was removèd thither; and it might have had a better seate, and more wholesome, and to the purpose for the trafficke of the South Sea, not [III. v. 883.] going very farre from whence the Citie now stands.

The Citie of Nombre de Dios, was by James of Nicuesa first planted 1510. and afterward by James of Albitez, by order of Pedrarias, and he was the first Admirall that discovered her port. It is removed to Portobelo, for *Portebello.* the first Admirall discovered it, and gave the name, because it was more wholesomer, and fitter for the loading and unloading of the Fleetes, and for their securitie, and of the new Citie of Saint Phillip, which is built there: the Inginer Baptista Antonelli, hath made a Castle, and appointed another on the other side the haven, for to keepe the entrie. The Merchandize are carried from Portobelo to Panama by two wayes, one by Land with carriage, which is eighteene leagues of lesse difficultie then by the way of Nombre de Dios: the other by Sea, and the River of Chagre, whose mouth is eighteene leagues from Portobelo, to the West, whereby the Merchandize goe up when the water reacheth to the vent of the Crosses, and from thence they go in carriages five leagues to Panama.

The Village of Nata stands thirtie leagues from Panama *Saint James of* to the West, in the Coast of the South Sea, Captaine *Nata.* Franciscus Companion peopled it, by order of Peter Arias, for the warre with the Casique Urraca. The inhabiting of Acla, and Captaine Gabriel of Rojas finished by commandement of Peter Arias, in the Coast of the North Sea, and entrance of the Gulfe of Uraba, right against the Iland of Pinos, whereof at this present there is no more memory then that there was the death of that famous Captaine, whose memory will last eternally, the President Basco Nunnez of Balboa, and of his company. In the breach of Almagro, and in the head of the River Chiepo, there is Gold, and in times past was much gotten. In all these Rivers are many Lizards or Crockadiles, and very great, which put the first discoverers and pacifiers to great trouble, and did devoure some men. It happened that a man being in a Boate neere to the Kings House

in Panama, a Lizard came and snatched him from the Stearne of the Boate, and carried him away to eate him on certaine Rockes, and having begunne to teare him in pieces, they shot at him with a Caliver and killed the Lizard, so that he before his death received the Sacraments of the Church.

The Province of Veragua, which stands in somewhat more then tenne degrees, doth confine with Costarica, on the West side: it hath in length East and West fiftie leagues, and in breadth five and twentie: a Mountainous Countrie, full of bushes, without Pastures or Cattle, Wheate, Barley, little Millet or little Pulse; but full of Gold with many vaines of it, and rich Mines in the Rivers, and breaches, and those Indians that are, are in

warre: it hath the Citie of the Conception fortie leagues from Nombre de Dios, to the West, where the Governour and the Officers (which they of Panama at this present

doe provide) are resident. The Village of Trinitie stands six leagues to the East of the Conception by Sea (for yee cannot goe by Land) neere to the River of Bethleem,

at three leagues from the Sea. The Citie of * Sancta Fe stands twelve leagues from the Conception to the South, with melting houses, and Deputie Officers. The Citie of

Charles, in the coast of the South Sea, neere to the Sea,

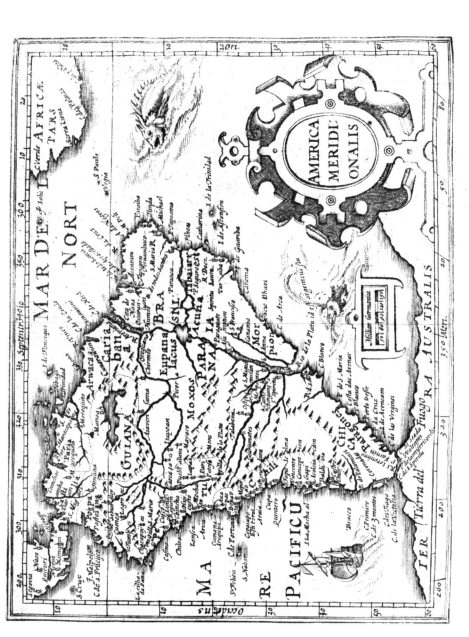

HONDIUS HIS MAP OF AMERICA MERIDIONALIS

fiftie leagues from the Citie of Sancta Fe, to the East: all the Indians of this government are in warre.

There is no Port of name in the two Coasts South, and North, of this government, and in all the bounds of the Counsell, are the Rivers, Ports, and points following. The Bay of Carabaco, or Saint Hierome, in the coast of the North Sea, and the confines of Veragua, and to the East of it, and of the River of the Trinitie, of the Conception, and of Bethlehem (where was the first inhabiting that the first Admirall made in Terra firme, of all that Orbe, in the yeare 1503. which continued not): and right against the Shield, an Iland, and the River of Chagre, and more to the East a league the Portete, to the place where the Admirall came discovering the same yeere, and the Ports of ^a Langostas twelve leagues from Nombre de Dios, to the West, and the Port de Gallinas or of Hennes nine degrees, and the Port of Bonaventure six, Portobelo five, and right against it the Ilands of the ^b Lookings, and those of the Provisions or Bastimentos: and having Nombre de Dios two leagues, the River of ^c Sardinilla, and the Iland of ^d Sardina, foure; and the River of Millet or Mayz, and the River of Snakes, or Culebras, eight; and at the entry of the Gulfe of Uraba, where in the yeare 1509. the Bachiller Enciso built the Citie of Sancta Marie of Darien. This Bachiller Enciso was he that published that in the Province which was called Castilla del Oro, there were places where the gold was fished with nets, which encouraged many people to goe to the Indies, which passed in the yeare 1514. with Peter Arias Danila: and the President Basco Nunnez of Balboa, went 1513. from the Darien in demand of the South Sea, and discovered it. The Point of the Iland of Captiva, stands right against the Mountaines of Saint Blas, and the Iland of Comagre, and the Iland of Pinos, more within the Gulfe of Uraba, and in the inward Port of it, the Port of Nilcos, neere to the mouth of the River of Darien, which divideth the bounds of this Counsell, and those of the Governement of Cartagena, and there is Culata

The Ports.

El Escudo.

^a *Or Locusts.*

^b *Las Miras.*

^c *Or Little Pilcherd.*
^d *Or Pilchard.*

de Uraba, where in the yeare 1510. Alonso of Oieda inhabited Saint Sebastian of Uraba. This Gulfe stands in 8. degrees, it hath foureteene leagues of longitude into the Lands, and in the entrie it hath six in breadth, and [III. v. 884.] a little forward fiftie, and at the end foure, and five leagues within was the Citie of Sancta Marie, the auncient of Darien.

In the South Sea stands the Cape of Sancta Marie, and point (de Guerra) of Warre, and toward Panama, the Gulfe of Parita, or Paris where stands Nata, the point of Chiame, the Countrie of that Cazique Chiapes, the friend of Basco Nunnez of Balboa, which holpe him in his discovery: and passed the Port of Panama, the River of Chepo, and the Balsa, or of Congos in the inner part of the Gulfe of Saint Michael, North and South from the Iland of Pearles, and the Point or Port of Pinyas, at the entrie of the Gulfe on the South side, which is fiftie leagues from Panama, and twentie overthwart to the Gulfe of Uraba, and Puerto Quemado, or Burnt Haven, neere to the Cape of Corrientes, in 5. degrees of altitude Septentrionall.

Chap. 16.
The limits of
the Counsell of
Sancta Fe of
Bogota: which
is the new
Kingdome of
Granada.

THe bounds of the Counsel of the New Kingdome hath in length East and West, three hundred leagues, and as many North and South, wherein are comprehended the Provinces of the New Kingdome, the governments of Sancta Martha, and Cartagena, and part of that of Popayan; & for borders the Provinces of the Dorado, or new Stremadura: the Province of New Kingdome, which is that which the Counsell governeth: it hath in length from East to West fourteen leagues, and eightie in breadth North and South of plaine ground, for the most part with Valleys and hils, and good Pastures for all sort of Cattle, which are in abundance, and in many places, Wheate, Millet, and the fruits of Castile, and generally much Gold and very fine, and Mines of Copper & Steele: and the Countrie men for the most part are able men, great traffickers, and doe weare Cotten cloath.

And the Townes that be in the Kingdome of Spaniards, are the Citie of * Sancta Fe of Bogota, which was built at the foote of Bogota, so called by the Cazique which was called Bogota, which the President Gonçalo Ximenez of Quesada built, and gave the name to the Citie and to the Kingdome, because he was of Granada, though in the discovery the President Belalcazar, and Nicholas Federman had part: it stands 72. degrees and a halfe of longitude from the Meridian of Toledo, which by a greater circle may be one thousand foure hundred and fortie leagues, and 4. degrees on this side of the Equinoctial, it hath more then six hundred housholds, in it is resident the Counsell, the Kings Officers and Royall treasurie, and Melting house, the Cathedrall Metropolitane, whose suffragans are, Popayan, Cartagena and Sancta Marta, with a Monasterie of Dominicke and another of Franciscane Friers, and in her borders more then fiftie thousand tributarie Indians and the Lake of Guatavita, which was a worshipping place of the Indians, where it is reported that they did cast great summes of Gold in offring to the Idols.

The Village of Saint Michael in the bounds of Sancta Fe, twelve leagues from it to the North, was built for trafficke with the Pauche Indians, because being of a hot Countrie it did them hurt to goe to Sancta Fe, which is cold. The Citie of Tocayma fifteene leagues from Sancta Fe, to the West, somewhat inclined to the North, with a Monasterie of Dominicke Friers, was inhabited the yeare 1545. by the Captaine Hernando Vanegas, in the border of the maine River Pati, which runneth into the River Magdalene. It hath no gold, and is most hot, and by night there falleth no Deaw in it. In all the Kingdome there is no generall tongue, that which is most understood, is that of the Pauches. In the Province of the Musos, and Colimas, which by another name are called Canupeis, five and twentie leagues in length, to the North-west of Bogota, a rough Countrie, sound, plentifull of Pastures, Gold, and Emeralds: there are two Townes; the Citie

Holy Faith.

Lake of Guatavita.

Saint Michael.

Tocayma.

The Trinitie. of the Trinitie twentie leagues from Sancta Fe, to the North-west, which the Captaine Lanchero inhabited the yeere 1582. when hee went to warre with the Indians
*Or Flies. * Moscas, a quicke and fearefull Nation: and in these bounds stands the rich Mine of the Emeralds, with many Indians which yet are peaceable, and in the Province of Chiagnachi, which signifieth Snailes, for there be many.

The Palma. The Village of Palma in the Colimas, of a temper hotter then cold, fifteene leagues from Sancta Fe to the North-west, the Captaine Don Gutierre of Ovalle built
Tunia. it 1572. in the Province of Tunia, which tooke the name of the Cazique, almost to the North, direct to that of Bogota, and in all like unto it: The Citie of Tunia stands two and twentie leagues from Sancta Fe, to the North-east, on a high hill, a strong scituation, for the warre with the Indians. There goe out of this Citie above two hundred Horse-men, and it is the most aboundant of Victuals of all the Borders, and there is the greatest Market in all the Realme: it hath one Monasterie of Dominicke, another of Franciscane Friers. The Captaine Gonçalo Xuarez Rondon built it, for the President
Pamplona. Gonzalo Ximenez of Pulsada. The Citie of Pamplona seventy leagues from Sancta Fe to the North-east, hath one Monasterie of Dominick Friers; much Gold is gotten in it, it hath abundance of Cattle: the Bachiller Michael Diaz of Armendariz peopled it. The Village of Saint Christopher is thirteene leagues from Pamplona to the North, the Captaine Franciscus of Caceres built it
*Or Crying. neere the Province of * Grita, so called because the Indians came out of the high wayes to shoute and crie after the Spaniards, and to kill them: little Gold is gotten in it, and it hath commoditie, for to breede Cattle.

Merida. The Citie of Merida, in the bounds of the government of Veneçuela and the New Kingdome, fortie leagues from Pamplona to the North-east: it is a plentifull Countrie of
[III. v. 885.] Mines of Gould, and of Wheate. The Citie of Belez
Belez. thirtie leagues from Sancta Fe to the North, and fifteene from Tunia, hath one Monasterie of Franciscane Fryers:

the Captaine Goncalo Ximenez Rondon inhabited it. It
is a Countrie where many thunderboults fell, and there *Thunderbolts.*
fall not so many since the holy Sacrament of the Altar
is there abiding: it hath one fierie mouth that casteth
many stones. The Citie of Mariquita of Ybague, by *Mariquita.*
another name Saint Sebastian of the Gould, is fortie
leagues from Sancta Fe to the North-west, the Captaine
Pedroso peopled it 1551. in certaine Meadowes, leaning
to the hill, the temper is very hot. The Citie of Ybague *Ybague.*
is three hundred leagues from Sancta Fe, almost to the
West: it is the first Towne of the New Realme, that
doth confine with Popayan, the Captaine Andrew Lopez
of Galarza peopled it 1551. by commission of the Counsell,
for to eschew the harmes these Indians did with those
of Tocayma, and Cartago, and for to open the way to
the government of Popayan, it hath a Monasterie of
Dominicke Friers.

The Citie of the Victorie of the Remedies, fiftie leagues *Victorie de los*
from Sancta Fe, to the North-west, is very rich of Mines. *Remedios.*
The Citie of Saint John of the Plaines, fiftie leagues *Saint John of*
from Sancta Fe to the South, is a Countrie of much *the Plaines.*
Gould. The Citie of Tudela which the Captaine Peter
of Ursua built, by order of the Bachiller Don Michael
Diuz of Armendariz was disinhabited, because the Indians
* Moxcas received hurt by it. And there are of the limits **Or Flyes.*
of the Counsell of the new Realme, seven Townes of
the government of Popayan, Sancta Fe of Antiochia,
Caramanta, Arma, Anzerma, Cartago, Saint Sebastian of
the Silver, and Saint Vincent de las Pazes.

The Merchandize enters this Kingdome, by the great
River of Magdalene, from the * Baranca of Malamba, of **Or Water-*
the jurisdiction of Cartagena, and the first that sent to *course.*
discover this River, was Garcia of Lerma, Governour of *Rio Grande or*
Magdilen
Sancta Martha 1531. It entreth into the Sea so broad *River.*
and strong, that at the passing, the Ships are wont to
be in danger, if they goe not somewhat distant, for the
combat of the current, and working of the Sea. It hath
an Iland in the mouth, it is navigated more then one

hundred and fiftie leagues, and in more then three hundred
it is not waded: it commeth from above Popayan from
two Fountaines that are fortie leagues distant, by which
joyning the River is made: it was called of Magdalene,
because on that day was the mouth discovered, in 12.
degrees of height, and six and twenty leagues from
Cartagena.

Sancta Martha. The Province and Government of Sancta Martha in
the coast of Terra firme is seventie leagues in breadth
and length, betweene Carthagena and the River of Hache:
it is a plentifull Countrie of Millet, and Potatoes, much
Gould, and Copper, and some Emeralds, and other Stones:
in it are five Spanish Townes; and though there be many
of the Countrie-men, the most are in warre. The President Bastidas peopled the Citie of Sancta Martha 1525.
neere to the Sea, in 10. degrees of latitude, and 74. of
longitude, one thousand foure hundred and twentie leagues
from Toledo, where is resident the Governour, and Officers
Royall, and the Cathedrall suffragan to the New Kingdome. The Port is reasonable. This Government hath
foure Provinces, Pozignay, Betona, Chimica, and Tayrona,
which signifieth a Forge, and with great reason, because
in that Countrie are an infinite quantitie of diversitie of
Mettals, and Stones of great esteeme and value.

Tenerife. Tenerife stands by the border of Rio Grande or the
great River (which is that of Magdelene) fortie leagues
from Sancta Martha to the South-west, part by the Sea,
and part by Land: Franciscus Euriques did people it,
by order of Gonçalo Perez which governed in Sancta
Tamala- Martha, by Commission of the President Lugo. Tama-
meque. lameque, or Village of the Palmes is sixtie five leagues
from Sancta Martha to the South, and twentie from
Tenerife, two leagues from the Great River: the Captaine
The Kings. Bartholomew Dalva peopled it 1561. The Citie of los
Reyes in the Valley of Upari, is plentifull of Millet,
Provision, and Cattle, and of much Copper, to the South-
east of Sancta Martha, fiftie leagues from it, and thirtie
from the River of Hache: the Captaine Sanct Anne

peopled it, by commandement of the Bachellor Michael Diuz, ^a La Ramada was built before, called first new Salamanca, fortie leagues from Sancta Martha to the East, and eight from the River of Plate, at the overflowings of the Snowie Mountaine. It stands in the Valley of Upani, where there is as much Copper as Stone. The Merchandize of this Government goeth up to the New Kingdome by the marsh of this Citie, which is eight leagues from it by the Sea, and afterward twelve unto the Barranca of Malambo, in the great River. Ocanna is also in this Government, which the Captaine Franciscus Hernandez inhabited 1572. and was first called Sancte Anne. There is in the Coast of this Government the River of Buhia, neere Ramada, and the River of Piras, and that of ^b Palomino, where a Captaine of this name was drowned, and the River of Don James, the ^c Ancones of Buritaca, and the Cape of ^d Aguia neere Sancta Martha, right against the hill of Bonda, and the River of Gayra, to the West.

The Province and Government of Cartagena, in the Coast of Terra firme, and the North Sea, hath in length East and West, from the River of the Magdalene, unto the River of Darien, eightie leagues North and South, and as many unto the confines of the New Kingdome, though men say it is more in Voyage. The Countrie is Mountainous of Hils and Valleys, of high Trees, rainie and moist: the seedes of Castile beare no seede, there is no Wheate, nor Gould, but in some places. There is much rozen made in some Mountaines of this Government, and Gums arromaticke, and other liquors which they get out of the Trees, and great quantitie of Sanguis Draconis, and a very fragrant balme of great vertues.

The Citie of Carthagena stands neare the Sea, two leagues from the Point of Canoa, to the West, in tenne degrees of latitude, and seventie six of longitude, one thousand foure hundred and sixtie leagues from Toledo, of more then five hundred housholds, among them above two thousand women. In it is resident the Governour, the Kings Officers, & treasurie Royall, and the Cathedrall

^a Sancta Ramada.

Ocanya.

^b Or Yong Pigeon.
^c Or Nookes.
^d Or the Needle.

Cartagena.

[III. v. 886.]

Citie of Cartagena.

suffragan to the New Realme, with Monasteries of Dominick and Franciscan Friers. The scituation is plain, and almost like an Iland, the Sea compasseth it on the North side, & it is a rough coast, and very shallow; and on the land side it hath an arme of the Sea which reacheth to a Marish, which is the Lake of Canapote, which ebbeth & floweth after the order of the Sea, & at the same houre, and they passe from the Citie to Terra firme, by a Bridge and a manner of a Causie, which hath about two hundred and fiftie paces. The Citie is built on Sand, & within two fathoms they finde fresh water, though sometimes it is unwholesome, not so much as the coast of Nombre de Dios; for the ayres in respect of the Marish are wont to cause diseases, but for the most part it is wholsome. The Haven is one of the least of the Indies, though the great Ships doe ride farre from the Citie. It hath at the entrie an Iland like that of Escombrera in Cartagena of Castile, whereby they called it Cartagena, and the Iland was called Codego, now they call it Caxes, it hath two leagues in length, & little more then halfe a league in bredth: it was wont to be inhabited with Indian Fishers, & it hath no water. The first that saw Carthagena, in the year 1502. was Roderick Bastidas, & the year 1504. Juan de la Cosa or John of the Thing went a shore, and found Lewes Guerra, and they were the first that began the warre with the Indians, which were proud and bould, and both men and women fought, with venomed arrows.

Amazonian women.

Afterward returned Alonso of Oieda with John of the Thing for Pilot Major, & Americo Vespucio for Mariner, & some years after Gregorie of Obiedo took upon him to inhabit Cartagena, & performed it not. The year 1532. went Don Pedro of Eredia born in Madrid, and inhabited it, and pacified a great part of the Countrie, though with labour and cunning, because the people were very warlike,

Valiant Virago.

and there was a woman that before they could take her, being about eighteene yeeres old, slew with her Bow eight Spaniards.

Saint James of Tolu.

The Village of Saint James of Tolu, is six leagues

from the Sea to the South-west of Cartagena two leagues from it, part by Sea (for by Land it cannot be gone) and part by the Marishes and Mountaines. It is a sound Countrie, of great breedings, and tillage, and fruits of Castile: the President Don Peter of Heredia peopled it. The Village of Marie thirtie two leagues from Cartagena, to the South, is also the inhabiting of Don Peter of Heredia, in the yeare 1534. The Village of * Sancta Cruz of Mopox is seventie leagues from Cartagena by the Sea and River of Magdalene, neere whose border it stands, & whereby they goe about more then halfe the way; it is not sound being among Quagmires. A Captaine of Don Peter of Heredia peopled it 1535. The yeare of 1509. the Bachiller Eusico (as hath been said) inhabited Sancta Marie, the auncient of the Darien, which is in this Government, forsaking the Village of Saint Sebastian of Bona vista, which the same Captaine Alonso de Oieda had inhabited, in the furthest place of Uraba: & afterward the Captain Alonso of Heredia inhabited Saint Sebastian againe, for the President his Brother, in certaine little hils, almost halfe a league from the Sea. And in the yeare 1537. the Bachiller John of Vadillo went out of Saint Sebastian with a good number of Souldiours, and passing many troubles, & most rough Mountains, & thick woods, came to the Citie of Antioquia, of the government of Popayan, & there was a Souldior that from thence came to the Citie of the Plate, in the Charcas, which is 1200. leag.

The * Barranca of Malambo, which is a Custome house of the jurisdiction of Cartagena, thirtie leagues from it, on the border of the great River, and twenty from Sancta Martha, & six from the Sea, where the Merchandize that are carried by Land to the New Realme are unloaden, & from the Barranca are carried up by the River in Canooes. Lower then Nopox entreth the River of Cauca into the River of Magdalene, which also springeth about Popayan: & more toward Cartagena and to the West, standeth the Knobbe, and the point of Zamba, and Butrio del gato or

The Village of Marie.

**Holy Crosse.*

Saint Sebastian.

*The Barranca. *Or Watercourse.*

Arbolera, and the seven Cottages, and the point of the Canowe, two leagues from Cartagena, and the point of Ycacos at the entrie of the port, right against the Iland of Carex, and the point of the Ship in Terra firme; at the other lesser entrie of the port, and almost to the North, is a little Iland which is called Sardina, and in the coast of Tolu the Ilands of Baru, which are six, and at the entrie of the Gulfe of Uraba the six, which are called of Saint Bernard, right against the River Zenu: and more within the Gulfe, the strong Iland, and the Tortoyse. The port of Zenu stands five and twenty leagues from Cartagena, it is a great Bay that hath his entrance by the East, it is secure: here they make store of Salt, and it tooke the name of the Towne Zenu, which standeth on the River.

El Darado.
Guiana.

In the Provinces of the Darade, or new Estremadura (which circuit pertaines to the bounds of the Counsell of the New Realme) many Captains have entred by Sea, and by sundry parts of the Land, and have never found the riches which the same promiseth. They fall on the other side of the River of Saint John of Amazones, by another name Orellana (which some erroniously wil have to be the Meranyon) and here is the Orinico, and other great Rivers, and the Gulfe of Paria which maketh the firme land, with the Land of the Trinitie, & the mouthes

[III. v. 887.] of the Serpent, & the Dragon, which the first Admirall named, where he saw himselfe in great danger, for the conflict which the fresh waters make there with the salt, whereof he had yet no notice, and here beginneth the

Great Tydes. flowing of the Sea to be very great, unto the streight of Magellan, and goeth continuing through all the coast of Piru, and New Spaine.

Piru, or Peru. The Provinces of Piru (whose name hath extended it selfe more then it was at the beginning) include all the Empire of the Ingas, or more; for when it was won it was divided in two governments, that of Don Franciscus Piçarro, called the New Castile, from the Quito unto the Cuzco, sixtie leagues below the Chincha: and that of

Don James of Almagro, called the New Toledo, two
hundred leagues toward the Streight from Chincha; which
governments were distinct until the Councell de los Reyes
was established, and a Vice-roy provided for the Kingdomes of Piru, in whose government are included, the
Councell of Saint Francis of the Quito, that of Lima
(or de los Reyes of the Kings) that of the Charcas, the
government of Chile, & countries of the Streights, the
Ilands of Salomon to the West, and for borders the
Provinces of the River of Plate, and that which determin-
ately is comprehended under the government of the
Vice-roy. It hath in length North and South from two
thousand leagues upward, and East and West, that which
is discovered from the South Sea to the North Sea. The
two Rowes that have beene spoken of, doe passe through
all the Provinces of Piru North and South, that of the
Andes from Popayan, and yet many will have, that from
Terra firme and New Spaine, till it ends in the * Streight,
and the other lesse, from the Quito unto Chile, along the
coast, twelve leagues distant, little more or lesse.

*The two Rowes
of the Indies of
the South.*

**Of
Magellan.*

The two wayes passed betweene these two Mountaines,
the one which they called of the Ingas, by the Andes from
Pasto unto Chile, which hath nine hundred leagues in
length, and five and twentie foote of Cawsie, and every
foure leagues very sumptuous houses, which they call
Tambos, where was provision of victuals and apparell,
and every halfe league men that were in postes for to
carry messages, and orders from hand to hand. The
other way went through the middest of the Playnes, along
the coast of five and twentie foote broad, betweene two
walls of a mans height, from Piru unto Chile, where
both the wayes met. And it is to be noted, that all the
Indies of the South are not to be understood by Piru, for
as hath beene said, it is not but that which beginneth
from Saint Francis of Quito, which is under the Equinoctiall Line, and runneth along unto Chile, going out
of the Tropicks, which may bee six hundred leagues,
and fiftie in breadth, though toward the Chachapoyas there

*The two great
wayes of Piru.*

Postes.

*Piru is not all
the Indies of
the South.*

Los Llanos.

Las Sierras.

Diversitie of
nature.

is more, and it is divided in three parts : The Playnes, which have ten leagues in breadth, and in parts lesse, they are the coast of the Sea : The Hills, which have about twentie, and is all Hills and some Valleys : and the Andes other twentie, which are most thicke Groves and Woods, and in so little space as fiftie leagues equally distant from the Line and Pole : there is so great diversitie, that in the one place almost it rayneth alwayes, and in the other almost never, which is the Coast, and in the third which is the Mountaines that fall in the middest of these extreames, sometime it rayneth, and sometime not, for it hath his Summer and Winter as in Castile : and the causes of not rayning in the Coast, and rayne in the Andes, are spoken of in the beginning of the Historie.

Chap. 17.
Of the
Councell of
Saint Francis
of the Quito.

THe bounds of the Councell resident in Quito, and confining Northward with that of Panama, in the Port of Bonaventura, and on the North-east with the New Realme, and on the South with that of Lima ; hath in length by the South coast, which is the place where it lengthens most, about two hundred leagues from the Port of Bonaventure, which is in the Gulfe of Panama, or of Saint Michael, the Port of Payta in the coast of Piru, and from thence crosse to the uttermost of Popayan, more then other two hundred and fiftie, the limits remayning open on the East side : in it is included three Governments, besides those of the Councell, which are Popayan,

*Or
Cynamon.
El Quito.

Quixos, la Canela,* and that of Juan de Salinas, of the Pacamoros, and Gualsango, divided in two Bishopricks.

The Province and Government of Quito, which the Councell governeth, hath in length eightie leagues, from neere the Equinoctiall to the other side, and in it these Townes of Spaniards following. The heaven and earth thereof, although it stands under the Equinoctiall, is like to that of Castile, cleere and faire, rather cold then hot,

Aire and
seasons.

and in parts where the snow continueth all the yeere, it rayneth from October to March, which they call the winter ; and in the other monoths they cut their Grasse, which though it be not long it is fit for the Cattell of Castile, whereof there is great store; and of Wheat and Barley, and gold in some places: and in this Region they live pleasantly, for there is nothing more pleasant for humane life, then to enjoy a wholesome and cleere skie, for they have no Winter to trouble them with cold, nor Summer to molest with heat. The Townes are, the Citie of Saint Franciscus of Quito, where Athavalpa Emperour of Piru was borne, it stands in halfe a degree of height from the Equinoctiall, and eightie two from the Meridian of Toledo, by a greater circle one thousand sixe hundred eightie sixe leagues from it, and sixtie from the South Sea; it is of five hundred housholds: In it is resident the Councell for matters of Justice, for those of the Government are at the Vice-roy his charge. There are also in this Citie the Officers of the Kings Rents and treasurie Royall, and the Cathedrall of this Bishopricke, Suffragane to the Archbishop of The Kings (los Reyes) there are three Monasteries of Dominicke, Franciscan, and Mercenarie * Friars: and in her jurisdiction eightie seven Townes, or parcialities of Indians. In the situation where this Citie was built, were certaine great lodgings which the King Topayuga built, and his sonne Guayvacapa beautified, and were called Quito, from whence the Citie tooke the name: the President Sebastian of Belalcaçar, a souldier of Don Franciscus Piçarro built it, a loyall man to the King, by order of the President Don James of Almagro, which left him for Governour of the Province when hee went unto it, having ended the agreement with the President Don Peter of Alvarado.

The River Bamba in the Province of the Purvaes, is a Countrie to Castile in the temperature, of herbes, flowres, and other things: it is a towne of shepheards, it stands five and twentie leagues to the South-west of Saint Francisce of Quito, the way to the Kings, wherein are fortie thousand head of cattell, the greatest part sheepe. Here the Yugas had certaine Royall houses, and here the President Belalcazar had a tedious battaile with the

Athavalpa or Atabaliba.

[III. v. 888.]

*Friars de la Merced, or our Lady of Grace.

River Bamba.

Indians, and overcame them, and in this place was the agreement rehearsed of Don James of Almagro and Don Peter of Alvarado, and in it was the Citie of Quito first built.

Cuenca. The citie of Cuenca (which the Marques of Cavyete commanded to be built, being Vice-roy of Piru, which by another name is called Bamba, one and fiftie leagues from Quito to the South) is a Corregidorship provided of the Vice-roy, with one Monasterie of Dominicke, another of Franciscan Friars. In her jurisdiction are rich mynes of gold, some of silver, and rich mynes of quick-silver, copper, Iron, and Brimstone. The citie of Loxa,

Loxa.
*Or Briar. otherwise called la Zarça eightie leagues from the citie of Quito toward the South, and thirtie from Cuenca, is a Governourship provided by the Vice-roy; it hath Monasteries of Saint Dominicke and of Saint Francis, it stands in the way from Cuzco to Quito, from whence it is eightie leagues, in the faire Valley of Cuxibamba, betweene two Rivers. Captaine Antonie of Mercadillo built it in the yeere 1546. for to pacifie the countrimen which were

Zamora. somewhat disordered. The citie of Zamora, which is called of the Alcaydes, is ninetie leagues from Quito South-eastward, having passed the Rowe of the Andez: it is a Government provided by the Vice-roy: it hath a Monasterie of Franciscans; they reape no Wheat because the countrie is very raynie: it hath rich Mynes of gold, wherin they find graines of foure pound waight and more: the Captaine Mercadillo peopled it the yeere 1549. by a covenant with Captaine Benavente: It stands twentie leagues from Loxa, having past the Rowe which divideth the bankes of the South Sea from the North, the Indians did call it Zamara: that part of the countrie is called Poroauca, which signifieth Indians of warre: much gold is gotten there, and there hath beene graines brought to his Majestie of twelve pound waight, and there are Salt-pits of salt-water.

Jaen. The citie of Jaen is five and fiftie leagues from Loxa, and thirtie from the Chachapoyas; Captaine James Palomino built it 1549. in the Provinces of Chuquimayo, in that of Chacaynga. The citie of Saint Michael of Piura is in the Province of Chila, one hundred and twentie leagues from Quito South-eastward, and five and twentie from the Port of Payta, where the bounds of this Councell doth end. It is a Government at the providing of the Vice-roy: it hath one Monasterie of Mercenaries. Though in this countrie rayne is holden for a wonder, there are good watered grounds, that beare good Wheat and Millet, and the seedes and fruits of Castile. The port of Payta stands in the jurisdiction of this Citie, in five Southerne degrees, which is good, great, and secure, where the ships that goe from Guatemala to Piru doe touch. The Marques Don Franciscus Piçarro built it in the yeere 1531. the first of these Kingdomes, and where the first Temple was erected in the honour of God, and the holy Mother Church of Rome. All the Province and borders of the Valleys of Tumbez are drie, and the high-way of the Ingas passeth through these Valleys of Piura, betweene trees and pleasant shadowes, and betweene the principall Valley are joyned two or three Rivers: the Citie was built at the first in Tangazala, from whence it was remooved because it was a sickly situation, and now it stands betweene two Valleys, and yet is somewhat sickly, especially for the eyes, for the great windes and dusts of the Summer, and great moistures of the Winter.

The Citie of Saint James of Guayaquil, by another name las Culata, sixtie leagues from Quito, and fifteene from the Sea to the South-west, it is a Government provided by the Vice-roy: the President Belalcazar peopled it, and many of the Indians having rebelled, and slaine many Spaniards, the Captaine Franciscus of Orellana peopled it againe 1537. it is a most plentifull and pleasant Countrie, and hath great store of hony in the hollow places of trees: The waters of this River which runne almost under the Equinoctiall, are thought healthfull for the French disease, and other such like. Many people

Saint Michael of Piura.

Raine a wonder.

Payta.

High-way admirable.

San Jago de Guayaquil.

The Rivers that goe to the North Sea are greater then those that goe to the South Sea.

went to the River to recover health, for the multitude
of the rootes of Zarçaparrilla that are in the River: it
is not very great, nor those that run to the South Sea are
so bigge as those that runne into the North Sea, because
they runne but a little way; but notwithstanding they
are strong and with sudden flouds, because they fall from
How the rivers the Mountaine. The Indians doe use many shifts for
are passed in to passe them; they have in some places a rope over it,
Piru. and a basket on it, and the passenger being put into it,
they pull him from the other side. In other Rivers the
Indian goeth riding on a trusse of straw, and carrieth
[III. v. 889.] the passenger behinde him: in other places they have a
great Net of gourds, upon the which they lay the cloathes
and the persons, and the Indians fastened with certaine
coardes goe swimming and pulling as coach-horses; and
a thousand other artes they use for to passe the Rivers.
The Port of this Citie stands neere unto it, for the River
is very broad, whereby they bring up the merchandise
from the Sea, and they goe by land to Quito. The yeere
Castro. 1568. Captaine Contero planted the citie of Castro, in
the Valley of Vili, the Licentiate Lope Garcia of Castro
Vili. beng Governour. Vili is in the Provinces of Bunigando,
Imdivono, and Gualapa, which they call the Province of
the Emeralds, and he went about it from Guayaquil, and
discovered all these Provinces from Passao unto the River
of Saint John, which entreth into the South Sea.
Or old Port. The Citie of Puerto Viejo is about eightie leagues
from Saint Francis of Quito to the West, though not of
open way, and other fiftie from Saint James of Guayaquil,
whereby yee goe from Quito: in her borders stands the
Passao, which is the first Port of the countrie of Piru,
and from it, and from the River of Saint James, began
the government of the Marques Don Franciscus Piçarro:
and because this countrie is so neighbour to the Equinoctiall line, that it stands in one degree; some beleeve it
is unwholsome, but in other parts as neere the Line men
live with much health, plentie and abundance of all things
for the sustenance of man, against the opinion of the

ancient: and so it is that the Indians of this countrie
doe not live long, and in many of them there breede
certaine red warts in the foreheads and noses, and other
parts, which beside the disease being grievous, it dis-
figureth them very much, and it is beleeved that it
proceedeth of eating some fish. In these bounds stands
the towne of Manta, whither great riches have beene *Manta.*
brought from within the Land; and it is held for certaine,
that here is a Myne of Emeralds, which are the best of
the Indies, and they grow in a stone like Cristall, and *How the*
they making like a veine, and by little and little congealing *Emeralds do*
and refining themselves, and of halfe white and halfe *grow.*
greene, they goe ripening and recovering their perfection.
The Captaine Franciscus Pacheco peopled this citie 1535.
by order of Don James de Almagro: it hath many Indians
in warre: there is in it a Monasterie of Mercenarie Friars,
they gather no Wheat, for it rayneth the eight moneths
in the yeere from October forward, and there are many
good showes of gold.

In the coast of this Government are the Ports, Ilands, *Ports &*
and Points following. The ᶜAucon of ᵈSar dinas, before *Points of the*
the Bay of Saint James, which is fifteene leagues from the *coast of this*
Point of Manglares to the South, and then the Bay of *government.*
Saint Matthew, and after the Cape of Saint Francis; and *ᵈOr Pilchers.*
past it Quiximies, foure Rivers before Portete, where the
blacke Moores that saved themselves of a ship that was *A towne of*
cast away, joyned with the Indians, and have made a *blacke Moores.*
towne; the Passao, a Point or Port of Indians, where they
say the Equinoctiall line passeth, neere the Mountaine of
Queaque, and the Bay of Carta which is before old Port,
one degree from the Equinoctiall to the South, and five
leagues from thence the Cape of Saint Laurence, and neere
from thence the Iland of Plate, and forward the Ports of
Callo, and Calango, before the Point of Saint Helen, in
two degrees hight; the River of Tumbez in foure degrees,
and the Iland of the Puna neere unto it, and the Iland
of Sancta Clara somewhat more to the Sea, and Cabo blanco
fifteene leagues from Tumbez to the South, and then the

e *Or white Cape.*

f *Or woolves.*

The Giants of the Point of Santa Helena.

Point of Parina, and to the South the Iland of e Lobos, foure leagues from the Port of Payta abovesaid, and la Silla, before the Point del Aguia, and the Port of Tangora.

The men of this countrie say, that in old time there came by Sea in Balsas (which are many pieces of timber fastened one upon another) men so bigge that had as much from the knee downward, as an ordinarie man in all his body, and that they made certaine Wells most deepe in a quicke Rocke, which at this day are seene very fresh and cold in the Point of Saint Helen, and that because that they used most abominable sinnes, fire fell from heaven and consumed them all, and now are found in that situation exceeding great bones of men, and pieces of teeth of fourteene ounces weight, and in New Spaine in the bounds of Tlascala, are bones found of the like bignesse. There are in this Point of Saint Helen, eyes and veine of Tarre, so perfect that they might calke with it, and it commeth out very hot.

Chap. 18. Of Popayon, Quixos, Canela, Pasamoros, and Gual- songo, which are the rest of the bounds of the Councell of Quito.

THe government of Popayan one hundred and twentie leagues North and South, from the confines of the Province of Quito, under the Equinoctiall unto the confines of Cartagena by the North, and another one hundred from the confines of new Realme by the East unto the South Sea, wherein are some Spanish townes, part of the Councell of Quito, and part of the new Realme. The countrie is commonly rough and very raynie, and therefore they have little Millet, and lesse Wheat, and no store of Cattell, but it is rich of Mynes of gold, and the Townes are these following.

The Citie of Popayan.

The citie of Popayan stands in two degrees and a halfe to the Septentrionall part of the Equinoctiall, and 78. and a halfe of longitude, one thousand five hundred and eightie leagues from Toledo : in it is resident a Lieftenant Governour, the Cathedrall, and one Monasterie of Mercenarie Friars. The President Sebastian of Belalcazar peopled this citie 1537. the people of these Provinces are farre different from that of Piru, for these are of greater understanding, and lived in more policie: the men of this government lived as in liberties. It was called Popayan, of the name of the Cazique Lord of it: it hath part in the [III. v. 890.] coast of the South Sea, and high Mountaines that goe Eastward: and on another side the Row of the Andes, and on both sides spring many Rivers, and the River of the Magdalene is one, which runneth into the North Sea: in this government are many coole and wholesome townes, and others hot and sickly.

The Citie of Cali stands in foure degrees, and two and *Cali.* twentie leagues from Popayan, and eight and twentie from the South Sea, it was inhabited 1537. by the Captaine Michael Munioz; and Sebastian of Belalcazar made it first in the townes which are called the * Gorroves; it *Or great hath the seate in a plaine Valley, leaning to the foot of a Cappes.* Hill, the temper is hot, the Governour, the Officers, and the Kings treasure are resident in it; a melting house, a Monasterie of Mercenaries, another of Augustine Friars. The Port of Bonaventure falleth in his jurisdiction in three degrees and a halfe of altitude: in it are some housholds resident for to receive the merchandize. The Indians of Cali are of a good condition, and good Christians, their old Lord was called Lisupete. The village of Saint Fè of Antiochia, is more then an hundred *Antiochia.* leagues from Popayan to the north-east, in the borders of the River Cauca, of the bounds of the Councell of the New Realme, and Bishopricke of Popayan, rich in Mynes of gold, neere to the Hill of Buritaca famous for the much gold that was in it: it is seated in certaine Plaines. The countrie people are good folkes, well made and white, and the temperature is such that they goe to sleepe on the houses, without any offence of the deaw: they breede much Cattell, many fruits, and fish in the Rivers and Plashes: the Captaine Gaspar of Rhodes inhabited it by commission of the President Belalcazar, the yeere 1541.

The Village of Caramanta is sixtie or seventie leagues *Caramanta.* from Popayan to the North-east, neere to the great River

515

Cauca, of the bounds of the New Realme, government and Bishopricke of Popayan, plentifull of Millet and other seedes, without Wheat, and with little Cattell, though they have many Swine, they goe by the River in five or sixe houres to Antiochia, though it bee fiftie leagues; for it runneth very swift: it is the plantation of the President Belalcazar. The village of Saint James of *Arma.* Arma, which hath many Mynes of gold, is fiftie leagues from Popayan to the North-east, declining to the East, it is of the Councell of the new Realme, the government and Diocesse of Popayan; without Wheat or seedes of Castile, but plentifull of the countrie seedes. The President Belalcazar inhabited this village, and here hee beheaded the Marshall George Robledo. It stands sixteene leagues from Ancerma: the people of the countrie *Canibals.* are so butcherly that the quicke are the sepulchre of the *Inhumanitie of* dead, for it hath beene seene the husband to eate the *the Indians of* wife, the brother the brother or sister, the sonne the father, *the borders of* and having fatned any captive, the day that they are to *Arma.* eate him, they bring him forth with many songs, and the Lord commandeth that an Indian doe goe cutting off every member, and so alive they goe eating him, and after the inhabiting of Arma they have eaten more then eight thousand Indians, and some Spaniards have also suffered this martyrdome.

Ancerma. The village of Saint Anne of Ancerma is fiftie leagues from Popayan to the North-east, in the border of Cauca, of the Councell of the new Kingdome, government and Bishopricke of Popayan, without Cattell or Wheat, very much annoyed with thunder-bolts: the Captaine George Robledo built it by order of Laurence of Aldana. Likewise the men of this countrie are eaters of humane flesh; they goe naked, they have no Idols, nor any thing to worship: there are in this jurisdiction good Mynes of gold; the climate is hot, and many thunder-bolts doe *Cartago.* fall. The citie of Cartago, five and twentie leagues from Popayan about the North-east, is of the Councell of the New Realme, Government and Bishoprick of Popayan,

without Wheat or any seedes of Castile: it is a temperate and wholesome countrie, of little gold, it rayneth much, they breede no other cattell but Kine, and Mares: they have many Mountaines, in the which breede many Lions, Tigres, Beares, and *Dantas, and wilde Boares: they *Or Buffes. have a Monasterie of Franciscan Friars: the Captaine George Robledo inhabited it, and it was called Cartaga, because all the inhabiters were of Cartagena. The village of Timana is fortie leagues from Popayan to the South- Timana. east, and sixtie from Santa Fè of Bogota, and thirtie from the Provinces of Dorado; here is a Lieftenant of the Governour, which also hath at his charge Saint Sebastian de la Plata: the Indians of their borders doe decay, for they are so inhumane that in many places they have Inhumanitie of publike shambles of men which they take captive. They these Indians. have their seate in the beginning of the Valley of Neyva, the temper is most hot: in their bounds is a Mountaine where they digge the Load-stone, and the Indian Paezes Where the are neere, and the Pixaos, which also are *Caribes. Load-stone is
found.
The Citie of Guadalajara of Buga, is fifteene leagues *Or eaters of from Popayan to the North-east, is of the bounds of the humane flesh. Councell of Quito, and Diocesse of Popayan. The Citie Buga. of Saint Sebastian of the Plate, in the confines of this Saint Sebas- Government is thirtie five leagues from Popayan, and tian of the thirtie to the South-west from Santa Fe, Diocesse of Plate. Popayan, where are many Mynes of silver, and in her borders twentie foure repartitions: it is three leagues from the Port of Onda, in the great River of Magdalen, where those that come up from Cartagena doe land: it is built in a Plaine, neere to the River Guala: there are many Earthquakes, and in Winter it is more hot then cold. The Countrymen goe to decay, because the ᶜCaribes which ᶜOr Canibals. they call del Rincon do eate them and have publike shambles of them, without any remedie for it: and the President Belalcazar built this Citie. The Citie of [III. v. 891.] Almaguer is twentie leagues from Popayan to the South- Almaguer. east; it is plentifull of Wheate and Millet, and other seeds, and cattle, and it hath Gold: the Captaine Alonso

of Fuenmayor, by order of the Licentiate Brizenyo Governour, and ^d Judge of Accounts, of Popazan peopled it,
being seated in a Hill of Zabana, and the climate is fresh,
and the people doe weare Cotton-cloth.

    S. John of Truxillo, and by another name Yscauce is
thirtie leagues from Popayan to the South-east. The
Citie of Madrigall, or Chapanchica, thirtie five from
Popayan about the South, a rough Countrey, where they
neither reape Wheate, nor breed cattell, though they gather
Millet twice a yeere in their jurisdiction: and for the
roughnesse of the Countrey, the men are evill to pacifie,

and in this Citie, and in the Citie of Agreda, and
Almaguer, are Mynes of Gold. Agreda, and by another
name Malga, stands fortie five leagues from Popayan to

the South-west. The Citie of Saint John of the Pasture,
so called because it is a Countrey of many Pastures, it
stands fiftie leagues from Popayan, about the South-west,
and as many from Quito about the North-east, and in
one degree from the Equinoctiall Diocesse of Quito, in
a good soyle, of a good climate, and plentifull of Millet,
and other provisions, with Mynes of Gold; In her borders
are 24000. Indians of fee, which are not Caniballs, but

of evill visages, filthy, and simple: they had no Idols
in the time of their Paganisme, they beleeved that after
death they should goe to live in more joyfull places. The
River which they call Whoate, is betweene Pasta, and
Popayan, it is of a very delicate water, and passed this
River is the Mountayne whither Gonçalo Piçarro did
follow the Vice-roy Blasco Nunyez Vela, and unto the
River Augasmayo, which is in this Province came the
King Guaynacapa.

    Beyond the River Caliente or hot River in a Moun-
tayne, is a firie mouth, that casteth store of smoake, and
it brake forth in ancient times, as the Countreymen doe

say. The Philosophers being willing to declare what
these firie mouthes or Ætnaes are, doe say, that as in the
Earth are places that have vertue to attract a vaporie
substance, and to convert it into water, whereof the con-

tinuall springs are made : there are also places that doe attract to themselves dry and hote exhalations, which are converted into fire and smoake, and with the force of them they cast also another grosse substance which is dissolved into ashes, or into stones, and these are the fierie mouthes. Saint John de Pasto hath Monasteries of Dominicke, Franciscan, and Mercenarie Friers : it is a cold Countrey, with abundance of victuals, it hath Sugar Mils, and many Fruites of the Countrey and of Castile : when the Captaine Lawrence of Aldona built it, hee called it ᵉ Villa viciosa de Pasto, it stands fortie leagues from the South Sea, towards the Iland Gorgova.

ᵉ *Or the ranke Village of Pasture.*

There hath beene disinhabited, or diminished in this Province, the Citie of Antiochia, the Village of Neyva in the Valley of Neyva, twentie leagues from Tumava, and it was through the rigour of the Indian Paezes, and Pixaos, and for the Manipos, in the Valley of Saldavya, and the Citie of Saint Vincent of the Paezes, sixtie leagues from Saint John of the Plaines, in the confines of Popayan, which Domingos Lozavo built, and the Citie of los Angelos, twentie two leagues from Tocayma, and nine from Neyva. There is in the Coast which this government extendeth on the South Sea, from the Cape of Corrientes, that stands in five degrees Septentrionall from the Line, the River of Solinas, betweene the Cape of Corrientes and the Iland of the Palmes in foure degrees one third part, and in the Coast that lyeth unto Gorgova, the River of Saint John among many other which make the Countrey boggie, and right against the mouth, the Iland of Gorgova, two leagues compasse, where Don Franciscus Piçarro was forsaken of all his men, with his thirteene companions. The River of Saint Lucar, and the River of Nicardo, before the River of ᶠ Zedros, in two degrees from the Line, in which stands the Ile del Gallo, and after the Port of the Crosse, and the point of Manglares, where beginneth the Coast of Quito.

Neyva.

Saint Vincent.

The Angels.

Rivers, Capes, and Points of the Coast of this government.

ᶠ *Or Cedars.*

Of the government of the Quixos, and Canela, there is no more notice, but that it falls to the East of the

Province of Quito, and part of the South, toward the
government of John of Salinas; there are in it three
Spanish Townes, with a Governour which the Vice-roy
of Piru provideth, and in spirituall respect it is of the
Bishopricke of Quito: the Countrey is rough and Mountaynous, without Wheate, and little Millet, with certayne
Trees which seeme of Cinamon. The first Towne is
Baeça eighteene leagues from Saint Francis of Juito,
toward the South-east, where the Governour is Resident:
the Citie of Archidova is twentie leagues beyond Baeça:
the Citie of Avila stands to the North of Archidova.

*Pacamores and
Gualsongo.* The government and Province of Pacamoros and
Gualsango, or of John of Salinas whose bounds and limits
are one hundred leagues, which were assigned him to
the East, from twentie leagues before the Citie of Zamora,
in the Rowe of the Andes, and as many more North and
South. It is a good Countrey in temper and disposition
for Wheate, seeds, and cattle, of rich Mynes of Gold
where they have pieces of great bignesse: there are
in it foure Townes of the Bishopricke of Quito, for
the Captaine John of Salinas did build them. The
Citie of Valladolid is in seven degrees height, twentie
leagues from Loxa to the South-east, having past the
Rowe of Piru, the Citie of Loyola, or Cumbruania is
sixteene leagues to the East from Valladolid: the Citie
of Saint James of the Mountaynes, fiftie leagues from
Loyola, toward the East, and in her borders much gold,
and very high in touch, and as touching the gold we
[III. v. 892.] need not intreat of his excellencies, being holden for
the Supreame power in the World. It is gotten in these
*In how many
sorts the gold
is gotten out
in Piru, and
other places.* Mynes in three manners: The first is in Pippens, which
are whole pieces without mixture of any other Metall,
that need not to be purified by fire, and these graines
commonly are like a Pompeon Seed, and sometimes
bigger: of this gold is found but litle, in respect of the
rest. The second sort is in stone, which is a vaine that
groweth in the stone it selfe, and these stones are found
in the government of John of Salinas very great, all

passed through with gold, and some which are halfe Gold, the which is found in Pits and Mynes, and it is hard to worke. The third, is gotten in powder, and is the greatest quantitie, and this is found in Rivers, or in places where some streame of water hath passed, and the Rivers of these Indies have many, especially in the Kingdoms of Chile, Quito, New Realme of Granada, and in the beginning of the Discoveries, there were many in the ^g Weather Ilands. The highest in touch is that of Carabaya in the Piru, and that of Valdivia in Chile, for it reacheth to twentie three Charracts and an halfe, and yet it passeth.

^g *Barlevento.*

THat which is called Piru, is proper and particularly the bounds of the Councell of los Reyes, and is comprehended North and South, from sixe unto seven Southerne degrees of altitude, which are two hundred and twentie leagues, though in Voyage they put three hundred from the point del Aguia, beyond Payta, whereby it joyneth with the Councell of Quito, till passing the Citie and Port of Arequipa, where beginneth the Councell of the Charcas, East and West. The inhabited part of this Councell hath about one hundred leagues from the Coast of the South Sea toward the East, whereby her bounds remayne open unto the Provinces of the River of Plate, and of Brasill, that which is from the Rowe, where, as hath beene said, it rayneth continually, unto the Sea, they call the Plaines of Piru, in the which it neither rayneth nor thundreth, because the great height of the Mountain doth shelter the Plaines in such sort, that it permitteth no wind from the Earth to blow, whereby the Sea wind reigneth, which having no contrary doth not represse the vapours that doe arise to make raine, in sort that the shelter of the Hill hindereth the thickning of the vapours: and this want of matter causeth that in that Coast the vapours are so thinne, that they make no more then a moyst or dankish mist, which is profitable for their sowings, which have not without the ^h mist so much

*Chap. 19.
Of the bounds
of the Councel
or Audience of
The Kings, or
los Reyes.
Mountaines
cause that it
rayneth not in
the Playnes of
Piru.
^h Some are of
opinion that
all plants and
trees are
nourished by
vapours: yea
that the
vapours of the
bloud nourish
living Crea-
tures. So Gen.
2. a mist in
Paradise, &c.
The Sunne as
Head of the
World, the
Hart as Sunne
in the Body,
causeth
nourishment
by vapours.*

vertue, be they never so much watered. The Countrey
is all sandie grounds, except the Valleyes which are made
by courses of the Rivers, that descend from the Mountayne, where much Corne is gathered by the waterings,
Wine, Oyle, Sugar, and the other Seeds, and Fruits, of
Castile, and of the Countrey. In the skirts and hils sides
of the Mountayne, are great Pastures and breedings of
cattell, and the temper variable, and as would be desired;
for the height is cold, and the low hot, and the middlemost
partakers of the extreames, as they are more or lesse neere
them. The government of this Councell, and of Quito,
and of the Charcas, is in the charge of the Vice-roy, and
there are the Townes following in the circuit of this
Councell.

*The Citie of
The Kings, or
los Reyes.*
The Citie of the Kings (or of Lima, because the Valley
is so called, which was the name of the Cazique, and it
is the greatest and broadest Valley, of all those that are
from Tumbez unto it) stands neere the South Sea, in
twelve degrees of Southerne altitude, and eightie two
from the Meridian of Toledo, distant from it about one
thousand eight hundred and twentie leagues by a greater
circle: it hath above three thousand housholds: the
Marques Don Franciscus Piçarro built it, in the beginning
of the yeere 1533. because suspecting that the President
Don Peter of Alvarado would come downe to the Sea
coast, when hee went with an Host from Guatemala
meanewhile that Don James of Alvarado went to resist
him to the Provinces of Quito, hee went to intercept
him the passages of the Sea. Neere this citie, on the
East side, passeth a River from whence all the houses
doe take water, and their gardens, wherein are excellent
fruits of Castile and of the Countrie, and it is one of the
best Climates of the World, seeing there is neither famine
nor pestilence; nor doth it rayne or thunder, nor fall
there any thunder-bolts or lightnings, but the Heaven
is alwayes cleere and very faire.

In this Citie is resident the Vice-roy, the Royall
Councell, an assembly of chiefe Justices, the Officers of

the Kings Rents, and treasurie Royall, the Tribunall of
the holy and generall Inquisition, which was founded
when the Inquisition of New Spaine was. The
Inquisitor generall in these Kingdomes was then the
Cardinall Don James of Espinosa Bishop of Siguença,
it having proceeded with mature deliberation, for the
augmenting of our holy Catholike Faith, and Christian
Religion. There is also in this Citie an Universitie,
where very learnedly the Sciences are read, and Schooles
of divers languages of the Indians, in the which the
Fathers of the Companie of Jesus are very diligent, to
reape fruit in the preaching of the Gospell. In this Citie
is the Archepiscopall resident, whose Suffraganes are the
Bishops of Chile, Charcas, Cuzco, Quito, Panama,
Nicaragua, and the River of Plate. There are three
Parishes, and five Monasteries of the foure Orders, and
of the Companie of Jesus, and two of Nunnes. Callao
which is her Port, is two leagues from it, great, capable,
and very good, where are store of houses, one of Justice,
a custome House, one Church, and one Monasterie of
Dominicke Friars: here hath beene seene the Wine and
the Water set to coole in the Sea in flaggons, whence
it is inferred that the Ocean hath the vertue to temper
and refresh the over-much heate. Many doe affirme that
in this Citie are twelve thousand Women of all Nations,
and twentie thousand blacke-Moores.

 The Village of Arnedo in the Valley of Chancai, is
ten leagues from The Kings, and halfe a league from
the Sea, with a Monasterie of Dominicke Friars, rich of
Vines: the Earle of Nieva built it. The Village of the
* Parrilla, or Santa, is by the Valley where it stands,
fiftie five leagues from The Kings, and fifteene from
Truxillo neere the Sea, neere to a great and faire River,
with a good Haven, in nine degrees, where the ships
that saile by the coast of Piru doe touch. The Citie of
Truxillo is in the Valley of Chimo, which Don James of
Almagro plotted first, and afterward the Marques Don
Franciscus Piçarro built it in the yeere 1533. It hath

*Such holinesse
of faith, such
meanes to
establish it,
force gluing
lips and Let-
tice together,
as Acosta
complayneth.
Universitie
and Jesuites.*

Sea cooleth.

[III. v. 893.]
*Women and
Negros.
Arnedo.*

*OrGridiron.

Truxillo.

523

many Vines and fruits of Castile, and Wheat: it is all watered ground, and a wholesome Countrie, and there bee great Orchards of Oranges, and breeding of Poultrie. It stands in seven degrees and a halfe, eightie leagues from Lima neere the Sea, with Monasteries of Saint Dominicke, Saint Francis, and Saint Augustine, and another of the Mercenaries, and Officers Royall, provided by the Vice-roy: and in her bounds about fiftie thousand tributarie Indians, in two and fortie repartitions. The Port is two leagues off in an open Bay, evill, and of little securitie.

Miraflores. The Village of Miraflores is in the Valley of Zava, ninetie five leagues from the Citie of The Kings to the North *Chachapoyas.* side, and neere to the Sea. The Citie of Chachapoyas, or Saint John of the Frontier, is about one hundred and twentie leagues from the Citie of The Kings to the North-east, it hath one Monasterie of the Mercenaries, and another of the Franciscans: in her bounds are Wheat, Millet, and Flaxe, many Mynes of gold, and more then twentie thousand tributarie Indians, which held out valorously a long time against the Ingas, but in the end they were over-come, and for greater quietnesse of the Countrie they carried many of them unto Cuzco, and they inhabited in a Hill which is called Carmenga. These *Faire Indians.* are the whitest and best favoured Indians of all the Indies, and the Women very faire. The Marshall Alfonsus of Alvarado, entred in this Province the yeere 1536. by order of the Marques Don Francisco Piçarro, and pacified it, and built the said Citie in a strong situation called Levanto, and afterward he passed to the Province of the Guancas.

Saint James of the Valleys. The Citie of Saint James of the Valleys, or Moyobamba, more then one hundred leagues from The Kings North-eastward, and five and twentie from Saint John of the Frontier, stands in a very raynie soile, and plentifull of *Lion of Guanuco.* Cattell. The Citie of Lion of the Guanuco, fiftie leagues from the Cite of The Kings to the North, neere the high-way of the Ingas, somwhat distant towards the East, hath Monasteries of Dominicans, Franciscans, and Mercen-

aries, and in her bounds thirtie thousand tributarie
Indians. Anno 1539. for the warre that the Tyrant
Yllotopa made to this Province, the Marques Don
Franciscus Piçarro sent Captaine Gomez of Alvarado
which built it, and afterward it was disinhabited, and
Peter Barroso reedified it, and after the battell of Chupas
the Licentiate Vaca de Castro, sent Captaine Pedro de
Puelles to make an end of the plantation. It stands in
a good and wholesome situation, abundant of victuals
and Cattell: it hath Mynes of silver, and the people is
of good capacitie. They reape much Wheat, for the
Indians have learned to be good husbandmen: for as
before in these Indies there was no Wheat, nor Barley,
nor Millet, nor Panick, nor any seede of the bread of
Castile of Europe, and they knew other kindes of Graine
and Rootes, only of the which Mayz or Millet was the
principall, being found in all the Indies; the Countrimen
have since delighted much in it, and have received it
well in those places where it is gathered, because the *Qualities of*
Mayz is not so strong nor of so much substance as the *the Millet.*
Wheat: it is fatter, and hot, and engendreth bloud, it
groweth in Canes, and beareth one or two bunches, and
some Spaniards doe eate it where they have no other
shift.

The Citie of Guamanga, or Saint Juan of the Victorie, *Guamanga.*
sixtie leagues from Lima to the South-east, in the way
of the Ingas, Bishoprick of Cuzco, hath Monasteries of
Dominicans, Franciscans, and Mercenaries, and one of
Nunnes, and in her bounds more then thirtie thousand
tributarie Indians: it is plentifull of Wheate and Wine,
and rich of silver Mynes. The Marques Don Franciscus
Piçarro built this Citie 1539. and placed it the first time
in a towne of Indians called Guamanga, neere to the great
Row of the Andes, and left for his Lieftenant the Captaine
Francisco de Cardenyas. Afterward it was removed to
the Playne where now it is, neere to certaine small Hills
on the South side, and nigh to a Brooke of good water.
In this Citie are the best houses in Piru, of stone and

bricke; the seate is healthfull, without offence of the
Sunne, the Aire, the Deaw, or the Moisture, or the Heate.

Great
buildings.

There are found in her borders certaine great buildings
(which the Indians say certaine white men with beards,
which came thither before the Ingas, did build) much
differing from the building of the Ingas: the most of
the Countrimen of this Countrie are Mitimaes, which

Transplanting
as of Egyptians
Gen. 42. 21.
the Israelites,
2. Reg. 17.
Jewes to Bab.
&c.

is to say, Transplanted, for the Ingas did use for the
greater securitie of the Empire, to take from one Province
the people they did not trust, and send them to live in
another.

Guamanga is sixtie leagues from Cuzco, and in the
way are the Hills and Playne of Chupas, where Vaca de
Castro, and Don James de Almagro the yonger did fight;
and forward are the buildings of Vilcaf, in the high way
in Andabaylas, eleven leagues from Guamanga, which was

Temple of the
Sunne.

the centre of the Ingas; and here was the great Temple
of the Sunne. The Province of the Andabaylas is long
and hath much tame Cattell, and victualls; from thence
they come to the River of Abancay, nine leagues neerer
Cuzco, where the President Don James of Almagro the

[III. v. 894.]

elder overthrew and apprehended Alfonso of Alvarado,
Generall of the Marques Don Francisco Piçarro. There
followeth the River of Apurima, eight leagues from
Passado, or the Passage, which is very great; and then
the Hill of Vilcaconga, where the said President Almagro
over-came a great battell of the Indians, before he won
Cuzco, and the Valley of Xaquixaguana is neere betweene
two rowes of Hills, not broad nor long, where the President Pedro la Gasca, by the vertue of those valiant and
faithfull Captaines Ynojosa, Peter of Valdibia, Gabriel
of Rojas, Alfonsus of Alvarado, and others (of the which
in their place shall be made mention particularly) did
over-throw Gonçalo Piçarro, and tooke him: and from this
Valley to the Citie of Cuzco are five leagues: and in this
Valley they gather great store of Wheat, and have great
store of Cattell

ANTONIO DE HERRERA

EIght or ten leagues from the Citie of Guamanga, somewhat North-westward, are the Mynes of Guan- cabelica, which they call El Assiento de Oropesa, where ordinarily are resident more then three hundred Spaniards. The Indians did worke in them to take out the red Oaker, to paint themselves when in the time of their Paganisme they went to warre, which is the Vermillion: and the Licenciate Lope Garcia of Castro, governing in Piru in the yeere 1566. a Portugall called Henrie Garces, considering that of the Vermillion the quick-silver is gotten, went to make a triall, and found it to be so. This metall the Romanes carried from Castile in stone, and out of it they got quick-silver, and held it for great riches. The Indians knew it not, nor minded any more then the ver- milion. The greatest profit it yeeldeth, is to purifie the *Profit of* silver from the earth, Lead, and Copper, wherewith it *quick silver.* groweth: it eateth all the other metals, and pierceth them as the Tin, Iron, and Lead, and therefore they carry it in leather, or vessels of earth. Quick-silver serveth also for other effects, and medicinall matters.

In this seat of Guania Velica is a spring, that as it *Spring turning* springeth it congealeth in a soft stone, of the which they *into stone, and* make their houses, and the Men or Beasts that doe drinke *killing.* it, die: for within the body it converteth into a stone. In the Bathes that are called of Inga neere the Cuzco, are two spouts of water the one neere the other, the first is hot, and the second cold, that it seemeth God did place *Hot and cold* them there for to temper themselves. In the same bounds *Bathes.* is a Spring, that as it springeth it becomes good and *Salt spring.* white salt: in this place the two great Rowes doe begin *Cordilleras or* to separate themselves, and make in the middest a great *rowes divided.* Champaine ground, which is called the Province of Collao, *Collao.* where are very many Rivers, and there is the great Lake of Titicaca, and great pasture grounds. Though it be a plaine Countrie, it hath the same height and distemperature of the Hills; it hath no Trees, nor Wood; the bread that is eaten are rootes that are called Papas, which grow also in all Piru; it is a healthfull Countrie, and much inhabited, and multiplieth every day; it hath store of Cattell of all sorts.

The Lake of Titicaca compasseth eightie leagues, and in some places it hath eightie fathom deepe, and in this, and in the waves are raysed when there is any winde, so that it seemeth as a Bay of the Sea, from which it stands about sixtie leagues, twelve or thirteene Rivers enter into it, and many Brookes, and from it goeth a River into another Lake, which they call the Aulagas, which hath no voyding place, though because some Eyes of water have beene seene that under ground goe into the Sea, it is judged that it might bee the water of these Lakes did goe, opening a way through the entrailes of the Earth unto the Sea. Round about the great Lake are many Townes, and in it great Ilands, with great Tillage in them, and there were the Indians wont to keepe their most precious things for greater securitie.

The great Citie of Cuzco, Seate Royall of the Ingas, and Head of their Empire (and now of the Kingdomes of Piru, by a Title which it hath of it from the Kings of Castile and Lion) stands in thirteene degrees and a halfe height, seventie eight of longitude, one hundred and five and twentie leagues from the Citie of The Kings to the South-east, of more then one thousand Spanish housholds; the Marques Don Franciscus Piçarro founded it. It hath eight Parishes, and foure Monasteries of the foure Orders, of Saint Dominicke, Saint Francis, Saint Augustine, the Mercenaries, and the Companie of Jesus, and one of Nunnes. Heere is resident the Cathedrall, Suffragane to the Archbishopricke of The Kings. There goe from this Citie since the time of the Ingas from the Market place foure high wayes towards the foure parts of the world; one called Chinchasuyo to the North, toward the Playnes and Provinces of Quito: another Condesuyo, to the West toward the Sea: the third called Collaosuyo, to the South and Chile: and the fourth to the East, which they call Andesuyo, which goeth to the Andes and skirts of the Mountaine. It stands in a soile of a good temper, moder-

ately fresh and healthfull, free from all venemous wormes, *No venemous*
and plentifull of all things, with a thousand kindes of *wormes.*
fruits of Castile, and smelling herbes and flowres at all
times which are of great delight.   In her jurisdiction is
the Valley of Toyma: there is great trafficke of Coca, and
showes of Gold, Silver, and Quick-silver; and there may
bee in her borders about an hundred thousand tributarie
Indians.   In all the parts of these Indies the Indians have
a great delight in carrying ordinarily in the mouth Rootes,
Boughes, or Herbes, and that which they most use in all
Piru, is the Coca, for as they say, they feele little hunger, *Coca a tree.*
and finde themselves with great vigour chewing it alwaies, [III. v. 895.]
though it rather seemeth a custome inherited, or a vice.
This is planted, and groweth to small trees, which are culti-
vated and cherished, and yeeld a leafe like myrtle, and
dried they carry it in baskets to sell, and much mony is
gotten by it.

In the Valley of Vilcabamba, stands Saint Francis of the *Saint Francis*
victorie in Andesuyo, between the Row of the Andes, *of the victorie.*
about twentie leagues from Cuzco to the East side, with
a Governour provided by the Vice-roy: it is of the
Bishopricke of Cuzco, in a rough ground, and of great
Mountaines.

The village of Saint John del Oro, is in the Province *Saint John of*
of Carabaya eightie leagues from Cuzco to the East South- *the Gold.*
east, and thirtie to the East from the Lake of Collao, and
it is called del Oro, of the Gold, for the great store that is
in her borders.   The Citie of Arequipa is in sixteen *Arequipa.*
degrees somewhat more, one hundred and thirtie leagues
from the Citie of The Kings, almost to the South-east as
the Coast runneth, and sixtie from the Citie of Cuzco, of
the Bishopricke of Cuzco: it hath Monasteries of
Dominicks, Franciscans, and Mercenaries; it hath fiftie
thousand tributarie Indians, and is of most pleasant
temperature to live in of all places in Piru.   They gather
in her borders great store of Wine, and Wheat.   The
Port is at the entrie of the River Chile, which passeth neere
the Citie where the merchandize is unladen.

Arequipa stands in the Valley of Quilca, fourteene leagues from the Sea. In her jurisdiction is the Province of Condesuyo, the Townes of the Hubinas, Gollaguas, Chiquiguanita, and Quimistaca; the Marques Don Francisco Piçarro built it 1534. it is very subject to earth-quakes as all these Indies, especially the Sea coasts. In the yeere 1582. there was an earth-quake that almost ruinated this Citie, and since there hath beene another, and a breaking out of a fierie mouth, whereof they tell strange things, in the yeere 1586. There was another in the Citie of the Kings the ninth of July, which ran one hundred and seventie leagues in length by the Sea side, and fiftie within the Land; it spoyled the Citie, indangered few people, because they went out into the fields, and a little after the earth-quake was past, the Sea went out of her bounds, and entred a great way within the Land fourteene fathom deepe. Such another earth-quake was in Quito the next yeere, in the Citie of la Paz in the yeere 1581. a great high Rocke fell which tooke under it a great many Indian witch trees, and the earth which fell did run one league and a halfe. In Chile was another great earth-quake that over-threw Mountaines and Valleyes, stopped the Current of the Rivers, brought the Sea out of her limits the space of some leagues, cast downe whole Townes, and slue many men. The Philosophers say that the earth-quake proceedeth from the heate of the Sunne, and of other celestiall Bodies, which not onely doe draw the exhalation to themselves, and the vapour of the super-ficies of the earth, but that also which is in the bowels of it, which comming out engendreth windes and raynes; and if it happen that the earth is so close that the exhalation cannot come out any way, then it mooveth from one part to another through the pores of the earth, with great violence breaking forth, as the powder in a Myne, tearing with such a furious rage, that it renteth the earth where it is, and openeth it selfe a way with great furie, and so much furious it is, how much more the exhalation inclosed is greater.

Earth-quakes in the Indies very terrible and strange.

From whence the earth-quakes doe proceede.

The Village of Saint Michael de la Ribera is sixe leagues *Saint Michael* from the Sea, in the Valley of Camana, one hundred and *of the Riber.* thirteene leagues from The Kings, two and twentie from Arequipa to the part of the Equinoctiall, of the Bishop-ricke of Cuzco. The Village of Valverde in the Valley *Valverde.* of Yca, five and thirtie leagues from the Citie of The Kings, ten from the Port of Saugalla, is of the jurisdiction of The Kings, and of the Archbishopricke; her borders are plentifull of Wheat, Millet, and Fruits, and of much Wine.

The Village of Cavyete, or of Guarco, by the Valley *Guarco.* where it stands, is distant from The Kings five and twentie leagues to the South, one league and a halfe from the Sea: her bounds are plentifull of bread the best of this King-dome, whence is carried great quantitie of meale to Terra firme. Before the comming to this Valley, are the Valleys of Chilca, and Mala; in the first it never rayneth, neither passeth any Fountaine nor Brooke through it, and they drinke of the Wells, and it is full of arable grounds, and fruits, which grow onely by the deaw of the Heaven. *Fertilitie* They catch many Pilcherds in the Sea, and with every *without raine.* graine of Millet they put into the hole where it is sowen *Pilchards.* one or two of the heads, and with that moysture it groweth well. In the Valley of Mala, Don James of Almagro, and Don Franciscus Piçarro being in quarrell, the father Bova-dilla of the Merced or Mercenarie Order, as an Arbitrator resolved their differences; through this Valley passeth a great River, which doth them great pleasure. Five leagues forward is the River of Guarco in a Valley most plentifull in all things, where the Countrimen maintayned the warre foure yeeres against the Ingas, and to preserve it they caused to build a Citie, and called it Cuzco, and erected for the triumph of the victorie a great Fortresse on a Hill, that the waves of the Sea doe beate upon the stayres. Six leagues from Guarco is the Valley of Chincha, famous, pleasant, and very plentifull, where a Monasterie of Dominicke Friars was built in stead of the Temple of the Sunne which the Indians had, with the

Monasterie of the Virgins. Then followeth the Valley of Yca, which is no lesse plentifull, going out of the Valleys, and Rivers of Nasca, and the principall is called Caxamalca, where excellent Wines are made. They goe *Ocanna.* from these Valleys to that of Hacari, where stands Ocanna, Camana, and Quilca, which is the Port of the Citie of Arequipa, and forward are the Valleys of Chuli, and [III. v. 896.] Tambopalla, and the Deylo, and them of Tarapaca, Rivers and plentifull, with good Mynes of silver, and neere the Sea: the Indians of the Ilands of The Seales doe carry great store of Fowles dung for their grounds, wherewith of a barren, they make a plentifull ground.

Ports, Capes, and Points of these Bounds of the Counsel of The Kings. There are in the coast of this Councel from the Point del Aguia, of the Needle, where it joyneth with that of Quito, in six degrees of Southerne altitude, the Ilands and Ports following; two Ilands which they call de Lobos in seven degrees, the one foure leagues from the Coast, and the other more to the Sea; and forward another called of Saint Rooke to the South-east, neere to Pazcamayo, and forward Puerto de Mal Abrigo, ten leagues before the Port of Truxillo, in seven degrees and a halfe, and seven leagues from the Port of Guanape; and of Sancta in nine degrees, and five leagues from this to the South, Porte Ferrol; and six from it that of Cazma; and afterward eight leagues the Port of Guarmey at the mouth of a River; and the Barranca twentie leagues to the South; and the Port of Gaura where is a very great Salt pit; and after this the Iland of Lima, at the entrie of the Port of Collao; and twentie leagues to the South the Point of Guarco, and one Iland de Lobos Marinos, or Seale fishes neere to it, and the Point of Chica in fifteene degrees, and neere to the Nasca; and forward the Point of Saint Laurence, in the Valley of Quilca, and neere the River of Arequipa, and the Creeke of Chulien; and afterward the River of Nombre de Dios, where the limits doe joyne by the Coast of the Counsels of The Kings, and of Charcas.

THe bounds of the Counsell of Charcas (which parteth limits with that of The Kings, stands in twentie degrees and a halfe of Southerne altitude, by the River of Nombre de Dios, and the beginning of the Lake of Collao) hath in length three hundred leagues unto the Valley of Copiapo, beginning of the Province of Chile in eight and twentie degrees of height, though in voyage they are reckoned neere foure hundred leagues East and West, that which is betweene of the South Sea unto the North Sea, or South which answereth to the Provinces of the River of Plate, which though it is not altogether discovered, it is understood that by placing all the Countrie of this Counsell in much altitude, it is more cold then hot.

Chap. 21.
Of the Bounds
of the Counsel
or Audience of
the Plate, or
of Charcas.

The Government of this Counsell, is at the charge of the Vice-roy of Piru, as that of the Counsell of Quito, and of The Kings: there are two Governours, and two Bishopricks, that of Charcas and Tucuman. The Province of the Charcas (which commonly is named that which is from the bounds of the Counsell of The Kings, till they passe Potosi) hath in length North and South about one hundred and fiftie leagues, and as many East and West; a Countrie not very plentifull, though abundant of Cattell, especially in Collao, that is from the Lake of Titicaca unto Charcas, where the Winter and Summer are contrarie to Europe : it is a plentifull Countrie of all Cattell, especially of sheepe, which are many, and of a very fine wooll.

In this Province are foure Townes of Spaniards of one Bishopricke, which are the Citie of the Plate, which the Captaine Peranzures inhabited, in the yeere 1583. by order of the Marques Don Franciscus Piçarro. It stands in seventie two degrees of longitude from the Meridian of Toledo, from whence it may be distant by a greater circle one thousand seven hundred and eightie leagues, and in nineteene degrees of latitude, one hundred seventie five leagues from Cuzco to the South, or Antartick Pole within the Tropicks, in the uttermost of the Torrid Zone. There are in the borders of this Citie in Chacaras (which are manured grounds) eight hundred Spanish housholds. It

*Heredades de
grangerias.*

is a Countrie extreme cold, whereas it should be temperate or hot, according to the height of the Pole it stands in : the Counsell and the Cathedrall is resident in this Citie, and there are Monasteries of Dominicke, Franciscan, Augustines, and Mercenarie Friars, and in her jurisdiction sixtie thousand tributarie Indians, divided in nine and twentie repartitions, and the seedes of Castile doe grow well, and there are many rich mynes of silver.

Our Lady of the Peace. The Citie of our Lady of the Peace, by another name the New Towne, and Chuquiabo, in the middest of the Collao, one hundred leagues from Cuzco, and eightie from the Plate, hath Monasteries of Franciscans, Augustines, and Mercenaries, with store of Wines and Cattell. Captaine Alfonsus of Mendoça built it 1549. when was President the Governour of Piru, the Licentiate Pedro de la Gasca, afterward Bishop of Siguença. The Province of *Chicuito.* Chicuito in Collao, somewhat North-east from the Province of Plata, more then an hundred leagues from it, inhabited by Indians, with a Spanish Governour, of the Bishopricke of Charcas, and one Monasterie of Dominicks, hath much Cattell, and it stands at the border of Titicaca. *Oropesa.* Oropesa, is a plantation of the Vice-roy Don Francisco de Toledo, in the Valley of Cochabamba, twentie leagues from the Citie of la Plata ; their husbandrie is crops of Wheat, Millet, and Cattell.

Potosi. The Imperiall Towne of Potosi is in nineteene degrees of altitude, eighteene leagues from the Citie of the Plate, and about eight from the Lake of the Aulagas to the East, in the skirt of the Hill of Potosi, that looketh to the North-east ; it hath five hundred housholds of Spaniards which doe attend the mynes, and of Merchants, and about 50000. Indians of ordinarie goers and commers to the trafficke of the silver. And though it be a Towne of it selfe, it hath no Ruler, but that of the citie de la Plata. There reside the Officers, and Royall treasurie of this Province, for the mynes of the Hill of Potosi, which a Castillane discovered 1545. called Villaroel, by meanes of [III. v. 897.] certaine Indians ; and it is called Potosi, because the

Indians doe so call Hills and high places; and the silver
was so much that they got at the beginning in the yeere
1549. every Saturday, that when they cast it, there came
to the Kings fifts from five and twentie to thirtie thousand
Pesos.   The Hill is flat and bare, their habitation drie and
cold, unpleasant, and altogether barren.   It bringeth forth
no fruit, graine or herbe, and because of the silver it is the
greatest inhabiting of the Indies, which hath about two
leagues in circuit, and where all kinde of dainties are
found, and plentie, though brought thither by carriages.
The colour of the ground of the Hill draweth towards red,
darke.   The forme is like a Sugar loafe, that over-peareth
all the other Hills that are neere it: the going up is rough,
and yet they goe up on horse-backe; it extendeth a league,
and from his top to the foote is about a quarter of a league.
It hath on all sides rich veines of silver, from the top to
the foote, and the Port of Arica whereby the merchandize *Arica.*
come, and the silver of this Hill is carried, is from it about
ninetie leagues, almost West.

Sixe leagues from the aforesaid Hill in the way of the
Port of Arica, is the Hill of Porco, an ancient seate of *Porco.*
Mynes of silver: whence it is affirmed the Ingas got the
greatest part of the silver that was in the Temple of the
Sunne of Curianche, whence yet is and will much silver be
gotten.

Santa Cruz de la Sierra stands one hundred leagues from *The holy crosse*
the Charcas to the East, in the way whereby they goe from *of the Hill.*
the Charcas to the Assumption, in the Provinces of the
River of Plate, whitherto they make three hundred leagues
journey, with a Governour provided by the Vice-roy, of
the Diocesse of the Charcas, and one Monasterie of Mercenaries, in a Countrie scarce of water, though plentifull **This Apostle*
of Wheat, Wine, and Millet.   This Province hath neigh-   *after his*
bourhood with many Nations of Infidell Indians, and many *miracles many,*
of them are alreadie baptized, and the first that strooke a *was for*
devotion in the Countrimen, was a Spanish Souldier,* that *wickednes*
                                                            hanged at
was among them, fled for faults; which for a great anguish *Potozi. See*
they were in for water made them a great Crosse, and *Ac. l.7.c.27.*

perswaded them to worship with great devotion that same
Crosse, and to aske water; and God for his mercy heard
them, and sent them much raine in the yeere 1560. The
Captaine Nuflo of Chaves went out of the Citie of the
Ascention in the River of Plate, to discover, and comming
to Sancta Cruz of the Hill, having made great discoveries,
the people came unto him, and seeming to him that hee
was neere to Piru, went to the Citie of The Kings, where
the Marques of Cavyete was Vice-roy, and with his order,
and for Lieftenant of his sonne Don Garcia of Mendoça,
the Captaine Nuflo of Chaves went againe to inhabit this
Citie, though he came out of the River of Plate, with
purpose to discover the Provinces of the Dorado.

*Ports &
Points of this
Counsell.*

In the Coast of this Councell, which beginneth in seventeene degrees and a halfe in the River of Nombre de Dios,
or Tambopalla, is the Port of Hilo neere to a River, in
eighteene degrees and a halfe, and more to the South, El
Morro de los Diablos, and the Port of Arica in nineteene
degrees one third part, and that of Tacama in one and
twentie, and the Point of Tarapaca to the South, and
more forward the River of Pica, and that de la Hoja, or of
the Leafe, and of Montelo, the Port of Mexillones, and

*Los Faral-
lones.*

*Punta Blanca.
Quebrada
Honda.*

more to the South the Point of the Beacones, or Morto
Moreno, before the Bay and River of Sancta Clara, and
more to the South the Breach, and the White point, and
the Deepe breach, and the River of Sancta Clara, about
thirtie leagues from the River of Copiapo, where the Coast
of Chile beginneth, and the Coast of the Charcas endeth.

*Province of
Tucaman.*

The Province and Government of Tucaman, is all Mediterrane; her bound begins from the Countrie of the
Chichas, which are of the jurisdiction of the Imperiall
village of Potosi: it stands in the same Line of the Citie
of the Assumption of the River of Plate, about an hundred
leagues from the South Sea coast; it doth confine with the
Province of Chile, it is a Countrie of a good temper,
reasonably plentifull, and untill now without Mynes of
silver, or gold. There is in it some Spanish Townes in
one Bishopricke, which are of the Citie of Saint Iago del

Estero, which at the beginning they named del Varco, or *Saint James of* of the Boate, in eight and twentie degrees of altitude, one *the Marsh.* hundred eightie five leagues from Potosi to the South, declining somewhat to the East: the Governour and the Officers of the goods, and treasurie Royall, and the Bishop, and the Cathedrall are resident here.

The Citie of Saint Marie of Talavera, is five and fortie *Talavera.* leagues from Saint James to the North, and fortie from Potosi in sixe and twentie degrees. The Citie of Saint *Saint Michael.* Michael of Tucuman eight and twentie leagues from Saint James to the West, in the way of the Charcas in seven and twentie degrees. There were inhabited in this Government in the time of Don Garcia of Mendoça, his father the Marques of Cavyete being Vice-roy, the New London, *New London.* and Calchaque, which they called [h]New wisedome, in the [h] *Hisp. Nueva* Province of the Jurias, and Draguita, which afterward were *Cordura.* dishabited within a few yeeres. The people of this Countrie goeth clothed in woollen, and in wrought leather, made by arte like the guilt or wrought leather of Spaine: they breed much Cattell of the Countrie, by reason of the profit of their wooll: they have the Townes very neere the one to the other, and the Townes are small, because there is but one kindred in every one, they are compassed round [1] *A kinde of* about with [1]Cardones, and thornie trees for the warres *Thistle that* that they had among themselves. They are great husband-*groweth every* men, and it is a people that is not drunke, for they are not *stemme foure* given to drinke, as other Nations of the Indies. There *inches square,* are in the Province seven mayne Rivers, and more then *and as high as* eightie Brookes of good waters, and great pastures: the *backe, and* Winter and the Summer are at such times as in Spaine: *taketh much* it is a healthfull Countrie and of a good temper, and the *ground, for* first that entred in it, were the Captaines Diego de Rojas, *there grow* Philip Gutterres, and Nicolas de Heredia; they dis-*one roote.* covered on this side the River of Plate unto the Fortresse [III. v. 898.] of Gabota.

Chap. 22.
Of the bounds
of the King-
dome of Chile.

DOn Diego de Almagro was provided the yeere 1534. in Toledo for Governour of two hundred leagues of ground beyond the Government of the Marques Don Francisco Piçarro, toward the Streight of Magellan, intituling this part, The new government of Toledo. Hee went to pacifie this Countrie, and because he forsooke it, it was given in charge to the Marques Don Francisco Piçarro 1537. and he commended it 1540. to the Captaine Peter of Valdinia; who went thither with one hundred and fiftie Spaniards. All the Countries of this Kingdome lye to the South of the Equinoctiall, in a more Southerne altitude then the Kingdome of Piru, and her Provinces within the Torride, from the Equinoctiall unto the Tropicke of Capricorne, which passeth a Desart, which they call of Atacama, which is from twentie three to twentie sixe degrees, and then beginneth the Kingdome of Chile, which the Indians call Chille, and before the inhabited *Rio de la Sal.* Countrie is the River of The Salt, in three and twentie degrees and three quarters, which from the East side of the Row of Mountaines, runneth to the West into the Sea, through a very deepe Valley, and though it hath the water very cleere; all that the Horses are wet with it when they drinke, is congealed with the heate of the Sunne; and it is so meere salt that it cannot bee drunke, and in the borders it is congealed: the River is before the entring in the first Province of Chile two and twentie leagues where the Xagueyes are, which are Wells of water, for there is no other in the two and twentie leagues, and all the Kingdome stands within the Zone, which the ancient men called Deserte, which is inhabited with white Indians, and it is situated on the borders of the South Sea, which is Mare Magnum, which is included betweene her Coast and the Coast of China.

This Government taken largely unto the Streight, hath in length North and South, from the Valley of Copiapo where it beginneth in seven and twentie degrees, five hundred leagues, and in breadth East and West, from the South Sea to the North Sea, from foure hundred to five hundred of ground to be pacified, which doth straighten it selfe, till it remayneth by the Streight in ninetie or in an hundred leagues. That which is inhabited of this Government, may bee three hundred along the North Sea coast, and the breadth of it twentie leagues and lesse, unto the Rowe of the Andes, which doe end neere the Streight, and it passeth through this Kingdome very high, and almost covered at all times with snow. All the Countrie is plaine, at the least there is no great roughnesse, except where the Rowe of Piru doth reach, and doth end within two or three leagues of the Coast.

The temper and qualitie of it (though it bee not without some difference for the varieties of the heights it standeth in altogether) is of the best, and most inhabitable that is in the Indies, in temperature like unto Castile, in whose opposite altitude it falleth almost all, and in abundance and goodnesse of victuals, and plentie of all things, riches of Mynes and Metals, and force and vigour of the Countrimen, which for being so great warriors have alwayes beene evill to pacifie, and there bee many out in the Mountaines, and Breaches of the end of the Rowe, the Provinces of Arauco, Tucapel, and the Valley of Puren, the bounds and borders betweene the Citie of the Conception, and los Confines, and la Imperial.

In this Government are eleven Spanish Townes, with a Governour placed in the matters of the Government to the Vice-roy, and Councell of Piru, after the Councell that was in the Countrie was taken away; and there is in it two Bishopricks Suffraganes to the Archbishoprick of the Kings. In the Bishopricke of Saint James are foure *Saint James.* Townes. The Citie of Saint James in the time of the first inhabiting of Chile, founded by Captaine Peter of Valdinia, it stands in thirtie foure degrees and a quarter of altitude, seventie seven of longitude, one thousand nine hundred and eightie leagues from Toledo by a direct Line, fifteene from the Sea, and ten beyond the Valley of Chile, which they named at the first New Extreame. In it is the Cathedrall resident with Monasteries of Dominicke,

Franciscan, and Mercenarie Friars, in a plentifull soile of wheat, Wine, and other things, and of very rich Mynes of gold, and in her jurisdiction more then eightie thousand Indians in sixe and twentie repartitions. This Citie is served of the Port of Valparayso at the mouth of the River Topocalma, which passeth neere unto it.

The Serena. Captaine Valdinia peopled also la Serena in the yeere 1544. neere to a good Haven; it is the first Towne of Spaniards, at the entrie of Chile sixtie leagues from the Citie of Saint James, somewhat North-west neere to the Sea in the Valley of Coquimbo, with Monasteries of *Raines seldom* Franciscan, and Mercenarie Friars. It rayneth in it but *and never.* three or foure times a yeere, and in the Countries before it, it never rayneth. The Port which they call of *Coquimbo.* Coquimbo, stands in two and thirtie degrees, it is a good Nooke where the ships of Piru doe make a stay. In the Province of Chucuito, which is on the other side of the Rowe of the Andes, in a cold and barren Countrie, doe *Mendoza.* stand the Citie of Mendoça, and of Saint John of the *Saint John of* Frontier; for Don Garcia of Mendoça peopled them both. *the Frontier.* The Citie of Mendoça is of the same height with Saint James, about fortie leagues from it, of a difficult way, for the snow that is in the Andes. The Citie of Saint John of the Frontier stands to the South of the Citie of Mendoça.

[III. v. 899.] In the Bishopricke of the Imperiall are seven Spanish Townes, which are the Citie of the Conception in seven and thirtie degrees of height, seventie leagues to the South of the Citie of Saint James, neere to the Sea, Peter Valdinia inhabited it in the yeere 1550. The Governours are resident in it, since the Councell (that was there from the yeere 1567. unto 1574.) was taken away. There are Monasteries of Dominicans, Franciscans, and Mercenarie Friars. The Port of this Citie stands in a nooke at the shelter of an Iland. The Citie of the new village of los *Now village of* Infantes, or los Confines; Don Garcia of Mendoça peopled *the Infants.* it, and the Governour Villagran commanded it to be called de los Confines. It stands sixteene leagues from the Conception to the side of the Streight, eight leagues from the Row of the Andes, and foure from that which goeth along the Coast. It hath one Monasterie of Dominicans, another of Franciscan Friars. The warlike Indians come to the bounds of this Citie, and the mayne River Biobio by them, and others which doe enter into it, and the River Ninequeten.

Peter of Valdinia peopled the Citie of the Imperiall *The Imperiall.* 1551. which is in nine and thirtie degrees of height, nine and thirtie leagues from the Conception toward the Streights side, three leagues from the Sea, where the Cathedrall is resident with one Monasterie of Franciscans, another of Mercenarie Friars; and in her bounds are more then eightie thousand Indians, with many other that in her bounds are in armes. The River Cauten passeth neere it, which is navigable to the Sea, though the Haven bee not good nor secure. Captaine Valdinia peopled also the * Rich Village, sixteene leagues from Imperiall, about the **Hisp.* South-eastward, and about foure and fortie from the Con- *Villarica.* ception, neere to the Snowy Row,[d] with one Monasterie *ᵈ Cordillera* of Franciscans, another of Mercenaries, in a Countrey cold *Nevada.* and barren of Bread and Wine.

The Citie of Valdinia is two leagues off the Sea, and *Valdinia.* fiftie from the Conception to the Streight ward: peopled also by Captaine Valdinia, with Monasteries of Domini- cans, Franciscans, and Mercenaries, in a plentifull Countrie of Wheat, and Seedes, and in place of good pastures for Cattell, and without Vines. The merchandize comes up by the River of Valdinia, which passeth neere it, and the Port stands in the mouth of it in fortie degrees of height. The Citie of Osorno, Don Garcia of Mendoça peopled, *Osorno.* sixtie leagues or more from the Conception to the port of the Streight, seven leagues from the Sea. It hath one Monasterie of Dominicans, another of Franciscans, with another of Nunnes, in a cold Countrie, scarce of victuals, but of much gold, and in her bounds two hundred thousand Indians of repartition. The Citie of Castro, which was inhabited by the Licenciate Lope Garcia de

Castro, being Governour of the Kingdomes of Piru, the which is called in the Indian tongue Chilue, which is the last of the inhabited in Chile, in an Iland of those that are in the Lake of Ancud, or Chilue, and the Archipelagus stands in three and fortie degrees of altitude, one and fortie leagues to the South of Osorno, with a Monasterie of Franciscans, with twelve thousand Indians of repartition in her bounds, for it is an Iland of fiftie leagues in length, and from two untill nine in breadth, which the Sea made with other great ones, tearing the Land unto the Row of the Andes. It is a mountaynous Countrey, and close, plentifull of Wheate, and of Millet, and Mynes of flying ᵍGold, on the Strand a thing fewe times, or seldome seene.

The Governour Villagran tooke away the name of the Citie which was Cavyete, that Don Garcia of Mendoça inhabited, and commanded to call it Tucapel, and afterward disinhabited it. There are in this Government which beginneth in two and twentie degrees, the Port and River of Copeapo, and to the South of it, the Port of Guascoin another River, and the River of Coquimbo in two and thirtie degrees: and past this the Port of the Cigua in the River, and the Port of Quintero at the mouth of the River of Concagua, before the Port of Saint James, or Valparayso, and the Port of Topocalma in the River of Maypa: and past the River of Maule the Port of the

ᶜHerradura, at the mouth of the River Itata, before the Port of the Conception in the great River of Biobio to the North, the Iland of Saint Marie right against the State of Aranco, and the Port of Cavyete, and the Iland of Mocha more to the South, and the Port of Cauten, which is that of the Imperiall, and to the South the landing place and the River of Tolten before the Port of Valdinia, and past this the Point of the Galley, and more to the South the great Bay or Port of Osorno in the River de las Canoas, and to the South of it about thirtie leagues to the Lake de los Coronados the broadest River of this Realme, and at the end of this Realme the Lake of Aucud.

MEn doe call the Streight of Magellanes, that which
is past the River of Plate by the South Sea; from
the last of Chile, unto the Streight two hundred leagues
before it, from two and fortie or three and fortie degrees
of altitude, unto two and fiftie and more, for although
men have sayled through both the Seas divers times, and
seene people in them unto the Streight it selfe, it hath not
beene pacified, nor made inhabiting, but that which the
fleete that Diego Flores de Valdes carried to the Streight
left in the mouth of the Streight on the North side, in the
yeere 1582. which was called the Citie of Saint Philip,
which for being in so much altitude could not be preserved
for the great cold, and therefore that navigation is difficult
and dangerous for the continuall tempests, and great
stormes of windes that are at all times.

*Chap. 24.
Of the Pro-
vinces of the
Streight.*

[III. v. 900.]

The Ports, Capes, and Points of the Coast of the one
and the other Sea unto the Streight, although they be
many, and some are not pointed in the Cardes of Navigation, it appeareth not wholly, neither is there any certaine
relation of all. And the most knowne of the Coast from
Chile unto the Streight, which runneth from Valdinia
about an hundred leagues to the West South-west are, the
Cape of Saint Andrew in seven and fortie degrees, from
whence the Coast turneth directly to the South unto the
Streight, by the Cape of Saint Roman in eight and fortie
degrees, and neere unto it the Iland of Saint Catalina,
neere to the great Bay which they call ᵍHartichoked, and
within it the Bay of our Lady, and the Iland of Santa
Barbara, and more forward the Ports of Hernan Gallego in
eight and fortie degrees two third parts, and the Bay of
The Kings eighteene leagues from the Port of Hernan
Gallego, and the Bay of Saint John in fiftie degrees one
third part, the Cape of Saint Francisco in one and fiftie,
whereby some Channels doe enter into the Land, and the
Iland de la Campana, or of the Bell, eleven leagues from
Saint Francis: also with some Channels which have not
beene navigated within the Land, and the Bay of Saint
Lazarus in two and fiftie degrees, with Channels on the

*Ports, Capes,
and Points of
these two
Coasts.*

ᵍ *Hisp.
Alcarchofado,
of the colour of
an Artichoke.
Or Ferdi-
nando of
Gallicia.*

543

sides, which enter very broad and long to the one and the other parts, which have not beene navigated, and a great Sea of Ilands which alwayes was said to bee at the South side neere to the mouth of the Streight, the which Sir Richard Hawkins denyeth; for hee saith, That at this mouth of the Streight on the South side, he found no more then foure small Ilands, and one in the middest like a Sugar loofe, and that at the least they are distant from the mouth of the Streight sixe leagues, and the great Sea is on the one side, and he holdeth for certaine it is that which they say is the firme Land of the South side of the Streight, and that there is no firme land. The Streight though they have past it from the South to the North side, by order of the Vice-roy Don Franciscus of Toledo, Peter Sarmiento, and Antonie Pablo Corso, and it is knowne it stands from 52. to 53. degrees of altitude, where it draweth most to the South, and that in length it hath one hundred and ten leagues, or one hundred and fifteene, little more or lesse, and in breadth from one to tenne: it hath never beene navigated to an end from the South Sea to the North Sea, nor the Pyrats that have past it from the North to the South, are understood to have returned by it. The above said Sir Richard Hawkins saith, that he sailed many dayes by the Straight, and affirmeth that all the Countrie on the South side is no firme Land, but many Ilands which reach to 56. degrees; the which he might know, because he sayled to the same 56. degrees through the middest of those Ilands, and seeing he found nothing but Sea, hee followed his course againe through by the Straight, and that this cannot be so farre, the differences of Seas, which the many entrings doe cause that are among those Ilands, and that the habiting of them is of people on the North side, which doe passe to those Ilands to sustaine themselves of fishings, and in their seasons returne to their Countries; and that he comprehended this of many things especially of not having seene any seated inhabitating, but some Cabbins which the Indians doe make for a time. The same said Sir Francis Drake, that it hapned him when he

Sir Richard Hawkins.

Streight of Magellan.

[III. v. 901.]

This is not true: for Captaine Winter & others have done it; which howsoever he cals Pirats, yet they have better descovered these Straights then the Spaniards.

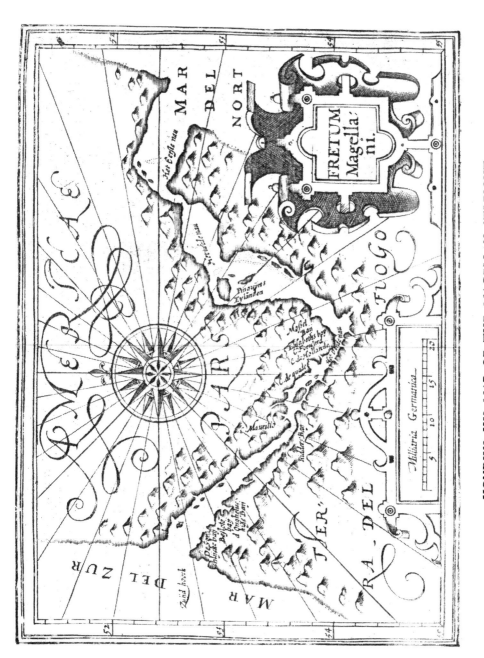

HONDIUS HIS MAP OF THE MAGELLAN STREIGHT

passed the Straight, the yeare 1579. who after his comming
out into the South Sea, he ran along with tempests compassing this Sea, unto the mouth of the North Sea, and
by the same way he had runne, he made sure his navigation
to the South Sea.

The parts most famous of the Straight at the entring
of the South are the Cape Desseado, or Desired, in 53.
degrees, and the Channell of all Saints, two and twentie
leagues from the mouth, very broad, and large, and past
it the port of the Treason, and afterward another great
large Channell which runneth to the North-west, and Row-
lands Bell, a great Rocke in the middest at the beginning
of a Channell. They gave it this name of one of
Magellanes fellowes called Rowland, who went to reack-
nowledge it, which was a Gunner: the point of possession
which is foure leagues from the Cape of Virgenes, at the
entring of the North Sea in 52. degrees and a halfe of
altitude, when Peter * Sarmiento, and Antonie Pablo Corso *Or *Vine*
by order which they had to reknowledge the Straight, for *Twig.*
it had beene commanded long before for to see if it were
a more easie navigation to the South Sea, then that of
Panama: they viewed the two narrow places, that at the
entrie of the North, and it seemed to Peter Sarmiento
that the one was so narrow, that with Artillerie it might Or *Ordi-*
be kept, and so much he perswaded it, that although the *nance.*
Duke of Alva affirmed it was impossible, the Armie which
James Flower carried unfruitfully was sent about it, and
in the end was knowne that that navigation is dangerous,
and the flowing of two Seas which come to meete in the
middest of the Straight, doe withdraw themselves with
such furie, ebbing in some places more then sixtie fathoms,
that when the Shippes did carry nothing but Cables to
preserve themselves from loosing that which they had
sayled, they would goe full froaghted.

In foure hundred leagues, there is of Coast from the
mouth of the Straight, unto the River of Plate, which
runneth altogether North-east and South-west, there is
the River of Saint Ilefonsus twelve leagues from the Cape

of the Virgenes, the [a] Gallizian River, and the Bay of Saint James, foureteene leagues from the River of Sancta Cruz, in 50. degrees, and at the mouth an Iland called of the Lyons, and the Port of Saint Julian in 49. degrees, and the River of John Serrana to the South of the Ilands of Duckes, in 47. degrees, the River of Cananor in 45. degrees, the Cape of Saint Dominicke, before the Cape of three Points, and the Land de los Humos or of the Smoakes, in 38. degrees, the Point of Sancta Hellene, and of Saint Apollonia, in 37. degrees before the White Cape, at the entrie of the River of Plate on the South side.

Chap. 24. Of the Provinces of the River of Plate, & of Brasile. Sebastian Gabote remaineth in the River of Solis, which is called of the Plate. He was an English-man by breeding, borne a Venetian, but spending most part of his life in England and English imployments. See the former Booke.

JOhn Dias de Solis discovered the River of Plate 1515. and Sebastian Gaboe an English-man, going with an Armie by order of the Emperour, in pursuit of the Fleete which Frier Garcia de Loaysa Commander, had carried to the Ilands of the Malucos, and conceiving hee could not overtake them, he thought good to busie himselfe in something that might be profitable; and entred the yeare 29. discovering the River of Plate, where he was almost three yeares; and being not seconded, with relation of that which he had found, returned to Castile, having gone many leagues up the River, he found Plate or Silver among the Indians of those Countries, for in the warres which these Indians had with those of the Kingdomes of Piru they tooke it, and from hence it is called the River of Plate, for before it was called the River of Solis. These Provinces are joyned with those of Brasil: by the line of the markes they have no determined bounds, but by the Coast of the Sea that falleth to the North, and entrance of the River of Plate, of the which the Countrie hath taken the name, and the mouth of this River may stand sixteene hundred leagues from the Bay of Saint Lucar of Barrameda.

Plentifulnesse of the Provinces of the River of Plate.

All these Provinces are very plentifull of Wheate, Wine, and Sugar, and all other seedes and fruites of Castile doe grow well: they have great Pastures for all sorts of Cattle, which have multiplied infinitely, especially the Horses, and though they have beene many yeares without thinking there were any Mines of Gold, or of Silver, they have already found a showe of them, and of Copper, and Iron, and one of very perfect Amathists. All these Provinces are of one Government, with title Royall, subordained for nearenesse to the Vice-roy of Piru, with one Bishopricke wherein are three Spanish Townes, and a great multitude of the Countrie men, of big bodies, and well conditioned. [III. v. 902.] And the Townes are; the Citie of our Lady of the Assumption, the first inhabiting, and the head of this *The Assumption.* Province, it stands in 25. degrees and a halfe of altitude: the Captaine John of Salazar built it by order of the Governour Don Peter Mendoça. The territory thereof was first called Gurambare: it hath Brasil at the right hand two hundred and eightie leagues, and in this compasse it hath the Citie Royall at eightie leagues, which the Indians call Guayra. And on the side of Piru, which is East and West, it hath at foure hundred and eightie leagues, the Citie of la Plata, and at two hundred and eightie, the Citie of Sancta Cruz de la Sierra or of the Hill, which Nuflo of Chanes built. To the South side which is toward the Straight of Magelane, it hath very great and rich Countries, and this Citie stands three hundred leagues from the mouth of the River of Plate, built neere to the River Paraguaye, on the East side, with foure hundred Spanish Housholds, and more then three thousand children of those that were borne to them in *Note.* the Countrie (which they call Mestizos) in it are resident the Governour, and Officers Royall, and the Cathedrall which is called the Bishopricke of the Plate, suffragan to the Archbishoprick of the Kings, and in her jurisdiction more then 400000. Indians, which doe increase daily.

Citie Royall was called by another name Ontiveros, *Ciudad real.* built by Ruidias de Melgareio; it stands eightie leagues from the Assumption North-east, toward the Land of Brasil, neere to the River Parana; it stands in a good soyle of Victuals, and Vines, and much good Copper, and

great number of Indians, which also doe much increase.
In this River Parana, neere the Citie Royall, there is a
great fall, that no man dare come neere it by Land within
two hundred paces, for the great noyse, and mist of the
water, and by the River no Canoe, nor Boate dare come
neere by a league; for the furie of the water doth carry
it to the fall, which is above two hundred fathomes off
a steep Rock, and it is so narrow, and the water goeth
so close, that it seemes ye may throw over it with a dart.

    * Buenos ayres is a Towne which in old time was
disinhabited neere the place where now it is built againe,
in the Province of the Morocotes, in the borders of the
River of Plate, in a plentifull soyle, where all things of
Castile doe grow very well; the Governor Don Peter of
Mendoça built it 1535. which caused all that which Gabote
forsooke to be discovered.   All this Countrie is commonly
plaine: for except the Cordilleras or Rowes (which are
on the Sea coast, and may be twentie leagues toward Brasil,
afterwards compassing all the Countrie toward the River
Maranyon) and the Rowes of the Kingdomes of Piru, all
is plaine, except some small hils.

    There are knowne in the Coast of these Provinces from
the Land of Brasil, unto the River of Plate five or six
reasonable Ports, the Port of Saint Vincent, in 33. degrees
height, right against Buenabrigo, an Iland where the line
of the repartition passeth; and six leagues to the South
the River Ubay, and the Port, and the Iland de la Cananea
in 35. degrees; and forward the River de la Barca, before
the Port of Bahia or River of Saint Francis, and the
Iland of Sancta Catalina, by another name the Port of
Vera, or Port of the Duckes (de Peros) and the Port of
Don Roderigo, twentie leagues to the South from Sancta
Catalina, an Iland 29. degrees and more to the South,
five leagues ª Close Haven, and fifteene the ᵇ Inhabited
River, and as much the Deepe-Bay from this, and the
River Tiraqueri, in 32. degrees and a halfe, before the
Cape of Saint Marie, which is in 35. degrees at the entrie
of the River of Plate.

ANTONIO DE HERRERA

The River is called in the Indian language Paranaguazu, and commonly Parana, hath his entrie and mouth in the South Sea, from thirtie five unto thirtie six degrees of altitude, between the Capes of Saint Marie, and Cape Blanke, which is from the one to the other about thirtie leagues of mouth, and from thence inward other tenne leagues in breadth, with many Ilands in the middest, and many very great maine Rivers, which enter into it by the East and West side, unto the Port of the Kings, which is a great Lake called of the Xarayes, little lesse then three hundred leagues from the River of Plate, where enter many Rivers that come from the skirts of the Andes and they may be of those Rivers that proceede in the Provinces of the Charcas and Cuzco, which runne toward the North, whereby entreth another maine arme into the said Lake, which hath given occasion to thinke that this River doth communicate with the River of Saint John of the Amazones; others say that it commeth from the Lake of the Dorado, which is fifteene journies from the Lake of the Xarayes, though there be opinions that there is no Darado.

The Captaine Salazar governing in these Provinces by the death of Don Peter Mendoça, in the yeare 1545. a Spaniard being in his bed and his wife by him on the out side, in the night there came a Tigre and gave the man a blow that he killed him, and carried him away, and betweene certaine Caves he did devoure him: in the morning the Captaine Salazar went forth with fiftie Souldiours to seeke the Tigre, and going through a wood, hee went alone by a path, and as soone as hee discovered the Tigre, hee being flesh set upon him, and at the time hee lifted up the pawe for to strike him, the Captaine let flee the Shaft out of his Cross-bowe, and strooke him to the heart, and it fell downe dead: an exploit of great courage, heede and dexteritie.

THe Provinces and Countrie of Brasil in the Coast of the North Sea, and Terra firme, is called all that which falleth to the East from the line of the repartition,

549

from twentie nine degrees of longitude from the Meridian
of Toledo, unto thirtie nine, which are two hundred
leagues from East to West, and foure hundred and fiftie
North and South, from two degrees of Southerne altitude,
by the Cape de Humos or of Smoakes, unto five and
twenty, by the Iland of Buenabrigo or Good-harbour.
And from the first inhabiting, unto the last of Brasil,
there are three hundred and fiftie leagues.   Vincent Yanes

Vincent Yanes
Pinzon, borne
in the Village
of Palos dis-
covered the
Brasil, and
then Diego de
Lepe.

Pinzon discovered first this Countrie by commandement
of the Kings Catholike, and presently after him James
of Lepe, in the yeare 1500. and six moneths after
Poralvarez Cabral, going with a Portugall armie to India,
which to avoide the Coast of Guinea did put so much to
the Sea that he found this Countrie, and called it Sancta
Cruz, because on that day he discovered it.   All of it is
very hot in Winter and Summer, and very rainie, and
compassed with Woods and Mists, unhealthfull, and full
of venemous Wormes, plentifull in Pastures for Cattle,
and not for Wheate, nor Millet; there are in it great
showes of Silver and Gold, but as the Portugals, have no
stocke to make any profit of the Mines, they leave them
as they are.

The principall foode of this Countrie is the Cazabi
which they make of the Yuca, and the greatest trafficke
is Sugar, and Cotten Bumbast, and Brasil Wood, which
was it that gave it the name.   There are in all the Province
nine Governments, which are called Captainships, and in
them seventeene Portugal Townes: in it may be about
three and thirtie hundred housholds, and great multitude
of warlike Indians, which have not suffered the Portugals
to build but on the Coast, in which are many Rivers,
Landings, and many Ports, and very safe, where any
Ships may come in, be they never so bigge.

Inhabitings of
the Coast of
Brazil.

The Colonie of the first Captainship, and the most
auncient is Tamaraca, the second Pernambuco, five leagues
from Tamaraca to the South, in eight degrees of altitude,
and there is a house of the Fathers of the Companie of
Jesus: the other is, that of all Saints, one hundred leagues

from Pernambuco in thirteene degrees, and there the Governour, the Bishop, and the Auditour generall of all the Coasts are resident, and it hath a Colledge of the *Many Jesuites* Company: the fourth Captainship of the Ilands is thirtie *Colledges.* leagues from the Bay of All Saints, in foureteen degrees & two third parts, it hath a House of the Fathers of the Companie. In this Captainship is found a Tree where out they take a precious Balme. The Captainship of the Sure-haven is thirtie leagues from the Ilands in sixteene *Puerto seguro.* degrees and a halfe: it hath three Inhabitings, and a House of the Fathers of the Companie. The Captaineship of the Holy-Ghost fiftie leagues from Puerto seguro, in twentie degrees, where they gather much Brasil, and there is one house of the Company. The Captainship of the River of Genero is sixtie leagues from the Holy-Ghost, in twentie three degrees and one third part, with a house of the Fathers of the Company, and they cut in their jurisdiction much Brasil Wood; the River is very faire, with fine and profitable borders. The last Captaineship is Saint Vincent, sixtie leagues from the River of Genero, in foure and twentie degrees, it hath a fortresse in an Iland for a defence against the Indians and Pirates, and a house of the said Fathers, which have done great profit in the inhabiting of this Countrie, and conversion of the Indians, and their libertie. The Cattle that are in these Provinces are many, and great breeding of Swine, and Hens, they gather much Amber which the Sea casteth *Ambar.* up with stormes at the spring tides, and many persons have inriched themselves with it. Their Summer is from September to February, and the Winter from March unto August; the dayes are almost as long as the nights, they increase and diminish onely an houre, in the winter the winde is alwaies at South and South-east, in Summer North-east and East North-east.

There are in this Coast eight or tenne Ports more *The princi-* principall then the rest, which are the River of Saint *pallest Ports of* Dominicke and de las Virtudes to the North-east of *this Coast.* Pernambuco, and Tamaraca, which is an Iland, and as it

is said, the first Plantation, and before the Cape of Saint
Austine, which stands in nine degrees, the River of Saint
Francis in ten degrees and a halfe, which is great and
mightie : the Bay of All Saints three leagues broad, and
thirteene into the Land unto Saint Saviour, the River and
Port Trevado, where the Ships doe touch that goe this
Voyage, and the River of Canamum in thirteene degrees
and a halfe, the River of the Beades or of Saint Austine
is foureteen degrees and a halfe ; and the River of the
Virgenes in sixteene. Portesecure in seventeen degrees :
the River of Parayua in twentie degrees, neere to Sancti
spiritus : the River of Genero neere to Saint Sebastian,
Cabo Frio.   and Cold Cape in three and twentie degrees beyond Saint
Vincent.

Chap. 26.
Of those which
men call the
Indies of the
West, which
are the Ilands
Philippinas,
coast of China,
Japan, and
the Lequias.

[III. v. 904.]

INdies of the West, are all the Ilands and firme Land
comprehended within the markes of the Crowne of
Castile and of Lyon, at the Occidentall end of the said
bounds ; whose line as is said passeth on the other side
the world, through the Citie of Malaca from whence
toward the East, and New Spaine, is a great Gulfe of
infinite Ilands great and small, and many pieces of Coasts,
and firme Land, which are divided into the Ilands of the
Spicerie, or of the Malucos, Ilands Philipinas, the Coast
of China, Ilands of the Lequios and Japones, Coast of
the new Guinea, Ilands of Salomon, and of Ladrones or
the Theeves : the temper of all these Ilands and Lands
in generall is moist, and temperately hot, plentifull of
Victuals, and Beasts, with some Gold, but base, no Silver,
store of Wax, and the people of sundry colours, and the
ordinary colour like Indians, and some white among them,
and some cole-blacke.

The Ilands of the Spicerie (which properly are called
so, because all the Pepper, Cloves, Sinamon, Ginger, Nutmegs, and Masticke that is spent in Europe, is brought
from them) are many, though the most famous of that
Gulfe are five small Ilands under the Equinoctiall in one
hundred nintie foure degrees from the Meridian of Toledo,

included in the morgage which the Emperor Charles the
fift made of them to the King of Portugall for three
hundred and fiftie thousand Duckets, which are Terrenate
of eight or nine leagues compasse, with a Port called
Talangame, and in it raigned Corala, which yeelded himselfe for subject to the King of Castile, when the Shippes
that remained of Magelanes fleete found these Ilands.
The Iland of Tidore stands one league from Terrenate to
the South, it hath tenne leagues compasse. The Iland
of Matil, or Mutier is of foure leagues compasse, and is
under the Equinoctiall, and Maquin three leagues to the
South, of seven in compasse, and tenne leagues to the South.
Batan or Baquian is twentie leagues in compasse. In the
Iland of Tidore raigned Almanzor, which also gave himselfe for subject of the King of Castile, the which, and
Carala did write and John Sebastian of the Cano, borne
in the Village of Guitarca, in the Province of Guipuzcoa
brought their Letters; the which departing from Tidore
in the yeare 1522. touched in the Iland of Zamatia, and
going up to almost fortie two degrees toward the Antar-
ticke Pole, he arrived at the Iland of Saint James of the
Greene Cape or Cabo Verde, and from thence to Sivill
with the Shippe called the Victorie, having spent seven
moneths time little lesse in comming from the Iland of
Tidore. Patian is the fift Iland like the other; Moores
inhabited in it, and Gentiles also, which knew not the
immortalitie of the soule. And when the Shippe of the
fleete of Fryer Garcia of Loaysa came, Roiami raigned
in Tidore of thirteene yeares of age, and againe acknowledged the King of Castile, and also the King of Gilolo
called Sultan Abderta meniani, and confirmed it with
an oath. Gilolo is an Iland under the line foure leagues
distant from those rehearsed; it is of two hundred leagues
compasse, without Spicerie: the Iland of Ambon in three
degrees and a halfe to the South, from the Iland of Gilolo
without Spicerie. The Ilands of Bandan are in foure
degrees of Southerne altitude, where the Nutmegge is
gathered, and Mace; and the Burro, which is to the West

*Of these see l.
4. c. 1. and
other English
voiages in the
first Tome.
See Magelanes
Voyage. Tom.
1. l. 2.
Certaine Tree
bearing a kind
of Date.*

of Ambon, and Timor, another Iland to the South-west
from Bandan, almost one hundred leagues, without
Spicery, but rich of Sandalo, Zeinda, fiftie leagues from
Timor, to the North-west of forty leagues compasse,
plentiful of Pepper, and the Iland of Celebes, which is
very great, & Borney greater, neere the straight of Malaca,
which is made in the firme Land; & Zamatia, which in
old time they called Taprobana. There be other manie
great Ilands, and small, which remaine to the South side,
neere Java Major & Minor, and to the North toward
the coast of Chyna: the Portugals have a fortresse in
Terrenate, and other in the Citie of Malaca at the entrie
of the Archipelagus.

The Ilands Philippinas are a Sea of thirtie or fortie
great Ilands, besides many other small ones which are
together in lesse then two hundred leagues in length North
and South, and one hundred in breadth betweene New
Spaine, and the Gulfe of Bengala, and they are about
seventeene hundred leagues from the Port of the Nativitie
in New Spaine, from six to fifteene or sixteene degrees
of Septentrional altitude, of a reasonable temperature,
and plentifull of victuals, specially of Rice, and some
base Gold in some places, and in some Ilands are Cinamon
Cinamon and long Pepper. trees, and long Pepper. The Countriemen are of a good
shape, and in some Ilands they are blacke, and those
which live in the center of the Countrie are whiter then
those that live in the Sea coasts. There are good Ports,
and Timber for Shipping, the names of the principallest
Ilands are Mindano, which is the greatest, and most
Southward, of a hundred leagues in length, and three
hundred in compasse, a rough Countrie, but plentifull
of Millet, Waxe, Rice, Ginger, and some Cinamon, and
Mines of Gold, with good Havens, and Rodes: the Iland
of Good-tokens, and Saint John leaning to Mindanao, on
the East side, of twenty leagues in length North and
South; Behol, ten leagues more to Mindanao on the
North side, nineteene leagues in length.

The Iland of Buglas or of Negros, by reason of those

that are in it, is in the middest of that Sea to the West, of fortie leagues in length North and South, and foureteen in breadth, and in her coast are some Pearles: the Iland of Zubu in the middest of all, of thirtie leagues in length North and South, and in it a Spanish Towne, called the Village of Jesus, on the East side, with one good Haven, besides other that are in the Iland, the Captaine Ferdinando Magellanes discovered this Iland, in the yeare 1520. the King yeelded then himselfe for subject to the Crowne of Castile, and before he discovered the Ilands, which he called de las Velas Latinas, because they sailed in their Shippes with sayles of Mats made of Palme tree leaves after the Latine fashion; and from Zubu Magellanes went with the King, to warre against the King of Matan, in *In Matan it* a little Iland close to that of Zubu on the South side, *was where* where being too valiant and confident he was slaine; and *Ferdinando* the Spaniards following their Voyage in demand of the *Magelanes* *was slaine.* Ilands of the Spicerie, they discovered Quepindo, Pulvan, and Burney, which is a great, rich, and plentifull Iland of Rice, Sugar, Goates, Swine, Cammels: it wants Wheate, Asses, and Sheepe; it hath Ginger, Camphire, Mirabolans, and other Drugges. Alvaro of Saavedra discovered also [III. v. 905.] the Phillippines, and tooke possession of them in the *Alvaro of* yeare 1527. for the Crowne of Castile, which by order *Saavedra* of the Marquesse of the Valley went from the Port of *tooke possession* *of the Philip-* Civitlanejo in New Spaine, in demand of the Ilands of *pine for the* the Spicerie, and particularly he was in Mindanao: and *Crowne of* this digression hath not bin out of purpose. *Castile, in the*

Returning to the order of the Phillippines, there *yeare 1527.* followeth the above said Abuyo, or Babay thirtie leagues in length North and South, and tenne in breadth, in which are good Mines, and Pearles, in her coast: Tandayala most famous of all, which for being first discovered, is called Phillipine, of which all take the name, in memory of the invincible King Don Philip the second, the Prudent. It hath fortie leagues on the North side, and of the East North North-east, and South South-west, and twelve leagues in breadth where most, with good Havens and

Roades: Masbat a meane Iland to the West of Tandaya, of seventeene leagues in length, and fifteene in breadth, with one Haven: Mindoro of five and twentie leagues in length North and South, and halfe in breadth; there is Pepper in it, and Mines of Gold: the Iland of Luzan, called the New Castile, as great or greater then Mindanao, the most Septentrionall of the Phillipines, in the which is built

*The Citie of
Manilla.*

Manila, a Citie of Spaniards, with title of Famous where the Governour, Officers of the goods, and chest Royall, and the Cathedrall are resident; it is a plentifull soyle of Victuals, with many Mines of Gold: the Haven of this Citie is bad, and for all that there is great trafficke with the Chynas, which bring Porcelane Vessell, Tinsels, coloured silkes, and other Merchandize: Luçon hath in length two hundred leagues, and it is very narrow.

In all these Ilands are many Mahometanes, whither they came by the East India, and could easily plant their falshood amongst those blinde Gentiles. Captaine Magellanes as above said discovered these Ilands, the yeare 1520. going with an Armie of the Crowne of Castile, in search of the Ilands of the Malucoes, and tooke possession of

*His voiage you
have before.*

them, and afterward Michael Lopez of Legazpi made an end of discovering them, the yeare 1564. with an Armie which hee tooke from New Spaine, by order of the Viceroy, Don Lewis of Velasco: it is judged that those Ilands

11000.
Ilands.

doe amount to eleaven thousand great and small. There are pacified about fortie of them, and converted more then a Million of men unto the Catholike Faith, with so many expences of the Crowne Royall, not having had untill now any profit from those Countries; for every Religious man of those that are sent thither, doth cost to set there one thousand Duckets. Those which hitherto have laboured in that Vineyard, with most great fruite of the soules, are the Religious Dominicans, Franciscans, Barefooted, and Austine Fryers, and the Company of Jesus; and from these Ilands hath beene begun to bridle the Mahometans, which from the Coast of Asia went by little and little extending through these, and other Ilands, and also to the

Chinas and Japones, and the Portugals had already lost the *Since, the* Ilands of the Malucos, if the Spaniards of the Provinces *Hollanders* of the Phillippines had not holpen and succoured them *have expelled the Portugals.* divers times and many wayes.

There is already a plainer notice had of the Chynas, by *China: see our* the commerce of the Phillippines, and their riches and *former Relation.* plenty is knowne : it is of the richest and mightiest King-domes of the World, and from Manila may be to the coast of China three hundred leagues, of eight dayes sayling, and the coast of that Countrie goeth running as to the North-east, more then seven hundred leagues, from twentie one to twenty two degrees of Septentrional lati-tude, and upward, and it is known that crosse over the Countrie inward is a Voyage of five or sixe moneths, to the confines of Tartaria ; being a Countrie of great Cities, with many Townes, and the people politicke, and prepared for their defence, but not warlike, and the Coast much inhabited with maine Rivers, and good Havens : it extends from seventeene unto fiftie degrees North and South, and East and West it occupieth two and twentie : the Citie of Paquin, where the King hath his Court, stands in fortie eight degrees of our Pole, it is divided in fifteene Pro-vinces, sixe Maritime, and nine Mediterrane, and the one are devided from the other with certaine Mountaines like the Pirineis, and there are but two passages whereby they doe communicate.

Thomas Perez Ambassadour of the King of Portugall, *The Provinces* was from Cantan to Nanqui foure Moneths, travelling *and Kingdoms of China.* always to the North : and to the largenesse of this King-dome is joyned the plentie of the Countrie, which is great, for the which the multitude of the navigable Rivers that do water it, are a help, wherewith it seemes a pleasant Forrest or Garden, and the abundance is doubled by many wayes, for the Kings spare no cost to make the Countrie watered in every place, cutting great hils, and making great Valleys plaine ; and the heate not wanting in any place, for all the Countrie almost is contained in the bounds of the temperate Zone, nor the moisture by the clemencie

of nature, and by the industrie of men it is incredibly all
multiplied, and all being compelled to busie themselves
in something, there is not one foote of ground left unpro-
fitable. In Canton among other notable things they say
there are a great number of blinde men that doe labour in
something, every one as he is able, and being forbidden
the going out of the Kingdome without licence, the which
is never granted, but for a limited time it is necessary
that the propagation increasing continually, the number
of the people be without end, especially that they hold for
a certaine, that for five persons that doe dye, there are
seven borne, and the purenesse of the ayre is so much,
that they doe not remember, there hath beene any universall plague, and with all these good things they have their
troubles also, for there are earthquakes that destroy whole
Cities, disinhabit the Countrie, and suppresse the auncient
Rivers, and raise others, and doe make great Mountaines
plaine, with a miserable misfortune of that people.

The yeare 1555. there burst out of the intrailes of the
earth such abundance of water, that it over-flowed the
space of sixtie leagues, and destroyed seven Cities with
their jurisdictions. And this as touching the continent
of China. There is through all the Coast a multitude of
Ilands, the greater part are unto us unknowne. Not farre
from Nanqui, is the Cape of Lampo, the Iland of Aveniga,
Abarda, Sumbar, Lanqui, and the Iland of Horses, of the
which no particular notice is had. Passing the Citie of
Chincheo, stands Lamao, and a great number of Ilands
are seene about Cantan, and these are the most celebrated,
Lantao, Macao, Veniaga, where is the Port of Tamo,
Lampacao, Sancoan, in all the which the King of China
hath Garrisons on Sea and Land, except in Lampacao
which is not inhabited.

Macao.   In Macao, by another name Macan, the Portugals have
a Towne, and the Chinas knowing the valour of the
Portugals, and the favour they have of the Castillans of
the Phillipines, suffer it with an evill will, but the
Portugals seeke to preserve themselves, for their profitable

commerce in China. Sancon is thirtie leagues from Cantan, where sometimes the Portugals have touched, and no Iland of China is of greater importance then Anian in the mouth of the Gulfe of Cauchinchina, five leagues from the * Firme Land, and one hundred and eightie from the Phillipines, and it is so bigge, that they affirme it to have thirtie Fortresses; in it is a fishing for small Pearles. It is aboundant of Victuals, and of many Fruits: under the Government of Cantan, the principall Port of China, and the Countrie men are grosse and rude people. *Ainan.*

*Or Terra firme.

Japan is many Ilands divided with small armes of the Sea, in three and thirtie Kingdomes, whose head is the Citie of Meaco, distant variable from China, and they count from the Iland of Goto in Japon to Liampo in China sixtie leagues, which is the neerest. The Japones doe greatly molest the Chinas, more with piracies, and thefts, then with just war, because Japan being divided in sundry Ilands, and divers Princes, they can make no warre against the Chinas, but with weake forces. They are more war-like and valiant then the Chinas: it is a temperate Countrie, plentifull of Seedes, Cattle and Fowle of Europe, it hath Mines of Iron and Steele: the Countrie men are strong, valiant, and for much labour: those Ilands stand in thirtie five degrees of the Pole, little more or lesse, according to the distance of every Iland. The Japones doe not understand the Chinas but by writing, because of the Characters, or Letters being one for them all, and though they signifie the same, they have not the same name, for they are to declare things, and not words, as the figures of Arithmeticke, that if a 9. be set, the French, the Castillan, and the English man doe understand it, that it signifieth 9. but every one doe name it after their owne fashion. *Japan.*

Characters as Ciphers.

By another side the Japones doe confine with the Phil-lipines, from whence there is commerce with them, and a great incouragement is given to the Fathers of the Company, for to labour in the conversion of the people of those Kingdomes, where notable fruite hath beene gotten, for the which these Ilands are much celebrated in the world, and by the comming of the Ambassadours of the new Christendome to the Pope, and to the King Phillip the second, the Prudent: and so as nature placed them in a scituation separated from the rest of the Land, the men of that Region are differing in customes from other people. In the yeare 1592. Nobunanga which caused himselfe to be called Emperour of Japan, interprised with eightie Vessels, and 20000. men, certaine Provinces tributarie unto China, and wan it.

From the Iland of Simo, which is among them of Japan the greatest, is extended a row of small Ilands, called the
Lequios.
Lequios, and doe prolong themselves toward the Coast of China; the two greater, which is every one of fifteene or twentie leagues, neere the Coast of Japan, are called the greater Lequio, and other two also great, though not so much, which are at the end of the Rowe, they call Lequio the lesser: some are inhabited of well shapen people, white, politicke, well apparelled, warlike, and of good reason, they abound in Gold more then others of that Sea, and not lesse in Victuals, Fruits, and good Waters. Neere unto the lesser Lequio stands Hermosa, or the beautifull Iland, which hath the same qualitie, and say it is as big as Sicilie.

Chap. 27.
Of the new
Guinea,
Ilands of
Salomon, and
the Theeves,
wherewith
endeth that
which they cal
West Indies.
The Lequios.
THe Coast of new Guiena beginneth one hundred leagues to the East of the Iland of Gilolo, in little more then one degree altitude, on the other side of the Equinoctiall, from whence it is prolonged toward the East three hundred leagues, till it come to five or six degrees. It hath beene doubted untill now, whether it be an Iland or firme Land, because it doth enlarge it selfe in so great a Voyage from being able to joyne with the Countries of the Ilands of Salomon, or Provinces of the Straight of Magellanes by the South side; but this doubt is resolved with that which those do affirme that sailed on the South side of the Straight of Magelanes, that that is not a continent, but Ilands, and that presently followeth a

spacious Sea, and among those that doe affirme it is Sir Richard Hawkins, an English Knight, which was five and fortie dayes among the same Ilands.

From the Sea the Land of this coast of Guinea seemeth good, and the men that have been seene are cole black, and in the coast are many Ilands with good roads, and ports whereof is no particular notice; for having sailed it few times, those which are found in some cards are Aguada or the watering to the East thirty five leagues from the first Land, is in one degree of Southern altitude; and eighteene forward the port of Saint James, and the Iland of the Crespos of sixteene leagues long neere the coast, right against the Port of Saint Andrew, and neere to it the River of Saint Peter, and Saint Paul, before the Port of Saint Jerom, and a small Iland neere the [a]thrust out Point, 40. leagues from S. Austin, which they call of Good-peace, and more forward from it, the [b]Shelter, and Evill people, two little Ilands, and the Bay of Saint Nicholas, fiftie leagues from Puntasalida, and among other Ilands one of white men, and the Mother of God before Good Baye, and of the Nativitie of our Lady, the last of that which is discovered, and as to the North from it the Caymana, an Iland without in the Sea among others which have no name.

[III. v. 907.]
*Ilands and
Ports of the
coast of Guine.*

[a] *Or Curled.*

[b] *Hisp.
Puntasalida.
Buena paz.*

[c] *Abrigo.*

The Meridionall coast is not yet known, the first that discovered the new Guine was Alvaro of Saavedra, being lost with many stormes from his course, returning to new Spain, when in the year 1527. the Marques of the Valley sent him that on that side he should seek the Ilands of the Spicerie.

The Ilands of Salomon are eight hundred leagues from Piru, & the opinion that is held of their riches, gave them this name, the which properly are called of the West, because they fal to the West from the Provinces of Piru, from the place that Alvaro of Mendoça made discovery of them by order of the Licentiate Lope Garcia de Castro his Unckle, Governor of the Kingdomes of Piru, in the yeare 1567. the first that saw the Land of these Ilands was a

yong man, called Trejo, in the top of a Ship: they are
from seven degrees of altitude on the other side of the
Equinoctiall about 1500. leagues from the Citie of the
Kings, they are many in quantity and greatnes, and
eighteen the most famous, some of 300. leagues in compasse, and two of 200. and of 100. and of 50. and thence
downward, besides many which are not yet made an end
of coasting, and they say that they might be a-continent
with the coast of the new Guiney, and the Countries to
be discovered toward the West of the straight: the
Countrie of these Ilands seemeth of a good temper, and
habitable, plentifull of victuals, and Cattell: there were
found in them some fruits like those of Castile, Swine &
Hens in great number: the Countrie men some of a
brown colour like Indians, others white & ruddie, and
some cole blacke, which is an argument of continuance
with the Countries of the new-Guinie, whereby there may
so many differences of people be mingled of those which
resort to the Ilands of the Spicery.

The greatest and most renowned are Sancta Ysabel,
from eight to nine degrees of altitude, of more then 150.
leagues in length, and eighteene in breadth, and one good
port called of the Star: Saint George or Borbi to the South
of S. Isabel one league and a halfe, of thirty leagues compasse. Saint Marcos, or Saint Nicholas of one hundred
leagues compasse to the South-east of Saint Isabel; the
Iland of ᶜShelves as great as the former to the
South of Saint Isabel, and Saint Jerome to the West of
100. leagues compasse; and Guadalcavall to the South-
west greater then all: and to the East of Saint Isabel, the
Iland of ᵈBuenavista, and Saint Dimas, and the Iland of
Florida of twenty leagues circuit every one; and to the
East of it, the Iland of ᵉRamos of 200. leagues compasse,
and neere to it Malayta, and ᶠAtreguada of thirty, and the
three Maries, certaine little Ilands, & the Iland of Saint
John of twelve leagues compasse betweene the Atreguada
and the Iland of S. James to the South. Malata of 100.
leagues circuit, and to the South-east of it, the Iland of

ᶜI. de
Atrazifes.

ᵈOr Good
sight.

ᵉOr Boughes.
ᶠOr Franticke.

Saint Christopher as bigge as it: and Saint Anne, and
Saint Catherine, two small Ilands fast by it: the Name of
God, a small Iland distant from the other fiftie leagues, in
seven degrees of altitude, and in the same Rumbe to the
North of Saint Isabel, the Shelves, which they call of
ᵍ Candelaria.

There is in the voiage that is made from Piru to the
Ilands of Salomon, an Iland called of S. Paul, in fifteen
degrees of altitude, 700. leagues from Piru, nineteen
degrees, 300. leagues of Land, others which may be those
that they called of Salomon, and they say also that they
might be others which this little while have beene discovered in the same Rombe of Chile.

The Ilands of the Theeves are a row of 16. smal Ilands
together which runne North and South, with the middest
of the coast of Guiney, from twelve degrees of altitude
unto seventeene Septentrionall or more, not farre from the
Phillippinas to the East. They are all barren ground,
and miserable, without Cattle, or Mettals, scarce of
Victuals, inhabited with poore people, well shapen, naked,
and much inclined to steale, even to the nayles of the
Shippes that came there, whereby Magelane named them
of the Theeves, in the yeare 1520. when he came to them
going in demand of the Spicerie. Their names are, the
English, the most North, and after it Ota Mao, Chemechoa
Gregua, Agan, or Pagan, Oramagan, Gugnan, Chareguan,
Natan, Saepan, Bota, Volia. There are among these
Ilands Phillipines, other eighteene or twenty, called of the
Kings, Archipelagus, or Ilands of the Corrall, and the
Gardens, another quantity of little Ilands, and Pialogo,
Saint Vilan, another little Iland, the Gardens, and the Iland
of the Matalotes, and that of the Shelves, and of Saint
John, or of Palmes, neere the Malucos, and on the North
side of the Theeves, five or six little Ilands together, called
the ᵍ Volcanes, where is store of Cochinilla; and ʰ Malpelo
another small Iland, where are * Civaloes very fine, and on
the East side of the Theeves, the two Sisters, two little
Ilands in ten degrees, and Saint Bartholomew in foureteene

and more toward new Spaine, the Shelves, Look how thou goest, Take away sleep, or See thou sleep not ; & neere to *Martin.* them the Iland of Martine, and Saint Paul, another small *Saint Peter,* Iland with shelves, and the inhabited the most Eastward *and Saint* toward new Spaine, Alvaro of Saavedra was also in the *Paul.* Iland of the Theeves, in the yeare 1527. returning from the Iland of Spicerie to new Spaine.

Chap. 28. THe Catholike King of Castile, and of Lyon continuing *Of the supreme* in their auncient, and Christian pietie, presently after *Counsel of the* these new Countries were discovered, and joyned with this *Indies, and of* faire Monarchie, procured to plant, and settle the Catholike *the spirituall* *government,* Religion in them, and temporall pollicie, with so much care *and Ecclesias-* and advice of the wisest men of these Kingdomes. For as *ticall Royall* the discoveries did increase the businesses, they formed a *Patronage.* particular Counsell with President and Councellours, that busying themselves in no other thing, with more diligence they might resort to that which so much pertained to the service of our Lord God, and government of that Orbe. And because hereafter mention shall be made of the persons which from the beginning have laboured, and *Counsell of the* served in the supreame Counsel of the Indies, which hath *Indies.* carried so great a waight unto this present houre, first shall be spoken of the spirituall and temporall government, and the rest worth the knowing, that the order of that Monarchie may be understood, with all brevitie.

The first thing that these godly Kings did charge and command the first Discoverer, and from man to man commanded the other Discoverers and Governours of that new World with very straight orders, was, that they should procure that the people which they carried, with the Christian life, and with their good customes, should give such example to the Indians, that they might be glad to imitate them, and should binde them unto it, entring first according to the Evangelicall Law, the religious men preaching it, that so rather with the sweetnesse of it, then with the force and noyse of Armes it should be admitted, and that justice should be administred with such equalitie to all men, that it might be much respected & esteemed. All went forward, the townes went augmenting in such manner, that with the zeale of the service of God, and good of the men it hath come to such a point, that at this day there are found built and established in all that Orbe of this Crowne possessed, as before hath beene seene, five Archbishopricks, twentie seven Bishopricks, two famous Universities, where with great learning and doctrine al the Sciences are read, more then foure hundred Monasteries of religious Dominicks, Franciscans, Augustines, Mercenaries, and the Companie of Jesus, with some Monasteries of Nunnes, and Colledges, infinite Hospitals, and Fraternities, innumerable store of beneficed Cures, which are called Doctrines, for to teach those new Converts, and Heremites, and Chappels in the high-way erected on pillars, having Crucifixes in them, without number. All the which was begun at the charge of the Crowne, and at this day it goeth forward where there is no maintenance for it. In effect, this Catholike pietie by the clemency of God goeth from good to better, augmenting with so much reverence and honour of God, that in no place of Christendome it is done with more order or care, by the care of the supreme Councell of the Indies. Of the which is inferred, that the Concession of the Apostolike Roman Sea made to the Crowne of Castile, and of Lion, of the Patronage Ecclesiasticall of that New World was a very great remedie, in the which our Lord God (as Hee which onely is Hee that seeth, and preventeth all things to come) did a thing worthy of His greatnesse, seeing Hee hath shewed the experience that if this had beene governed otherwise, it had beene impossible to have proceeded with the harmonie, and even concent as it hath, of Religion, Justice, and Government, with so much obedience and quietnesse.

The Ecclesiasticall Patronage is governed in the same manner that in the Kingdome of Granada, the Kings Catholike presenting to the chiefe Bishop onely the Archbishops, and Bishops, that from his holy hand they may

How many Archbishopricks, Bishopricks, Monasteries, and Schooles of Doctrine are in the Indies. So Humilladeros is said to signifie, the translator had Shrines: the latine hath Pœnitentiarii.

How the Ecclesiasticall Patronage is governed.

receive these Prelacies, and may dispatch their Bulls, procuring alway that they be persons of a religious life, and great learning. All the other Dignities and Benefices are provided by the King, and consultation of the supreme Councell of the Indies, and they go not to Rome for Buls: and their rents consist in tithes and first fruits which arise of the Spanish inhabiters. For in the most places of these Indies the Countrie men paie not, and where the tithes are wanting, it is supplied out of the goods royall: and touching the tithes and first fruits that are to be paied, many ordinances and rates are made according to the stile of these Kingdomes, that the men of each Colony, it is just it should follow her customes. And though the Kings of Castile, and of Lyon, are Lords of the tithes by Apostolike concession, & might take them to himselfe, supplying where it wanteth with that which in other places doth exceede, he leaveth them to the Prelates & Churches, providing of his own goods Royall with the liberality of so Catholik Princes, to all the necessities of the poore Churches, giving to every one that is built anew the greatest part of that which is spent in the building, with *Of Images* *or Pictures.* a Chaliz, a Bell, and a painted * Table.

That the distribution of that which proceedeth of the tithes, and of that which is bestowed out of the goods Royall in maintenance of the Prelates, Dignities, and Canons of the Cathedrall Churches, and Benefices, Cures, and persons that are occupied in the divine Service, and instructing of the Indians, may be fruitfully imploied according to the holy intention of the Kings; the supreme Counsell hath made good ordinances. First, that all the said persons be of an approved life and customes, & especially those that doe meddle in the Doctrines, being [III. v. 909.] first examined touching * learning, and after in the *Las Letras.* language of the Indians; for it would little availe, that the Disciples should not understand the Maister: and that these do continually reside: and that no Curate, or Teacher may have two Benefices; and that those which shall from these parts passe to the Indies be more

566

approved, it is commanded that no Priest doe passe without licence of his Prelate and of the King, and that if any
be there found without it, presently they should send him
to Spaine.

And that the manner how the Royall Patronage is *He continueth*
governed may better be understood, seeing it appertaineth *the governe-*
to this Crowne, because that it hath discovered and *ment of the*
acquired that New World; and hath also built and *Ecclesiasticall*
endowed, out of the goods Royall, so many Churches, & *Patronage.*
Monasteries, as by the Apostolike concession, that for no
cause the said patronage, nor any part of it, either by
custome, or prescription, or other title may be separated
from it: it is ordained what care the Vice-roies, Counsels,
Governors, & Rulers, are to have in it, and what penalties
the transgressors should incur. First, that no Cathedrall
or Parish Church, Monasterie, Hospitall, nor votive
Church, should be founded without consent of the King.
That when in the Cathedrall Churches there are not foure
* Beneficed men resident, provided by royall presentation, **Or Pen-*
& canonicall provision of the Prelate, because the other *tioners.*
Prebends be voide, or absent for more then eight moneths
(though for a lawfull cause.) The said Prelate, till such
time as the King doth present, may chuse to the accomplishing of the foure Clarks (besides those that are
provided and resident) of the most sufficient of those that
shall offer themselves, without that the said provision be
in Titulo (to be removeable at pleasure) & that they have
no seate in the Quire, nor voice in Counsell. That no
Prelate may make canonicall institution, nor give possession of any Prebend, or Benefice, without presentation
Royall, & in such a case that without delay they make the
provision, and command to resort with the fruits. That
in all the dignities, & Prebends, the learned be preferred
before the unlearned, and those which have served in the
Cathedral Churches of Castile, and have more exercise
of the service of the Quire, before them that have not
served in them. That at the least there be presented for
every Cathedrall Church a graduate Lawyer, & a Divine

for the Pulpet, with the obligation that in these Kingdoms
the doctoral Canons, & Magistrates have; & another
learned Divine to read the sacred Scripture : and another
Lawyer or Divine for the Cannonship of Pennance,
according to the sacred Counsell of Trent. That all the
other Benefices, Cures, and simples, secular, and regulars,
and the Ecclesiasticall Offices that shall be voide, or provided anew. That they may be made with lesse delay,
and the Royall patronage may be preserved, it is commanded that they be made in the forme following. That
any of the abovesaid Benefices, or Offices being voide, the
Prelate shall command to make edicts with a competent
tearme, and of those that shall offer themselves having
examined them, and being informed of their behavior,
shall name of the best ; and the Vice-roy or Governor of
the Province, shal chuse one and remit the election to
the Prelate, that he make the provision, Collation, and
Cannonicall institution by way of recommendation, and
not in a perpetuall title, so that when the King doth make
the presentation, and in it shal be expressed that the
collation be made in a perpetuall title, the Canonicall
institution shall be in title, and not in recommendation :
and the presented by the King be alwayes preferred before
the presented by his Ministers.

Provision of
the Prebends,
and Benefices.
That in the repartitions, and Towns of the Indians,
and other places where they have no benefice to elect, or
means to place one to administer the Sacraments, the
Prelates shall procure there be one to teach the Doctrine,
making an Edict, and having informed himselfe of his
sufficiency and goodnes, he shall send the nomination to
the Ministers Royal, that they do present him one of the
two nominated, and if there be but one, that, and in the
vertue of such a presentation the Prelate shall make the
provision, giving him the instruction how he is to teach,
and commanding him to give notice of the fruits. That
in the presentations of all the dignities, offices, and benefices, the best deserving, and that most exercised in the
conversion of the Indians, and the administration of the

Sacraments shall be provided; which, & those that best speak the language of the Indians, shall be preferred before the other. That he which shall come or send to request his Majestie to present him to some dignitie, office, or benefice, shall appeare before the Ministers of the Province, and declaring his petition, he shall give information of his kindred, learning, customes & sufficiency, and the Minister shall make another of his office, and with his opinion to send it, and that the pretendant do bring also an approbation from his Prelate; for without these diligences those that come shall not be admitted. That none may obtaine two Benefices, or dignities in one, or in sundry Churches. That the presented not appearing before the time contained in the presentation before the Prelate, it shall be voide, and they may not make him a Cannonicall institution.

BEsides that which is rehearsed, it is provided that they doe not permit any Prebendary in the Cathedrall Churches, to enjoy the rents of it, except it be serving & being resident; and that the Benefices of the Indians be Cures, and not simples, and that in the new discoveries, and plantations that shall be made, there be presently an Hospitall built for the poore, and sicke persons, of sicknesses that are not contagious, which shall be placed neere the Temple, and for a Cloyster of the same; that for the sicke of contagious diseases, the Hospitall shall be set that no hurtfull winde passing by it doe strike in the other inhabiting, and if it be built on a high place it will be better. And because the King being informed that goods of the deceased in those parts do not come so wholly as they might, nor so soone to the hands of the heyres, by will of the said deceased, for many causes, whereby the heires received great damage, and the testaments were not performed: for a remedy, it was provided, that whatsoever Spaniard shall come to any Village, or Towne of those parts, he shall present himselfe before the Clarke of the Counsell, where he shall Register the

*Chap. 29.
Of the
Spirituall
Governe-
ment, Goods of
Men deceased:
of the married:
and of the holy
office of the holy
and general
Inquisition.
Building of an
Hospitall.*

[III. v. 910.]

*Orders for the
goods of the
deceased.*

569

name, and surname of such a one, with the place of his
aboad or birth, that his death happening, it may be
knowne where those that are to be his heires may be
found. That the ordinary Justice, with the most auncient
Ruler, and the Clark of the Counsell shall take charge of
the goods of the persons that shall dye, and shal set them
in an Inventorie, before a Scrivener and Witnesses: and
the debts that he did owe, and were owing him, and that
which is in Gold & Silver, small Pearle, and other things
shall be sold, and put in a Chest of three Locks, whose
Keyes the three persons abovesaid shall keepe. That the
goods be sold in a publike out-cry, with the Testimony
of a Scrivener: that if neede be, an Atturney shall be
constituted. That the said Justices doe take accompt of
all those that have charge of dead mens goods, and recover
all that they are behinde hand without any appeale, and
doe put it in the Chest of the three Keyes. That having
any Will of the deceased where he dyeth, and the Heires
or Executors, the Justice shall not meddle in any thing,
neither take the goods, taking only notice who be the
Heires of the said deceased. That the said Justices,
Rulers, and Scriveners doe send also to the Contractation-
house of Sevill, all that which they shall recover of the
goods of the deceased, declaring the name, surname, and
aboad of every one deceased, with the Copy of the
Inventory of his goods, that they may be given to his
Heires, by the order that touching the same is given.
That when they take accompt of those that have had
goods of men deceased, it shall be sent to the supreme
Counsell of the Indies, with a very particular relation, and
reason of all. That the Justices doe with care enforme
themselves carefully of those which have in possession the
goods of men deceased, whether they have done any
fraude, and prejudice to the goods they have had in possession, & send to the Counsel notice thereof, that they
may give accompt with paiment to the Justices above said.
That accompt be given every yeere, and the memoriall of
the dead that have beene that yeere shall be shewed to the

Governor of the Country, & of the goods they had, that they may be sent to Sevill, & be given to his heires, and the Testaments be fulfilled, with good accompt and reason that is behoovefull. For in every Counsell, one of the Justices is Judge of the goods of the deceased, the one succeeding another, from the yongest to the eldest, by their turne, which doth send his Commissaries through the bounds to take accompt of the houlders, and there be any carelessenesse, the Justices are charged therewith in the visitations which are made of them, and before when there are any Plaintifes.

Those Catholike Kings being informed that in the Indies were many married Spaniards, which lived separated from their wives, of the which, besides the offence that was done to our Lord God, there followed a great inconvenience to the Plantation of those Countries, for that such not living seated in them, were not continued, neither did they attend to build, plant, breed, nor sowing, nor doing other things, which the good inhabiters are wont to doe, whereby the Townes doe not increase, as is behoofefull, and as they would do if there came inhabitors with their wives & children, as true Townsmen; being willing to remedy the abovesaid, commanded that all and every person or persons that should be found to be married, or betrothed in these Kingdomes, should come unto them for their wives, and not returne to the Indies without them, or with sufficient proof that they are dead. And the same order was given for all the Kingdomes, of that new world, and sundry times hath beene reiterated, and commanded to be executed upon grievous penalties.

Touching married men.

Proceeding from the yeare 1492. when the discovery of this Orbe was begun, in directing and setling the spirituall government, as hath beene seene, for greater perfection, and enduring of it: The Catholike King Don Phillip the second, called the Prudent, considering that among the great benefits that the Indians have received, their illumination to receive the Evangelicall Doctrin was the greatest, which hath extended it selfe, and con-

The holy Office of the Inquisition.

sidering also the singular grace which God for his mercy hath used with them, in giving them knowledge of our holy Catholike Faith; that it was necessary to have a speciall vigilancy in the conserving of the devotion, and reputation of the inhabitors, and Castillane pacifiers, which with so many labours procured the augmenting of the Religion, and exalting of the Catholike Faith (as in those parts like faithful & Catholik Christians, and good naturall and true Castillans they have done) & seeing that those which are out of the holy Catholike & Apostolic Roman Church, obstinate, and stubborne in their errors, and heresies, do alwayes procure to pervert the faithful Christians, labouring to draw them to their false opinions, scattering certain damned Books, whereof hath followed great hurt to our sacred Religion; and having so certain experience that the best meanes to prevent these evils, consisteth in the separating the communication of heretical persons, punishing their errors, according to the disposition of the sacred Canons & laws of these Kingdoms (which by this holy means, by the divine clemency have beene preserved from this wicked contagion, and is hoped they will be preserved hereafter) to the end that the Orbe doe not receive so much hurt, where the inhabiters of these Kingdomes have given so good example of Christianity, & the Country-born have not perverted themselves with erronious doctrines of the hereticks: It seemed good to his Majestie, with the advice of the Cardinal D. James of Espinosa, Bishop of Siguença, Inquisitor generall in these
[III. v. 911.] Kingdoms, a man of great prudence, and of many rare parts and vertues, for the which he made election of his person, to help him to beare the burden of so many Kingdomes, and Lordships, and of the Counsels of the holy, and generall Inquisition, and of the supreame Counsell of the Indies (for it behoved to place one Counsell of the holy Office in Mexico; for the Kingdomes of New Spaine, and the rest of the Indies of the North, and another in the Citie of the Kings, for the Kingdomes of Piru, and the adherents, which are called the Indies of the South)

which the authority that the Councels of these Kingdomes have, so that as yet they should not meddle with the cases of the Indians, but onely of the Castillanes, & other Nations that should be found in the Indies, and so that the appeals should come to the supreame Counsell that is resident in this Court, as it is done in Spaine, and in the accomplishing thereof, in the yeare 1570. the King Don Phillip the second, called the Prudent, gave a generall power to the Towne of Madrid, the 16. of August, that the Apostolike Inquisitours that should be named for the present, and for hereafter against the hereticall perversnesse, & Apostacie; and the Officers and Ministers necessary for this holy Office, which was commanded to be seated in the Cities of Mexico, and of the Kings, should exercise & use their Offices, and royall warrants, that Don Martin Enriques, and Don Franciscus of Toledo, Viceroyes, and Captains generall in the Kingdomes of New Spaine, and Piru, and the Counsels, and Justices, Governours, and other persons should give all aide, and favour to the holy Officio, and the Inquisitors, and Officers were nominated, as in their owne place shall be spoken more at large.

THese Catholike Kings, most wisely constituted the Supreme Counsell of the Indies, that they might helpe them to beare so great a burden, as is already the government of that Orbe, and the Counsell consisteth in one President, and eight or more Counsellors, as necessitie requireth with one Atturney, Secretaries, Clerkes of the Chamber, Relators, and other Officers, and an Office of Accompts, where a notice is had of all the goods Royall of those parts. And that proceeding might be according to rule and order, they declared first that the Counsell should meet three houres every day in the morning, and two in the afternoone, three dayes in the weeke that bee no holy dayes, and that they should firme the Warrants that should be delivered for these Kingdoms; but that those that were for the Indies, should have the seale Royall: and

Chap. 30. Of the forme of the government of the supreame Counsell of the Indies, and of the Institution of the Counsels, and Chanceries royall of those parts.

that in those parts it should have supreme jurisdiction, and might make Lawes, and Decrees, to see and examine whatsoever Statutes, Constitutions of Prelates, Senates, Chapters, and Convents of the Religious, and of the Vice-royes, Courts, and Counsels; and that in the Indies, and in these Kingdoms, in matter dependant of them it should bee obeyed: that the government of the Indies should bee like this of these Kingdomes, and that more in particular the Counsell doe occupie it selfe in the matters of

Appeales. government. That in Suites remitted those of the Counsell Royall shall come to give their voyces to that of the Indies, and that two voyces shall make a Sentence in suites

ᵈ Which is 100. pound English, taking two Ryals for one shilling. of 500. ᵈ Pesos, or under. That there be a second Supplication in a case of 10000. Pesos: that they deale not in the repartitions of the Indians in those parts, but the Processes well perused in the Courts according to a Law, called of Malinas (for there it was made) they shall come to the Supreme Counsell: touching order to be held in matters of services, that the Counsell doe see them all; and in matters of rewards, that which the greatest part doth determine, shall be done, and that in these there be a Supplication, and that no expedient suite be seene the third time: and that in the matters they doe resolve with brevitie, that the charges be given to the best deserving, and that they be not given to the allied and kinsmen of them of the Counsell; neither may such bee Solicitors, nor Atturneys; in the providings of the Office no price shall be admitted: nor that they of the Counsell have any Indians of repartition, and they shall assist in their houses, that the Suiters may find them there, when they goe not to Counsel: and that due secrecy be kept in all things, and above all that the Counsell have a particular care of the Conversion and good Instruction of the Indians, and

ᵉ Which as we accompt 441. pound 3 shillings and one third part of a pennie. of the spirituall government; and that of ᵉ600000. Marmediz upward the appeale shall come to the Counsell; that they may appeale from the Sentences in the five Cases of naturall death, or mayming of a member, or other bodily punishment, publike shame, or racking, and the appeales shall come to the Counsell, with many other laudable orders, which are omitted for brevities sake.

That the President being a learned man, shall have a voice in matters of Government, gratuities, and favours, visitations, and accompts, and not in suits, because he may be the more free for the government of the Counsell; and being unlearned he shall have no voice, but in matters of grace, government, and favour, and that he may assemble the Counsell in his owne house, and have a noate of the businesses, and that the Counsellours doe not accompany with the Suitors. And because it seemed a necessary thing that one Fiscad or Atturney should assist in Counsell, it was commanded he should have the same stipend that the Counsellours, and that they deliver him the dispatches of the Office, that he have a care to know how that is accomplished which is provided for the Indies; that necessary Papers be given him for his Office, that he doe see the visitations before Counsell: that he have a book to register all the capitulations that are taken with the King, another wherein he may set down the Atturneys Pleas: that he delay not the suits: that his demands, or those that are against him be admitted, if the Counsel think it good: that he keep a book of that which is concluded for the cases; that he have a care to know the Officers that doe omit to send a relation every yeere to the Counsell.

He continueth the orders of the supreame Counsell.

Having ordained all that which appertaineth to the Counsell, which is the head of this Government, with many other orders which are not rehearsed for brevitie; they proceeded in ordering all the Provinces of the Indies, in the matters of justice, as neede required: and these Catholike Kings desiring the common good of that new world, that their subjects that should possesse it, having a zeale to the service of our Lord God, good, profit, & ease of the said Subjects, & to the peace, and quitenesse of the Towns, as the King is bound unto God, and to them, for to accomplish with the Office that he hath in earth, hee thought good to command to place the Courts and

[III. v. 912.]
Institution of the Courts royall of the Indies.

Royall Chanceries, that (as hath beene said) are in the Indies, with the Statutes, and orders that hath beene given them, that the Ministers may doe their office, and justice be well administred, and the Townes obtained the benefit pretended.

The Court of the Hispanyola.

The first Court that was established, was in the Citie of Saint Dominicke in the Iland of Hispaniola, with one President a learned man, though now because of the warre he is a Souldiour, with title of Captaine Generall, and

ᵃ*Or Ordinary Justice, &c.*

foure Justices that beare rods, like an ᵃAlcalde, and deale in civill and criminall matters, in a degree of apeale, and in the instance in matter of Court, and the Government is onely commended to the President (which now is in Don Antonio Ossorio) and the limits thereof. The

The Court of Mexico.

second Court was established in the Citie of Mexico, in New Spaine: the first President which was Nunyo of Guzman, had no authoritie, for he was placed but for a season: with the second Court, the Bishop D. Sebastian Ramirez (for he was so in the Court of Hispanyola) he had the Government of the Kingdomes, and the supreame authoritie, and hee left that, established that which belonged unto it, and unto justice, as at this present it is. The President of this Court is the Vice-roy (which now is the Earle of Monterrey) there are eight Justices, which doe judge in civill matters, and in the appeale of the cases of government which the Vice-roy establisheth. There are three Justices of criminall cases, which beare rods, and deale in criminal cases, and two Atturnies, one of civill, another of criminall causes, and hee provideth the Rulers charges that are not reserved to the King, and the other Officers, and helpes of cost in releases, and vacations in the limits of this Court of Mexico, and in that Counsell of new Galicia.

The Court of Panama.

The third Court was that of Panama in Terra firme (for this name was given to it, because it was the first

Wherefore it was called Terra firme.

place where from the Ilands the Castillanes went to inhabit, and as their common speech was to say that they went and came from the Firme Land, though other Provinces were

found in the firme land of that Orbe) this Province continued this name, loosing that of Castilla del Oro,
wherewith the Kings commanded it should be called: and
when the affaires of Peru grew greater, in the yeare 1542.
it was thought good that this Court should be removed
to the Citie of The Kings, where the Vice-roy (which now
is Don Lewis of Velasco) hath at his charge the government of these limits, and that of the Courts of the Charcas
and Quito. There is in this Court of the Kings eight *Court of the*
Justices, three Justices of Court, and two Atturneys, in *Citie of the*
the same order as in Mexico: and the Vice-roy is resident *Kings.*
in the Citie of the Kings, and is the President of this
Court, and shall be in the other two, when he is present in
them, and doth divide all the repartitions of Indians that
are voide in the bounds of them.

The fourth Court was established in the Province of
the Confines, and seeming it was needlesse it was dissolved, and the yeare 1570. it was established againe in
the Citie of Saint James, of the Kingdome of Guatemala: *The Court of*
in it is one President which is the Doctor Criado of *Guatemala.*
Castile: foure Justices with rods, and one Attorney.
They sit on civill and criminall cases, in appeales, and in
the first instance: in matters of Court the President onely
hath the Government, and assigneth the Indians, provideth the Rulerships, and other Offices temporall. The
fift Court was established in the Citie of Sancta Fe de
Bogata, in the new Kingdome of Granada, with one *The Court of*
President (which now is the Doctor Francisco de Sande) *the new*
foure Justices with rods, and one Atturney, with the same *Kingdome.*
authority that the former. The sixt was established in
the Citie of Guadalajara, of the new Kingdome of Gallicia, *The Court of*
with one Regent, three chiefe Justices, which dispatched a *the new*
great while without Seale, and the matters increasing, the *Kingdome of*
Seale was given, and a Register, and a President was *Galicia.*
placed, which now is Doctor Sanctiago de Vera: and three
Justices with rods, one Atturney, and the Viceroy of New
Spaine hath the Government. The seventh Court, was *The Court of*
placed in the Citie of Saint Francis of Quito, of the *Quito.*

Province of Piru, where there was also a Regent, chiefe
Justices without Seale, and afterward the Court was established with a President (which now is the Licentiat Miguel
de Vuarar) with three Justices with rods, & one Atturny
with the same faculty of Guadalajara, the government,
& the rest remaining to the Vice-roy of Piru, as abovesaid.

The Court of the Charcas. The eight Court was in the Citie of the Plate, in the
Province of the Charcas, with a Regent and chiefe
Justices: after there was placed a President, foure
Justices with rods, Atturney, Seale, and Register, and
now is President the Licentiat Cepeda, with reservation of
the providing the charges, and the rest to the Vice-roy of
Piru. The ninth Court, is that which was established

Counsell of Panama.
*Sc. a Soldiour.
againe in the Citie of Panama, with a President of * Sword
and Cloake, because of the matters of warre, which is
now Don Alonso de Sotomayor, with the title of Captaine
Generall of Terra firme: there are three Justices with
roddes, which doe deale in Appeales of civill and criminall
cases, and at first instance in matters of Court, and it
hath onely the Government. In the Citie of Saint
James, of the Province of Chile, was placed the tenth

[III. v. 913.] Court, and because it seemed needelesse, it was dissolved,
and a Governour was provided, which dependeth on the

The Court of the Phillipines. Viceroy of Piru. In the Citie of the Philippinas, called
Manila, was a Court, and it was dissolved, because it
seemed needelesse: a few yeares since it was established
againe, with a Captaine Generall which is Don Peter of
Acunya which is President, and foure Justices, and one
Atturney, with the same authoritie that the other Courts.
For the Catholike Kings of Castile, with the advise of
the supreme Councell of the Indies, doe alwayes provide
with a sincere and just minde, that which is convenient
for the preservation, and augmenting of the spirituall and
temporall things of those parts, without any spare of
expences, or labor: and every Court hath according to
the use of these Kingdomes, Secretaries, Relators, Ser-
geants, Porters, and the Officers which are necessarie.

THe harmonie and agreement of this great Monarchie, is such, that to every Minister hath beene given the authoritie that as well by reason of estate, as for the reputation of justice hath seemed to be convenient, reserving to the supreme Majestie that which hath beene judged to be necessarie to his authoritie. For to the Vice-royes and Presidents, that they may have to reward the well-deserving, and they be more respected, there are Offices assigned which they may provide, and matters wherein they may gratifie, and to the providing of the Person Royall have remayned, with consultation of the supreme Councell of the Indies the offices following.

Chap. 31. Of the things that are provided in the supreme Councell of the Indies with consultation of the Kings.

For the Kingdome of Chile a Governour and a learned Justice, with facultie to incommend or authorise the Indians: another for Tucuman, with tne same facultie: another for the Provinces of the River of Plate, for Popayan, Sancta Martha, Cartagena, and Veragua, with their Governour in every one with the same power. In the Provinces of Nicaragua, and the Rich Coast, one: in the Iland of Cuba, one Governour, and Captaine which is resident in the Citie of Saint Christopher of the Avana: there are besides the Governours of the Iland of Saint John of Porte-rico, Venezuela, Soconusco, Yutacan, Cozumel, and Tabasco, which is all one government with authoritie to commend the Indians. His Majestie provideth also the governments of Honduras, the Margarite, Florida, new Bisquie, Dorado, those of the new Realme of Lion, and that of Pacamoros, Ygualsango, which are for terme of life, and the same in the Provinces of Choco, Quixos, the Cynamom, Ilands of Salomon, Sancta Cruz of the Hill, and the last is that of the new Andalusia.

The governments which the King provideth in the Indies.

Likewise there are provided by his Majestie the Ruler-ships following. The Cuzco, the Citie of the Plate, and the seate of the mynes of Potosi, and the Province of Chicuito, the Andes of Cuzco, the citie of Truxillo, Arrequipa, Saint James of Guayaquil, Guamanga, the citie of the Peace, Chiquiabo, Saint John of the Frontier, Lion of Guanuco, Old Haven, Zamora, the inhabiting of

The Ruler-ships that his Majestie doth provide.

the mynes of the Zacatecas in new Galicia, Cuenca, Loxa, Tunja, the citie of Mexico, the citie of the Kings, the province of Nicoya. Chiefe Justiceships, are those of the village of Saint Saviour of the province of Guatemala, *Or the name* the inward part of Hispaniola, *Nombre de Dios, the *of God.* village of Chuluteca, province of the Chiapa, Zapotlitan, the village of Nata, Sancta Marie of the victorie in Tabasco. And the chiefe Bayliwickes are, in the citie of Saint Dominicke in Mexico, in Guadalajara, Saint James of Guatemala, Panama, holy Faith of Bogota, Saint Francis of Quito, the citie of the Kings, the Plata. In the Cities recited in every one is a chiefe Bayliefe, which hath a voice in Councell as a Ruler, and Deputies named, for the use of his Office, and in every Court is another chiefe Bayliefe with facultie to name other two Deputies.

For the government of the goods Royall are provided by his Majestie, with the opinion of the supreme Councell of the Indies, many Officers, Factors, Treasurers, Tellers, and Over-seers, which all doe give assurance in Castile and in the Indies, of good and faithfull administration: and because this new Commonwealth doth augment so much, it seemed behoofefull to the service of God, and of the King, to ennoble and authorize it more, with placing two Vice-royes, one in New Spaine, another in the King-domes of Piru, that in the Kings name they should governe and provide the things belonging to the service of God, and of the King, and to the conversion and instruction of the Indians, sustayning, continuing, inhabiting, and ennobling of the said Kingdomes, which experience hath shewed, that it hath beene convenient: to the which Vice-royes instructions are given very particular of that which is recited, and that they may have in protection the holy office of the Inquisition, and with their strong arme to defend and protect it, that this con-formitie as a fast knot, may be the pure and true preservation of the spirituall and temporall Estate, which is the best and truest estate, and most according to the Evangelicall estate.

The Vice-royes are commanded also, and likewise the *That which is* Judges, not to have houses proper, nor to trafficke, nor *forbidden the* contract, nor be served of the Indians, neither have any *Vice-royes,* * Grangeries, nor meddle in Armies, nor Discoveries; that *and Judges.* they receive no guifts nor presents of any person; nor *of Cattell are* borrow mony, nor any thing to eate; nor pleade, nor *bred.* receive arbitrements. That no Lawyer may plead where his father, father in law, brother in law, cousin, or sonne is Judge. That no Vice-roy, President, Justice, Judge of the criminall Cases, Solicitor, nor their children may marry in the Indies. That no Governours, Rulers, nor their Deputies, may buy Lands, nor build Houses, nor trafficke in their jurisdiction. That they may not farme the Bayli-wickes, nor Jaylorships, nor other offices. That no Governour, Ruler, nor chiefe Bayliefe, during the time of his office, may marry in the bounds of his jurisdiction. That no Judge be provided for a Ruler, neither shall the said Judges, or Bayliefs, have any charge in which they [III. v. 914.] are to make any absence from their offices: neither shall any office of justice be given to the sonnes, sonne in law, brothers in law, nor fathers in law of Presidents, Justices, nor Solicitors, nor to the Officers of the Courts, and of the goods Royal, neither to servants not allied of theirs: and the same is commanded the Vice-royes. And that none of the abovesaid Ministers, doe accept warrant for recoveries nor other things, nor serve themselves of the Indians without paying them. That no Advocate, Scrivener, nor Relator, doe dwell in the house of Judge, nor Bayliefe, nor the Suiters serve the Judges. That the Judges of Panama, doe not accompanie themselves with the Dealers, nor give leave to their wives to accompanie them. And that no Justices of all the Courts, shall have much communication with the Suiters, Advocates, nor Atturneys: neither in body of a Court to goe to Marriages, Funerals, nor Spousals, except it be a very weighty matter: neither visite any Neighbour for any cause. That they doe not meddle in matters of the Common-wealth, nor any Justice, nor other minister of the Court.

may have two offices in it.   And besides these many other Ordinances, and good Lawes, which are all concerning administration of justice.

*Chap. 32.
Wherein hee
continueth the
matter of the
good govern-
ment of the
Indies.*

ANd because these Catholike Kings have left nothing which most wisely they have not provided for according to their dutie, the first thing they command the Vice-royes, and all the Ministers in generall and particular is, the good usage of the Indians, and their preservation, and the accomplishing of the Orders which are made as touching this, for to punish the Offenders with great rigour: and as the Indians doe learne the Castillan policie, and can complaine, and know in what things they receive wrong, for their greater ease it is provided, that they give no place that the ordinarie writings be made in the suites betweene, or with the Indians, neither make any delayes, as it is wont to happen, by the malice of some Advocates, and Atturneys, but that summarily they be determined, keeping their uses and customes, not being manifestly injust, and that by all meanes possible, they doe provide the good and short dispatch of them.   And having notice that in the interpretation of the Indians languages, there were some fraudes; for to prevent all, it was ordayned, that every

interpretation be made by two Interpreters, which shall not confer both together about that which is controverted by the Indian: and that before they be received to the use of the office, they shall take their oath to administer it faithfully, and that they receive no guifts of the Indians suiters, nor of others.   That they doe assist at the Agreements, Courts, and visitations of the Prisons.   That in their houses they heare not the Indians, but to carry them to the Court.   That the Interpreters be not Solicitors, not Atturneys of the Indians.   That they aske them nothing. And for their greater good, it is provided, that the Atturney of the supreme Councell of the Indies, bee Protector of the Indians, and defend them in their suites, and aske in the Councell all the necessarie things for his instruction, preservation, and politike life: and now there are appointed Protectors in the Kingdomes of Piru, and New Spaine, with new orders for their better usage.

It is also commanded, to set up Schooles of the Castillane tongue, that the Indians may learne it, and may doe it from their childhood; and that no vagabond Spaniard doe dwell or remayne in the Townes of the Indians, nor among them, but that the Vice-royes and the Courts, doe put all diligence in driving such out of the Land, shipping them for Castile: and the * Countrie borne be compelled to serve and to learne Trades. And as well to the Prelates, as to the Vice-royes, Courts, Governours, and Rulers, and other whatsoever Justices, is ordayned, and particular care is had they doe accomplish it, that they doe provide how the offences that were done to God may cease, in the Indians marrying whiles they are children, without having respect of age: the Caziques marrying with more than one woman, though he be an Infidel: in hindering that when some Cazique did die they should kill another to bee buried with him, and other like abominable uses. That it be permitted to the Indians that they may dispose of themselves what they list, as free men, and exempted from all manner of labour, though it shall bee procured that they doe labour and not be idle, and may have libertie to dispose of their goods, the Lands being set to sale by out-cry thirty dayes, and the moveable nine, the Justice being present. That the Lands remayning of any Indian deceasing without a Will, shall remayne in the Townes where they dwelt. That they make the Markets freely, and sell in them their merchandize. That their good uses and ancient customes be approved. That they may send to these Kingdomes Indian Atturneys for three yeeres. That the * Residencies be published in the Indian Townes, to see if any will demand justice. That in every Towne of the Indians there bee an Hospitall with the things necessarie.

In this matter of the Indian slaves, there were in the beginning of the Discoveries divers opinions, and orders,

governing themselves as the time required and the state
of the things: but after the Bishop Don Sebastian
Ramirez came for President of New Spaine, this use was
absolutely abolished, notwithstanding the ancient one
which the Indians had to make themselves slaves one to
another: neither might they buy of them, nor receive
them, neither that any person may bring to these Kingdomes any Indian in title of a slave, though he be taken
in lawfull warre: and for this are so straight orders given
that they are effectually kept, and so in no place of the
[III. v. 915.] Indies are Indian slaves, though they be out of the
bounds of Castile and Lion. And to eschew this inconvenience the more, the bringing Indians to these parts for
whatsoever title it bee, is forbidden.

About unquiet
persons.
And the quietnesse for the Commonwealth being above
all very necessarie, facultie is given to the Vice-royes,
Presidents, Governours, and other Justices, that they may
drive away, and banish from the Indies all unquiet
persons, and send them to these Kingdomes, judging
it so to bee convenient for the quietnesse of those, but
that it bee not for hatred or passion, nor for any such
reason.

And that it may be some bridle to the Superiors, they
are commanded, that they hinder no man the writing to
the King, to his Councell, and to other persons, what they
will: neither open, nor take any papers, or letters, under
great penalties, and that they permit to passe and repasse
through the Countrie them that will, providing wayes
and bridges in the places where they are wanting.

Matters of
warre.
As touching the matters of Warre, it is also provided
with great deliberation, for the Vice-royes greater
authoritie, facultie is given them to have a Guard on foot,
and on Horse-backe: to make a casting place for
Ordnance and Bullets, and a building for munitions, to
levy men, arme ships, and make fortifications, and provide
all the rest convenient for the defence of those Kingdomes,
and how the excesses of the Souldiers may be eschewed,
as well by Land as by Sea, and to them that goe in the

fleetes, committing the punishing of them to whom it belongeth, for to excuse competencies of jurisdiction.

It hath already beene said how all the Government of this Orbe, depends of the supreme and Royall Councell of the Indies, that are neere the Person Royall. But as it is necessarie that the executions of those parts have correspondence in these; and here also there be they that may provide in effecting that is behoofefull for the matters there: it was necessarie to place in Sivil, where all the trafficke of the Indies doth come, a house Royall of contractation of it, that medleth not but in the dispatching of those businesses, and dependants of them, without any person nor Justice doe intermeddle in any thing belonging to the Indian affaires: and it is in substance, a Tribunall of great authoritie, in the which is a President, which now is Don Bernardino Delgadillo of Avellaneda, a Teller, a Treasurer, one Factor, three learned Judges, one Solicitor, one Relator, one Sergeant, Scriveners, Porter, Jaylor, and other Officers. In the Ilands of Tenerife and Palma, are placed two learned Judges, called Officers Royall, or Judges of the Registers, to cause Orders to be kept that are given for the lading and Registers of those Ilands, and Navigation of that voyage. The house of the Contractation hath her instruction and ordinances, how her jurisdiction is to be governed and exercised, and the learned Judges have it also for their use and exercise, keeping in the seeing of the plea, betweene parties, the order that is held in the Courts of Valladolid, and Granada: and because the particular care of the officers of this house, is the dispatch of the Fleetes and Armies, that they may depart in due times, they employ themselves in it with great diligence, and in receiving them that come, and setting in safeguard the Gold, Silver, Jewels, and other things that doe come, with a distinction of the waight and carracts, charging themselves with all, that there may be more account and reason, and for to make the provisions of the Fleetes and Armies. There are so good orders given, that neither the Ministers doe

The house of contractation of Sivil.

exceed, nor the Subjects receive wrong, for all passeth very conformable to the intention of these Godly and Catholike Kings, by meanes of the great diligence of the supreme Councell of the Indies.

Instruction of the Councell of Camara, or of Houshold.

And because the businesses of the Indies have increased so much, that the supreme Councell could not dispatch them with the brevitie convenient to the good government of that Orbe, and the benefit of the Suiters, with the advice of the President and supreme Councell; the King Don Philip the third our Lord, in imitation of his Catholike and Godly Predecessors, for the greater good of his subjects, hath instituted a Privie Councell, where all the businesses of spirituall and temporall warrants, favours and rewards may bee conferred and dispatched: and besides this, there are two Halls instituted, where on dayes appointed they may intreat of matters of warre, with the President and three Counsellors of the Indies, and two or three of the Counsell of warre, and other dayes, of the matters of the goods, by the President and Counsellors of Indies, and two of the Counsell of the goods, Atturney, and Secretarie of the Counsell of the Indies, the President naming those that he shall thinke best for it.

That the Indies shall not bee alienated.

And as these Catholike Kings doe alwayes looke to the benefit of the people of that Orbe, considering that the propagation of the holy Gospell in no part of it could goe more prosperously by any other hands then his, nor bee attended for his preservation, and to have the Conquerours and Inhabiters of those parts more satisfied, seeing all were his Subjects, and borne in these Kingdomes, declared by their Royall warrants, dated the yeere 1520. in Valladolid, and in the yeere 1523. in Pamplona, that their Majesties, nor any of their Heires, in no time shall alienate from the Crowne Royall of Castile and Lion, the Ilands and Provinces of the Indies, Towne, or any part of them, and so they promised it and gave their Royall word.

ANTONIO DE HERRERA

The Presidents, Counsellors, Secretaries, and [III. v. 916.]
Atturneys, which unto this present day have
served, and doe serve in the Supreme Councell
of the Indies, from their first Discoverie.

PRESIDENTS.

JOhn Rodriguez of Fonseca, brother to the Lord of
Coca and Alaejos, Archbishop of Rosano, and Bishop
of Burgos, being Deane of Sivil, governed that which
appertayned to the dispatching of the Fleets and Armies
of the Indies, till the Catholike King Don Fernando V.
called him, to the end that in his Court hee might take
charge of the Indian affaires, and he did it till the Emperor
came to reigne, which commanded that the Doctor
Mercurino Gatinara his great Chancellor, should be
Superintendent of all the Councels, and all the dispatches
passed through his hands, and intermedled in all the
Assemblies that were made.

Friar Garcia of Loaysa Generall of the Order of Saint
Dominicke, the Emperours Confessor, Bishop of Osma,
which was Archbishop of Sivil, and Cardinall.

Don Garcia Maurique, Earle of Osorno, which being
Assistant of Sivil, did governe till the Cardinall came
from Rome.

Don Lewis Hurtado of Mendoça, Marques of Mondejar, which after was President of the Royall and supreme
Councell of Castile.

The Licenciate Don Franciscus Tello of Sandoval,
which having beene of the Councell of the Indies, went
for President of the Royall Chancerie of Granada, and
from thence came to governe in the Councell of Indies.

The Licenciate Don John Sarmiento was also of the
Councell of the Indies, and after went to governe in
the Royal Chancerie of Granada, from whence he returned
to be President of the Royall and supreme Councell of
the Indies.

Lewis Quixada, Lord of Villagarcia, and of the Councell
of Warre.

The Licenciate John of Obando, of the supreme
Councell of the holy Inquisition, did preside in the
Councell of the Indies, and of the goods Royall.

The Licenciate Don Antonio de Padilla, of the Royal
and supreme Counsell of Castile, passed to be President
of the Councell of the Orders, and after to the supreme
Councell of the Indies.

The Licenciate Hernando of Vega and Fonseca, of the
supreme Councell of the holy and generall Inquisition,
passed to the Councell of the goods Royall, and from it
to the Royall and supreme Councell of the Indies.

The Licenciate Don Pedro de Moya of Contreras, the
first Inquisitor that went to Mexico for to seate the holy
Office in that Citie. Hee was Archbishop of that Citie,
and President of the supreme Councell of the Indies.

The Licenciate Paul of Laguna, of the Royall and
supreme Councell of Castile, and of the holy and generall
Inquisition, passed to governe in the Councell of the
goods Royall and Tribunals of it, and was after President
of the supreme Councell of the Indies: and in his time
began the Royall Councell of the House-hold.

COUNSELLORS.

HErnando of Vega, Lord of Grajal, which was chiefe
Knight of Lion, and President of the Councell of
Orders. Licenciate Lewis Zapata. Licenciate Moxica.
Doctor S. James. Doctor Palacios Penbios. Doctor
Gonçalo Maldonado, which was Bishop of the citie
Rodrigo. Master Lewis Vaca, Bishop of Canarie.
Doctor Aguirre. Doctor Mota, Bishop of Badajoz.
Doctor Sosa. Doctor Peter Martyr of Angleria, Abbot
of Jamayca. Mosiur of Lassao, of the Emperours
Chamber, and of the Councell of Estate. Licenciate
Garcia of Padilla, of the habit of Calatrana. Doctor
Beltran. Doctor Galindez of Carvajal. Doctor Bernal.
Licenciate Peter Manuel. Licenciate Rodrick of the

Court.   Licenciate   Montoya.   Licenciate   Mercado.
Licenciate Antonie of Aguilera.   Licenciate Don Her-
nando of Salas.   Licenciate John Thomas.   Doctor
Villafanye.   Licenciate Bottelbo Maldonado.   Licenciate
Otalora.   Licenciate James Gasca of Salazar.   Licenciate
Gamboa.   Doctor Gomez of Santillana.   Licenciate
Espadero.   Licenciate Don James of Zunnigo.   Licen-
ciate Lopez of Sarria.   Licenciate Enao.   Doctor Lope
of Bayllo.   Licenciate Gedeon of Ynojosa, of the habit
of Saint James.   Licenciate Villafanne.   Doctor Antonie
Gonçalez.   Licenciate   Franciscus   Balcazar.   Licenciate
Medina of Sarauz.   Licenciate Don Lewis of Mercado.
Doctor Peter Gutierrez Flores.   Licenciate Peter Dayes
of Tudança.   Licenciate Benitte Rodriguez Valtodano.
Licenciate   Austine   Alvarez   of   Toledo,   and   of   the
Chamber.   Doctor Don Roderick Zapata.   Licenciate
Peter Brano of Sotomayor.   Licenciate Molina of
Medrano, of the habit of Saint James, & of the
Chamber, Commissioner of this Historie.   Licenciate
James of Armenteros.   Licenciate Alonso Perez of
Salazar.   Licenciate Gonçalo of Aponte, and of the
Chamber.   Licenciate Don John of Ocon, of the habit
of Calatrana.   Licenciate Hernando of Saanedra.   Licen-
ciate Don Thomas Ximenez Ortiz.   Licenciate Eugenius
of Salazar.   Licenciate Don Franciscus Arias Maldonado.
Licenciate Andrew of Ayala.   Licenciate Benavente of
Benavides.   Licenciate Roocke of Villagutierre Chuma-
zero.

SECRETARIES.

JOhan Colona.   Michael Perez of Almazan.   Gaspar
of Gricio.   The Knight Lope of Conchillos.   Franciscus of the Cobos, chiefe Commander of Lion.   John
of Samano.   The Commander Franciscus of Eraso.   [III. v. 917.]
Antonie of Eraso.   The Commander John of Ybarra.

THe Licenciate Franciscus of Vargas. Licenciate Prado. Licenciate Martin Ruyz of Agreda. Doctor Franciscus Hernandez of Liebana. Licenciate Jerome of Ulloa. Licenciate Gamboa. Licenciate Lopez of Sarria. Licenciate Scipion Antolinez. Licenciate Negron. Doctor Valençuela. Doctor Marcus Caro. Licenciate Bennet Rodriguez of Valtodano. Licenciate Alonso Perez of Salazar. Licenciate Roocke of Villagutierre Chumazero.

The Governours, and Vice-royes, which have governed untill this time, the Kingdomes of New Spaine, and of Piru.

In New Spaine.

DOn Fernando Cortes Marques of the Valley, Governour, chiefe Justice, and Captaine generall.

The Licenciate Lewis Pance, of the House of the Duke of Arcos, Judge of * Residencie, with facultie to take the government, and by his death the Licenciate Marcus of Aguilar, naturall of the Citie of Ezija, was subrogated his Deputie, and because of his death succeeded within two moneths; hee substituted his authorities in the Treasurer Alonso of Estrada, borne in Citie Royall: and the death of Lewis Pance being knowne in Castile, it was provided that Marcus of Aguilar should governe, and in defect of him, Alonso of Estrada, till the first Court came, with order that Nunno of Guzman, Knight of Guadalajara, Governour of Panuco, a President did come: and because it was convenient to take away those Judges, others were sent in their places, and for President in the government universall of New Spaine, Don Sebastian Ramirez of Fuenleal, Bishop of Saint Dominicke, and of the Conception, late President of the Court of Saint Dominicke, a man of great learning, and that after many dignities died in Castile Bishop of Cuenca, and then the charge of Captaine generall was given anew to the Marques Don Hernando Cortes, that he might governe the matters of warre, with the advise of Don Sebastian Ramirez.

The first that had title of Vice-roy and Captaine generall of New Spaine, was Don Antonie of Mendoça, brother of the Marques of Mondejar.

Don Lewis of Velasco, a Gentleman of the House of the high Constable of Castile.

Don Gaston of Peralta, Marques of Falces.

Don Martine Enriquez of Almansa, brother of the Marques of Alcannizes, the Kings Steward.

Don Laurence Xuarez of Mondoça, Earle of Corunya, which deceased being provided for Piru, and by his death Don Peter Moya of Contreras, Archbishop of Mexico, governed in the meane while.

Don Alvaro Manrique of Zunniga, Marques of Villamamuque, brother of the Duke of Bojar.

Don Lewis of Velasco, sonne to the abovesaid Don Lewis of Velasco, which passed to governe the Kingdomes of Piru, where at this present hee is.

Don Gaspar of Zunniga and Fonseca, Earle of Monterrey, which governeth at this day.

In the Kingdomes of Piru.

DOn Franciscus Piçarro, Marques of the Charcas, Governour, chiefe Justice, and Captaine generall.

The Licenciate Vaca of Castro, of the habit of Saint James, of the supreme Councell of Castile, carried Title of Governour generall.

Blasco Nunnez Vela, a Gentleman of Avila, was the first that carried the Title of Vice-roy and Captaine general of the Kingdomes of Piru.

The Licenciate James de la Gasca, of the Councell of the holy and generall Inquisition, carried the Title of President of the new Court that was sent to the Citie of The Kings, and of Governour generall, with facultie to give the government of Armes to whom hee thought

Or of the examination of a Judge or Justice, or other Officer after their time is expired, to see if any will complaine of any wrong done to him in that time, and to pay the damage so sustained by his default.

best. He died Bishop of Siguença, and his Funerall and Trophees are seene in Magdalene Church in Valladolid, and in his absence the government remayned to the Court of the Citie of The Kings.

The second that carried Title of Vice-roy and Captaine generall, was Don Antonie of Mendoça, that governed the Kingdoms of New Spaine.

Don Andrew Hurtado of Mendoça, Marques of Cauyete.

Don James of Zunyga and Velasco, Earle of Nieva.

The Licenciate Lope Garcia of Castro, of the Royall and supreme Councell of the Indies, caried title of President and Governor general.

Don Franciscus of Toledo, brother to the Earle of Oropesa, Steward to the King.

Don Martin Enriquez, from the charge of New Spaine, passed to governe the Kingdomes of Piru.

Don Garcia of Mendoça, Marques of Cavyete.

Don Lewis of Velasco, from the charge of New Spaine, passed to the Kingdomes of Piru, where now he is, and at the instant of the impression of this Worke, is provided for Vice-roy and Captaine generall of those Kingdomes, Don John Pacheco, Duke of Escalona.

Printed at Madrid by Juan Flamenco. An. 1601.

END OF VOLUME XIV.

CPSIA information can be obtained at www.ICGtesting.com
Printed in the USA
LVOW06s0107150115

422697LV00004B/387/P